McGraw-Hill Ryerson

DATA MANAGEMENT

12

Authors

Wayne Erdman, B.Math, B.Ed.
Markham, Ontario

Mariarosa Criscuolo, B.A., B.Ed., M.Ed., OCT
York Region Catholic District School Board

Roland W. Meisel, B.Sc., B.Ed., M.Sc.
Port Colborne, Ontario

David Petro, B.Sc (Hons.), B.Ed., M.Sc.
Windsor Essex Catholic District School Board

Jacob Speijer, B.Eng., M.Sc.Ed., P.Eng.
District School Board of Niagara

Wendy Telford, B.Sc. (Hons.), B.Ed., M.A.
Peel District School Board

Senior Project Consultant

Wayne Erdman, B.Math, B.Ed.
Markham, Ontario

Assessment and Student Success Consultant

Antonietta Lenjosek, B.Sc. (Hons.), B.Ed.
Ottawa Catholic School Board

Pedagogy Consultant

Larry Romano, B.A. (Hons.)., B.Ed.
Toronto Catholic District School Board

Technology Consultant

Sam Garrison, B.Sc (Hons.)., B.Ed.
Toronto District School Board

Advisors

Emidio DiAntonio, B.Sc., B.Ed., M.A.
Dufferin-Peel Catholic District School Board

Michael Lieff, B.Sc. (Hons.), B.Ed.,
Upper Canada District School Board

Paul Alves, B.A.Math, B.Ed.
Peel District School Board

Anthony Meli
Toronto District School Board

Michael Campbell
Ottawa-Carleton Distrist School Board

Mathematical Literacy Reviewer

Mark Bouwmeester, B.Math., B.Ed.
Dufferin-Peel Catholic District School Board

COPIES OF THIS BOOK
MAY BE OBTAINED BY
CONTACTING:
McGraw-Hill Ryerson Ltd.

WEB SITE:
www.mheducation.ca

E-MAIL:

canada.cs.queries@
mheducation.com

TOLL-FREE FAX:
1-800-463-5885

TOLL-FREE CALL:
1-800-565-5758

OR BY MAILING YOUR
ORDER TO:
McGraw-Hill Ryerson
Order Department
300 Water Street
Whitby, ON L1N 9B6

Please quote the ISBN and
title when placing your order.

McGraw-Hill Ryerson
Data Management 12

ISBN-13: 978-1-25-925636-3
MHID: 1-25-925636-7

www.mheducation.ca

1 2 3 4 5 6 7 8 9 10   TCP   1 0 9 8 7 6 5 4

Printed and bound in Canada

Care has been taken to trace ownership of copyright material contained in this text. The publishers will gladly accept any information that will enable them to rectify any reference or credit in subsequent printings.

Statistics Canada information is used with the permission of Statistics Canada. Users are forbidden to copy the data and redisseminate them, in an original or modified form, for commercial purposes, without permission from Statistics Canada. Information on the availability of the wide range of data form Statistics Canada can be obtained from Statistics Canada's Regional Offices, its World Wide Web site at http://www.statscan.ca, and it toll-free access number 1-800-263-1136.

Microsoft® Excel is either a registered trademark or trademarks of Microsoft Corporation in the United States and/or other countries.

TI-83™ is a registered trademark of Texas Instruments.

PUBLISHER: Jean Ford
PROJECT MANAGER: Christine Arnold
DEVELOPMENTAL EDITORS: Christine Arnold, Jean Ford
MANAGER, EDITORIAL SERVICES: Crystal Shortt
SUPERVISING EDITOR: Janie Deneau
COPY EDITOR: Kelli Howey
PHOTO RESEARCH AND PERMISSIONS: Linda Tanaka
EDITORIAL ASSISTANT: Erin Hartley
MANAGER, PRODUCTION SERVICES: Yolanda Pigden
PRODUCTION COORDINATOR: Sheryl MacAdam
INSIDE DESIGN: Michelle Losier
COVER DESIGN: Cathie Ellis
ART DIRECTION: Tom Dart/First Folio Resource Group, Inc.
ELECTRONIC PAGE MAKE-UP: Tom Dart/First Folio Resource Group, Inc.
COVER IMAGES: Main image: © Sergey Nivens/Shutterstock
          Bar graph: © Ersin Kurtdal/Shutterstock
          Lightening: © Stephen Cullum/Shutterstock
          Coin toss: © pogonici/Shutterstock
          Combination lock: © Aaron Amat/Shutterstock
          Dice: © Carrie's Camera/Shutterstock

Acknowledgements

The publisher, authors, and editors of *Data Management 12*, wish to extend their sincere thanks to the teachers, consultants, and reviewers who contributed their time, energy, and expertise to the creation of this textbook. We are grateful for their thoughtful comments and suggestions. This feedback has been invaluable in ensuring that the text and related teacher's resource and digital products meet the needs of students and teachers.

Reviewers

Kirsten Boucher
Durham District School Board

Lida Fiala Chiarelli
Ottawa Catholic District School Board

Mike DePelsmaeker
Halton Catholic District School Board

Barry Driscoll
Kawartha Pine Ridge District School Board

Vikki Dunn
Kawartha Pine Ridge District School Board

Steve Etienne
District School Board of Niagara

Shaun Hussain
Toronto Catholic District School Board

Rina Hyland
Windsor-Essex Catholic District
  School Board

Joanne Milligan
Peel District School Board

Patricia Misner
Grand Erie District School Board

Aaron Neal
Halton District School Board

Breeann Staibano
Hamilton-Wentworth Catholic District
  School Board

Christine Siwy
Ottawa-Carleton District School Board

Wendy Telford
Peel District School Board

Justin Van Horn
Lambton-Kent District School Board

Chris Wadley
Grand Erie District School Board

Contents

Introduction to Probability

When and where a bolt of lightning will strike is difficult to predict. How likely do you think it is that you will be struck by lightning at some point in your life? Would this change if you decided to go golfing in a thunderstorm?

Meteorology is the study of Earth's atmosphere as a way to forecast weather. Although advances in technology have made weather predictions more reliable, there is still a level of uncertainty involved. Meteorologists often use probability, which is the mathematics of uncertain events, in their work. In this chapter, you will learn how to use probability to solve problems involving unknown outcomes in mathematics and in other fields of study.

Key Terms

probability	odds in favour
outcome	odds against
experimental probability	mutually exclusive events
subjective probability	non-mutually exclusive events
theoretical probability	
sample space	compound events
event	independent events
complement	dependent events
	conditional probability

Career Link

Insurance Underwriter

An insurance underwriter provides automobile insurance to licensed drivers. The terms and cost are determined by a number of factors, such as the driver's age, gender, marital status, and driving record, and the type of vehicle. Who do you think would pay more for insurance, a 30-year-old male with two accidents, or a 20-year-old female with two years of clean driving? Why do you think this is? How are these factors related to probability?

Most insurance underwriters have a bachelor's degree in business, mathematics, or statistics.

Literacy Strategy

A Venn diagram is a way to compare the characteristics of a group of objects, which is important when exploring probability. For example, you can use a Venn diagram to compare and sort cards in a standard deck of cards. What do you think the overlap represents?

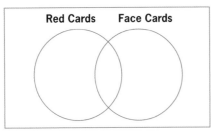

Red Cards   Face Cards

Chapter Problem

Game Analysis

Most games usually involve a combination of strategy and chance. The uncertain outcome when you throw a die or spin a spinner adds suspense and excitement. Some games, such as the card game War, are based almost purely on luck. Other games, such as chess, are based almost purely on skill. These games can be very mentally stimulating, but they tend to always favour the more skillful player.

A good game involves an appropriate balance of luck and strategy that matches the entertainment needs of its players. Pick two or three games to research as you study this chapter. At the end of the chapter, you will have the opportunity to share your analysis.

1. What elements of the game involve strategy?
2. What elements of the game involve chance or probability?
3. What is the relative balance of strategy versus chance in this game?

Fractions, Decimals, and Percent

1. Express each fraction as a decimal and as a percent.

   a) $\frac{1}{4}$

   b) $\frac{5}{6}$

   c) $\frac{2}{3}$

   d) $\frac{13}{20}$

2. Express each fraction in lowest terms.

   a) $\frac{9}{12}$

   b) $\frac{13}{52}$

   c) $\frac{22}{35}$

   d) $\frac{16}{36}$

3. Add or subtract the following. Express your answer as a fraction in lowest terms, as a decimal, and as a percent.

   Example:

   $\frac{2}{3} + \frac{1}{4} = \frac{8}{12} + \frac{3}{12}$ Express fractions with a common denominator. Add numerators. Is the fraction in lowest terms?

   $= \frac{11}{12}$

   To express a fraction as a decimal, divide the numerator by the denominator.

   $11 \div 12 = 0.91\overline{6}$

   To express a decimal as a percent, multiply by 100%.

   $0.91\overline{6} \times 100\% = 91.\overline{6}\%$, or approximately 92%

   a) $\frac{1}{6} + \frac{1}{3}$

   b) $\frac{1}{4} + \frac{4}{6}$

   c) $\frac{3}{4} - \frac{1}{3}$

   d) $1 - \frac{1}{4}$

4. Multiply. Express your answer as a fraction in lowest terms, as a decimal, and as a percent.

   Example:

   $\frac{3}{4} \times \frac{1}{6} = \frac{3}{24}$ Multiply numerators and denominators. Is the fraction in lowest terms?

   $= \frac{1}{8}$

   To express as a decimal, divide the numerator by the denominator.

   $1 \div 8 = 0.125$

   To express as a percent, multiply by 100%.

   $0.125 \times 100\% = 12.5\%$

   a) $\frac{1}{6} \times \frac{1}{2}$

   b) $\frac{1}{4} \times \frac{2}{3}$

   c) $\frac{2}{3} \times \frac{5}{6}$

   d) $\frac{5}{12} \times \frac{3}{10}$

Ratio and Proportion

5. A bag contains 3 red counters, 2 blue counters, and 5 yellow counters.

   a) Write a ratio that expresses the number of red counters to the total number of counters.

   b) Repeat a) for the other two colours. Write each ratio in lowest terms.

   c) What percent of the total number of counters does each colour represent?

6. A baseball player has 10 hits in 35 times at bat.

   a) Express the ratio of hits to times at bat in fraction form.

   b) Convert the fraction to a decimal, rounded to three decimal places.

   c) Use proportional reasoning to estimate the number of hits this player would have in 400 times at bat.

Randomization

A random act is an occurrence in which the outcome is unpredictable.

7. Classify each act as either random or non-random. Explain your reasoning.

  a) Flipping a coin

  b) Safely entering a traffic intersection

  c) Looking into a box and picking your favourite candy

  d) Reaching into a box and picking a candy without looking

8. a) Describe a random act scenario in a board game.

  b) Describe a scenario that involves a non-random act.

Playing Cards and Dice

9. A standard deck of playing cards has four suits: clubs, diamonds, hearts, and spades.

  a) What fraction of the deck are spades?

  b) Face cards are any cards showing a face, namely a jack, queen, or king. What percent of the deck are red face cards?

10. When you throw a pair of standard dice, the value shown on the upper faces gives the outcome of that throw. The following table illustrates all possible outcomes.

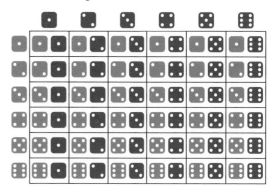

List and count all the ways each of the following sums could occur.

  a) 2   **b)** 7   **c)** 1

  d) doubles (both dice produce the same value)

  e) a perfect square

Organizing, Presenting, and Analysing Data

A class was surveyed to determine the students' favourite cafeteria menu items. The tally sheet shows the results.

Menu Item	Favourite
Lasagna	⦀⦀⦀ |
Meatloaf	⦀⦀⦀
Fish	⦀⦀⦀
Pork chops	⦀⦀⦀
Chicken	⦀⦀⦀ ⦀⦀⦀

Use this information to answer #11 and #12.

11. Construct a bar graph to represent the data.

12. a) Which meal is the class's favourite? What percent of the class chose this meal?

  b) What fraction of the class did not choose lasagna?

  c) **Open Question** Ask and answer a question related to the data.

Simple Probabilities

Learning Goal

I am learning to

- use probability to describe the likelihood of something occurring
- measure and calculate simple probabilities

> ## Minds On...

The students know there are 10 coloured counters in the bag; however, they do not know how many of each colour there are.

- How could they estimate the number of each colour?

- What mathematical processes could they use to determine the bag's contents?

> ## Action!

Probability involves making predictions about uncertain situations (or events). A probability experiment is a specific action that has at least two possible results, or **outcomes**. The probability of a certain outcome represents how likely it is to occur.

One way to measure probability is to carry out a probability experiment several times and analyse the results using statistics. Statistics involves working with large amounts of data. Probability and statistics are closely related and are often studied together. The **experimental probability** of an outcome is a measure of how frequently it occurs in a probability experiment. You can express probability as a fraction, decimal, or percent.

probability
- likelihood of something occurring

outcome
- a possible result of an experiment

experimental probability
- probability based on experimental trials
- number of times an outcome happens divided by total number of trials
- sometimes called *statistical probability* or *empirical probability*

Experimental Probability

$$P(A) = \frac{n(A)}{n(T)}$$

where $P(A)$ is the probability that outcome A occurs, $n(A)$ is the number of times that outcome A occurred, and $n(T)$ is the total number of trials.

Investigate Experimental Probability

1. Work with a partner. Secretly create a "mystery bag" of 10 counters using a combination of three different colours of your choice. Your partner does the same.

2. Take turns drawing a single counter at random from your partner's mystery bag. Replace the counter after each draw and shake the bag. No peeking! Record your results in a table, like the one shown.

Colour	Outcomes
Blue (B)	|||
Red (R)		
Yellow (Y)	|||||	

3. **a)** Carry out 10 trials.

   b) Determine the experimental probability of drawing each colour listed in your table. Use these values to make a prediction about the contents of your partner's mystery bag.

   c) How confident are you with your prediction? Explain.

4. **a)** Reveal the contents and check your prediction. How close was it?

   b) Compare results with your partner and with other classmates. Did everyone have the same results? Explain.

5. **Reflect**

   a) Explain why using experimental probability is not always an accurate method of predicting.

   b) Can you think of some ways to improve the accuracy of experimental probability? Explain.

6. **Extend Your Understanding** How accurate would the experimental probability values be if none of the 10 counters drawn were replaced before drawing the next counters? Explain.

Materials

- coloured counters (e.g., tiles, cubes, etc.)
- paper bag or envelope

Literacy Link

At random means that each counter has an equal likelihood of being chosen.

Processes

Selecting Tools and Computational Strategies

To calculate the experimental probability, use

$P(A) = \dfrac{n(A)}{n(T)}$.

For example, from the table,

$P(B) = \dfrac{n(B)}{n(T)}$

$= \dfrac{3}{10}$

So, the probability of selecting a blue counter is $\dfrac{3}{10}$.

Example 1

Calculate Experimental Probability

A student spins a mystery spinner 24 times. The table shows the results.

Colour	Favourable Outcomes, $n(A)$
Red	12
Yellow	4
Blue	8

a) Determine the experimental probability of the spinner landing on each colour. Express your answers as a fraction, a decimal, and a percent.

b) Determine the sum of the probabilities and explain what it means.

c) What could this spinner look like? Can you be certain this is what the spinner looks like?

Solution

a) To calculate the experimental probability, divide the number of favourable outcomes by the total number of trials.

The total number of trials is:

$$n(T) = 12 + 4 + 8$$
$$= 24$$

The experimental probability of the spinner landing on red is

$$P(R) = \frac{n(R)}{n(T)}$$
$$= \frac{12}{24}$$
$$= \frac{1}{2}$$

The experimental probability of the spinner landing on red is $\frac{1}{2}$, or 0.5, or 50%.

Similarly,

$$P(Y) = \frac{n(Y)}{n(T)} \qquad\qquad P(B) = \frac{n(B)}{n(T)}$$
$$= \frac{4}{24} \qquad\qquad\qquad = \frac{8}{24}$$
$$= \frac{1}{6} \qquad\qquad\qquad\quad = \frac{1}{3}$$

The experimental probability of the spinner landing on yellow is $\frac{1}{6}$, or $0.1\overline{6}$, or approximately 17%. The experimental probability of the spinner landing on blue is $\frac{1}{3}$, or $0.\overline{3}$, or approximately 33%.

b) Add all the probability values. Use the unreduced forms since they already have a common denominator.

$$P(R) + P(Y) + P(B) = \frac{12}{24} + \frac{4}{24} + \frac{8}{24}$$
$$= \frac{24}{24}$$
$$= 1$$

Why does this result make sense?

c) Based on the statistical probabilities, the spinner could be one-half red, one-sixth yellow, and one-third blue.

This spinner design may or may not look like the real spinner because it is based on experimental probability. Later in this chapter you will learn how to improve the accuracy of experimental probability.

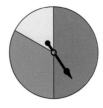

Processes

Reflecting and Representing

How is a spinner related to a pie graph? What does a spinner or pie graph show more clearly than a table does?

Your Turn

A mystery spinner produces these results.

Colour	Favourable Outcomes, $n(A)$
Orange	8
Red	4
Purple	8
Green	12

a) Determine the experimental probability of the spinner landing on each colour. Express your answers as a fraction, a decimal, and a percent.

b) What could this spinner look like?

c) Is it possible that there is a fifth colour? Explain your answer.

If you add all probabilities in an experiment, the total will always equal 1. Each probability represents the fraction of times an outcome occurred. All the fractions combined make up the whole set of outcomes that occurred during the experiment.

Sum of Probabilities

For a probability experiment in which there are n outcomes,

$$P_1 + P_2 + P_3 + \dots P_n = 1$$

where $P_1, P_2, P_3, \dots P_n$ are the probabilities of the individual outcomes.

Experimental probability is a useful tool for making predictions. Although the predictions may not always be perfectly correct, they can be close enough to help with decision making.

Example 2

Apply Experimental Probability

Tia is the manager of a pizza shop. The table shows the number of pizza slices ordered during the lunch rush over several days.

Pizza Type	Number of Slices
Pepperoni	98
Hawaiian	48
Vegetarian	51

a) Determine the experimental probability that a customer will order each type of pizza slice.

b) Based on this information, what advice should Tia offer her chef in order to be ready for the lunch rush?

Solution

a) Determine the total number of slices ordered.

$n(T) = 98 + 48 + 51$
$= 197$

Use this value to determine the experimental probability for each type of pizza.

Pizza Type	Number of Slices	Experimental Probability, $\frac{n(A)}{n(T)}$
Pepperoni	98	$\frac{98}{197} = 0.497...$
Hawaiian	48	$\frac{48}{197} = 0.243...$
Vegetarian	51	$\frac{51}{197} = 0.258...$

The probability of a customer choosing a pepperoni slice is about 50%, a Hawaiian slice is about 24%, and a vegetarian slice is about 26%.

b) These results show that the shop sells about the same number of Hawaiian and vegetarian pizza slices and about twice as many pepperoni slices. Tia should advise her chef to bake two pepperoni pizzas for every Hawaiian pizza and vegetarian pizza in order to be ready for the lunch rush.

Your Turn

A market researcher is conducting a telephone poll to gather data about which type of television service families use the most. The table illustrates the results.

Television Service	Tally
Cable	48
Satellite	42
Internet	15
Antenna	4
None	6

a) Determine the experimental probability of using each television service the most.

b) Who might be interested in these results, and for what purpose?

c) Suggest how these results may change over time. Explain why you think so.

Probability is often used outside of mathematics, both formally and informally. Suppose your friend tells you, "I'm 99% certain I just aced my history test!" It is quite likely that she did. This is an example of **subjective probability**. In this case, your friend most likely felt that she knew the answers to all or most of the questions on the test.

Subjective probability has no mathematical definition. This use of probability is related to relative certainty. The probability of an outcome can range anywhere between 0 (impossible) and 1 (certain).

subjective probability

• a probability estimate based on intuition

• often involves little or no mathematical data

Example 3

Estimate Subjective Probability

Match each scenario with its most likely subjective probability.

Scenario	Subjective Probability, $P(A)$
a) A person randomly selected from your high school is a student.	
b) A shaker randomly picked from a dining room table contains pepper.	0.2 0.9 0.5
c) You turn on the radio at some random time and an advertisement is playing.	

Solution

Consider the likelihood of each scenario.

a) Most high schools have far more students than teachers and other staff. Therefore, the probability of randomly selecting a student will be close to 1. A good subjective probability of this event occurring is 0.9.

b) Most dining room tables have the same number of salt and pepper shakers. Therefore, a reasonable subjective probability of randomly picking a pepper shaker is 0.5.

c) Advertisements are played often on most radio stations, but not nearly as much as music. Therefore, a subjective probability of randomly encountering a radio advertisement could be around 0.2.

Your Turn

Estimate the subjective probability of each of the following outcomes. Justify your estimates.

a) You will have a snow day in July where you live.

b) The sun will set in the west tonight.

c) The next person to enter the school cafeteria will be female.

Key Concepts

- The probability of an outcome is a measure of how likely it is to occur in a probability experiment.
- The experimental probability of an outcome is based on experimental data. It is defined as the number of favourable outcomes divided by the total number of trials.

$$P(A) = \frac{n(A)}{n(T)}$$

- Subjective probability is an estimate of how likely it is something will occur, based largely on intuition.

Reflect

R1. a) What is meant by the term "experimental probability"? Explain how it is calculated.

b) Explain why experimental probability is a useful strategy for making predictions.

c) Explain why experimental probability is not a perfect strategy for making accurate predictions.

R2. a) The probability of an outcome is 0. What does this mean?

b) The probability of an outcome is 1. What does this mean?

c) Why does the probability of an outcome always have a value between 0 and 1?

R3. a) Write a tweet that explains the concept of subjective probability.

b) Write another tweet that provides an example of subjective probability.

Literacy Link

A *tweet* is a message that is no longer than 140 keystroke characters. Hashtags are sometimes used to identify and flag important words, such as #probability.

Practise

Choose the best answer for #1.

1. A standard die is rolled 12 times and a 2 comes up 3 times. The experimental probability of rolling a 2 with this die is

   A 0.17

   B 0.20

   C 0.25

   D 0.33

2. A coin is tossed 10 times and comes up heads 4 times. What is the experimental probability of this coin coming up

   a) heads?

   b) tails?

Apply

3. **a)** Helena successfully made 21 out of 30 free throw attempts. What is the experimental probability that she can make a successful free throw?

   b) If Helena makes 5 out of the next 10 shots, what is her new overall experimental probability of scoring?

   c) Helena says that she typically makes 80% of her free throws. How accurate would you say this statement is? Justify your answer.

4. **Communication** The table shows the results for a mystery spinner.

Colour	Favourable Outcomes, n(A)
Yellow	6
Green	2
Purple	3
Blue	1

   a) Determine the experimental probability of the spinner landing on each colour.

   b) Draw what the spinner could look like, based on the given data.

   c) Could the real spinner look different? Explain.

5. **Open Question**

   a) Create the results for a mystery spinner where the experimental probability of the spinner landing on green is twice as great as landing on orange.

   b) Draw what the spinner could look like, based on your data.

6. An ice-cream stand owner keeps track of his cone sales over a period of several days. The table shows the results.

Flavour	Number of Sales
Vanilla	9
Chocolate	21
Raspberry ripple	43
Pralines and cream	78

   a) Determine the experimental probability of a random customer ordering each flavour.

   b) How could this information be useful for the ice-cream stand owner?

7. Application A weather report claims that the PoP of a rainy day in the previous April was 70%. How many rainy days were there in April?

Literacy Link

In meteorology, the study of weather, *PoP* means the probability of precipitation. It represents the probability that precipitation (rain, snow, etc.) will occur.

8. Application A pitcher throws the following pitches in a game.

Pitch	Count
Fast ball	86
Curve ball	8
Knuckle ball	0

a) Determine the experimental probability that the pitcher will throw each type of pitch.

b) How could this information be useful to the batter?

9. When Sandeep makes her first serve in tennis, she aims for one of the three regions indicated below.

The table shows the ball placements for several of her previous first serves, not counting missed serves.

Serve	Count
Down the line	3
Middle	12
Outside	25

a) Determine the experimental probability of each of Sandeep's serve locations.

b) How could this information be useful to Sandeep's opponent?

10. Communication Estimate the subjective probability of each event. Justify your reasoning.

a) You will earn an A in this course.

b) You will pass this course.

c) It will snow tomorrow.

d) You will hear your favourite song on the radio within the next week.

11. Open Question Pick a favourite sports team or athlete. Identify an upcoming competition (e.g., the Stanley Cup playoffs or the next Olympics). Estimate the subjective probability that your team or athlete will win their competition. Justify your estimate.

12. Thinking The experimental probability of randomly choosing a male from a litter of puppies is $\frac{1}{4}$. If there are 6 female puppies in the litter, how many males are there?

✓ Achievement Check

13. A paper bag contains 10 coloured counters. A counter is randomly drawn and then replaced for several trials. The table shows the results.

Colour	Frequency
Red	22
Green	75
Orange	64
Blue	39

a) Construct a bar graph or pie chart of the data, with or without technology.

b) Determine the experimental probability of randomly drawing each colour.

c) Use these results to predict the contents of the bag. Explain your reasoning.

d) Is it possible that your answer to c) could be incorrect? Explain.

14. Thinking A spinner has four colours: red, yellow, green, and purple. The experimental probability of spinning a red is 0.2, of spinning a yellow is 0.3, and of spinning a green is 0.4. If the spinner was spun 30 times, how many times did it land on purple?

15. You can use a graphing calculator to generate random numbers to simulate a probability experiment. Suppose you wish to simulate rolling an 8-sided die 20 times. Follow these instructions to carry out this experiment:

- Press **MATH**. From the PRB menu, choose **5: randInt(**.
- Enter the following:

```
randInt(1,8,20)
```

The calculator will randomly produce 20 integer values between the values of 1 and 8.

a) Carry out the experiment described above by pressing **ENTER**.

b) Tally the outcomes. Use the left ← and right → arrow keys to scroll through the trials.

c) Determine the experimental probability of rolling each value from 1 to 8.

d) Are these values all equal? Do you think they should be? Why or why not?

16. Use the random number generator of a graphing calculator to determine the experimental probability of rolling a 2 with a 4-sided die, using 10 trials.

Extend

17. Open Question Design a probability experiment that will reveal purchasing trends at your school cafeteria. Carry out the experiment and calculate experimental probabilities related to your study. You may wish to focus your study on one particular area, such as drink purchases or main menu selections. Write a brief report of your findings, including how the information could be useful.

18. A grocery store manager recorded these data at various times during a typical weekday.

Time of Day	Customers per Hour	Cash Registers Open
Morning	99	5
Afternoon	204	8
Evening	58	4
Overnight	16	1

On average, it takes 3 min to check out a customer. Use experimental probability to determine whether these staffing levels are appropriate or whether some changes should be made. Justify your reasoning.

Theoretical Probability

Learning Goal

I am learning to

• calculate theoretical probability

> **Minds On...**

Board games usually involve a combination of strategy and luck. Some board games use a pair of standard dice.

• How many possible outcomes are there when rolling a pair of standard dice?

• Suppose you are playing a game involving the sum of two dice. Do you think all sums are equally likely?

• Are there different outcomes that can produce a sum of 2?

• What about a sum of 7?

> **Action!**

The **theoretical probability** of an outcome is one based on analyzing all possible outcomes. Unlike experimental probability, no experiment is carried out. All possible outcomes combined make up the **sample space**. It is often useful to combine different outcomes that have something in common. An **event** occurs when any of these similar outcomes occur. For example, the dice pictured above show a sum of 7. But this is not the only outcome that can result in a sum of 7. What are some others?

If all outcomes are equally likely, then the theoretical probability of an event, A, is a measure of the ratio of the number of ways it can occur compared to the entire sample space. You can express this probability as a fraction, decimal, or percent.

theoretical probability

• probability based on analysis of all possible outcomes

• also called *classical probability*

sample space

• collection of all possible outcomes

• sometimes called *sample set*

event

• set of outcomes that have a common characteristic

Theoretical Probability

$$P(A) = \frac{n(A)}{n(S)}$$

where $P(A)$ is the probability that event A can occur, $n(A)$ is the number of ways it can occur, and $n(S)$ is the total number of possible outcomes in the sample space.

Investigate Outcomes and Events

1. This table illustrates the possible outcomes when two standard dice are thrown.

Materials
- 2 standard dice

a) Which sum or sums has the greatest theoretical probability? What is the value of this probability?

b) Which sum or sums has the lowest probability? What is the value of this probability?

2. What is the probability of rolling a 9 or greater?

3. **Open Question**

a) Create your own probability problem based on the data in the table.

b) Trade problems with a classmate and solve each other's problems. Compare your solutions.

4. **Reflect** Explain how the table in this investigation was useful for calculating theoretical probabilities.

5. **Extend Your Understanding** Suppose 8-sided dice were used instead, numbered 1 through 8. Would the theoretical probability of rolling each of the following sums increase, decrease, or stay the same? Explain your answers.

a) 2

b) 9

c) doubles

In the investigation, you used a table to represent the sample space of the probability experiment. You can also use tree diagrams and Venn diagrams to help organize the outcomes of a sample space. The choice of strategy to use often depends on the situation.

You can also represent a sample space and event of a probability experiment using set notation. Suppose, for example, that a number cube is rolled and the favourable event, A, is rolling an even number. The sample space is all six possible outcomes:

$S = \{1, 2, 3, 4, 5, 6\}$

The event of rolling an even number includes these three outcomes:

$A = \{2, 4, 6\}$

You can use a Venn diagram to represent this relationship visually.

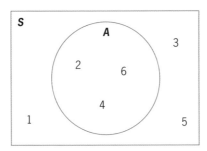

Example 1

Calculate Theoretical Probability

Fiona has two shirts and three pairs of pants that she can wear to her co-op placement.

a) Suppose Fiona randomly picks a shirt and a pair of pants. Identify the sample space for this probability experiment.

b) Fiona does not like to wear blue and green together, nor does she like orange and red together. What is the theoretical probability that she will randomly pick a shirt and pants combination that she does not like?

c) Suppose Fiona wants to decrease the probability of drawing a combination she does not like. If Fiona buys another pair of pants, which colour should she choose—green, white, or orange—and why?

Solution

a) Construct a tree diagram to organize all possible outcomes. Then analyse the results. Fiona has two shirts, which you can represent using two branches.

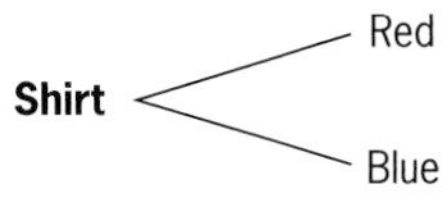

Shirt
- Red
- Blue

Fiona also has three pairs of pants, which you can represent using three branches.

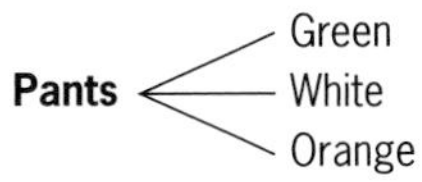

Pants
- Green
- White
- Orange

Combine these to illustrate all possible outcomes.

Shirt	Pants	Outcomes
Red	Green	Red, Green (RG)
	White	Red, White (RW)
	Orange	Red, Orange (RO)
Blue	Green	Blue, Green (BG)
	White	Blue, White (BW)
	Orange	Blue, Orange (BO)

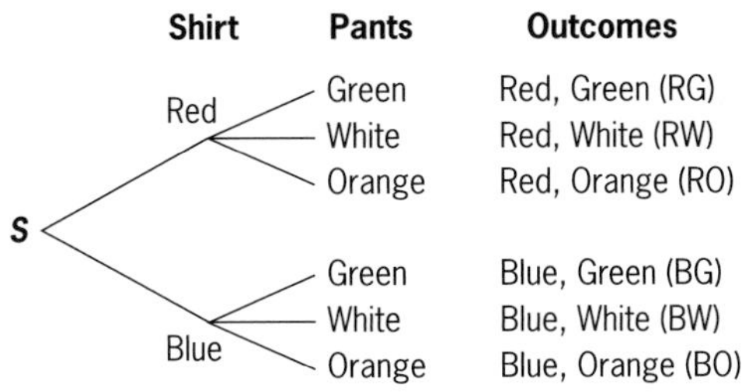

Read the sample space by following each branch in turn.

$S = \{$RG, RW, RO, BG, BW, BO$\}$

b) The sample space is all six possible outcomes. The event of drawing a combination Fiona does not like, C, consists of two outcomes: the red-orange combination and the blue-green combination.

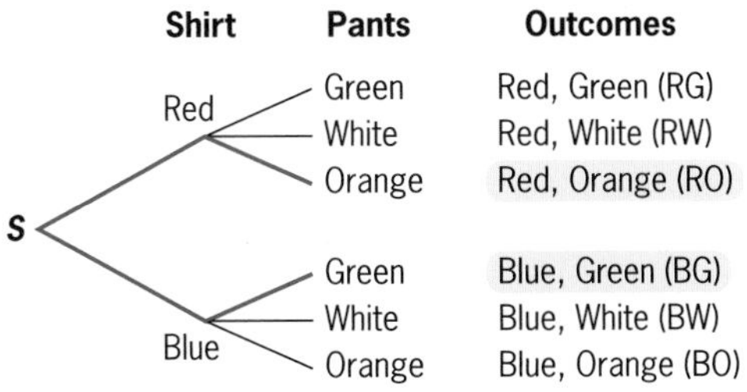

Shirt	Pants	Outcomes
Red	Green	Red, Green (RG)
	White	Red, White (RW)
	Orange	Red, Orange (RO)
Blue	Green	Blue, Green (BG)
	White	Blue, White (BW)
	Orange	Blue, Orange (BO)

The tree diagram shows two out of six possible outcomes resulting in a combination Fiona does not like.

$C = \{$BG, RO$\}$

The probability of having a combination Fiona does not like, $P(C)$, is

$$P(C) = \frac{n(C)}{n(S)}$$

$$= \frac{2}{6}$$

$$= \frac{1}{3}$$

Therefore, there is a $\frac{1}{3}$, or approximately 33%, theoretical probability that Fiona will randomly draw a combination she does not like.

c) If Fiona buys a fourth pair of pants from among the same colours that she already has, she should buy a pair that she can wear with all her shirts. Green and orange both produce a combination she does not like, but white does not. The tree diagram shows the sample space if she buys a second pair of white pants.

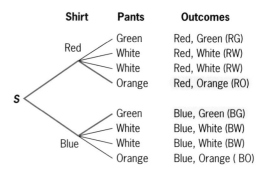

Shirt	Pants	Outcomes
Red	Green	Red, Green (RG)
	White	Red, White (RW)
	White	Red, White (RW)
	Orange	Red, Orange (RO)
Blue	Green	Blue, Green (BG)
	White	Blue, White (BW)
	White	Blue, White (BW)
	Orange	Blue, Orange (BO)

In this scenario, a combination she does not like can occur in two possible ways out of eight. Therefore, the probability of Fiona randomly drawing an outfit she does not like decreases from 33% to 25%.

Your Turn

Lee has a green hat, a black hat, and a grey hat. She also has green gloves, black gloves, and red gloves. In a hurry, Lee randomly grabs a hat and gloves. Determine the theoretical probability that the hat and gloves are the same colour.

Sometimes you need to know the probability that one event happens compared to all others. If one event is A, then the event A' is all of the possible outcomes not in A. This is known as the **complement** of A. Because the sum of all probabilities in a sample space must equal 1, there is a useful relationship between $P(A)$ and $P(A')$.

complement

• set of possible outcomes not included in an event

Literacy Link

The event A' is called "A prime."

$$P(A) + P(A') = 1$$

This relationship can be rearranged into two other useful forms.

$$P(A') = 1 - P(A) \quad \text{or} \quad P(A) = 1 - P(A')$$

Example 2

Probability of a Complement

Battleship is a game in which two opponents use a coordinate grid to try to guess the location of each other's ships.

Examine the board shown. Suppose a location is guessed at random.

a) What is the theoretical probability of hitting a ship on the first guess?

b) What is the probability of a miss on the first guess?

> Solution

a) Let A represent the event of hitting a ship.

Determine the number of locations covered by ships, $n(A)$.

$$n(A) = 2 + 3 + 3 + 4 + 5$$
$$= 17$$

The grid has dimensions 10 by 10. So, there are $n(S) = 100$ locations in total.

The probability of hitting a ship is

$$P(A) = \frac{n(A)}{n(S)}$$

$$= \frac{17}{100}$$

The theoretical probability of randomly hitting a ship on the first guess is 17%, or 0.17.

b) A random guess will result in either a hit, A, or a miss, A'. These are complementary events. One way to calculate the probability of missing the ships on the first guess is to count all locations not covered by a ship and divide by 100. A more efficient strategy, however, is to apply complementary reasoning.

$$P(A') = 1 - P(A)$$
$$= 1 - 0.17$$
$$= 0.83$$

Therefore, there is an 83% chance of randomly missing the ships.

Your Turn

A box contains 3 bran, 4 banana, 5 blueberry, and 3 carrot muffins. What is the theoretical probability that you will not randomly choose a blueberry muffin?

Processes

Representing
You can visually represent the relationship between A and A', as in the Venn diagram shown. The two regions combined make up the sample space representing all outcomes.

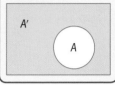

One application of probability, often used in sports, is odds. Odds can be expressed as the **odds in favour** of an event occurring or the **odds against** an event occurring. In sports it is actually more common to give the odds against something happening.

Odds

The odds in favour of $A = P(A) : P(A')$

The odds against $A = P(A') : P(A)$

Sports analysts often make predictions about a player's or team's chances for winning a tournament or championship. Often these predictions involve subjective probability based on the analyst's understanding of the player's or team's relative skill level.

odds in favour

• ratio of the probability that an event will happen to the probability that it will not

odds against

• ratio of the probability that an event will not happen to the probability that it will

Example 3

Odds of an Event

a) A hockey analyst gives the Canadian women's hockey team a 75% probability of winning the gold medal in the next Winter Olympics. Based on this prediction, what are the odds in favour of Canada winning Olympic gold?

b) A local sports journalist estimates that the high school boys' soccer team has a 40% probability of going to the OFSAA championship tournament. What are the odds against the boys making OFSAA?

Solution

a) The subjective probability of Canada winning the gold medal, $P(A)$, is given as 75%, or 0.75. The probability that Canada does not win is

$$P(A') = 1 - P(A)$$
$$= 1 - 0.75$$
$$= 0.25$$

Use the definition of odds to calculate the odds of Canada winning gold.

$$\frac{P(A)}{P(A')} = \frac{0.75}{0.25} \quad \text{How can you express as a ratio in lowest terms?}$$
$$= \frac{3}{1}$$
$$= 3:1$$

The odds in favour of the Canadian women's hockey team winning the gold medal at the next Winter Olympics are $3:1$, based on the analyst's estimate.

b) Let A represent the event that the boys' soccer team makes it OFSAA. The probability that the boys' team goes to OFSAA, $P(A)$, is 40%, or 0.4. The probability that the team does not make OFSAA is

$$P(A') = 1 - P(A)$$
$$= 1 - 0.4$$
$$= 0.6$$

Calculate the odds against the boys' team making the OFSAA tournament using the definition

$$P(A'):P(A) = 0.6:0.4$$
$$= 6:4 \qquad \text{Reduce to lowest terms.}$$
$$= 3:2$$

The odds against the high school boys' soccer team going to OFSAA are $3:2$.

Your Turn

a) A sports commentator claims that the Toronto Raptors have a 60% probability of making the playoffs. Based on this estimate, what are the odds in favour of the Raptors making the playoffs?

b) It is estimated that a golfer has a 20% chance of winning a tournament. What are the odds against this golfer winning the tournament?

Consolidate and Debrief

Key Concepts

- The theoretical probability of an event occurring is a measure of its likelihood based on analysis of all possible outcomes.

- The theoretical probability of an event is calculated by dividing the total number of favourable outcomes by the total number of outcomes in the sample space.

- The probability of the complement of an event is the probability that the event will not occur.

- The odds in favour of an event is the ratio of the probability that the event will happen to the probability that it will not happen.

- The odds against an event occurring is the ratio of the probability that the event will not occur to the probability that it will.

Reflect

R1. a) Describe how the terms outcome, event, and sample space are related in terms of theoretical probability. Use a diagram, mind map, or other visual organizer to support your explanation.

    b) Create an example that illustrates your answer to a).

R2. a) Explain how an event is related to its complement.

    b) Create an example of an event and its complement, and determine their theoretical probabilities.

R3. a) What does odds in favour of an event mean?

    b) What does odds against an event mean?

    c) How are these concepts similar? How are they different?

Practise

Choose the best answer for #1 to #3.

1. Yuri is playing a card game. He will lose if he draws a face card (J, Q, or K) from a full deck of standard playing cards. What is the theoretical probability that Yuri will win his first draw?

   A 6%   **B** 9%

   C 23%   **D** 77%

2. A weather forecast predicts a 33% chance of rain tomorrow. What are the odds in favour of it raining tomorrow?

   A 1:2   **B** 1:3

   C 2:1   **D** 3:1

3. Susie is drawing toothpicks with four co-workers to see who will go on a snack run. What are the odds against Susie having to go get the snacks?

   A 1:4   **B** 1:5

   C 4:1   **D** 5:1

Apply

4. Two standard dice are thrown. Determine the theoretical probability that the sum is

   a) 4   **b)** 7

   c) an even number   **d)** not a 6

   e) not a perfect square

5. A drawer contains 3 black socks, 1 white sock, and 2 grey socks, all of the same style. Two socks are chosen from the drawer at random.

   a) Describe the sample space using set notation.

   b) Use set notation to show the different ways of choosing two socks that are the same colour.

   c) What is the theoretical probability that two randomly chosen socks will be the same colour?

   d) What are the odds in favour of two randomly chosen socks being the same colour?

6. In a lab study of learned behaviours, monkeys are taught to reach into a box and randomly choose a shape from the ones shown. If the monkey chooses any shape that is not red, he gets a reward. If he chooses a red shape, he gets nothing. By monitoring the monkey's behaviour as several trials are carried out, scientists can see whether there is any evidence that the monkey is able to recognize red.

   a) Determine the theoretical probability that the monkey will be rewarded on any given trial, assuming that he randomly chooses a shape.

   b) Determine the theoretical probability that the monkey in this example does not randomly choose a star.

7. **Communication** Refer to #6. Suppose that after several trials, the experiment is modified to allow the monkey to look into the box while choosing a shape. The table shows the results.

Colour Chosen	Count
Red	2
Not red	58

   a) Determine the experimental probability that the monkey will choose a red shape.

   b) Determine the experimental probability of the complementary event.

   c) What might this suggest to the science researchers? Explain your reasoning.

8. Emily estimates that the odds against Paulo asking her to the prom are 4:1.

   a) What type of probability is Emily applying?

   b) What is the probability that Paulo will ask Emily to the prom, based on her estimate?

9. Chelsea is trying out for her school play. Using subjective probability, she estimates that she has an 80% chance of getting a part and a 25% probability of landing a lead role.

   a) What are the odds in favour of Chelsea getting a part in the play?

   b) What are the odds against her landing a lead role?

✔ Achievement Check

10. Kwon is answering four true or false questions on a quiz. Assume that he randomly guesses each answer.

   a) Draw a tree diagram to illustrate all possible outcomes.

   b) What is the theoretical probability that he gets

   • all four correct?
   • exactly three correct?
   • fewer than two correct?
   • not all incorrect?

11. **Communication** Use a form of electronic (e.g., Internet) or print (e.g., newspaper) media to find an example in which the term "odds" is used. Describe the context and interpret the meaning of the information in terms of probability.

12. **Thinking** Puddles the frog is jumping around in Halls Lake. Sometimes she lands on a lily pad, and sometimes she falls into the water. Assume that on her next jump Puddles is equally likely to land anywhere in the square region shown below, including on top of the lily pad.

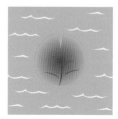

   a) Estimate the theoretical probability that Puddles will land on the lily pad.

   b) How many more times is she likely to fall into the water instead?

13. **Thinking** Suppose there are k possible outcomes to a certain probability experiment, all equally likely. Use algebraic reasoning to prove that the sum of the theoretical probabilities for all possible outcomes for this experiment must equal 1.

14. **Communication** A panel of hockey analysts gives 8 to 1 odds against the Montréal Canadiens winning the Stanley Cup and 17 to 2 odds against the Vancouver Canucks winning the Cup. Based on this information, which team is more likely to win the Stanley Cup? Explain your reasoning.

15. **Communication** A TV reporter states that "The chances of the Ottawa Senators winning against the Vancouver Canucks are 3 : 1 because they have won only one of their three meetings so far this year."

   a) Describe the mathematical errors made by this reporter.

   b) Reword the statement so it is mathematically correct.

Extend

16. **Application**

   a) A fair coin is tossed n times. Determine an algebraic formula that will give the theoretical probability that all tosses will result in heads.

   b) Use the formula to determine the theoretical probability of tossing 10 heads in a row.

17. **Thinking**

   a) Explain how the odds in favour of an event occurring is related to the odds against the event occurring.

   b) Provide an example to illustrate your answer.

   c) Use algebraic reasoning to prove your answer to a).

1.3

Compare Experimental and Theoretical Probabilities

Learning Goal

I am learning to

* recognize the difference between experimental probability and theoretical probability

> ## Minds On...

Have you ever wondered what it would be like to fly in space? Not many people get the opportunity to do that, but technology can be used to simulate the real experience. In fact, astronauts spend far more time preparing in a flight simulator than they actually do in space. What other types of simulators have you heard about?

> **Literacy Link**
>
> A *simulator* is a tool or machine that can be used to provide a sensation that is close to a real experience.

> ## Action!

Technology can also be used to simulate a probability experiment, such as flipping a coin or rolling a pair of dice. This is particularly useful when carrying out a large number of trials. Flipping a coin 1000 times seems rather tedious when a graphing calculator or a computer program can simulate the task in a matter of seconds.

Investigate 1 Three-Coin-Flip Simulation

Materials

* coins
* graphing calculator with Probability Simulation application or
* computer with spreadsheet software

In this activity you will compare the experimental probability to the theoretical probability when three fair coins are flipped.

1. Draw a tree diagram to show all possible outcomes. Examine the sample space. How many possible outcomes are there?

2. What is the theoretical probability that there will be:
   a) exactly three heads
   b) exactly two heads
   c) exactly one head
   d) no heads

3. Choose one of the following three methods to conduct this simulation for a large number of trials.

Method 1: Use a Graphing Calculator

a) • Press **APPS** and choose **Prob Sim**.
   • From the main menu choose **1. Toss Coins**.

Note that you will be using the graphing calculator keys along the top row for a number of the menu choices.

 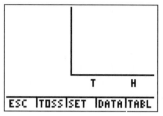

b) • Choose **SET** by pressing the **ZOOM** key and change the number of coins from 1 to 3.
   • Choose **OK**.

 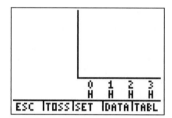

   • Choose **TOSS** by pressing the **WINDOW** key to simulate one trial.

c) Repeat for a few trials and note how the results are tallied in the bar graph. Based on the theoretical probability values calculated earlier, create a sketch of what this bar graph should look like after a large number of trials are carried out.

d) Carry out 100 trials. Here are some helpful tips:
   • Use **+10** or **+50** to conduct 10 or 50 trials at a time.
   • Use the left ← and right → arrows to inspect the frequencies of each outcome.
   • Choose **ESC** and then **TBL** to check the total number of trials carried out.
   • Choose **GRPH** to return and conduct more trials.

How does the graph compare to the theoretical prediction?

e) Carry out 1000 trials. Describe how the bar graph changes.

Method 2: Use a Spreadsheet

a) Open a spreadsheet and label eight columns as shown.

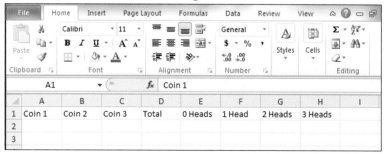

Processes

Selecting Tools and Computational Strategies and Representing

In this simulation, the spreadsheet randomly generates an integer between 0 and 1.

A 1 represents heads, and a 0 represents tails.

What does the sum of any row of columns A to C represent?

b) Program the spreadsheet to simulate three coin tosses:
- Type the following in cell A2: =RANDBETWEEN(0,1)
- Copy the contents of cell A2 into cells B2 and C2.

c) Program the spreadsheet to calculate the total number of heads for a given trial:
- Type the following in cell D2: =SUM(A2:C2)

d) Carry out 10 trials:
- Highlight cells A2 to D2.
- Drag the small square in the bottom right corner of D2 down to cell D11.

e) Program the spreadsheet to count the number of heads in each trial. For example, type "=COUNTIF(D:D,0)" into E2 to count how many trials included 0 heads. Use this command for counting 0, 1, 2, or 3 heads.
- Type the following in cell E2: =COUNTIF(D:D,0)
- Type the following in cell F2: =COUNTIF(D:D,1)
- Type the following in cell G2: =COUNTIF(D:D,2)   What do these
- Type the following in cell H2: =COUNTIF(D:D,3)   commands do?

f) Create a bar graph to represent the frequency of each outcome:
- Highlight cells E1 to H2.
- Choose the **Insert** tab.
- From the **Column** menu, choose **Clustered Column**.

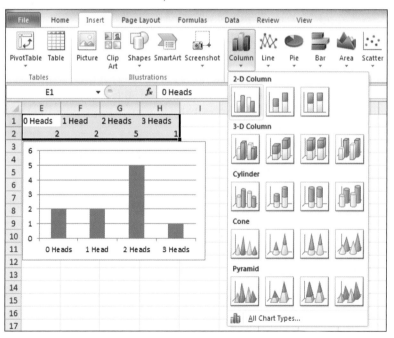

Processes

Reflecting

Why is it necessary to go to row 101? Why not row 100?

g) Carry out 100 trials:
- Highlight cells A11 to D11.
- Click and drag the bottom corner of cell D11 to cell D101.
  How does the graph compare to the theoretical prediction?

h) Carry out 1000 trials. Describe how the bar graph changes.

Method 3: Combine Real Trials

a) Flip three coins 10 times. Determine the experimental probability of each outcome based on these 10 trials. Compare these values with the theoretical probabilities calculated in #2 above. How close are they?

b) Combine trials with your classmates until you have 100 trials in total. Sketch a bar graph of the results. How does the graph compare to the theoretical prediction?

c) Combine with your classmates' data from part b) to carry out 1000 trials and sketch a new graph. Describe how the bar graph changes as the number of trials increases.

4. Reflect Explain what happens to the statistical probabilities of this experiment as the total number of trials increases.

5. Extend Your Understanding Suppose this experiment were modified to include five coins, instead of three.

a) Do you think it would take more, fewer, or about the same number of trials for the statistical probabilities of the outcomes to match the theoretical probabilities? Explain your reasoning.

b) Design and carry out this experiment and write a brief report of your findings.

Investigate 2 Dice Simulation

The table below illustrates all possible outcomes for the sum of the dice when two standard dice are thrown.

Materials

- 2 dice
- graphing calculator with Probability Simulation application or
- computer with Fathom™

	Outcome	Die 1					
		⚀	⚁	⚂	⚃	⚄	⚅
Die 2	⚀	2	3	4	5	6	7
	⚁	3	4	5	6	7	8
	⚂	4	5	6	7	8	9
	⚃	5	6	7	8	9	10
	⚄	6	7	8	9	10	11
	⚅	7	8	9	10	11	12

1. What is the theoretical probability of rolling each sum?

2. Sketch a bar graph showing the theoretical probability of rolling each sum.

3. Choose one of the following three methods to conduct this experiment for a large number of trials.

Method 1: Use a Graphing Calculator

a) • Press **APPS** and choose **Prob Sim**.
  • From the main menu choose **2. Roll Dice**.

b) • Choose **SET** by pressing the **ZOOM** key and change the number of dice from 1 to 2.
  • Choose **OK**.

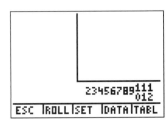

c) Carry out more trials, 50 at a time, and describe how the graph is changing. Keep adding more trials until the statistical probabilities look very similar to the theoretical probabilities.
  • Choose **ROLL** to carry out one trial.
  • Use **+10** and **+50** to carry out several trials at a time.

Method 2: Use Fathom™

a) Open Fathom™ and create a new collection by dragging the **Collection Box** into the workspace.

b) Create the dice simulation:
  • Double click on **Collection 1** to open the **Inspector**.
  • In the Attribute column, enter "Die_1", "Die_2", and "Sum" as shown.
  • Double click under **Formula** and type the following for each die and then choose **OK**:
    randomInteger(1,6)   What do these commands do?
  • Enter the formula for **SUM** as follows:
    – Click on **Attributes**.
    – Double click on **Die_1**.
    – Click on the **+** key.
    – Double click on **Die_2** and choose **OK**.

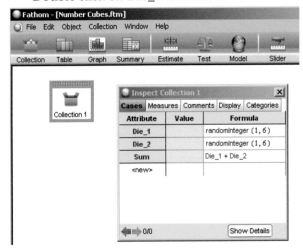

c) Simulate 10 trials:
- Right click on **Collection 1**.
- From the Collection menu, choose **New Cases**.
- Type 10 and choose **OK**.

Use the left and right arrows in the **Inspector** to view the outcomes.

d) Construct a bar graph to illustrate the outcomes:
- Click and drag a **Graph** into the workspace.
- Click on the **Sum** attribute in the **Inspector** and drag it onto the horizontal axis of the graph.
- Click on **Dot Plot** and change the graph to **Histogram**.

e) Conduct several trials. From the **Collection** menu, choose **New Cases**. Enter 90 and click **OK** to generate a total of 100 cases. Describe how the shape of the graph has changed.

f) Add new cases, 100 at time, and describe how the graph changes Keep adding cases until the statistical probabilities look very similar to the theoretical probabilities. How many cases did you have to use?

Literacy Link

A *histogram* shows the distribution of outcomes in an experiment. Although a histogram looks similar to a bar graph, it represents continuous data, so the bars are always placed side by side. You will learn more about histograms and their uses later in this course.

Method 3: Combine Real Trials

a) Roll two dice 10 times. Determine the experimental probability for each event. Are the statistical probabilities for these trials very useful? Explain why or why not.

b) Combine trials with your classmates until you have 100 trials in total. Sketch a bar graph of the results. How does the graph compare to the theoretical prediction?

c) Combine with your classmates' data from part b) to carry out 1000 trials and sketch a new graph. Describe how the bar graph is changing as the number of trials increases.

4. Reflect Explain what happens to the statistical probabilities of this experiment as the total number of trials increases.

5. Reflect Approximately how many trials did it take before the statistical probabilities closely agreed with the theoretical probabilities? Why do you think this is so?

6. Extend Your Understanding How would the outcomes of this experiment change if you used three dice instead of two? Design and carry out an experiment to find out. Describe your findings.

Project Prep

If your project involves probability, what elements of statistical, subjective, or theoretical probability could be relevant? Which tools and strategies could be useful for comparing experimental probability and theoretical probability?

Key Concepts

- Probability experiments can be carried out using physical materials or technology-based simulations. Technology-based simulations are useful for carrying out very large numbers of trials.

- Experimental probability approaches theoretical probability as a very large number of trials are conducted.

Reflect

R1. Why is theoretical probability not a perfect predictor of the outcome of a probability experiment? Why is experimental probability not a perfect predictor of the outcome of a probability experiment?

R2. Why is it usually necessary to conduct a very large number of trials in order for experimental probability to reasonably agree with theoretical probability?

Practise

Choose the best answer for #1 and #2.

1. A die is rolled once and turns up a 4. Which statement is true about rolling a 3?

   A The experimental probability is 0 and the theoretical probability is $\frac{1}{6}$.

   B The experimental probability is 1 and the theoretical probability is $\frac{1}{6}$.

   C The experimental probability is $\frac{1}{6}$ and the theoretical probability is $\frac{1}{6}$.

   D The experimental probability is 1 and the theoretical probability is 1.

2. Which of the following statements is true?

   A Experimental probability is always equal to theoretical probability.

   B Experimental probability approaches theoretical probability when a very large number of trials are carried out.

   C Experimental probability is always a more reliable predictor than theoretical.

   D Theoretical probability is always a more reliable predictor than experimental.

Apply

3. **Application**

   a) Use the *Spin Spinner* simulation in the graphing calculator Probability Simulator to construct a mystery spinner:
   - From the main menu, choose **4. Spin Spinner**.
   - Choose **SET**. Design your spinner
   - Choose **ADV**. Change the probability values. Note that the sum of these values must equal 1.
   - Choose **OK** twice.

   b) Trade with a classmate. Work with your partner's mystery spinner. Look at the spinner. Estimate the theoretical probability of each outcome.

   c) Carry out several trials to determine the experimental probability of each outcome. When you are confident that you have solved the mystery spinner, check the spinner's design by choosing **SET** and then **ADV**.

4. Application

a) Use the *Pick Marbles* simulation in the graphing calculator Probability Simulator to construct a mystery bag of marbles.
 - From the main menu, choose **3. Pick Marbles**.
 - Choose **SET**. Design your mystery bag.

b) Trade with a classmate. Try to guess each other's mystery bag using experimental probability.

5. Suppose you rolled two 8-sided dice, each having values from 1 to 8 on their faces.

a) What sums are possible? What is the theoretical probability of rolling each sum?

b) Sketch a bar graph showing the theoretical probability of rolling each sum.

c) Conduct a large number of trials of this probability experiment using a simulation tool or strategy of your choice. Discuss how the statistical and theoretical probabilities compare over:
 - a few trials
 - a very large number of trials

d) About how many trials did it take for the statistical and theoretical probability values to agree closely?

✓ **Achievement Check**

6. Two fair coins are tossed at the same time.

a) Identify the sample space that represents all possible outcomes.

b) Determine the theoretical probability of
 - no heads
 - exactly one head
 - two heads

c) Draw a bar graph that predicts how the statistical probabilities for a large number of trials will look.

d) Use a technology-based simulation tool to carry out a very large number of trials.

e) Compare the resulting graph to the one you drew in c). How close are they? How many trials did you use to get them to look very similar?

7. Open Question

a) Design a probability experiment involving coins and/or dice. Determine the theoretical probability of each event.

b) Use a simulation tool or other strategy to carry out a very large number of trials.

c) Describe the trend behaviour of the statistical probabilities as the number of trials increases.

8. Thinking Two dice are thrown and the sum is recorded.

a) If 20 trials are carried out, is it possible for the statistical probabilities of each value to be equal to the corresponding theoretical probabilities? Explain why or why not.

b) What is the minimum number of trials necessary for statistical and theoretical probability values to perfectly agree in this case? Justify your answer.

Extend

9. Thinking

a) Choose one of the graphing calculator probability simulations that was not explored in this section. Briefly describe what it simulates.

b) Create and solve a probability problem that can be done with this simulation.

c) Trade with a classmate and solve each other's problems.

10. Open Question

a) Find an online probability simulator on the Internet. Briefly explain what it does.

b) What are some things you like about this simulator?

c) What are some things you wish it did better?

Mutually Exclusive and Non-Mutually Exclusive Events

Learning Goal

I am learning to

- describe how an event can represent a set of probability outcomes
- recognize how different events are related
- calculate the probability of an event occurring

> ## Minds On...

Playing cards has been a popular source of entertainment for hundreds of years. Simple games such as Snap and Crazy Eights can be easily learned by young children. More complex strategy-based games such as bridge can be more challenging.

- What are some card games that you have heard of?
- What makes them interesting or fun to play?
- How are the games related to probability?

Literacy Link

Unless otherwise noted, we will use the term "probability" to refer to *theoretical* probability from this point onward.

> ## Action!

Investigate Counting Cards

Materials

- standard deck of playing cards
- Venn diagram

A standard deck of playing cards is represented below.

A♣ 2♣ 3♣ 4♣ 5♣ 6♣ 7♣ 8♣ 9♣ 10♣ J♣ Q♣ K♣
A♦ 2♦ 3♦ 4♦ 5♦ 6♦ 7♦ 8♦ 9♦ 10♦ J♦ Q♦ K♦
A♠ 2♠ 3♠ 4♠ 5♠ 6♠ 7♠ 8♠ 9♠ 10♠ J♠ Q♠ K♠
A♥ 2♥ 3♥ 4♥ 5♥ 6♥ 7♥ 8♥ 9♥ 10♥ J♥ Q♥ K♥

1. a) How many cards are clubs?

  b) How many cards are spades?

2. Add the answers to 1a) and 1b).

3. Create a Venn diagram by placing or listing all of the cards that are either a club or a spade.

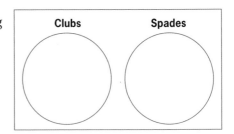

4. How many total cards are in the Venn diagram?

5. Reflect Are the answers to step 2 and step 4 the same? Explain why or why not.

6. a) How many cards are diamonds?

  b) How many cards are face cards?

7. Add the answers to 6a) and 6b).

8. Create a Venn diagram by placing or listing all of the cards that are a diamond, a face card, or both.

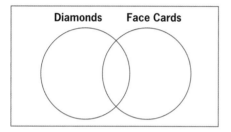

Processes

Selecting Tools and Computational Strategies
How is a Venn diagram useful for comparing the attributes of cards?

9. How many total cards are in the Venn diagram?

10. Reflect Are the answers to step 7 and step 9 the same? Explain why or why not.

11. Extend Your Understanding

  a) Determine the probability of randomly drawing either a club or a spade from a standard deck of cards.

  b) Determine the probability of randomly drawing either a diamond or a face card.

  c) Explain your methods.

Literacy Link

Unless otherwise noted, we will use the term "probability" to refer to *theoretical* probability from this point onward.

When calculating the probability of either one event happening or another happening, it is important to carefully count the outcomes. This is relatively easy to do when the events have completely different characteristics. Such events are said to be **mutually exclusive events**, because you can have either one event or the other, but not both.

When you flip a coin, it comes up either heads or tails. It cannot be both. Similarly, a newborn is either a boy or a girl. When a card is drawn from a standard deck of cards, it will be a club, a diamond, a heart, or a spade. All of these are examples of mutually exclusive events.

mutually exclusive events

- events that have different attributes
- cannot occur simultaneously

Example 1

Probability of Mutually Exclusive Events

A picnic basket of sandwiches contains 3 ham, 2 turkey, 1 chicken, and 4 egg salad sandwiches. What is the probability of reaching in and randomly choosing either a ham or an egg salad sandwich?

Solution

Method 1: Examine the Sample Space

Use a Venn diagram to illustrate all possible outcomes. The favourable outcomes are H or E.

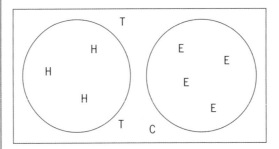

There are 7 out of 10 favourable outcomes. The probability of randomly choosing a ham or an egg salad sandwich is

$$P(H \text{ or } E) = \frac{7}{10}$$
$$= 70\%$$

Method 2: Add the Probabilities

Determine the probability of each favourable event and add them together. There are 3 ham sandwiches and 4 egg salad sandwiches, out of a total of 10.

$$P(H) = \frac{3}{10} \text{ and } P(E) = \frac{4}{10}$$

Add the probabilities.

$$P(H) + P(E) = \frac{3}{10} + \frac{4}{10}$$
$$= \frac{7}{10}$$
$$= 70\%$$

Therefore, the probability of randomly drawing a ham or an egg salad sandwich is 70%.

Your Turn

A cooler contains the following juice bottles: 3 orange, 5 apple, 3 citrus blend, and 4 grape. What is the probability of reaching in and randomly choosing an apple or grape juice?

The second method used in Example 1 shows the additive principle for mutually exclusive events. You can use algebraic reasoning to show that this method is valid for any such situation. In Method 1, all favourable events were counted and divided by the total number of possible outcomes:

$$P(A \text{ or } B) = \frac{n(A \text{ or } B)}{n(S)}$$

In how many ways can A or B occur?

$$= \frac{n(A) + n(B)}{n(S)}$$

$$= \frac{n(A)}{n(S)} + \frac{n(B)}{n(S)}$$

Write as separate fractions and apply the definition of probability.

$$= P(A) + P(B)$$

This result represents the approach that was used in Method 2.

Additive Principle (Rule of Sum) for Mutually Exclusive Events

The probability of either of two mutually exclusive events, A or B, is:

$$P(A \text{ or } B) = P(A) + P(B)$$

Literacy Link

In this resource, we will call the additive principle the *rule of sum*.

Example 2

Apply the Rule of Sum for Mutually Exclusive Events

A number of actors have starred as James Bond over the years. The table summarizes Rolly's Bond movie collection, tallied by actor.

Actor	Number of Movies
Sean Connery	6
George Lazenby	1
Roger Moore	7
Timothy Dalton	2
Pierce Brosnan	4
Daniel Craig	2

Sometimes Rolly likes to pick a Bond movie to watch at random. What is the probability that Rolly will randomly pick either a Connery, C, or a Dalton, D, film from his shelf?

Solution

There are two favourable outcomes. Determine their probabilities and apply the rule of sum for mutually exclusive events. There are 22 movies in total. Therefore:

$$P(C) = \frac{n(C)}{n(S)} \qquad\qquad P(D) = \frac{n(D)}{n(S)}$$

$$= \frac{6}{22} \qquad\qquad\qquad = \frac{2}{22} \qquad \text{Why should these fractions be left unreduced?}$$

Add the probabilities of the two favourable outcomes:

$$\begin{aligned} P(C \text{ or } D) &= P(C) + P(D) \\ &= \frac{6}{22} + \frac{2}{22} \\ &= \frac{8}{22} \\ &= 0.3636\ldots \end{aligned}$$

The probability of Rolly randomly picking a Connery or a Dalton movie is approximately 36%.

Your Turn

What is the probability that Rolly will randomly pick either a Brosnan or a Moore movie?

In some situations, it is possible for different events to occur simultaneously. For example, in a standard deck of cards, let $n(D)$ represent the number of diamonds and $n(F)$ represent the number of face cards.

A♣ 2♣ 3♣ 4♣ 5♣ 6♣ 7♣ 8♣ 9♣ 10♣ J♣ Q♣ K♣
A♦ 2♦ 3♦ 4♦ 5♦ 6♦ 7♦ 8♦ 9♦ 10♦ J♦ Q♦ K♦
A♠ 2♠ 3♠ 4♠ 5♠ 6♠ 7♠ 8♠ 9♠ 10♠ J♠ Q♠ K♠
A♥ 2♥ 3♥ 4♥ 5♥ 6♥ 7♥ 8♥ 9♥ 10♥ J♥ Q♥ K♥

From the diagram, $n(D) = 13$ and $n(F) = 12$. Adding these gives

$$\begin{aligned} n(D) + n(F) &= 13 + 12 \\ &= 25 \end{aligned}$$

non-mutually exclusive events

- different events that can happen at the same time

This sum includes three cards that belong to both sets, J♦, Q♦, and K♦, which have been counted twice. This represents an example of **non-mutually exclusive events**.

A♣ 2♣ 3♣ 4♣ 5♣ 6♣ 7♣ 8♣ 9♣ 10♣ J♣ Q♣ K♣
A♦ 2♦ 3♦ 4♦ 5♦ 6♦ 7♦ 8♦ 9♦ 10♦ J♦ Q♦ K♦
A♠ 2♠ 3♠ 4♠ 5♠ 6♠ 7♠ 8♠ 9♠ 10♠ J♠ Q♠ K♠
A♥ 2♥ 3♥ 4♥ 5♥ 6♥ 7♥ 8♥ 9♥ 10♥ J♥ Q♥ K♥

To obtain the correct number of diamonds and face cards, subtract the three cards that were counted twice from the sum found above:

$$25 - 3 = 22$$

This counting strategy is known as the principle of inclusion and exclusion.

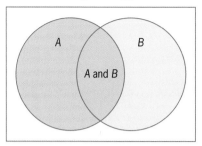

Literacy Link

When counting outcomes from different sets, the following notation is sometimes used:

The *union set*, $n(A \cup B)$, is the combined set of elements contained in either sets A or B.

The *intersection set*, $n(A \cap B)$, is the overlapping set of elements contained in both sets A and B.

Principle of Inclusion and Exclusion

If A and B are non-mutually exclusive events, then the total number of favourable outcomes is:

$n(A \text{ or } B) = n(A) + n(B) - n(A \text{ and } B)$

Example 3

Principle of Inclusion and Exclusion

In a room with 30 students, 10 play basketball and 15 play volleyball. If 7 students play both sports, what is the probability that a student chosen at random plays basketball or volleyball?

Solution

Apply the principle of inclusion and exclusion to count the number of students who play basketball $n(B)$ or volleyball $n(V)$. Then divide by the total number of students, $n(S)$.

$$\begin{aligned} n(B \text{ or } V) &= n(B) + n(V) - n(B \text{ and } V) \\ &= 10 + 15 - 7 \\ &= 18 \end{aligned}$$

The probability of randomly choosing a basketball or volleyball player is

$$\begin{aligned} P(B \text{ or } V) &= \frac{n(B \text{ or } V)}{n(S)} \\ &= \frac{18}{30} \\ &= \frac{3}{5} \end{aligned}$$

Therefore, there is a $\frac{3}{5}$, or 60%, probability of choosing a basketball player or volleyball player.

Your Turn

Miranda is part of a gift exchange with 24 other family members and friends. Of the 24 family members, 10 like to ski, 12 like to cycle, and 6 like to ski and cycle. If Miranda randomly draws a name, what is the probability that she will pick someone who likes to ski or cycle?

To calculate the probability of two non-mutually exclusive events, A and B, add the probability of each event and subtract the probability of both events occurring simultaneously.

Probability of Non-Mutually Exclusive Events

The probability of either of two non-mutually exclusive events, A or B, is:

$$P(A \text{ or } B) = P(A) + P(B) - P(A \text{ and } B)$$

Example 4

Probability of Non-Mutually Exclusive Events

The playing tokens and their characteristics for a role-playing game are shown below.

	Dragon	Hawk	Knight	Lion	Princess	Witch	Wizard	Unicorn
Human			✔		✔	✔	✔	
Animal	✔	✔		✔				✔
Supernatural	✔					✔	✔	✔
Can fly	✔	✔				✔		
Can cast spells						✔	✔	

If Jozo is randomly assigned a playing token, what is the probability that it will be either an animal or a supernatural creature?

Solution

Calculate the probability that Jozo randomly picks an animal or a supernatural creature by applying either the probability of non-mutually exclusive events or the principle of inclusion and exclusion.

There are 4 animals: dragon, hawk, lion, and unicorn. There are 8 tokens in total.

$$P(A) = \frac{4}{8}$$
$$= \frac{1}{2}$$

There are 4 supernatural creatures: dragon, witch, wizard, and unicorn.

$$P(S) = \frac{4}{8}$$
$$= \frac{1}{2}$$

There are 2 supernatural animals: dragon and unicorn.

$$P(A \text{ and } S) = \frac{2}{8}$$
$$= \frac{1}{4}$$

The probability that Jozo will randomly choose an animal or a supernatural creature is

$$P(A \text{ or } S) = P(A) + P(S) - P(A \text{ and } S)$$
$$= \frac{1}{2} + \frac{1}{2} - \frac{1}{4}$$
$$= 1 - \frac{1}{4}$$
$$= \frac{3}{4}$$

Therefore, Jozo has a $\frac{3}{4}$, or 75%, probability of randomly picking an animal or a supernatural creature.

Your Turn

What is the probability that Jozo will randomly pick a flying creature or one that can cast spells?

Consolidate and Debrief

Key Concepts

- Mutually exclusive events cannot occur at the same time.
- To calculate the probability of either mutually exclusive events A or B occurring, use the additive principle (rule of sum) for mutually exclusive events:

  $$P(A \text{ or } B) = P(A) + P(B)$$

- Non-mutually exclusive events can occur at the same time.
- To calculate the number of outcomes included in non-mutually exclusive events A and B, use the principle of inclusion and exclusion:

  $$n(A \text{ or } B) = n(A) + n(B) - n(A \text{ and } B)$$

- To calculate the probability of either non-mutually exclusive events A or B occurring, use the additive principle for non-mutually exclusive events:

  $$P(A \text{ or } B) = P(A) + P(B) - P(A \text{ and } B)$$

R1. Copy and complete the Frayer model shown for the term "mutually exclusive events."

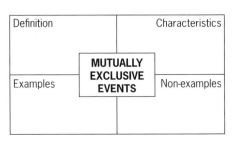

Definition		Characteristics
	MUTUALLY EXCLUSIVE EVENTS	
Examples		Non-examples

R2. a) What is the principle of inclusion and exclusion?

b) When and why is it important to use it?

R3. Provide an example of non-mutually exclusive events that are different from those already shown.

Practise

Choose the best answer for #1 and #2.

1. What is the probability of rolling a 3 or 4 using a standard die?

A $\frac{1}{6}$ **B** $\frac{1}{4}$ **C** $\frac{1}{3}$ **D** $\frac{1}{2}$

2. The card game euchre uses only the cards shown from a standard deck of playing cards.

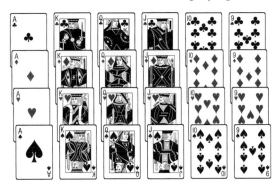

What is the probability of randomly drawing an ace or a king from a euchre deck of cards?

A $\frac{5}{12}$ **B** $\frac{1}{2}$ **C** $\frac{7}{12}$ **D** $\frac{1}{3}$

Apply

3. Communication Kara's shirt collection is shown below.

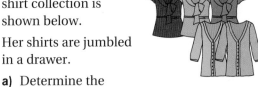

Her shirts are jumbled in a drawer.

a) Determine the probability that Kara randomly draws each of the following:
- a pink shirt or a purple shirt
- a pink shirt or a short-sleeved shirt

b) Which of the scenarios in a) represent:
- a mutually exclusive event?
- a non-mutually exclusive event?

Explain your answers.

4. Application Every Friday night, Rutger's family orders take-out. The table shows their ordering habits for the past several weeks.

Type of Food	Tally
Pizza	IIII
Mexican	II
Burgers	IIII
Chicken	III

Rutger's favourites are Mexican and chicken. What is the experimental probability that Rutger will get one of his favourites next Friday?

5. What is the probability of rolling a sum that is not a 7 or an 11 with a pair of dice?

6. Refer to the euchre deck of cards in #2.

a) Determine the probability of randomly drawing either an ace or a spade from the deck.

b) What is the probability of randomly drawing a red card or a diamond from the deck?

c) What is the probability of not drawing a face card or a club?

7. Refer to the euchre deck of cards in #2.

a) What is the probability of randomly drawing a 9 or a 10 or a diamond from the deck?

b) Explain how you solved this problem.

8. **Thinking** Deer Button is a game played by people of the Woodland Nations. Players use eight two-colour counters made from deer's antlers, like the ones shown below.

Players take turns throwing all eight deer buttons at the same time. They win beans according to this scoring table:

Number of Buttons of the Same Colour	Beans Awarded
8	10
7	4
6	2
other	0

a) Determine the probability that a player will score 10 points on a given throw.

b) What is the probability of scoring at least 4 points on a throw?

c) Explain how you solved this problem.

Achievement Check

9. Juliette puts these letter tiles into her handbag.

a) If Juliette then reaches into the handbag and randomly takes out one tile, determine the probability of each of the following occurring:
   • She chooses an "e" or a "t."
   • She chooses a red letter or an "e."
   • She chooses a capital letter or a vowel.
   • She does not choose a yellow letter or a "t."

b) Draw a Venn diagram to represent each scenario in part a).

c) **Open Question** Create a probability question using these tiles for which the answer is between 25% and 40%.

10. **Open Question** A bag contains three blue marbles and some other marbles. There is a 50% probability that a randomly chosen marble is either green or yellow.

a) What could the contents of the bag be?

b) Provide a different answer that is also correct.

11. **Thinking** Marie is playing a board game and can win if she rolls a sum of either 6 or 8 or doubles with a standard pair of dice. What are the odds against Marie winning on a given throw?

12. **Open Question** Create and solve a probability problem involving mutually exclusive events.

Extend

13. Use algebraic reasoning to prove that the probability of two non-mutually exclusive events, A and B, can be calculated using $P(A \text{ or } B) = P(A) + P(B) - P(A \text{ and } B)$.

14. **Application** Renzo knows that his first-semester timetable will include biology, chemistry, English, and a study period, but he does not know when each will occur during the day. Two periods run in the morning and two periods run in the afternoon. The time of day for each course does not change.

a) What is the probability that Renzo will have both science classes in the morning or both in the afternoon?

b) Explain how you solved this problem.

c) Discuss any assumptions you made in your solution.

15. **Thinking**

a) Use algebraic reasoning to develop the additive principle for three non-mutually exclusive events.

b) **Open Question** Design a question that can be solved using the result from part a). Then solve the problem.

1.5

Independent and Dependent Events

Learning Goal

I am learning to

- describe and determine how the probability of one event occurring can affect the probability of another event occurring
- solve probability problems involving multiple events

> ## Minds On...

Modern technology allows doctors to predict the gender of a baby long before it is born. Some parents like to know this information as soon as possible, while others prefer to keep it a surprise.

Look at the family pictured.

- Do you think having three boys and three girls is very likely?
- Do you think the gender of one birth will have an effect on the gender of a following birth? Why or why not?

When multiple events occur in a probability experiment, these events are called **compound events**.

compound events

- multiple events in a probability experiment
- may or may not affect each other

> ## Action!

Example 1

Simple Compound Events

a) The Archers currently have no children, but would like to have three children. Assuming that they do have three children and there is an equal probability of any birth resulting in a boy or a girl, what is the probability that they will all be boys?

b) The Burnell family has two sons. What is the probability that their third child will be a boy?

c) Why are the answers to a) and b) different?

> **Solution**

a) The sample space for the Archers is shown.

1st Child	2nd Child	3rd Child	Outcomes
		G	GGG
	G	B	GGB
G		G	GBG
	B	B	GBB
		G	BGG
	G	B	GBG
B		G	BBG
	B	B	BBB

Processes

Selecting Tools and Computational Strategies
A tree diagram is a useful way to clearly identify and organize all possible outcomes.

The tree diagram shows that there are eight possible outcomes, only one of which results in three boys. The probability of the Archers having three boys is

$$P(A) = \frac{n(A)}{n(S)}$$
$$= \frac{1}{8}$$

The probability that the Archers will have three boys is $\frac{1}{8}$, or 12.5%, assuming that they have three children.

b) Assume that there is an equal probability of any birth resulting in a boy or a girl. The fact that the Burnells already have two sons has no impact on the outcome of their third birth. The sample space for the gender of the third child is shown.

Therefore, the probability that the third Burnell child will be a boy is 50%.

c) The answers to a) and b) are different because they represent different situations. In the case of the Archers, the probability of multiple events is being considered. The Burnell case involves just a single event.

Your Turn

The Singh family currently has no children but hopes to have four children. Assuming they do have four children, what is the probability that they will all be girls?

independent events
• situations in which the occurrence or non-occurrence of one event has no influence on the probability of the other event occurring

Sometimes the probability of one event depends on whether another event occurs, and sometimes it does not. When one event has no effect on the probability of another, the events are **independent**.

Example 2

Probability of Independent Events

Olivia has four highlighting pens in her pencil case: two yellow, one orange, and one blue. She reaches into her pencil case and randomly chooses a highlighter. After she uses it, she immediately replaces it in the case so it can be used again. What is the probability that she will choose

a) two yellow highlighters in a row?

b) a yellow highlighter followed by a blue highlighter?

Solution

a) Use a tree diagram to illustrate all possible outcomes. Since the highlighters are replaced into the case immediately after being used, these are independent events.

Olivia can choose two yellow highlighters in a row 4 out of 16 ways. Therefore,

$$P(YY) = \frac{4}{16}$$

$$= \frac{1}{4}$$

The probability of Olivia choosing two yellow highlighters in a row is $\frac{1}{4}$.

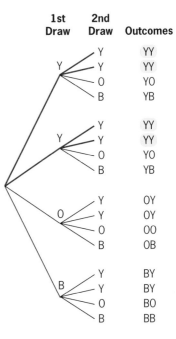

b) Inspect the tree diagram and identify the ways in which a yellow highlighter can be followed by a blue highlighter.

Olivia can choose a yellow highlighter followed by a blue highlighter in a row 2 out of 16 ways. Therefore,

$$P(YB) = \frac{2}{16}$$

$$= \frac{1}{8}$$

The probability of Olivia choosing a yellow highlighter followed by a blue highlighter is $\frac{1}{8}$.

1st Draw	2nd Draw	Outcomes
Y	Y	YY
	Y	YY
	O	YO
	B	YB
Y	Y	YY
	Y	YY
	O	YO
	B	YB
O	Y	OY
	Y	OY
	O	OO
	B	OB
B	Y	BY
	Y	BY
	O	BO
	B	BB

Your Turn

Three green marbles and two yellow marbles are placed into a bag. What is the probability of randomly drawing a green marble followed by a yellow marble, assuming that the first marble is replaced before the second marble is drawn?

Another way to determine the probability of compound independent events is to multiply the probability of the first event by the probability of the second event. In Example 2, the probability of Olivia choosing a yellow highlighter is 2 out of 4 or $\frac{1}{2}$, and the probability of choosing a blue highlighter is 1 out of 4 or $\frac{1}{4}$.

Using this method, the probability of choosing two yellow highlighters in a row is

$$P(YY) = \frac{1}{2} \times \frac{1}{2}$$
$$= \frac{1}{4}$$

Similarly, calculate the probability of choosing a yellow highlighter followed by a blue highlighter.

$$P(YB) = \frac{1}{2} \times \frac{1}{4}$$
$$= \frac{1}{8}$$

Note that these values agree with the ones obtained from analysing the tree diagram.

This result is an illustration of the multiplicative principle for independent events.

Literacy Link

In this resource, we will refer to the multiplicative principle as the *fundamental counting principle*. You will learn more about this principle in a later chapter.

> **Multiplicative Principle (Fundamental Counting Principle) for Independent Events**
>
> The probability of two independent events, A and B, occurring is
>
> $$P(A \text{ and } B) = P(A) \times P(B)$$

Example 3

Different Compound Events

A game is played in which a standard die is rolled and a spinner is spun.

Player A wins a point if the spinner lands on red and an even number is rolled. Player B wins a point if the spinner lands on yellow or green and a composite number is rolled. Is this a fair game? Explain.

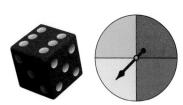

Solution

Assume that the spinner and the die are fair. Determine the probability of each player's winning compound event.

Player A wins a point if the spinner lands on red, R, and the die turns up even, E. Since one-quarter of the spinner area is red,

$$P(R) = \frac{1}{4}$$

Since three of six possible outcomes for a standard die are even,

$$P(E) = \frac{3}{6}$$
$$= \frac{1}{2}$$

The spinner and die results are independent events.

The compound probability of Player A winning a point, $P(A)$, is
$$\begin{aligned} P(A) &= P(R \text{ and } E) \\ &= P(R) \times P(E) \\ &= \frac{1}{4} \times \frac{1}{2} \\ &= \frac{1}{8} \end{aligned}$$

Player A has a $\frac{1}{8}$, or 12.5%, probability of winning a point on a given trial.

You can use a probability tree diagram to illustrate this solution.

Player B wins a point if the spinner lands on yellow or green, YG, and the die turns up a composite number, C. Since half of the spinner area is yellow or green,

$$P(YG) = \frac{1}{2}$$

There are two composite numbers on a die: 4 and 6. The probability of rolling a composite number is

$$P(C) = \frac{2}{6}$$
$$= \frac{1}{3}$$

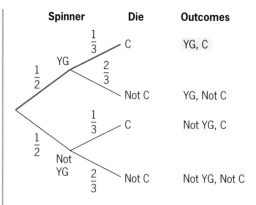

Since the spinner and die results are independent events, the compound probability of Player B winning a point, $P(B)$, is

$$P(B) = P(YG \text{ and } C)$$
$$= P(YG) \times P(C)$$
$$= \frac{1}{2} \times \frac{1}{3}$$
$$= \frac{1}{6}$$

Therefore, Player B has a $\frac{1}{6}$, or approximately 17%, probability of winning a point on a given trial. This game is not fair. Player B has an advantage over Player A, who has just a 12.5% probability of winning a point.

Your Turn

What is the probability of flipping heads with a fair coin and rolling a prime number with a fair die?

Sometimes the probability of one event occurring has an effect on another event occurring. When this happens, the events are said to be **dependent**.

dependent events

- the occurrence or non-occurrence of one event influences the probability of the other event occurring

Example 4

Probability of Dependent Events

Two red checkers and two black checkers are placed into a bag. What is the probability that a red checker is randomly chosen, followed by a second red checker, assuming that the first checker drawn is not replaced?

Solution

Let $P(R)$ represent the probability of choosing a red checker and $P(RR)$ represent the probability of choosing two consecutive red checkers. Two out of four checkers are red.

Therefore, $P(R) = \frac{1}{2}$.

1st Draw

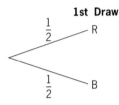

After the first checker is chosen, there will be three left.

In this case, the probability of choosing a second red checker, given that the first checker chosen was red, is $\frac{1}{3}$.

If the first checker chosen is black, then the bag will have three checkers.

In this case, given that the first checker chosen was black, the probability of drawing a red checker is $\frac{2}{3}$. Use these values to complete the probability tree diagram.

1st Draw	2nd Draw	Outcomes
$\frac{1}{2}$ R	$\frac{1}{3}$ R	R, R
	$\frac{2}{3}$ B	R, B
$\frac{1}{2}$ B	$\frac{2}{3}$ R	B, R
	$\frac{1}{3}$ B	B, B

To determine the probability of randomly choosing two consecutive red checkers, multiply the probabilities along the RR branch.

$$P(RR) = \frac{1}{2} \times \frac{1}{3}$$
$$= \frac{1}{6}$$

Therefore, there is a $\frac{1}{6}$, or approximately 17%, probability of randomly choosing a red checker followed by another red checker.

Your Turn

A bag contains two apples, one orange, and two peaches. Suppose Jelena reaches in and chooses a piece of fruit at random, and then selects another piece of fruit without replacing the first one. What is the probability that she will choose two peaches?

The previous example illustrates how the outcome of one trial can affect the probable outcome of a subsequent trial. When the first checker was chosen and not replaced the sample space was reduced, which changed the probability values for the second trial.

When the outcome of one trial has been determined, then the **conditional probability** of a subsequent trial can be calculated based on the result of the first trial. If the first event is A and the second event is B, then $P(B|A)$ represents the conditional probability that B will occur, given that A has occurred. To calculate the probability of both dependent events occurring, apply the multiplicative principle for dependent events.

conditional probability

- probability of a second event occurring, given that a first event occurred
- the sample space for the second event is reduced from the first event

Multiplicative Principle for Dependent Events

To calculate the probability of two dependent events, A and B, occurring, multiply the probability that A occurs by the conditional probability that B occurs, given that A occurred.

$P(A \text{ and } B) = P(A) \times P(B|A)$

Example 5

Conditional Probability in Telemarketing

A study of a telemarketing company's data showed that of 1000 calls placed:
- The experimental probability of a call receiver staying on the line for at least a minute was 16%.
- The conditional probability of a call resulting in a sale, given that a receiver stayed on the line for at least a minute, was 10%.
- No sales were made if the receiver did not stay on the line for at least a minute.

How many sales were made?

Solution

Construct a probability tree diagram to represent the data. There is a 16% experimental probability of having a long call, L, and therefore an 84% chance the caller will hang up, H.

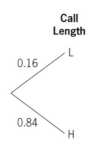

Call Length

If the caller hangs up early, the probability of a sale is 0. If the caller stays on the line, there is a 10% experimental probability of a sale. Add this information to the tree diagram.

Multiply the experimental probability that a customer stays on the line by the conditional probability that the call results in a sale, given that the customer stays on the line.

$$P(L \text{ and } \$) = P(L) \times P(\$|L)$$
$$= 0.16 \times 0.1$$
$$= 0.016$$

Therefore, there is a 0.016, or 1.6%, experimental probability that a random call will result in a sale. Use the definition of experimental probability to calculate the number of sales.

$$P(\$) = \frac{n(\$)}{n(S)}$$

where $n(\$)$ is the number of sales made and $n(S)$ is the total number of calls made. Solve for the unknown, $n(\$)$.

$$P(\$) \times n(S) = \frac{n(\$)}{n(S)} \times n(S) \qquad \text{Multiply both sides by } n(S).$$
$$n(\$) = P(\$) \times n(S) \qquad \text{Substitute and solve.}$$
$$= 0.016 \times 1000$$
$$= 16$$

Therefore, 16 sales were made from the 1000 calls that were studied.

Your Turn

Lars is offering juice samples at a shopping mall. The experimental probability of a randomly chosen shopper accepting a sample is 15%. The conditional probability of a customer purchasing some juice given that he or she tried a sample is 20%. No one purchases juice without trying a sample. If Lars offers 500 people juice samples, how many sales will he make?

Consolidate and Debrief

Key Concepts

- Compound events involve more than one event for a given trial of a probability experiment.

- Independent events have no influence on each other's probability of occurring.

- To calculate the probability of two independent events, A and B, both occurring, multiply the probability of each of them occurring:

  $$P(A \text{ and } B) = P(A) \times P(B)$$

- When the occurrence or non-occurrence of one event influences the probability of a second event occurring, the events are dependent.

- To calculate the probability of two dependent events, A and B, both occurring, multiply the probability of the first event occurring by the conditional probability of the second event occurring, given that the first event occurred:

  $$P(A \text{ and } B) = P(A) \times P(B|A)$$

Reflect

R1. a) What is the difference between independent events and dependent events?

  b) Provide an example of each.

R2. Which of the following scenarios is most likely to occur, and why?
  - a coin is flipped three times and comes up heads every time
  - after coming up heads four times, a coin comes up heads on the fifth toss

R3. a) Explain what is meant by conditional probability.

  b) Describe a situation in which conditional probability
   - applies
   - does not apply

R4. What are some advantages of using a probability tree diagram in solving problems involving dependent events?

Practise

Choose the best answer for #1 to #3.

1. A fair coin is flipped twice. What is the probability that it will come up heads followed by tails?

  A 0   **B** $\frac{1}{8}$ **C** $\frac{1}{4}$ **D** $\frac{1}{2}$

2. Hanna forgot to study for her math quiz. In the multiple-choice section there are two questions, each with four answer choices. If Hanna randomly guesses the answer to both questions, what is the probability that she will get them both correct?

  A 0%   **B** 6.25%   **C** 12.5%   **D** 25%

3. A fair coin is flipped twice. What is the probability that it will come up once heads and once tails, in either order?

   A 0

   B $\frac{1}{8}$

   C $\frac{1}{4}$

   D $\frac{1}{2}$

Apply

4. Two green tiles, one red tile, and a blue tile are put into a paper bag.

   a) What is the probability that a green tile is drawn, followed by a blue tile, assuming the first tile is replaced before the second tile is drawn?

   b) How does the answer to part a) change if the first tile drawn is not replaced?

   c) Explain why these answers are different.

5. **Thinking** Crazy Spinners is a game in which the two spinners below are spun at the same time.

   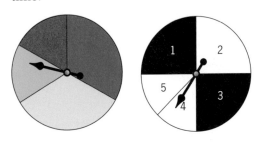

   a) Player A wins a point if the result is Red-1. Player B wins a point if the result is Blue-4. Is this a fair game? Explain.

   b) **Open Question** Change the rules so that this game is almost but not quite fair.

6. Kevin works in car sales. Over a period of time he spoke with 400 customers. The experimental probability of a customer going for a test drive was 20%. If a customer went for a test drive, there was a 5% conditional probability that Kevin made a sale. Assuming that Kevin did not make a sale if there was no test drive, how many sales did Kevin make over this time period?

7. **Application** While playing an online adventure game, Briony finds herself lost in the Maze of Misfortune, as shown below:

   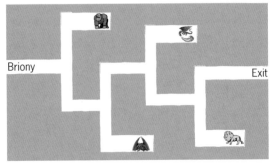

   Briony is being pursued and has no time to second-guess any of her path decisions.

   a) Assuming she has no knowledge of the maze, what is the probability that Briony will successfully escape the Maze of Misfortune?

   b) What is the conditional probability that Briony will successfully navigate the maze given that she makes

   • her first path decision correctly?
   • her first two path decisions correctly?

8. Refer to Rolly's James Bond movie collection from page 37.

Actor	Number of Movies
Sean Connery	6
George Lazenby	1
Roger Moore	7
Timothy Dalton	2
Pierce Brosnan	4
Daniel Craig	2

   Suppose Rolly randomly picks a movie to watch, and then randomly picks a second movie without putting the first movie back on the shelf. Determine the probability of each of the following scenarios:

   a) Rolly will watch a Connery movie followed by a Moore movie.

   b) Rolly will watch two consecutive Dalton movies.

   c) Rolly will watch three consecutive Craig movies.

9. Petra wants to borrow her dad's car on Saturday, but so does her brother Alek. They decide to play Rock-Paper-Scissors to settle the dispute. Petra decides to go with Rock.

a) What is the probability that she will win the car on the first trial?

b) Assuming Petra continues with Rock, how likely is Petra to win the car if she and Alek play until a winner is declared?

c) Explain why these answers are different.

d) Is there any single choice that gives an advantage over any other? Explain using probability. What assumptions did you make?

Literacy Link

Rock-Paper-Scissors is a game in which two opponents each make one of the hand signals shown at exactly the same time. The winner is declared as follows:

• Paper covers Rock: Paper wins
• Scissors cuts Paper: Scissors wins
• Rock smashes Scissors: Rock wins

If both players make the same signal, the result is a draw and another trial is conducted.

10. **Thinking** Siko is a contestant on a TV game show called *Win a Million*. Each time she answers a multiple-choice question correctly, she wins money. If she picks a wrong answer, she is eliminated. If Siko does not know the right answer, she can use one of the following Helping Hands:

• *Quiz the Crowd*: She can poll the audience. The crowd has an experimental probability of being correct 85% of the time.

• *Double Up*: She can give two answers, instead of just one. If either is correct she stays in the game.

• *Rule One Out*: One of the incorrect answers is removed, leaving three choices.

Suppose Siko encounters three questions in a row to which she does not know the answers.

a) Assuming that she can use each Helping Hand only once during the game, and only once per question, what is the best estimated probability Siko has of staying

alive through the three questions? What assumptions did you make.

b) How many more times is Siko likely to stay in the game if she uses all three Helping Hands than if she simply guesses at random on all three questions?

Extend

11. **Thinking** The Toronto Maple Leafs are facing the Montréal Canadiens in a best of seven playoff series. The first team to win four games wins the series. Ties are broken through sudden decision overtime. Assuming that the teams are evenly matched,

a) what are the odds in favour of either team sweeping the series, in which one team wins four consecutive games?

b) what are the odds against the series going a full seven games?

12. **Open Question** Refer to #11. How would your answers change if the teams were not very evenly matched? Pick one team as superior to the other to support your reasoning.

13. Suppose A and B are two dependent events. In general, will $P(A|B) = P(B|A)$? Use a bag of coloured tokens or an alternate scenario to illustrate your answer.

Processes

Reasoning and Proving
Can you use algebraic reasoning to prove that something is true? Can you use a counter-example to prove that something is not true?

14. **Application** In business, a common planning strategy is to use a decision tree.

a) Research this topic and write a brief report that addresses:
• What is a decision tree?
• What elements can it contain?
• How is it related to probability?
• Why is it a useful business strategy tool?

b) Include a real example of a decision tree and use it to support your answers to a).

Chapter 1 Review

Learning Goals

Section	After this section, I can
1.1	• use probability to describe the likelihood of something occurring • measure and calculate simple probabilities
1.2	• calculate theoretical probability
1.3	• recognize the difference between experimental probability and theoretical probability
1.4	• describe how an event can represent a set of probability outcomes • recognize how different events are related • calculate the probability of an event occurring
1.5	• describe and determine how the probability of one event occurring can affect the probability of another event occurring • solve probability problems involving multiple events

1.1 Simple Probabilities, pages 6–15

1. A mystery spinner is spun several times, producing the results shown in the table.

Colour	Count
Blue	24
Green	48
Yellow	51
Purple	26

   a) Calculate the experimental probability of the spinner landing on each colour.

   b) Sketch what this spinner could look like. Explain your reasoning.

   c) Could the spinner look differently? Explain.

2. A quarterback successfully completed 21 of 35 pass attempts.

   a) What is the experimental probability that the quarterback will complete a pass?

   b) Suppose the quarterback throws 280 pass attempts over the course of a season. How many is he likely to complete, based on your answer to part a)?

3. Match each scenario with its most likely subjective probability. Justify your answers.

Scenario	Subjective Probability, P(A)
a) Canada will win at least one medal at the next Olympics.	0.1 0.25 0.9
b) A person selected at random will be left-handed.	
c) A randomly chosen high school student will be in grade 10.	

1.2 Theoretical Probability, pages 16–25

4. What is the theoretical probability of rolling each of the following sums with a pair of dice?

   a) 2   b) 9

   c) not 7   d) not a perfect square

5. A card is randomly drawn from a standard deck of cards. What is the theoretical probability that it will be

   a) a club?   b) an ace?

   c) a face card?

6. A sports analyst predicts that a tennis player has a 25% chance of winning a tournament. What are the odds against winning?

1.3 Compare Experimental and Theoretical Probabilities, pages 26–33

7. A standard die is rolled 24 times and turns up a 3 six times.

a) What is the experimental probability of rolling a 3 on a given trial?

b) What is the theoretical probability of rolling a 3?

c) Explain why these answers are different.

8. Suppose two fair coins are flipped.

a) Draw a tree diagram to illustrate all possible outcomes.

b) Sketch a bar graph that shows the predicted relative frequency of each of the following events when a very large number of trials is carried out
- no heads • one head • two heads

c) Explain why your graph has the shape that it does.

1.4 Mutually Exclusive and Non-Mutually Exclusive Events, pages 34–43

9. A graphing calculator is programmed to randomly generate an integer value between 1 and 8. Determine the probability that the number will be

a) a five or an eight

b) a prime number or a perfect square

c) an even number or a seven

d) not a composite number or an odd number

10. A small vehicle rental company randomly assigns its vehicles to customers based on whatever happens to be available. The fleet is shown below.

Assume that each vehicle has an equal probability of being available at any given time. Determine the probability that a customer will randomly be assigned:

a) a coupe or a mini-van

b) a blue vehicle or a mini-van

c) a grey vehicle or a sedan

d) not a red vehicle or a coupe

> **Literacy Link**
>
> A *coupe* is a car with two passenger doors.
> A *mini-van* is larger than a car but smaller than a van.
> A *sedan* is a car with four passenger doors.

1.5 Independent and Dependent Events, pages 44–55

11. A standard die is rolled and a card is drawn from a standard deck of playing cards.

a) Which of the following is more likely to occur?
- an even value will be rolled and a heart will be drawn
- a composite value will be rolled and a face card will be drawn

b) Justify your answer with mathematical reasoning.

12. A bag has 3 red tiles, 1 yellow tile, and 2 green tiles.

a) What is the probability that a red tile is drawn, followed by a second red tile, if the first tile is replaced?

b) How does this value change if the first tile drawn is not replaced?

c) Explain why these answers are different.

13. Josiah has a 20% experimental probability of hitting the snooze button any morning when his alarm goes off. When he hits the snooze button, there is a 25% conditional probability that he misses his bus. He has never missed the bus when he has not hit the snooze button. If Josiah's alarm woke him 120 times over the course of the semester, how many times did Josiah miss his bus?

Chapter 1 Test Yourself

✓ Achievement Chart

Category	Knowledge/Understanding	Thinking	Communication	Application
Questions	1, 2, 3	6, 10	5, 7	4, 8, 9

Multiple Choice

Choose the best answer for #1 to #3.

1. A married couple decides to have two children. Assuming that they do, what is the probability that they will either have two boys or two girls?

    A 0.125
    B 0.25
    C 0.5
    D $0.\overline{6}$

2. Natalie logged on to a social media website 50 times. Fifteen of those times she encountered a pop-up advertisement. What is the experimental probability that Natalie will see a pop-up at this site?

    A 7.5%
    B 15%
    C 30%
    D 70%

3. This spinner is spun 20 times and lands on green 5 times. Identify the true statement.

    A The theoretical probability of landing on green is 20% and the experimental probability of landing on green is 20%.

    B The theoretical probability of landing on green is 20% and the experimental probability of landing on green is 25%.

    C The theoretical probability of landing on green is 25% and the experimental probability of landing on green is 20%.

    D The theoretical probability of landing on green is 25% and the experimental probability of landing on green is 25%.

Short Answer

4. A fair coin is flipped four times. What is the probability that it will land heads exactly once?

5. Marlis feels 80% confident that she will pass her driver's exam.

    a) What type of probability is Marlis using? Explain your choice.

    b) What are the odds in favour of Marlis passing her driver's exam, based on her probability estimate? Justify your reasoning.

6. Tenzin is playing a carnival game in which he throws a dart at the target shown below. Assuming that he is equally likely to hit any point on the target, what is the probability Tenzin wins the following on a given throw?

    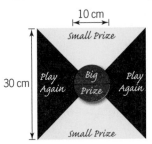

    a) a big prize

    b) a small prize

7. In a game involving two standard dice, you win if you roll a sum of 7 or 11, or if you roll doubles (both dice showing the same number).

    a) What are the odds against you winning this game?

    b) Explain how you solved this problem.

8. Mr. Dobson's tie rack is shown below.

What is the probability that Mr. Dobson randomly selects

a) a solid blue tie or a polka dot tie?

b) a striped tie or a solid coloured tie?

c) a solid black tie or a striped tie?

d) a solid coloured tie or a solid blue tie?

9. Bao has two pencils, a blue pen, and a red pen in his pencil case. Suppose he randomly withdraws one writing tool, followed by another, without replacing the first one. What is the probability that Bao will randomly draw

a) a red pen followed by a blue pen?

b) a pen followed by a pencil?

10. Abia is one of three servers who work at a restaurant that is open from Tuesday to Sunday. Every week the servers randomly draw slips of paper from a hat to decide which two days they will not have to work, in addition to Monday.

One week Abia gets to draw her two days first.

a) What is the probability that Abia will draw a weekend day (Saturday or Sunday) on her first draw?

b) What is the conditional probability that Abia will draw a second weekend day, given that her first draw was a weekend day?

c) What is the probability that Abia will get to enjoy a three-day weekend (Saturday to Monday)?

Chapter Problem

Game Analysis

At the beginning of this chapter you were asked to pick two or three games to analyse and report on the following questions:

1. What elements of the game involve strategy?

2. What elements of the game involve chance or probability?

3. What is the relative balance of strategy versus chance in this game?

Select at least three outcomes that are unique to the game, such as landing on a specific square, or rolling doubles twice in succession. Calculate the probability of each of these events occurring.

Present all of your findings for this project in one of the following formats:

- Written report
- Electronic slideshow
- Podcast
- Poster
- Other

Permutations

You can think of a permutation as a way to arrange objects. We use the power of permutations on a regular basis in everyday life. Encryption is a way of coding messages so that only people who know the code can read the message. Companies use encryption to ensure online payments and passwords are secure. Randomization of electronic game content forces players to make wise choices when playing. Route planners need to determine the most efficient route for garbage and recycling pickup, as well as street cleaning. Toys such as the Rubik's Cube® rely on permutations to make them challenging. Composers explore the permutations of rhythms and notes to create music. Brainstorm other ways in which people use permutations on a regular basis.

Key Terms

fundamental counting principle	factorial
arrangement	permutation
	indirect method

Literacy Strategy

A Frayer model is a visual organizer that helps you understand key words and concepts. Copy and complete this organizer as you learn about permutations in this chapter.

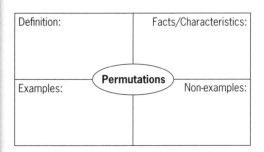

Definition:	Facts/Characteristics:
Examples:	Non-examples:

Permutations

Career Link

Computer Programmer

Public key encryption allows people to encrypt and decrypt messages without sharing passwords. Encryption is used in automated banking machine (ABM) security, cell phone security, Internet purchases, smart card applications, and hard disk protection. Its use has allowed Internet commerce to flourish. Dan is a computer programmer who specializes in encryption code. He has a degree in computer science and has taken mathematics courses in combinatorics and set theory. For a debit card, how many four-digit passwords are possible? What about for an eight-character password that includes digits, capital letters, and lower-case letters?

Password Encryption

Consider the passwords you use for your bank card, the Internet, and so on. What are the rules for creating them? What must be included? What may be included? What must not be included? What is the probability of someone guessing a password on the first try? How long, on average, do you think it would take for a good password cracking program to break each of your passwords? In this chapter problem, you will analyse passwords and learn how to create a good password.

Prerequisite Skills

Decimals and Fractions

1. Order each list from least to greatest.

   a) 0.5, 0.24, 0.718, 0.039

   b) 3.78, 3.078, 3.0078

   c) $\dfrac{1}{2}, \dfrac{1}{3}, \dfrac{1}{6}, \dfrac{1}{5}, \dfrac{1}{4}$

   d) $\dfrac{5}{8}, \dfrac{3}{4}, \dfrac{5}{6}, \dfrac{7}{12}$

2. Convert to a percent.

   > **Example:** To change 1.5 to a percent, multiply by 100.
   >
   > $1.5 \times 100 = 150\%$
   >
   > To change $\dfrac{3}{5}$ to a percent, determine the decimal and multiply by 100.
   >
   > $3 \div 5 = 0.6$
   >
   > $0.6 \times 100 = 60\%$

   a) 0.275

   b) 4.9

   c) 125.62

   d) $\dfrac{2}{5}$

   e) $\dfrac{57}{12}$

3. Find the next number in the sequence $\dfrac{2}{8}, \dfrac{7}{12}, \dfrac{33}{36}, \dfrac{20}{16}.$

Number Patterns

34 Describe each pattern and extend it for three more terms.

   a)

   b) 12, 9, 6, 3, ...

   c) $n - 2, n - 3, n - 4, ...$

   d) $\dfrac{1}{2}, \dfrac{1}{4}, \dfrac{1}{8}, ...$

5. You can use the diagram to illustrate patterns.

   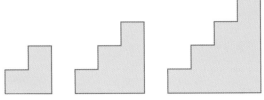

   a) Identify at least two number patterns from the diagram.

   b) Extend each sequence of numbers by two more terms.

Order of Operations

6. Use the order of operations to evaluate.

   a) $(12)(11)(10) - (9)(8)(7)$

   b) $\dfrac{5 \times 4 \times 3 \times 2 \times 1}{3 \times 2 \times 1} + \dfrac{6 \times 5 \times 4}{4 \times 3}$

   c) $9(9 - 1)(9 - 2)(9 - 3)(9 - 4)$

   d) $5^5 - (3^5 + 2^5)$

   e) $1 - \left(\dfrac{2}{3}\right)^4$

   f) $\left(\dfrac{1}{2}\right)^2\left(\dfrac{1}{4}\right)^3$

Evaluating Expressions

7. Evaluate each expression.

   a) $n(n - 1)(n - 2)(n - 3)$ for $n = 6$

   b) $(a + 3)(a + 2)(a + 1)$ for $a = 10$

   c) $\dfrac{x(x - 1)(x - 2)(x - 3)(x - 4)}{(x + 1)(x + 2)}$ for $x = 7$

   d) $n^r \times m^q$ for $m = 0.4$, $n = 0.6$, $r = 3$, and $q = 4$

8. Evaluate for $n = 5$ and $m = 3$.

   a) $n(n - 1)(n - 2)$

   b) $(n + 2)(m + 6)$

   c) $\dfrac{n(n - 1)(n - 2)}{m + 1}$

   d) $(n + 5)(n + 4)(n + 3) + (m - 1)(m - 2)$

Simplifying Expressions

9. Simplify.

 a) $x(x-1)(x-2)$

 b) $(x+1)(x+2) + (x-1)(x-2)$

 c) $\dfrac{(x+5)(x+4)}{x+4}$

 d) $\dfrac{x(x-1)(x-2)(x-3)}{x(x-1)}$

10. Evaluate each expression as written. Then, simplify the expression before evaluating.

 a) $\dfrac{8 \times 7 \times 6 \times 5 \times 4 \times 3 \times 2 \times 1}{5 \times 4 \times 3 \times 2 \times 1}$

 b) $\dfrac{8 \times 7 \times 6 \times 5 \times 4 \times 3 \times 2 \times 1}{2 \times 2 \times 2}$

 c) $\dfrac{5 \times 4 \times 3 \times 2 \times 1}{5 \times 4}$

 d) $\dfrac{11 \times 10 \times 9 \times 8 \times 7 \times 6}{5 \times 4 \times 3 \times 2 \times 1}$

Probability

11. State the probability of each event.

 a) Rolling a 4 on a single die.

 b) Rolling a sum of 6 on a pair of dice.

 c) Flipping tails with a coin.

 d) Flipping two heads with two coins.

 e) Selecting a blue ball from a bag containing a red, a blue, a green, a yellow, a brown, and a purple ball.

12. State whether the events are independent. Justify your reasoning.

 a) Flipping a coin and rolling a die.

 b) Dealing a card to one person and a second card to another person.

 c) Rolling two dice.

 d) Randomly selecting a date from a calendar. Randomly selecting someone's name from a list.

13. An icosahedron die has 20 faces labelled from 1 to 20. When rolled, what is the probability that the upper face is

 a) 3?

 b) 4?

 c) 3 or 4?

 d) even?

 e) a prime number?

 f) greater than 6?

14. Classify each pair of events as mutually exclusive or non-mutually exclusive.

	Event A	Event B
a)	rolling a 3 with a single die	rolling an even number with a single die
b)	randomly selecting a student with blue eyes	randomly selecting a student with brown hair
c)	selecting a face card from a deck	selecting a numbered card from a deck
d)	selecting a red sweater	selecting a wool sweater
e)	randomly selecting a vowel from the alphabet	randomly selecting "A" or "E" from the alphabet

Drawing Diagrams

15. There are four daily flights available from Waterloo region to Ottawa, and two from Ottawa to Sudbury. There is also one direct flight from Waterloo to Sudbury. Draw a route map and a tree diagram illustrating a passenger's choices to fly from Waterloo to Sudbury.

16. Make a chart and draw a tree diagram illustrating the sums when rolling two standard dice.

Organized Counting

Learning Goal

I am learning to

- make lists, charts, and tree diagrams to organize counting

Minds On...

A store is offering a promotion on cell phones. Three different models are on sale. Each model is available in two different colours. How many different choices are available?

Action!

Investigate Illustrating and Counting Outcomes

On a TV game show, a contestant must pick one of three doors, labelled 1, 2, and 3. Behind each door are two boxes to choose from. Boxes A and B are behind Door 1, boxes C and D are behind Door 2, and boxes E and F are behind Door 3.

1. Illustrate all the possible outcomes in each of the following ways:
   a) a chart
   b) a set of ordered pairs

2. How many possible outcomes are there?

3. Draw and describe what a tree diagram would look like for this situation.

4. **Reflect** How does the tree diagram show the number of possible outcomes?

5. **Extend Your Understanding** Describe how the tree diagram would change if there were a third set of choices after the contestant selects the box.

Example 1

Illustrating Possible Outcomes

Little Red Riding Hood knows there are three paths from her house: one going to a pond, one going to a field, and one going to the wolf's lair. From the pond, there are two paths to Grandma's house. From the field, there are three paths, and from the wolf's lair there is one path.

a) Illustrate Little Red Riding Hood's choices with a map and a tree diagram.

b) How many different routes are there for Little Red Riding Hood to take to Grandma's house?

Solution

a)

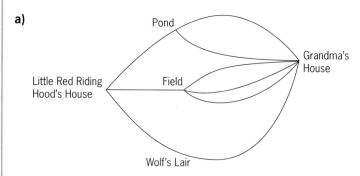

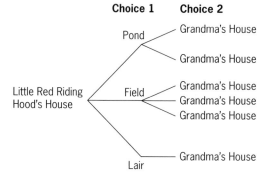

b) There are six branches in the final stage. So, there are six different routes that Little Red Riding Hood could take.

Your Turn

Abby makes two stops on her way to school. She stops to pick up her friend Regan, and then stops to get breakfast at a coffee shop. There are three routes from her house to Regan's house, and two routes from Regan's house to the coffee shop. There is one route between the coffee shop and school.

a) Make a map and a tree diagram illustrating all the possible routes Abby can take to school.

b) How many possible routes are there?

Example 2

Illustrating Replacement and Non-Replacement of Items

A jar contains a red, a blue, and a yellow ball. A student removes three balls one after the other. Draw a tree diagram to illustrate and count the number of outcomes. Highlight the path illustrating (yellow, red, blue) if

a) the balls are replaced after each selection.

b) the balls are not replaced after each selection.

Solution

a)

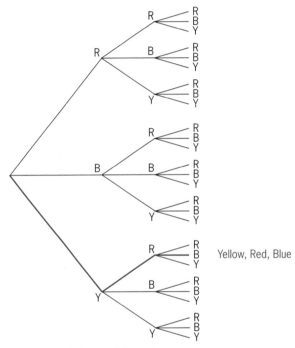

There are 27 possible outcomes.

b)

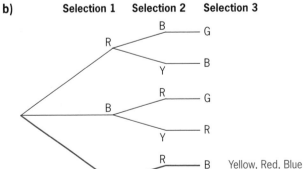

Without replacement, there is one fewer choice at each stage.

There are 6 possible outcomes.

Your Turn

A family has four boys, Zach, Dylan, Ben, and Rhys. Each morning, there are four chores to do: set the table, help make breakfast, wash the dishes, and sweep the floor. Each boy does one chore.

a) Make a tree diagram illustrating the different options for doing the chores.

b) Highlight the path that illustrates Zach setting the table, Ben helping make breakfast, Rhys washing the dishes, and Dylan sweeping the floor.

c) What is the total number of different arrangements for doing the chores?

Consolidate and Debrief

Key Concepts

- You can illustrate a sequence of events using multiple methods, including a list, a chart, and a tree diagram.

- In a tree diagram, each stage in the event is illustrated with a new set of branches extending from the end of each branch in the previous stage.

- To identify a given outcome in a tree diagram, read across a distinct path.

- To determine the number of outcomes in a tree diagram, count the number of distinct end paths across the tree diagram.

Reflect

R1. Consider a spinner with four sections. Is a tree diagram an efficient way of illustrating the outcomes of three spins? Explain.

R2. a) Ken shows all the outcomes of rolling two dice using a table of values. Barb uses a tree diagram. Which method do you prefer? Why?

b) When is a chart less efficient than a tree diagram?

Practise

Choose the best answer for #3 and #4.

1. Make a list and a tree diagram illustrating the outcomes on a true or false quiz with five questions. How many different ways are there to answer the five questions?

2. A spinner is divided into three equal sections. Make a tree diagram and state the number of outcomes if the spinner is spun

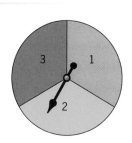

a) twice

b) three times

3. In the game Rock-Paper-Scissors, two competitors use hand signals to indicate either rock, paper, or scissors. Consider each competitor as a stage. Which tree diagram correctly illustrates the outcomes of the game?

A

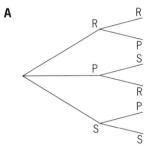

B

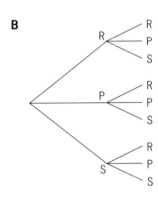

C

D

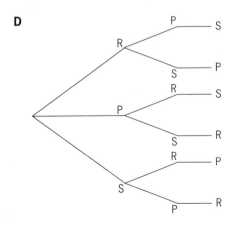

4. A single die is rolled twice. What is the best description of the tree diagram illustrating this event?

A six stages, two branches per stage, 36 outcomes

B two stages, six branches per stage, 12 outcomes

C two stages, six branches per stage, 36 outcomes

D six stages, six branches per stage, 36 outcomes

Apply

5. Draw a family tree, starting with your parents. Work back four generations to illustrate the number of direct ancestors you have.

6. Application In a best-of-five hockey playoff, the winner of the series is declared once a team wins three games. Ties are not allowed.

   a) Draw a tree diagram illustrating all the possible outcomes in a best-of-five series.

   b) List all the outcomes.

   c) How many outcomes are possible?

7. Two people will be chosen to be on a dance committee from Alicia, Benoit, Chantel, Daniqua, Eddie, and Farid.

   a) Make a chart to illustrate this situation.

   b) How many outcomes are possible?

   c) Communication How many outcomes are truly different if order is not important? Explain.

8. Communication For her probability project, Ming designs a game that requires a player to roll a die and flip a coin. Does it matter whether the die is rolled first or the coin is flipped first? Support your decision with a diagram.

9. A teacher allows his students to write a test up to three times. Draw a tree diagram to illustrate the possible sets of results for a given student. How many different sets of results are there?

10. To get from her house to the shopping mall, Cathie can walk along Main Street, through the park, or along a path out of her subdivision. From Main Street, there are two streets that go to the mall. From the park, there are four streets that go to the mall. From the path, there is only one street that goes to the mall.

a) Illustrate Cathie's choices with a map and a tree diagram.

b) How many different routes are there for Cathie to get to the shopping mall?

✓ **Achievement Check**

11. The jack, queen, king, and ace of diamonds are removed from a standard deck of cards. One card is selected at random from these four cards, returned to the deck, and then another is selected.

a) Illustrate the outcomes using a list, a tree diagram, or a chart.

b) Repeat with repetition of cards not permitted.

c) Explain the difference in the resulting number of outcomes.

12. Thinking Pinetree Homes builds new homes with white, grey, or tan siding. The trim is white, black, almond, brown, or grey. Garage doors are painted white, grey, or tan.

a) How many different colour configurations does Pinetree Homes offer?

b) Which would increase the number of choices by a greater amount—an additional siding colour or an additional trim colour? Justify your answer.

> **Processes**
>
> **Selecting Tools and Computational Strategies**
> Which method is the best for solving this problem? How did you decide?

13. A coin is flipped five times. How many results are possible in which there are

a) no consecutive flips of heads or tails?

b) at least two consecutive flips of tails?

c) two flips of two consecutive tails?

Extend

14. A telephone number has 10 digits and consists of a 3-digit area code, a 3-digit local prefix, and 4 more digits. From her house, Sarah can make local calls to area codes 519 and 226. Within area code 519, there are 80 local prefixes. Within area code 226, there are 39 local prefixes. How many different local phone numbers can Sarah call?

15. A checkerboard is an 8 by 8 grid. You can move a checker diagonally left or right forward one square until it reaches the opposite side of the board. For a checker in the fourth square on the near side of the board, draw a tree diagram to determine the total number of possible moves to the opposite side of the checkerboard.

16. In the game of Plinko, a disc is fed into a slot at the top of a board and can go either left or right as it proceeds down the board, as shown.

a) How many paths are there to the bottom of the board?

b) How many paths would there be if the board were extended to five rows?

c) How many paths would there be if the board were extended to n rows?

2.2

The Fundamental Counting Principle

Learning Goal

I am learning to

- use the fundamental counting principle for counting and to solve problems

 Minds On...

There are many different types of random number generators. At their simplest, dice and spinners are used in many board games. On a graphing calculator, randInt(*lower,upper*) returns a random integer between the lower and upper values.

- How many different outcomes (ordered pairs) are possible when rolling two dice?

- How many different outcomes are possible when spinning the pictured spinner twice?

- How many different outcomes are possible when generating a random number twice on a calculator using randInt(1,100)?

- What operation did you use to do your calculations?

 Action!

Investigate Determining the Number of Outcomes

Materials

- 1 die
- 1 coin
- spinner with four equal sections

1. a) Roll one die and flip a coin. Make a list or a diagram to illustrate all the possible outcomes.

  b) How many outcomes are possible?

2. Roll one die, flip a coin, and spin a spinner with four equal sections. Without making a list or diagram, determine how many outcomes are possible. Describe your method.

3. Randomly select a number between 1 and 100, and a letter from the alphabet. How many outcomes are possible? How did you know this without counting all the outcomes?

4. **Reflect** Events A and B are independent. Event A has m outcomes. Event B has n outcomes. How many outcomes are possible, in total, if both events occur together?

5. **Extend Your Understanding** Explain why your method in step 4 works.

Example 1

Use the Fundamental Counting Principle

At an ice-cream stand, customers have a choice of a plain cone or a sugar cone. There are six choices for ice-cream flavours: vanilla, chocolate, strawberry, butterscotch, lemon, and raspberry. How many different single-scoop ice-cream cones can be made?

Solution

You can use a tree diagram to illustrate the outcomes. The flavours are labelled with their initial letters.

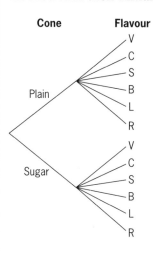

For each of the two types of cone, there are six choices for flavours of ice cream. You can use the **fundamental counting principle**, sometimes called the multiplicative counting rule, to determine the number of outcomes. Multiply to get the total number of choices.

$2 \times 6 = 12$

There are 12 different ways to make a single-scoop ice-cream cone.

fundamental counting principle

• if one event can occur in m ways and a second event can occur in n ways, then together they can occur in $m \times n$ ways

Your Turn

When buying a new smartphone, Li Ming has the following choices:
• 2 GB, 4 GB, or 8 GB of memory
• 64 GB or 128 GB of storage
• 10 colours

How many different configurations of the smartphone are available?

Example 2

Counting Repeated Independent Trials

You roll a standard die. How many outcomes are possible with

a) two rolls? **b)** three rolls?

> ### Solution

A standard die has six faces. For each die, there are six choices for the upper face. Use squares to help visualize the number of trials.

a)

6	6

$6 \times 6 = 36$

There are 36 different outcomes with two rolls.

b)

6	6	6

$6 \times 6 \times 6 = 216$

There are 216 different outcomes with three rolls.

Processes

Representing
Why would a tree diagram be hard to use here?

Your Turn

A password consists of six letters of the alphabet, with repetition permitted.

a) How many different passwords are possible?

b) How many passwords are possible if the letters can be capitals or lower case?

Example 3

Counting Repeated Trials Without Replacement

Two cards are chosen from a standard deck without replacement. How many possible outcomes are there?

> ### Solution

A deck of cards contains 52 cards. So, there are 52 choices for the first card. Since the card is not replaced for the second draw, there are now only 51 cards remaining.

52	51

$52 \times 51 = 2652$

There are 2652 possible outcomes when choosing two cards without replacement.

Your Turn

From a class of 25 students, in how many ways could three of them be selected to attend a workshop—one as a speaker, one as a videographer, and one to take notes?

Consolidate and Debrief

Key Concepts

- If one event can occur in m ways and a second event can occur in n ways, then together they can occur in $m \times n$ ways. This is called the fundamental counting principle.

- The fundamental counting principle can be used for multiple trials. For example, events can occur in $m \times n \times p$ ... ways.

Reflect

R1. Johnny wants to go see a movie in Toronto. He is considering four different movies and notices they are each showing at eight different theatres, and at three different times. Johnny thinks he has 15 choices in total, because $4 + 8 + 3 = 15$. Is he right or wrong? Explain.

R2. Explain the fundamental counting principle, using an example to support your explanation.

Practise

Choose the best answer for #5 and #6.

1. Determine the number of possible outcomes when a coin is tossed
   a) twice
   b) three times
   c) four times
   d) n times

2. A committee has 15 people.
   a) In how many ways could a president and vice president be chosen?
   b) In how many ways could a president, vice president, and secretary be chosen?

3. When selecting patio stones, the customer has 10 choices for the type of bricks, 8 choices for colours, and 3 choices for layout. How many choices does the customer have in total?

4. A set, three-course menu in a restaurant allows the customer to select from four appetizers, five main courses, and three desserts.
   a) How many options are there?
   b) How many choices are there for each option?
   c) What is the total number of meal choices for the customer?

5. A computer randomly selects three different numbers from between 1 and 100. In how many ways can this be done?
   A 3^{100}
   B 100^3
   C $100 \times 99 \times 98$
   D 3×100

6. On a TV game show, a contestant spins a spinner to randomly select a letter of the alphabet. At the same time, the contestant rolls a standard die. What is the total number of possible outcomes?

   A 32

   B 156

   C 308 915 776

   D 52

7. How many two-digit numbers can be formed from the digits 1, 2, 3, 4, 5 if repetition is

   a) permitted?   b) not permitted?

Apply

8. How many different outcomes are possible when rolling

   a) two 4-sided dice?

   b) three 4-sided dice?

   c) two 8-sided dice?

   d) four 8-sided dice?

   e) two 12-sided dice?

   f) five 12-sided dice?

   g) k n-sided dice?

9. A business card design software package provides 25 templates, 38 fonts, and 20 colour combinations. How many different business card designs are available to the user?

10. Tonya has a job wrapping gifts during the holiday season. There are five colours of paper, six choices for ribbon, and three choices for bows. How many choices does the customer have in total?

11. In the game of Yahtzee, five dice are rolled. How many outcomes are there for rolling the five dice once?

12. **Application** A radio station plays a winning song once per hour at a randomly selected time (in minutes). During an announcer's four-hour show, how many different arrangements of winning times could occur if

   a) repetition of times during each hour is permitted?

   b) repetition of times during each hour is not permitted?

13. A combination lock uses the numbers from 0 to 59. Three numbers are dialled in the correct sequence. How many unique lock combinations are possible

   a) if repetition is permitted?

   b) if repetition is not permitted?

✔ Achievement Check

14. An eight-character password has been randomly assigned, containing digits and capital and lower-case letters, with repetition permitted.

   a) How many passwords are available in total?

   b) In how many ways could the password begin with four different capital letters, followed by four different digits?

   c) In how many ways could the password contain one digit and seven letters?

15. Licence plates consist of letters and/or digits. Calculate the number of licence plates that could be formed in each province or territory. Assume all numbers and letters are possible.

   a) Ontario, with four letters followed by three digits

   b) Québec, with three letters followed by three digits

   c) Northwest Territories, with six digits

16. Alberta licence plates have three letters followed by four digits. Is this approximately the same number of licence plates as Ontario? Explain without calculating the total number of Alberta plates.

17. When flying from Halifax to Vancouver on his preferred airline, Angus needs to stop over in Toronto. He has a choice of four morning flights to Toronto and six connecting afternoon flights to Vancouver. In how many ways could Angus travel from Halifax to Vancouver via Toronto?

18. Communication Will the number of outcomes for the following events be the same or different? Explain.

- A red die, a green die, and a white die are rolled at the same time.
- Three white dice are rolled at the same time.
- A die is rolled three times.

19. a) Application Simulate trying to break a security code using a graphing calculator. Think of a three-digit security code. On a graphing calculator, press MATH. From the PRB menu, choose **5: randInt**. Enter randInt(0,9,3) and press ENTER repeatedly until your security code comes up. How does that compare with the total number of possible three-digit security codes?

b) How long do you think it would take to break a five-digit security code?

20. Thinking At Triple Pizza, every pizza has three different toppings. Triple Pizza advertises that you can choose from 4080 different pizzas. How could this be so?

21. Application Each question on a 10-question multiple choice test has four possible answers. In how many ways could the questions be answered if

a) all questions must be answered?

b) the student is permitted to leave answers blank?

Extend

22. Thinking An Ontario licence plate consists of four letters followed by three digits. Plates are assigned in numeric order, then alphabetic order. Assume all letters of the alphabet and all digits can be used. How many licence plates were assigned between the ones shown?

23. If repetition is not permitted, how many even three-digit numbers can be formed from the digits

a) 1, 2, 3, 4, 5, 6?

b) 0, 1, 2, 3, 4, 5?

24. There are three grade 9, five grade 10, six grade 11, and nine grade 12 students on a student council. A committee is being formed with one student from each grade, plus an additional student from either grade 11 or 12. In how many ways could this committee be formed?

25. How many strings of five different letters can be formed from the alphabet if they must begin with a vowel and end with a consonant?

Permutations and Factorials

Learning Goals

I am learning to

- see how using permutations has advantages over other counting techniques
- solve simple problems using techniques for counting permutations
- write permutation solutions using proper mathematical notation

> ## Minds On...

A game involves placing three different coloured balls under three different cups, then quickly mixing them up. The player must correctly identify the final order of the three colours. In how many different orders could the colours finish? Describe at least two ways to figure this out.

> ## Action!

Investigate The Number of Arrangements of Coloured Blocks

Materials

- 5 different coloured blocks or linking cubes

arrangement

- an ordered list of items

1. Select any three blocks and place the others aside.

   a) Use the blocks to make a list or a tree diagram of all the possible **arrangements** of three blocks in a row.

   b) How many arrangements are there?

   c) Use the fundamental counting principle to verify your answer in part b).

2. Select any four blocks and place the other aside.

   a) Make a list or a tree diagram to show all of the possible arrangements of four blocks in a row.

   b) How many arrangements are there?

   c) Use the fundamental counting principle to verify your answer in part b).

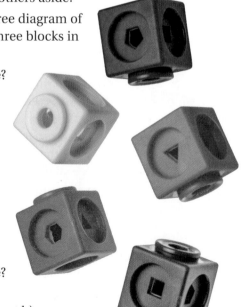

3. How many arrangements are there with five blocks?

4. Reflect Explain a method of calculating the number of arrangements of n different items.

5. Extend Your Understanding Use your method to determine the number of arrangements of 15 different items.

Example 1

Evaluating Factorial Expressions

Evaluate each **factorial**.

a) 3!   **b)** 5!   **c)** 10!   **d)** $\frac{6!}{4!}$

Solution

a) $3! = 3 \times 2 \times 1$ Explore how to use the factorial
$= 6$ key on your calculator.

b) $5! = 5 \times 4 \times 3 \times 2 \times 1$
$= 120$

c) $10! = 10 \times 9 \times 8 \times \dots \times 1$ Why do the values increase quickly
$= 3\,628\,800$ as the value of n increases?

d) $\frac{6!}{4!} = \frac{6 \times 5 \times \cancel{4} \times \cancel{3} \times \cancel{2} \times \cancel{1}}{\cancel{4} \times \cancel{3} \times \cancel{2} \times \cancel{1}}$
$= 6 \times 5$
$= 30$

factorial

- a product of sequential natural numbers with the form
$n! = n(n - 1)(n - 2)$
$\dots \times 2 \times 1$
- $n!$ is read "n factorial"

Your Turn

Evaluate each factorial.

a) 4!   **b)** 6!   **c)** $\frac{11!}{7!}$ **d)** $\frac{6! \times 4!}{5!}$

Permutations of *n* Items

When an arrangement of items needs to appear in order, it is called a permutation.

There are n ways of selecting the first item, $n - 1$ ways of selecting the second item, $n - 2$ ways of selecting the third item, and so on, until there is only one way of selecting the last remaining item. Using the fundamental counting principle, multiply these numbers together: $n(n - 1)(n - 2)(n - 3) \dots \times 3 \times 2 \times 1$, which is n factorial.

The number of permutations of n items is $_nP_n = n!$.

permutation

- an arrangement of n distinct items in a definite order
- the total number of these permutations is written $_nP_n$ or $P(n, n)$

Example 2

Counting Permutations

A photographer lines up six people. How many different arrangements could she make?

> Solution

Since all six people are to be arranged, use a factorial.

$6! = 6 \times 5 \times 4 \times 3 \times 2 \times 1$
$\quad = 720$

The photographer can arrange the people in 720 ways.

Your Turn

A half-hour TV show has eight 30-second advertisement time slots. In how many ways could the eight advertisements be assigned a time?

Example 3

Permutations of Some Items in a Set

There are 12 people on a swim team. Four will be chosen to take part in a relay, racing in a given order. In how many ways could the four swimmers be selected?

> Solution

Method 1: Use the Fundamental Counting Principle

There are four positions to fill.

| 12 | 11 | 10 | 9 |

$12 \times 11 \times 10 \times 9 = 11\ 880$

The positions can be filled in 11 880 ways.

Method 2: Use Factorials

Start with 12! because there are 12 people on the swim team. Divide by the number of arrangements of the non-chosen swimmers, 8!.

$\dfrac{12!}{8!} = \dfrac{12 \times 11 \times 10 \times 9 \times \cancel{8} \times \cancel{7} \times \cancel{6} \times \cancel{5} \times \cancel{4} \times \cancel{3} \times \cancel{2} \times \cancel{1}}{\cancel{8} \times \cancel{7} \times \cancel{6} \times \cancel{5} \times \cancel{4} \times \cancel{3} \times \cancel{2} \times \cancel{1}}$
$\quad = 12 \times 11 \times 10 \times 9$
$\quad = 11\ 880$

The positions can be filled in 11 880 ways.

Your Turn

Forty athletes are entered in a triathlon. Medals are presented to the top three finishers. In how many ways could the gold, silver, and bronze medals be awarded?

Permutations of *r* Items Out of *n* Items

The number of permutations of r items from a collection of n items is

$$_nP_r = n(n-1)(n-2)\cdots(n-r+1)$$
$$= \frac{n!}{(n-r)!}$$

Note that $n \geq r$.

Applying the formula to Example 3,

$$_{12}P_4 = \frac{12!}{(12-4)!}$$
$$= \frac{12!}{8!} \qquad \text{If your calculator has an } _nP_r \text{ function, explore how to use it.}$$
$$= 11\,880$$

Processes

Reasoning and Proving
How could you develop the permutation formula algebraically?

Example 4

Permutations With Restrictions

A librarian wants to display 10 books by Canadian authors on a bookshelf. There are three books by Joseph Boyden, and the rest are by different authors. In how many ways could he arrange the books if the Joseph Boyden books must remain side-by-side?

Solution

Use the fundamental counting principle. First, arrange the books with the three Joseph Boyden books together. Consider the Joseph Boyden books as a single book with the others. This can be done in 8! ways.

The three Joseph Boyden books can be arranged in 3! ways.

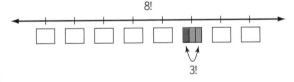

$8! \times 3! = 241\,920$

The books can be arranged in 241 920 ways.

Your Turn

Six team photos are hanging on the wall outside a high school gym. Two of the photos are of the junior and senior football teams. In how many ways could they be arranged in a straight line if the two football photos must be beside each other?

Project Prep

This example may help you with your probability project. How can you count the results when there is a restriction on the selection of items?

Key Concepts

- The number of permutations of n items is n factorial,

  $$n! = n(n-1)(n-2)(n-3) \ldots \times 3 \times 2 \times 1$$

- You can use factorials as a counting technique when repetition is not permitted.

- The number of r-permutations of n items can be calculated by

  $$_nP_r = n(n-1)(n-2) \cdots (n-r+1)$$
  $$= \frac{n!}{(n-r)!}$$

Reflect

R1. Which would have more possibilities, arranging r people from a group of n people **with** regard to order or **without** regard to order? Explain your reasoning.

R2. Use your calculator to determine the value of 0!. Explain why it would have this value. Include an example to support your explanation.

Practise

Choose the best answer for #4 and #5.

1. Evaluate.

   a) 9!

   b) $\dfrac{12!}{5!}$

   c) $_7P_7$

   d) $_8P_5$

2. Write in factorial form.

   a) $_6P_4$

   b) $_{15}P_6$

   c) $7 \times 6 \times 5 \times 4 \times 3 \times 2 \times 1$

   d) $8 \times 7 \times 6 \times 5$

   e) $n(n-1)(n-2)(n-3)$

   f) $(n+1) \times (n) \times (n-1) \times \ldots \times 3 \times 2 \times 1$

3. Express in the form $_nP_r$.

   a) 6!

   b) $91 \times 90 \times 89 \times 88 \times 87 \times 86$

   c) $\dfrac{18!}{12!}$

4. Which is the correct simplification of $\dfrac{96!}{24!}$?

   A 4!

   B 4

   C $_{96}P_{72}$

   D $_{96}P_{24}$

5. Which is the correct number of permutations of five items from a list of nine items?

   A 126

   B 15 120

   C 45

   D 59 049

6. There are 15 teams competing in a synchronized swimming competition. In how many ways could first, second, and third place be awarded?

7. A club has 18 members. In how many ways could a president, vice president, treasurer, and secretary be elected?

Apply

8. There are 22 players on a baseball team. In how many ways could the batting order of nine players be assigned?

9. Write in simplest factorial form.
   a) $10 \times 9 \times 8 \times 7!$
   b) $99 \times 98 \times 97!$
   c) $90 \times 8!$
   d) $n(n-1)!$
   e) $(n+2)(n+1)n!$

10. **Application** A salesperson needs to visit 15 different offices during the week.
    a) In how many ways could this be done?
    b) In how many ways could she visit four different offices on Monday?
    c) In how many ways could she visit three different offices each day from Monday to Friday?

11. a) How many 10-digit numbers are there with no digits repeated?
    b) How many 7-digit numbers are there with no digits repeated?

12. Caleb needs to create an 8-digit password using only numbers. How many different passwords are there if he wants to use 00 exactly once?

✔ Achievement Check

13. The six members of the student council executive are lined up for a yearbook photo.
    a) In how many ways could the executive line up?
    b) In how many ways could this be done if the president and vice president must sit together?
    c) In how many ways could this be done if the president and vice president must sit together in the middle of the group?

14. How many ways are there to seat six boys and seven girls in a row of chairs so that none of the girls sit together?

15. **Thinking** Twenty figure skaters are in a competition. In the final round, the bottom five competitors skate first in a random order. The next five do likewise, and so on until the top five skate last in a random order. In how many ways could the skating order be assigned?

Extend

16. Solve for n.
    a) $_nP_2 = 110$
    b) $P(n, 3) = 5!$

17. Ten couples are being seated in a circle. How many different seating arrangements are there if each couple must sit together?

18. The names of the Knights of the Round Table at Winchester, UK, were engraved on the table, but they are no longer visible. There are 23 knights, plus King Arthur himself. In how many ways could King Arthur and the knights be seated at the Round Table?

19. A double factorial represents the product of all odd, or even, integers up to a given odd number, n. For example, $9!! = 1 \times 3 \times 5 \times 7 \times 9$.
    a) Express $9!!$ as a quotient of factorials.
    b) Express $(2k + 1)!!$ as a quotient of factorials.
    c) Simplify $(2n)!!$, writing it in simple factorial form.

20. Without using a calculator, determine how many zeros occur at the end of $30!$.

The Rule of Sum

Learning Goal

I am learning to

• use the rule of sum to solve counting problems

> ## Minds On...

Many grade 12 students consider attending university. Sidney is applying to Waterloo for math or engineering, Queen's for physics, chemistry, or engineering, and Laurentian for science or engineering. How many program choices does Sidney have in total?

Jenna is applying to Windsor for business or economics, York for commerce or business, and Ottawa for economics, political science, or business. How many program choices does Jenna have in total?

Describe how you calculated the number of choices Sidney and Jenna each have.

> ## Action!

Investigate The Rule of Sum

The fundamental counting principle is used when one event **and** another event occur together. This activity investigates when one event **or** another event occurs.

1. Make a tree diagram of the outcomes for the following activity.

   Imagine you are picking coloured balls out of bins.
   • For your first selection, you can choose a red or a green ball.
   • If your first ball is red, you can choose blue, yellow, or orange for your second ball.
   • If your first ball is green, you can choose white or black.
   • Regardless of the colour of the first or second ball, you can choose orange, pink, or brown for your third ball.

2. How many outcomes are possible if you choose red as your first selection?

3. How many outcomes are possible if you choose green as your first selection?

4. How many outcomes are there in total?

5. What is the relationship that connects your answers to steps 2, 3, and 4?

6. Reflect If you know the number of outcomes for each of events A **and** B, how many outcomes are there for event A **or** B?

7. Extend Your Understanding

   a) If you are allowed to either roll a die or toss a coin, how many possible outcomes are there?

   b) Compare the results in part a) to the number of outcomes when you roll a die and toss a coin.

Example 1

Use the Rule of Sum

At an international conference, either eight or nine countries may attend. In how many different arrangements could the countries' flags be flown?

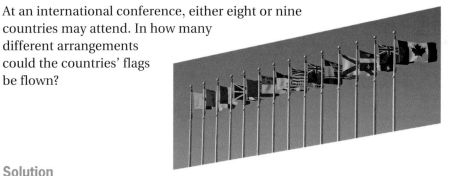

Literacy Link

In chapter 1, you learned about the *rule of sum*, which is also called the additive principle for mutually exclusive events. It states that if one mutually exclusive event can occur in m ways, and a second can occur in n ways, then one or the other can occur in $m + n$ ways.

Solution

Use the rule of sum because either eight **or** nine countries' flags will be flown.

$8! + 9! = 403\,200$

The flags could be arranged in 403 200 ways.

Your Turn

At the conference in Example 1,

a) in how many different arrangements could the flags be flown if seven, eight, or nine countries attend?

b) in how many different arrangements could the flags be flown if the host country's flag is always on the far left?

Example 2

Use the Principle of Inclusion and Exclusion

Three players are playing the card game Pass the Ace. Each player receives one card. In how many ways could the cards all be face cards or red cards?

Solution

Because each player receives a different card, order is important.

There are $_{12}P_3$ ways to select three face cards.

There are $_{26}P_3$ ways to select three red cards.

The events "face cards" and "red cards" are not mutually exclusive, since there are six red face cards, which have been counted twice.

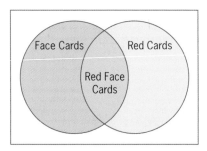

Apply the principle of inclusion and exclusion, $n(A \text{ or } B) = n(A) + n(B) - n(A \text{ and } B)$, to determine the number of red cards or face cards.

There are $_6P_3$ ways to deal three red face cards.

$$\text{Number of ways to deal three face cards or red cards} = {_{12}P_3} + {_{26}P_3} - {_6P_3}$$
$$= 1320 + 15\,600 - 120$$
$$= 16\,800$$

There are 16 800 ways to deal three face cards or three red cards.

Your Turn

Three players each cut one card from a standard deck. If order is important, in how many ways could they be

a) all hearts?

b) all aces?

c) all aces or hearts?

Example 3

Use the Indirect Method

The 12 members of a basketball team are lining up for their medals after a tournament. In how many ways can this be done

a) if there is no restriction?

b) if the captain and assistant captain must be together?

c) if the captain and assistant captain must not be together?

Solution

a) With no restriction, it is a permutation of all 12 players.

$12! = 479\ 001\ 600$

They could line up in 479 001 600 ways.

b) Treat the captain and assistant captain as a single person, making 11 players. Then arrange the two of them among themselves.

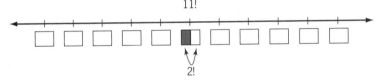

$11! \times 2! = 79\ 833\ 600$

They could line up in 79 833 600 ways.

c) There are numerous positions in which the captain and assistant captain could be apart, so the solution is the sum of many different scenarios. You can use the **indirect method** to subtract the number of ways they are together from the total without restrictions. In other words, part a) minus part b).

$$\begin{aligned}
\text{Total} - \text{together} &= 12! - 11! \times 2! \\
&= 479\ 001\ 600 - 39\ 916\ 800 \times 2 \\
&= 479\ 001\ 600 - 79\ 833\ 600 \\
&= 399\ 168\ 000
\end{aligned}$$

They can be apart in 399 168 000 ways.

indirect method

- subtract the number of unwanted outcomes from the total number of outcomes without restrictions

Your Turn

In how many ways could the letters in the word FACTOR be arranged so that the vowels are not together?

How is the indirect method is similar to the probability of a complement that was introduced in chapter 1?

Processes

Connecting
How could you determine the number of girls in a class?

Directly: count the girls

Indirectly: subtract the number of boys from the total number in the class

Key Concepts

- The rule of sum states that if one mutually exclusive event can occur in m ways, and a second can occur in n ways, then one **or** the other can occur in $m + n$ ways.

- If two events are not mutually exclusive, the principle of inclusion and exclusion needs to be considered:

  $n(A \text{ or } B) = n(A) + n(B) - n(A \text{ and } B)$.

- To reduce calculations, consider using the indirect method, which involves subtracting the unwanted event from the total number of outcomes in the sample space: $n(A) = n(S) - n(A')$.

Reflect

R1. A student council has five executive positions: president, vice president, secretary, treasurer, and assistant treasurer. There are six female and seven male candidates. It is important that at least one male and one female be on the executive. Explain why the indirect method is useful in determining the number of possible outcomes.

R2. Write a general guideline explaining when to use the fundamental counting principle and when to use the rule of sum for permutations. Include a similar example for each.

Practise

Choose the best answer for #3 and #4.

1. Determine the total number of arrangements of three or four toys from a basket of eight different toys.

2. a) How many ways are there to roll a sum of 7 or 11 on two dice?

   b) How many ways are there to roll doubles or a sum divisible by three on two dice?

3. A game has players roll either one or two standard dice. Which is the total number of possible different outcomes?

   A 42

   B 36

   C 18

   D 12

4. Which is the total number of arrangements of the digits 1, 2, 3, 4, 5, if the even digits must not be together?

   A 120

   B 24

   C 48

   D 72

Apply

5. a) How many even numbers can be formed from the digits 1, 2, 3, 4, 5?

   b) How many of these numbers are greater than 3000?

6. **Application** A motorcycle licence plate consists of two or three letters followed by four digits. How many licence plates can be made?

7. A security code consists of either five or six different letters. How many distinct security codes are possible?

8. Communication Suppose a country has a rule that a newborn child may have either one, two, or three names.

   a) If parents were to choose from a list of 50 names, how many choices would they have when naming their child?

   b) What if they could choose from 100 names?

   c) Explain why the total in part b) is more than 2 times the total in part a).

9. Open Question Five speakers, P, Q, R, S, and T, have been booked to address a meeting.

   a) In how many ways could the speakers be ordered if speaker P must go before speaker Q?

   b) Make up your own problem about these five speakers. Solve it, share it with a classmate, and check his or her solution.

10. How many five-digit numbers include the digits 4 or 6 or both?

11. Ten names are placed into a hat. In how many ways could they be pulled from the hat so they are not in alphabetical order?

12. A spinner has six equally spaced sections numbered 1 to 6 as shown. You spin the spinner four times.

   a) In how many ways could the spinner result in the same colour on all four spins?

   b) In how many ways could the spinner result in an even number or the same colour on all four spins?

13. Thinking In the game of Monopoly, you can get out of jail by rolling doubles. If you are unsuccessful on the first roll you may try again, up to a total of three attempts. In how many ways could this occur? Explain your solution.

14. Communication Morse code uses dots and dashes to represent letters, digits, and eight punctuation symbols. Use the fundamental counting principle and the rule of sum to help explain why a maximum of six characters is needed.

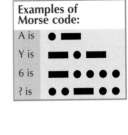

Examples of Morse code:

A is ● ▬
Y is ▬ ● ▬ ▬
6 is ▬ ● ● ● ●
? is ● ● ▬ ▬ ● ●

✔ **Achievement Check**

15. A password must be 6, 7, or 8 characters long, and may include capital letters, lower-case letters, or digits. In how many ways could this be done

   a) with no restriction?

   b) with no repetition permitted?

   c) if at least one of the characters in part a) must be a digit?

Extend

16. How many different numbers can be formed by multiplying some or all of the numbers 2, 3, 4, 5, 6, 7, 8?

17. A derangement is a permutation of a set of numbers in which no item remains in its original position. For the set {1, 2, 3}, the derangements are {2, 3, 1} and {3, 1, 2}. The permutation {1, 3, 2} is not a derangement because 1 is in its original position. Determine the number of derangements of each set.

   a) {1, 2, 3, 4}

   b) {1, 2, 3, 4, 5}

18. The labels from six different cans of soup have come off. If you were to replace them at random, in how many ways could this be done so that

   a) none of the cans will be labelled correctly?

   b) at least one of the cans will be labelled correctly?

   c) all of the cans will be labelled correctly?

Probability Problems Using Permutations

Learning Goal

I am learning to

- solve probability problems using counting principles for situations with equally likely outcomes

Minds On...

In chapter 1, you investigated simple probabilities. Match each event with its appropriate description.

Event	Description
hoping for a king to be dealt, given that a king has already been dealt	Independent
Jonathan Toews has a 17.6% probability of scoring	Dependent
two rolls of a single die	Mutually exclusive
a number is even, a number is odd	Complements
dealing three cards from a standard deck	Statistical
the results on a green die or a red die	Rule of sum
the results on a green die and a red die	Fundamental counting principle
a card is a heart, a card is a spade	Mutually exclusive

Describe a different event that would be categorized by

- independent events
- dependent events
- mutually exclusive events
- complements

Action!

In this section, you will be extending probability to more complex problems. It will be important to list or describe the event and the sample space and then calculate the number of elements in each. Multiple choice tests are used not only by teachers, but also by testing sites for things like driver's licences. How would probability play a role in multiple choice tests?

Example 1

Independent Trials

Software for generating multiple choice tests randomly assigns A, B, C, or D as the correct answer. On a 10-question test, what is the probability that all 10 questions have C as the correct answer?

Solution

Method 1: Use the Theoretical Probability

There are four choices for each correct answer. There are 10 questions, so there are 10 trials.

$$n(S) = 4^{10}$$
$$= 1\ 048\ 576$$

There is only one successful outcome: all Cs. So, $n(A) = 1$.

$$P(\text{all Cs}) = \frac{n(A)}{n(S)}$$
$$= \frac{1}{1\ 048\ 576}$$

The probability that all 10 questions have C as the correct answer is $\frac{1}{1\ 048\ 576}$.

Method 2: Use the Independent Event Probability

These trials are independent, so the probability of a C on each question is $\frac{1}{4}$.

| $\frac{1}{4}$ | $\frac{1}{4}$ | $\frac{1}{4}$ | $\frac{1}{4}$ | $\frac{1}{4}$ | $\frac{1}{4}$ | $\frac{1}{4}$ | $\frac{1}{4}$ | $\frac{1}{4}$ | $\frac{1}{4}$ |

There are 10 trials, so

$$P(\text{all Cs}) = \left(\frac{1}{4}\right)^{10}$$
$$= \frac{1}{1\ 048\ 576}$$

The probability that all 10 questions have C as the correct answer is $\frac{1}{1\ 048\ 576}$.

> **Processes**
>
> **Selecting Tools and Computational Strategies**
> How are these strategies the same? How are they different?

Your Turn

A street illusionist asks five people to each secretly write a number between 1 and 100 on a card. Incredibly, they all write the same number.

a) What is the probability of this occurring?

b) Relate your answer to part a) to the probability of rolling a six on a standard die five times in a row.

Example 2

Dependent Trials

Eight people on a waiting list for advance tickets to a concert have been selected to choose their seats. What is the probability they will have been notified in order from youngest to oldest?

Solution

Method 1: Use Factorials

The trials are dependent, since a person cannot be selected more than once.

You can use factorials.

$n(S) = 8!$

There is only one successful outcome, the single order from youngest to oldest, so $n(A) = 1$.

$P = \dfrac{1}{8!}$

$\quad = \dfrac{1}{40\ 320}$

The probability of notifying the people in order from youngest to oldest is $\dfrac{1}{40\ 320}$.

Method 2: Use Individual Probabilities

Since the people are notified without replacement, the events are dependent.

The probability of selecting the youngest first is $\dfrac{1}{8}$.

The probability of notifying the next youngest on the second choice is $\dfrac{1}{7}$.

Following a similar process for all eight people gives the probability of notifying people in order from youngest to oldest of

$P = \dfrac{1}{8} \times \dfrac{1}{7} \times \dfrac{1}{6} \times \dfrac{1}{5} \times \dfrac{1}{4} \times \dfrac{1}{3} \times \dfrac{1}{2} \times 1$

$\quad = \dfrac{1}{40\ 320}$

The probability of notifying the people in order from youngest to oldest is $\dfrac{1}{40\ 320}$.

Your Turn

Four students, one from each of grades 9, 10, 11, and 12, line up to pose for a photograph. What is the probability that they will be in order of their grades?

Example 3

Ordered Selections

Logan selects three cards in order, without replacement, from a standard deck. What is the probability that he selects a king, then two queens?

Solution

Since the Logan selects the cards without replacement, the trials are dependent.

$$n(S) = {}_{52}P_3$$

Select one king from 4 and two queens from 4.

$$n(A) = {}_4P_1 \times {}_4P_2$$

$$
\begin{aligned}
P(\text{king, queen, queen}) &= \frac{{}_4P_1 \times {}_4P_2}{{}_{52}P_3} \\
&= \frac{4 \times 12}{132\ 600} \\
&= \frac{48}{132\ 600} \\
&= \frac{2}{5525}
\end{aligned}
$$

The probability of selecting a king and then two queens is $\frac{2}{5525}$.

> **Processes**
>
> **Representing**
> Why does
> $\frac{4}{52} \times \frac{4}{51} \times \frac{3}{50}$
> give the same answer?

Your Turn

Kylie selects five cards.
a) What is the probability that she selects three aces followed by two jacks?
b) What is the probability that Kylie selects two hearts followed by three clubs?

Example 4

The Birthday Problem

There are 30 students in Wayne's class.
a) What is the probability that no two people have the same birthday?
b) What is the probability that at least two students share the same birthday?

> Solution

a) There are 365 days in one year. So, for the sample space, each of the 30 students has 365 choices for their birthday. There are 30 trials, so $n(S) = 365^{30}$.

If everyone must have a different birthday, the successful outcomes are dependent and 30 days are selected from 365 days.

So, $n(A) = {}_{365}P_{30}$.

$$P(\text{all different}) = \frac{{}_{365}P_{30}}{365^{30}}$$
$$\approx 0.2937$$

The probability that no two people have the same birthday is approximately 0.2937.

b) Use the indirect method, $P(A) = 1 - P(A')$.

$P(\text{at least two the same}) = 1 - P(\text{no two the same})$

$n(A') = {}_{365}P_{30}$

$$P(A) = 1 - \frac{{}_{365}P_{30}}{365^{30}}$$
$$\approx 0.7063$$

Why would the probability be this great with only 30 people?

It is likely someone in the classroom has the same birthday as you?

The probability that at least two students have the same birthday is approximately 0.7063.

Your Turn

From a group of 16 people, what is the probability that
a) none share a birthday?
b) at least two of them share the same birthday?

Consolidate and Debrief

Key Concepts

- You can calculate the probability of an event using $P = \dfrac{n(A)}{n(S)}$, where $n(A)$ is the number of successful outcomes and $n(S)$ is the number of outcomes in the sample space.

- If the trials are dependent, you can use permutations in the calculations.

- To use the indirect method, subtract the probability of the complement from 1.

$$P(A) = 1 - P(A')$$

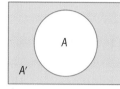

$P(A) = 1 - P(A')$

Reflect

R1. A tour guide bet her group of 27 tourists that at least two people have the same birthday. Should they accept the wager? Explain.

R2. Describe the clues you should look for to identify that a probability problem involves permutations. Include an example.

R3. How is $_{12}P_3$ different from $_{12}P_1 \times 3$? Use examples to help distinguish between the two.

Practise

Choose the best answer for #3 and #4.

1. Three cards are drawn from a deck without replacement. What is the probability that they will be a king, a queen, and a jack, in that order?

2. Abby, Chantral, Dougie, Kajan, Minh, and Zara are all in a race and are considered to be equally fast. What is the probability that Abby and Chantral will be the first two finishers?

3. Five names are selected at random from a list of 25 names. What is the probability that they will be in alphabetical order?

   A $\dfrac{1}{_{25}P_5}$ **B** $\dfrac{5!}{_{25}P_5}$

   C $\dfrac{1}{25^5}$ **D** $\dfrac{5}{25!}$

4. A standard die is rolled four times. What is the probability that it shows a number divisible by three all four times?

   A $\dfrac{1}{3}$ **B** $\dfrac{1}{6}$

   C $\dfrac{1}{81}$ **D** $\dfrac{1}{12}$

Apply

5. There are 15 numbered balls on a pool table. What are the odds against them falling in order from 1 to 15? Remember, odds against is the ratio $P(A') : P(A)$.

6. **Communication** A charity lottery uses a random number generator to choose three different days from the calendar. These are days on which grand prizes will be awarded.

   a) What is the probability that all three days fall in the month of April?

   b) Explain the method you used.

7. In the game of backgammon, when you roll doubles with two dice you can double the total on the dice.

a) What is the probability of rolling doubles?

b) What is the probability of rolling doubles on two consecutive rolls?

c) Which has a greater probability: rolling consecutive doubles, or rolling consecutive sums of 7 on two rolls of the dice?

8. What is the probability that a family has all boys, in a family of

a) 3 children? **b)** 4 children?

c) 5 children? **d)** n children?

9. A four-letter word jumble is being formed from the letters in the word LOGARITHM.

a) What is the probability it spells MATH?

b) What is the probability it includes the letters M, A, T, and H?

c) What is the probability it includes the letter M?

10. Application One card is dealt from a standard deck to each of seven players.

a) What is the probability that the cards are dealt in ascending order?

b) What is the probability that none of the cards are of the same denomination?

11. What is the probability that two or more people in a party with 20 people will have the same birthday?

12. Thinking How many students are needed in a class for the probability of the "birthday problem" in Example 4 on page 92 to reach 0.5?

13. Your MP3 player is set to random and will play 10 of your favourite songs. What is the probability that

a) the songs are played in your order of preference?

b) your two favourite songs are first and second?

14. Five people each choose a card from a standard deck. They replace the card after making their choice.

a) What are the odds against at least two people choosing the same card?

b) What are the odds against at least two people choosing the same denomination?

> **Processes**
>
> **Selecting Tools and Computational Strategies**
> How does the tool you selected help you understand the birthday problem?

15. To simulate the results of the birthday problem in Example 4 on page 92, use either a spreadsheet or a graphing calculator to generate 30 random integers between 1 and 365. Repeat this 10 times and determine the number of classes in which at least two people share the same birthday.

- In a spreadsheet, enter **=randbetween(1,365)** in cell A1. Fill down to cell A30. To identify the most frequent number, or mode, in cell A31, enter **=mode(A1:A30)**.

- Using a graphing calculator, press STAT then select **1:Edit**. Place the cursor in the heading for list **L1**. Press MATH then select **PRB** and **5:randInt(1,365,30)**. Press ENTER. Sort the data by pressing STAT, then **2:SortA(L1)** and ENTER. Press STAT, then **1:Edit**. Scroll down to see which numbers repeat.

16. a) Find the probability of cracking a combination lock on a safe if five different numbers are used from

i) 1 to 35

ii) 1 to 40

iii) 1 to 45

b) Communication Compare the results and explain the differences.

17. On a TV game show, the contestant is asked to pick one of three doors. Behind each door are two large boxes to choose from. The grand prize is in one of the boxes behind Door 1. There are good prizes in one box behind Door 2 and one box behind Door 3. The other boxes all contain gag prizes.

a) Make a tree diagram showing the possible outcomes.

b) Assign a probability to each branch in the tree diagram.

c) What is the probability of winning the grand prize?

d) What is the probability of winning a good prize?

e) What is the probability of winning a gag prize?

f) What is the sum of all the probabilities? Explain the result.

18. Which of the following scenarios could be modelled using the "birthday problem"? Solve it using the appropriate techniques.

• The probability that at least two people receive hearts when each of six people are dealt five cards.

• The probability that at least two people roll double sixes, from a group of 10 people.

• The probability that at least two people, from a group of 25 people, have the same birthday as you.

19. Thinking Which is more likely?

a) Throwing a sum of 7, or not throwing a sum of 7, on six consecutive rolls of a pair of dice.

b) Five different digits being arranged in descending order, or three different letters being arranged in alphabetical order.

c) At least two out of 20 friends having the same birthday, or at least two out of five friends having the same birth month.

Extend

20. A lottery ticket contains five numbers chosen from the numbers 1 to 40. The winning ticket is the one that matches all five numbers in the correct order. The second prize winner matches four of the five numbers in the correct order. What is the probability of winning the first or second prize?

21. Open Question Create your own probability example that has $\dfrac{1}{{}_{15}P_7}$ as its solution. Provide a rationale.

22. A computer screen is divided into a 16 by 9 grid with grid points defined by ordered pairs, using whole numbers, from $(0, 0)$ to $(16, 9)$. A segment is drawn joining two randomly chosen points.

a) What is the probability the segment is horizontal?

b) What is the probability the segment is on one of the screen's diagonals?

23. A game involves making a 3 by 3 grid with nine cards from a standard deck. You win if three cards in a row (horizontally, vertically, or diagonally) are the same denomination or are consecutive (in any order).

a) What is the probability that there is exactly one winning set of the same denomination?

b) What is the probability that there is exactly one winning set of consecutive cards?

24. In the card game, Six in a Row, six cards are dealt in a row. Points are given for the number of consecutive cards. What is the probability that the six cards are

a) consecutive and in order (e.g. 4, 5, 6, 7, 8, 9)?

b) consecutive, but in any order?

Learning Goals

Section	After this section, I can
2.1	• make lists, charts, and tree diagrams to organize counting
2.2	• use the fundamental counting principle for counting and to solve problems
2.3	• see how using permutations has advantages over other counting techniques • solve simple problems using techniques for counting permutations • write permutation solutions using proper mathematical notation
2.4	• use the rule of sum to solve counting problems
2.5	• solve probability problems using counting principles for situations with equally likely outcomes

2.1 Organized Counting, pages 64–69

1. Draw a tree diagram showing all the possible outcomes (win, loss, or tie) in three games between two hockey teams. How many possible outcomes are there?

2. Octahedral dice have eight faces. Make a chart showing the sums of the faces on two dice. Which sum occurs most frequently? Which sums occur least frequently?

3. The heart honour cards (10, J, Q, K, A) are removed from a standard deck. Three cards are randomly selected from the heart honour cards without replacement.

   a) Illustrate all the possible outcomes using a tree diagram.

   b) Highlight the path that indicates the run queen of hearts, king of hearts, ace of hearts).

   c) How many possible outcomes are there?

2.2 The Fundamental Counting Principle, pages 70–75

4. A home security code requires five digits to be entered on a keypad.

   a) How many distinct security codes are possible?

   b) Sarah reset her security code but has forgotten it. If it takes her eight seconds per attempt, what is the maximum time it would take for her to find the correct code?

5. When ordering a gaming computer online, Ryan has three choices for processors, four choices for size of RAM, five choices for the video card, three choices for the hard drive, and two choices for the sound card.

   a) How many choices does Ryan have when configuring his computer?

   b) If there were an additional choice for the video card, how would it affect the total number of choices? Explain the difference.

6. Barb knits socks for a charity supporting homeless and low income people. She likes to make striped socks and selects from six different colours. The top stripe can be any colour. The second stripe may not match the first colour. The bottom colour may not match the second, but may match the first. How many distinct pairs of socks could Barb make?

2.3 Permutations and Factorials, pages 76–81

7. How many ways are there for a company to assign three different jobs to three of its five employees?

8. a) Evaluate each permutation and place them in the array as shown.

$$_1P_1$$
$$_2P_1 \qquad _2P_2$$
$$_3P_1 \qquad _3P_2 \qquad _3P_3$$
$$_4P_1 \qquad _4P_2 \qquad _4P_3 \qquad _4P_4$$
$$_5P_1 \qquad _5P_2 \qquad _5P_3 \qquad _5P_4 \qquad _5P_5$$

b) Extend the array by one row without using factorials. Explain how you did this.

c) Identify and describe two other patterns in the array.

9. A bookstore clerk is arranging seven novels, four plays, and five poetry books in a display case. Each type of book remains in its own group, but the groups can be in any order. In how many ways could she arrange the books?

2.4 The Rule of Sum, pages 82–87

10. In how many ways could the letters in the word STORAGE be arranged if the vowels must remain in
  a) even positions?
  b) odd positions?
  c) even or odd positions?

11. In how many ways can you rearrange the letters in the word NATIVE if the vowels must not be together?

12. How many five-digit even numbers can be formed using all the digits 0, 1, 2, 3, and 4?

2.5 Probability Problems Using Permutations, pages 88–95

13. For a gift exchange, 10 people's names are written on slips of paper and placed in a bowl. The slips of paper are mixed up, and each person selects one name.
  a) What is the probability that everyone selects their own name?
  b) What is the probability that nobody selects his or her own name?

14. Six different coloured balls are placed in a box. Kendra and Abdul each select a ball without replacement.
  a) What is the probability that Kendra selects the green ball and Abdul selects the red ball?
  b) What is the probability that Kendra selects the green ball and Abdul does not select the red ball?
  c) What is the probability that Kendra does not select the green ball and Abdul does not select the red ball?

15. If five people each select a letter from the alphabet with repetition permitted, what is the probability that they are
  a) all the same?
  b) all different?

Chapter 2 Test Yourself

Category	Knowledge/ Understanding	Thinking	Communication	Application
Questions	1, 2, 3, 4, 7, 8	11, 13, 14	4, 14	5, 6, 9, 10, 12

Multiple Choice

Choose the best answer for #1 to #3.

1. How many orders of faces are possible when a standard die is rolled four times?

   A 16

   B 24

   C 1296

   D 4096

2. Which of the following is equivalent to $_{101}P_{98}$?

   A 3!

   B $101 \times 100 \times 99 \times 98$

   C $\dfrac{101!}{98!}$

   D $\dfrac{101!}{3!}$

3. When flipping a coin five times, what is the probability that heads turns up every time?

   A $\dfrac{1}{32}$

   B $\dfrac{5}{32}$

   C $\dfrac{1}{10}$

   D $\dfrac{1}{25}$

4. Which of the following is not defined? Explain your reasoning.

   - $_{12}P_8$
   - $_9P_{10}$
   - $_7P_0$
   - $_{100}P_{100}$

Short Answer

5. Rosa is getting dressed and has decided that her shirt, pants, and socks are not to be the same colour. She has red, green, black, and blue of each.

   a) Draw a tree diagram illustrating her choices.

   b) How many choices does she have if she starts with a red pair of pants?

6. A hockey team has four left wingers, three right wingers, four centres, three left defence, four right defence, and two goalies. To create a starting lineup, a coach needs one player in each position. In how many ways could the starting lineup be chosen?

7. How many ways are there to assign five different roles in a play to the 12 members of a drama club?

8. There are three Canadians in the finals at a ski competition. Assuming all eight competitors are equally likely to win, what is the probability that the three Canadians will win gold, silver, and bronze?

Justine Dufour-Lapointe

Extended Response

9. a) How many arrangements are there of the letters in the word COMPUTER?

b) How many of them begin with a consonant?

10. In how many ways could the 11 members of a soccer team line up if the captain and assistant captain must remain apart?

11. There are 25 men and 20 women who belong to a club. An executive panel consisting of a president, vice president, secretary, and treasurer is being chosen.

a) In how many ways could the executive panel be chosen with no restrictions?

b) In how many ways could the executive panel be chosen if it must include at least one woman and one man?

c) In how many ways could the executive panel be chosen if the president and vice president must have different genders?

12. Four letters are randomly selected from the alphabet. What is the probability that they are A, B, C, and D, in that order,

a) if repetition is permitted?

b) if repetition is not permitted?

13. Ten people each randomly select a number between 1 and 20. What is the probability that at least two of them select the same number?

14. To determine who should be the first dealer in a card game, one card is dealt to each of five players. The player with the card of the highest denomination gets to deal first.

a) How many different results are possible when dealing to the five players?

b) In how many ways could all players receive cards of different denominations?

c) What is the probability that four players receive cards of the same denomination?

d) How would the solution to part c) change if players each chose a card from a full deck instead of being dealt one?

Chapter Problem

Password Encryption

Consider four passwords you use, for bank cards, websites, and so on.

a) What are the rules for each? What must be included? What may be included? What must not be included?

b) What is the probability of someone guessing each password on the first try?

c) At 90 000 codes per second, how long, on average, would it take for a good password cracking program to break each of your passwords?

d) Some passwords require at least one digit and at least one capital letter. Why?

e) Develop a set of guidelines to identify a good, poor, or average password. Back it up with examples and calculations.

Combinations

There are 100 letter tiles in the popular word game Scrabble®. Of these, 42 are vowels. A player chooses seven tiles to begin the game. What is the probability that the player will select only vowels?

Key Terms

combination

null set

Pascal's triangle

binomial theorem

Literacy Strategy

You can solve counting problems using powers, permutations, and/or combinations. As you work through this chapter, you will learn the difference between permutations and combinations. Make a summary and a flowchart to help you decide whether you should solve a problem using powers, permutations, the rule of sum, or the fundamental counting principle. Include simple examples to support your summary.

Career Link

Management Science

Eleanor has a career in management science; she uses advanced analytics to improve decision making. Her position requires university courses in mathematics, including combinatorics. One project she worked on involved designing a panel for a bank of elevators in a 75-storey building. A passenger enters the destination floor into the software and it analyses the variables and combinations of routes. The software then indicates which elevator will be quickest to reach the destination. For example, if there are people on eight different floors requesting elevators, and three elevators can reach each floor, how many different ways can the elevators pick up the passengers?

Counting Story

Children's stories are often about a problem that needs to be solved. Some problems may involve math. For example,

> When Goldilocks entered the Three Bears' home, she went into the kitchen. There, she saw three pots of porridge (a blue pot, a red pot, and a green pot). She wanted to try the porridge and looked in the cupboard for a bowl. Goldilocks found a small bowl, a medium bowl, and a large bowl. In how many ways could she serve herself some porridge?

At the end of this chapter, your task will be to rewrite a children's story by including counting techniques.

Prerequisite Skills

Factorials

1. Evaluate.

   a) $8!$

   b) $\dfrac{9!}{3!}$

   c) $3! \times 4!$

   d) $_{10}P_6$

   e) $_{12}P_3$

   f) $\dfrac{_7P_3}{3!}$

   g) $\dfrac{_{11}P_4}{4!}$

   h) $\dfrac{14!}{2!\,5!\,6!}$

2. a) Define $n!$ in words and with a formula.

   b) Define $_nP_r$ in words and with a formula.

3. Express each permutation in factorial form.

   a) $_7P_3$

   b) $_{100}P_{92}$

   c) $_nP_6$

   d) $_{15}P_r$

Permutations

4. How many ways are there to arrange

   a) 8 objects?

   b) 5 of 8 objects?

   c) 3 of 13 objects?

5. a) In how many ways could five girls and six boys line up in one row?

   b) In how many ways could they line up with the girls in the front row and the boys in the back row?

6. a) How many permutations are there of all the letters in TRIANGLE?

   b) How many arrangements are there of any three of the letters in TRIANGLE?

Pascal's Triangle

7. This array of numbers is called Pascal's triangle.

$$
\begin{array}{ccccccccc}
 & & & & 1 & & & & \\
 & & & 1 & & 1 & & & \\
 & & 1 & & 2 & & 1 & & \\
 & 1 & & 3 & & 3 & & 1 & \\
1 & & 4 & & 6 & & 4 & & 1
\end{array}
$$

   a) Investigate the terms and describe how to determine the next row. Continue Pascal's triangle for two more rows.

   b) Describe any patterns you see in the triangle.

Probability

8. A coin is flipped three times. Calculate the probability of each event.

   a) heads, heads, heads

   b) heads, heads, tails

   c) heads, tails, heads

   d) two heads and one tail in any order

9. Two cards are dealt from a standard deck. Determine each probability.

   a) The first card is a king and the second card is an ace.

   b) The first card is red and the second card is black.

   c) The first card is a heart or the second card is a king.

10. There are 18 students in a class. Their names are drawn, at random, to determine the order in which they will present their projects. Determine each probability.

    a) Jacob is first.

    b) Caryn is last.

    c) Jacob is first or Caryn is last.

    d) The names are in alphabetical order.

Tree Diagrams

11. The tree diagram illustrates all the possible outcomes when a standard die and a coloured die are rolled.

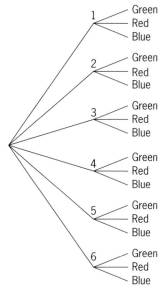

a) Describe the faces of the coloured die.

b) How many different outcomes are there?

c) Determine the probability $P(5, \text{Red})$.

d) What is the probability $P(\text{Green or Blue})$?

Principle of Inclusion and Exclusion

12. Use the Venn diagram to help you explain the principle of inclusion and exclusion.

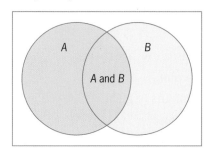

13. In a game of cards, a hand contains five red cards and four face cards. Two cards are red face cards. How many cards are in the hand?

14. Draw a Venn diagram to illustrate each of the following.

a) Face cards and numbered cards from a standard deck.

b) Prime and even whole numbers. Remember, 0 is neither prime nor even.

c) Vowels and consonants.   What can be said about "Y"?

d) The set of integers and the set of natural numbers.

Simplifying Expressions

15. Simplify.

a) $(x^2)^3$

b) $(2a)^2$

c) $(5m^3)^2$

d) $(3k^3)^4$

16. Expand and simplify.

a) $(x + y)^2$

b) $(a + b)^3$

c) $(2p + q)^2$

17. Simplify by reducing.

a) $\dfrac{(n - 1)(n - 2)(n - 3)(n - 4)}{(n - 3)(n - 4)}$

b) $\dfrac{n(n - 1)(n - 2) \cdots 3 \times 2 \times 1}{(n - 2)(n - 3)(n - 4) \cdots 3 \times 2 \times 1}$

c) $\dfrac{n!}{(n - 1)!}$

Permutations With Non-Ordered Elements

Learning Goals

I am learning to

- recognize the advantages of different counting techniques
- make connections between situations that involve permutations and combinations

> **Minds On...**

In the previous chapter, the objects in each set were always different. This is not always the case. Sometimes, there are objects that are identical.

- Do you think this will increase (or decrease) the number of different arrangements? Why?

- There may be some objects that cannot be rearranged. Do you think this will increase (or decrease) the number of arrangements? Why?

> **Action!**

Investigate Permutations With Identical Elements

Materials

- 6 coloured blocks or linking cubes (3 of one colour, 2 of a second colour, 1 of a third colour)

1. Select the coloured blocks as indicated. Set the others aside. For each set of blocks, answer the following questions:
   - What are the possible permutations?
   - How many arrangements of blocks in a row are there?

   a) two of one colour, one of another colour

   b) two of one colour, two of different colours (e.g., blue blue yellow red)

   c) two of one colour, two of another colour

   d) two of one colour, three of another colour

2. What would you multiply by to get the total number of arrangements if the blocks were all different?

3. **Reflect** Raj counted all of the permutations of 3 red, 2 blue, and 2 yellow blocks and found there were 210 possible arrangements. Explain how the number of arrangements relates to the types of blocks in the set.

4. **Extend Your Understanding** Assume you know the number of arrangements of n objects when p, q, r, ... of them are alike. Make a hypothesis of what you would multiply by to get the total number of arrangements if the objects were all different. Test your hypothesis.

Example 1

Permutations With Like Elements

Compare the number of arrangements of the sets of letters A_1A_2BC and AABC.

Literacy Link

The subscripts make the letters A_1 and A_2 distinct.

> **Solution**

List all of the possible arrangements of A_1A_2BC and AABC.

Arrangements of A_1A_2BC		Arrangements of AABC
A_1A_2BC	A_2A_1BC	AABC
A_1A_2CB	A_2A_1CB	AACB
A_1BA_2C	A_2BA_1C	ABAC
A_1CA_2B	A_2CA_1B	ACAB
A_2BCA_1	A_1BCA_2	ABCA
A_1CBA_2	A_2CBA_1	ACBA
BA_1A_2C	BA_2A_1C	BAAC
CA_1A_2B	CA_2A_1B	CAAB
BA_1CA_2	BA_2CA_1	BACA
CA_1BA_2	CA_2BA_1	CABA
BCA_1A_2	BCA_2A_1	BCAA
CBA_1A_2	CBA_2A_1	CBAA

In each case, there are 2! permutations of A_1A_2BC for each AABC arrangement. This is because there are 2! permutations of A_1A_2.

Your Turn

Compare the number of arrangements of the sets of letters.

a) $AB_1B_2B_3$ and ABBB

b) $A_1A_2B_1B_2$ and AABB

Processes

Representing
How else could you display the arrangements?

Permutations With Like Objects

In Example 1, you can multiply the number of arrangements of AABC by 2! to determine the number of arrangements of A_1A_2BC. You can also divide the number of arrangements of A_1A_2BC by 2! to determine the number of arrangements of AABC.

The number of permutations of n elements, when p of one type are identical, q of another type are identical, r of another type are identical, and so on, is $n(A) = \dfrac{n!}{p!\,q!\,r!\dots}$.

Example 2

Permutations With Several Identical Elements

A hockey team ended its season with 12 wins, 8 losses, and 4 ties. In how many orders could these outcomes have happened?

Processes

Selecting Tools and Computational Strategies
Why wouldn't you choose to solve the problem by listing all of the orders?

Solution

Apply the formula.

$n = 12 + 8 + 4$ $p = 12$ $q = 8$ $r = 4$
$\quad = 24$

Number of permutations $= \dfrac{24!}{12!\,8!\,4!}$ When using a calculator, enter the denominator in brackets.
$\qquad\qquad\qquad\qquad = 1\ 338\ 557\ 220$

These outcomes could have happened in 1 338 557 220 ways.

Your Turn

Compare the number of orders of this hockey team's wins, losses, and ties with those of a team that had eight wins, eight losses, and eight ties. Would you expect the number of orders to be higher or lower in the second scenario? Why?

Example 3

Distinct Objects in a Fixed Order

How many ways are there to arrange the letters in the word NUMBER if the consonants must remain in the original order?

Solution

You can place the consonants in any position but you must keep them in the order NMBR.

Some of the possible arrangements include:

NMBEUR
UNEMBR
NUMEBR
NEMUBR

Since you cannot arrange the consonants in a different order, treat them as like elements, using C for each consonant. Rewrite the letters as CUCCEC.

$n = 6$
$p = 4$

The number of arrangements of CUCCEC is

$\frac{6!}{4!} = 30$

There are 30 ways to arrange the letters, keeping the consonants in the original order.

Your Turn

How many permutations are there of the letters in the word EXPLAIN if the vowels must be in alphabetical order?

Consolidate and Debrief

Key Concepts

- The number of permutations of n objects, when p of one type are identical, q of another type are identical, r of another type are identical, and so on, is $n(A) = \dfrac{n!}{p!\,q!\,r!\dots}$.
- If a number of distinct objects need to remain in a specific order in a permutation, divide by the factorial of that number.

Reflect

R1. Explain why you need to divide by 4! when calculating the number of arrangements of the digits 1, 2, 2, 2, 2, 3, 4.

R2. Is the number of permutations of three girls and four boys the same as the number of permutations of three red balls and four green balls? Explain.

R3. Why is it easier to use the formula $n(A) = \dfrac{n!}{p!\,q!\,r! \ldots}$ than to use a tree diagram or chart?

Practise

Choose the best answer for #2 and #3.

1. Simplify.

   a) $\dfrac{10!}{2!\,3!\,5!}$

   b) $\dfrac{9!}{3!\,3!\,3!}$

   c) $\dfrac{7!}{2!\,3!}$

   d) $\dfrac{120!}{115!\,3!\,2!}$

2. What is the number of arrangements of five small tiles and three large tiles?

   A 20

   B 56

   C 720

   D 40 320

3. Dana has 12 pens. There are four blue, three red, and the others are different colours. Which set of values for the variables in a permutation calculation is correct?

   A $n = 12, p = 4, q = 3, r = 5$

   B $n = 7, p = 4, q = 3$

   C $n = 12, p = 4, q = 3, r = 0$

   D $n = 12, p = 4, q = 3$

4. How many permutations are there of all the letters in each name?

   a) WATERLOO

   b) TORONTO

   c) MISSISSAUGA

   d) OTTAWA

5. How many five-digit numbers can be formed using each set of numbers?

   a) 1, 2, 2, 3, 4

   b) 1, 2, 2, 2, 3

   c) 1, 1, 2, 3, 3

   d) 1, 2, 2, 2, 2

Apply

6. Sam has four different types of fruit. He has three pieces of each type. In how many ways could he arrange them on a platter

   a) in a line?

   b) in three rows of four?

   c) in two rows of six?

7. In a panel of eight light switches, half are on and half are off. In how many ways could this be done?

8. In one of her tricks, a clown rearranges two identical quarters, three identical loonies, and five identical toonies in a row. In how many ways can the clown arrange the coins?

9. How many arrangements are there of 15 flags in a row if five are red, four are green, two are blue, and four are yellow?

10. **Communication** When applying the formula $n(A) = \dfrac{n!}{p!\,q!\,r!\ldots}$, will the result ever not be a natural number? Justify your explanation. Hint: A natural number is a whole number greater than zero.

11. **Application** When travelling from home to school, Minh travels five blocks north and six blocks west. How many different routes can he take? What assumptions did you make?

12. **Thinking** In how many ways could 12 volleyball players be assigned to

    a) four triple rooms?

    b) six double rooms?

13. In how many ways could the letters in the word PROBLEM be arranged if the consonants must remain in the original order?

14. In how many ways could the digits in the number 458 978 be arranged if the prime digits must remain in the original position?

✔ Achievement Check

15. In the opening credits of each episode of the TV show *Fawlty Towers*, the sign on the front of the hotel rearranged the letters in the hotel's name.

    a) How many arrangements are there of all the letters in FAWLTY TOWERS?

    b) How many arrangements of these letters are possible if the A, Y, O, and E must remain in their original order?

    c) How many arrangements of these letters are possible if the vowels must remain in the second, sixth, eighth, and tenth positions?

    d) How many arrangements of these letters are possible if the consonants (excluding Y) must remain in alphabetical order?

16. **Thinking** An Ontario licence plate contains four letters followed by three digits. Derek noticed that the four letters on his licence plate were all different and in alphabetical order. Similarly, the three digits were all different and in numerical order.

    a) How many licence plates have all different letters and digits and just the letters in alphabetical order?

    b) How many licence plates have all different letters and digits and just the digits in numerical order?

    c) How many have all different letters and digits and both the letters in alphabetical order and the digits in numerical order?

    d) Mathematically, how does the number of licence plates in part c) compare to the total number of licence plates with no restrictions?

17. **Open Question** Design an example that has $\dfrac{12!}{2!\,3!\,4!\,3!}$ as its solution. Justify your reasoning.

Extend

18. How many 7-digit even numbers can be formed using all of the digits 0, 1, 1, 2, 3, 4, 5?

19. How many four-letter "words" can be made from the letters of the word APPLE?

20. A dart board has the numbers from 1 to 20 around the circumference. In how many ways could the numbers be arranged if pairs of numbers on opposite sides of the board must add to the same value?

3.2

Combinations

Learning Goals

I am learning to

- recognize the advantages of using permutations and combinations over other counting techniques
- apply combinations to solve counting problems
- express combinations in standard notation, $C(n, r)$, $_nC_r$, $\binom{n}{r}$

> ## Minds On...

Often a set of objects is selected from a larger set, and the order is not important. Selecting pizza toppings and forming teams for a sports game are two examples. Can you describe a situation in which the order of selecting objects does matter and one in which the order does not matter for these activities?

- cooking
- forming teams
- cleaning
- packing for a trip

> ## Action!

Investigate Non-Ordered Selections

1. **a)** List all of the arrangements of two letters in the word MATH.

   b) List all the combinations of two letters in the word MATH, with no regard to order.

   c) Compare the results.

2. Sanjit, Dennis, Mia, and Kelsey volunteer to be on a dance committee.

   a) Make a list of all possible ways a chair, a secretary, and a treasurer could be chosen.

   b) Make a list of all possible ways the committee could be formed without assigning positions.

   c) Compare the results.

3. **Reflect**

   a) Write the formula for the number of arrangements of r objects, taken from a set of n elements.

   b) How would you change the formula to calculate the number of ways of selecting r objects without regard to order?

4. **Extend Your Understanding** You have a toonie, a loonie, a quarter, a dime, and a nickel. How many different sums of money could you form by selecting three of the coins?

Combinations

In the previous section, you divided the permutation formula by the number of ways of arranging the identical items to account for identical items. Similarly, when choosing r items from a set of n items, without regard to order, divide the permutation formula by $r!$.

The number of **combinations** of r objects chosen from a set of n items is

$$_nC_r = \frac{_nP_r}{r!}$$

$$= \frac{\frac{n!}{(n-r)!}}{r!}$$

$$= \frac{n!}{(n-r)!\,r!}$$

Other standard combination notation is $\binom{n}{r}$ and $C(n, r)$. This is read as "n choose r."

combination

• a selection from a group of objects without regard to order

Example 1

Choose Items From a Set

How many ways can a five-card hand be dealt from a standard deck?

> **Solution**

Order is not important when combining cards to form a hand. For example, king, queen, 9, 8, 3 is the same hand as 3, queen, 9, king, 8.

$$_nC_r = \frac{n!}{(n-r)!\,r!}$$

$$_{52}C_5 = \frac{52!}{(52-5)!\,5!}$$ Explore how to use the combinations key on your calculator.

$$= \frac{52!}{47!\,5!}$$

$$= 2\,598\,960$$

A five-card hand can be dealt in 2 598 960 ways.

Your Turn

In a competition, junior chefs make a gourmet soup by selecting from 10 different ingredients. How many different soups can the chefs make if the soup must include

a) four of the ingredients?   **b)** five of the ingredients?

c) six of the ingredients?

Example 2

Choose More Than One Group

A committee of 3 men and 3 women is formed from a group of 8 men and 10 women. How many ways are there to form the committee?

Solution

Choose each group of three men and three women separately. Since the two groups are being selected together, the fundamental counting principle applies.

Choices for men × choices for women = $_8C_3 \times {}_{10}C_3$ Because you are choosing
$$= 56 \times 120 \quad \text{3 men } and \text{ 3 women,}$$
$$= 6720 \quad \text{multiply.}$$

The committee can be chosen in 6720 ways.

Your Turn

Erica is making a platter of four types of cheese and four types of crackers. She has seven different cheeses and six different crackers. In how many ways can Erica make the platter?

Example 3

Interpret a Diagram

The seven points represent cabins at a lodge. How many paths can be drawn by joining pairs of cabins?

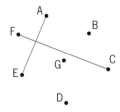

Solution

Choosing any two points from the seven will produce a unique path. Note: Path AE is the same as path EA.

$$_7C_2 = \frac{7!}{(7-2)!\,2!} \quad \text{Why is it important that no}$$
      three points are collinear?
$$= \frac{7!}{5!\,2!}$$
$$= 21$$

A total of 21 different paths can be made between cabins in the lodge.

Your Turn

How many triangles can be drawn using the seven points as vertices?

Key Concepts

- A combination is a set of items taken from another set in which order does not matter. In a permutation, the order of the items matters.
- The number of combinations of r items taken from a set of n items is

$$_nC_r = \frac{n!}{(n-r)!\,r!}.$$

Reflect

R1. Five people are chosen from a group of eight people. Describe a situation for this set that involves

a) permutations

b) combinations

R2. Describe two everyday situations in which items are chosen and the order of the selections does not matter.

R3. Which situation has a greater number of possibilities, one in which order matters or one in which order does not matter? Explain why.

Practise

Choose the best answer for #2 and #3.

1. Convert to factorial form, then evaluate.

   a) $_9C_5$

   b) $_8C_4$

   c) $C(12,3)$

   d) $\binom{11}{5}$

   e) $_7C_2 \times _6C_3$

   f) $\binom{101}{98} \times \binom{101}{3}$

2. Which is an incorrect way of writing $_{10}C_3$?

   A $\dfrac{_{10}P_3}{3!}$

   B $\dfrac{_{10}P_3}{7!}$

   C $\dfrac{10!}{7!\,3!}$

   D $\dfrac{10!}{3!\,7!}$

3. How many three-member committees can be formed from a group of nine people?

   A 27

   B 84

   C 504

   D 729

4. In how many ways could 6 online magazine subscriptions be chosen from a set of 10 magazines?

5. In how many ways could you choose 4 packages of pasta from a bin containing 11 different packages of pasta?

6. In how many ways could you reach into a bag containing 10 marbles and pull out none of them?

7. Refer to #6. Evaluate each combination by first writing in factorial form. Remember, $0! = 1$.

   a) $_1C_0$

   b) $_2C_0$

   c) $_3C_0$

   d) $_{15}C_0$

   e) $_nC_0$

Apply

8. **Application** On an English exam, students need to answer six out of eight questions in Part A and two out of four questions in Part B. The order in which they answer the questions does not matter. In how many ways could a student answer the questions on this exam?

9. From a standard deck, how many five-card hands contain the following?

   a) only black cards

   b) all face cards

   c) no hearts

   d) two red and three black cards

   e) one face card

10. **Communication** Juries are chosen from large pools of people selected at random from the local population. A jury pool has 40 people.

   a) How many ways are there to form a 12-person jury in a criminal case?

   b) How many ways are there to form a 6-person jury in a civil case?

   c) Which situation gives a larger number of ways? Explain why this is to be expected.

11. A dealership has six models of trucks and five models of cars for sale. Wayne sells four vehicles this week. How many of the following combinations of four can be formed?

   a) no restrictions

   b) two trucks and two cars

   c) three cars and one truck

   d) only cars

   e) only trucks

   f) How are the answers to parts b) to e) related to part a)? Explain why this is true.

12. **Communication** Fourteen family members have a one-on-one video chat with each other to wish each person happy new year.

   a) Is this situation a permutation or a combination? Explain.

   b) How many video chats will occur? Express your answer using standard combinatorial notation and then evaluate.

13. Ten points are drawn on the circumference of a circle. Using these points as vertices,

   a) how many quadrilaterals can be drawn?

   b) how many pentagons can be drawn?

   c) how many polygons of n sides can be drawn?

14. **Thinking**

   a) Compare each pair of values.

   i) $_7C_2$ and $_7C_5$

   ii) $_4C_3$ and $_4C_1$

   iii) $_{12}C_4$ and $_{12}C_8$

   b) State a hypothesis from your observations in part a). Explain why this makes sense when you are thinking about groups.

   c) Prove your hypothesis algebraically, using $_nC_r$ in your proof.

15. **Communication** In a drama class of 18 students, nine are selected to be actors in a play, five will build sets, and four will be stage hands. In how many ways could the class be divided up?

   a) Make your calculations by selecting the actors first.

   b) Make your calculations by selecting the set builders first.

   c) Compare your answers. Explain the results.

16. a) How many diagonals are there in any convex octagon?

Literacy Link

Convex means curved out. Concave means curved in. A convex octagon has all vertices pointing outward.

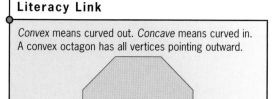

b) How many diagonals are there in a convex polygon with n sides? Explain your reasoning.

✔ **Achievement Check**

17. Ten identical playing pieces are placed on a 5 by 5 game board.

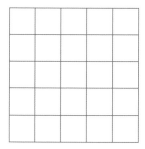

a) In how many ways could 10 playing pieces be placed on the board if there are no restrictions?

b) In how many ways could 10 playing pieces be placed on the board if there must be two pieces in each row?

c) Describe how the results would change if the playing pieces were all different.

18. In how many ways can 15 people be divided into three identical groups of five?

19. In how many ways can a team of 20 hockey players be accommodated in 10 two-person hotel rooms? Assume that the order of assigning the rooms does not matter.

20. Compare your technique in #18 and #19 to the one you used in #12 in section 3.1 on page 109.

21. Show that the number of ways of dividing a class of 30 students into six teams of five members is the same as the number of ways of arranging five red, five green, five purple, five blue, five white, and five black balls.

22. Communication For $r > 0$, will there always be more r-permutations of n items or r-combinations of n items? Why?

23. Thinking Five points are drawn horizontally, and four points are drawn vertically, with the top one overlapping the point on the right side. How many triangles can be formed using the points as vertices?

• • • • •

•

•

•

Processes

Problem Solving
How would you solve a simpler version of this problem?

Extend

24. a) Show that the product of three consecutive numbers is divisible by 3!.

b) Show that the product of r consecutive numbers is divisible by $r!$.

25. Solve for n in $n! = 12 \times {}_nC_2$.

26. How many ways are there to choose three numbers from 1 to 20 so that no two are consecutive?

Problem Solving With Combinations

Learning Goals

I am learning to

- distinguish situations that use permutations from those that use combinations
- solve counting problems using the rule of sum and the fundamental counting principle

> ## Minds On...

You have learned techniques for counting items in which order does and does not matter. How many possible sums are there if you have

- one nickel and one toonie
- three dimes and two quarters

How can you be sure you did not miss any amounts? Explain.

> ## Action!

Investigate The Number of Sums of Money

1. For each set of coins,
   - list the different sums of money you could make,
   - record the number of sums, and
   - verify your answer using combinations and the rule of sum.
   a) dime, quarter
   b) nickel, dime, quarter
   c) nickel, dime, quarter, loonie

2. Describe the pattern in the results.

3. **Reflect** Predict the total number of sums of money (including no money) that could be made from a nickel, a dime, a quarter, a loonie, and a toonie.

4. **Extend Your Understanding** How would you change your methods if you are not allowed to choose zero coins?

Total Number of Subsets of a Set

When building subsets of a given set, you can choose from 0 to n elements to be in the subset. The total number of subsets of a set of n elements is $_nC_0 + \,_nC_1 + \cdots + \,_nC_n$.

Another way of looking at this is that each given element of a set could be either included or excluded, which can be counted as two different ways. Since there are n elements, this could be done in $2 \times 2 \times 2 \ldots \times 2 = 2^n$ ways. The total number of subsets of a set of n elements is 2^n.

Null sets have zero elements. If the null set is excluded from the tally, the total number of subsets would be $2^n - 1$.

Literacy Link

A *subset* is a set whose elements are also elements of another set.

null set

• a set with no elements

Example 1

Determine the Total Number of Subsets

Apples, grapes, peaches, plums, and strawberries are available for dessert. How many different combinations of fruit can be made for dessert?

Solution

Method 1: Use Combinations

Since dessert must include at least one fruit, determine the number of combinations of 1, 2, 3, 4, and 5 fruits.

$$_5C_1 + \,_5C_2 + \,_5C_3 + \,_5C_4 + \,_5C_5$$
$$= \frac{5!}{(5-1)!\,1!} + \frac{5!}{(5-2)!\,2!} + \frac{5!}{(5-3)!\,3!} + \frac{5!}{(5-4)!\,4!} + \frac{5!}{(5-5)!\,5!}$$
$$= \frac{5!}{4!\,1!} + \frac{5!}{3!\,2!} + \frac{5!}{2!\,3!} + \frac{5!}{1!\,4!} + \frac{5!}{0!\,5!} \qquad \text{What does 0! equal?}$$
$$= 5 + 10 + 10 + 5 + 1$$
$$= 31$$

Dessert can be made in 31 ways.

Method 2: Use the Indirect Method

Dessert must include at least one fruit. So, subtract 1 from the total number of possible desserts. The 1 represents the number of desserts with no fruit (null set).

$$2^5 - 1 = 32 - 1$$
$$\qquad\quad = 31$$

The value 2^5 indicates that each of the 5 fruits has the possibility of being selected in 2 ways, either *in the dessert* or *not in the dessert*.

Dessert can be made in 31 ways.

Your Turn

A bag contains eight different-coloured marbles. Use two methods to determine the number of ways to reach into the bag and pull out one or more marbles.

Processes

Connecting
Why is the rule of sum applied here?

Processes

Selecting Tools and Computational Strategies
Which method is more efficient for this problem? When might you choose to use method 1? method 2?

Example 2

Count Cases

The card game euchre uses only the 9s, 10s, jacks, queens, kings, and aces. Five-card hands are dealt to the players. How many euchre hands contain

a) at least three queens?

b) at least two black cards?

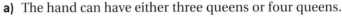

Solution

There are 6 cards in each suit and 24 cards in total.

a) The hand can have either three queens or four queens.

Case 1: Three Queens and Two Other Cards

$$\text{choices for queens} \times \text{choices for other cards} = {}_4C_3 \times {}_{20}C_2$$

$$= \frac{4!}{(4-3)!\,3!} \times \frac{20!}{(20-2)!\,2!}$$

$$= \frac{4!}{1!\,3!} \times \frac{20!}{18!\,2!}$$

$$= 4 \times 190$$

$$= 760$$

Case 2: Four Queens and One Other Card

$${}_4C_4 \times {}_{20}C_1 = \frac{4!}{0!\,4!} \times \frac{20!}{19!\,1!}$$ The first factor represents the number of ways of
$$= 1 \times 20$$ selecting 4 queens. The second factor represents
$$= 20$$ the number of ways of selecting 1 card from the 20 remaining cards used in euchre.

Because either Case 1 **or** Case 2 applies, use the rule of sum.

Total number of possibilities $= 760 + 20$
$$= 780$$

In euchre, 780 hands contain at least three queens.

b) Use the indirect method by subtracting the number of hands with 0 or 1 black card from the total number of hands. Since euchre uses 24 cards, the total number of hands possible is ${}_{24}C_5 = 42\,504$.

Case 1: Zero Black Cards and Five Red Cards

$$\text{Choices for black cards} \times \text{choices for red cards} = {}_{12}C_0 \times {}_{12}C_5$$ Why
$$= \frac{12!}{12!\,0!} \times \frac{12!}{7!\,5!}$$ does ${}_{12}C_0$
$$= 1 \times 792$$ represent
$$= 792$$ only one choice for the black cards?

Case 2: One Black Card and Four Red Cards

$${}_{12}C_1 \times {}_{12}C_4 = \frac{12!}{11!\,1!} \times \frac{12!}{8!\,4!}$$

$$= 12 \times 495$$

$$= 5940$$

The number of possible hands is $42\,504 - 792 - 5940 = 35\,772$.

In euchre, 35 772 hands contain at least two black cards.

Processes

Reflecting
Could you solve part a) using the indirect method? Which method do you predict will be easier? Why?

Your Turn

In the game of hearts, the entire deck of cards is dealt. If you have a hand with 13 cards, in how many ways could the hand contain

a) at least two hearts?

b) at least ten hearts?

c) five clubs and five spades?

d) three diamonds?

e) five clubs or five spades?

Example 3

Choose, Then Arrange

Christine has 10 pictures of family and 8 pictures of friends to put on her wall. She installs shelves to display the pictures. The shelves can fit only four of the family pictures and three of the friends pictures. In how many ways can Christine arrange the pictures on the shelves?

Solution

First, determine the number of ways of choosing the two types of pictures. The number of ways to choose the four family pictures and the three friends pictures is $_{10}C_4 \times _8C_3$.

Once Christine chooses the seven pictures, she must decide how to arrange them. This can be done 7! ways.

The total number of arrangements is

$$_{10}C_4 \times _8C_3 \times 7! = \frac{10!}{(10-4)!\,4!} \times \frac{8!}{(8-3)!\,3!} \times 7!$$

Multiply each factor because Christine chooses 4 family pictures and 3 friends pictures. Then, arrange all of them.

$$= \frac{10!}{6!\,4!} \times \frac{8!}{5!\,3!} \times 7!$$

$$= 59\ 270\ 400$$

There are 59 270 400 ways to arrange four of Christine's family pictures and three of her friends pictures on the shelves.

Your Turn

a) How many five-letter codes can be formed from two different vowels and three different consonants? Consider Y a vowel.

b) How many of these codes contain the letter C?

Key Concepts

- The total number of subsets of a set of n elements is $_nC_0 + {_nC_1} + \ldots + {_nC_n} = 2^n$.

- In some cases the null set is not considered. In such cases, $_nC_1 + {_nC_2} + \ldots + {_nC_n} = 2^n - 1$.

- Consider using the indirect method, especially if it involves fewer cases, such as when you need to choose at least one or two items.

- If the order is important, consider selecting the items first and then arranging them in order.

Reflect

R1. When determining the total number of subsets of a set, you add the number of possibilities in each case. Explain why you add instead of multiply.

R2. When using cases to determine the number of ways of selecting objects from different sets, do you multiply or add? Explain your reasoning.

R3. You can solve counting problems using powers, permutations, combinations, or both. Make a summary and a flowchart to help decide which method(s) to use. Include simple examples to support your summary.

Practise

Choose the best answer for #2 and #3.

1. How many different sums of money can be made from a $5 bill, a $10 bill, a $20 bill, and a $50 bill?

2. In how many ways could a group of 10 people form a committee with at least 8 people on it?

   A 45   **B** 56   **C** 450   **D** 1016

3. If a set has 12 elements, how many subsets can be formed?

   A 12   **B** 24   **C** 4095   **D** 4096

4. A judging panel will have 6 members chosen from 8 teachers and 10 students. There must be at least 3 students on the panel. In how many ways could there be

   a) 3 students on the panel?

   b) 4 students on the panel?

   c) 5 students on the panel?

   d) least 3 students on the panel?

Apply

5. **Communication** Identify whether the following situations involve permutations, combinations, or both. Justify your choice.

   a) forming a committee of 5 people from a group of 12 people

   b) choosing a president, a vice president, and a treasurer from a committee of 12 members

   c) choosing 4 men and 4 women to be on a basketball team from among 6 men and 6 women, and assembling the athletes for a team photo

   d) naming 3 people from among 15 contestants to win 3 different prizes

6. You receive requests to connect with people every day on your social media account. If you have 15 requests to be "friends" with people, in how many ways could you respond by either accepting or rejecting each request?

7. Tonya has the following toppings available for her sandwich: lettuce, tomatoes, onions, olives, sprouts, peppers, mustard, and shredded cheese. She can use up to three toppings. How many different sandwiches can Tonya make?

8. Rohan is shopping for new pants. Six different styles are available. How many different purchases could Rohan make?

9. You can factor the number 210 into prime factors as $2 \times 3 \times 5 \times 7$. The products of prime factors form divisors (e.g., $2 \times 3 = 6$). Determine the total number of divisors of 210.

10. A board of directors needs to assign a chair, vice chair, treasurer, secretary and communications officer. There are four women and six men on the board. There will be two women and three men on the executive. In how many ways could this be done?

11. Thinking In cribbage, each player is dealt six cards from a standard deck. In how many ways could a hand contain

  a) at least two queens?

  b) more than three red cards?

  c) at least two hearts and at least two spades?

12. Application A telemarketer will call 12 people from a list of 20 men and 25 women. In how many ways could he select

  a) 12 men or 12 women?

  b) 6 men and 6 women?

13. A cabin has two rooms with three single beds each, one room with four single beds, and one room with two single beds. Six girls and six boys are assigned to rooms with people of the same gender. In how many ways can the rooms be assigned?

14. Six students from each of grades 9 to 12 have been pre-selected to win eight different prizes as students of the month. In how many ways could two students from each grade be selected to win these prizes?

15. Thinking Given the numbers –6, –5, –4, –3, –2, –1, 1, 2, 3, 4, 5, in how many ways could four different numbers be chosen so that their product is negative?

✓ **Achievement Check**

16. On a crown and anchor wheel, a crown, an anchor, and the four suits from a deck of cards are displayed in slots around the wheel.

  a) Each three-of-a-kind (e.g., ♚♚♚) occurs twice. Calculate the number of slots with three-of-a-kind.

  b) Determine the number of slots with two-of-a-kind.

  c) The following restrictions are in place when all three symbols are different:
  • A crown and an anchor do not occur together (e.g., ♚⚓♦ cannot occur).
  • Three different suits do not occur together (e.g., ♦♥♠ cannot occur).
  • If a crown occurs with two different suits, an anchor may not also occur with the same two suits, and vice versa (only one of ♠⚓♦ or ♠♚♦ can occur).
  Calculate the number of slots with three different symbols. Use your calculations to verify the total number of slots on the wheel.

Extend

17. There are 10 points in a plane. No three points are collinear. How many convex polygons can be drawn using these points as vertices?

18. Five men and five women are selected from eight men and nine women and then seated around a circular table. In how many ways can this be done if their particular seat at the table does not matter?

3.4

Combinations and Pascal's Triangle

Learning Goal

I am learning to

- make connections between combinations and Pascal's triangle

Minds On...

Scholars in many different cultures have known about **Pascal's triangle** for thousands of years. The modern version is attributed to Blaise Pascal, a 17th-century mathematician and philosopher. He discovered numerous patterns in the triangle, including those relating it to combinatorics and probability.

Pascal's triangle

- a triangular array of numbers in which each term is the sum of the two terms above it

The top rows of Pascal's triangle are shown, along with the term references. The terms are designated by $t_{n,r}$, where n is the row number, starting at zero, and r is the diagonal number, also starting at zero.

			1			**Row 0**
		1		1		**Row 1**
	1		2		1	**Row 2**

$$
\begin{array}{ccccccccc}
 & & & & 1 & & & & \textbf{Row 0} \\
 & & & 1 & & 1 & & & \textbf{Row 1} \\
 & & 1 & & 2 & & 1 & & \textbf{Row 2} \\
 & 1 & & 3 & & 3 & & 1 & \textbf{Row 3} \\
1 & & 4 & & 6 & & 4 & & 1 \quad \textbf{Row 4}
\end{array}
$$

$$
\begin{array}{ccccccccc}
 & & & & t_{0,0} & & & & \\
 & & & t_{1,0} & & t_{1,1} & & & \\
 & & t_{2,0} & & t_{2,1} & & t_{2,2} & & \\
 & t_{3,0} & & t_{3,1} & & t_{3,2} & & t_{3,3} & \\
t_{4,0} & & t_{4,1} & & t_{4,2} & & t_{4,3} & & t_{4,4}
\end{array}
$$

- Describe how to generate any given row.
- What are the terms of row 5?

Action!

Investigate Connecting Pascal's Triangle With Combinations

1. a) Build a triangular array of terms by calculating each combination.

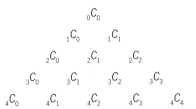

$$
\begin{array}{ccccccccc}
 & & & & {}_0C_0 & & & & \\
 & & & {}_1C_0 & & {}_1C_1 & & & \\
 & & {}_2C_0 & & {}_2C_1 & & {}_2C_2 & & \\
 & {}_3C_0 & & {}_3C_1 & & {}_3C_2 & & {}_3C_3 & \\
{}_4C_0 & & {}_4C_1 & & {}_4C_2 & & {}_4C_3 & & {}_4C_4
\end{array}
$$

b) Describe any observations.

c) Use two methods to determine the next row of Pascal's triangle.

2. How do combinations of the form $_nC_r$ relate to the terms in row 4 of Pascal's triangle?

3. a) Determine the sum of each row.

   b) Reflect Relate the results to a previous observation in this chapter.

4. Extend Your Understanding

   a) What is the sum of the terms in row 10? How do you know?

   b) What is the sum of the terms in row n? How do you know?

Pascal's Method

The terms of Pascal's triangle are generated by adding two adjacent terms and placing the result immediately below them in the next row.

$t_{n,r} + t_{n,r+1} = t_{n+1,r+1}$

Using combinations, $_nC_r + {_nC_{r+1}} = {_{n+1}C_{r+1}}$

Example 1

Diagonal Patterns in Pascal's Triangle

Calculate the sum of the first four terms of diagonal 2. Find this sum in Pascal's triangle and relate it to $_nC_r$.

Solution

For diagonal 2, which is outlined in the diagram, $r = 2$.

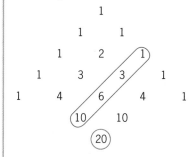

The sum of the first four terms is $1 + 3 + 6 + 10 = 20$.   This value is circled in the diagram.

Comparing the terms in Pascal's triangle to combinations gives $_2C_2 + {_3C_2} + {_4C_2} + {_5C_2} = {_6C_3}$.

Your Turn

Calculate the sum of the first five terms of diagonal 6. Find this value in Pascal's triangle and relate it to $_nC_r$.

Example 2

Routes on a Grid

To get from home to work, Hannah travels four blocks south and five blocks east. How many different routes can she take, travelling only south and east?

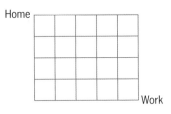

> **Solution**

Method 1: Use Pascal's Method

Each point of intersection can be reached only when Hannah travels south or east. Add the number of paths to the adjacent grid points to determine the number of paths to the given point. Continue until the diagram is complete.

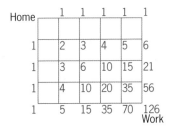

Hannah can take 126 different routes to work.

Method 2: Use Combinations

Hannah needs to travel nine blocks to work. Select any four of these nine blocks to travel southbound. The remaining five blocks will be eastbound.

$$_9C_4 \times {}_5C_5 = \frac{9!}{5!\,4!} \times \frac{5!}{0!\,5!}$$

Why do you not simply use $_{14}C_9$?

$$= 126$$

Hannah can take 126 different routes to work.

Your Turn

Bill rides his bike to school and travels four blocks west and six blocks north. Use two methods to determine the number of different routes Bill could take to school if he travels only north and west.

Example 3

Pascal's Triangle and the Binomial Theorem

a) Expand and simplify $(x + y)^2$ and $(x + y)^3$.

b) Relate the coefficients in the binomial expansion to Pascal's triangle and to combinations.

c) State the degree of each term and describe the pattern in the exponents.

> **Solution**

a)
$$(x + y)^2 = (x + y)(x + y)$$
$$= x^2 + 2xy + y^2$$

$$(x + y)^3 = (x + y)(x + y)(x + y)$$
$$= (x^2 + 2xy + y^2)(x + y)$$
$$= x^3 + x^2y + 2x^2y + 2xy^2 + xy^2 + y^3$$
$$= x^3 + 3x^2y + 3xy^2 + y^3$$

b) For $(x + y)^2$, the coefficients 1, 2, and 1 are the terms in row 2.

These terms correspond to combinations $_2C_r$, where $r = 0$ to 2.

$$(x + y)^2 = {_2C_0}x^2y^0 + {_2C_1}xy + {_2C_2}x^0y^2$$

For $(x + y)^3$, the coefficients 1, 3, 3, and 1 are the terms in row 3.

These terms correspond to combinations $_3C_r$, where $r = 0$ to 3.

$$(x + y)^3 = {_3C_0}x^3y^0 + {_3C_1}x^2y + {_3C_2}x^1y^2 + {_3C_3}x^0y^3$$

c) For $(x + y)^2$, the degree of each term is 2, which is the exponent of the binomial. For $(x + y)^3$, the degree of each term is 3, which is the exponent of the binomial.

For the first term, the exponent of x is n and the exponent of y is 0. For each successive term, the exponent of x decreases by 1, while the exponent of y increases by 1.

Literacy Link

The *degree* of a term is the sum of the exponents of its variables.

Binomial Theorem

You can use the binomial theorem to expand any power of a binomial expression.

$$(x + y)^n = {_nC_0}x^ny^0 + {_nC_1}x^{n-1}y^1 + {_nC_2}x^{n-2}y^2 + \dots + {_nC_{n-1}}x^1y^{n-1} + {_nC_n}x^0y^n$$

The general term is $_nC_r x^{n-r}y^r$.

binomial theorem

- a formula used to expand $(a + b)^n$

Your Turn

Use the binomial theorem to expand each binomial, relating it to both Pascal's triangle and combinations. State the degree of each term.

a) $(a + b)^4$ **b)** $(p + q)^5$

⟫⟫⟫ Consolidate and Debrief ⟫⟫⟫

Key Concepts

- The terms in row n of Pascal's triangle correspond to the combinations $t_{n,r} = {_nC_r}$.

- A given term in Pascal's triangle equals the sum of the two terms directly above it in the previous row. They can be generated using the relationship $t_{n,r} + t_{n,r+1} = t_{n+1,r+1}$. This is known as Pascal's method.

- Using combinations, $_nC_r + {_nC_{r+1}} = {_{n+1}C_{r+1}}$.

- The coefficients in the binomial expansion of $(x + y)^n$ are found in row n of Pascal's triangle.

- According to the binomial theorem,
  $$(x + y)^n = {_nC_0}x^ny^0 + {_nC_1}x^{n-1}y^1 + {_nC_2}x^{n-2}y^2 + \dots + {_nC_{n-1}}x^1y^{n-1} + {_nC_n}x^0y^n.$$

- Pascal's method can be applied to counting paths in arrays.

Reflect

R1. Explain why the term labels of Pascal's triangle begin at $t_{0,0}$.

R2. Describe how Pascal's triangle and combinations are related. Use one row as a reference.

R3. Sam is working through Example 2. He calculates the number of arrangements of the letters SSSSEEEE (S for south, E for east) to solve the problem. Is this a valid solution? Justify your reasoning.

Practise

Choose the best answer for #3 and #4.

1. a) Write each term in row 9 of Pascal's triangle using $_nC_r$.

   b) Write the first five terms in diagonal 4 of Pascal's triangle using $_nC_r$.

2. Use Pascal's method to complete the array.

```
78      286     b
     a      1001
         c
```

3. The first three terms in the expansion of $(x + y)^7$ are

   A x^7, x^6y, x^5y^2

   B x^7, x^6, x^5

   C $xy^7, 7xy^6, 21xy^5$

   D $x^7, 7x^6y, 21x^5y^2$

4. Point B is four blocks east and three blocks south of point A. How many routes are possible from A to B, travelling only south and east?

   A 220

   B 35

   C 12

   D 7

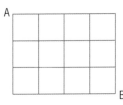

5. Write the first nine rows of Pascal's triangle. Circle the given terms in Pascal's triangle, then circle the correct answer to help use Pascal's method to rewrite each of the following:

   a) $_5C_2 + _5C_3$ **b)** $_7C_3 + _7C_4$

   c) $_5C_4 - _4C_4$ **d)** $_8C_6 - _7C_5$

Apply

6. Communication

   a) Evaluate each of the following:

   i) $_2C_2 + _3C_2$

   ii) $_3C_2 + _4C_2$

   iii) $_4C_2 + _5C_2$

   b) Describe the results.

   c) Identify the terms from part a) in Pascal's triangle.

   d) Summarize the results, in general, as they apply to combinations and Pascal's triangle.

7. a) Calculate the sum of the first four terms of diagonal 7 (diagonals begin at zero). Locate the sum in Pascal's triangle and relate it to $_nC_r$.

   b) Generalize by stating the sum of the first k terms of diagonal r in Pascal's triangle and relating it to $_nC_r$.

8. Application A checker is placed on a checkerboard in the top right corner. The checker can move diagonally downward. Determine the number of routes to the bottom of the board.

9. A black checker is placed in the bottom-right corner of a checkerboard. The checker can move diagonally upward. The black checker cannot enter the square occupied by the red checker, but can jump over it. How many routes are there for the black checker to the top of the board?

10. Determine the number of paths from A to B, travelling downward and to the right.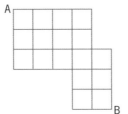

11. Determine the number of paths that spell PASCAL. Can combinations be used to solve each question?

a)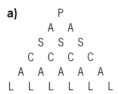
```
        P
      A   A
    S   S   S
  C   C   C   C
A   A   A   A   A
L   L   L   L   L   L
```

b)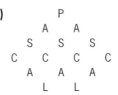
```
        P
    A       A
  S   S       S
C   C   C       C
  A   A       A
    L       L
```

12. Application Investigate the sums of the first n natural numbers. For example, $1 + 2 = 3$, $1 + 2 + 3 = 6$, ...

a) Locate the results in Pascal's triangle.

b) Summarize the results using combinations.

c) Refer to Example 1 on page 123. Explain why the results are similar.

13. Use Pascal's triangle to expand and simplify.

a) $(x + y)^8$ **b)** $(x - y)^5$

c) $(2a + b)^4$ **d)** $(x^2 - 2)^3$

14. Drawing a line through a circle divides it into two regions.

a) If n lines are drawn through a circle, what is the maximum number of regions formed? Develop a formula using Pascal's triangle.

b) Twenty lines are drawn through a circle. What is the maximum number of regions inside the circle?

15. a) Investigate the sum of the squares of the natural numbers from 1 to n by copying and completing the chart up to $n = 6$.

n	Sum of Squares $1^2 + 2^2 + \ldots + n^2$	$t_{n+1,3} + t_{n+2,3}$
1		
2		

b) Describe the results.

c) Generalize using combinations.

d) State the sum of the squares of the first 50 natural numbers.

16. Thinking Investigate the number of oranges needed to stack the fruit in a tetrahedron.

a) Complete a chart showing the total number of oranges needed relative to the number of layers.

b) Identify the results in Pascal's triangle and describe your findings.

c) Write a relationship involving $_nC_r$.

d) How many oranges are needed for a 10-layer stack in a tetrahedral shape?

✓ **Achievement Check**

17. a) Calculate the sum of the squares of the terms in rows 2 to 5 of Pascal's Triangle.

Row n	Sum of Squares	Term in Pascal's Triangle
2		
3		

b) Identify the sums from part a) in Pascal's triangle. Describe your findings.

c) Rewrite each of the sums using combinations.

d) Generalize the relationship using a formula involving $_nC_r$.

18. Thinking Explain how $(h + t)^5$ could be used to show the different combinations of heads and tails when a coin is tossed repeatedly.

Extend

19. Expand and simplify.

a) $\left(p - \dfrac{1}{p}\right)^5$

b) $\left(3m^2 + \dfrac{2}{m^2}\right)^4$

Probabilities Using Combinations

Learning Goal

I am learning to

- solve probability problems using counting principles

Minds On...

Experienced card players usually consider probability. For example, a player has the king of spades, king of hearts, queen of diamonds, jack of clubs, and 9 of hearts. She needs to determine whether it is more likely that the next card will be another king, for three-of-a-kind, or a 10 for a five-card run (i.e., 9, 10, J, Q, K). How can she determine the likelihood of drawing each card?

Action!

Investigate Winning a Lottery

To win a particular lottery, your ticket must match five different numbers from 1 to 30, without regard to order.

1. How many winning combinations are there?

2. How many ways are there of choosing five different numbers from 1 to 30?

3. What is the probability of winning this lottery?

4. **Reflect** Research a lottery based on matching numbers.
   a) How does the probability of winning this lottery compare to the one analysed above?
   b) Would the probability of winning affect which lottery ticket you would buy? Explain.

5. **Extend Your Understanding** Some lotteries sell a specified number of tickets, and the winning ticket is drawn from those sold. Does the probability of winning increase as you buy more tickets? Make up an example to explain your answer.

Example 1

Chances of Winning

A scratch and win contest at a store allows you to scratch five numbers. If all of your numbers match the winning set of five numbers, chosen from 1 to 25 without regard to order, you win the grand prize.

a) What is the probability of winning the grand prize?

b) To win second prize, four of the five winning numbers must match. What is the probability of winning second prize?

Solution

a) The total number of possible outcomes is $n(S) = {}_{25}C_5$. There is only one successful outcome: matching all five of the winning numbers.

$n(A) = {}_5C_5$
$\quad\;\; = 1$

$$P(\text{all five selected}) = \frac{n(A)}{n(S)}$$
$$= \frac{1}{{}_{25}C_5}$$
$$= \frac{1}{53\ 130}$$
$$\approx 0.000\ 018\ 821$$
$$\approx 0.001\ 882\%$$

There is approximately a 0.001 882% chance of having all five winning numbers.

b) The total number of possible outcomes is $n(S) = {}_{25}C_5$. Four of your numbers will match the winners, but the fifth does not, so it needs to be chosen from the remaining 20 numbers.

$n(A) = {}_5C_4 \times {}_{20}C_1$

$$P(\text{four successes}) = \frac{{}_5C_4 \times 20}{{}_{25}C_5}$$
$$= \frac{100}{53\ 130}$$
$$\approx 0.001\ 882$$
$$\approx 0.1882\%$$

There is approximately a 0.1882% chance of winning second prize.

Your Turn

To win the grand prize in a fundraising draw, you need to match seven numbers from 1 to 27, without regard to order.

a) What is the percent chance of winning the grand prize?

b) What is the percent chance of winning second prize, which involves matching six of the seven winning numbers?

c) What is the probability of not winning first or second prize?

d) Comment on how difficult it is to win lottery prizes.

Example 2

Choose From Groups

A university task force of 8 people is to be formed from 16 members of the student government and 10 professors. Each person is equally likely to be chosen.

a) What is the probability that there is an equal number of students and professors?

b) What is the probability that at least six members are students?

c) Which outcome is more likely to occur?

Solution

Eight members are chosen, without regard to order, from a total of 26 people: $n(S) = {}_{26}C_8$.

a) Four students and four professors are chosen. *The use of **and** tells you to multiply.*

$$n(A) = {}_{16}C_4 \times {}_{10}C_4$$

$$P(\text{equal number}) = \frac{{}_{16}C_4 \times {}_{10}C_4}{{}_{26}C_8}$$

$$\approx 0.244\ 64$$

The first factor represents the choices for students. The second factor represents the choices for professors.

The probability that an equal number of students and professors is chosen is approximately 0.24.

b) There could be six, seven, or eight students. The remaining members are professors.

*The use of **or** tells you to use the rule of sum.*

$$n(A) = \left({}_{16}C_6 \times {}_{10}C_2\right) + \left({}_{16}C_7 \times {}_{10}C_1\right) + \left({}_{16}C_8 \times {}_{10}C_0\right)$$

$$P(\text{at least 6 students}) = \frac{\left({}_{16}C_6 \times {}_{10}C_2\right) + \left({}_{16}C_7 \times {}_{10}C_1\right) + \left({}_{16}C_8 \times {}_{10}C_0\right)}{{}_{26}C_8}$$

$$= \frac{360\ 360 + 114\ 400 + 12\ 870}{1\ 562\ 275}$$

$$\approx 0.312\ 12$$

The probability that there are at least six students on the task force is approximately 0.31.

c) $P(\text{at least 6 students}) > P(\text{equal number})$. Therefore, it is more likely that there will be at least six students than an equal number of students and professors.

Your Turn

A teacher uses a random name generator to select six students to present their projects. In a class of 23 students, 12 are male and 11 are female.

a) What is the probability that an equal number of male and female students will present?

b) What is the probability that more female than male students will present?

c) Which outcome is more likely?

Example 3

Apply Pascal's Triangle to Probability

In the game of Plinko, a disc is dropped into a slot at the top of a board. When it hits a peg, it falls to the left or right as it travels down the board. State the probability of the disc ending up in each slot at the bottom of the board.

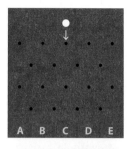

Solution

Using Pascal's triangle, the total number of paths to the bottom of the board is $1 + 4 + 6 + 4 + 1 = 16$.

$P(C) = \dfrac{6}{16}$

$P(B) = P(D)$

$\qquad = \dfrac{4}{16}$

$P(A) = P(E)$

$\qquad = \dfrac{1}{16}$

Processes

Reflecting
Could you have used combinations to solve this problem?

The probability of the disc ending up in each slot from the left is $\dfrac{1}{16}, \dfrac{4}{16}, \dfrac{6}{16}, \dfrac{4}{16}, \dfrac{1}{16}$.

Your Turn

State the probability of the disc ending up in each slot at the bottom of this Plinko board.

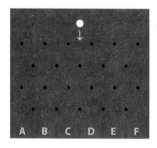

> ## Consolidate and Debrief

Key Concepts

- You can sometimes use combinations or Pascal's triangle to determine probabilities.

- The numerator, $n(A)$, represents the number of successful outcomes, usually involving restrictions.

- The denominator, $n(S)$, represents the total number of outcomes, with no restrictions.

Reflect

R1. Using cards from a standard deck, provide an example of a situation in which permutations are used to calculate probabilities. Change the example so it involves combinations.

R2. Tim and Ginny are solving the following problem:

In a race of eight runners, what is the probability that Jake and Hamid are the top two finishers?

Tim solves the problem using permutations: $P(A) = \dfrac{_2P_2}{_8P_2}$

Ginny solves it using combinations: $P(A) = \dfrac{_2C_2}{_8C_2}$

Are both solutions valid? Why?

Practise

Choose the best answer for #3 and #4.

1. What is the probability that a hand of five cards contains only
   a) hearts?
   b) red cards?
   c) face cards?

2. In the story of the Three Little Pigs, the big bad wolf was able to blow down the two houses made of straw and of sticks, but not the house made of bricks. If the wolf chose two houses at random, what is the probability that it would be able to blow them both down?

3. A department has 10 employees. Two will be chosen at random to attend a conference. What is the probability that both Sarah and Dan will be selected?

   A $\dfrac{1}{5}$ B $\dfrac{1}{45}$

   C $\dfrac{2}{45}$ D $\dfrac{1}{90}$

4. To win the grand prize in a hospital lottery, you must match six different numbers chosen from the numbers 1 to 45. What is the probability of winning the grand prize?

   A $\dfrac{1}{5\ 864\ 443\ 200}$

   B $\dfrac{6}{5\ 864\ 443\ 200}$

   C $\dfrac{1}{8\ 145\ 060}$

   D $\dfrac{6}{8\ 145\ 060}$

Apply

5. **Application** In the game of rummy, a player wins with a hand of three-of-a-kind or a run of three or more cards in the same suit. What is the probability that a hand of seven cards will be dealt
   a) three kings?
   b) three-of-a-kind?
   c) the 4, 5, and 6 of spades?
   d) a run of exactly three cards?

6. In the game of hearts, each of four players receives 13 cards. What is the probability that each player receives 13 cards of the same suit?

7. Six girls and five boys wish to join a committee. Four of them will be selected. What is the probability that three girls and one boy will be selected?

8. Four different numbers are selected at random from 1 to 15. What are the odds in favour of exactly two of the numbers being divisible by 5?

9. A spider walks from point A in its web always moving outward from the centre, until it reaches the perimeter. What is the probability that the spider will reach point B?

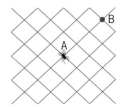

10. Communication Kayla is playing checkers on her smartphone. A checker is in the bottom square of the third column. It will randomly move diagonally left or right one space forward, for a total of seven moves.

a) Which space has the greatest probability as the destination for the checker?

b) If the checker begins in a different position, will it affect the results? Explain.

11. A four-member curling team is randomly chosen from six grade 11 students and nine grade 12 students. What is the probability that the team has at least one grade 11 student?

12. Thinking A Plinko board has six rows of pegs. The top slots are numbered 1–6. The bottom slots are labelled A–G. Contestants choose the slot into which they drop the disc. What is the best strategy for releasing the disc and for predicting its landing location?

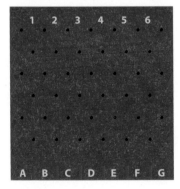

13. Five children are selected at random from a group of eight children. What is the probability that Fariba or Sana, but not both, is selected?

14. Adrian has 15 classmates. He selects four of them to form a study group. What is the probability that Reg or Carlos is selected?

✔ **Achievement Check**

15. A fast-food restaurant is running a scratch and win contest. Customers scratch six squares on a card and try to match the six numbers, randomly selected from 1 to 20, that are printed across the top of the card.

- First prize is awarded if all six numbers match.
- Second prize is awarded if five of the six numbers match.
- Third prize is awarded if four of the six numbers match.

a) What is the probability of winning first prize?

b) What is the probability of winning second prize?

c) What is the probability of winning third prize?

d) What are the odds against winning a prize?

e) Predict the number of fast-food meals a person would need to buy in order to have a relatively good chance of winning a prize. Do you think this strategy is sensible? Why?

Extend

16. In the binomial expansion of $(x - y)^8$, what is the probability that a randomly selected term is divisible by x^2?

17. Three different numbers are randomly chosen from the numbers 2 to 10. What is the probability that the product is

a) even? **b)** divisible by 2?

c) divisible by 6?

18. An unknown card has been lost from a standard deck. Two cards are dealt and both turn out to be spades. What is the probability that the lost card is also a spade?

Learning Goals

Section	After this section, I can
3.1	• recognize the advantages of different counting techniques • make connections between situations that involve permutations and combinations
3.2	• recognize the advantages of using permutations and combinations over other counting techniques • apply combinations to solve counting problems • express combinations in standard notation, $C(n, r)$, $_nC_r$, $\binom{n}{r}$
3.3	• distinguish situations that use permutations from those that use combinations • solve counting problems using the rule of sum and the fundamental counting principle
3.4	• make connections between combinations and Pascal's triangle
3.5	• solve probability problems using counting principles

3.1 Permutations With Non-Ordered Elements, pages 104–109

1. How many ways are there to arrange four boys and three girls in a line for a photo if the girls must be in order of height from shortest to tallest?

2. How many arrangements are there of the letters in each word?

   a) ANAGRAM

   b) EXPRESSIONS

   c) ENGINEERING

3.2 Combinations, pages 110–115

3. The rooms in Kendra's apartment have 14 walls in total. She has enough paint to cover 10 of these walls in one colour and the rest in another colour. In how many ways could Kendra paint her apartment?

4. a) Determine the value for r that has the greatest number of combinations.

   i) $C(8, r)$ ii) $C(10, r)$

   iii) $C(7, r)$ iv) $C(15, r)$

   b) Generalize your findings.

5. A school choir has 10 sopranos, eight altos, seven tenors, and five basses. How many ways are there to select

   a) an octet of three sopranos, two altos, two tenors, and a bass?

   b) a barbershop quartet of two tenors and two basses?

6. A committee of four people is to be chosen from a list of 10 people.

   a) In how many ways could this be done?

   b) Rewrite the problem so that it requires permutations in its solution.

   c) Solve the new problem.

3.3 Problem Solving With Combinations, pages 116–121

7. In how many ways could five different envelopes be distributed into three mailboxes?

8. You have one each of $5, $10, $20, $50, and $100 bills in your wallet. How many different sums of money could you form by reaching into your wallet and pulling out some bills?

9. You are selecting an 8-character password using 26 letters and numbers 0 through 9. In how many ways could your password contain

a) at least two letters?

b) at least two numbers?

c) at least two letters and two numbers?

3.4 Combinations and Pascal's Triangle, pages 122–127

Refer to Pascal's triangle on page 122.

10. Some entries of two rows of Pascal's triangle are given. Determine the unknown entries.

330   462   b

     a   924

11. A circle is drawn with n points situated on its circumference.

a) Using these points as vertices, how many quadrilaterals can be formed if

  i) $n = 4$?

  ii) $n = 5$?

  iii) $n = 6$?

b) Identify these numbers in Pascal's triangle. Describe their location.

c) Relate these numbers to combinations in terms of $_nC_r$.

d) How many quadrilaterals can be formed if $n = 12$?

12. Determine the row in Pascal's triangle that has a sum of

a) 512

b) 4096

13. Stephen's school is four blocks west and seven blocks south of his home. Use two methods to determine the number of routes he could take to school, travelling west or south at all times.

14. Use Pascal's triangle and combinations to expand and simplify.

a) $(a + b)^5$

b) $(2x + y)^4$

3.5 Probabilities Using Combinations, pages 128–133

15. A poker hand of five cards is dealt from a standard deck.

a) What is the probability that the jack, queen, and king of hearts, but no other hearts, are in the same hand?

b) What is the probability that the hand contains five hearts?

16. Five students are randomly selected from seven boys and six girls to join a ski trip. What is the probability that

a) all are girls?

b) there are more boys than girls?

17. A total of 25 photos have been submitted for a photo competition, three of which were submitted by you. From the submissions, five photos will be chosen as finalists.

a) What is the probability that all of your photos will be chosen as finalists?

b) What is the probability that none of your photos will be chosen as a finalist?

c) What is the probability that at least one of your photos will be chosen as a finalist?

Chapter 3 Test Yourself

Multiple Choice

Choose the best answer for #1 to #4. Refer to Pascal's triangle on page 122 as needed.

1. How many ways are there to select four people from a group of nine people, without regard to order?

   A 36

   C 126

   B 262 144

   D 3024

2. What is the total number of subsets of a set of 10 elements?

   A 1024   B 1023   C 100   D 20

3. Using Pascal's method, what is $_7C_3 + _7C_4$?

   A $_8C_3$ B $_8C_4$ C $_8C_5$ D $_7C_5$

4. What is the number of arrangements of three red and two green blocks?

   A $\dfrac{5!}{3!\,2!}$

   C $5!$

   B $3! \times 2!$

   D $\dfrac{6!}{3!\,2!}$

Short Answer

5. In how many ways could a 6-member committee be formed from a 16-member club, if the president and secretary must be on the committee?

6. You found seven library books that you would like to take out, but the maximum is four. In how many ways could you select the four books?

7. How many quadrilaterals can be formed from the vertices of an octagon?

8. How many permutations are there of the letters in the word RELATIONS, if the vowels must be in alphabetical order?

9. a) How are $_8C_3$ and $_8P_3$ related?

   b) Explain this relationship. Include an example to support your explanation.

10. Two balls are selected from a bag with five white and nine black balls. What is the probability that both balls are black?

11. What is the coefficient of p^4q^6 in the expansion of $(p + q)^{10}$?

Extended Response

12. Use two methods to show the number of ways 18 members of a rugby team could be assigned to six triple hotel rooms.

13. a) Describe the relationship between Pascal's triangle and combinations.

    b) Write Pascal's method as it relates to both the entries in Pascal's triangle and to combinations.

14. Alternately subtract and add successive terms in a row of Pascal's triangle. For example, in row 4, $1 - 4 + 6 - 4 + 1$.

    a) Investigate a few rows and describe the results.

    b) Relate the results to combinations and provide a formula in terms of $_nC_r$.

15. Mario orders a pizza with 3 toppings, chosen from 15 available toppings.

    a) In how many ways could mushrooms or olives be included in his toppings?

    b) Would the result in part a) be greater or less if he orders 4 toppings? Explain.

16. A package of 50 computer chips contains 45 that are perfect and 5 that are defective. If 2 chips are selected at random, what is the probability that

a) neither is defective?

b) both are defective?

c) only one is defective?

17. The tens, jacks, queens, kings, and aces are removed from a standard deck of cards. From these cards, four are chosen. What is the probability that

a) all are queens?

b) all are red?

c) two are face cards?

d) there is at least one ace?

e) there are at least one ace and one king?

Chapter Problem

Counting Story

One day, when Goldilocks was out for a walk in the woods, she came upon a house and wondered if anybody was home. The door was not locked so she went inside. As soon as she closed the door, Goldilocks smelled something wonderful and it made her feel very hungry.

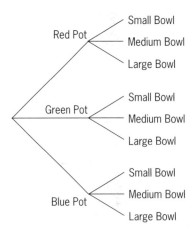

She went into the kitchen and found porridge in three pots (one blue, one red, and one green) on the stove. There were three empty bowls (one small, one medium, and one large) on the table. Goldilocks wanted some porridge but realized there were so many choices available to her. She could have porridge from the blue pot, the red pot, or the green pot; in a small bowl, a medium bowl, or a large bowl. Goldilocks couldn't think straight, so she drew a diagram.

There were so many decisions to make! Goldilocks could serve herself porridge in $3 \times 3 = 9$ different ways.

a) Rewrite a children's story such as Rumpelstiltskin or the Three Little Pigs to involve permutations, combinations, or Pascal's triangle. Make the math an integral part of the story line, where the character is facing difficult decisions involving large numbers. Carry the problem through the story plot. Use diagrams to illustrate the choices to be made, but do not use combinatorial symbols, such as factorials, $_nP_r$ or $_nC_r$, in the story.

b) Then, write a mathematical summary of your story, connecting the story to permutations, combinations, or Pascal's triangle. In this summary, use combinatorial symbols.

Chapters 1 to 3 Cumulative Review

1. In a taste-test survey, 140 people out of 210 picked Koala Cola over Brand X. What is the experimental probability that a randomly selected taster will pick

   a) Koala Cola?

   b) Brand X?

2. Selia likes to listen to blues, country, and hard rock music. The table shows the songs loaded on her MP3 player.

Type of Song	Number of Songs
Blues	20
Country	30
Hard Rock	50

   Selia's player is set to random shuffle, which means that the player randomly plays a song. What are the odds in favour of the player randomly playing

   a) a blues song?

   b) a hard rock song?

3. **a)** A standard die is rolled 10 times. Explain why it is impossible that the experimental and theoretical probabilities will be perfectly equal.

   b) How can this experiment be changed so that they become very close to being equal?

4. Determine the probability of rolling a sum of 7 or 11 using a standard pair of dice.

5. What is the probability of randomly drawing an ace or a red card from a standard deck of playing cards?

6. Consider the bag of marbles.

   a) What is the probability of selecting a yellow marble followed by another yellow marble if the first marble is replaced?

   b) How does this answer change if the first marble chosen is not replaced?

   c) Explain why these answers are different.

7. Kaan lives in Orillia and will be flying to Jamaica on vacation. To get to Toronto Pearson International Airport, he can drive, take a bus, or take a taxi. He can fly non-stop to Jamaica or he can go via New York, Miami, Atlanta, or Philadelphia. Draw a map, a tree diagram, and make a list of all possible routes Kaan can take to Jamaica.

8. How many different outcomes are there when rolling

   a) three standard dice?

   b) four standard dice?

   c) two 8-sided dice?

   d) three 12-sided dice?

9. **a)** In how many ways could four adjacent countries on a map be coloured if eight colours are available? Adjacent countries must be different colours.

   b) Why is it important that the countries are adjacent?

10. A total of 500 people enter a draw in which there is a first prize, a second prize, and a third prize. In how many ways could the prizes be awarded?

11. In how many ways could a president, vice president, secretary, and treasurer be elected from a condominium board that has 8 members?

12. In how many ways could 12 people be seated at a rectangular table if the two hosts must not sit together?

13. To win a school fundraising lottery, you need to correctly select five different digits in the correct order.

    a) What is the probability of winning?

    b) Would winning be more or less probable if the digits could be repeated? Why?

14. Find the prime factors of 255 255. What is the total number of divisors of 255 255, excluding 1 and itself?

15. Before a school dance, students tweeted requests to the DJ for five hip hop, seven R&B, eight rock, and nine pop songs. The DJ will play three requested songs from each genre. How many different playlists could the DJ generate?

16. To get to school, you travel six blocks west and four blocks south.

    a) Use permutations, combinations, or Pascal's method to determine the number of routes you could take to school.

    b) Relate your method to one of the other methods.

17. **Communication** Copy the table and extend it by six rows.

    a) Use a calculator or refer to Pascal's triangle to complete the chart up to $n = 9$.

n	$_nC_2 \div {_nC_1}$	Result
2		
3		

    b) For which values of n is $_nC_2$ divisible by $_nC_1$?

    c) Generalize your findings as they relate to combinations and Pascal's triangle.

    d) Is $_{15}C_2$ divisible by $_{15}C_1$? How do you know, without actually calculating it?

18. In how many ways can eight tickets be put into two envelopes if one envelope is to contain five tickets and the other envelope is to contain three tickets?

19. How many different sums of money can be made from a $5, a $10, a $20, a $50, and a $100 bill?

    a) Use the direct method.

    b) Use the indirect method.

20. A spider walks from one corner of a cube to the diagonally opposite corner.

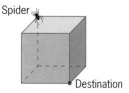

    a) If the spider walks along the edges only, and never backtracks, how many different paths can it take?

    b) Can combinations be used to solve this problem? Why or why not?

21. A jury of 12 people is chosen from 20 men and 30 women. What is the probability that

    a) there is an equal number of men and women on the jury?

    b) there are at least two men on the jury?

Probability Distributions for Discrete Variables

In the study of probability, the mathematical models used to analyse data are called distributions. They describe the probabilities that arise under particular situations. Insurance companies use probabilities to calculate the expected cost of health insurance for different age groups. Game show producers consider both probabilities and payouts when designing the rules of the game.

Key Terms

probability distribution
random variable
discrete random variable
continuous random variable
probability histogram
weighted mean

expectation
uniform distribution
binomial probability
 distribution
hypergeometric probability
 distribution

Literacy Strategy

A compare and contrast graphic organizer helps organize and connect ideas and compare concepts and strategies. As you complete the chapter, compare binomial and hypergeometric distributions.

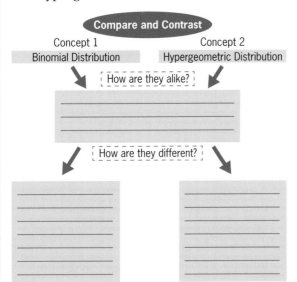

Career Link

Rainfall Forecast
THURSDAY - FRIDAY

Meteorologist

A meteorologist uses probability and statistics to analyse weather patterns and make predictions. For example, under a given set of conditions, there may be an 80% chance of rain in about 50% of the area. The meteorologist multiplies the numbers to estimate a 40% chance of rain in the given area (80% × 50% = 40%). Meteorologists also often predict an expected amount of precipitation, such as 8 mm of rain over the next 24 hours. What other factors does a meteorologist consider, and how are they related to probability?

Chapter Problem

Painted Cube

A large cube is painted on all six faces. It is then cut into 27 smaller, congruent cubes as shown. These smaller cubes have a variety of paint patterns. You will calculate the probabilities associated with each number of painted faces. You will also design a simulation to help compare the theoretical to the statistical probability. How many patterns of painted faces do you think there are?

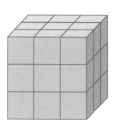

Prerequisite Skills

Simple Probability

1. When selecting a card from a standard deck, what is the probability that it is
   a) a king?
   b) a red card?
   c) a spade?

2. An experiment involves rolling three dice and recording the sum.
   a) Calculate the probability of each sum.
   b) Verify that the sum of the probabilities is 1.

3. In an experiment, a lab rat searches for food behind one of eight doors. Three doors are red, and the remaining doors are green.
   a) What is the probability that the food was placed behind a red door?
   b) What is the probability that the rat will select the correct door?

Mutually Exclusive Events

4. A bag contains six red, one green, four blue, and three yellow marbles. A marble is selected at random. What is the probability that the marble is
   a) red or green?
   b) neither red nor blue?

5. If a deck containing only the face cards is shuffled and one card is selected, what is the probability that the card is
   a) a queen or a king?
   b) a red card or the queen of spades?
   c) a red card and a spade?

Independent and Dependent Events

6. Classify each pair of events as independent or dependent.
   a) rolling two dice

   b) selecting two cards at the same time from a standard deck
   c) flipping a head on one coin and a tail on another
   d) selecting two males from a list of four males and five females

7. a) Use a tree diagram to illustrate the probabilities associated with the number of heads when three coins are flipped.
   b) Are the events (head, tail, tail) independent or dependent? Explain.

8. A card game uses only the hearts. Players select two cards without replacement. What is the probability that a player will
   a) select a queen followed by a king?
   b) select a queen and a king?
   c) not select a face card on either draw?

Combinations

9. Twelve men and 10 women apply to attend a special event. Six names are selected.
   a) In how many ways could three men and three women be selected?
   b) In how many ways could more men than women be selected?

10. A cookie jar contains three chocolate chip, four peanut butter, and six butterscotch cookies. Hansa reaches in and grabs a handful of five cookies. In how many ways could she select
    a) two chocolate chip, two peanut butter, and one butterscotch cookie?
    b) no chocolate chip cookies?
    c) at least one of each type of cookie?

11. In how many ways could 15 different books be divided equally
    a) among five different people?
    b) among three different people?

Evaluating Expressions

12. Evaluate.

a) $_{12}C_5 \times {}_8C_3$

b) $\dfrac{_8C_5}{_{12}C_7}$

c) $\dfrac{_7C_3 \times {}_9C_5}{_{16}C_8}$

d) $_5C_2(0.6)^2(0.4)^3$

e) $_6C_4\left(\dfrac{1}{3}\right)^4\left(\dfrac{2}{3}\right)^2$

Binomial Theorem

13. Use the binomial theorem to expand.

> **Example:**
> $$(a + b)^3 = {}_3C_0a^3 + {}_3C_1a^2b + {}_3C_2ab^2 + {}_3C_3b^3$$
> $$= a^3 + 3a^2b + 3ab^2 + b^3$$

a) $(x + y)^4$

b) $(4x + 3y)^5$

c) $(0.3 + 0.7)^6$

d) $\left(\dfrac{1}{4} + \dfrac{3}{4}\right)^5$

Graphing Calculator Keystrokes

14. Use a graphing calculator to make a frequency histogram of the data:

Homework Hours	0	1	2	3	4	5	6	7	8
Frequency	24	35	30	18	12	1	0	2	2

> **Example:**
>
> | Student Age | 14 | 15 | 16 | 17 | 18 | 19 | 20 |
> |---|---|---|---|---|---|---|---|
> | Frequency | 18 | 22 | 25 | 34 | 19 | 12 | 4 |
>
> **a)** Setting up lists:
> - To clear all lists, press **2ND** **MEM**. Then select **4:ClrAllLists** and press **ENTER**.
> - To enter the data in the lists, press **STAT**, then select **1:Edit**.
> - Enter the ages individually from 14 to 20 in list **L1**.

- Enter the frequency of each age in list **L2**.

b) Graph a frequency histogram of the ages.

- To access the statistical plot, press **2ND** **STAT PLOT** and select **Plot 1**.
- Set the plot parameters as shown.

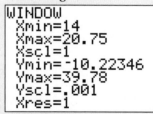

- To set the appropriate parameters for the graph, press **ZOOM**, then select **9:ZoomStat**.
- To adjust the scale so that the x-axis counts by 1, press **WINDOW** and change Xscl to 1.

```
WINDOW
 Xmin=14
 Xmax=20.75
 Xscl=1
 Ymin=-10.22346
 Ymax=39.78
 Yscl=.001
 Xres=1
```

- Press **TRACE** to see the frequency histogram and to read the values associated with each bar.

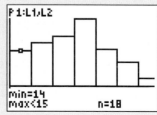

Probability Distributions

Learning Goals

I am learning to

- recognize and identify a discrete random variable
- generate a probability distribution by calculating the probabilities for all values of a random variable
- represent a probability distribution using a table and a probability histogram
- make connections between the frequency histogram and the probability histogram
- calculate and interpret the expected value for a probability distribution
- make connections between the expected value and the weighted mean of the values of the discrete random variable

Minds On...

When a seemingly rare event occurs, we often wonder, "What are the chances?"

- In a family with five children, what is the probability of having three boys?

- What about all the other possibilities, such as five boys? Are they equally rare?

- When rolling two dice, double ones and double sixes are rare, but are they any rarer than other doubles or other combinations of the dice?

Action!

Investigate Probability Distributions

A relative frequency histogram shows the probability of each outcome as the height of each bar in the histogram.

Sicherman dice have faces as shown. They were invented by George Sicherman, an American military strategist. Consider all the possible sums when rolling the two dice.

1. Copy and complete the table showing the sums of the two dice.

		Die 1					
		1	**2**	**2**	**3**	**3**	**4**
	1						
	3						
Die 2	**4**						
	5						
	6						
	8						

2. Make a table of values showing the probability of each sum.

3. Construct a histogram to illustrate the probability distribution.

Method 1: Use a Graphing Calculator

Refer to the Prerequisite Skills on page 143 to review how to use a graphing calculator.

a) Enter the data into the lists.
   - Enter the sums in list **L1**. Enter the frequencies in list **L2**.
   - To calculate the probability of each sum, enter L2÷36 in the **L3** column heading.

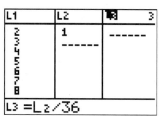

b) Graph a frequency histogram of the sums.
   - Press **2ND** **STAT PLOT** and select **Plot 1**.
   - To adjust the scale, select **9:ZoomStat**, then **WINDOW**. Set the scale as shown.
   - Press **TRACE** to see the frequency histogram.
   - Use the left and right arrows to see how the frequency ($n = ?$) changes for each sum.

The parameters provide a range of x between 0 and 13 with a scale of 1 unit. The range of y is 0 to 7, but –0.1 is the lower limit so you can easily view the x-axis.

c) Describe the graph. What does it tell you?

d) Graph a relative frequency histogram.
   - Press **2ND** **STAT PLOT** , then select **Plot 1** and change it to **Off**.
   - Select **Plot 2** and set the plot parameters as shown.
   - To adjust the scale, select **9:ZoomStat**, then **WINDOW**. Set the scale as shown.
   - Press **TRACE** to see the relative frequency histogram.
   - Use the left and right arrows to see how the frequency ($n = ?$) changes for each sum.

Change the scale and range of y-values to reflect that relative frequencies are between 0 and 1.

probability distribution
- the probabilities for all possible outcomes of an experiment or sample space
- often shown as a graph of probability versus the value of a **random variable**

random variable
- a quantity that can have a range of values
- designated by a capital letter X, with individual values designated by a lower-case x

Method 2: Use Fathom™

a) Set up the lists.
- Drag a new **Collection** to the workspace and name it Dice.
- With the Collection highlighted, drag a new **Table** down.
- Double click on **<new>** and rename it **SUM**.
- Enter all 36 sums in the list, making sure you enter each sum the appropriate number of times (e.g., 4 occurs three times).

b) Graph a frequency histogram of the sums.
- With the **Collection** highlighted, drag a new **Graph** down.
- Drag the **SUM** attribute from the table to the x-axis of the graph.
- At the top right, select **Histogram**.

c) Describe the graph. What does it tell you?

d) Graph a relative frequency histogram.
- With the graph highlighted, in the **Graph** menu select **Scale**, then **Relative Frequency**.

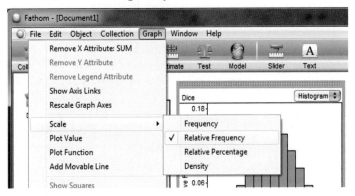

4. Reflect How are the relative frequency histogram from step 3d) and the frequency histogram from step 3b) the same? different?

5. Extend Your Understanding How is this distribution similar to the probability distribution of the sum of two standard dice? How is it different?

Discrete Sample Space

discrete random variable

- a variable that can have only certain values within a given range, such as the sum of two dice

A discrete sample space is the set of all values of a discrete random variable. In the Investigation, you created a discrete probability distribution to show the probabilities of the discrete sample space. A discrete probability distribution maps each value x, of a discrete random variable X, to a corresponding probability.

Continuous Sample Space

continuous random variable

- a variable that can have an infinite number of possible values in a given range, often measurements, such as volume or time

A continuous sample space is the set of all values of a continuous random variable. A continuous probability distribution shows the probabilities of a continuous sample space. You will investigate continuous probability distributions in chapter 7.

Example 1

Constructing a Probability Histogram

The table gives the probability distribution of the number of digits in street addresses of a large city.

Number of Digits, x	Probability, P(x)
1	14%
2	31%
3	42%
4	11%
5	2%

a) Identify the random variable.

b) Construct a **probability histogram**.

c) Explain the meaning of the individual bars in the histogram.

d) Describe the distribution.

e) Calculate the sum of the probabilities. Comment on the result.

probability histogram

- a graph of a probability distribution in which equal intervals are marked on the horizontal axis and the probabilities associated with these intervals are indicated by the areas of the bars

Solution

a) The random variable, X, is the number of digits used in a street address.

b) Label the horizontal axis with the digits from 1 to 5, equally spaced. Centre each bar on the discrete variable it represents.

c) The area of each bar represents its probability. The width of each bar is 1, so the probability is shown on the vertical axis.

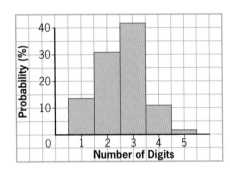

Why would the distribution look the way it does? Consider how street numbers are assigned.

d) Three-digit numbers occur most frequently, and the probability decreases as the digit value increases or decreases from three digits.

e) The sum of all the probabilities in any distribution is 1 because the distribution covers 100% of all cases.

Your Turn

The table gives the percent breakdown of the number of rooms in apartments in a particular complex.

Number of Rooms, x	Percent, P(x)
2	15
3	30
4	42
5	10
6	3

a) Identify the random variable.

b) Construct a probability histogram.

c) Explain the meaning of the individual bars in the histogram.

d) Describe the distribution.

e) Calculate the sum of the probabilities. Does this confirm the results in the example?

Project Prep

Your probability project may involve a probability distribution. How do you know the difference between discrete and continuous random variables?

Example 2

Expectation of a Probability Distribution

a) Make a tree diagram and show the probability distribution for the number of girls in a family of three children.

b) Make a probability histogram for this distribution.

c) Calculate the **weighted mean** number of girls in a "typical" family of three children.

d) Calculate the **expectation** for the number of girls in a family of three children. Compare it to the weighted mean.

e) Interpret the results in parts c) and d).

> **Solution**

a) Boys and girls are equally likely, so each branch in the tree diagram has a probability of $\frac{1}{2}$.

There are eight strings of branches and each has a probability of $\left(\frac{1}{2}\right)^3 = \frac{1}{8}$.

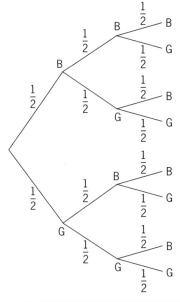

Number of Girls, x	Distribution of Girls	Frequency	Probability, P(x)
0	BBB	1	$\frac{1}{8}$
1	GBB BGB BBG	3	$\frac{3}{8}$
2	GGB GBG BGG	3	$\frac{3}{8}$
3	GGG	1	$\frac{1}{8}$

b)

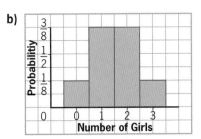

Sidebar:

weighted mean

- the mean of a set of numbers that are given weightings based on their frequency
- multiply each number by its weight (or frequency) and divide by the sum of the weights

expectation (expected value)

- written $E(X)$
- $E(X)$ of a probability distribution is the predicted average of all possible outcomes
- $E(X)$ is equal to the sum of the products of each outcome, x, with its probability, $P(x)$
- $E(X) = \sum_{i=1}^{n} x_i \cdot P(x_i)$

c) To determine the weighted mean, use the values in the table in part a). For each row, multiply the number of girls, x, by the frequency, since this is how many times the outcome can occur. Then, find the sum of the products and divide by the total frequency.

Weighted mean

$$= \frac{(x_1 \cdot \text{frequency}) + (x_2 \cdot \text{frequency}) + (x_3 \cdot \text{frequency}) + (x_4 \cdot \text{frequency})}{\text{total frequency}}$$

$$= \frac{(0 \times 1) + (1 \times 3) + (2 \times 3) + (3 \times 1)}{8}$$

$$= 1.5$$

d) Add a fourth column to the chart and multiply each value of the random variable with its probability.

Number of Girls, x	Distribution of Girls	Frequency	Probability, P(x)	x·P(x)
0	BBB	1	$\frac{1}{8}$	0
1	GBB BGB BBG	3	$\frac{3}{8}$	$\frac{3}{8}$
2	GGB GBG BGG	3	$\frac{3}{8}$	$\frac{6}{8}$
3	GGG	1	$\frac{1}{8}$	$\frac{3}{8}$
Sum		8		$\frac{12}{8}$

Literacy Link

Capital sigma

$\sum_{i=1}^{n} f(x_i)$ is a symbol for the sum of the values of the function $f(x)$. The limits below and above the sigma show that the sum is from the first term ($i = 1$) to the nth term. For example,

$$\sum_{i=1}^{5} i^2 = 1^2 + 2^2 + 3^2 + 4^2 + 5^2.$$

$$\sum_{x=0}^{3} x \cdot P(x) = \frac{12}{8}$$
$$= 1.5$$

The expected number of girls in a family of three children is 1.5. The expectation equals the weighted mean of the outcomes.

e) On average, a family of three would have 1.5 girls.

Although it is impossible to have 1.5 children, do not round because this is a predicted average value.

Your Turn

A spinner has two equal sectors, coloured red and blue.

a) Make a tree diagram to show the probability distribution for the number of times the spinner lands on blue when it is spun four times.

b) Make a probability histogram for this distribution.

c) Calculate the expected number of times the spinner lands on blue.

d) Interpret the results in part c).

Example 3

Expected Value

A hospital is having a fundraising lottery to raise money for cancer research. A ticket costs \$10, and 2 000 000 tickets are available. There are four levels of prizes: one \$5 000 000 grand prize, three \$100 000 second prizes, ten \$1000 prizes, and 2000 free tickets for next year's lottery.

a) What is the expected value of each ticket?

b) Explain its meaning.

Solution

a) Method 1: Use the Equation for the Expectation of a Probability Distribution

$$E(X) = x_1 \cdot P(x_1) + x_2 \cdot P(x_2) + \cdots + x_n \cdot P(x_n) - \text{price per ticket}$$

$$E(X) = 5\,000\,000 \times \frac{1}{2\,000\,000} + 100\,000 \times \frac{3}{2\,000\,000} + 1000 \times \frac{10}{2\,000\,000}$$

$$+\; 10 \times \frac{2000}{2\,000\,000} - 10$$

$$= 5\,330\,000 \times \frac{1}{2\,000\,000} - 10$$

$$= 2.665 - 10$$

$$= -7.335$$

Method 2: Subtract the Cost of the Ticket From the Expected Payout

$$E(X) = \frac{\text{total value of all the prizes}}{\text{the number of tickets sold}} - \text{price per ticket} \qquad \text{What is the value of a free ticket?}$$

$$E(X) = \frac{(5\,000\,000 + 3 \times 100\,000 + 10 \times 1000 + 2000 \times 10)}{2\,000\,000} - 10$$

$$= 2.665 - 10$$

$$= -7.335$$

The expected value per ticket is –\$7.335.   Just as with averages, expected values should not necessarily be rounded.

b) On average, a ticket is worth a loss of \$7.335.

Processes

Connecting
Why might someone choose to buy a ticket for this lottery knowing they probably will not win?

Your Turn

A lottery has a \$10 000 000 grand prize, a \$500 000 second prize, and ten \$50 000 third prizes. A ticket costs \$5, and 4 000 000 tickets were sold.

a) What is the expected value of each ticket?

b) Using the results of this question and of Example 3, are lottery tickets a good investment?

c) How could the lottery be adjusted to make buying a ticket more attractive?

Key Concepts

- A probability distribution shows the probabilities of all possible outcomes in an experiment.

- The sum of all probabilities in any distribution is 1.

- A probability histogram graphs the relative frequency of the random variable. The area of each bar represents the probability of the variable.

- Expectation, or expected value, is the weighted average value of the random variable.

$$E(X) = x_1 \cdot P(x_1) + x_2 \cdot P(x_2) + \cdots + x_n \cdot P(x_n)$$

$$= \sum_{i=1}^{n} x_i \cdot P(x_i)$$

  The expectation can be a non-integer value.

Reflect

R1. The expected number of children in a Canadian family is 1.8. Should this be rounded to 2 or left as is? Explain.

R2. Give two examples of a discrete probability distribution. Explain what makes them discrete.

R3. Describe the steps in setting up a probability distribution for the sum of two 12-sided dice.

Practise

Choose the best answer for #2 and #3.

1. Classify each of the random variables as discrete or continuous:

   a) the number of points scored in a basketball game

   b) the length of time players played in a basketball game

   c) the mass of the weights in a weight room

   d) the number of windows in the classrooms in a school

   e) the area of the windows in the classrooms in a school

2. Which of the following is a false statement about expectation?

   A The sum in the expected value calculations is equal to 1.

   B $E(X) = \sum_{i=1}^{n} x_i \cdot P(x_i)$

   C It is the predicted average of all possible outcomes.

   D It is equal to the mean of the outcomes weighted according to their respective frequencies.

3. In Example 2 on page 148, what is the discrete random variable?

   A x

   B $P(x)$

   C the number of girls in a family of three children

   D the expected number of girls in a family of three children

4. Draw a probability histogram for each of the distributions.

a)

x	P(x)
1	0.35
2	0.42
3	0.11
4	0.12

b)

x	P(x)
5	$\frac{1}{8}$
10	$\frac{1}{4}$
15	$\frac{5}{12}$
20	$\frac{1}{12}$
25	$\frac{1}{8}$

5. Calculate the expectation for each of the distributions.

a)

x	P(x)
1	0.3
2	0.2
3	0.1
4	0.4

b)

x	P(x)
0	$\frac{1}{5}$
2	$\frac{3}{10}$
4	$\frac{1}{5}$
6	$\frac{1}{10}$
8	$\frac{1}{10}$
10	$\frac{1}{10}$

Apply

6. Communication The distribution of marble sizes in a bag is shown in the table.

Diameter (mm)	Frequency
12.0	5
13.0	11
14.0	24
20.0	15
25.0	5

a) Identify the random variable.

b) Is the random variable discrete? Explain.

c) Draw a probability histogram for this distribution.

d) Describe what each bar in the histogram represents.

e) Calculate the weighted mean of the diameters. How does this relate to the expectation?

7. Application Two 8-sided dice are rolled.

a) Show the probability distribution for the sums of the two dice.

b) Draw a probability histogram by hand or using technology.

c) Calculate the expectation. Explain its meaning in this context.

8. A rectangle is to be drawn on a grid with perimeter of 24 cm. The dimensions are integers, and are randomly selected. Show the probability distribution for either the dimensions or the area. Include a probability histogram.

9. Thinking A school is holding a fundraising raffle. The first prize is $500, the three second prizes are $100 each, and the five third prizes are $50 each. A total of 2000 tickets were sold at $5 each.

a) What is the probability of winning a prize?

b) What is the expected payout per ticket?

c) What is the expected profit per ticket?

d) What price should have been charged to have a 90% profit per ticket?

10. A card is chosen from a standard deck, replaced, then another is chosen. This process is repeated three times.

    a) Show the probability distribution for the number of face cards in three trials.

    b) Sketch a graph of this distribution.

    c) Is the number of face cards a discrete random variable? Justify your response.

    d) Calculate the expected value. Explain its meaning.

11. In many games, rolling doubles has beneficial results. Three people are playing a board game in which two dice are rolled.

    a) Use a tree diagram to illustrate the probability distribution of the number of doubles in three rolls of two dice.

    b) Calculate the probability of each outcome in the sample space.

    c) What is the expected number of doubles in the three rolls?

12. Build a probability distribution for the sums of three dice. Include all pertinent components of a distribution, and appropriate explanations.

13. **Open Question** A random device is one that generates a random result. Spinners and dice are typical random devices. Design a random device that has at least four outcomes with non-equal probabilities. Develop the probability distribution for your device and illustrate it using a probability histogram.

> **Project Prep**
>
> You may need to make a random device in your probability project. Think of an appropriate device that you can use.

14. **Communication** The graph shows the percent of numbers that start with each digit when applied to many different data sets, such as hydro bills, addresses, stock prices, population sizes, death rates, and lengths of rivers.

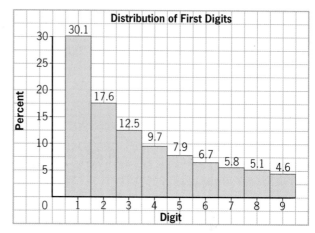

    a) Why would the distribution look this way?

    b) Calculate the expectation. Explain what it means.

Extend

15. When continuously cutting a card from a deck with replacement, what is the probability that the first ace will be cut

    a) on the first try?

    b) on the second try?

    c) on the third try?

    d) on the nth try?

16. Use technology to show the probability histogram for a spinner with five unequal sectors, labelled 1 to 5, respectively. The sectors are proportionally equal in arc length to their labelled numbers.

17. What is the expected sum of two weighted dice on which the number 5 occurs twice as often as the other numbers?

4.2

Uniform Distributions

Learning Goal

I am learning to

- solve problems involving uniform probability distributions

> ### Minds On...

On a TV game show, Allie has the option of taking home $750 or guessing which one of 26 briefcases contains $1 000 000.

- What are her chances of winning?

- Is each briefcase equally likely to hold the money? What would you do?

- How would all of this change if she were allowed a second chance after checking the contents of five briefcases?

> ### Action!

Investigate Uniform Distributions

1. Create the probability distribution for each experiment.

   a) the upper face on a single roll of a die

   b) the result of a single spin of the spinner

   c) the position a person could be assigned when the eight runners in a race are randomly assigned a starting lane from lanes 1 to 8

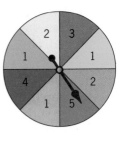

2. Sketch a probability histogram for each distribution in step 1.

3. Compare the three distributions. How are they different? the same?

4. **Reflect** Which distribution(s) would be considered a **uniform distribution**? Why?

5. **Extend Your Understanding** Rewrite the descriptions of the non-uniform examples so they are uniform.

uniform distribution

- occurs when, in a single trial, all outcomes are equally likely

- for all outcomes, x, $P(x) = \frac{1}{n}$, where n is the number of possible outcomes in the experiment

Example 1

Uniform Distribution

A calculator has been programmed to generate a random number between 1 and 5.

a) Classify this distribution.

b) Calculate the probability distribution.

c) Sketch a graph of the distribution. Comment on the shape of the graph.

d) Calculate the expectation. Interpret its meaning.

> **Solution**

a) Each random number is equally likely and there is a single trial. So, this is a uniform distribution.

b)

Random Number, x	$P(x)$	$x \cdot P(x)$
1	$\frac{1}{5}$	$\frac{1}{5}$
2	$\frac{1}{5}$	$\frac{2}{5}$
3	$\frac{1}{5}$	$\frac{3}{5}$
4	$\frac{1}{5}$	$\frac{4}{5}$
5	$\frac{1}{5}$	$\frac{5}{5}$

c) Since this is a uniform distribution and all the probabilities are equal, the bars all have the same dimensions.

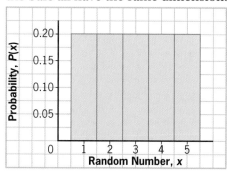

d) Method 1: Use the Sum of the Values of $x \cdot P(x)$

$$E(X) = \frac{1}{5} + \frac{2}{5} + \frac{3}{5} + \frac{4}{5} + \frac{5}{5}$$
$$= \frac{15}{5}$$
$$= 3$$

Method 2: Use the Common Fraction $\frac{1}{5}$

$$E(X) = \frac{1}{5}(1 + 2 + 3 + 4 + 5)$$
$$= \frac{1}{5}(15)$$
$$= 3$$

You can use $\frac{n(n+1)}{2}$ to calculate the sum of the numbers from 1 to n. Show how this works.

The expectation is 3. The predicted average value of the random number will be 3.

Your Turn

A screen saver has been programmed to draw a circle with a randomly chosen radius of integer length between 1 and 8 cm.

a) Is the probability distribution of areas uniform? Explain.

b) Calculate the probability distribution.

c) Sketch a graph of the distribution. Comment on the shape of the graph.

d) Calculate the expectation. Interpret its meaning.

Example 2

Fair Game

A game involves rolling a die. A player who rolls an even number receives points equal to two times the face value of the die. If the player rolls an odd number, the player loses three times the face value of the die. Is this a fair game?

Solution

Calculate the expectation. Points received indicate a positive value for the random variable, x. Points lost indicate a negative value for x.

$$E(X) = \sum x \cdot P(x)$$
$$= -\frac{3}{6}$$
$$= -0.5$$

Roll	Point Value, x	$P(x)$	$x \cdot P(x)$
1	−3	$\frac{1}{6}$	$-\frac{3}{6}$
2	4	$\frac{1}{6}$	$\frac{4}{6}$
3	−9	$\frac{1}{6}$	$-\frac{9}{6}$
4	8	$\frac{1}{6}$	$\frac{8}{6}$
5	−15	$\frac{1}{6}$	$-\frac{15}{6}$
6	12	$\frac{1}{6}$	$\frac{12}{6}$
		Sum	$-\frac{3}{6}$

A fair game will have an expectation equal to 0. This is not a fair game because the player will lose 0.5 points on each turn, on average.

Project Prep

Your culminating probability project may require you to calculate the expectation and to determine whether it is a fair game. How would you make those calculations for any particular game?

Your Turn

A spinner has eight equally spaced sectors labelled from 1 to 8. In a particular game, a player wins points equal to double the sector's face value if a power of two is spun. For all other spins, the player loses the face value of the spin. Is this a fair game?

Key Concepts

- A uniform distribution occurs when, in a single trial, all outcomes are equally likely.
- For a uniform distribution, $P(x) = \frac{1}{n}$, where n is the number of possible outcomes in the experiment.
- When calculating expectation for a uniform distribution, you can factor $\frac{1}{n}$ to make the calculations easier: $E(X) = \frac{1}{n} \sum_{i=1}^{n} x_i$
- When calculating expectation, you can calculate the sum of the numbers from 1 to n using the expression $\frac{n(n+1)}{2}$.
- The expected outcome of a fair game is equal to 0.

Reflect

R1. A school board randomly selects students by their student number to take part in a survey. Is this process a uniform distribution? Explain.

R2. A spinner has 10 equally spaced sectors. Draw an example of a spinner with

a) a uniform distribution

b) a non-uniform distribution

R3. A school raffle has payouts totalling $1500. The school expects 2000 tickets to be sold. Will a price of $2 per ticket give an advantage to the school, to the customers, or will it be a fair game? Justify mathematically.

Practise

Choose the best answer for #2 and #3.

1. Explain whether each of the following is a uniform distribution:

   a) recording the sum of two dice

   b) cutting a card from a well-shuffled deck

   c) an MP3 player randomly selecting a song from a playlist

   d) the number of boys in a family of five children

   e) randomly selecting five students to be members of a committee

2. Which of these is not a uniform distribution?

   A political parties using robo-callers to telephone all constituents in a riding

   B three people being selected at random from a group of four girls and five boys

   C dealing one card, face down, to each of five players

   D a school randomly selecting a student to attend a conference

3. A random number generator provides a number between 1 and 10. What is the expected outcome?

   A 5   **B** 50

   C 55   **D** 5.5

4. A jar contains red and green balls. A person reaches in and randomly selects a ball to indicate the number of points earned or lost. There are four red balls, each labelled +3 points. How many green balls, each labelled –2 points, would be required for this to be a fair game?

5. Given the probability distributions, determine the expected values.

a)

x	P(x)
5	$\frac{1}{5}$
10	$\frac{1}{5}$
15	$\frac{1}{5}$
20	$\frac{1}{5}$
25	$\frac{1}{5}$

b)

x	P(x)
0	12.5%
1	12.5%
2	12.5%
3	12.5%
4	12.5%
5	12.5%
6	12.5%
7	12.5%

Apply

6. A random number between 1 and 12 is generated to decide on the hour during which a special contest will be played on a radio station.

a) Develop the probability distribution for the contest hour, and calculate the expected outcome.

b) Does this mean that the time represented by the expectation is the most likely to be selected? Explain.

7. Communication A card is randomly selected from a deck.

a) What is the probability that it is any specific card?

b) Is this an example of a uniform distribution? Explain.

c) The card is not placed back into the deck and a second card is selected. What is the probability it is any specific card?

d) Are the two card choices an example of a uniform distribution? Explain.

8. A multiple choice test has five possible answers, labelled A, B, C, D, E. If the position of the correct answer is to be chosen at random, draw a probability histogram for this distribution.

9. The Prisoner's Dilemma involves two prisoners, P and Q, who are being held for a crime. If both P and Q confess to the crime, each of them goes to prison for two years. If P confesses but Q denies the crime, P will be set free but Q will serve three years in prison (and vice versa). If P and Q both deny the crime, both will serve only one year in prison.

a) If each prisoner's decision is randomly chosen, show the probability distribution for the number of years in prison for prisoner P.

b) If you were prisoner P, what would your decision be? Base your decision on mathematical reasoning.

10. Application There are only five platonic solids: tetrahedron (4 faces), cube (6 faces), octahedron (8 faces), dodecahedron (12 faces), and icosahedron (20 faces).

Literacy Link

A *platonic solid* is a regular, convex polyhedron with congruent faces.

a) Predict the expected outcome for each die.

b) Check your prediction with appropriate calculations for the four smallest platonic solids.

c) Use your findings to confirm or refine your prediction for the icosahedron die.

11. On a TV game show, a giant wheel has 10 equally spaced sectors as shown. To play the game, contestants must risk a certain amount of their previous winnings. What amount of risk money would make this a fair game?

12. **Thinking** A target contains circles with radii of 8 cm, 12 cm, and 20 cm.

    a) If a dart randomly lands on one of the three regions, show mathematically that this is not a uniform distribution.

    b) Assign points to each area to make this a fair game.

    c) Create a similar target with a uniform distribution.

13. In its Flip Your Lid contest, a coffee chain offers prizes of 50 000 free coffees, each worth $1.50; two new TVs, each worth $1200; a snowmobile worth $15 000; and a sports car worth $35 000. A total of 1 000 000 promotional coffee cups have been printed for this contest. Coffee sells for $1.50 per cup. What is the expected value of a cup of coffee to the consumer?

14. A charity raffle offers a first prize of $1 000 000, a second prize of $100 000, and a third prize of $10 000. A total of 500 000 tickets will be sold. What price should be charged for a ticket in order for the charity to make a 60% profit on this raffle?

✔ Achievement Check

15. Describe or draw an example of a random number generator to be used in a uniform distribution that

    a) has $P(x) = \frac{1}{9}$ for each value of x.

    b) has an expected outcome of 8.

    c) provides an outcome for an unfair game.

16. The game show Deal or No Deal involves trying to guess which of 26 briefcases contains $1 000 000. Each briefcase contains a different amount of money. Your teacher will direct you to a website where you can read the rules of Deal or No Deal and play the game yourself online.

    a) What is the expectation of this game? How does it compare to the offer given to "quit now"?

    b) Calculate the expectation after each of the next two rounds. How does it compare to the offers given to quit?

    c) Is this a fair game? Explain.

Extend

17. A uniform distribution has possible outcomes from 1 to n. Develop a formula to calculate the expected outcome.

18. A contest involves a contestant choosing a number between 1 and 10. One of two cards, each containing a formula, is selected at random. The first card indicates that the contestant will win $40 plus double the contestant's chosen number. The second card indicates that the contestant will win $100 minus the square of the contestant's chosen number. Describe an appropriate strategy to win the most money.

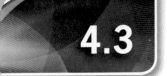

4.3

Binomial Distributions

Learning Goals

I am learning to

- recognize conditions that give rise to a binomial probability distribution
- make connections among the table, histogram, and algebraic representation of a binomial probability distribution
- solve problems involving binomial probability distributions

Minds On...

Many events in games and industry rely on success or failure, and these often can be quantified with probabilities. For example, in the game of Monopoly, success in getting out of jail means rolling doubles, and failure means any other roll. When measuring the fit of car doors, success could be being within a given gap tolerance. Think of other examples where success or failure could be quantified by probability.

Action!

Investigate Binomial Distributions

Materials

- 4 red tiles and 3 green tiles
- computer with Fathom™ software (optional)

binomial probability distribution

- a distribution with independent trials whose outcomes are either success or failure
- the random variable is the number of successes in a given number of trials

In this activity, you will develop a binomial probability distribution for the number of red tiles selected in four independent trials. Randomly select one tile from four red and three green tiles. Repeat four times with replacement.

1. What is the probability of drawing a red tile on a single draw?

2. Make a tree diagram that illustrates the probability distribution for the number of red tiles selected in four trials. Label each branch with the outcome and its independent probability.

3. **a)** How many paths represent two red tiles?

   b) How is this related to $_nC_r$ and/or Pascal's triangle?

4. Copy and complete the table for 0 to 4 red tiles.

Number of Red Tiles	Number of Paths	Number of Paths in $_nC_r$ Form	Probability	Probability in the form $axbxc$
0				
1				

5. How could you use your understanding of independent probabilities with $_nC_r$ to determine the probability of exactly two red tiles?

6. Describe the relationship between the probability column and the other columns.

7. Make a probability histogram for this distribution.

8. Reflect

   a) Write a formula for calculating the probability of x red tiles in four independent trials.

   b) Write a formula for calculating the probability of x red tiles in n independent trials.

   c) Use your formula to calculate the probability of selecting two red tiles in five independent trials.

9. Extend Your Understanding Your teacher will provide you with a file called **BinomialProbability Distribution.ftm**. When you open the file, you will see four open collections.

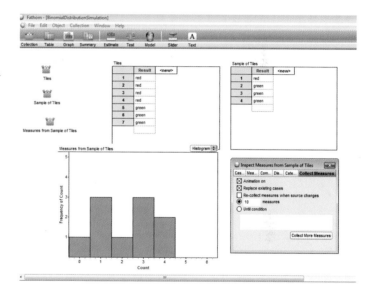

   - The "Tiles" collection gives the tiles available for selection.
   - "Sample of Tiles" simulates the results when four independent trials are completed.
   - "Inspect Measures from Sample of Tiles" allows you to simulate any number of experiments of four trials each, and is set to 10.
   - The graph is a histogram of the results from these 10 experiments.

   a) Press **Collect More Measures**. You can repeat this any number of times. Describe what happens to the graph.

   b) De-select **Replace existing cases** and change 10 measures to 100. You may wish to turn off animation to speed up the process. Press **Collect More Measures**. How closely does the graph resemble your histogram in step 6? Explain.

Example 1

Counting Successes

Two dice are rolled five times. What is the probability that doubles occur twice?

Solution

The probability of success (rolling doubles) on any individual roll of two dice is $\frac{1}{6}$. The probability of failure is $\frac{5}{6}$.

There will be two successes and three failures in the five rolls. So, there is some combination of $\left(\frac{1}{6}\right)\left(\frac{1}{6}\right)\left(\frac{5}{6}\right)\left(\frac{5}{6}\right)\left(\frac{5}{6}\right) = \left(\frac{1}{6}\right)^2\left(\frac{5}{6}\right)^3$

The two doubles can occur on any two of the five rolls, in $_5C_2$ ways. The three non-doubles can occur in the remaining $_3C_3$ ways.

The probability of success on two dice and failure on the other three is $_5C_2\left(\frac{1}{6}\right)^2 \times {}_3C_3\left(\frac{5}{6}\right)^3$.

$$P(x = \text{doubles}) = {}_5C_2\left(\frac{1}{6}\right)^2\left(\frac{5}{6}\right)^3 \quad \text{Remember, } _3C_3 = 1.$$
$$\approx 0.1608$$

The probability that doubles occur twice in five rolls is about 0.1608.

Your Turn

A card is repeatedly cut from a deck and replaced each time. What is the probability that, in 10 tries, an ace is cut

a) once? **b)** three times?

The method used in Example 1 can be applied to the general case.

Probability in a Binomial Distribution

The probability of x successes in n identical independent trials is $P(x) = {}_nC_x p^x q^{n-x}$, where p is the probability of success in an individual trial, and $q = 1 - p$ is the probability of failure.

Each term in the expansion of $(p + q)^n$ represents the probability of one possible outcome in the probability distribution.

Expectation for a Binomial Distribution

When determining the expectation for a binomial distribution, you can multiply the number of trials by the probability of success in an individual trial instead of using the standard process.

$$E(X) = np$$

Example 2

Binomial Distribution

A random number generator provides a number between 1 and 100 over a total of five trials with repetition permitted. Calculate a probability distribution for the number of times a prime number is output.

a) Identify the discrete random variable.

b) Calculate the probability distribution.

c) Verify that the sum of the probabilities is 1.

d) Graph the probability distribution.

e) Describe the shape of the probability histogram.

f) What does $P(5)$ tell you?

g) Calculate the expectation. Interpret its meaning.

Solution

a) X = the number of occurrences of a prime number

b) The 25 prime numbers between 1 and 100 are 2, 3, 5, 7, 11, 13, 17, 19, 23, 29, 31, 37, 41, 43, 47, 53, 59, 61, 67, 71, 73, 79, 83, 89, and 97.

Method 1: Use a Scientific Calculator

Each trial is independent, and on each trial the probability of a prime number is $\frac{25}{100} = 0.25$.

Number of Primes, x	Probability, $P(x)$	$x \cdot P(x)$
0	$_5C_0(0.25)^0(0.75)^5 = 0.2373$	0
1	$_5C_1(0.25)^1(0.75)^4 = 0.3955$	0.3955
2	$_5C_2(0.25)^2(0.75)^3 = 0.2638$	0.5273
3	$_5C_3(0.25)^3(0.75)^2 = 0.0879$	0.2637
4	$_5C_4(0.25)^4(0.75)^1 = 0.0146$	0.0586
5	$_5C_5(0.25)^5(0.75)^0 = 0.0010$	0.005

Method 2: Use a Graphing Calculator

Refer to the Prerequisite Skills on page 143. After setting up the lists, complete the following steps:

- In the **L1** column, enter the x-values, 0 to 5. To program $_5C_x(0.25)^x(0.75)^{5-x}$ in the **L2** column heading, enter
5 **MATH** **PRB 3:nCr** **ENTER** **2ND** **L1** **×**
0.25 **^** **2ND** **L1** **×** 0.75 **^** **(** 5
− **2ND** **L1** **)** **ENTER**

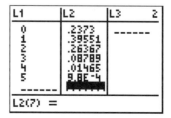

c) $0.2373 + 0.3955 + 0.2638 + 0.0879 + 0.0146 + 0.0010 = 1$

The sum of the probabilities is 1.

d) Method 1: Use Paper and Pencil

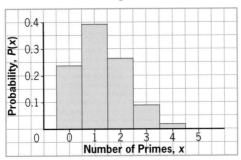

Method 2: Use a Graphing Calculator

Refer to the Prerequisite Skills on page 143.

- Set up your Stat Plot screen as shown. Make sure all other Stat Plots have been turned off.

- Press **WINDOW** and change the parameters as shown.

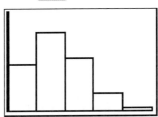

- Press **GRAPH**.

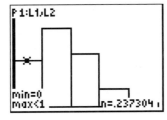

- Press **TRACE** to read the coordinates for each bar.

e) The probability is somewhat bell-shaped, with the mode at $x = 1$ prime. It is skewed to the right.

Literacy Link

A graph is *skewed* when the data are spread out more on one side of the median than the other.

f) $P(5) = 0.001$, which means that selecting five prime numbers is extremely rare.

g) Method 1: Use the Sum of the $x \cdot P(x)$ Values

$$\sum_{x=0}^{5} x \cdot P(x) = 0(0.2373) + 1(0.3955) + 2(0.2638) + 3(0.0879) +$$
$$4(0.0146) + 5(0.001)$$
$$= 1.2501$$

Method 2: Use a Graphing Calculator

- In the column heading of list **L3**, enter
  2ND **L1** **×** **2ND** **L2** **ENTER**.

- In the bottom cell of list **L3**, enter
  2ND **LIST** **MATH** **Sum** **(** **2ND** **L3** **)** **ENTER**.

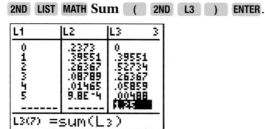

Method 3: Use the Formula

$E(X) = np$
$\quad = (5)(0.25)$
$\quad = 1.25$

On average, you can expect 1.25 prime numbers out of 5 randomly chosen numbers.

Your Turn

A family has six children. Consider a probability distribution for the number of girls in the family.

a) Identify the discrete random variable.

b) Calculate the probability distribution.

c) Verify that the sum of the probabilities is 1.

d) Graph the probability distribution. Compare the shape of the probability histogram to the one in Example 2.

e) Calculate the expectation. Interpret its meaning.

Example 3

Apply the Binomial Distribution

The failure rate is 5% in the initial production run of a new computer chip. A quality control inspector selects 30 chips for testing.

a) What is the probability that more than two of them are defective?

b) What is the expected number of defective chips?

Solution

a) In this case, the probability of success means the *failure* of the chip, so

$$p = 5\% \qquad q = 1 - 0.05$$
$$= 0.05 \qquad = 0.95$$

You could add the probabilities of having exactly 3, 4, 5, ..., 30 failures. It is easier to use the indirect method, $P(x > 2) = 1 - P(x \le 2)$.

Method 1: Use a Scientific Calculator

$$P(x > 2) = 1 - P(0) - P(1) - P(2)$$
$$= 1 - {}_{30}C_0(0.05)^0(0.95)^{30} - {}_{30}C_1(0.05)^1(0.95)^{29} - {}_{30}C_2(0.05)^2(0.95)^{28}$$
$$\approx 0.1878$$
$$= 18.78\%$$

Method 2: Use a Graphing Calculator

Use **2ND** **DISTR** **A:binomcdf(n, p, x)**. This returns the cumulative probability of x successes on n trials with probability of success on each trial of p.

$$P(x > 2) = 1 - P(0) - P(1) - P(2)$$
$$= 1 - \text{binomcdf}(30, 0.05, 2)$$
$$= 0.1878$$

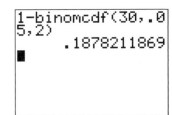

There is about an 18.78% chance that more than two chips are defective.

b) $E(X) = np$
$$= (30)(0.05)$$
$$= 1.5$$

On average, there will be 1.5 defective chips in a selection of 30 chips.

Your Turn

With a certain set of atmospheric conditions, the probability of rain is 40%. During a one-month period, eight days had those conditions.

a) What is the probability that it rained on fewer than six of those days?

b) What is the expected number of rainy days?

Consolidate and Debrief

Key Concepts

- A binomial distribution has a specific number of identical independent trials in which the result is success or failure.

- You can represent a binomial distribution using a table, a histogram, and a formula.

- The probability of x successes in n independent trials is $P(x) = {}_nC_x p^x q^{n-x}$, where p is the probability of success in an individual trial, and $q = 1 - p$ is the probability of failure.

- The expectation for the binomial distribution is $E(X) = np$.

Reflect

R1. The formula for the binomial distribution is $P(x) = {}_nC_x p^x q^{n-x}$. What is the purpose of the ${}_nC_x$ coefficient?

R2. In a binomial distribution, how are p and q related? Include an example using a deck of cards.

R3. About 11% of Canadians are left-handed. A newspaper columnist interpreted this to mean that there is an 11% chance that any one of the newspaper's 25 reporters will be left-handed. Discuss the accuracy of this statement.

Practise

Choose the best answer for #1 to #3.

1. Which expression best represents the probability of three successes in seven independent trials in a binomial distribution?

   A ${}_7C_3 p^3 q^4$ **B** ${}_7C_3 p^4 q^3$
   C ${}_7C_4 p^3 q^4$ **D** ${}_7C_4 p^4 q^3$

2. What is the expectation for a binomial distribution with $p = 0.5$ and $n = 8$?

   A 0.4   **B** 4
   C 16   **D** 0.0625

3. Which of the following is an example of a binomial distribution?

   A probabilities of the number of queens in a five-card hand

   B probability of each sum when two dice are rolled

   C probability of each lane for a 100 m race

   D probabilities of the number of times a 5 occurs when spinning a spinner six times

4. A tetrahedral die has four triangular faces. Three faces are labelled **1** and the fourth is labelled **2**. The die is rolled four times.

   a) Draw a tree diagram to illustrate the possible outcomes.

   b) Use the tree diagram to assign probabilities for this distribution.

   c) Verify these probabilities using the binomial distribution formula.

   d) Substitute values for p and q and expand $(p + q)^4$, but do not simplify. How does the expansion relate to the above results?

5. Prepare a probability table and a graph for a binomial distribution with

   a) $n = 6$ and $p = 0.3$

   b) $n = 8$ and $p = \frac{1}{9}$

6. What is the expected number of times a 6 appears when rolling a die 2000 times?

7. In a family of five children, what is the probability that there are exactly

   a) two girls?

   b) three boys?

Apply

8. Six people are asked to choose a number between 1 and 20. What is the probability that

   a) two people choose the number 9?

   b) at least two people choose the number 9?

9. Two dice are rolled repeatedly and their sum is recorded.

   a) Show the probability distribution for the number of sums of 7 in five rolls.

   b) Graph the distribution with a probability histogram.

   c) Verify the formula $E(X) = np$.

10. In archery competitions, Paul hits the bull's-eye 45% of the time.

    a) Show the probability distribution for the number of bull's-eyes in eight attempts.

    b) What is the expected number of bull's-eyes in eight attempts?

    c) What does $P(8)$ tell you?

11. a) You roll five dice at the same time. What is the probability that you roll two 3s?

    b) Expand the binomial $\left(\frac{1}{6} + \frac{5}{6}\right)^5$.

    c) Which term in the expansion matches the answer in part a)?

    d) How does the binomial probability distribution relate to the binomial theorem?

12. **Application** A machine makes light bulbs, and 6% do not meet the specifications. An inspector randomly chooses 10 light bulbs for testing.

   a) What is the probability that three bulbs do not meet specifications?

   b) What is the probability that seven bulbs do not meet specifications?

   c) What is the probability that between three and seven bulbs do not meet specifications?

   d) What method did you use in part c)? Describe an alternate method.

   e) Should the inspector be concerned if two bulbs do not meet specifications? Explain your reasoning.

13. **Thinking** On a game show, five contestants are each given a box containing 10 car keys, one of which fits their assigned new car. Each contestant is allowed to choose one key and try to start their car. If no car starts, or only one car starts, nobody wins their car. If two or more cars start, then those contestants win their car. Do the results of the game favour the contestants or the game show? Justify mathematically.

14. Jamaal is successful on basketball free throws 80% of the time.

    a) How likely is he to be successful on eight of 10 free-throw attempts?

    b) How likely is he to be successful on at least eight of 10 free-throw attempts?

15. Jean forgot to study for an eight-question multiple choice quiz. Each question contains four possible answers. Jean will guess the answer to each question.

    a) What is the probability that she will get only two questions correct?

    b) What is the probability that she will pass?

    c) What is the expected number of correct answers on the quiz?

    d) Predict the shape of the probability histogram for this distribution. Explain your reasoning.

    e) Describe how the graph will change if Jean feels that she has a 40% chance of guessing correctly on each question.

    f) Use technology to check your predictions to parts d) and e).

16. **Communication** A jar contains 12 red balls and eight green balls. Six balls are removed without replacement. What is the probability that four of the balls are red?

    a) Explain why the binomial distribution is not a suitable model for this problem.

    b) Write a new question using the same set of balls so it can be modelled using a binomial distribution.

    c) Solve the new problem.

17. Opinion polls based on small samples often yield misleading results. In a particular city, 65% of residents are opposed to a new light rail transit system.

    a) If a poll were taken, calculate the probabilities of a majority of people approving the transit system with a sample of
       • 7 people
       • 100 people
       • 1000 people

    b) Explain any differences in the results.

18. **Thinking** A store offers a scratch and win discount for each customer who spends over $100. Each card has six spots that give a discount of $10, three spots that give a discount of $25, and one spot that gives a discount of $50. What is the expected cost to the store if it has 200 customers one particular day?

19. Your teacher will provide you with the file **BinomialProbabilityDistribution.ftm** that was used in the Investigation at the beginning of this section.

    a) Edit the file to simulate the success and failure options for your choice of questions 8, 10, 11, 15, 16, or 18.

    b) Try the simulation for 5 experiments, 10 experiments, 100 experiments, and so on, until the graph becomes close to matching the theoretical probabilities.

    c) How many experiments did it take for the simulation to come close to the theoretical probabilities?

20. **Open Question** Use one of the following rates to develop your own problem involving the binomial distribution. Then, trade problems with a classmate.

    • 19% of the Canadian population live in rural areas
    • 39% of the Canadian population live in Ontario

Extend

21. A standard die is painted so that opposite faces are green, red, and yellow, respectively. In 10 rolls of this die, how many could be red or green or yellow? This leads to what could be a trinomial distribution.

    a) Develop a formula to calculate the probability distribution in which there are three outcomes with individual probabilities of p, q, and r.

    b) Use your formula to determine the probability of rolling three reds, two greens, and five yellows in 10 rolls of the die described above.

22. Derive the formula for expectation of a binomial distribution $E(X) = np$ algebraically.

4.4

Hypergeometric Distributions

Learning Goals

I am learning to

- recognize conditions that give rise to a hypergeometric distribution
- calculate the probability associated with each random variable of a hypergeometric distribution
- represent the hypergeometric distribution using a table and a probability histogram
- solve problems involving hypergeometric probability distributions

Minds On...

The binomial distribution involves independent trials. This section develops a distribution involving dependent trials. Cutting cards with a standard deck provides independent trials, whereas dealing the cards involves dependent trials. Similarly, selecting a jury pool and catching and tagging animals for scientific research involve dependent trials. Brainstorm other examples of dependent trials.

Action!

Investigate Hypergeometric Distributions

Materials

- 4 red tiles and 3 green tiles
- computer with Fathom™ software (optional)

hypergeometric probability distribution

- a distribution with dependent trials whose outcomes are either success or failure
- the random variable is the number of successes in a given number of trials

In this activity, you will develop a **hypergeometric probability distribution** for the number of red tiles selected in four dependent trials. Randomly select one tile from four red and three green tiles. Repeat four times without replacement.

1. What is the total number of ways of selecting four tiles from seven tiles, without replacement?

2. Make a tree diagram that illustrates the probability distribution for the number of red tiles selected in four trials. Label each branch with the outcome and its dependent probability.

3. **a)** How many paths represent two red tiles?
   b) How is this related to $_nC_r$ and/or Pascal's triangle?

4. Copy and complete the table for 0 to 4 red tiles.

Number of Red Tiles	Number of Paths	Number of Paths in $_nC_r$ Form	Probability	Probability as $\frac{a \times b}{c}$, where a, x, b, c are written as $_nC_r$
0				
1				

5. Describe the relationship between the probability column and the other columns.

6. Make a probability histogram for this distribution.

7. Reflect

   a) Write a formula for the probability of choosing three red tiles in four dependent trials.

   b) Write a formula for calculating the probability of x red tiles in four dependent trials.

   c) Write a formula for calculating the probability of x red tiles in r dependent trials.

   d) Use your formula to calculate the probability of selecting two red tiles in five dependent trials.

   e) Compare your answer to that in section 4.3 Investigate Binomial Distributions, step 7c) on page 161.

8. Extend Your Understanding Your teacher will provide you with a file called **Hypergeometric ProbabilityDistribution.ftm**. When you open the file, you will see four open collections.

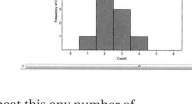

   • The "Tiles" collection gives the tiles available for selection.
   • "Sample of Tiles" simulates the results when four dependent trials are completed.
   • "Inspect Measures from Sample of Tiles" allows you to simulate any number of experiments of four trials each, and is set to 10.
   • The graph is a histogram of the results from these 10 experiments.

   a) Press **Collect More Measures**. You can repeat this any number of times. Describe what happens to the graph.

   b) De-select **Replace existing cases** and change 10 measures to 100, then to 1000. You may wish to turn off animation to speed up the process. Press **Collect More Measures**. How closely does the graph resemble your histogram in step 6? Explain.

Example 1

Hypergeometric Probability

A committee of six people is to be formed from a pool of six grade 11 students and seven grade 12 students. Determine the probability that the committee will have two grade 11 students.

Solution

The population size is 13 students. The size of the sample space is six students.

$$n(S) = {}_{13}C_6$$

For the successful outcome, select two of the six grade 11 students and four of the seven grade 12 students.

$$n(2 \text{ grade 11s}) = {}_6C_2 \times {}_7C_4$$

$$P(2 \text{ grade 11s}) = \frac{{}_6C_2 \times {}_7C_4}{{}_{13}C_6}$$

$$= \frac{525}{1716}$$

$$\approx 0.3059$$

The probability of having two grade 11 students on the committee is about 30.6%.

Your Turn

On a team of 15 astronauts, six are women and nine are men. If four astronauts are selected at random for a flight simulation, what is the probability that two men and two women are selected?

Probability in a Hypergeometric Distribution

The probability of x successful outcomes in r dependent trials is

$$P(x) = \frac{{}_aC_x \cdot {}_{n-a}C_{r-x}}{{}_nC_r}$$

where a is the number of successful outcomes available in a population of size n.

Expectation for a Hypergeometric Distribution

The ratio of the expectation to the number of trials is proportional to the ratio of the number of available successes to the size of the population.

$$\frac{E(x)}{r} = \frac{a}{n}$$

So, $E(X) = \frac{ra}{n}$.

Example 2

Hypergeometric Distribution

A five-card hand is dealt from a standard deck of cards.

a) Show the probability distribution for the number of hearts in the hand.

b) Illustrate the distribution with a probability histogram.

c) Describe the shape of the graph.

d) What does $P(5)$ tell you?

e) Calculate the expectation and explain its meaning.

Solution

a) $n(S) = {}_{52}C_5$

$\qquad = 2\ 598\ 960$

There can be 0 to 5 hearts in the hand. The number of ways the hearts can be chosen is ${}_{13}C_x$. The number of ways of choosing the remaining cards is ${}_{39}C_{5-x}$.

$P(x) = \dfrac{{}_{13}C_x \times {}_{39}C_{5-x}}{{}_{52}C_5}$, where x is the number of hearts in the hand.

Method 1: Use Paper and Pencil

Number of Hearts, x	Probability, $P(x)$	$x \cdot P(x)$
0	$\dfrac{{}_{13}C_0 \times {}_{39}C_5}{{}_{52}C_5} \approx 0.2215$	0
1	$\dfrac{{}_{13}C_1 \times {}_{39}C_4}{{}_{52}C_5} \approx 0.4114$	0.4114
2	$\dfrac{{}_{13}C_2 \times {}_{39}C_3}{{}_{52}C_5} \approx 0.2743$	0.5486
3	$\dfrac{{}_{13}C_3 \times {}_{39}C_2}{{}_{52}C_5} \approx 0.0815$	0.2445
4	$\dfrac{{}_{13}C_3 \times {}_{39}C_1}{{}_{52}C_5} \approx 0.0107$	0.0428
5	$\dfrac{{}_{13}C_5 \times {}_{39}C_0}{{}_{52}C_5} \approx 0.0005$	0.0025

Method 2: Use a Graphing Calculator

Refer to the Prerequisite Skills on page 143.

- In list **L1**, enter the x-values, 0 to 5.

- To program $\dfrac{{}_{13}C_x \times {}_{39}C_{5-x}}{{}_{52}C_5}$ in the **L2** column heading,

  enter 13 **MATH** **PRB 3:nCr** **ENTER** **2ND** **L1** **×** 39 **MATH**
  PRB 3:nCr **(** 5 **−** **2ND** **L1** **)** **÷** 52 **MATH** **PRB**
  3:nCr 5 **ENTER**

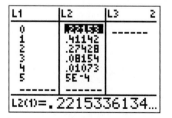

b) Method 1: Use Pencil and Paper

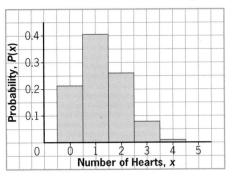

Method 2: Use a Graphing Calculator

Refer to the Prerequisite Skills on page 143.

- Set up your **Plot1** screen as shown. Make sure all other Stat Plots have been turned off.

- Press **WINDOW** and change the parameters as shown.

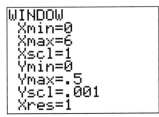

- Press **GRAPH**.

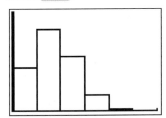

- Press **TRACE** to read the values associate with each bar.

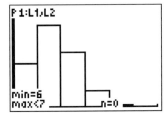

c) The graph has the shape of a bell curve with the mode at $x = 1$. It is skewed to the right.

d) $P(5) = 0.0005$
$\qquad\ \ = 0.05\%$

Getting five hearts is extremely rare.

e) Method 1: Use the Sum of the $x \cdot P(x)$ Values

$$\sum_{x=0}^{5} x \cdot P(x) = 0(0.221\ 53) + 1(0.411\ 42) + 2(0.274\ 28) + 3(0.081\ 54) +$$
$$4(0.010\ 73) + 5(0.0005)$$
$$= 1.2498$$

Method 2: Use a Graphing Calculator

- In the column heading of list **L3**, enter `2ND` `L1` `×` `2ND` `L2` `ENTER`
- In the bottom cell of list **L3**, enter `2ND` `LIST` `MATH` Sum `(` `2ND` `L3`
  `)` `ENTER`

L1	L2	L3 3
1	.41142	.41142
2	.27428	.54856
3	.08154	.24463
4	.01073	.04292
5	5E-4	.00248
------	------	------

L3(7) =sum(L3)

Method 3: Use the Formula

$E(X) = \dfrac{ra}{n}$

$\qquad = \dfrac{(5)(13)}{52}$

$\qquad = 1.25$ Do not round this value, since it represents an average.

On average, there will be 1.25 hearts in a five-card hand.

Your Turn

A bag contains 10 jellybeans. Four are blue and six are green. Four jellybeans are selected at random.

a) Show the probability distribution for the number of green jellybeans selected.

b) Illustrate the distribution with a probability histogram.

c) Compare the shape of the graph to the one in Example 2. Explain any differences.

d) What does $P(0)$ tell you?

e) Calculate the expectation and explain its meaning.

Project Prep

You might use cards when designing your probability project. Will they involve a hypergeometric distribution? How can you use cards appropriately?

Example 3

Apply the Hypergeometric Distribution to Selections

In a class of 30 students, 18 have a driver's licence. Ten students are selected at random.

a) What is the probability that at least four have their driver's licence?

b) What is the expected number of students with their driver's licence?

Solution

a) $n = 30$, $r = 10$, $a = 18$

You could add the probabilities of 4, 5, … 10 students with their driver's licence. It is easier to use the indirect method by subtracting the probabilities of 0, 1, 2, and 3 students with their driver's licence from 1. $P(x \geq 4) = 1 - P(x \leq 3)$.

Method 1: Use a Scientific Calculator

$$P(x \geq 4) = 1 - P(0) - P(1) - P(2) - P(3)$$
$$= 1 - \frac{{}_{18}C_0 \times {}_{12}C_{10}}{{}_{30}C_{10}} - \frac{{}_{18}C_1 \times {}_{12}C_9}{{}_{30}C_{10}} - \frac{{}_{18}C_2 \times {}_{12}C_8}{{}_{30}C_{10}} - \frac{{}_{18}C_3 \times {}_{12}C_7}{{}_{30}C_{10}}$$
$$\approx 0.9758$$

The probability that at least four students will have a driver's licence is about 0.9758.

Method 2: Use a Graphing Calculator

A graphing calculator can combine operations on sets of numbers by placing them in lists using curly brackets {} for both the x values of 0, 1, 2, and 3, and the $10 - x$ values of 10, 9, 8, and 7. Use the sum command to add the results. To enter $1 - {}_{18}C_x - {}_{12}C_{10-x} - {}_{30}C_{10}$, type

1 − **2ND** **LIST** **MATH 5:sum(** **ENTER** 18 **MATH**
PRB 3:nCr **ENTER** **2ND** **{** 0,1,2,3 **2ND** **}**
× 12 **MATH PRB 3:nCr** **ENTER** **2ND** **{**
10,9,8,7 **2ND** **}** **)** **÷** 30 **MATH PRB**
3:nCr **ENTER** 10 **ENTER**

```
1-sum(18 nCr {0,
1,2,3)*12 nCr {1
0,9,8,7))/30 nCr
10
       .9758351593
```

The probability that at least four students will have their driver's licence is about 0.9758.

b) $E(X) = \dfrac{ra}{n}$
$$= \frac{(10)(18)}{30}$$
$$= 6$$

On average, six students will have their driver's licence in a selection of 10 students.

Your Turn

Twenty-four students have signed up to attend a workshop. Fourteen are female and ten are male. Seven are randomly chosen to attend.

a) What is the probability that at least three are male?

b) What is the expected number of male and female students chosen?

Example 4

Apply the Expectation Formula

Wildlife officials tagged 350 seals from a particular colony. Forty seals were caught later, and 17 of them had been tagged. What is the approximate size of the seal population in this colony?

Solution

The 40 seals caught were all independent from each other, so the trials were dependent. If they were tagged, the trial was deemed a success; if not, the trial was deemed a failure. This is represented by a hypergeometric distribution.

n = size of seal population

a = number originally tagged (number available)
  $= 350$

r = number later caught (sample size)
  $= 40$

$E(X)$ = number of seals that had been tagged (expectation from the sample)
  $= 17$

Method 1: Use the Expectation Formula

$$E(X) = \frac{ra}{n}$$
$$17 = \frac{(40)(350)}{n}$$
$$n = \frac{(40)(350)}{17}$$
$$n = 823.53$$

The seal population is about 824 seals.

Method 2: Use a Proportion

$$\frac{E(X)}{r} = \frac{a}{n}$$
$$\frac{17}{40} = \frac{350}{n}$$
$$n = \frac{(40)(350)}{17}$$
$$n = 823.53$$

When a whole number answer is needed, rounding the expectation is appropriate.

Your Turn

During one summer, 500 foxes were caught and vaccinated against rabies. At that time, they were also tagged. Eighty foxes were later caught to estimate the size of the fox population, and 34 of them had been tagged. Estimate the size of the fox population.

Key Concepts

- A hypergeometric probability distribution occurs when there are two outcomes, success and failure, and all trials are dependent. The random variable is the number of successes in a given number of trials.

- You can represent a hypergeometric distribution using a table, a probability histogram, or a formula.

- The probability of x successes in r dependent trials is $P(x) = \dfrac{{}_aC_x \cdot {}_{n-a}C_{r-x}}{{}_nC_r}$, where a is the number of successful outcomes available in a population of size n.

- Expectation $E(X) = \dfrac{ra}{n}$.

Reflect

R1. For each example of a hypergeometric distribution, identify the random variable, the size of the sample space, the size of the population, and the range of the random variable.

a) A bag contains six red and four green marbles. Five marbles are randomly selected from the bag. The number of red marbles is recorded.

b) A seven-card hand is dealt from a standard deck. The number of hearts is recorded.

R2. A standard die is rolled five times and the number of 3s is noted. Explain why this would or would not be a valid hypergeometric probability situation.

Practise

Choose the best answer for #1 to #2.

1. A bag contains five red and six blue blocks. What is the probability of getting three red blocks if four blocks are randomly selected?

A $\dfrac{{}_{11}C_3 \times {}_6C_4}{{}_{18}C_4}$ **B** $\dfrac{{}_5C_3}{{}_{11}C_4}$

C $\dfrac{{}_5C_3}{{}_6C_4}$ **D** $\dfrac{{}_5C_3 \times {}_6C_1}{{}_{11}C_4}$

2. Which is an example of a hypergeometric distribution?

A probability of the number of aces in a seven-card hand

B probability of each sum when two dice are rolled

C probability of a number being randomly chosen from the numbers 1 to 10

D probability of the number of times a 3 occurs when rolling a die six times

3. Each expression represents the probability of a hypergeometric probability. State the values of the unknowns.

a) $\dfrac{{}_6C_3 \times {}_9C_2}{{}_nC_r}$ **b)** $\dfrac{{}_aC_5 \times {}_7C_b}{{}_{10}C_6}$

c) $\dfrac{{}_6C_3 \times {}_cC_2}{{}_{25}C_d}$

4. Show the hypergeometric probability distribution for an experiment with

a) $n = 15$, $r = 4$, $a = 7$.

b) $n = 8$, $r = 4$, $a = 4$.

Apply

5. A five-card hand is dealt from the honour cards in a standard deck (10, J, Q, K, A).

  a) Show the probability distribution for the number of hearts in the hand.

  b) Calculate the expectation in two ways.

6. In a box of 20 light bulbs, five are defective. Three light bulbs are selected at random.

  a) What is the probability that at least one is defective?

  b) What is the expected number of defective light bulbs?

  c) What is the meaning of $P(3)$ in this context?

7. In the card game of bridge, 13 cards are dealt to each player. Find the probability of each of the following hands:

  a) 4 aces   **b)** at least 1 king

  c) 5 clubs, 8 diamonds

8. **Communication** A laboratory has 30 mice, eight of which have a specific genetic mutation. A lab assistant randomly selects 10 of the mice. Which has a greater probability of the mice having the genetic mutation, fewer than three, or more than seven? Explain.

9. In a provincial park, 200 foxes are tagged. In 100 sightings, 14 were tagged. Estimate the size of the fox population.

10. **Application** Wildlife officials tagged 80 deer in an area that had approximately 120 deer.

  a) If they later took a sample of 25 deer, how many would they expect to have been tagged?

  b) Should the officials be surprised if the sample has fewer than 13 tagged deer? Explain your thinking.

11. **Thinking**

  a) Which will have a greater probability, a seven-card hand with no spades, or a five-card hand with no spades.

  b) Verify mathematically and explain any discrepancies with your prediction.

✔ Achievement Check

12. The members of an antique car club own one car from the 1920s, two cars from the 1930s, four cars from the 1940s, six cars from the 1950s, and seven cars from the 1960s. They have been invited to send four cars to a car show and will choose them at random.

  a) Compare the probabilities of sending all four cars from any given decade.

  b) Show the probability distribution for the number of cars selected from the 1950s or 1960s, in table form and graphically.

  c) What is the expected number of cars sent from the 1940s?

  d) How would the graph of the distribution in part b) change if there were an additional three cars from the 1920s?

13. A jury of 12 people is to be chosen from a pool of 9 men and 11 women.

  a) Graph the probability distribution for the number of men on the jury.

  b) Simulate the probability distribution by using 9 red and 11 black playing cards. Perform 10 trials, then combine your results with other classmates. Alternatively, use the file **HypergeometricProbability Distribution.ftm** that was used in the Investigation on page 170. Make appropriate changes to accommodate the different choices available. Run the simulation for 10 experiments, then 100, and so on.

  c) After how many experiments did the simulation reasonably match the theoretical probabilities?

Extend

14. Calculate the probability that a bridge hand of 13 cards contains four cards of one suit and three of each other suit.

15. A bag contains three nickels, five dimes, and four quarters. Three coins are removed at random. What is the probability that the value of the coins will total 75 cents?

4.5

Comparing and Selecting Discrete Probability Distributions

Learning Goals

I am learning to

- compare the probability distributions of discrete random variables
- solve problems involving uniform, binomial, and hypergeometric distributions

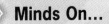

Minds On...

In earlier chapters, you looked at independent and dependent events. When determining the appropriate probability distribution, this is an important criterion to consider. How would you differentiate between independent and dependent events? Come up with two or three examples of each. Consider board games, card games, or other types of games.

Action!

Investigate Comparing Binomial and Hypergeometric Distributions

Consider the binomial and hypergeometric distributions.

1. If you have not already done so, complete the compare and contrast graphic organizer on page 140. Consider the following criteria: population, discrete or continuous, independence of trials, counting outcomes, number of trials, random variable, what needs to be known?, expectation, parameters (n, r).

2. **Reflect** Use your graphic organizer to help classify each of the probability distributions as binomial, hypergeometric, or neither. Justify your classification.

   a) the probability of successfully shooting 13 free throws in 15 tries given the probability of success on a free throw

   b) the probability of each possible outcome when a card is drawn from a standard deck

   c) selecting 25 grizzly bears at random and determining how many of them were tagged with radio chips over the last year

   d) the probability that three or more batteries are defective in a batch of 35 batteries when batteries have a rate of defect of 0.05%

3. **Extend Your Understanding** Compare and contrast the uniform distribution with the binomial and hypergeometric distributions.

Example

Compare Two Similar Distributions

a) Compare and contrast the following probability distributions. Include the values of the parameters.
  - cutting five cards from a standard deck, with replacement, and counting the number of face cards
  - dealing five cards at the same time from a standard deck and counting the number of face cards

b) Graph the two probability histograms.

c) How are the graphs alike? How are they different?

Literacy Link

A *parameter* is a constant that can have different values in an expression, but that does not change the form of the expression. For example, in $y = mx + b$, m and b are parameters, while x and y are variables.

Solution

a) Use a Venn diagram to compare and contrast.

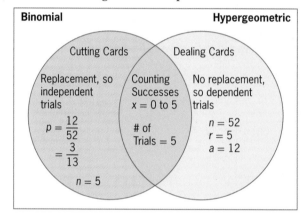

b) Method 1: Use a Graphing Calculator

Refer to the Prerequisite Skills on page 143.

  - In list **L1**, enter the x-values, 0 to 5.

  - For the binomial distribution, to program $_5C_x\left(\frac{3}{13}\right)^x\left(\frac{10}{13}\right)^{5-x}$ in the **L2** column heading, enter:

5 MATH PRB 3:nCr ENTER 2ND L1 ×
(3 ÷ 13) ^ 2ND L1 × (
10 ÷ 13) ^ (5 − 2ND L1
) ENTER

L1	L2	L3	3
0	.26933	▓▓▓▓	
1	.40399	.42197	
2	.2424	.2509	
3	.07272	.06603	
4	.01091	.00762	
5	6.5E⁻⁴	3E⁻⁴	
------	------	------	

L3(1)=.2531812725...

  - For the hypergeometric distribution, to program $\frac{_{5}C_x \times {_{40}}C_{5-x}}{_{52}C_5}$ in the **L3** column heading, enter:

5 MATH PRB 3:nCr ENTER 2ND L1 × 40 MATH PRB 3:nCr ENTER (5
− 2ND L1) ÷ 52 MATH PRB 3:nCr ENTER 5 ENTER

To see the graphs, press: 2ND STAT PLOT 1:Plot 1 ENTER

- Set up your **Plot1** screen as shown. Make sure all other Stat Plots have been turned off.

- Press **WINDOW** and change the parameters as shown.

- Press **TRACE**. Use the left and right arrows to read the coordinates of each bar.

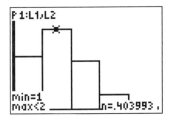

For the hypergeometric distribution, turn off **Plot1** and, when setting up the Stat Plot, use **Plot2** and **Freq:L3**.

- Press **TRACE**. Use the left and right arrows to read the coordinates of each bar.

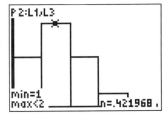

Method 2: Use a Spreadsheet

Open a spreadsheet.

- Create three columns called **Number of Face Cards**, **Probability With Replacement**, and **Probability Without Replacement**.

- In the **Number of Face Cards** column, enter the values from 0 to 5.

- In the **Probability With Replacement** column, enter the binomial formula in B2:
  =COMBIN(5,A2)*(3/13)^A2*(10/13)^(5−A2).
  Copy it from B2 to B7.

- In the **Probability Without Replacement** column, enter the hypergeometric in C2:
  =COMBIN(12,A2)*COMBIN(40,5−A2)/COMBIN(52,5).
  Copy it from C2 to C7.

	A	B	C
	Number of Face Cards	Probability With Replacement	Probability Without Replacement
1			
2	0	0.269329074	0.253181273
3	1	0.403993612	0.421968788
4	2	0.242396167	0.25090036
5	3	0.07271885	0.066026411
6	4	0.010907828	0.007618432
7	5	0.00065447	0.000304737

- Highlight columns B and C, select **Insert** from the ribbon, and then select **Clustered Column**.

- Right click on the chart and click on **Select Data…** .

- Under Horizontal (Category) Axis Labels, click **Edit**. Highlight cells A2 to A7 for the axis label range. Click **OK**. Click **OK** again.

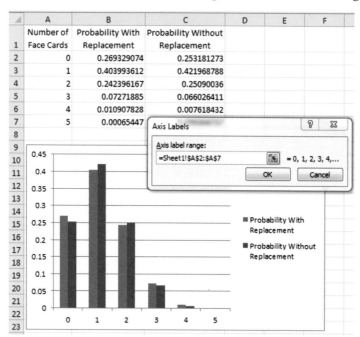

c) The graphs have the same bell-like shape, with the $x = 1$ face card being the most likely outcome. The hypergeometric graph is slightly taller than the binomial graph at $x = 1$ (0.422 vs 0.404) and $x = 2$ (0.251 vs. 0.242), and shorter at the other values of x. This occurs due to the dependent nature of the hypergeometric distribution, causing probabilities to increase when fewer choices are available.

Your Turn

a) Use a Venn diagram to compare and contrast the probability distributions if a hat contains five male and six female names.
- Selecting four names with replacement, and counting the number of female names.
- Selecting four names without replacement, and counting the number of female names.

b) Graph the two probability histograms.

c) How are the graphs alike? How are they different?

Consolidate and Debrief

Key Concepts

- The chart summarizes the general conditions of the distributions.

	Uniform	Binomial	Hypergeometric
Parameters and What They Represent	n = number of items	n = number of trials p = probability of success on an individual trial q = probability of failure on an individual trial	n = size of the population r = number of trials a = number of successful items available
Definition of Random Variable, x	Value of the outcome	Number of successful outcomes	Number of successful outcomes
Range of Values for x	Depends on the situation	$x = 0, 1, 2, ..., n$	$x = 0, 1, 2, ..., r$
Probability Formula	$P(x) = \dfrac{1}{n}$	$P(x) = {}_nC_x p^x q^{n-x}$	$P(x) = \dfrac{{}_aC_x \cdot {}_{n-a}C_{r-x}}{{}_nC_r}$
Expectation Formula	$E(X) = \dfrac{1}{n}\displaystyle\sum_{i=1}^{n} x_i$	$E(X) = np$	$E(X) = \dfrac{ra}{n}$
Identifying Characteristics	All items are equally likely A single trial	Trials are independent Successes are counted	Trials are dependent Successes are counted

Reflect

R1. Refer to the graphic organizer in the Investigation on page 180, and to the general conditions chart in the Key Concepts above. Make a Venn diagram or a graphic organizer to compare and contrast the general conditions for the binomial and hypergeometric probability distributions.

R2. Sam wrote that the difference between binomial and hypergeometric distributions is that with the binomial distribution each trial has the same probability, but with hypergeometric the individual probabilities change with the sampling. Is this an accurate statement? Explain.

Practise

Choose the best answer for #2 and #3.

1. State which type of probability distribution (uniform, binomial, hypergeometric, none of these) would model each situation.

   a) A health inspector is in charge of inspecting 75 restaurants, 15 of which have had health code violations in the past. The inspector randomly selects 10 of the 75 restaurants for inspection. What is the probability that four of these will have had health code violations?

   b) It is estimated that 12% of all restaurants in a city have had health code violations. Ten restaurants are selected at random for inspection. What is the probability that four of these will have had health code violations?

   c) For a charity lottery, you picked 1, 2, 3, 5, and 8 from the numbers 1 to 20. Five different winning numbers are selected at random. What is the probability of three of your numbers matching the five winning numbers?

   d) For a school fundraising draw, 1000 tickets are sold, each with a number from 0001 to 1000. The winning ticket is drawn from a bin. What is the probability of winning the draw?

2. If, in a probability distribution, the number of successes is counted, then the distribution

   A must be binomial

   B must be hypergeometric

   C may be either binomial or hypergeometric

   D may be neither binomial nor hypergeometric

3. On a TV game show there are nine squares, five of which have a winning sum of money. The contestant selects four different squares. The probability distribution for the number of squares chosen that contain money is

   A uniform

   B binomial

   C hypergeometric

   D none of the above

4. Identify possible random variables for the following experiments and the values the variables may take:

   a) dealing five cards from a deck

   b) naming four members of a committee selected from five grade 11 and seven grade 12 students

   c) cutting a card from a deck

   d) rolling a die 10 times

   e) testing 20 bottles of ginger ale for quality control

   f) selecting a winning square on a TV game show

Apply

5. **Communication** Make a flowchart to help you decide when to use each type of distribution (uniform, binomial, hypergeometric, neither).

6. A game consists of randomly selecting a number from 1 to 15. Your favourite number is 13, and you are hoping your number will come up.

   a) Is this a uniform or binomial distribution? Explain.

   b) Rewrite the situation to convert it to uniform or binomial, as appropriate.

7. At Bill's Burger Barn, there is a one in eight chance of winning a free hamburger. Nicolas bought a hamburger every day for five days, hoping to win as many free hamburgers as possible.

a) Is this a binomial or hypergeometric distribution? Explain.

b) Rewrite the situation to convert it to binomial or hypergeometric, as appropriate.

8. For a random draw, 20 slips of paper containing people's names are placed into a bin. Barb noted that four of the names were her friends. Five names will be selected to win a prize, and Barb is hoping at least one of the prizes goes to a friend.

a) Is this a binomial or hypergeometric distribution? Explain.

b) Rewrite the situation to convert it to binomial or hypergeometric, as appropriate.

c) Calculate the probability of success for Barb in each distribution.

d) Which distribution would make Barb happier? Why?

9. a) With or without technology, simulate the binomial and hypergeometric distributions in #8. See the Investigates in section 4.3, page 160, and section 4.4, page 170, for instructions on using Fathom™ to simulate probability distributions.

b) Compare the theoretical probabilities to the simulation.

c) What would make the simulation closer to the theoretical?

d) What would make the binomial and hypergeometric close to being the same?

10. Application Compare the expectations for cutting a card from a deck four times and for dealing four cards. Then, explain the results

a) for the number of aces

b) for the number of red cards

c) for the number of hearts

✔ Achievement Check

11. A basket contains 20 slips of paper, each with a different student's name on it. Eight of the names are boys and 12 are girls. Six different names are selected at random, and those students will win fantastic prizes!

a) Explain why this scenario can be modelled using a hypergeometric distribution.

b) Show a full probability distribution for the number of girls who win prizes.

c) Determine the expected number of girls who win prizes using two methods and confirm that they are equal. If not, explain any differences.

d) Rewrite the situation described above to change it to a binomial distribution.

12. Thinking At a fall fair, players in a ring-toss game are successful 8% of the time.

a) Design a problem that would involve a binomial distribution.

b) Design a problem that would involve a hypergeometric distribution.

c) Design a problem that would involve the uniform distribution.

13. **Thinking** An activity involves selecting six people from a population in which six are males and the rest are females. The results will be different if the population is 10 people than if it is 200 people. Use technology to develop solutions to the questions:

a) Make graphs for the two population sizes using the hypergeometric distribution.

b) Make graphs for the two population sizes using the binomial distribution.

c) Compare the two distributions for $n = 10$ and for $n = 200$.

d) Comment on the accuracy of using the binomial distribution to approximate the hypergeometric distribution when r is small in relation to n.

Extend

14. When the population in a binomial distribution is very large and p is very small, it can be modelled using the Poisson distribution, named for the French mathematician Siméon-Denis Poisson (1781–1840). It uses the formula $P(x) = \dfrac{e^{-np}(np)^x}{x!}$, where e is the irrational number 2.718 28…. An estimated 1.5% of the world's population has green eyes. If 2000 people were selected at random, use the Poisson distribution to calculate the probability that fewer than 10 have green eyes. Compare the results using a graphing calculator. How close is the approximation?

15. a) Determine the expected values of the following:

   i) a single trial in which the random variable can take the values $1, 2, 3 \ldots n$

   ii) multiple independent trials in which there are a successful items in a population of n items, and the random variable can take the values $1, 2, 3 \ldots n$

   iii) multiple dependent trials in which there are a successful items in a population of n items, and the random variable can take the values $1, 2, 3 \ldots n$

b) Compare the results and explain any similarities or differences.

> **Processes**
>
> **Representing**
> How can you represent these expected values algebraically?

16. The geometric probability distribution involves the probability that a given waiting time will occur before success. A certain traffic light is programmed to be red 40% of the time.

> **Literacy Link**
>
> *Waiting time* refers to the number of failures before success.

a) What is the probability that your first red light will be on

   i) your first trip through the intersection?

   ii) your second trip through the intersection?

   iii) your third trip through the intersection?

   iv) your nth trip through the intersection?

b) Describe how to calculate the probability of an event occurring for the first time after n initial failures, involving independent trials.

c) Derive a formula that calculates this probability.

d) You repeatedly roll a pair of dice until you roll doubles. Build a probability distribution for up to eight rolls of the dice.

e) Compare and contrast the geometric distribution with the binomial and hypergeometric distributions.

Learning Goals

Section	After this section, I can
4.1	• recognize and identify a discrete random variable • generate a probability distribution by calculating the probabilities for all values of a random variable • represent a probability distribution using a table and a probability histogram • make connections between the frequency histogram and the probability histogram • calculate and interpret the expected value for a probability distribution • make connections between the expected value and the weighted mean of the values of the discrete random variable
4.2	• solve problems involving uniform probability distributions
4.3	• recognize conditions that give rise to a binomial probability distribution • make connections among the table, histogram, and algebraic representation of a binomial probability distribution • solve problems involving binomial probability distributions
4.4	• recognize conditions that give rise to a hypergeometric distribution • calculate the probability associated with each random variable of a hypergeometric distribution • represent the hypergeometric distribution using a table and a probability histogram • solve problems involving hypergeometric probability distributions
4.5	• compare the probability distributions of discrete random variables • solve problems involving uniform, binomial, and hypergeometric distributions

4.1 Probability Distributions, pages 144–153

1. Classify each random variable as discrete or continuous.

   a) length of time you play in a hockey game

   b) number of times you successfully shoot a basket in a basketball game

   c) number of candies in a bag

   d) mass of candies in a bag

2. Graph each distribution using a probability histogram.

   a)

x	P(x)
0	$\frac{1}{12}$
1	$\frac{5}{12}$
2	$\frac{1}{3}$
3	$\frac{1}{6}$

   b)

x	P(x)
2	0.05
4	0.13
6	0.24
8	0.38
10	0.12
12	0.05
14	0.03

3. Calculate the expectation for each distribution in #2.

4.2 Uniform Distributions, pages 154–159

4. Describe the criteria for a distribution to be uniform.

5. A spinner has six equal sectors, numbered from 1 to 6.

   a) Show the probability distribution for a single spin, using a table and a graph.

   b) Calculate the expected outcome. Interpret its meaning.

6. An urn contains 25 balls, 40% of which are green. A contestant reaches in the urn to choose three balls; the contestant will win $200 if he or she selects a green ball, but will lose $120 for any other colour. Is each version of the game a fair game? Justify your response.

a) The ball is replaced after each draw.

b) The ball is not replaced after each draw.

4.3 Binomial Distributions, pages 160–169

7. Prepare a distribution table and probability histogram for the number of 5s when a die is rolled six times.

8. The chart shows the percent of Canadians with each blood type.

Blood Type	Percent
O	46
A	42
B	9
AB	3

a) If 120 people are donating blood, what is the expected number of people with type O blood? Why would this be considered a binomial distribution?

b) Calculate the expected number of people with each of the other types of blood.

9. A restaurant gives customers a card with each purchase; customers scratch a box to see if they have won a prize. Twelve percent of the cards are winners.

a) What is the probability of winning a prize only once in 10 tries?

b) What is the probability of winning a prize at least three times in 10 tries?

c) What is the expected number of winning cards in 10 tries?

4.4 Hypergeometric Distributions, pages 170–179

10. a) Prepare a table and a graph for a hypergeometric distribution with $n = 25$, $a = 10$, and $r = 7$.

b) Calculate the expected outcome using two methods.

11. In a collection of 56 coins, 18 are rare. If you select 10 of the coins, what is the probability that

a) all of them are rare?

b) none of them is rare?

c) at least two of them are rare?

12. The fisheries department caught and tagged 420 seals. Recently, 100 seals were caught and 42 had been tagged. Estimate the size of the seal population.

4.5 Comparing and Selecting Discrete Probability Distributions, pages 180–187

13. Classify each situation as uniform, binomial, hypergeometric, or none of these.

a) Forty-five percent of women aged 18 to 25 are currently enrolled in post-secondary education. The random variable is the number of women between the ages of 18 and 25, out of 25 polled, who attend post-secondary education.

b) Twenty out of 30 people at a party are non-smokers. The random variable is the number of smokers in a selection of 8 partiers.

c) The flaws in pieces of timber average 0.2 per metre. The random variable is the number of flaws in the next 50 m of timber.

d) A spinner has 20 equally likely spaces, numbered from 1 to 20. The random variable is the number on which the spinner lands.

14. a) Seven cards are dealt from a standard deck. What is the probability that five are face cards?

b) Seven cards are chosen from a standard deck, with replacement. What is the probability that five are face cards?

c) Compare the two answers in parts a) and b). Explain any differences.

✓ **Achievement Chart**

Category	Knowledge/ Understanding	Thinking	Communication	Application
Questions	1, 2, 3, 4, 5	8, 12, 14, 15, 16	8, 14, 15	6, 7, 9, 10, 11, 13

Multiple Choice

Choose the best answer for #1 to #5.

1. An 8-sided die has its faces numbered 2, 4, 6 ... 16. What is the expected outcome on a typical roll?

   A 7   **B** 8

   C 9   **D** 16

2. The binomial and hypergeometric distributions are similar in that

   A they both use independent trials

   B they both use dependent trials

   C they use the same formula for calculating the expectation

   D they both involve counting successes

3. The expectation for a uniform distribution is calculated using

   A $\frac{1}{n}\sum_{i=1}^{n} x_i$ **B** $\frac{ra}{n}$

   C np **D** $\frac{x}{n}$

4. Counting the number of tails when a coin is flipped 20 times is an example of a

   A binomial distribution

   B hypergeometric distribution

   C uniform distribution

   D none of the above

5. The probability that exactly two students will be selected when five people are selected from four students and three teachers is

   A $\frac{2}{5}$ **B** $\frac{{}_4C_2 \times {}_3C_3}{{}_7C_5}$

   C ${}_5C_2\left(\frac{4}{7}\right)^2\left(\frac{3}{7}\right)^3$ **D** $\frac{5 \times 4}{7}$

Short Response

6. A particular traffic light is programmed to be red 40% of the time. On his daily Monday to Friday commute to and from work, what is the expected number of times Jack can expect to have a red light?

7. Three cards are selected, without replacement, from the honour cards (10, J, Q, K, A) in a standard deck. What is the probability that two of them are face cards?

8. **a)** Is the situation in #7 modelled by a binomial or a hypergeometric distribution? Explain.

   b) Describe how to change the situation to the binomial or hypergeometric distribution, as appropriate.

9. The beaver population in a particular provincial park is known to be 452. Two hundred beavers were caught and tagged. If 65 beavers were later caught and checked for tags, how many would you expect to be tagged?

Extended Response

10. Two dice are rolled a total of eight times, and the sum is recorded each time.

    a) Show the probability distribution for a sum of 7.

    b) Make a probability histogram of the distribution.

    c) Determine and interpret the expected outcome.

11. A certain cell phone provider's help line is busy 95% of the time.

   a) In 15 calls to the help line, what is the probability that it will be busy every time? at least 12 times?

   b) What is the expected number of times a caller should expect the line to be busy in 15 attempts?

12. Ten males and five females applied for four job promotions. The union's affirmative action committee is concerned that no females were hired, saying that at least one should have been female. Use appropriate calculations to support or refute their claim.

13. The incidence of a disease in the population is 12%. Six people are in an elevator.

   a) What is the probability that at least two of them will have the disease?

   b) What is the expected number of these people with the disease?

14. Eighteen of thirty players selected in the NHL first–round draft were Canadian. If seven drafted players are randomly selected, what is the probability that

   a) only one is Canadian?

   b) all are Canadian?

   c) most of them are Canadian?

15. If $n \div r > 200$, the binomial distribution can be used to approximate the hypergeometric distribution. Why would this be?

16. Four numbers are chosen from six positive and eight negative numbers. What is the probability that the product of these four numbers will be positive, given that

   a) there is no repetition of numbers?

   b) repetition of numbers is permitted?

Chapter Problem

Painted Cube

A large cube is painted on all six faces. It is then divided into 27 smaller, congruent cubes.

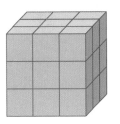

a) Use a table and a histogram to show the probability distribution for the number of painted faces on a randomly selected cube.

b) If you select 10 of the cubes at the same time, what is the probability that at least half of them will have two painted faces?

c) If you select a cube 10 times, with replacement, what is the probability that at least half of them will have two painted faces?

d) Justify your choice of distributions in parts a), b), and c).

e) For each distribution, calculate the expectation and interpret its meaning.

f) A person is blindfolded and then randomly selects one cube and rolls it. What is the probability that it lands paint side up?

g) Design a simulation that models the distribution in either part b) or c). Conduct 10 trials and compare the results to the theoretical probability that at least half will have two painted faces. Comment on any differences.

Organization of Data for Analysis

In the 21st century, farming has evolved to use data in order to maximize crop yield. For example, machines can sort green tomatoes from red ones at a rate of more than 3000 tomatoes per minute. Fertilizer spreaders use GPS and soil sample data to customize how much fertilizer is applied to specific parts of a field.

Key Terms

numerical (quantitative) data

categorical (qualitative) data

ordinal data

nominal data

population

sample

variability (in samples)

treatment group

control group

bias

primary source data

microdata

secondary source data

aggregate data

response bias

sampling bias

measurement bias

non-response bias

Career Link

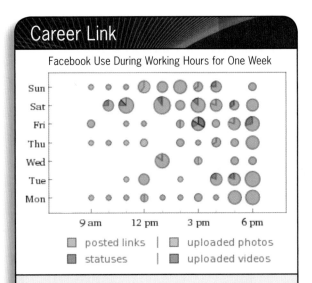

Facebook Use During Working Hours for One Week

☐ posted links | ☐ uploaded photos
☐ statuses | ☐ uploaded videos

Literacy Strategy

You can use a mind map to organize the different ways that data can be displayed and situations where one method is better than another. As you complete the chapter, you will learn about different types of data. Create a mind map to show how to display different types of data graphically. Include information about when to use each type of graph.

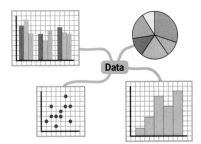

Data

Data Miner

A data miner takes a large set of data and "mines" it for patterns, trends, and relationships. Often data miners do not collect the data themselves but rather "dig in" to large sets of data that others have created. For example, social media websites such as Facebook use data mining to customize advertising for each user. Although computers do the actual "mining" of a user's Facebook page, data miners and others develop the algorithms that make it work. How do you think the ads on your Facebook page might differ from the ones on your friends' or parents' pages?

Chapter Problem

Food Production

It is estimated that by 2050 there will be over 9 billion people living on the planet. Some estimates suggest that by then we will need 30–70% more food and 40% more water. Imagine you have been hired by Agri-Research Consultants, a firm that helps farmers maximize the yield of various crops. List some ways data could help farmers increase their yields.

Identifying and Analysing Graphs

1. Name each type of graph.

a)

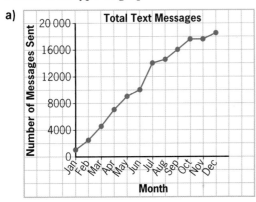

Total Text Messages

b)

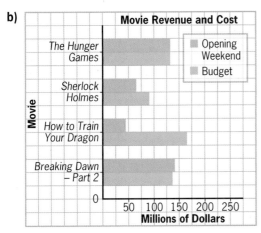

Movie Revenue and Cost

c)

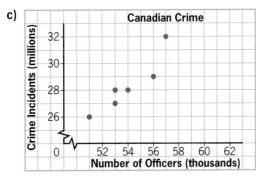

Canadian Crime

d) Favourite Game Console

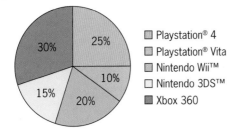

□ Playstation® 4
□ Playstation® Vita
□ Nintendo Wii™
□ Nintendo 3DS™
■ Xbox 360

e)

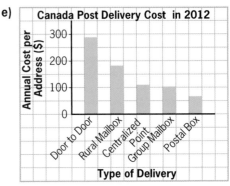

Canada Post Delivery Cost in 2012

f)

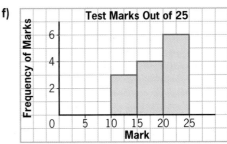

Test Marks Out of 25

2. Use the graphs in #1 to answer the questions.

   a) What intervals does the histogram show?

   b) Approximately how much does it cost to deliver mail to a centralized point?

   c) What trend seems to exist between number of officers and crime incidents?

   d) What is the most popular game console?

   e) During which month do you think students had their cell phones taken away?

   f) Which movie made the most money on its opening weekend?

3. What is the difference between a bar graph and a histogram?

Use a Spreadsheet to Create Graphs

4. Create a bar graph to represent the data in the table. Include a title and label the axes.

TV Show	Viewers (millions)
America's Got Talent	9.8
Big Bang Theory	18.6
The X Factor	4.9
Elementary	9.1

5. Create a circle graph to represent the data in the table.

Favourite Food	Amount of People
Spaghetti	20%
Pizza	40%
Hamburgers	15%
Subs	25%

Example: Create a bar graph and a circle graph to represent the data in the table.

Console	Preferred Console (%)
Xbox	34
PlayStation	29
Wii	24
Other	13

Enter the data in a table in a spreadsheet.

To create a bar graph, highlight the data. Then select **2-D Clustered Column** from the **Insert** menu.

Under **Chart Tools**, click **Layout**. Label the axes by clicking on **Axis Titles**.

To create a circle graph, highlight the data. Then select **2-D Pie Chart** from the **Insert** menu.

Under **Chart Tools**, choose the **Design** tab to show the labels on the graph.

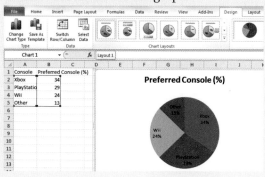

6. Use the same steps as above to create a scatter plot. Instead of selecting **Column** or **Pie** on the **Insert** menu, choose **Scatter**. Then, select **Scatter with only Markers**.

Year	2007 Toyota Camry Value ($)	2007 Ford Fusion Value ($)
2010	15 575	13 997
2011	14 230	12 924
2012	13 107	11 308
2013	12 224	9 831

7. The data describe the change in population in New York and Toronto since 2001. Create a cluster bar graph to display the data.

City	Population in 2001 (millions)	Population in 2012 (millions)
Toronto	2.25	2.73
New York	7.86	8.34

Example: Create a cluster bar graph to compare the changes in price.

	2003 Price ($)	2012 Price ($)
Gasoline (1 L)	0.76	1.25
Milk (1 L)	2.20	2.45

Enter the data in a table in a spreadsheet.

Highlight the data. Then select **Clustered Column** from the **Insert** menu.

Reformat the chart to compare the price change in gas and milk independently. Right click on the chart and click on **Select Data**. Click on **Switch Row/Column**. The chart will now directly compare the price of each item.

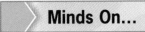

5.1

Data Concepts and Graphical Summaries

Learning Goals

I am learning to

- show how data are used and misused in statistical studies
- identify different types of data
- understand that there is variability in data
- see that you can analyse single sources of data or related sources

Minds On...

Data are everywhere. What story does the data in the image tell?

Action!

Investigate Interpreting Data

Materials

- calculator
- grid paper and ruler or graphing software
- computer with Internet access

On its maiden voyage in 1912, the RMS *Titanic* struck an iceberg and sank in less than three hours. The table shows survival statistics.

| Category | Survivors | | Deceased | | Total |
	Women and Children	Men	Women and Children	Men	
First Class	145	54	11	119	329
Second Class	104	15	24	142	285
Third Class	105	69	119	417	710
Crew	214		685		899
Total	706		1517		2223

Source: Statistics of Passengers Rescued and Lost, White Star Momentos

1. Create a graph that lawyers could use to help families of the affected passengers. Explain what type of graph you chose and why.

2. The cruise line released a statement with the headline, "Hundreds of Lives Saved in *Titanic* Mishap." Create a graph or highlight some data that the cruise line could use to justify this headline.

3. **Reflect** How do the graphs from steps 1 and 2 show that the way in which you represent information can change people's perceptions?

4. **Extend Your Understanding** Search the Internet for some examples of data displays that are accurate but misrepresent the information.

Example 1

Variability in Data

Sometimes people can use accurate information to tell different stories. Probability of precipitation (PoP) is a common measurement used in weather forecasts. The graph shows the accuracy of a national weather website and local news channels compared to perfect accuracy.

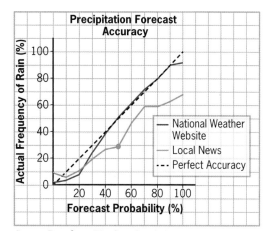

a) What does the yellow dot indicate?

Source: Data from *The Signal and the Noise: Why So Many Predictions Fail—But Some Don't*

b) Which outlet is more accurate, the national weather website or the local news?

c) If both outlets base their forecasts on information collected by Environment Canada, what reasons can you suggest for their differences?

Solution

a) This data point shows that when the local news predicted a 50% chance of precipitation, it actually rained only about 30% of the time.

b) For most of the predictions, the national weather website was closer to perfect than the local news. The local news consistently overestimated the chance of rain, in some cases by as much as 30 percentage points. The national weather website's predictions were more accurate than the local news except where their predictions were between 0% and just over 20% PoP.

c) Environment Canada collects weather data at many locations in small geographic areas. The national weather website may be forecasting for a larger area than the local news. If precipitation is recorded in a localized region, it may be outside the area forecast by the local news, but included in the forecast for the national weather website. Also, although the raw data come from the same source, the calculations used to make the predictions may be different. This results in different analyses of the same data.

Your Turn

Researchers often have conflicting opinions even though they use the same data. Research one of the following topics to find conflicting opinions:
- climate change
- vaccinations
- fluoridated water

numerical (quantitative) data

- data in the form of any number

categorical (qualitative) data

- data that can be sorted into distinct groups or categories

There are two main types of data: numerical (quantitative) and categorical (qualitative). Numerical data are either continuous or discrete.

Continuous data can have any value in a range (including decimal numbers). For example, the weight of a person or the amount of time an experiment takes could have any value in a range. We often use a histogram to display continuous data. When the bars in a histogram are touching, it means that the data can be any value in a range.

Discrete data are data that only have specific values (usually whole numbers). We often represent discrete data with a bar graph. The bars do not touch, indicating that there are no possible values in between.

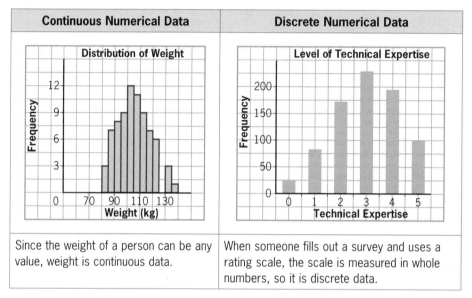

Continuous Numerical Data	Discrete Numerical Data
Since the weight of a person can be any value, weight is continuous data.	When someone fills out a survey and uses a rating scale, the scale is measured in whole numbers, so it is discrete data.

ordinal data

- qualitative data that can be ranked
- examples: poor, fair, good, very good

nominal data

- qualitative data that cannot be ranked
- examples: blue eyes, green eyes, brown eyes

There are two main types of categorical data: ordinal data and nominal data.

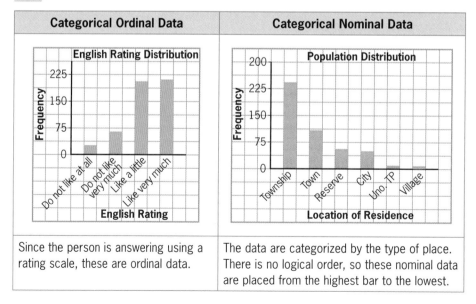

Categorical Ordinal Data	Categorical Nominal Data
Since the person is answering using a rating scale, these are ordinal data.	The data are categorized by the type of place. There is no logical order, so these nominal data are placed from the highest bar to the lowest.

Example 2

Comparing Types of Data

For each graph, identify the type of data, give reason(s) for your choice, and write one statement about what the data show.

a) A survey asks people to rate how concerned they are with Internet privacy on a scale where 1 is not concerned and 5 is very concerned.

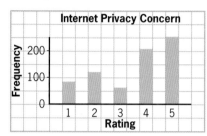

b) A survey asks 1000 people how many hours a week they watch TV.

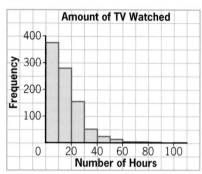

c) A town planner records how many floors each apartment building has.

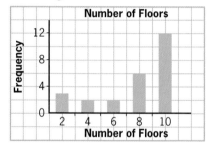

d) The songs in a digital music library are sorted by genre.

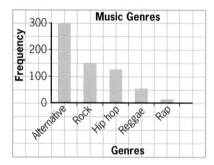

Solution

a) • categorical, ordinal data since they are non-numerical and ranked
   • most people are concerned with Internet privacy

b) • numerical, continuous data since the numbers can be any value
   • more than one-third of the respondents watch 0–10 hours of TV

c) • numerical, discrete data since each value can be only a distinct whole number
   • most apartment buildings in the town have 10 floors

d) • categorical, nominal data since they are non-numerical and not ranked
   • the owner of the library likes alternative music more than any other

> **Project Prep**
> Being able to identify types of data will be useful in organizing the information for your project.

Your Turn

Your teacher will provide you with a file called **YouthSurvey.ftm**. Create one graph for every type of data. Are there any types of data that could not be represented as a graph? Explain.

Example 3

Data With More Than One Variable

Literacy Link

Per capita means per person.

Researchers often measure more than one variable of a particular item. Then, they can analyse the data to see if the measurements are connected to each other. The table shows the life expectancy in years and the health care spending per capita in dollars from various countries. Your teacher will provide you with a Fathom™ file called **HealthCare.ftm** to use if you wish.

Country	Spending per Capita ($)	Life Expectancy (years)	Country	Spending per Capita ($)	Life Expectancy (years)
Australia	3734	81.6	Japan	3025	83
Austria	4345	80.4	Korea	1895	80.4
Belgium	3874	80.1	Luxembourg	4755	80.7
Canada	4309	81	Mexico	957	74
Chile	1283	78.8	Netherlands	4870	80.8
Czech Republic	2039	77.4	New Zealand	2984	80.8
Denmark	4390	79	Norway	5300	81
Estonia	1371	75	Poland	1356	75.8
Finland	3259	80.1	Portugal	2692	79.6
France	3962	81.5	Slovak Republic	2063	75.3
Germany	4187	80.3	Slovenia	2470	79.3
Greece	2977	80.3	Spain	3080	81.8
Hungary	1567	74.4	Sweden	3703	81.5
Iceland	3597	81.8	Switzerland	5157	82.3
Ireland	4037	80.2	United Kingdom	3456	80.4
Israel	1991	81.5	United States	8006	78.5
Italy	3030	82			

Source: Table 2: Total expenditure on health per capita, OECDiLibrary, October 11, 2013 and Table 11: Life expectancy at birth, total population, OECDiLibrary, December 6, 2013

a) Which country spends the most per person on health care? the least? Where is Canada on the list?

b) The dot plots show the spending per capita and the life expectancy of each country. In each plot, each dot represents one country.

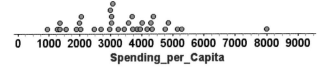

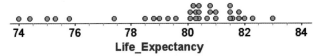

For each graph, identify the lowest and highest ranked country, as well as Canada and the United States. What story does the data seem to tell?

c) Create a scatter plot of life expectancy versus health care spending. Which countries lie outside the general trend? How do you know?

d) In what area of the graph would a country want to be located? Why?

e) In Canada, everyone has access to health care services. This is not the case in the United States. How can these data be used to argue against more health care spending? How can they be used to argue in favour of more health care spending?

Solution

a) The United States spends the most per person on health care ($8006). Mexico spends the least ($957). Canada is in the middle, at $4309.

b) The United States has the highest health care spending, but is in the middle in terms of life expectancy. Mexico has the lowest life expectancy and the lowest spending per person. Japan has relatively low health care spending yet it has the highest life expectancy.

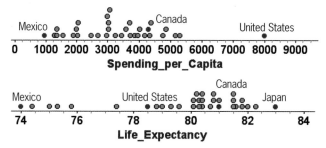

c) You can use technology to create the scatter plot. Your teacher will provide you with a Fathom™ file called **HealthCare.ftm** or a CSV file called **HealthCare.csv**. Refer to the Prerequisite Skills section on page 195 for help creating a scatter plot using technology.

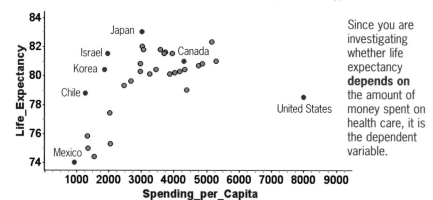

Since you are investigating whether life expectancy **depends on** the amount of money spent on health care, it is the dependent variable.

Literacy Link

CSV stands for *comma-separated values*. Data in a list are separated by commas, which then instructs the spreadsheet that the data entry belongs in the next cell of the column.

The country clearly outside of the trend is the United States, since it spends almost twice as much as every other country. Chile, Korea, Israel, and Japan could also be considered outside the trend since they all seem to have a higher life expectancy than many of those in the trend that spend similar amounts.

d) The top left area of this graph indicates that countries have a high life expectancy with low spending per capita.

e) Someone who is in favour of spending less on health care could argue that Americans are already paying almost twice as much per person for health care as many countries, yet their life expectancy is in the middle of the range. It would be hard for someone in favour of more health care spending to use the data. However, these data show that other factors must affect life expectancy since spending in the United States is so high and life expectancy is not affected. Perhaps the issue is less about the amount of money being spent and instead is about how that money is being spent. Or, perhaps it is about lifestyle choices, diet, exercise, and other environmental factors.

Your Turn

The graphs show the number of tweets at various times of day that contain the hashtags #vacation, #math, and #Junos.

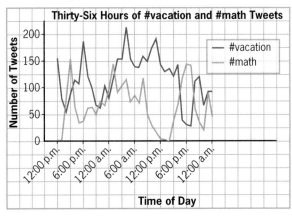

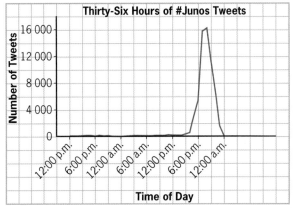

a) What do these graphs tell you about the frequency of tweets with each type of hashtag?

b) What do the data seem to indicate about #math and #vacation as Twitter topics?

c) The Juno Awards is the Canadian music industry's yearly award show. When do you think the show was broadcast?

d) Could these graphs be compared to each other as they are? Explain why or why not.

Key Concepts

- Depending on who is analysing the data and their intention, the information taken from the data can be very different.

- Variability in data exists due to errors in measurement or varying conditions in experiments.

- Different people can interpret data in different ways.

- There are two main types of data: numerical and categorical. Numerical data may be classified as continuous or discrete. Categorical data may be classified as ordinal or nominal.

- When researchers collect data on more than one variable, they can compare the data to see if there is a relationship.

Reflect

R1. Studies show that political experts' predictions are correct or mostly correct 46% of the time and incorrect or mostly incorrect 47% of the time. The remaining 7% are a mix of correct and incorrect predictions. What does this suggest about how reliable experts might be when making predictions?

R2. In the last 20 years, the amount of data being moved and stored online has become staggeringly large. In 2012 alone, almost 3 zetabytes of information moved online. Discuss the positives and negatives of collecting this large amount of data each year.

Literacy Link

A *terabyte* is 10^{12} bytes. A *petabyte* is 10^{15} bytes. A *zetabyte* is 10^{21} bytes.

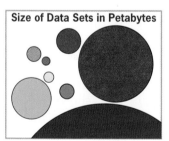

Size of Data Sets in Petabytes

- Business emails sent each year (2986)
- Content uploaded to Facebook each year (182)
- Google's search index (97)
- Kaiser Permanente's digital health records (31)
- Large Hadron Collider annual data output (15)
- Videos uploaded to YouTube each year (15)
- National Climatic Data Center database (6)
- Library of Congress digital database (5)

Practise

1. Use examples to describe similarities and/or differences between the two types of data.

   a) continuous versus discrete

   b) ordinal versus nominal

   c) numerical versus categorical

2. List the different types of data.

a)

	A	B	C	D	E	F
1	Province	Height	Armspan	Handedness	Eye Colour	Fav Sport
2	Ontario	156.5	122	Right	Green	Dancing
3	Ontario	156	139	Right	Blue	Swimming
4	Ontario	163.5	163	Right	Brown	Hockey
5		.	.	.	.	.
6		.	.	.	.	.

b)

	A	B	C	D	E	F
		Number of Languages Spoken	Reaction Time	Mode of Travel	Travel Time	Number of Siblings at Home
1	Province					
2	Ontario	1	0.33	Bus	15	2
3	Ontario	2	0.485	Walk	10	3
4	Ontario	1	0.28	Car	25	1
5		.	.	.	.	.

3. In 2012, the Council of Ontario Universities published a report showing the average annual salary for different university majors two years after graduation. The table shows the 10 lowest paid majors. Create a graph that unfairly shows how poorly someone with a major in Fine and Applied Arts will be paid.

Rank	Major	Salary
1	Fine & Applied Arts	$35 539
2	Humanities	$38 696
3	Theology & Religious Vocations	$39 333
4	Kinesiology/Recreation/ Phys-Ed	$39 779
5	Architecture & Landscape Architecture	$40 733
6	Social Sciences	$42 585
7	Journalism	$42 901
8	Agricultural & Biological Services	$43 466
9	Forestry	$43 889
10	Food Science & Nutrition	$43 952

Source: 2012 Grad Survey, Council of Ontario Universities

Apply

4. A teacher creates a new blog about mathematics and statistics. She collects data showing the number of pageviews in the first few months.

Month	Pageviews
Jan	120
Feb	315
Mar	434
Apr	502
May	596
Jun	537
Jul	472
Aug	645
Sept	848

a) Create a graph of the data.

b) What is the general trend for the traffic on this blog?

c) The graph shows a dip in pageviews. Suggest reasons why this might happen.

d) Predict the number of pageviews expected in December.

5. Consider the headline and graph from *Maclean's*:

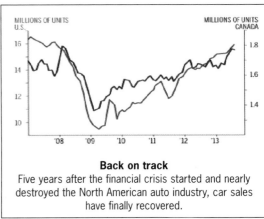

Back on track
Five years after the financial crisis started and nearly destroyed the North American auto industry, car sales have finally recovered.

Source: "Chart of the Week," *Maclean's*, September 30 2013, p. 36

a) The graph uses real data. How have the data been presented to increase impact of the statement?

b) This graph shows the same data. What is it about the original statement that this graph does not show as well?

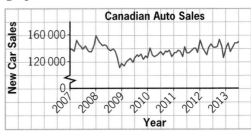

Source: CANSIM Table 079-0003, Statistics Canada, April 11, 2014

6. **Thinking** The graph in #5 shows the seasonal adjusted data. This graph shows the actual number of sales.

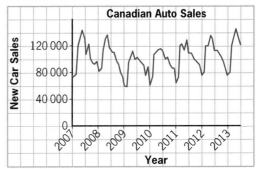

Source: CANSIM Table 079-0003, Statistics Canada, April 11, 2014

a) Why do you think *Maclean's* chose to show seasonally adjusted data?

b) Why do you think auto sales are compared to the same month in the previous year rather than to the previous month?

Literacy Link

When data are *seasonally adjusted*, they are changed so that fluctuations due to seasonal factors are removed. For example, some farm workers will be unemployed during the winter months, so unemployment rates will be higher in the winter.

✔ **Achievement Check**

7. The table shows some statistics for superhero searches on YouTube.

Superhero	Views	Hours Watched
Batman	3 000 000 000	71 000
Thor	2 100 000 000	66 000
Superman	1 700 000 000	14 000
Iron Man	1 400 000 000	20 000
The Avengers	1 000 000 000	31 000
Wolverine	540 000 000	7 800
Spider-Man	340 000 000	7 400
Captain America	280 000 000	4 900
Justice League	220 000 000	3 200
Deadpool	200 000 000	8 900

a) Create a graph that tells a story about the data. Your teacher will provide you with a file called **Superheros.csv**.

b) How can the large numbers be expressed so that they have more meaning?

c) Your teacher will direct you to a website that creates graphs based on search criteria. Enter three superheroes as separate search items. Describe the graphs.

Extend

8. Your teacher will direct you to a website that shows the popularity of various names.

a) Search for your name and describe how its popularity has changed over the years.

b) Enter a common name at your school. Is it just as popular on this site? Explain.

c) Determine three names that are currently not popular but were at one time.

d) Determine three names that were not popular until the last decade.

9. Communication The graph shows the results of EQAO tests at three schools.

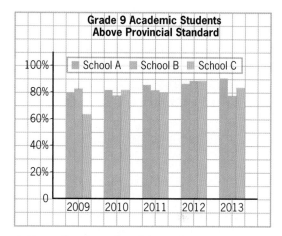

a) Describe the schools' results over time. Which school is doing the best?

b) Some people prefer to compare the results of the same cohort of students. The circle graphs show the cohort data for 2013 from the three schools.

Literacy Link

A *cohort* is a group of people.

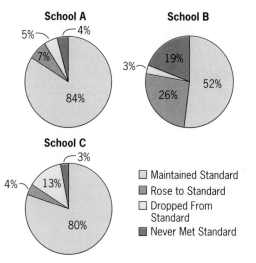

Describe some positive and negative results for each school. Based on this data, which school appears to have the best results?

Principles of Data Collection

Learning Goals

I am learning to

- distinguish between a population and a sample
- understand why sampling a population can give information about that population
- understand that when sampling data the results can vary
- sample data in various ways

Minds On...

What if your job were to test the quality of french fries? At a french fry factory, quality control experts measure and assess batches of fries. Why do you think this is done?

Action!

Investigate Political Party Support

population
- all the individuals in a group that is being studied

sample
- a group of items or people selected from the population

variability (in samples)
- shows how samples are different from each other
- the more similar the samples are to each other, the lower the variability and the more accurately the samples represent the population

In the months leading up to an election, media outlets often predict which party will get the most votes from the **population**. They use the results published by polling firms, which contact a **sample** of the registered voters to try to predict who will win.

1. Work in groups or as a class to design a survey to determine which political party people would vote for.

2. Have everyone in the class answer the survey anonymously.

3. In small groups, choose several other groups of people to sample. What are some factors you might want to consider to get a sample that represents the voting population?

4. Survey the rest of your groups.

5. Compare the results of your surveys between the sample groups. Are the responses similar or is there **variability** in the samples?

6. **Reflect**
   a) Is this is an accurate method to measure the support for political parties?
   b) When polls are conducted, the number of people polled is often a very small proportion of the voting public. How will this affect the accuracy of the estimates?

c) What if only one sample were done? How would this affect the accuracy?

d) What if the sample were much smaller? How would this affect the accuracy?

7. **Extend Your Understanding** Research the results of a recent political poll for Ontario. Your teacher will provide you with a list of websites. Are the results of the poll similar to the results from your investigation? Why or why not?

For a sample to be representative of a population, each member of the population must have an equally likely chance of being selected in the sample. So, selection for the sample must be random. If the sample is not random, it is biased and not as reliable. There are different types of sampling methods. Some are better than others.

Type of Sample	Example
Simple Random • randomly choose a specific number of people • examples: stratified samples and systematic samples	Put all the names in a population into a hat and draw one or several names. Each person has an equal chance of being chosen.
Systematic • put the population in an ordered list and choose people at regular intervals	Order all the patients of a doctor in some way (e.g., alphabetically) and choose one randomly. Select the rest of the data at regular intervals from the original starting point (e.g., every tenth name after the original).
Stratified • divide the sample into groups with the same proportions as those groups in the population • time- and cost-efficient to conduct	Survey factory employees about new safety initiatives. There are 1000 employees in the factory, of which 633 are women and 367 are men. Randomly select 63 women and 37 men to take the survey.
Cluster • divide the population into groups, randomly choose a number of the groups, and sample each member of the chosen groups	Survey Little League Canada baseball players. Randomly select five districts in each province and give the survey to every player in those districts.
Multistage • divide the population into a hierarchy and choose a random sample at each level	Conduct an employee wellness survey by randomly selecting 10 stores. Randomly select three departments in each store, and randomly select 10 employees in each of those departments.
Convenience • choose individuals from the population who are easy to access • can yield unreliable results since it inadvertently omits large portions of the population • often very inexpensive to conduct	To get the public's input on a new pet by-law, a local politician goes to a local park and asks people their opinion.
Voluntary • allow participants to choose whether or not to participate • often the only people who respond are either heavily in favour or heavily against what the survey is about	Conduct an online poll asking people whether banning junk food in schools will fight obesity.

Example

Types of Samples

For each situation, identify the type of sample and discuss whether each member of the population is equally likely to be chosen.

a) A teacher wishes to get feedback from the class about a recent presentation. He plans to draw five students' names out of a hat. All 30 students' names will be in the hat.

b) A telephone company wants to determine whether a fitness centre would be used by its 3000 employees. The company plans to survey 300 employees by interviewing every tenth person on the payroll list.

c) A chain store is trying to decide whether to open a store in Huntsville, Ontario. The company decides to survey 25% of the population of Huntsville and three nearby towns. The table shows the population of each location.

Location	Population
Huntsville	19 056
Kearney	841
Emsdale	2 317
McMurrich	779

d) A market research company mails surveys to all of the adult residents in a town. The survey asks about brands of consumer products. The residents are asked to mail back their responses in a prepaid envelope.

e) A reporter stops people on a downtown street to ask what they think of the city's waterfront.

f) Researchers want to investigate the use of pesticides by apple farmers in Ontario. They divide the province into 10 sections and choose five sections at random. They sample all farms within the five sections.

g) The province wants to randomly choose 250 students. It randomly selects five school boards from the 72 in Ontario. Then it randomly selects five schools in each of those boards. Finally, it randomly chooses 50 students in each of those schools.

Solution

a) This is a simple random sample. The draw includes all possible students, so each person has an equally likely chance of being selected.

b) Since the employees are ordered, and every tenth person is chosen, this is a systematic sample. As long as the first person is chosen randomly, everyone has an equal chance of being selected.

c) If 25% of each town is sampled, this is a stratified sample since the number from each town in the sample would be in the same proportion as in the population (the company would survey 4764 people from Huntsville, 210 from Kearney, 579 from Emsdale, and 195 from McMurrich). Everyone has an equal opportunity to be selected since the 25% of people being sampled are randomly selected from each town.

d) Since the residents choose whether or not they respond to the survey, it is a voluntary response survey. Even though all residents received the survey, the data will reflect responses only from those who are interested. Usually only people who feel strongly one way or another will respond. Thus, the entire population will not be represented in the sample.

e) Since the reporter surveys anyone who is walking on the street, the data are collected in a way that is easily accessible. So, this is a convenience sample. The entire population is not represented since only people in that area at that time are surveyed.

f) This is a cluster sample because the population is divided into groups, a number of sections are randomly chosen, and all farms in those sections are surveyed. Since there is random selection in the first set of groups and sections, all groups and sections are equally likely to be chosen. It is more efficient for the researchers to visit the farms within five areas than it would be to travel to different farms throughout the whole province.

g) This population has a hierarchy of organization and random sampling occurs at each level of the organization, so this is multistage sampling. Each student is equally likely to be chosen since there is random sampling at every level.

Your Turn

In each case, identify the type of sample.

a) You want to find out if your town is in favour of starting a composting pickup service. You ask everyone on your street.

b) A university is polling its students. It selects 200 students at random in the same proportions as the enrollment in each department.

c) There are 139 swim clubs in Ontario. Swim Ontario conducts a survey to vote on its new logo. The organization randomly selects 10 swim clubs and surveys every member in each of those clubs.

d) A coach puts the names of all the basketball players into a hat and draws one name for a free basketball.

e) A questionnaire is sent to every ninth person on an alphabetical list of a store's credit card customers. The first person chosen from the list is picked randomly.

f) The student council invites all students to provide ideas for activities.

g) A marketing firm wants to collect information on certain products in a city of 800 000 people. The researchers randomly select 10 neighbourhoods. In each neighbourhood they randomly select five streets, and on each street they randomly select 10 households.

Key Concepts

- A population is the entire group of a set of people or things. A sample is a smaller portion of that population.

- You can learn a lot about a population by examining samples of that population, as long as all members of the population are equally likely to be part of the sample.

- When multiple samples are taken from the same population, they are different from each other. This is called variability of samples. The smaller the differences in the samples, the more likely the sample closely represents the population.

- There are many types of sampling techniques. Some types of samples work better in certain situations. A good sample is random, and each person in the population has an equally likely chance to be chosen.

Reflect

R1. What are the differences and similarities between a cluster sample and a multistage sample?

R2. If a population is either heavily in favour or heavily against a certain topic, the sample size for a survey does not need to be as large as it would if the opinions were mixed. Why might this be?

Practise

1. Describe the sampling method used.
   a) A seat belt factory randomly selects a time each hour and then tests the next 10 seat belts on the factory line.
   b) A city randomly selects 500 residential addresses from its database.
   c) A charity mails a survey to its 450 members.
   d) The manager of a golf course knows that about 40% of the members are female. He randomly selects 75 females and 112 males to survey.

2. What is the difference between a population and a sample? Use examples to explain.

3. Write several tweets (140 characters or less) to describe each type of sampling method.

Apply

4. Use the data to describe three sampling methods you could use to conduct a survey.

Grade 9		Grade 10		Grade 11		Grade 12	
Girls	Boys	Girls	Boys	Girls	Boys	Girls	Boys
78	91	102	95	91	95	68	62
Classes		Classes		Classes		Classes	
7		8		7		7	

5. **Open Question** A candy factory wants to do some quality control on its production line to see if it has the right proportion of each flavour in its coloured candy mix. Outline a possible plan to sample the product.

6. Use the Internet to research Audrey Tobias and her connection to the Canadian census.

Literacy Link

A *census* is a count or survey of a population. For example, surveying everyone at your school.

7. Describe how each pair of sampling methods are similar and different. Provide examples to support your answers.

a) multistage versus stratified

b) convenience versus voluntary

Processes

Representing
How could you show your answer? Think about visual ways to compare.

8. A car dealership conducts a phone survey to determine customer satisfaction. The dealership will like to use a stratified sample based on the type of vehicle purchased.

Type of Vehicle	Number of Customers
SUV/truck	858
Minivan	1213
Midsize car	478
Economy car	987
Sports car	221

a) What is the population?

b) If the dealership wishes to conduct 250 surveys, how many calls should it make for each type of vehicle?

c) Why would the dealership choose to do a phone survey rather than mailing a survey to each customer?

d) What else can be done to ensure the survey results represent the population?

✓ **Achievement Check**

9. Tomato farmers use an automated tomato picker to pick the tomatoes and eliminate non-ripe tomatoes. The machine works very quickly but the elimination of non-ripe tomatoes is not perfect.

a) The farmer sells a 41.9915-tonne load to a buyer who takes a single scoop of tomatoes from a random spot in the load. If the sample has approximately 300 tomatoes and 92% are acceptable, how much is the load worth? Tomatoes sell for $94.40 per tonne.

b) At least 67% the tomatoes in a load must be acceptable for the buyer to purchase the load. If the farmer expects to get 150 loads from his fields each year, by how much could the farmer's income vary? How do you think the variability in the yields affects how the farm's finances are managed?

c) What type of sampling method is used? Do you think it is accurate enough to be reliable? Explain.

Extend

10. Communication Prior to 2011, the Canadian census required approximately 80% of households to complete the short form questionnaire and about 20% to complete the long form (more detailed) questionnaire. In the 2011 census, the long form was replaced by the National Household Survey, which was no longer mandatory. Describe some pros and cons of this change.

11. Thinking It is estimated that there are over 4000 moose in Algonquin Provincial Park. Research how the moose count is done. Does it use a sampling method similar to those described in this section? Explain.

Collecting Data

Learning Goals

I am learning to

- collect primary data by designing surveys and experiments
- describe the characteristics of an effective survey

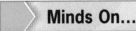

Minds On...

People are asked survey questions all the time. Sometimes the way the question is asked or the subject matter of the question can influence the results of the survey.

- If you were asked whether you would help at the local food bank, how would you answer?

- How might the question itself influence your answer?

Action!

Investigate Conducting an Experiment

Materials

- wastepaper basket, bucket, or other container
- at least 3 different types of balls

Conduct an experiment to determine which combination of ball and throwing style will yield the highest probability of a basket. Follow the steps to complete the table.

	Ball 1		Ball 2		Ball 3	
Distance	Underhand	Overhand	Underhand	Overhand	Underhand	Overhand
1 m						
3 m						
5 m						

1. Place the empty basket against a wall.

2. Stand 1 m from the basket. Use an underhand throw to toss one type of ball into the basket. Repeat 10 times and record how many times you got the ball in.

3. Repeat step 2 from a distance of 3 m and 5 m. Record your results.

4. Repeat steps 2 and 3 using an overhand toss.

5. Repeat steps 2 to 4 using a different type of ball. Then repeat steps 2 to 4 using the third type of ball.

6. Based on your data, which type of ball and throwing style combination gives you the best chance of getting the ball in the basket?

7. How is organizing your information in a table helpful for answering the question?

8. When researchers conduct experiments, they often try to keep all variables constant while changing only one thing at a time. How did this experiment follow that model?

9. **Reflect** Why is changing only one variable at a time a good thing to do, in general, when conducting experiments?

10. **Extend Your Understanding** You are planning an experiment involving measuring the time it takes for a soup can to roll down ramps with different angles of elevation. Which variables do you need to keep constant?

There are two different types of experiments: observational studies and experimental studies.

In observational studies, researchers look at situations that are already occurring and try to make inferences. For example, a researcher might compare two groups of people, one with members who exercise and another with members who do not exercise, to see if one group is healthier than the other.

In experimental studies, researchers control what is going on and make inferences based on those controls. For example, a researcher might randomly choose two similar groups and have members of one group perform rigorous exercise once a day for 30 days while members of the other group continue with their normal lifestyle. The researchers would then measure the fitness of both groups at the end of the month.

In this example, the group that exercises is the treatment group while the one that does not exercise is the control group. In an experimental study there is a greater chance of determining the cause of a particular behaviour. Three things need to occur to determine the cause:

- Control: as many aspects of the experiment need to be controlled as possible so that if there is an effect, the researchers know what caused it.

- Randomization: when groups are chosen, subjects need to be randomized so that no biases occur in any of the groups.

- Replication: even though the groups are random, when researchers repeat an experiment they should be similar in make-up so that changes from one group to another are easier to detect.

Literacy Link

An *inference* is a conclusion based on reasoning.

treatment group

- the participants in an experiment who receive the specific treatment being measured

control group

- the participants in an experiment who do not receive the specific treatment being measured

- compared to the treatment group

Example 1

What Type of Study?

For each case, answer the following questions:

a) Is it an experimental study or an observational study? Give reasons why.

b) If it is an experimental study, what is the control group and the treatment group? What effect is being studied? If it is an observational study, what are some things that could cause the effect to happen?

Case 1: People with headaches are randomly divided into two groups. One group gets pain medication, and the other does not. One hour later, the participants are asked about their pain.

Case 2: You go to all of the houses in your neighbourhood and ask whether they use fertilizer on their lawns. You then check if their grass is green.

Solution

Case 1:

a) Since there is randomization and some aspect of control (some are given the medicine while the others are not), this is an experiment. Even though you cannot tell if the two groups have similar make-up, the other two criteria are met, so this is a well-designed experimental study.

b) Control group: those who did not get medication
Treatment group: those who did get medication
Effect being studied: whether medication decreases headache pain

Case 2:

a) This is an observational study. There are no controls for who used fertilizer and who did not, and subjects are not randomized.

b) The effect being studied is whether fertilizer makes lawns green. Factors other than fertilizer, such as watering, can affect the colour of a lawn. Without good control, it is hard to know what causes any effect.

Your Turn

1. A researcher interviews people as they leave the gym and finds that they get fewer colds compared to people who do not go to the gym.

   a) Why is this an observational study?

   b) What could be done to turn this into an experimental study?

2. A botanist is studying the effects of acidity on rate of growth. She grows one group of plants using water with neutral pH. She grows each other group using water with increasingly acidic pH levels.

   a) Which are the control and which are the experimental groups?

   b) Why do you think groups of plants were used rather than one single plant for each pH level?

Example 2

Survey Questions

Conducting surveys is another way to collect primary data. Surveys are less controlled than experiments, but a well-written survey can provide useful information. The following survey is being distributed to 100 students:

School Feelings Survey

Name: _____ Age: ☐ 10–12 ☐ 12–16 ☐ 16–17 ☐ Over 18

Gender: ☐ Male ☐ Female

1. Would you like to have the freedom to use your cell phone in class or would you rather be alone with no communication? ☐ Cell phones ☐ No cell phones

2. Which of the following is your favourite subject? ☐ Math ☐ English ☐ Drama

3. Do you think it's important for students to attend church? ☐ Yes ☐ No

4. How do you like the new cafeteria menu?
   ☐ Pretty good   ☐ Good   ☐ Great   ☐ Fantastic   ☐ Awesome

5. How do you like the new school logo and mascot at the school?
   ☐ Like them   ☐ Do not like them

Check to make sure the survey asks appropriate questions.

a) Is the survey anonymous? Why might anonymity be important?

b) Are the choices for ages appropriate and clear? If not, how can you fix this section? Why is this important information to collect?

c) Is #1 a leading question? If so, explain why this is a problem and rewrite the question.

d) Do any questions provide a limited number of options? If so, rewrite the question.

e) Does the survey ask any personal questions that people might prefer not to answer?

f) Is the rating scale in #4 a well-written scale? If not, rewrite it.

g) Question #5 asks for an opinion about two things in one question. Explain why this is a problem and rewrite the question.

Literacy Link

A *leading question* is phrased so that it could influence the way a person answers.

Solution

a) No, the survey asks for a name. People may be less likely to answer truthfully, especially if the questions are personal or embarrassing.

b) No. There are several issues with the age range boxes:
- The ranges overlap: 12 and 16 are both covered in two boxes.
- The ranges vary: the 12–16 age group is larger than the others.
- There is no box for an 18-year-old to check.

Use individual ages:

   ▪ 12 and under ▪ 13 ▪ 14 ▪ 15 ▪ 16 ▪ 17 ▪ 18 ▪ 19 and over

Demographic information can reveal trends within the population.

Literacy Link

Demographic information includes things like age, gender, level of education, income, residency, ethnicity, and so on.

bias

- occurs when there is a prejudice for or against an idea or response

- biased samples can result from problems with either the sampling technique or the data collection method

- example: a survey question that asks whether you agree that the government should continue to waste money is biased because it leads people to change their opinion toward government spending

c) The cell phone question suggests that having a cell phone is better than not having one. This is a **biased** question. Phrase questions in a way that is neutral and does not reveal your personal opinion. When asking for an opinion, include a "No Opinion" option.

> Should cell phones be allowed in class? ■Yes ■No ■No opinion

d) The question about a favourite subject includes only three options. Instead, allow respondents to fill in the blanks.

> What is your favourite subject? _____

Open questions can sometimes result in unexpected answers. For example, if a respondent says Shakespeare is his favourite subject, you might choose to categorize that as English.

e) The question about going to a church is unethical. By asking only about church, the question is excluding a potentially large number of people who attend a different place of worship. It is also unrelated to the topic of School Feelings. Consider whether you really need the question in the survey. If you do, rephrase the question and include a third option:

> Do you think it is important for students to attend a place of worship?
> ■Yes ■No ■Prefer not to answer

f) The scale gives only positive choices. Also, the choices are vague. Use clear wording and put the worst option at one end of the scale and the best option at the other end. Place the other choices evenly between.

> How do you like the new cafeteria menu?
> ■Dislike ■Do not like or dislike ■Like

g) A person who likes either the mascot or the logo, but not both, has nowhere to answer. Either ask two separate questions, or give options that cover all the situations.

> How do you like the new school logo and mascot at the school?
> ■I like both ■I like the logo but not the mascot
> ■I like the mascot but not the logo ■I dislike both

Your Turn

In each case, identify the problem with the question and rewrite it so that it is more appropriate.

a) What is your favourite game system?
■Xbox ■PlayStation® ■Wii™

b) Running a business is hard. Leadership training will help your business run smoother.
■Agree fully ■Somewhat agree ■Agree a little

c) How important do you think speed and quality of service are?
■Very important ■Important ■Modestly important
■Of little importance ■Unimportant

Example 3

Create a Survey Using Technology

Create a survey to compare how much males and females like baseball.

> Solution

Method 1: Use Fathom™
- Open Fathom™.

- Drag a new **Collection** to the workspace. Double click on the icon and name it "Baseball Survey." With your collection selected, from the **Collection** menu choose **Create Survey**.

- Fill in the **attribute** name, "Gender." Under **Format**, choose **Define a New Category Set**. Type in "Male, Female" (a comma separates each choice). Click OK. Under **Question,** type: "What is your gender?"

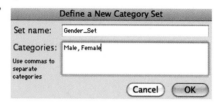

- Fill in the next **attribute** name, "Baseball." Under **Format**, choose **Define a New Category Set**. Type: "Like a lot, Like a little, Do not like or dislike, Dislike a little, Dislike a lot." Click OK. Under **Question,** type: "Do you like baseball?" In the **Instructions** box, type the instructions for the survey: "Please fill out this survey honestly."

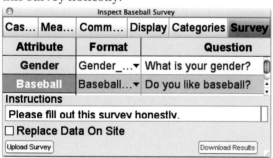

- Click **Upload Survey** to create the online portion of your survey. Your teacher will provide you with a login and password.

- Once uploaded, press **View Survey** to see the survey and get the link. Anyone taking the survey will need the same login and password.

- Once your survey is filled out, click **Download Results** to gather the information in Fathom™.

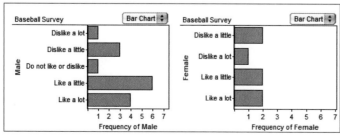

Method 2: Use Google Docs

- Sign in to or create a Google account and click on **Google Drive**.
- Click on **Create** and then select **Form** from the drop down list.
- Call the form "Baseball Survey."
- Title question 1: "What is your gender?" Select **Multiple Choice** and enter the two options as "Female" and "Male." Click **Done**.
- Click **Add Item**. Then title question 2: "Do you like baseball?" Select **Choose from a list** and enter the following five options: "Like a lot," "Like a little," "Do not like or dislike," "Dislike a little," "Dislike a lot." Click **Done**.

- Click on **Send form**. You can send the survey by entering email addresses, posting a link to the survey on Facebook or Twitter, or embedding it in a website.
- After getting several responses, log in to your Google Drive account and click on **Baseball Survey form (Responses)** to open the spreadsheet that contains all the survey responses. You can cut and paste the data into a spreadsheet or into a Fathom™ collection.
- To get a visual representation of the data, click on the **Form** menu and select **Show Summary of Responses**.

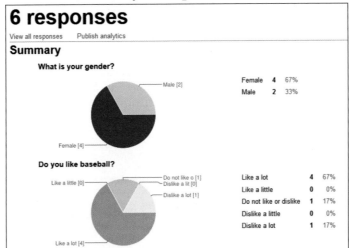

Your Turn

Use a technology of your choice to create a survey with two questions. Share your survey with your classmates.

Key Concepts

- In an observational study, the researcher records behaviour and tries to draw conclusions based on the observations.

- Experimental studies try to determine the cause and effect relationship between two variables by controlling for one variable to see what effect it has on the other variable.

- Effective experiments have good control, randomize the members of the treatment and control groups, and try to have a similar demographic make-up in each group.

- Surveys are a powerful way to gain information about a group of people.

- Surveys should be anonymous but can ask for precise demographic information.

- Items on surveys should be clear, concise, and ask only one question that is free of bias.

- Rating scales on a survey should be evenly distributed between good and bad outcomes.

- Data from surveys can be efficiently collected using technology.

Reflect

R1. Why do you think asking clear and concise survey questions is important for gaining information about people?

R2. Clinical tests of medication use a third experimental group called the placebo group. This group takes a medication that has no active ingredient. Members of the placebo group do not know that they are not getting the real medication. Why do you think this group is also studied?

R3. Researchers want to determine whether smoking causes decreased lung capacity. They gather two randomly chosen groups of 100 people. One group smokes one pack of cigarettes a day while the other group does not smoke at all. After two years, the researchers assess the lung capacity in both groups. This is called a longitudinal study. Discuss any possible ethical issues with this study.

Literacy Link

A *longitudinal study* is a type of observational study where researchers measure the same variables over a long period of time, often years or decades.

Practise

Choose the best answer for #1 and #2.

1. Which of the following is an unacceptable rating scale?

   A ■Agree ■Undecided ■Disagree

   B ■Frequently ■Occasionally ■Rarely

   C ■Usually true ■Occasionally true ■Sometimes true

   D ■Important ■Moderately important ■Unimportant

2. Which of the following statements is true?

   A Observational studies are used to determine the cause of various events.

   B Experimental studies must have variables controlled throughout the study.

   C Observational studies should have all of their participants randomized.

   D Experimental studies keep track of the behaviour of groups that are created by the participants.

3. For each of the survey questions, explain how the question could be improved. Then, rewrite it.

a) Do you exercise daily and get enough sleep at night? ■Yes ■No

b) The *Star Wars* saga is one of the best science fiction stories of all time. How do you feel about Disney taking over the franchise?
■Strongly agree ■Agree ■Don't know
■Disagree ■Strongly disagree

c) Which is your favourite type of music?
■Rap ■Electronic ■Pop

d) How do you feel about the following statement: We should not reduce the number of recycling days in the school.
■Strongly agree ■Agree ■Don't know
■Disagree ■Strongly disagree

4. Use the scale to write a survey question.
■Very frequently ■Frequently
■Occasionally ■Rarely ■Never

5. Identify each case as an observational or experimental study. Indicate what relationship is being studied.

a) People are asked if they have had magnetic therapy and whether their pain is reduced.

b) As part of a study to gain information regarding travel to Mars, NASA is paying subjects $18 000 to lie in bed for 70 days.

c) Two randomly selected groups of 100 students are studied. One group has all left-handed students while the other has right-handed students. Their math grades are collected and analysed.

Apply

6. In 2000, a survey was given to 1000 Canadians about their use of technology. The results for two of the questions are shown. The red bars show people who answered no when asked whether they had used the Internet.

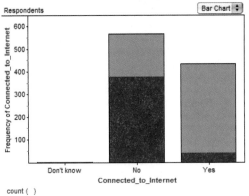

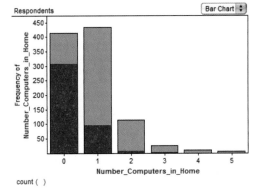

a) Approximately how many people had no computers in their home?

b) Why do you think a large portion of the people who had no computers are highlighted in red?

c) This survey was a cross-sectional study. How do you think these graphs would change if the same questions were asked now?

Literacy Link

A *cross-sectional study* is a type of observational study where researchers measure the variables from a population at one specific point in time.

d) Your teacher will provide you with a file called **TechUse.ftm**. Create three graphs using the data in it. Describe the story those graphs tell.

7. **Open Question** Write three ineffective survey questions. Exchange with a partner and fix each other's questions.

8. Your teacher will provide you with a file called **2001CensusOntario.ftm**.

   a) Double click on the collection and click on the Comments tab. What kind of information is provided?

   b) Create two different graphs using location data. Describe what each graph shows.

   c) Create three graphs using ethnicity data. What does each graph show?

   d) Why is it important to have these data?

9. **Open Question** Create a survey with five questions. Make each question collect a different type of data (categorical, nominal, discrete, numerical, etc.). You could use a situation such as entertainment, sports, the environment, school, or technology.

10. **Open Question** Create a survey with five questions that ask for opinions. Use a different rating scale for each one.

11. For #9 and #10, use technology to create a survey. Have your classmates fill it out. Create a graph to show the results for each question.

12. Organic farmers grow their crops using only natural fertilizers, while traditional farmers use chemical fertilizers. Researchers decide to contact 24 farmers and collect data on the yields of corn grown on 11 organic farms and 13 traditional farms. They find that the organic farms tend to have between 5% and 34% lower crop yields than the traditional farms.

   a) What kind of study did they likely conduct?

   b) Describe a study that could more formally test whether organic crops yield less than traditional farms.

✔ Achievement Check

13. You want to find out if there is a link between eating habits and grades at your school.

   a) **Application** Write 5 to 10 questions to collect data on this topic.

   b) Create this survey using technology and have your classmates complete it.

   c) Create three or more graphs that compare eating habits and grades.

   d) **Thinking** Design an experimental study to see if there is a link between eating habits and grades.

14. **Thinking** A researcher wants to determine whether there is a connection between academic success and birth order. Explain why this could not be done as an experimental study.

Extend

15. **Thinking** The effects of coffee on the human body and mind are widely studied.

   a) Search the Internet for three to five different studies on the effects of drinking coffee. Do any of the studies seem questionable? In what way?

   b) For each study, identify the type of study and what effect was being measured.

   c) Search online for a 2013 study called "Association of Coffee Consumption with All-Cause and Cardiovascular Disease Mortality." What type of study was this? What were the conclusions? What kind of evidence, if any, exists that suggests the conclusions could be reliable?

16. **Communication** Clinical trials often use placebos to help determine if the medication is working. Search for studies that have used placebos. Find at least one where the placebo helped to show the medication worked and one where it did not.

Interpreting and Analysing Data

Learning Goals

I am learning to

- distinguish between primary and secondary sources of data
- distinguish between microdata and aggregate data
- collect and analyse data from primary and secondary sources
- collect and analyse data obtained through experimentation

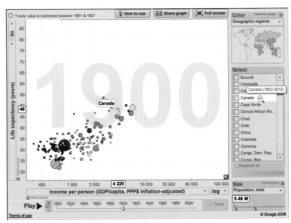

Source: Free material from Gapminder World

> **Minds On...**

The graphs show data about life expectancy and income per person for 200 countries. In 1900, Canadians had a life expectancy of 48 years, the average income per person was $4225 per year, and there were 5.46 million people in the country. In 2012, Canadians had a life expectancy of 81 years, the average income per person was $35 993 per year, and there were 35 million people in the country. What kind of stories do these data tell about Canada compared to other countries?

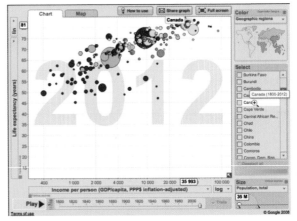

Source: Free material from Gapminder World

> **Action!**

Investigate Statistics Canada Data

The branch of the Canadian government that is in charge of the census and all the other data collection is called Statistics Canada. The public can access much of the information through CANSIM (Canadian Socio-Economic Information Management System) or actual census data. In this investigation, you will explore how to get the price of goods and services from CANSIM.

1. Go to the Statistics Canada website and choose **Browse by subject** from the menu. Choose **Prices and price indexes**, then **Consumer price indexes**, and then **Detailed tables from CANSIM**.

2. Scroll down the list until you see **Table 326-0020** on the Consumer Price Index. This table contains information on the price of over 280 goods and services. Click on **Description** and determine the range of years these data cover and what year equals 100. These values do not represent the price of these items but instead the price index.

3. Click on **Table 326-0020**. Describe what you see. Click on the **Add/Remove data** tab.

> **Table 326-0020** [1, 2, 3, 4, 5, 6, 7, 9, 10]
> **Consumer Price Index (CPI), 2011 basket**
> monthly (2002=100)
>
> | Data table | Add/Remove data | Manipulate | Download | Related information | Help |
>
> The data below is a part of CANSIM table 326-0020. Use the Add/Remove data tab to customize your table.

Source: CANSIM Table 326-0020, Statistics Canada

4. Scroll down and click on **+Expand** from **Step 2-Select: Products and product groups**. Deselect anything currently checked. Put a check beside Fresh milk, Water, and Gasoline.

> | ☐ Dairy products and eggs | ☐ Water, fuel and electricity | ☐ Rental of passenger vehicles |
> | ☐ Dairy products | ☐ Electricity [20] | ☐ Operation of passenger vehicles |
> | ☑ Fresh milk | ☑ Water | ☑ Gasoline |

5. From **Step 3-Select the time frame**, choose the earliest possible year and month and the latest possible year and month.

6. From **Step 4-Select the Screen output format**, choose **HTML table, time as rows**. Then choose **Apply**.

7. What is the earliest date for which data exist for these items? Choose **Add/Remove data** and change the beginning date to the actual time when the data start and choose **Apply**. Be sure to select **HTML table, time as rows** after changing the dates.

8. Select all the data and paste them into a spreadsheet program. Create a single graph that has all three sets of data on it. Refer to the Prerequisite Skills on page 195 for help on plotting multiple series using spreadsheet software.

9. Which set of data did not have data for the entire time frame?

10. **Reflect** Compare how each set of data changed its value over time. Which one seems to vary the most? What is the general trend for all three?

11. **Extend Your Understanding** Determine the current price of each item. Use the Consumer Price Index and the fact that the prices will be proportional to the Consumer Price Index to estimate the cost of each item over this time span. How does this affect the graph of your data?

Literacy Link

The *Consumer Price Index (CPI)* is a value that represents a "basket" of goods that are typically purchased by consumers. The prices are averaged with each item being weighted by importance. When the CPI is high it means that prices in general are high, and vice versa.

Project Prep

Statistics Canada is a huge resource that includes many topics and years. When looking for information for your project, you may wish to search there for the most up to date Canadian data.

primary source data

- data that have been collected directly by the researcher and have not been manipulated or summarized

microdata

- an individual set of data about a single respondent

secondary source data

- data used by someone other than those who actually collected them

aggregate data

- data that are combined or summarized in such a way that the individual microdata can no longer be determined

When you collect and analyse data, it is considered **primary source data**. The individual responses in a survey are called **microdata**. Each line in the table is microdata about each person. The entire table is the researcher's primary data about a group of people.

	A	B	C	D	E
1	Person ID	Gender	Age	Marital Status	Employment
2	1224	Male	43	Married	Employed
3	1225	Female	25	Single	Employed
4	1226	Male	17	Single	Student
5	1227	Male	35	Divorced	Unemployed

Any data that you have not collected on your own represent **secondary source data**. These are often in aggregate form, meaning they have been manipulated in some way. For example, if you collect data about the height of each person in your class, the individual heights are microdata, while the summary of the heights in the form of an average is **aggregate data**.

Example 1

Interpreting Data from Statistics Canada

The table shows the average domestic airfares for 10 Canadian cities.

	2010	2011	2010 to 2011
City	**Dollars**		**% Change**
Canada	182.5	190.7	4.5
Calgary	165.5	176.2	6.5
Edmonton	160.8	170.0	5.7
Halifax	172.0	179.3	4.2
Montréal	191.1	194.1	1.6
Ottawa	196.0	194.8	–0.6
Regina	168.1	177.8	5.8
Saskatoon	170.2	178.8	5.1
Toronto	205.2	214.9	4.7
Vancouver	199.2	206.7	3.8
Winnipeg	181.0	189.4	4.6

Source: Table 1 Average domestic air fares for 10 major Canadian cities, *The Daily*, Wednesday, January 9, 2013, Statistics Canada

a) Does this table show microdata or aggregate data? How do you know?

b) Is this table a primary or secondary source of data? Justify your answer.

c) Identify the independent and dependent variables.

d) What kind of story do the data in this table tell?

e) Locate this report from *The Daily* archive on the Statistics Canada website. What other types of things are mentioned in the report?

f) What type of sampling was used? Where did you find that information?

Solution

a) The data represent averages, so this table shows aggregate data.

b) The table is primary data for Statistics Canada, because Statistics Canada collected the data. It is secondary data for anyone else.

c) The independent variable is the city and the dependent variable is the average airfare.

d) Create a graph to help see a pattern in the data.

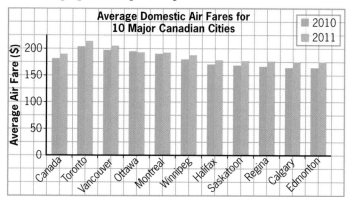

When organizing categorical data, often it is appropriate to arrange in order of size. Note that Canada goes first because it is not a city.

Except for Montreal and Ottawa, all the cities have a similar increase in ticket cost. Montreal's increase was half as large as the next highest, and Ottawa had a drop in price.

e) Besides a brief summary of the data, there is also a link to the summary table as well as links to the four sets of data that were used to create the table. There is also a link to the actual survey information.

f) A stratified random sample was used. The survey method was found under the section titled "Definitions, data sources and methods."

Your Turn

One of the tables that was used to collect the above data was CANSIM Table 401-0004. A condensed version of the table is shown.

a) Can you see any patterns in the data?

b) What kinds of comparisons could be made between 2008 and 2011?

Average Domestic Fares for Canada and 10 Major Cities

Geography	2008	2009
Canada	196.30	173.00
Halifax	197.20	170.80
Montréal	194.30	177.80
Ottawa	205.80	189.30
Toronto	219.80	194.40
Winnipeg	191.50	169.90
Saskatoon	184.00	160.50
Regina	x	160.00
Calgary	185.20	156.40
Edmonton	180.50	154.20
Vancouver	209.10	182.60

Symbol legend: x Suppressed to meet the confidentiality requirements of the *Statistics Act*

Source: CANSIM Table 401-0004, Average domestic fares for Canada and ten major cities, Statistics Canada, February 18, 2014

Example 2

Analysing a Database

A music library has the attributes shown in the table. Use the table and the graphs to answer the following questions:

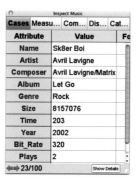

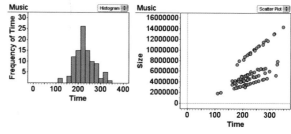

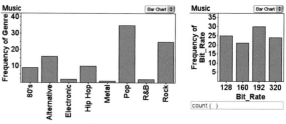

a) What type of data are these?

b) How many songs are in this library?

c) What is a more appropriate arrangement of the Genre graph?

d) What kind of story or stories do the data in the graphs show?

e) How does bit rate relate to the scatter plot of Size vs. Time?

f) Your teacher will provide you with a file called **Music.ftm**. Use it to determine which song(s) is the most played.

Solution

a) These are microdata. Since they come from a personal library of music, they are also primary data.

b) There are 100 songs in the library.

At the bottom of the attribute list, 23/100 means you are looking at the 23rd piece of data out of 100. How could you use the graphs to see how many songs there are?

c) Since they are non-ordinal, categorical data, it makes the most sense to arrange the bars from largest to smallest.

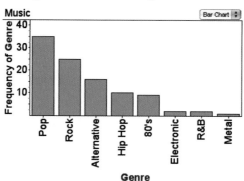

To move the bars around on a categorical plot, drag the names with your mouse.

d) Pop and Rock music make up more than half of the songs, and there are more than twice as many Pop songs as there are Alternative songs. In general, the longer the song, the larger the size of the song.

e) Since there are four distinct "lines" of data on the scatter plot, each must correspond to a specific sample rate. For example, if the data with 160 bits per second are selected, you can see their distinct line on the graph. The higher the bit rate, the steeper the line (and the larger the files for the same length of song).

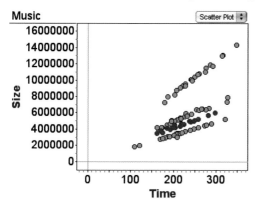 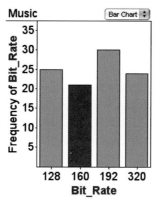

f) Use the attribute called Plays to create a tally of how many times each song was played. Drag a **Graph** from the tool bar and drag the Plays attribute to the horizontal axis. Click on each dot plotted at 13. The name of the song will appear in the list.

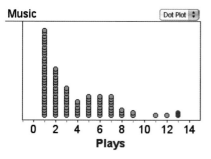

Two songs have been played 13 times each: "I Kissed a Girl" and "Remember the Name."

Your Turn

Using the data set from the example, determine the following:

a) What information is given about each song?

b) What kind of story does the Time histogram tell you?

c) Are each of the artist genres equally distributed in terms of the bit rate?

d) If you knew how long a song was, could you determine its size? Explain.

Example 3

Interpreting a Trend on a Time Graph

One of the gases directly linked to the greenhouse effect and climate change is carbon dioxide (CO_2). Keeping track of the amount of carbon dioxide in the atmosphere is an indirect method of measuring the potential for climate change. At the Mauna Loa Observatory in Hawaii, scientists have been collecting atmospheric data since the 1950s. Due to its remote location and minimal influence from vegetation or human activity, this site has become important in the collection of many types of atmospheric data.

Year	CO$_2$ Reading (ppm)
1993	355.97
1994	356.90
1995	359.57
1996	361.02
1997	362.02
1998	364.16
1999	367.52
2000	368.36
2001	369.61
2002	371.43
2003	373.65
2004	376.03
2005	377.61
2006	380.10
2007	381.80
2008	384.06
2009	385.66
2010	387.51
2011	390.06
2012	392.17
2013	394.66

Source: National Oceanic and Atmospheric Administration, August 28, 2013

a) This data set shows the average monthly carbon dioxide levels (in parts per million) in January of each year for two decades. What type of data are these? Explain.

b) Without graphing, suggest what appears to be happening over time.

c) Create a graph showing these data. Your teacher will provide you with a file called **MaunaLoaSmall.csv** if you wish to use technology. What story do the data tell?

d) Your teacher will provide you with a file called **MaunaLoa.csv**. This is a more complete set of data. Create a graph of the data. Compare the story this graph tells to that of your graph from part c).

Solution

a) Since these are monthly averages, the data have been manipulated. So, they are aggregate data. Although the researchers collected the readings and thus used primary data to generate the summary, these are secondary data for anyone else who uses them.

b) The carbon dioxide levels appear to be rising. At the beginning of the data, the CO_2 level was at 355.97 ppm in 1993, and it was at 394.66 ppm in 2013. That is a rise of 38.69 ppm, or 11%.

c) The graph confirms there has been a fairly steady rise in CO_2 readings in the past two decades that does not appear to be slowing down.

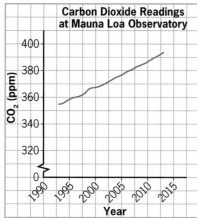

Why is it appropriate to use a line graph rather than a scatter plot?

d) This file has seasonal data rather than the annual data, so the graph shows more detail. Although the CO_2 levels are going up as in part c), they are fluctuating as they go up. A closer look seems to indicate that the levels may fluctuate with the seasons.

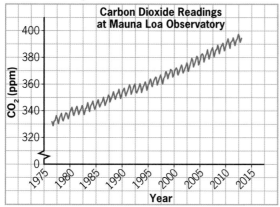

Your Turn

A student drops a ball from various heights and measures the height of the bounce. The table shows the results.

a) Is this a study or an experiment? Explain.

b) What is being controlled and what is being changed in this activity?

c) What is the relationship between the drop height and the bounce height?

d) Create a graph of the data. Describe the relationship in the graph.

e) If you dropped the ball from a height of 130 cm, could you use this information to predict its bounce height? If so, explain how.

Drop Height (cm)	Bounce Height (cm)
0	0
10	7
20	14
30	21
40	30
50	38
60	46
70	51
80	60
90	62
100	70

Key Concepts

- Primary sources of data are collected directly from the source and are not manipulated or summarized in any way.

- Microdata are the individual pieces of data that make up all of the primary data.

- Secondary sources of data are used by someone who did not collect them. Often these data have been manipulated and summarized. Data found in the media often are secondary data.

- Data that are summarized in some way are called aggregate data.

- Large sources of data are available for analysis on the Internet.

- Sources of data also are hidden in digital items like songs and photos.

Reflect

R1. How are websites for the NHL, MLB, NBA, and NFL like databases?

R2. Which is more visible to the public, primary or secondary data? Why do you think this is?

Practise

Choose the best answer for #1 and #2.

1. Which of the following is microdata?
   - A batting averages for a baseball team
   - B the height of each person in your class
   - C monthly sales for each store in a chain
   - D number of births in each country in 2013

2. Go to the Statistics Canada website and search the CANSIM database. Which of the following tables contain information about vacations?
   - A 128-0014
   - B 203-0026
   - C 427-0004
   - D 361-0013

3. For each of the CANSIM tables in #2, describe the topic of the data.

4. In each of the following cases, determine whether the data are primary or secondary.
   a) Your town sends a survey to each household and collects the data.

   b) After collecting the survey from part a), your town publishes the average number of people per house on each street.

   c) The newspaper reports the salary of every city council member.

   d) A magazine lists the total number of home sales each month for the last year.

   e)

Person ID #	Age	Job	Hours Worked
345	24	Shipper	38
231	38	Custodian	42
124	29	Mail clerk	40

   f)

	Percent of Students Who Take the Bus to School	
Grade	Male	Female
9	78	82
10	85	80
11	74	81
12	65	64

Apply

5. Go to the Statistics Canada website and choose **Census of Canada**, **Data products**, and **Census Profile**. Search for the city or town closest to where you live.

   a) What percent of people are in your age group?

   b) What is the largest age group in your city or town?

   c) Answer parts a) and b) again, for Toronto. If you live in Toronto, use Sarnia.

   d) Compare the population, population density, and percent of married people between the two cities.

6. **Thinking** The data below represent all the earthquakes over magnitude 4 on the Richter scale that occurred in North or South America in 2012.

Month	Day	Name	Depth (km)	Magnitude
1	30	Peru: ICA	43	6.4
3	20	Mexico: Guerror, Oaxaca	20	7.4
3	25	Chile: Parral, Santiago	41	7.2
4	17	Chile: Valparaiso	29	6.7
5	14	Chile: Arica; Peru: Tacna	10	6.3
5	19	Brazil: Montes Claros	10	4.1
8	27	El Salvador: Off the coast	28	7.3
9	5	Costa Rica: Nicoya	35	7.6
10	28	Canada: Queen Charlotte Islands	14	7.7
11	7	Guatemala: San Marcos, San Cristobal Cochu	24	7.3

Source: National Geophysical Data Center

   a) A total of 48 earthquakes over magnitude 4 occurred all over the world. What percent were in North or South America?

   b) Where in Canada did the only earthquake above magnitude 4 occur? Was this a big earthquake in comparison to the others?

   c) Represent this information in a graph. Why did you choose that graph type?

   d) Your teacher will provide you with a file called **Earthquake2012.ftm**. It contains more detailed, world-wide data about all of the earthquakes over magnitude 4 in 2012. Use Fathom™ to create a new graph. Drag the **Longitude** to the horizontal axis and the **Latitude** to the vertical axis. What does this graph represent? Drag the **Magnitude** onto the centre of this graph to create a "heat map." Why do you think this is called a heat map?

   e) Where is there a concentration of large magnitude earthquakes?

   f) Search the Internet for the Significant Earthquake Database. Get all of the earthquake data for the last complete year available. Create a graph and compare to 2012.

7. **Thinking** Every time you take a picture, your camera records details about the photo. These data are called the Exif information.

   a) Your teacher will provide you with a file called **Images.ftm**. It contains Exif information for over 500 images. What kind of information is stored about each image?

   b) Create three graphs that use numerical data and three graphs that use categorical data. Why do you think this sort of information would be important to a photographer?

   c) Create a scatter plot comparing file size to the number of pixels in the image. Some cameras predict how many more photos you can take before the memory card runs out of space. How can this comparison be used by your camera to make this prediction?

8. Some of the largest databases are weather-related. One of the wettest places in Canada is Henderson Lake, BC. Weather stations there measure an average of 9082 mm of rain every year. Consider some of the wettest communities listed below.

Canada's Wettest Communities	
Location	Rain (mm)
Hartley Bay, BC	4549
Holberg, BC	3912
Port Renfrew, BC	3671
Tofino, BC	3306
Prince Rupert, BC	3111
Gold River, BC	2846
Wreck Cove Brook, NS	1945
Pools Cove–Fortune Bay, Nfld	1829
Louisbourg, NS	1599
Sydney, NS	1505
Alliston, PEI	1182
Charlottetown, PEI	1173
Sept-Iles, Que	1156
Stratford, Ont	1064
Cameron Falls, Alta	1103

Source: "Rainiest Places in Canada" Current Results

a) Are these data primary or secondary? Give reasons.

b) People in Stratford probably think they get a lot of rain. Compare Stratford, Hartley Bay, and Henderson Lake to get a sense of how much rain these places are getting.

c) Create a graph of the data. How does the graph indicate that BC is likely the wettest province? Your teacher will provide you with a file called **WettestCommunities. csv** if you wish.

✔ Achievement Check

9. There are over 180 known meteor craters on the planet. Most of these impact sites are millions of years old. The graphs show some data that scientists have collected about them.

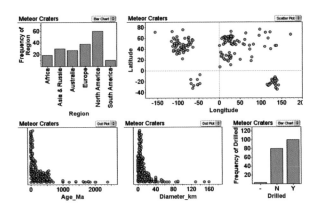

a) Is this is a primary or secondary source of data? Justify your answer.

b) Are these data the result of a study or an experiment? Justify your answer.

c) North America has had a substantially larger number of impact craters than other regions. Why might this be of interest to scientists? Is there any reason why this could be perfectly normal?

d) Your teacher will provide you with a file called **MeteorCraters.ftm**. Which region has had the lowest proportion of craters drilled to have their rocks tested? Why might this make sense?

e) Does it appear that the older the impact, the larger the diameter? Justify your answer. Create a new graph to demonstrate your point.

Extend

10. **Thinking** Go to the Gapminder website. From the **Menu** choose **Data** and in the search enter "life." From the options for the indicator named "Life Expectancy (Years)," choose **Visualize** 🔘 . Slide the slider back to 1800 and click on the Play button.

a) Describe what happens to the graph.

b) Explain what the size and colour of the circles represents. What else can the size of the circle represent?

c) What kind of story is told by the data? How is Canada part of the story?

d) Go back to the Data page and find a different data set. What story does your new set tell?

5.5

Bias

Learning Goals

I am learning to

- distinguish among types of bias when sampling data
- analyse and interpret statistics presented by the media to judge their validity
- identify different ways that graphical data can be misleading

Minds On...

On competitive reality shows, the audience often votes for contestants. But phone voting systems are often overwhelmed. In one instance, two contestants both had about 24 million votes, but over 200 million calls did not get through. What does this say about the reliability of the voting system?

Action!

response bias
- when respondents change their answers to influence the results, to avoid embarrassment, or to give the answer they think the questioner wants

sampling bias
- when the sample does not closely represent the population

measurement bias
- when the collection method is such that the characteristics are consistently over- or under-represented

non-response bias
- when the opinions of respondents differ in meaningful ways from those of non-respondents

Certain types of bias make it difficult to get a representative sample or truthful responses.

Type of Bias	Example
response bias	A teacher asks students to raise their hand if they cheated on last week's test. Students will not want to admit to cheating on a test so it is unlikely that many will raise their hand.
sampling bias	A politician goes back to the farming community she grew up in to ask for opinions on her latest initiative for the agriculture industry. It is likely that a larger proportion of the people she speaks to would support the initiative, both because it would benefit them and because she grew up in the area. This would not accurately represent the entire population.
measurement bias	A survey question asks, "A lot of people do not like math. How would you feel being referred to as a math geek?" This is a leading question; the wording of the question can affect the outcome by influencing someone's answer. Other types of measurement bias can occur when the collection method affects the results, for example when the options in a multiple choice question are too limited for an honest response.
non-response bias	A mail-in survey asked respondents about their drinking habits. Only 3% of the surveys were returned. Such a small return rate would likely not yield a representative sample. In fact, those who respond often have very strong opinions about the subject matter and so the results could easily over- or under-estimate the feelings of the population.

Example 1

Identifying Bias

A large sample does not guarantee good data. This is especially true if the method of data collection has some bias associated with it. Identify the type of bias that may occur in each situation.

a) Families in a neighbourhood are told they are part of a study about healthy eating habits.

b) You ask only students on sports teams how to spend the school fundraising money.

c) A survey question asks, "Who is the best basketball player of all time, Michael Jordan or LeBron James?"

d) A radio call-in show asks callers to answer the question, "Are you in favour of a law that would ban pitbulls from the city?"

Solution

a) This is response bias. Because the families are told the study is looking at healthy eating habits, it is likely they will start eating better because they are being watched and want to give a good impression.

b) Since you are only asking students who play sports, it is likely the respondents will overwhelmingly want to spend the money on sports-related things. This is sampling bias.

c) This is measurement bias, because there are only two choices.

d) Usually, the people who call in to radio shows have extreme opinions. People who are indifferent or do not think the topic is important may not vote, so a large proportion of listeners choose not to respond. This is non-response bias. Also, since only listeners of the radio show will call in, it is also sampling bias since the respondents likely would not properly represent the population.

Your Turn

Identify the type of bias that may occur in the following situations.

a) A survey question asks, "How many words per minute can you read?"

b) A survey is sent to parents of school-age children that asks whether bus safety lanes should be installed.

c) A phone company surveys its customers via text message about which services people like the best.

d) A survey asks, "Now that the city is in debt, do you think the current mayor will win the next election?"

Project Prep

When collecting your own data or using a secondary source of data, it is important to make sure the data are free of bias. If you fail to do this, the integrity of your project will be compromised.

Example 2

Misleading Statistics

Explain how each case uses misleading or questionable statistics.

a) The *Daily Mirror* and *The Times* retweeted this tweet about a British high-speed rail project (HS2) that is expected to take 20 years to complete.

> Interesting stat: 93% of today's UK population will be dead by the time HS2 is finished. Wow. #bbcqt

b) In 2005, the British Cheese Board conducted a study to show that eating cheese does not give you nightmares.

c) Classmates' Eye Colour

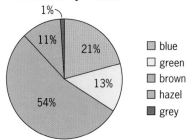

- blue
- green
- brown
- hazel
- grey

d) A newscaster reports about a survey that asked, "Did scientists falsify research to support their own theories on climate change?" and shows the following summary:

59% Somewhat likely
35% Very likely
26% Not very likely

e) Research shows that if you eat a sausage a day, your risk of a certain type of cancer goes up by 20%.

Solution

a) The original figure was mathematically implausible since it is unlikely that such a high proportion of the population will die in the next 20 years. The media outlets did not check whether the statistic was true before they retweeted it.

b) When a company or organization conducts research to disprove negative effects, the method of collection and validity of the data should be studied closely. In this case, the subject of the study is nightmares, which are intangible and hard to quantify and verify.

c) Circle graphs are hard to visually interpret if the sizes of the wedges are similar because judging the size of areas is difficult. In this graph, you know how big each section is because the percents are shown. A bar graph would allow people to more easily compare the sizes of the bars even without the percents labelled.

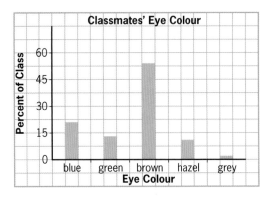

Classmates' Eye Colour

d) The values in this summary add up to more than 100%. This mistake was made by a major news service. When you refer to the original survey, you can see the results were different.

Newscast	Actual Survey
59% Somewhat likely	35% Very likely
35% Very likely	24% Somewhat likely
26% Not very likely	21% Not very likely
	5% Not at all likely
	15% Not sure

The newscast combined the top two percents and combined the third and fourth responses. But they also included the data for "Very likely" again, skewing the data further.

e) When dealing with percents, it is often important to have more information to determine whether the number is significant. In this case, 20% sounds like it could be a significant increase. However, you need to know the current rate of this type of cancer. If about five people in 100 will have it, a 20% increase is actually only going from five out of 100 to six out of 100.

Your Turn

Explain how each case uses misleading or questionable statistics.

a) A news report on jobs lost shows this graph.

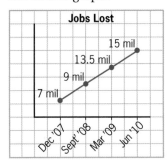

b) A newspaper headline states "Unemployment Dropping" and includes this graph.

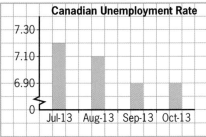

c) A yogurt manufacturer states that 67% of customers surveyed claimed they lost weight while eating its brand of yogurt.

Example 3

Some Numbers Are Bigger Than Others

Sometimes numbers that seem big are really small, and other times numbers that seem big truly are. When you see big numbers, try to put them into perspective.

a) A recent settlement of $52.5 million was awarded to 970 000 households from Québec affected by the 1998 ice storm. Is this a big settlement?

b) Switzerland has the highest consumption of chocolate per person. The population is 8.0 million people and they eat about 82 million kg of chocolate each year. Is that a lot of chocolate?

Solution

a) Determine the amount of money awarded to each household.

$$\frac{52\ 500\ 000}{970\ 000} = 54.1237\ldots$$

Each household will get $54.12.

At first $52.5 million sounds like a lot of money, but when you consider all the households that received money, it seems much less significant.

b) First, determine the amount of chocolate eaten per person.

$$\frac{82\ 000\ 000}{8\ 000\ 000} = 10.25$$

Each person in Switzerland eats 10.25 kg of chocolate per year.

Next, get a sense of how much that is. One chocolate bar is about 50 g.

$$\frac{10\ 250\ \text{g}}{50\ \text{g}} = 205\ \text{bars}$$

$$\frac{205\ \text{bars}}{52\ \text{weeks}} = 3.9\ \text{bars/week}$$

The average person in Switzerland eats approximately four chocolate bars per week. Someone who does not eat chocolate regularly would consider this a lot of chocolate, but someone who eats chocolate every day would not.

Your Turn

a) Every year, Canadians and Americans spend over $8 billion on Halloween. Do you think this is a lot of money? Justify your response.

b) In 2011, Apple Corporation's profit grew by almost $19 000 000 000 from 2010. Do you think this is a large increase? Justify your response.

Example 4

Interpreting Infographics

Infographics combine both visual and text-based representations of data. In some cases the representations are standard, while others are more unique or stylish.

a) Describe how this infographic was constructed.

b) Why do you think this representation is called a heat map?

c) The scale represents the ranking. How does this show that ranking is a problem (especially if that is all you know about the data)?

d) What kind of story is told by the data?

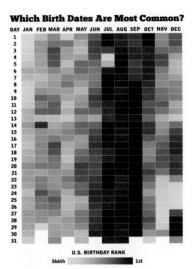

Which Birth Dates Are Most Common?

U.S. BIRTHDAY RANK
366th — 1st

Source: NYTimes, Amitabh Chandra, Harvard University. Photo from the Daily Viz.

Solution

a) Each rectangle represents a day of the year. The data are based on the number of birthdays each day. The day with the most birthdays is ranked 1st and has the darkest colour. The day with the fewest birthdays is ranked 366th and has the lightest colour.

b) This is called a heat map because colour coding is often used to represent temperature. The data are represented by the shade of colour. Instead of representing heat or temperature, these data show rank on a list.

c) This method only ranks the data, it does not show how significant the differences are between the data. Consider the two fictional classes below.

Rank		1	2	3	4	5	6	7	8	9	10
CLASS A	Student	T	A	D	F	S	G	H	U	E	O
	Mark	93	89	88	87	87	85	84	82	81	80
CLASS B	Student	Z	B	R	M	K	N	L	J	X	W
	Mark	95	87	83	77	72	68	67	60	59	51

Both classes have 10 students ranked from highest to lowest. In Class A, all of the marks are 80 or above. In Class B, student Z has the highest mark of both classes, but student W has the lowest mark of both classes. Student Z's mark of 51 is significantly lower than the lowest mark in Class A of 80. If you consider only rank, you see only the order of the marks and do not know that even though Student O is ranked last in Class A, the mark of 80 is actually a fairly high mark.

d) Even though you don't know the actual number of birthdays on each day, you can see that the highest numbers of birthdays are around September.

Your Turn

Consider the infographic from CBC's *Hockey Night in Canada*.

a) How are Canadian teams distinguished from other teams?

b) How could you determine which team had the fewest North American players?

c) How could you use the data to argue that hockey is Canada's pastime, but not the pastime of the United States?

d) What information is difficult to determine from this representation?

e) Is this infographic free of bias? Explain.

f) Write a tweet (140 characters or less) that is related to this infographic.

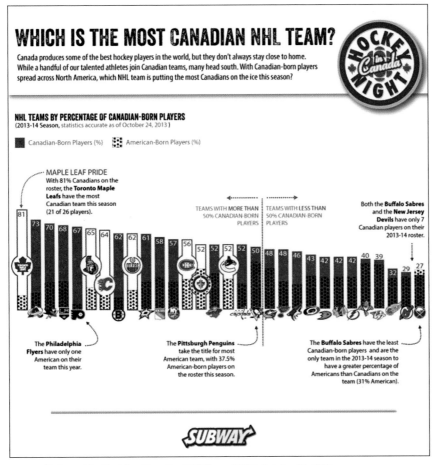

Source: "Infographic: The Most Canadian NHL Team," CBC, October 25, 2013

Key Concepts

- For data to be valid, collection methods must be free from bias.

- The data can be affected if the collection methods suffer from sampling, measurement, response, or non-response bias.

- Different ways of displaying data can distort it and make it biased.

- Large numbers should always be put in context.

- Infographics can be dense with information or convey an idea with unique methods.

Reflect

R1. Companies often want to back up their product with scientific claims. Is it possible to make misleading claims even if the data are free from bias?

R2. How is it possible for someone to "lie" with statistics yet still be telling the truth?

R3. In recent years, many soft drink companies have developed vitamin-enriched drinks, claiming they have health benefits. When the owners of vitaminwater® were sued for making false health claims, part of their defence was that

"no consumer could reasonably be misled into thinking vitaminwater was a healthy beverage or was composed only of vitamins and water because the sweet taste of vitamin water puts consumers on notice that the product contains sugar."

Source: Gleeson, John, "Memorandum and Order," CV-09-0395 (JG) (RML).

What is the company claiming and why should it make you wary as a consumer?

Practise

Choose the best answer for #1.

1. Which of the following is not a leading question?

   A We have recently upgraded SurveyMakers to become a first-class tool. What are your thoughts on this first-class site?

   B Should the mayor fix the dirty, potholed streets in the city?

   C As a good patriotic citizen, do you think you should buy an imported car?

   D How important is health care compared to other social issues?

2. Identify the type of bias and suggest how the same data could be researched without bias.

   a) Your teacher asks you to raise your hand if you understood the lesson.

   b) City council conducts a survey about the police force by asking everyone who comes to the next council meeting.

   c) The local news posts a poll on its website asking if climate change is real.

   d) An application to join a gym asks how much you like exercising.

   e) A store that sells hunting gear petitions to lower the cost of registering a gun.

3. **Open Question** Choose one of the four types of bias and develop a situation that would result in biased data. Trade with a classmate and identify each other's type of bias.

4. Identify the problem with the graph or situation.

a) A drug company states that in its clinical trials, patients had 20% fewer headaches.

b)

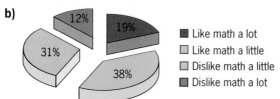

- Like math a lot — 19%
- Like math a little — 38%
- Dislike math a little — 31%
- Dislike math a lot — 12%

c)

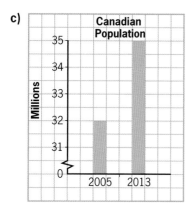

Canadian Population graph, y-axis Millions (0, 31–35), bars for 2005 (32) and 2013 (35).

d) Teens were surveyed to see which social media sites they use. The following results were given:

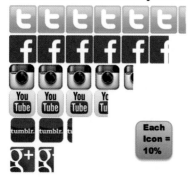

Which social media outlets do you use?

Each Icon = 10%

e)

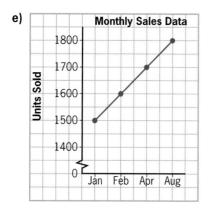

Monthly Sales Data graph, y-axis Units Sold (0, 1400–1800), x-axis Jan, Feb, Apr, Aug.

Apply

5. Elections are integral to democracy.

a) In an election, the polls are open for a particular period of time. In some cases, the party in power drops the number of polling booths in areas where they have low support and increases the number of polling booths in areas where they have more support. Describe how this may affect the results and how it is biased.

b) In 2011, Canada held a federal election. The results were:
Conservative Party: 39.6%
NDP: 30.6%
Liberal Party: 18.9%
Bloc Québécois: 6.0%
Green Party: 3.9%

If you wanted to make the Conservative win sound bigger, would you use percents or percentage points to compare the results? Explain.

c) Voter turnout for the 2011 election was 61.1%. The population eligible to vote was 24 257 592. What percent of Canadians actually voted for each party? How does that compare to the percent that did not vote? What type of bias could this represent?

d) In the 1898 election only 44.6% of the population voted. What implications might this have had on the actual results of the election?

e) **Thinking** Your teacher will provide you with a file called **VoterTurnout.csv**. It contains data from all of Canada's past elections. Create an infographic that displays some aspects of the data.

6. Determine if the number is significant.

a) Canada Post delivers 9.8 billion pieces of mail each year.

b) Over 70 billion hours of video are watched on YouTube each year.

c) Clayton Kershaw earns $30 000 000 a year to play baseball.

d) In 2013, the Canadian national debt was over $650 billion.

7. *Maclean's* magazine published an infographic about solar energy.

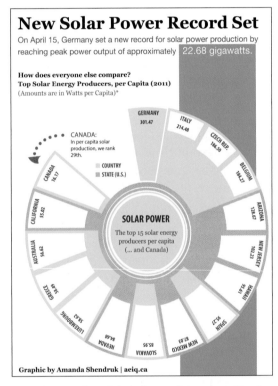

New Solar Power Record Set

On April 15, Germany set a new record for solar power production by reaching peak power output of approximately **22.68 gigawatts.**

How does everyone else compare?
Top Solar Energy Producers, per Capita (2011)
(Amounts are in Watts per Capita)*

CANADA:
In per capita solar production, we rank 29th.

■ COUNTRY
■ STATE (U.S.)

SOLAR POWER
The top 15 solar energy producers per capita (... and Canada)

GERMANY 301.47
ITALY 214.48
CZECH REP. 186.50
BELGIUM 184.27
ARIZONA 128.67
NEW JERSEY 102.23
HAWAII 95.61
SPAIN 93.27
NEW MEXICO 87.03
SLOVAKIA 85.95
NEVADA 84.48
LUXEMBOURG 58.82
GREECE 56.49
AUSTRALIA 56.62
CALIFORNIA 55.02
CANADA 16.17

Graphic by Amanda Shendruk | aeiq.ca

a) What makes this infographic appealing?

b) How does Canada rank as a solar-energy producing nation? Why might this be?

c) How does the way the data are displayed visually connect them to the topic of solar power?

d) What do you think the editors are trying to convey with the statement in the centre of the circle: "The top 15 solar energy producers per capita (… and Canada)."

8. Communication In 2013, the Canadian Cancer Society reported a 1.6% rate of a certain type of cancer in women. If this were to rise to 2% in 2014, create two headlines to relay this information. Make one headline shocking and one neutral.

9. Communication Research "push polling" and explain how it affects elections.

10. Research the Hawthorne effect and give an example of when it might occur.

11 Communication There are types of bias other than the four types described in this chapter. Research the following types of bias and describe whether you have experienced any of them.

a) confirmation bias

b) observational selection bias

12. An agricultural research firm conducts a survey of local farmers.

a) One of the questions on the survey asks, "The use of high-tech farming methods increases yields by up to 20%. How important is it for you to use high-tech farming methods?" What type of bias does this question have? Rewrite it so it is free of bias.

b) The brochure includes this graph. Why do you think the firm presents the information this way?

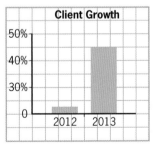

13. The table shows the all-time North American box office Top 20 up to 2013.

Rank	Released	Film Name	Total Box Office
1	2009	*Avatar*	$760 507 625
2	1997	*Titanic*	$658 672 302
3	2012	*Marvel's The Avengers*	$623 279 547
4	2008	*The Dark Knight*	$533 345 358
5	1999	*Star Wars Ep. I: The Phantom Menace*	$474 544 677
6	1977	*Star Wars Ep. IV: A New Hope*	$460 998 007
7	2012	*The Dark Knight Rises*	$448 139 099
8	2004	*Shrek 2*	$441 226 247
9	1982	*ET: The Extra-Terrestrial*	$435 110 554
10	2006	*Pirates of the Caribbean: Dead Man's Chest*	$423 315 812
11	1994	*The Lion King*	$422 780 140
12	2010	*Toy Story 3*	$415 004 880
13	2013	*Iron Man 3*	$408 992 272
14	2012	*The Hunger Games*	$408 010 692
15	2002	*Spider-Man*	$403 706 375
16	2009	*Transformers: Revenge of the Fallen*	$402 111 870
17	1993	*Jurassic Park*	$395 708 305
18	2011	*Harry Potter and the Deathly Hallows: Part II*	$381 011 219
19	2003	*Finding Nemo*	$380 529 370
20	2005	*Star Wars Ep. III: Revenge of the Sith*	$380 270 577

a) What is surprising about the data?

b) The graph shows the movies organized by the year of their release. What does it say about the fairness of this comparison?

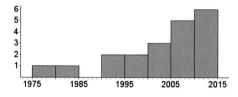

c) This graph is adjusted for inflation. How is it different? Why does it make more sense?

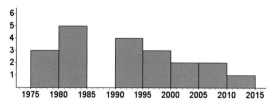

Literacy Link

Inflation is an increase in prices over time. When comparing dollar amounts from different time periods, it is important to *adjust for inflation*.

d) Your teacher will provide you with a file called **Top20Movies.csv**. It contains both the adjusted for inflation and non-adjusted Top 20 movies. How does the list change when comparing the unadjusted to the adjusted movies?

e) **Thinking** Create an infographic that displays the information provided above.

Extend

14. **Thinking** Even though celebrities may or may not be experts, they can often be influential because they are visible in the media. Vaccines have had some controversy associated with them.

a) Research how these two facts are connected.

b) Why is there such caution about vaccines and why might this be unfounded?

15. **Communication** When medication is being developed, pharmaceutical companies use complex procedures to verify that the drugs actually work. To be completely sure, they use a procedure called a double blind study. Research double blind studies and explain why they are so important.

Learning Goals

Section	After this section, I can
5.1	• show how data are used and misused in statistical studies • identify different types of data • understand that there is variability in data • see that you can analyse single sources of data or related sources
5.2	• distinguish between a population and a sample • understand why sampling a population can give information about that population • understand that when sampling data the results can vary • sample data in various ways
5.3	• collect primary data by designing surveys and experiments • describe the characteristics of an effective survey
5.4	• distinguish between primary and secondary sources of data • distinguish between microdata and aggregate data • collect and analyse data from primary and secondary sources • collect and analyse data obtained through experimentation
5.5	• distinguish among types of bias when sampling data • analyse and interpret statistics presented by the media to judge their validity • identify different ways that graphical data can be misleading

5.1 Data Concepts and Graphical Summaries, pages 196–205

1. Give an example of a variable that could be measured using each type of data.

   a) numerical, discrete

   b) numerical, continuous

   c) categorical, ordinal

   d) categorical, nominal

2. The graph shows the Internet usage of a family of five for one month.

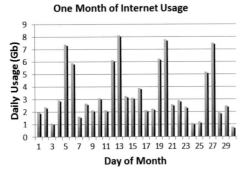

One Month of Internet Usage

3. a) Account for the peaks in the data. Justify your answer.

   b) The family's Internet plan has a 100 Gb monthly data limit. Estimate whether they went over their limit.

   c) Your teacher will provide you with a file called **InternetUsage.csv**. Check your answer from part b).

   d) Determine the average daily Internet usage. Do you think this number is useful for the family? Explain why or why not.

5.2 Principles of Data Collection, pages 206–211

3. Determine the type of sampling.

   a) Your favourite social networking site asks what your favourite band is.

   b) The Pelee Island Bird Observatory does its annual bird count every December. Researchers set up traps in the trees in three locations to gather the birds.

5.3 Collecting Data, pages 212–221

4. For each survey question, identify the problem with the question and rewrite it.

  a) How old are you?
  ▇ 15 and below ▇ 15–20
  ▇ 20–35 ▇ 35–60 ▇ Above 60

  b) Violence in video games could cause people to be violent in real life. How do you feel about a violence rating system for video games?
  ▇ Strongly agree ▇ Agree
  ▇ Agree a little ▇ Don't agree

  c) Do you like the new logo for the school?
  ▇ Yes ▇ No

5. Determine whether each study is observational or experimental.

  a) In 2006, a research team asked nearly 5000 households for charitable donations to see which methods produced higher amounts. When the solicitor was an attractive female, the average donation increased by 50–135%, especially if a male answered the door.

  b) A teacher looks at class averages over the last 10 years and sees that the smaller the class size, the higher the class average.

5.4 Interpreting and Analysing Data, pages 222–232

6. In each case, determine whether the data are from a primary or secondary source.

  a)

Percent of Students Achieving at or Above Provincial Standard in Grade 9 Math				
	School		School Board	
Year	Applied	Academic	Applied	Academic
2011	66	92	45	85
2012	43	86	49	86
2013	56	91	58	87

  b) Your classmates fill out a survey that asks for their age, height, gender, eye colour, and favourite food.

  c)

Late Night TV Hosts' Yearly Salaries (millions)	
Jon Stewart (*The Daily Show*)	$35
Jimmy Fallon (*The Tonight Show*)	$12
Jimmy Kimmel (*Jimmy Kimmel Live*)	$10

5.5 Bias, pages 233–243

7. Give an example to show each type of bias.

  a) sampling **b)** measurement

  c) response **d)** non-response

8. In each case, indicate how the representation is misleading.

  a)

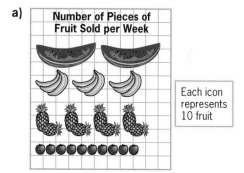

Number of Pieces of Fruit Sold per Week

Each icon represents 10 fruit

  b) Energy Usage per Year

  ▇ Dishwasher
  ▢ 42" TV
  ▇ Fridge
  ▇ Clothes Dryer
  ▢ Tablet Computer
  ▢ Hair Dryer

9. Create an infographic of the Canadian data.

Total area = 9 985 000 000 km²	
Land area = 9 094 000 000 km²	
Population = 35 million people	
Population density = 3.95 people per km²	
Population growth = 1.05% per year	
Life expectancy = 81.2 years	
Median age = 40.4 years	
Internet usage = 30.26 million people	
Mobile phone usage = 26.26 million people	
Number of students = 6.188 million people	
Number of teachers = 278 000 people	
Health spending = $3895 per person per year	

Chapter 5 Test Yourself

Achievement Chart

Category	Knowledge/ Understanding	Thinking	Communication	Application
Questions	1, 2, 3, 4, 5	9, 10	5, 6, 7, 8, 9, 10	6, 7, 8

Multiple Choice

Choose the best answer for #1 to #4.

1. Which of these are significant numbers?

   A Facebook surpasses 1 trillion page views per month.

   B Health care spending in Ontario will go up by $2.1 million.

   C On average, a person will breathe about 500 million times in their life.

   D Approximately $135 million is donated to the Canadian Cancer Society each year.

2. Which of the following is not a valid sampling method?

   A Order data from highest to lowest, randomly select one item, and then choose every fifth value after that.

   B Put all the data into a bin and randomly select as many as you wish.

   C Arrange the data into demographic groups and pick 100 from each group.

   D Send out a survey and ask people to fill it out and send it back.

3. Which of these is a good survey question?

   A Where do you get most of your information on video games and movies?
   ■Friends ■Game store ■Internet ■TV

   B Should formula sheets be allowed on math exams?
   ■Strongly agree ■Agree ■Don't know
   ■Disagree ■Strongly disagree

   C Which uniforms do you prefer for the football team, the new modern style or the old style?
   ■New ■Old

   D What is your favourite sport?
   ■Soccer ■Tennis ■Volleyball ■Golf

4. Which situation comprises microdata?

   A the average height of students in each class in your school

   B the height of every student in your school

   C the total number of recycled cans collected by each school

   D the average annual salary of citizens in different cities

Short Answer

5. Describe why these situations have bias and what you could do to eliminate it.

   a) A company comes door-to-door selling rooftop solar panels. The sales representative claims that by the end of the third year you will be making more than $500 per month.

   b) Your teacher explains a difficult topic and then asks the students if they understand.

6. Your teacher will provide you with a file called **Waste.csv**.

   a) Create a graph of these data.

   b) What story is told by the data?

7. Create a short survey that you could give to your classmates on one of the following topics:
   • Internet usage
   • climate change
   • poverty

8. The table shows data on energy production in Ontario.

Type	Nuclear	Gas	Hydro	Coal	Wind	Other
Energy Produced (MW)	12 998	9987	7939	3293	1725	122

a) Create a graphical representation of the data that is not misleading.

b) Create a graphical representation of the data that is misleading. Explain why it is misleading.

Extended Response

9. Researchers surveyed 881 people to find out what province each person was born in.

NFLD	PEI	NS	NB	QUE
18	10	36	16	225

ONT	MAN	SASK	ALTA	BC
301	29	33	80	133

a) Graph these data.

b) What type of sampling method was likely used? Why?

c) The researchers also collected data from a much larger group about the number of trips people made.

NFLD	PEI	NS	NB	QUE
3500	1091	8115	5458	60 169

ONT	MAN	SASK	ALTA	BC
90 174	7984	8624	21 558	22 380

A newspaper published the headline "Ontarians travel much more than people from other provinces." Why might this headline be incorrect?

d) How could the data be displayed more accurately?

10. a) Collect data on a topic of your choice.

b) Consider sampling methods, non-biased techniques, and good survey questions to develop a strategy that would lead to collecting data that are
- highly credible
- not very credible

Chapter Problem

Food Production

It is estimated that by 2050 there will be over 9 billion people living on the planet. Some estimates suggest that by then we will need 30–70% more food and 40% more water. As the population continues to increase, why is it important for farmers to use data management techniques to help them grow their crops? To justify your answer, think about ways farmers can use
- primary data collection
- experimental design
- interpretation of data from the media or advertising
- sampling techniques

One-Variable Data Analysis

Athletes are often compared to one another. Team managers make generalizations about players' abilities to decide what they are worth. What statistical calculations could help the manager
- determine the value of a player's contract?
- decide which player to hire for their team?
- decide how much money to pay a player for a five-year contract?

Popular musicians are compared with artists from the past and present. What statistical calculations could you use to compare
- the number of days on the top 10 charts?
- the most listened to genre of music?
- songs that have lasted the test of time?

In this chapter, you will learn various methods of statistical analysis and assess their strengths and weaknesses.

Key Terms

mean	variance
median	standard deviation
mode	z-score
outlier	multiple bar graph
percentile	split bar graph
quartile	relative split bar graph
range	reliable data
interquartile range (IQR)	valid data

Literacy Strategy

A mathematics word wall identifies words and phrases that you need to understand to develop mathematical skills and reasoning. Careful use of visuals helps support understanding of key words. How does this image convey the meaning of the word "median"?   **median**

As you work through this chapter, think about some of the key words you encounter. Use visuals and letters to show the meaning of words for a classroom word wall.

Career Link

Risk Assessment Manager

In the financial services industry, many careers involve assessing business risks and taking measures to control or reduce the risk. Victoria is a risk management analyst who assesses the risks related to defaults on loans. It is her job to assess whether borrowers will be able to repay the loans they receive and whether her firm will get enough return on investment.
- Who do you think would be a lower risk, a young employed couple buying a house, or a startup company in the information technology field?
- How do you think risk level affects the type of loan that each could get?

Chapter Problem

Used Car Lot Business Report

Retail sales outlets regularly use statistics to describe their products, and used car lots are no exception. The amount of time a car sits, unsold, on the lot can affect the value of the car. In this exercise, you will analyse time spent on the lot and present a report of your findings.

a) List some pros and cons of buying a used car.

b) List three things car buyers look for when purchasing a used car.

c) A typical used car may take about a month to sell. What do you think would happen to the price of a used car after it has been on the lot for three months?

d) What other statistics will affect the price of the car?

Prerequisite Skills

Measures of Central Tendency

The three most common measures of central tendency are mean, median, and mode.

Mean

Example: To determine the mean of the numbers 15, 21, 12, 4, 13, and 5, add all the data values within the set:

$15 + 21 + 12 + 4 + 13 + 5 = 70$

Divide the total by the number of values.

$\frac{70}{6} \approx 11.7$

Mode

Example: The mode is the number that appears most often. There can be one mode, more than one mode, or no mode. If no numbers repeat, then there is no mode.

In the following data set, the mode is 11.

11 3 4 9 25 8 1 11 3 4 11

Median

Example: To find the median, put the data set in order from least to greatest. Find the value(s) in the middle of the data set.

2 4 5 5 6 7 9 12 15 15 16 17 20 25

There are two middle values. Determine the average of the two values.

$\frac{9 + 12}{2} = 10.5$

1. Determine the mean, median, and mode of each set of data points.

   a) 45, 24, 62, 12, 43, 73, 98, 58, 12, 81, 25, 12, 43, 52

   b) 6, 14, 3, 14, 21, 20, 14, 16, 19, 6, 7

   c) 12.3, 15.8, 9.9, 13.0, 12.7, 16.1, 20.0, 8.3

   d) 102, 134, 187, 155, 142, 134, 134, 156, 181

2. The mean of the set of numbers is 15. What is the missing number?

   13, 16, 15, 20, 14, ▪

Types of Data

Categorical data can be sorted by category. Ordinal data can be ranked. Numerical or quantitative data are in the form of any number.

3. Identify each type of variable as categorical, ordinal, or quantitative.

   a) hair colour

   b) salary

   c) gender (M, F)

   d) rating scale (low, medium, high)

   e) level 1, 2, 3, or 4 on a standardized test

   f) temperature

Graphical Summaries

You can use a variety of graphical summaries to display data. Some are better for discrete data, while others are better for continuous data. You will often need to judge which option is the most meaningful way to display your data.

Bar Graph

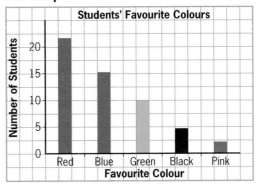

Pictograph

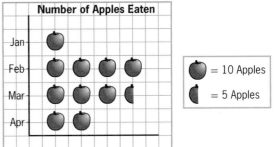

Circle Graph

Favourite Type of Movie

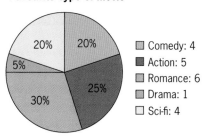

- ☐ Comedy: 4
- ■ Action: 5
- ☐ Romance: 6
- ☐ Drama: 1
- ☐ Sci-fi: 4

Example: To determine the central angle, multiply the percent of the data for each category by 360 degrees. For example, 25% of those surveyed preferred action movies.

$0.25 \times 360° = 90°$

Histogram

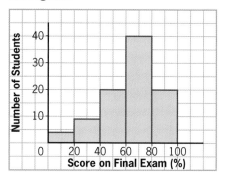

Stem and Leaf Plot

Example: Create a stem and leaf plot for the following data:

170 173 173 175 179 179 179 181 181 182
183 187 188 188 189

Represent the hundreds and tens digits as the stem. Represent the ones digits as the leaves. Enter all values in numerical order.

Stem	Leaf
17	0 3 3 5 9 9 9
18	1 1 2 3 7 8 8 9

4. Match each description with the appropriate type of graph. Some graph types can be used more than once.

Description

a) Displays discrete data in separate columns.

b) Organizes data by representing part of each number as a stem and the other part as a leaf.

c) Uses pictures or symbols to represent data.

d) Displays data as a percent of the whole.

e) Uses proportional areas of the bars to show frequencies of the values of the variables.

f) Represents data using a circle that has been divided into sectors.

g) Represents nominal data, such as days of the week.

Graph

Bar graph
Histogram
Circle graph
Stem and leaf plot
Pictograph

5. A survey asked grade 12 students to state their first choice for the university they would like to attend from the list given.

University	Frequency
Queen's University	33
University of Waterloo	32
University of Toronto	41
York University	35
University of Ottawa	40
McMaster University	31
University of Western Ontario	33

Illustrate the data using two graph types of your choice. Justify your choices.

6. Create a stem and leaf plot for each list of student averages. Compare with a histogram.

a) 78, 83, 77, 73, 61, 99, 65, 80, 55, 67, 52, 79, 43, 59

b) 63.2, 71.4, 79.5, 50.0, 93.7, 44.5, 87.6, 65.7, 54.9, 92

Measures of Central Tendency

Learning Goals

I am learning to

- interpret the mean, median, and mode of a set of data
- choose the measure of central tendency that best describes the data

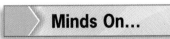

Minds On...

It is important to collect and organize data in a way that helps you understand where the majority of the numbers are found. This clustering of data is referred to as measures of central tendency. The three most commonly used measures of central tendency are **mean**, **median**, and **mode**.

Think about the following situations:

- A post-secondary admissions board uses students' individual averages to decide who will be most successful in a particular field of study. How might a post-secondary admissions board analyse the cluster of applicants' grades to help its decision-making process?

- How might coaches of a sports team use averages to determine how well a player is performing in the season and how much money she should be paid?

- How might economists use median household income to divide the country into equal income distribution groups?

- How might shoe and clothing store managers use the mode to make decisions about which products to stock?

mean
- the sum of the data entries divided by the number of entries

median
- the middle value of all the data points when the data values are listed in order from least to greatest
- if there is an even number of data points, then the median is the average between the two middle values

mode
- the data value that occurs most often in the list of data points
- it is possible to have no mode, one mode, or more than one mode

Action!

The Greek letter *μ*, pronounced "mu," is used to represent the population mean. x̄, read as "x-bar," is used to represent the sample mean.

In statistics, you can find the mean of a population and the mean of a sample of that population. A sample mean will approximate the actual mean of the population.

Population Mean	**Sample Mean**
$\mu = \dfrac{x_1 + x_2 + \ldots + x_N}{N}$	$\overline{x} = \dfrac{x_1 + x_2 + \ldots + x_n}{n}$

where N is the size of the population and n is the sample size.

Although the calculations are the same, different symbols are used to indicate whether it represents a population or a sample.

Investigate Where the Money Falls

Sport Tech, a sporting goods company, is deciding how it should spend its advertising funds this year. Accountants analyse the company's largest sporting goods accounts for each season. They decide, based on the data presented in the table below, to spend the bulk of this year's budget on advertising winter sports gear.

Season	Sport	Revenue ($)
Winter	Skiing	1 000 000
	Skating	120 000
	Snowboarding	1 200 000
	Snowmobiling	525 658
	Ice fishing	455 200
Spring	Baseball	200 120
	Soccer	450 000
	Tennis	250 000
	Golf	1 000 000
Summer	Surfing	750 000
	Skateboarding	345 200
	Swimming	120 000
	Beach volleyball	120 000
Fall	Football	1 100 000
	Swimming	120 000
	Golf	1 000 000
	Soccer	450 000

1. Refer to the information in the table. Do you agree with the accountants' conclusion? Explain why or why not.

2. What data values may have contributed to the accountants' decision?

3. Determine the mean revenue for each season. Show how you calculated this value.

4. What is the median revenue for each season?

5. Determine the mean and median for the overall sports revenues.

6. **Reflect** What data values may have contributed to the differences in mean and median values between each season and overall? Do these data values have a greater effect on the mean or the median?

7. **Extend Your Understanding** Write a proposal to describe where you think the funds should be distributed. Consider whether you would choose one season or more than one season. What factors might contribute to why a particular sports season generates more revenue than another?

The measures of central tendency of a data set can be affected by the presence of **outliers**.

outlier

- an element of the data set that is significantly different from the rest of the data points

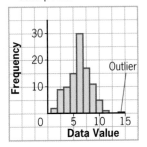

- In a symmetric distribution such as the uniform distribution, the mean, median, and mode will all be equal.

- In a non-symmetric or skewed distribution, the mean, median, and mode will differ.

- In a positively skewed distribution, the mode will be the lowest of the three values and the mean will be the highest.

- In a negatively skewed distribution, the mode will be the highest of the three values and the mean will be the lowest.

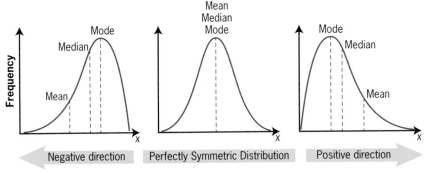

Recall that you studied uniform distributions in section 4.2. Why are the mean, median, and mode all equal in a uniform distribution?

Example 1

Evaluating Measures of Central Tendency

You are interviewing for an internship at a risk assessment firm to gain experience for your post-secondary program. The interviewer tells you that the average annual income of the 15 employees at the company is $73 518.27. The chart shows the actual incomes of the 15 employees.

$34 983	$18 980	$12 500	$48 980	$478 320
$17 305	$36 540	$12 500	$250 921	$32 654
$45 678	$33 855	$25 676	$33 450	$20 432

a) Determine the mean, median, and mode of the incomes.

b) Use the measures of central tendency to decide whether the interviewer's statement is accurate.

c) What is the effect of the outliers on the measures of central tendency?

d) Which measure of central tendency best represents the "average" income of the employees?

> Solution

a) **Method 1: Use Paper and Pencil**

Determine the mean of the 15 income values.

Recall that the Greek letter Σ, pronounced "sigma," is used to represent the sum of a series of numbers. $\sum x$ means $x_1 + x_2 + x_3 + \ldots + x_n$.

$$\mu = \frac{\sum x}{n}$$

$$= \frac{34\ 983 + 18\ 980 + 12\ 500 + 48\ 980 + \ldots + 20\ 432}{15}$$

$$= \frac{1\ 102\ 774}{15}$$

$$\approx 73\ 518.27$$

The mean income is $73 518.27.

There are an odd number of data points. To determine the median, place the values in order from least to greatest. Then, locate the 8th term because it is the middle of the 15 data points.

$12 500 $12 500 $17 305 $18 980 $20 432 $25 676 $32 654
$33 450 $33 855 $34 983 $36 540 $45 678 $48 980 $250 921
$478 320

The median is $33 450.

The mode is $12 500 because it occurs twice in the set of data points.

$12 500   **$12 500** $17 305 $18 980 $20 432 $25 676 $32 654
$33 450 $33 855 $34 983 $36 540 $45 678 $48 980 $250 921
$478 320

Method 2: Use a Graphing Calculator

- Press **STAT**, then **1:Edit…**. Enter the salaries in list **L1**.

- Press **2ND** **QUIT**.

- Press **STAT**. Use the arrow keys to choose **CALC**, then **1:1-Var Stats**. Press **ENTER**.

- Scroll down to read the mean and median, along with numerous other statistics. The calculator will not identify the mode.

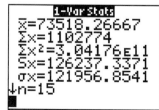
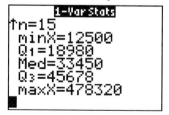

The mean income, $\bar{x}$, is $73 518.27, and the median income, Med, is $33 450. You can see the mode of $12 500 by inspecting the table.

Method 3: Use a Spreadsheet

Open a spreadsheet and enter the data as shown.

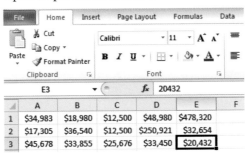

Remember that commands may vary from one spreadsheet to another. Explore the spreadsheet you are using and record any variations to the commands for measures of central tendency.

To find the mean, click on an empty cell and enter the formula **=average(A1:E3)**. Repeat this step using the command **=median(A1:E3)** and **=mode(A1:E3)** to find the median and mode of your data.

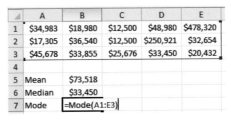

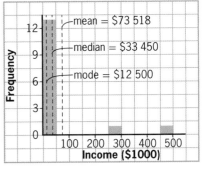

This gives a final mean income of $73 518, a median of $33 450, and a mode of $12 500.

b) If you look only at the calculation of the mean, the interviewer's statement is accurate because the average of a set of data is usually defined as the mean. However, when analysing all three measures of central tendency—mean, median, and mode—it is evident that the mean is affected by the two outliers, $250 921 and $478 320, and the mode is the smallest income. So the median is more representative of the data. Therefore, the interviewer's statement is not an accurate reflection of the income of an average employee.

c) The outliers cause the location of the cluster of the data to be skewed. As a result, the mode is the least of the three measures, and the mean is the greatest. The outliers cause the mean to be inflated because the two highest incomes are much larger than the rest of the data set.

Calculate the mean without the outliers of $250 921 and $478 320.

$$\mu = \frac{\sum x}{n}$$

$$= \frac{34\,983 + 18\,980 + 12\,500 + 48\,980 + \ldots + 20\,432}{13}$$

$$= \frac{373\,533}{13}$$

$$\approx 28\,733.31$$

Without the two outliers, the mean income is $28 733.31.

d) The mean is significantly affected by the outliers, the mode is the smallest income of all the employees, and the median is the middle income of all the employees. The median would be the best measure to represent the average income. Looking at the data, this median appears to be fairly close to many data points and provides a description of the data without taking the outliers or repeated values into effect.

Your Turn

Before heading on vacation to Mexico, you observe the actual high temperatures for seven days. The table shows the temperatures.

Day	Temperature (°C)
1	27
2	29
3	32
4	29
5	45
6	29
7	31

a) Determine the mean, median, and mode of the temperatures.

b) The weather report predicts that based on the previous seven-day forecast, the temperature on the day of your arrival should be 36 °C. Use the measures of central tendency in part a) to determine whether the weather report is accurate.

c) Is there an outlier in the data? How does it affect the measures of central tendency?

d) Which measure of central tendency would best represent the temperatures in this Mexican location? Explain.

When the quantity of data is large, you can group the data into intervals to make them easier to analyse. When data are grouped into intervals, you can only approximate the centre of the data. To do this, assume that the data are evenly spaced in each interval, and use the midpoint to represent the values in each interval. Multiply the data values by their respective frequencies. Then, add these products and divide by the total frequency. You can use the following formula to approximate the mean for grouped data.

Mean for Grouped Data

$$\bar{x} = \frac{\sum f_i m_i}{\sum f_i}$$

where m_i is the midpoint of each interval and f_i is the frequency of each interval.

You can use a frequency distribution table to help organize your data.

Example 2

Using Grouped Data

The time taken to complete a chess game was recorded, to the nearest minute. The frequency table shows the data.

Time (min)	10–15	15–20	20–25	25–30	30–35
Frequency	2	20	18	10	5

a) Calculate the estimated mean, median, and mode times, in minutes, to complete a chess game.

b) Describe potential issues with finding the measures of central tendency of grouped data.

c) Graph the data using a histogram. Mark the measures of central tendency on the graph.

d) Discuss any skewing of the data with respect to the measures of central tendency.

Solution

a) **Method 1: Use Paper and Pencil**

Use the following table.

Number of Minutes	Midpoint, m_i	Number of Games, f_i	$m_i f_i$	Cumulative Frequency
10–15	12.5	2	25	2
15–20	17.5	20	350	22
20–25	22.5	18	405	40
25–30	27.5	10	275	50
30–35	32.5	5	162.5	55

$$\sum f_i = 2 + 20 + 18 + 10 + 5$$
$$= 55$$

$$\sum m_i f_i = 25 + 350 + 405 + 275 + 162.5$$
$$= 1217.5$$

Calculate the grouped mean.

$$\bar{x} = \frac{\sum m_i f_i}{\sum f_i}$$
$$= \frac{1217.5}{55}$$
$$\approx 22.14$$

Therefore, the mean number of minutes is approximately 22 min per game.

To determine the median, look for the interval in which the middle value occurs. There are 55 data values in this example, so the median will be the $\frac{55 + 1}{2} = 28$th term. The frequency table shows that the 28th term occurs within the 20–25 min interval. Therefore, the estimated median is 22.5 min.

When working with grouped data, use a modal interval in place of a mode. The modal interval is the interval with the greatest frequency, namely 15–20 min.

Method 2: Use a Spreadsheet

Enter the data into a spreadsheet.

	A	B	C	D
1	Time(min)	Midpoint	Frequency	Midpoint x Frequency
2	10-15	12.5	2	
3	15-20	17.5	20	
4	20-25	22.5	18	
5	25-30	27.5	10	
6	30-35	32.5	5	

When entering the first column of data, change the cell format to text to avoid having an interval (such as 10-15) converted to a date (such as Oct 15).

In cell D2 enter the formula **=B2*C2**, and copy this entry from cell D2 to D6.

To find the mean, divide the sum of column D by the sum of the frequencies in column C. Click on an empty cell. Enter **=Sum(D2:D6)/ Sum(C2:C6)**. This yields a grouped mean of approximately 22 min.

=SUM(D2:D6)/SUM(C2:C6)

	A	B	C	D
1	Time(min)	Midpoint	Frequency	Midpoint x Frequency
2	10-15	12.5	2	25
3	15-20	17.5	20	350
4	20-25	22.5	18	405
5	25-30	27.5	10	275
6	30-35	32.5	5	162.5
7				
8			Grouped Mean	=SUM(D2:D6)/
9				SUM(C2:C6)

Determine the median and mode by inspection. Since there are 55 data values in this example, the median will be the $\frac{55 + 1}{2} = 28$th entry, which occurs in the 20–25 min time interval. Its midpoint is 22.5 min. The modal interval is the most frequent interval, which occurs in the 15–20 min time interval.

b) Since grouped data use the midpoint of the interval, your calculations could be less accurate when the interval size is quite large. Also, the actual data values in each interval could lie anywhere within the interval. So, the actual values may be closer to the boundaries of the interval and using the midpoint could provide inaccurate results.

c) Enter the data into your spreadsheet as shown. Highlight the frequency column, select the **Insert** tab, and then choose **Column, Clustered Column** from the drop-down menu.

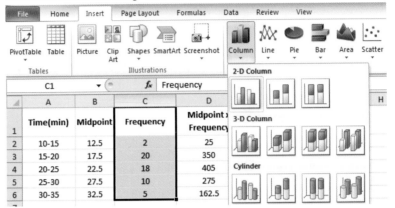

Right click on the x-axis and choose **Select Data…**. Under the options for **Horizontal (Category) Axis Labels**, select **Edit** and highlight the data for your time intervals from A2:A6.

Change the title of your graph to **Frequency of Chess Game Length**. With your graph selected, click on the **Layout** tab and choose **Axis Titles**, then choose **Primary Horizontal Axis Title – Title Below Axis**. Rename the axis title **Time (min)**.

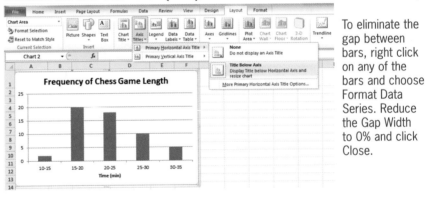

To eliminate the gap between bars, right click on any of the bars and choose Format Data Series. Reduce the Gap Width to 0% and click Close.

d) Since the data are positively skewed, the modal interval is the least appropriate measure of central tendency. The median and mean are very close together, so either one would be an appropriate measure.

Your Turn

A group of children were asked how many hours a day they spend playing video games. The table shows the data.

a) Determine the estimated mean, median number of hours, and modal interval for the above distribution.

b) Discuss any skewing of the data with respect to the measures of central tendency.

Number of Hours	Number of Children
0–2	3
2–4	11
4–6	7
6–8	2
8–10	1

Certain values in a data set are sometimes of greater relative importance than others. In these cases, it is useful to calculate a weighted mean. To do this, multiply the weighting by the corresponding data value, find the sum of these products, and then divide by the total weighting.

Weighted Mean

$$\mu = \frac{\sum x_i w_i}{\sum w_i}$$

Where x_i represents each data value in the data set and w_i represents its weight or frequency.

Example 3

Using a Weighted Mean

A teacher is calculating the marks for the students in her Data Management class. She assigns the following values to each category:

Knowledge: 25%   Thinking: 10%
Application: 20%   Culminating Project: 15%
Communication: 15%   Final Exam: 15%

Kyle has not yet written his final exam, but his marks in the first five categories are 90, 79, 82, 70, and 85.

a) Determine the weighted mean for Kyle before the final exam.

b) How does this weighted mean differ from the unweighted mean?

c) What mark must Kyle receive on the final exam to finish the course with 84%?

Solution

a) Calculate the weighted mean:

$$\mu_w = \frac{90(0.25) + 79(0.20) + 82(0.15) + 70(0.10) + 85(0.15)}{0.85}$$

$$= \frac{70.35}{0.85}$$

$$\approx 82.76$$

b) Calculate the unweighted mean:

$$\mu = \frac{90 + 79 + 82 + 70 + 85}{5}$$

$$= \frac{406}{5}$$

$$= 81.2$$

Without the weighted mean, Kyle would receive a lower average mark because the categories he excels in are worth more when calculated using the weighted mean.

c) The final exam is worth 15%. Determine the final exam score, E, needed for Kyle to receive 84% in the course.

$$84 = \frac{90(0.25) + 79(0.20) + 82(0.15) + 70(0.10) + 85(0.15) + E(0.15)}{1.00}$$

$$84 = 70.35 + E(0.15)$$
$$84 - 70.35 = 0.15E$$
$$13.65 = 0.15E$$
$$91 = E$$

Kyle must receive 91% on his final exam to finish the course with an 84%.

Your Turn

A math department assigns the following weights for each category in its Advanced Functions course:

Knowledge: 25%   Thinking: 10%
Application: 15%   Culminating Project: 10%
Communication: 10%   Final Exam: 30%

Catherine's marks in the course so far are 87, 90, 76, 78, and 84 in each of the first five categories. She still needs to write the final exam.

a) Determine the weighted mean for Catherine before writing her final exam.

b) Is it possible for Catherine to receive a final mark of 90% in the course? Justify your answer.

Consolidate and Debrief

Key Concepts

- Three measures of central tendency are mean, median, and mode.
- The mean represents the average of a set of data.
- The median is the middle number when the numbers are arranged in numerical order.
- The mode is the number that occurs most often; it is possible to have one, more than one, or no mode.
- Outliers have a greater effect on the mean than other measures and either pull the mean up or drag the mean down.
- A weighted mean accounts for the relative importance of each value in the average.
- Grouped data are organized into intervals. Use the interval midpoints and frequencies to estimate the measures of central tendency.

Reflect

R1. Which measure of central tendency is most affected by extreme values? Explain using specific examples to justify your answer.

R2. Describe a situation in which it would be necessary for you to use
- **a)** the mean
- **b)** the weighted mean
- **c)** grouped data

R3. Which measure of central tendency is being used in each situation? Explain.
- **a)** The average person has two hands, two eyes, two ears, and two legs.
- **b)** The average time it takes to get to school is 38 min.
- **c)** Johnny is an above average student.

Practise

Choose the best answer for #3 and #4.

1. Determine the mean, median, and mode for each set of data.
   - **a)** 4 6 9 12 15 7 13 4 7 10 3 8 15
   - **b)** 9 8 20 23 12 12 9 9 12 9 20 21 9
   - **c)** 110 152 112 124 110 134 138 127 118 110 114 162

2. Nina runs the 400-m race for Mustang High School. Her times in the last six track meets were 1.45 min, 1.50 min, 1.42 min, 1.41 min, 1.42 min, and 1.48 min.
   - **a)** What are the mean and median for her running times?
   - **b)** Which measure of central tendency best describes Nina's average time? Explain.

3. The observation that occurs most frequently in a data sample is the
   - **A** mean
   - **B** weighted mean
   - **C** mode
   - **D** median

4. What is the median of the sample 5, 5, 11, 9, 8, 5, 8?
   - **A** 9
   - **B** 6
   - **C** 5
   - **D** 8

Apply

5. The mean of Daniel's marks on five tests was 77.4. His marks on the first four tests were 88, 77, 70, and 72. Calculate Daniel's mark on the fifth test.

6. The average daily snowfall for the first week of December was 2.5 cm. In each of the first two days, 2.5 cm fell. In each of the next four days, 2 cm fell. What was the snowfall for the last day of the week?

7. **Communication** Determine whether the argument is valid for each situation. Explain your thinking.
   - **a)** An advertising company has a mean monthly sales record of $16 235. Therefore, half the team members sold more than $16 235.
   - **b)** A survey shows that 78% of all salaries are below the mean. Therefore, there must be a mistake.
   - **c)** The mean mark of one class is 71, while the mean mark of another class is 76. Therefore, the mean of the two classes is 73.5.
   - **d)** My median monthly expenses total $850. Therefore, my total expenses for the year must be $10 200.

8. Communication Which measure of central tendency would be best suited for each situation? Explain why you chose the measure that you did.

a) a summary of a class's report card marks

b) an award for the most popular movie of the year

c) an employer budgeting for the average salary of its employees

d) a potential employee looking for the typical salary among current employees

9. Thinking Create a data set of at least seven values that satisfies each of the conditions. Use the context of marks, salaries, sports statistics, or choose a context of your own.

a) The mean, median, and mode are all 15.

b) The median is 7.5 and the mean is greater than 15.

c) The mean is 7.5 and the median is greater than 15.

d) Explain why the mean is more affected by outliers than the median.

10. Michael surveyed the grade 12 students at his school to research the number of hours of sleep they got. He asked them how many hours of sleep they got last night. The table shows his results.

Time (h)	4–5	5–6	6–7	7–8	8–9
Frequency	32	50	125	67	108

a) Make a histogram of these data.

b) Estimate the mean, median, and modal interval for the hours of sleep by grade 12 students.

c) Mark the measures of central tendency on your histogram.

d) Discuss any skewing of the data and how it relates to the measures of central tendency.

11. Application Your teacher will provide you with a file called **Nobel Winners.csv**, listing the Canadian or Canadian-born Nobel Prize winners up to 2013. Use appropriate technology to answer the questions.

a) Make a histogram of the winners' ages.

b) Calculate the mean, median, and mode ages.

c) Describe the "average" age of a Canadian Nobel Prize winner. Explain why this age would not be younger.

12. Application Your teacher will provide you with a file called **Olympics 2014.csv**, listing the medal counts and populations of winning countries in the 2014 Sochi Winter Olympics. The file ranks countries by number of gold medals, followed by silver and bronze. Use appropriate technology to answer the questions.

a) Re-rank the countries by total medals relative to the population.

b) Re-rank the countries using a weighted mean, with each type of medal having a different weighting.

c) Which system do you prefer? Write a paragraph supporting your choice.

13. Karen's term mark is 82%. The term counts for 70% of the final mark. What mark must Karen achieve on the exam to earn a final mark of

a) 80%?   b) 85%?

c) at least 75%?

d) Can Karen achieve 88%? Explain.

14. Thinking Using the data provided in the frequency table, describe a context that the mean, median, and mode could represent.

Age in Years	20–30	30–40	40–50	50–60	60–70
Frequency	14	15	28	19	5

15. The table shows student absences from Lakeside High School during the first semester. Assume that the absences located exactly on the endpoints of an interval were placed in the lower interval.

Student Absences	Number of Students
0–3	47
3–6	89
6–9	33
9–12	102
12–15	24
15–18	19
18–21	6
21–24	8
24–27	0
27–30	2

a) Calculate the estimated mean, median, and modal interval of student absences.

b) Does there appear to be an outlier? If so, how does it affect the mean and median of the data set?

c) Which would be the most reliable measure of central tendency if you were trying to make a generalization to someone about the data presented? Justify your response with calculations.

16. On a fishing trip with his father, Alex caught eight bass with a mean mass of 1.2 kg and five trout with a mean mass of 2.9 kg. What was the mean mass, in kilograms, of all the fish Alex caught?

17. a) Create a frequency distribution table of the number of vowels and consonants found in the names of the students in your class.

b) Make appropriate graphs of the data.

c) Calculate the measures of central tendency of each type of letter and mark them on your histograms.

d) Decide which measure of central tendency would be best to make an assumption based on the data presented.

e) Summarize your findings.

Extend

18. A trimmed mean removes a small percent of the largest and smallest values before calculating the mean. This is to reduce the effects of outliers. At a diving competition, the marks for Competitor A were 8.7, 8.9, 8.1, 8.6, 8.5, 8.8, and 8.0. The marks for Competitor B were 8.4, 8.6, 8.6, 8.5, 8.5, 8.4, and 8.9.

a) Using the marks as given, which competitor would have the higher mean mark?

b) To reduce the influence of biased judging, the highest and lowest marks are deleted for all competitors. Which competitor has the higher average mark under this system?

19. The harmonic mean is defined as $\dfrac{n}{\dfrac{1}{x_1} + \dfrac{1}{x_2} + \dfrac{1}{x_3} + \cdots + \dfrac{1}{x_n}}$, where n is the number of values in the set of data. It is also defined as the reciprocal of the mean of the reciprocals.

a) Find the harmonic mean of the numbers 1, 4, and 7.

b) Find the mean of the reciprocals of 1, 4, and 7. What is the reciprocal of the result?

c) The harmonic mean can be used to find the mean of a set of rates. The harmonic mean will give you the average price between two rates. What is the average price between $1.25/kg and $1.38/kg?

20. The geometric mean is defined as $\sqrt[n]{x_1 \cdot x_2 \cdot x_3 \cdots x_n}$, where n is the number of values in the set of data.

a) Find the geometric mean of the numbers 2, 8, and 9.

b) The geometric mean can be used to calculate the average annual rate of change when rates are compounded on each other. Calculate the average annual rate of change if inflation were at 2%, then 4%, then 3%, respectively, over a three-year period.

6.2

Measures of Spread

Learning Goals

I am learning to

- describe the variability in a sample or population using measures of spread
- calculate the range
- understand how to use quartiles and percentiles to analyse data

> ## Minds On...

The fuel economy of various cars in a given class will vary significantly. Cars can be rated anywhere from 4 L/100 km to 9 L/100 km. Understanding where most of the data occur using the measures of central tendency is sometimes not enough to make a broad generalization of the data. Why is it also important to know the distance associated with each data value and the centre of the data? The measure of how widely the data vary around their central location is referred to as the measure of spread or dispersion.

> ## Action!

Investigate Percentiles

An automotive publication ranked the following 2013 subcompact cars based on their fuel economy in the city. The chart shows the cars' fuel economy in the city and on the highway. Your teacher will provide you with the data in a file called **Fuel Economy.csv**.

| Make/Model | L/100 km | |
	City	Hwy
TOYOTA PRIUS C	3.5	4.0
SCION iQ	5.5	4.7
SMART FORTWO	5.8	4.2
CHEVROLET SPARK	6.3	5.1
FIAT 500	6.4	4.9
TOYOTA YARIS	6.7	5.5
MINI COOPER	6.8	5.2
KIA RIO	6.8	5.4
FORD FIESTA	6.9	5.1
HONDA FIT	7.1	5.4
MAZDA 2	7.1	5.8
HYUNDAI ACCENT	7.2	5.2
SCION xD	7.4	5.9
NISSAN VERSA	7.4	5.4
CHEVROLET SONIC	7.7	5.5
VOLKSWAGEN BEETLE	9.5	7.1
SUBARU BRZ	9.6	6.6

Source: "Fuel Consumption Ratings," Natural Resources Canada, February 5, 2014.

1. **a)** Identify the car with the median city fuel economy in city driving.

   b) The median is also called the 50th **percentile**. Why would that be?

2. The 80th percentile would be the car whose fuel economy in city driving is greater than 80% of all others. Which car would that be?

3. What percent of the cars have a better fuel economy than a Fiat?

4. **a)** Identify the car with the best fuel economy in the city and the car with the best fuel economy on the highway. What percent of the cars have a worse fuel economy?

   b) Identify the car with the worst fuel economy in the city and the car with the worst fuel economy on the highway. What percent of the cars have a worse fuel economy?

5. **Reflect** Describe how you can use percentiles to compare data.

6. **Extend Your Understanding** If you were comparing your marks to those of your classmates, would you rather be in the 95th percentile or the 5th percentile? Explain.

To help analyse the spread of data, you may need to identify the percentile rank or calculate percentiles.

Percentile Rank

$R = \frac{p}{100}(n + 1)$

where p is the percentile, n is the size of the population, and R is the whole number rank of the data point. If R is not a whole number, round R down.

Percentile

$p = 100\frac{(L + 0.5E)}{n}$

where p is the percentile, L is the number of data less than the data point, E is the number of data equal to the data point, and n is the size of the population.

Example 1

Percentiles

The list shows the marks for 25 students on a recent test out of 40.

31 28 28 30 20 25 38 40 26 28 15 21 28
36 25 16 21 34 37 30 23 24 36 32 25

a) Calculate the 80th percentile.

b) What percentile is a mark of 25?

c) What percentile is a mark of 40?

Solution

Order the data from least to greatest.

15 16 20 21 21 23 24 25 25 25 26 28 28
28 28 30 30 31 32 34 36 36 37 38 40

a) There are 25 data values. To calculate the 80th percentile, use the formula for percentile rank.

$$R = \frac{p}{100}(n + 1)$$

$$= \frac{80}{100}(25 + 1)$$

$$= 20.8$$

Round down to 20. Determine the midpoint of the 20th and 21st measurements.

Why do you round down to 20?

$$80\text{th percentile} = \frac{34 + 36}{2}$$

$$= 35$$

The 80th percentile is a mark of 35. This means that 80% of the data are below 35.

b) A mark of 25 is the 8th ranked mark. It is also the 9th and 10th marks.

There are 7 data values less than 25, so $L = 7$.

There are 3 data values equal to 25, so $E = 3$.

$$p = 100\frac{(L + 0.5E)}{n}$$

$$= 100\frac{(7 + 0.5(3))}{25}$$

$$= 34$$

A mark of 25 is in the 34th percentile. This means that 34% of the data are below 25.

c) A mark of 40 is the 25th ranked mark.

There are 24 data values less than 40, so $L = 24$.

There is 1 data value equal to 40, so $E = 1$.

$$p = 100\frac{(L + 0.5E)}{n}$$

$$= 100\frac{(25 + 0.5(1))}{25}$$

$$= \frac{100(24.5)}{25}$$

$$= 98$$

A mark of 40 is in the 98th percentile.

Your Turn

The mean playing times per game for the 22 hockey players on a team are given.

16.4, 18.3, 21.7, 18.5, 9.2, 17.9, 12.0, 15.2, 23.4, 20.5, 16.7, 13.4, 8.3, 17.9, 22.6, 18.1, 21.7, 14.6, 13.8, 24.3, 12.4, 17.4

a) Determine the 40th and 95th percentiles.

b) Determine the percentile rank of the player who averaged

   i) 9.2 min per game

   ii) 21.7 min per game

   iii) 18.1 min per game

To better understand the variability of a data set, you can use a variety of measures of spread. You can use a box and whisker plot to visually demonstrate the spread of a distribution along a number line.

To construct a box and whisker plot:

- Draw a rectangle whose ends are the first (lower) and third (upper) **quartiles**.

- Draw the median within the rectangle.

- Add "whiskers," which are horizontal line segments connecting the box to the extremes of the data, covering the entire **range**.

Each of the four zones illustrated by a box and whisker plot contains 25% of the data. The difference between the first and the third quartiles is known as the **interquartile range (IQR)**. The interquartile range represents the "middle half" of the data.

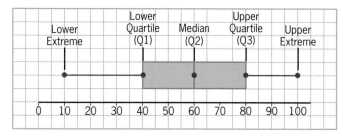

Because of the nature of the calculations, box and whisker plots are appropriate only for quantitative data.

quartiles
- three points that divide the data set into four equal groups
- the first quartile (Q1) is the middle number between the smallest number and the median; it is also the 25th percentile
- the second quartile (Q2) is the median of the data set; it is also the 50th percentile
- the third quartile (Q3) is the middle number between the median and the largest number in a data set; it is also the 75th percentile

range
- the difference between the highest value and the lowest value of a data set
- range = highest value – lowest value

interquartile range (IQR)
- the difference between the first and third quartiles
- IQR = Q3 – Q1

Example 2

Interquartile Range and Box and Whisker Plots

The table lists the heights of the 20 girls who signed up to try out for their school basketball team.

Height (cm)	Frequency	Cumulative Frequency
155–160	1	1
160–165	3	4
165–170	4	8
170–175	7	15
175–180	3	18
180–185	1	19
185–190	0	19
190–195	1	20

a) Determine the median, range, first and third quartiles, and interquartile range. Create a box and whisker plot of the data.

b) Describe the data in each zone of the plot.

c) Identify any outliers, if they exist.

Solution

a) **Method 1: Use Paper and Pencil**

The median is the 50th percentile. Calculate the percentile rank.

$$R = \frac{p}{100}(n + 1)$$
$$= \frac{50}{100}(20 + 1)$$
$$= 10.5$$

The median is the midpoint of the 10th and 11th measurements.
The median lies within the 170–175 cm interval.
The median height is 172.5 cm.

The range is the difference between the highest and lowest values.

Range $= 195 - 155$
$\qquad = 40$

The range is 40 cm.

The first quartile is the 25th percentile. Use the percentile rank formula.

$$R = \frac{p}{100}(n + 1)$$

$$Q1 = \frac{25}{100}(20 + 1)$$
$$= 5.25$$

Q1 is the midpoint of the 5th and 6th measurement. Looking at the cumulative frequency column, we can see that this lies within the 165–170 cm interval.

Q1 is 167.5 cm.

The third quartile is the 75th percentile. Use the percentile rank formula.

$$R = \frac{p}{100}(n + 1)$$

$$Q3 = \frac{75}{100}(20 + 1)$$

$$= 15.75$$

Q3 is the midpoint of the 15th and 16th measurements. Looking at the cumulative frequency column, we can see that this lies on the border between the 170–175 cm and 175–180 cm intervals.

Q3 is 175 cm.

Interquartile range = 175 – 167.5

$$= 7.5$$

The interquartile range is 7.5 cm.

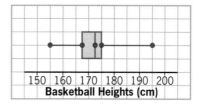
Basketball Heights (cm)

Method 2: Use Fathom™

Begin a new collection and name it **Basketball Heights**. Open a table and name the first attribute **Height_cm**. Enter all 20 values from the table, using the midpoint of each interval, and based on the individual frequencies. For example, in the 2nd interval, enter 162.5 a total of 3 times.

Under the **Graph** menu, select **Graph**. From the upper right, select **Box Plot**.

Making sure the Graph window is selected, under the **Graph** menu, select **Plot Value**. When the calculator window pops up select **Statistical**, then from **One Attribute** select **Median**. Then, from the **Attributes** category, select **Height_cm**. Press **OK**. Repeat the process for Q1, Q3, Max, and Min.

Because Fathom™ only works with raw data, not intervals or grouped data, use the midpoint of the interval for each data point in the interval.

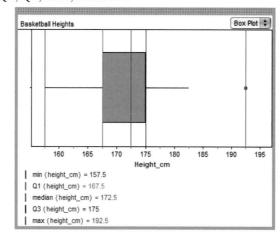

Method 3: Use a Graphing Calculator

Enter the midpoints in list **L1** and the frequencies in list **L2**.

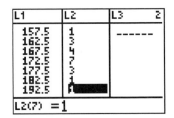

Press **STAT**, select **CALC**, and select **1:1-Var Stats**. Press **ENTER**.

Now you need to tell the calculator that the data are in **L1** and the frequency is in **L2**. Select **2ND** **L1** **,** **2ND** **L2** and press **ENTER**.

Scroll down to see the quartiles.

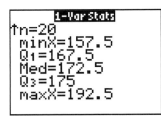

Set up Plot1 as shown.

Use the following **WINDOW** settings.

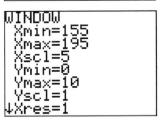

Press **GRAPH**.

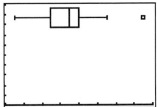

Press **TRACE** and use the arrow keys to scroll through the values on the graph.

b) 25% of the data are contained in each of the intervals 155 to 167.5 cm, 167.5 to 172.5 cm, 172.5 to 175 cm, and 175 to 195 cm.

c) An outlier is identified as being more than 1.5 times the interquartile range (IQR) below Q1 or above Q3.

Lower Extreme:

$$Q1 - 1.5(IQR)$$
$$= 167.5 - 1.5(7.5)$$
$$= 156.25$$

Upper Extreme:

$$Q3 + 1.5(IQR)$$
$$= 175 + 1.5(7.5)$$
$$= 186.25$$

No data point is less than 156.25 cm, but one is greater than 186.25 cm. Therefore, one outlier of approximately 192.5 cm exists in this data set.

Your Turn

A summer camp activity involves measuring the distance travelled by 50 turtles in 15 min. The table shows the results.

Distance (m)	Frequency
0–5	1
5–10	0
10–15	6
15–20	12
20–25	15
25–30	5
30–35	7
35–40	1
40–45	3

a) Determine the median, range, first and third quartiles, and interquartile range. Make a box and whisker plot of the data.

b) Describe the data in each zone of the plot.

c) Identify any outliers, if they exist.

Example 3

Interpreting Quartiles

The box and whisker plots illustrate the spread of Canadian full-term male and female baby masses, in kilograms, at birth.

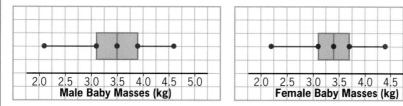

Compare the spreads of birth masses for boys and girls.

Solution

	Boys (kg)	Girls (kg)
Median	3.5	3.4
Range	4.6 – 2.1 = 2.5	4.4 – 2.2 = 2.2
Q1	3.1	3.1
Q3	3.9	3.7
IQR	3.9 – 3.1 = 0.8	3.7 – 3.1 = 0.6

The median birth mass for boys is 0.1 kg greater than the median birth mass for girls. The middle 50% of the birth masses for boys lie between 3.1 kg and 3.9 kg, for an IQR of 0.8 kg. The middle 50% of the birth masses for girls lie between 3.1 kg and 3.7 kg, for an IQR of 0.6 kg. Both the range and the IQR for boys are greater than for girls. So, the birth masses for boys are more spread out.

Your Turn

The box and whisker plots illustrate the spread of Canadian full-term male and female baby lengths, in centimetres, at birth. Compare the spreads of birth lengths for boys and girls.

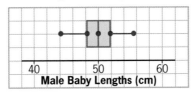
Male Baby Lengths (cm)

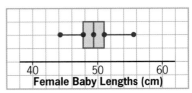
Female Baby Lengths (cm)

Consolidate and Debrief

Key Concepts

- A measure of spread helps you understand how closely a set of data is clustered around its centre.

- The range is the difference between the maximum value and minimum value.

- A percentile is the percent of all the data that are less than or equal to the specific data point.

- Quartiles divide the data set into four equal parts. Q1 is the 25th percentile, Q2 is the median (or 50th) percentile, and Q3 is the 75th percentile.

- The interquartile range (IQR) is the distance between the first and third quartiles. To calculate, subtract the value for Q1 from the value for Q3. The interquartile range contains the middle 50% of the data.

- A box and whisker plot uses a rectangle to visually demonstrate the spread of the distribution along a number line by displaying the median, quartiles, and upper and lower extremes.

- An outlier exists if it is less than Q1 – 1.5 × IQR or greater than Q3 + 1.5 × IQR.

Reflect

R1. Consider the information in the table regarding two data sets. Compare their spreads.

	Data Set 1	Data Set 2
Median	56.3	57.1
Min	32.1	24.2
Max	65.9	71.1
Q1	43.2	34.5
Q3	60.2	63.2

R2. What problems can occur if the range is used to measure the spread of a set of data?

R3. What information does the interquartile range provide?

Practise

Choose the best answer for #4 and #5.

1. Calculate the percentile rank for each student's quiz result in a grade 12 math class.

Mark	Frequency
4.0	2
5.0	6
6.0	8
7.0	13
8.0	4
9.0	3
10.0	2

2. What is the range of the data set?

   23 56 45 65 59
   55 62 54 85 25

3. Calculate the median, range, Q1, Q3, and interquartile range of each set of data. Identify any outliers.

   a) 39 51 35 22 28 67 57
   42 56 74 51 87 99 48
   36 28 57 23 53 74

   b) 245 264 222 213 243
   215 467 264 276 199
   127 216 233

   c) 5 7 9 4 5 7 3 2 6
   2 8 5 9 1 3 3 0 4
   6 8 5 9 2 3 4 5 0
   4 2 4 6 2 5 6

   d) 6213 7985 3426 5134
   7659 3462 5348 6213
   5968 7659 3567

4. If each number in a set is increased by two, which of the measures of spread would remain unchanged?

   A the range

   B the interquartile range

   C the percentiles

   D all of the above

5. Which is an incorrect statement about the interquartile range?

   A It contains the middle 50% of the data.

   B An outlier lies more than 1.5 times the IQR from Q1 or Q3.

   C To calculate the interquartile range, subtract Q3 – Q1.

   D The median always lies at the middle of the interquartile range.

Apply

Use the table for #6 to #8.

The infant mortality rate represents the number of children, per thousand, who die before the age of one year.

Infant Mortality Rates by Province and Territory

	2007	2008	2009	2010	2011
Newfoundland and Labrador	7.5	5.1	6.3	5.3	6.3
Prince Edward Island	5.0	2.0	3.4	3.6	4.2
Nova Scotia	3.3	3.5	3.4	4.6	4.9
New Brunswick	4.3	3.2	5.8	3.4	3.5
Québec	4.5	4.3	4.4	5.0	4.3
Ontario	5.2	5.3	5.0	5.0	4.6
Manitoba	7.3	6.5	6.3	6.7	7.7
Saskatchewan	5.8	6.2	6.7	5.9	6.7
Alberta	6.0	6.2	5.5	5.9	5.3
British Columbia	4.0	3.7	3.6	3.8	3.8
Yukon	8.5	5.4	7.8	5.2	0.0
Northwest Territories	4.1	9.7	15.5	1.4	7.2
Nunavut	15.1	16.1	14.8	14.5	26.3
Canada	5.1	5.1	4.9	5.0	4.8

Source: Infant mortality rates, by province and territory (both sexes), Statistics Canada.

6. a) Rank the provinces in ascending order by their 2011 infant mortality rates.

   b) Determine the percentile ranks for five provinces or territories of your choice.

7. a) Determine the median and interquartile range for the infant mortality rate in each year.

   b) Compare these measures across the years.

   c) Why would the medians not be the same as the mortality rate for all of Canada?

8. a) Are the 2011 mortality rates for Yukon and Nunavut outliers?

   b) Explain the variability of the mortality rates in Yukon, Northwest Territories, and Nunavut as compared to Ontario.

9. Application The table shows the size of each age group in Canada in 2009 and 2013.

Population of Canada by Age Group

Age Group (years)	2009	2013
All Ages	33 628 571	35 158 304
0 to 10	3 626 272	3 804 924
10 to 20	4 253 528	4 048 205
20 to 30	4 608 623	4 855 939
30 to 40	4 534 301	4 762 084
40 to 50	5 251 373	4 940 356
50 to 60	4 798 598	5 256 870
60 to 70	3 299 618	3 857 403
70 to 80	1 994 853	2 202 364
80 to 90	1 075 522	1 181 124
90 to 100	180 409	242 124
100 or over	5 474	6 911

Source: Estimates of population, by age group and sex for July 1, Canada, provinces and territories, annual, Statistics Canada.

   a) Rank the age groups in ascending order by size for each year. Calculate the percentile rank for three different age groups in each year.

   b) Describe the changes in population breakdown from 2009 to 2013.

10. Communication The table shows the average net worth of Canadian families, as a percent of total, in 1999 and 2005.

Quintile	Net Worth (% of total)	
	1999	2005
1st	0.1	0.1
2nd	2.5	2.3
3rd	8.8	8.4
4th	20.1	20.2
5th	68.5	69.2

Source: Drummond, Don and David Tulk, "Lifestyles of the Rich and Unequal: An Investigation Into Wealth Inequality in Canada," TD Economics Special Report, December 13, 2006.

   a) Describe what is meant by quintile.

   b) Describe the change in distribution of incomes from 1999 to 2005.

11. A consumers group recently tested 100 compact fluorescent light bulbs and recorded their lifetimes. The chart shows the results.

Lifetime (h)	Frequency
5000–6000	7
6000–7000	12
7000–8000	34
8000–9000	27
9000–10 000	10
10 000–11 000	8
11 000–12 000	2

a) Make a box and whisker plot of the data.

b) Make a histogram of the data and mark the quartiles on it.

c) Describe the middle 50% of the data.

d) Identify any outliers.

12. Agencies track airline flight delays to help consumers compare airlines. The table outlines the number of delayed flights per month for one major airline. Determine whether December's results are an outlier. If so, what might have caused it?

Month	Number of Delayed Flights
Jan	288
Feb	295
Mar	274
Apr	280
May	246
Jun	251
Jul	218
Aug	221
Sep	246
Oct	264
Nov	257
Dec	459

Extend

13. Your teacher will provide you with a file that shows the percentiles for body mass index of boys ages 2 to 20.

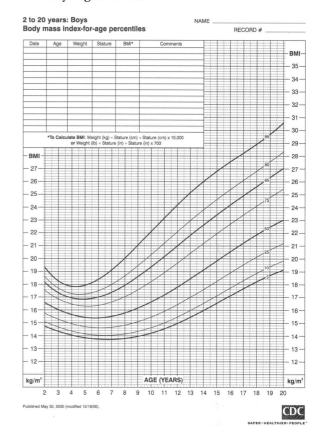

Source: National Center for Health Statistics and National Center for Chronic Disease Prevention and Health Promotion, "2 to 20 years: Boys Body mass index−for−age−percentiles," CDC, May 30, 2000.

a) Describe how to use this chart.

b) Make an accompanying table listing the body mass index values for ages 2, 10, and 20, organized by percentiles.

14. An alternate method of calculating Q1 and Q3 is to use the midpoints of the median and the minimum value and the median and the maximum value, respectively. Use any set of data in the questions above to verify that this method works.

Standard Deviation and z-Scores

Learning Goals

I am learning to

- use technology to calculate the variance and standard deviation of a data set
- calculate and understand the significance of a z-score
- relate the positive or negative scores to their locations in a histogram
- develop significant conclusions about a data set

> ## Minds On...

The ozone layer protects Earth's surface from much of the Sun's destructive radiation. Unfortunately, the ozone layer is being destroyed, in part by chlorofluorocarbons such as coolants in old refrigerators. The ozone layer's thickness can vary significantly over periods as short as a week. What other parts of our environment are changing due to pollutants?

> ## Action!

Investigate Standard Deviation

Literacy Link

A *Dobson unit (DU)* measures the thickness of the ozone layer. It is equivalent to the number of molecules of ozone that would be required to create a layer of pure ozone 0.01 mm thick at a temperature of 0 °C and a pressure of 1 atmosphere.

The table shows the thickness of the ozone layer on each day of a given week.

Day	Thickness, x (DU)	Deviation from the Mean $x - \bar{x}$	Squared Deviation $(x - \bar{x})^2$
1	152		
2	158		
3	151		
4	153		
5	159		
6	158		
7	152		
Sum			

1. Calculate the mean thickness, $\bar{x}$.

2. a) Calculate the deviation from the mean for each day. Enter the results in the third column.

   b) Enter the sum at the bottom of the column.

   c) Explain the resulting sum.

3. a) Calculate the squares of the deviations from the mean. Enter the results in the fourth column.

   b) Enter the sum at the bottom of the column.

4. Divide the sum of the squares by 7. This is called the **variance**.

5. Take the square root of the variance. This is called the **standard deviation**.

6. **Reflect** The standard deviation is the average difference of all the measurements from the mean. What other formula does this resemble?

7. **Extend Your Understanding** For the previous week, the mean thickness was 158.2 DU, with a standard deviation of 4.8 DU. Compare these two weeks' measurements.

Standard deviation is used more commonly than variance as a measure of spread because it is expressed in the same units of measure as the data, whereas variance is expressed in square units.

variance

- the average squared difference of the scores from the mean

standard deviation

- the square root of the variance
- the average distance of the scores from the mean

The variance and standard deviation of a data set allow you to determine how close the values in a distribution are to the middle of the distribution. You can calculate the variance and standard deviation of a data set using the following formulas.

The Greek letter σ (lower case), pronounced "sigma," is used to represent the population standard deviation, while the letter s is used to represent the sample standard deviation. Remember that capital sigma, Σ, is used to denote a sum.

Population Variance

$$\sigma^2 = \frac{\sum(x - \mu)^2}{N}$$

Sample Variance

$$s^2 = \frac{\sum(x - \bar{x})^2}{n - 1}$$

Population Standard Deviation

$$\sigma = \sqrt{\frac{\sum(x - \mu)^2}{N}}$$

Sample Standard Deviation

$$s = \sqrt{\frac{\sum(x - \bar{x})^2}{n - 1}}$$

where the population deviation is represented by $(x - \mu)$ and the sample deviation is represented by $(x - \bar{x})$.

Samples rarely contain extreme values when compared to entire populations. As a result, the variance and standard deviation are less than would be expected. To use the sample variance and standard deviation to model a population, divide by $n - 1$ instead of n. This slightly increases their values.

Calculating the variance alone is not a perfect measure of spread. First, because the deviations of each value are squared in the formula, more "weight" is given to extreme values. Therefore, data sets with extreme values or outliers will skew the validity of the result. Second, the variance is calculated in units squared, which is not the same units as the scores in the data set. This means that you cannot show the variance on a frequency distribution and cannot make a direct correlation between its value and the values of your data set. This problem is easily corrected by calculating the standard deviation.

Example 1

Visualizing the Spread of Marks

The graphs represent the scores on two quizzes. The mean score for each quiz is 7.0.

a) Which quiz would have a greater standard deviation? Why?

b) The variance of Quiz 1 is 1.5. What is the standard deviation?

c) What would the Quiz 1 graph look like if the standard deviation were 1.6?

d) What would the graph look like if the standard deviation were 0?

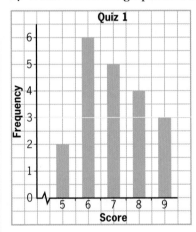

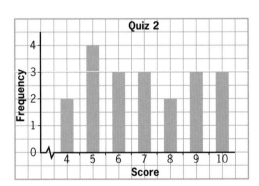

Solution

a) As can be seen on the graphs, Quiz 2 is more spread out than Quiz 1. As a result, its standard deviation will be greater.

b) The standard deviation is the square root of the variance.
$$\sigma = \sqrt{1.5}$$
$$\approx 1.22$$

c) Since 1.6 > 1.22, a standard deviation of 1.6 would result in a wider spread, such as that in Quiz 2.

d) A standard deviation of 0 means there is no spread. All data would consist of the same value.

Your Turn

Sketch examples of two histograms that show the distribution of two sets of girls' heights with the same mean but with different standard deviations. Indicate which histogram will have a greater standard deviation.

Example 2

Calculating Variance and Standard Deviation

The ages of participants in a school's talent contest are listed below.

16 17 18 16 15 16 17 15 18 14
17 19 18 16 17 17 17 14 15 18

Use technology to answer the questions.

a) Plot a histogram of the data.

b) Calculate the mean and standard deviation.

c) What would happen to the standard deviation if the first person's age were 18?

d) What would happen to the standard deviation if the second person's age were 16 instead of 17?

e) What would happen to the standard deviation if each person were one year older?

f) Which ages are more than one standard deviation from the mean?

Solution

a) and **b)** Enter the data into list **L1**. Set up Plot1 as shown.

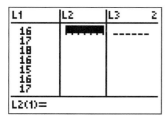 

Press **ZOOM** and then select **9:ZoomStat**.

Press **TRACE** to view the histogram. Scroll left and right to view the coordinates of each bar. Press **STAT** **CALC** and select **1:1-Var Stats**.

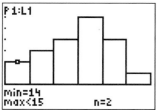 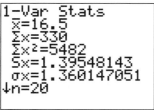

The mean, $\bar{x}$, is 16.5 years and the standard deviation, σ, is approximately 1.360 years.

c) $\sigma = 1.429$ years

The standard deviation would increase because age 18 is farther from the mean and the spread of the data would increase.

Population formulas were used here because all participants were included.

d) $\sigma = 1.359\,23$ years

The standard deviation would decrease because age 16 is closer to the mean and the spread of the data would decrease.

e) $\sigma = 1.395\,48$ years

Since values increase by the same amount, the spread will not change. The standard deviation would be unchanged.

f) $\mu + \sigma = 17.86$ years

$\mu - \sigma = 15.14$ years

Ages greater than 17 or less than 16 are more than one standard deviation from the mean.

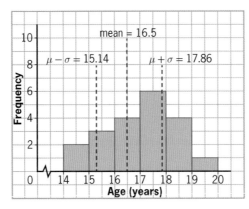

With which type of data (ordinal, quantitative, categorical) is it appropriate to calculate a standard deviation?

Your Turn

The increases in sound volume from a TV program to the advertisements were measured in decibels during a one-hour TV show. The results were as follows:

1.7 1.9 1.5 2.0 2.1 1.8 2.2 1.9 2.0
1.4 1.7 1.8 1.8 2.1 2.7 1.0 0.6 1.8

a) Plot a histogram of the data.

b) Calculate the population mean and standard deviation.

c) Predict what would happen to the standard deviation if the first measurement were 1.5 dB.

d) Predict what would happen to the standard deviation if the second measurement were 1.7 dB.

e) What would happen to the standard deviation if each measurement were 0.5 dB quieter?

f) Which measurements are within one standard deviation of the mean?

A **z-score** indicates how many standard deviations a data value lies from the mean. In Example 2, part f), the z-score would be 1. You can calculate a z-score using one of the following formulas:

z-score

• the number of standard deviations an observation is from the mean

Population z-Score	Sample z-Score
$z = \dfrac{x - \mu}{\sigma}$	$z = \dfrac{x - \bar{x}}{s}$

You can derive computational standard deviation formulas from the given formulas. These formulas simplify the calculations of standard deviation using a scientific calculator.

You will explore the derivation of the computational formulas in Extend #19.

Population Standard Deviation	Sample Standard Deviation
$\sigma = \sqrt{\dfrac{\sum x^2 - N \cdot \mu^2}{N}}$	$s = \sqrt{\dfrac{\sum x^2 - n \cdot \bar{x}^2}{n - 1}}$

Example 3

Analysing z-Scores

A food manufacturer makes 2-L jars of pasta sauce. Samples are tested for how close to 2 L the jars are filled. Fifteen samples were taken and their volumes, in litres, were as indicated:

2.11 2.02 2.10 1.99 1.92 2.01 1.89 1.96
2.00 1.96 1.98 2.02 2.08 2.15 2.03

a) Determine the sample mean and standard deviation.

b) Calculate the z-score of the jar that was filled to a volume of 2.02 L. Interpret its meaning.

c) Calculate the z-score of the jar that was filled to a volume of 1.98 L. Compare its distance from the mean to that of 2.02 L.

d) The manufacturer rejects any jars that are filled to less than 1.5 standard deviations below the mean. Which jars would be rejected?

Solution

a) Method 1: Use a Scientific Calculator

Sample mean:

$$\bar{x} = \frac{\sum x}{n}$$
$$= \frac{30.22}{15}$$
$$\approx 2.014\,67$$

The sample mean is approximately 2.014 67 L.

To calculate the sample standard deviation, first add the squares of the measurements:

$$\sum x^2 = 60.955$$

$$s = \sqrt{\frac{\sum x^2 - n \cdot \bar{x}^2}{n-1}}$$

$$= \sqrt{\frac{60.955 - 15(2.014\ 67)}{14}}$$

Most scientific calculators have built-in functions to calculate mean and standard deviation. Refer to your user manual to explore how to calculate the mean and standard deviation on your device.

$$\approx 0.0716$$

The sample standard deviation is approximately 0.0716 L.

Method 2: Use a Graphing Calculator

Enter the values into list **L1**. Press **STAT** **CALC** and select **1:1-Var Stats**.

```
1-Var Stats
x̄=2.014666667
Σx=30.22
Σx²=60.955
Sx=.0716007449
σx=.0691728913
↓n=15
■
```

Sample mean, $\bar{x} = 2.014\ 67$ L.

Sample standard deviation, $s = 0.0716$ L.

b) Use the z-score formula.

$$z = \frac{x - \bar{x}}{s}$$

$$= \frac{2.02 - 2.014\ 67}{0.0716}$$

$$\approx 0.0744$$

A jar filled to a volume of 2.02 L is 0.0744 standard deviations greater than the mean. This means that it is very close to the mean.

c) Use the z-score formula.

$$z = \frac{x - \bar{x}}{s}$$

$$= \frac{1.98 - 2.014\ 67}{0.0716}$$

$$\approx -0.4842$$

If a positive z-score indicates a standard deviation greater than the mean, what does a negative z-score indicate?

A jar filled to a volume of 1.98 L is 0.4842 standard deviations less than the mean. It is farther from the mean than is 2.02 L.

d) Determine the volume of 1.5 standard deviations below the mean.

$$\bar{x} - 1.5s = 2.014\ 67 - 1.5(0.0716)$$

$$= 1.9073$$

Any jars that are filled to less than 1.9073 L would be rejected. Therefore, the jar containing 1.89 L of sauce would be rejected.

Your Turn

A car manufacturer tested the gap between the doors and the body of a car. Eighteen samples were taken. Their gaps, in millimetres, are shown:

1.7 1.9 1.4 1.4 1.5 1.7 1.1 1.6 1.9
1.4 1.5 1.5 1.6 1.5 1.3 1.8 1.6 1.2

a) Determine the sample mean and standard deviation.

b) Calculate the z-score of a door with gap of 1.6 mm. Interpret its meaning.

c) Calculate the z-score of a door with gap of 1.4 mm. Compare its distance from the mean to that of 1.6 mm.

d) The manufacturer rejects any cars with door gaps that are not within two standard deviations of the mean. Which cars would be rejected?

> > > ## Consolidate and Debrief

Key Concepts

- The variance and standard deviation are measures of spread. The standard deviation is the square root of the variance.

  Population variance:
  $$\sigma^2 = \frac{\sum(x - \mu)^2}{N}$$

  Population standard deviation:
  $$\sigma = \sqrt{\frac{\sum(x - \mu)^2}{N}}$$

  Sample variance:
  $$s^2 = \frac{\sum(x - \bar{x})^2}{n - 1}$$

  Sample standard deviation:
  $$s = \sqrt{\frac{\sum(x - \bar{x})^2}{n - 1}}$$

- You can use the following computational formulas to calculate standard deviation more easily.

  Population standard deviation:
  $$\sigma = \sqrt{\frac{\sum x^2 - N \cdot \mu^2}{N}}$$

  Sample standard deviation:
  $$s = \sqrt{\frac{\sum x^2 - n \cdot \bar{x}^2}{n - 1}}$$

- The standard deviation of a set of data determines the average distance of the measurements from the mean. The larger the value, the greater the spread of the data. The units of the standard deviation are the same as for the mean.

- The z-score tells you the number of standard deviations that an observation in a data set is from the mean.

  Population z-score: $z = \frac{x - \mu}{\sigma}$ Sample z-score: $z = \frac{x - \bar{x}}{s}$

Reflect

R1. The mean of a set of data is 23.5, with standard deviation of 3.1.

    a) What does a z-score of –2 mean for a given data point?

    b) What does a z-score of 1.5 mean for a given data point?

R2. Before investing in stocks, you read an analysis that includes the standard deviation of its price over a given period of time. Two stocks have the same mean price of $15.43 over the past 10 days. Stock A has a standard deviation of $0.56 and stock B has a standard deviation of $1.22. What does this mean to you as an investor?

R3. Explain how x relates to the mean if the z-score corresponding to x is

    a) positive

    b) negative

    c) zero

R4. Explain how to decide whether the population or sample formulas need to be used for mean and standard deviation.

Practise

Choose the best answer for #1 and #2.

1. Adam is building a doorway and wants the height of the door to be three standard deviations above the mean Canadian height. How high must the door be if the mean is 210 cm with a standard deviation of 10 cm?

    A 230 cm

    B 250 cm

    C 200 cm

    D 240 cm

2. Which is an incorrect statement about standard deviation?

    A The variance is the square root of the standard deviation.

    B The standard deviation is often called the average distance of the measurements from the mean.

    C The standard deviation is expressed in the same units as the data.

    D The standard deviation is always a positive quantity.

3. The mean of a data set is 25.3 cm, and the standard deviation is 3.6. Determine the z-score of each of the following and interpret the results.

    a) 27.2

    b) 24.1

    c) 21.9

    d) 29.8

4. Calculate the standard deviation for each data set and interpret the results.

    a) Lengths, in centimetres, of fish caught on a fishing trip.

        15.4   12.3   18.2   9.9
        17.4   12.6   16.3   11.8
        12.3   12.6   16.7

    b) Number of home runs in a season by the players on a team.

        3 10 0 12 5 6 10 16 34 11
        6 7 21

    c) Final scores by the figure skaters in a competition.

        168.3   178.2   186.1   134.5
        156.7   156.4   167.1   132.0
        154.7   149.8   126.2   134.8
        154.0   175.2   159.2

5. For each of the situations, decide whether you would use the sample or population standard deviation formula. Explain your decisions.

a) A researcher recruits females ages 35 to 50 years old for an exercise training study to investigate risk markers for heart disease (e.g., cholesterol).

b) One of the questions on a national survey asks for the respondent's age. Researchers want to describe the variability in all ages received from the survey.

c) A teacher administers a test to her students. The teacher wants to summarize the results the students attained as a mean and standard deviation.

6. As part of a report on its employees, a company published this graph.

a) The standard deviation is given as 4.1 years. Identify which numbers of years worked are within one standard deviation of the mean.

b) What percent of the employees are within two standard deviations of the mean?

c) How does this graph help to explain z-scores?

Apply

7. The chart shows the waiting times for customers while having winter tires installed on their cars.

Time (min)	Frequency
30–35	10
35–40	16
40–45	21
45–50	17
50–55	19
55–60	8
60–65	2

When calculating the standard deviation for data in intervals, use the following formulas:

$$\sigma = \sqrt{\frac{\sum(f_i \cdot m_i^2) - N \cdot \mu^2}{N}} \text{ and}$$

$$s = \sqrt{\frac{\sum(f_i \cdot m_i^2) - n \cdot \bar{x}^2}{n - 1}},$$

where f is the respective frequency of each interval and m is the interval midpoint.

a) Using the midpoints of the intervals as the measurements, estimate the mean and standard deviation of the wait times.

b) Did you use the population or sample formulas? Why?

c) Calculate the z-scores of each of the midpoints.

d) Draw a histogram and mark the information from part c) on the graph.

8. **Application** The mean size of Canada's 308 electoral districts or ridings is 102 639.28 people, with a standard deviation of 21 855.384. In 2006, Mississauga-Erindale had a population of 143 361. Parkdale-High Park had a population of 102 142.

a) Compare the z-scores for these ridings.

b) What argument could the citizens of Mississauga-Erindale make about their representation in the House of Commons?

9. Maria handed in her final data management project last week. The class mean was 83% with a standard deviation of 8. If Maria's mark produced a z-score of 1.09, what was her grade?

10. The actual volume of milk in 1-L cartons of milk was checked by measuring a selection of 120 cartons. The chart shows the results.

Volume (L)	Frequency
0.98	6
0.99	18
1.00	30
1.01	35
1.02	19
1.03	9
1.04	0
1.05	3

a) Calculate the mean and standard deviation, accurate to three decimal places.

b) Did you use the population or sample formulas? Why?

c) The company has decided that a sample that is within two standard deviations of the mean is acceptable. A random sample was taken and the volume was 0.98 L. Would this be an acceptable sample?

d) On the following day, the mean volume of milk per carton was 1.012 L, with a standard deviation of 0.009 L. Compare the two days' test results.

11. The table shows the lengths of logs shipped to a lumber mill on a particular day.

Length (m)	Frequency
3.5–4.5	3
4.5–5.5	20
5.5–6.5	17
6.5–7.5	38
7.5–8.5	31
8.5–9.5	19
9.5–10.5	15

a) Calculate the mean and standard deviation of the logs, accurate to three decimal places.

b) How does this data set compare to the previous day, with a mean of 8.44 m and standard deviation of 1.836 m?

c) Why would the standard deviation be important to the operators of the lumber mill?

✔ **Achievement Check**

12. Along with their application to a particular university, students were instructed to submit a 700-word essay. The table shows the lengths of 16 of the essays that were submitted.

Student	Number of Words in Essay
Alex	709
Christian	743
Maria	810
Hasanika	900
Daniel	1112
Barb	568
Brian	804
Cathie	951
Wayne	643
Shaniqua	829
Jiang	674
Bill	769
Mohammed	781
Farah	735
Tim	700
Guido	583

a) Calculate the mean, variance, and standard deviation to the nearest whole number for the data set.

b) Did you use the sample or population formulas? Why?

c) Make an appropriate graph of the data. Mark the interval that is within one standard deviation of the mean.

d) Use z-scores to determine whether Cathie's or Wayne's essay length is closer to the mean.

e) Compare this group's essays to the essays in the previous year, with a mean of 712.1 words and standard deviation of 23.2 words.

13. Communication When is it possible for the standard deviation to be larger than the variance?

14. After graduating from university, Yee Ping hopes to get a job in a career with a mean starting salary of $56 000. Compare the salary ranges for standard deviations of $15 000 and $5000, knowing that 95% of the starting salaries are within two standard deviations of the mean.

15. Communication When buying an investment such as a mutual fund, investors look at its volatility. Volatility is measured by calculating the standard deviation of the returns over a given period of time.

a) What will the standard deviation show an investor if the mean rate of return of a particular mutual fund unit is 14.37% with a volatility of 6.54%?

b) How would the standard deviation change for a riskier investment?

16. Thinking A set of five whole numbers is arranged in order from least to greatest. The fifth number is decreased by one. Would the interquartile range or standard deviation be more affected? Explain.

Extend

17. The mean of a sample of n values is $\bar{x}$ and the standard deviation is s. Suppose you add a constant value a to each observation so that the new data values are

$$x_1 + a, x_2 + a, ..., x_n + a.$$

Determine the new mean and standard deviation.

18. The mean of a sample of n values is $\bar{x}$ and the standard deviation is s. Suppose the observations are multiplied by a constant value c so that the new data values are

$$cx_1, cx_2, ..., cx_n.$$

Determine the new mean and standard deviation.

19. Algebraically derive the computational formula

$$\sigma = \sqrt{\frac{\sum x^2 - N \cdot \mu^2}{N}}$$

from the defined standard deviation formula

$$\sigma = \sqrt{\frac{\sum (x - \mu^2)}{N}}.$$

Interpreting Statistical Summaries

Learning Goals

I am learning to

- interpret statistical summaries to describe a one-variable data set and to compare two related one-variable data sets
- understand whether the data presented are valid and reliable
- describe how statistical summaries can misrepresent one-variable data
- make inferences and make and justify conclusions from statistical summaries of one-variable data
- interpret statistics in the media, assess the validity of conclusions made, and explain how statistics are used to promote a certain point of view

Minds On...

Suppose you read this statement online.

- How would you interpret it? Would you agree or disagree?

- Would you like to know who collected the data to be able to make such an inference with confidence?

Chinchilla Kittykat
Today at 10:55 AM

Significantly more women than men spend time using social media.

2 Likes   15 Comments

👍 Like   💬 Comment   ➡ Share

Action!

How you collect data is important. How you organize and display data helps you analyse and make conclusions. Finally, how you summarize data determines whether you can make valid generalizations.

Investigate Statistical Claims in the Media

The headline "Significantly more women than men spend time using social media" came from an article about a survey of 900 men and 1100 women on their use of social media. The survey asked the question, "Do you use social media every day?"

The information was compared using a **multiple bar graph**, a **split bar graph**, and a **relative split bar graph**.

multiple bar graph

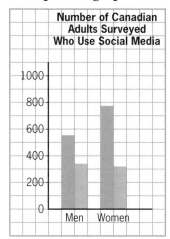

split bar graph

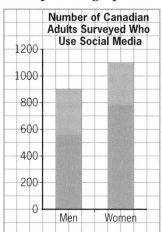

multiple bar graph

- different quantities are represented by different colours and lengths of bars that are placed side by side

split bar graph

- different quantities are represented by different colours and lengths of bars that are placed one above the other

relative split bar graph

- different percents, totalling 100, are represented by different colours and lengths of bars that are placed one above the other

relative split bar graph

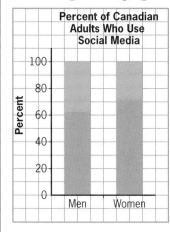

☐ Use Social Media
☐ Do Not Use Social Media

1. What does the multiple bar graph tell you?

2. What do the split bar graph and relative split bar graph tell you?

3. Which graph helps summarize the information best? Why?

4. Describe any sampling or measurement bias.

5. **Reflect** Does the Facebook post in the introduction accurately reflect the results of the survey? Explain.

6. **Extend Your Understanding** Is it appropriate to extend the results of this survey to the entire population? Explain.

As a society, we collect data to acquire information. As seen in the above investigation, one method of collecting information is through the process of conducting surveys. In chapter 5, you learned that a sample is usually used because it is difficult to survey an entire population.

reliable data

- results of a study that can be duplicated in another study
- repetition of trials will produce more accurate data

valid data

- results that accurately represent the entire population

It is important that the data gathered are both **reliable** and **valid**.

For example, suppose you want to know how many 15- to 18-year-olds in Ontario choose to play Xbox over PlayStation®. You sample students from Aurora, Newmarket, and Stouffville, which are all north of Toronto. Your results are reliable but not necessarily valid, due to sampling bias. Marketing or availability of the units may be different in other parts of Ontario.

Why would these survey results be reliable, but not valid?

How could you improve the validity of the results?

Example 1

Interpreting Measures of Central Tendency

A recent headline read, "Americans are significantly wealthier than Canadians." The article indicated that, in 2011, the income per capita in Canada was about $38 000, and in the United States was about $42 000.

Another publication showed the following graph. Both cited Statistics Canada and the US Census Bureau as their sources.

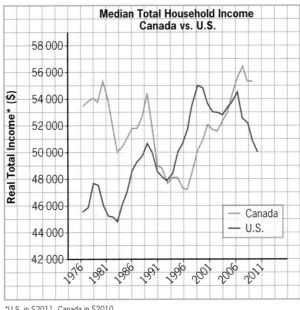

The footnote "*U.S. in $2011, Canada in $2010" indicates that the incomes were adjusted to discount the effects of inflation, using 2011 in the United States and 2010 in Canada as reference years. This is often a challenge when using secondary data to make comparisons. Analysts use whatever statistical summaries are available at the time.

*U.S. in $2011, Canada in $2010
Source: U.S. Census Bureau, Statistics Canada

a) Interpret these statements and explain what might cause the discrepancy.

b) Compare the two countries' median household incomes over the years.

c) Discuss the vertical scale of the graph and how it may influence the reader.

a) The graph indicates that the median income in Canada in 2011 was about $55 500, and in the United States it was about $50 000. Income per capita represents the mean income per person. The mean is influenced by outliers, so extremely wealthy individuals will significantly increase the mean. This results in income per capita being greater in the United States than in Canada. Both articles use reliable sources, but the interpretation in the first article is inaccurate. It is important for the reader to critically analyse claims in the media.

b) The graph shows that the median annual income is greater in Canada than in the United States for most years, with the exception of about 1992 to 2005. For an analysis to be accurate, many years of data must be analysed because the datum for a single year could be an outlier. The use of two different base years could be an issue if there were not such a marked difference between the two countries' results.

c) The vertical scale begins at $42 000. As a result, the differences between the graphs of Canadian and American incomes seem to be greater than in reality. For a more accurate view of the data, the vertical scale should begin at 0.

Your Turn

The graph below was included in a report by an Internet service provider.

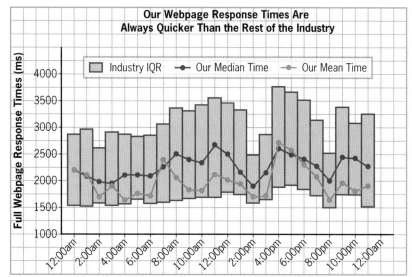

a) What statistical measures does the graph show?

b) Which measures of central tendency are used in the Internet service provider's analysis?

c) Discuss whether the Internet service provider's claim is accurate.

d) Discuss the vertical scale of the graph and how it may influence the reader.

Example 2

Comparing Groups Graphically

The Athletic Council of Reliable College wants to know whether males or females play more tennis at their school. They decide to poll the grade 11 and 12 students to organize, display, and draw conclusions about their data.

The following table lists the data they gathered.

	Frequency	
	Male	**Female**
Plays tennis	87	112
Does not play tennis	52	94

a) Create a multiple bar graph, a split bar graph, and a relative split bar graph to display the data.

b) Which graph more clearly shows which gender plays tennis more often?

c) Can you draw any other conclusions by looking at the visual representations of the data?

Solution

a) Create a multiple bar graph using the above data.

- Open a spreadsheet.
- Enter the following data:

	Male	**Female**
Plays tennis	87	112
Does not play tennis	52	94

- Highlight the data in the table. Select **Insert**, then select **Column**.
- Choose the first option, **2D Clustered Column**.
- The program will create the chart for you.

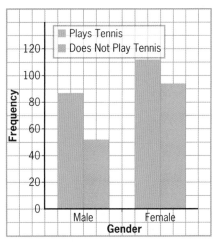

Some spreadsheet software refers to a multiple bar graph as a clustered column graph and a stacked bar graph as a stacked column graph. Explore the options in your spreadsheet software to see how these graph types are referred to.

- Create a split bar graph by following the same steps as above, but this time choosing the second option, **2D Stacked Columns**.

- Create a relative frequency stacked graph by selecting **100% Stacked Column**.

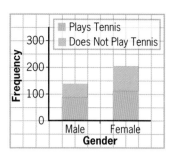

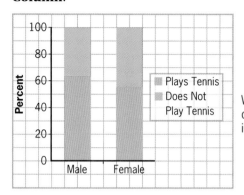

Which type of data (categorical, ordinal, quantitative) can be illustrated using these graphs?

b) The multiple bar graph and the split bar graph both show the breakdown of tennis players within the given gender. However, the sample sizes are different, so the relative frequency graph needs to be used to compare how well tennis is liked by males versus females. It indicates that tennis is more popular among males than females in the sample. Looking only at the relative frequency graph, you may not question the sampling method that was used. However, when looking at the multiple bar graph and the split bar graph, you might wonder how likely this gender proportion would be if a good random sample were carried out.

c) The green parts of the relative frequency split bar graph show that more than 50% of both males and females polled play tennis.

Your Turn

You work at StatSmart and your manager wants to determine how the store is performing on sales based on each quarter year, by region. The following sales data were gathered for the store during the year. Organize, display, and draw conclusions about the data to help show the manager how the store is performing.

	StatSmart Sales ($ millions)			
Region	Quarter 1	Quarter 2	Quarter 3	Quarter 4
North	100	200	230	185
South	200	137	164	123
East	231	70	110	228
West	125	210	246	166

a) Organize and display the data using a multiple bar graph, a split bar graph, and a relative split bar graph.

b) What can you conclude from the data? Explain.

Example 3

Critical Analysis of Claims in the Media

Can You Recall The Last Time Your Phone Was *Not* Within Ear Shot?

63% of smartphone owners keep their phone with them *for all but an hour of their waking day.* 79% keep it with them for all but two hours of their day.

1 out of 4 of all respondents didn't recall a time in their day when their phone was not within reach or in the same room.

Whether it is a weekday or weekend, the amount of time away from one's phone didn't vary—it is a *critical tool* for connecting with friends, family and colleagues *every day.*

17% 3 hours or more

9% 2-3 hours

19% 1-2 hours

23% 30 minutes to 1 hour

24% Less than 30 minutes throughout the day

25% Never that I can recall was it not close to me

Source: WorkSmart: 10 Surprising Social Media Statistics That Will Make You Rethink Your Social Strategy; 25% of Smartphone Owners Ages 18–44 Say They Can't Recall the Last Time Their Smartphone Wasn't Next to Them.

a) What message do these statistics convey?

b) What techniques are used to influence the reader with statistics?

c) What questions need to be answered about the data collection to critically analyse the results of the survey?

d) What questions need to be asked to check the reliability of the source?

> ## Solution

a) The statistics suggest that a smartphone is a critical tool for communicating and being in close contact with others all day long.

b) The following techniques were used to influence the reader:
- Coloured highlighting is used for emphasis.
- Circles are used instead of bar graphs, so it is very difficult to see area differences.
- The intervals of time are not equal.
- The sentence "63% of smartphone owners keep their phone with them *for all but an hour of their waking day...*" infers the results of a survey to the entire population.

c) The following questions need to be answered to critically analyse the results:
- How large was the sample?
- How was the sample chosen and was it a random selection?
- What questions were asked in the survey?

d) To check the reliability of the source, the following questions should be asked:
- What was the source of the data?
- Were the data primary or secondary?
- Who sponsored the survey?

Your Turn

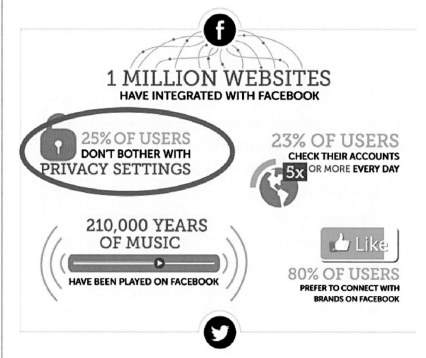

Source: WorkSmart: 10 Surprising Social Media Statistics That Will Make You Rethink Your Social Strategy; 25% of Facebook Users Don't Bother With Privacy Settings.

a) What messages do these statistics convey?

b) What techniques are used to influence the reader with statistics?

c) What questions need to be answered to critically analyse the results of the survey?

d) What questions need to be asked to check the reliability of the source?

Consolidate and Debrief

Key Concepts

- When you compare data values, it is possible to draw conclusions based on the data set results.

- There may or may not be a relationship between compared values.

- In some instances, graphs provide a stronger visual of the conclusion.

- You can use multiple bar graphs, split bar graphs, and relative split bar graphs to compare two similar data sets.

- Statistics are often used to represent certain points of view by manipulating graph axes, by citing only one measure of central tendency, or through measurement or sampling bias.

- It is key to perform a critical analysis of any statistical report.

Reflect

R1. How are multiple bar graphs, split bar graphs, and relative split bar graphs different? How are they similar?

R2. a) Why is it important to critically analyse a statistical summary?

b) What are some important questions that would need to be asked?

Practise

Choose the best answer for #3 and #4.

1. Grade 12 students were divided into two groups, male and female, and asked if they have successfully acquired a G2 driver's licence. Based on the results shown below, does gender appear to have an effect on whether or not a grade 12 student has their licence? Explain your reasoning.

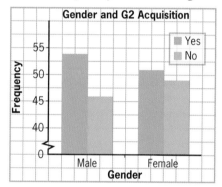

2. To decide on a reasonable price for a bottomless cup of hot chocolate, a cafe owner recorded the number of cups each customer ordered on a winter morning.

2	1	2	3	0
1	1	1	2	2
1	3	1	4	2
0	1	2	3	1

a) Will these data offer a reliable data set? Explain.

b) How might the cafe owner ensure a reliable and valid source of data?

3. In a split bar graph,

A the parts are compared to the whole

B the bars are divided into categories

C each bar displays a total

D all of the above

4. Which of the following best describes reliable data?

A represents the entire population

B can be duplicated

C you can trust the sample responses

D none of the above

5. Identify the information provided in the following statistical summary:

Total length of rainbow trout ($n = 128$) averaged 50.4 cm ($s = 12.4$ cm) in June 2014 samples from Lake Ontario.

6. Students were asked whether they ate their lunch in the school cafeteria. The table summarizes their responses.

	No	Yes
Grade 9	21	79
Grade 10	36	54
Grade 11	59	41
Grade 12	84	16

a) Create a multiple bar graph, a split bar graph, and a relative split bar graph to represent the data.

b) Which graph is more informative? Why?

Apply

7. The United Nations published a statement that 2% of the world's population has more than half the world's wealth, whereas half the world's population has only 1% of the world's wealth. In 2013, the world's population reached 7 100 000 people, while the world's total wealth reached $231 trillion. Analyse the United Nations' announcement in context.

8. Application The graph below had the headline, "Is climate change really happening?"

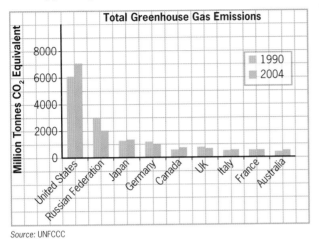

Source: UNFCCC

a) What do you think the author is trying to illustrate with this graph?

b) Is there enough evidence to suggest Russia is one of the most polluting countries on the list?

c) Is there enough evidence to suggest Russia has done the most to reduce greenhouse gases?

d) Critically analyse the information in the graph and the headline.

9. Thinking The side-by-side box plots were provided as part of a report on the results of a mathematics aptitude test involving 200 boys and 200 girls.

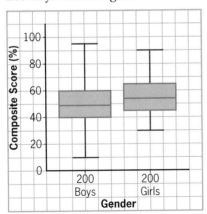

a) Write a paragraph summarizing the results, using proper mathematical terminology.

b) Evaluate the strength of the evidence that girls are better than boys at math.

10. An article on child development included the statement that, on the height-for-age distribution for a 36-month-old boy, the mean height is 96 cm and the difference between a z-score of -2 and a z-score of -1 is 3.8 cm. The same difference is found between a z-score of 0 and a z-score of $+1$ on the same distribution. Interpret the meaning of this statement.

11. Application A group of grade 12 male and female students were asked how many minutes they think they will spend getting ready for the school prom. The chart lists their responses.

a) Calculate the measures of central tendency.

b) Display the data with an appropriate graph.

c) Write a headline and a one-paragraph article for the school newspaper based on parts a) and b).

Number of Minutes	
Male	**Female**
60	94
64	128
68	54
59	102
74	108
66	120
88	79
97	87
54	111
51	51

12. Communication The graph shows the number of NFL football playoff telecasts for each US network, broken down by the league's conferences. Write a brief summary of the information provided in the graph from the point of view of CBS.

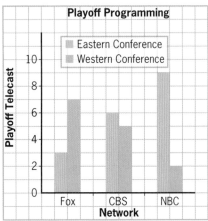

13. a) What is implied by this graph?

b) Where would you look if you were to try to validate the data?

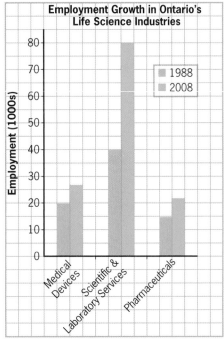

Source: Statistics Canada (Labour Force Survey) and Ontario Ministry of Finance.

14. This diagram was used in an article to illustrate the cross section of a river. Perform appropriate calculations and provide a statistical summary of the depth of the river.

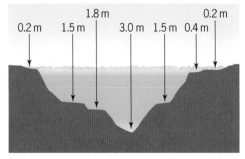

15. A common belief among fitness trainers is that you should do cardiovascular exercises to warm up before weight training. Trainers believe that a warm-up helps the elasticity of the arteries, which is beneficial before resistance training. One study among 15 male power lifters showed that cardio warm-ups caused fatigue among the athletes. The report concluded that cardiovascular training should not occur before weight training. Outline the steps that would be needed to validate this claim.

16. A store manager wants to show head office that sales are increasing dramatically, given that the sales for six months are $321 587, $335 892, $336 998, $340 256, $348 640, and $359 361.

a) Draw a graph to accurately represent the data.

b) Draw a graph to show a dramatic increase in sales.

17. Your teacher will provide you with a file called **WorldHealthStatistics2013.pdf**. It is a summary of a report by the World Health Organization.

   a) Describe the main points of the article.

   b) What are the sources of the data? Are they reliable? Explain.

   c) What types of graphs are used to present the data? Do the graphs distort the information? If yes, how would you change them to make them more accurate?

   d) Would you consider the data and sources to be reliable? Explain.

   e) Is there sufficient evidence to conclude that most people have access to clean drinking water, and that access is continuing to improve? Explain.

18. The rate of return on investments is very important to investors. Comparisons to other similar investments are often done. Instead of providing detailed statistics, they are usually summarized by indicating in which quartile the rate of return falls. However, in financial circles, quartiles are listed in reverse, so Q1 would mean the 75th percentile and Q4 the 25th percentile. The following table compares the returns of three mutual funds, by quartile.

Fund	2014	2013	2012	2011	2010
Global Science & Technology Fund	Q4	Q2	Q3	Q3	Q1
Canadian Mineral Resource Fund	Q1	Q2	Q3	Q1	Q2
North American Growth Fund	Q3	Q2	Q2	Q3	Q3

   a) Which fund had the most consistent ratings? Explain.

   b) Which fund would you recommend as an investment? Explain.

19. Do a search on the Internet for examples of misrepresentations of statistics in the media. Print out three or more of them and describe how statistics are misrepresented.

Extend

20. The diagram shows the percent of bird strikes on Canadian aircraft by phase of flight.

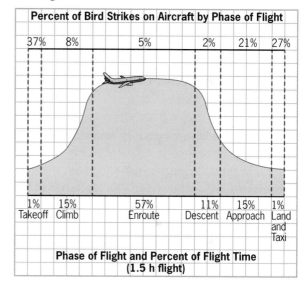

   a) Rank the bird strike percents from least to greatest.

   b) Consider the number of bird strikes in 100 flights. Rewrite the bird strike percents as percentiles.

   c) Recalculate the bird strike percents as bird strike risk, relative to the flight phase. Then re-rank them and change to percentiles.

6.5

Analysing Data from Statistics Canada

Learning Goals

I am learning to

- collect data through secondary sources
- generate, using technology, the relevant graphical summaries of one-variable data
- interpret statistical summaries
- assess the validity of conclusions presented in the media
- draw conclusions from the analysis of data and evaluate the strength of the evidence

Minds On...

Statistics Canada is the country's national statistics agency. It collects statistics on Canadians and Canadian issues through the national census and through regular surveys. The data tables are published online at CANSIM (Canadian Socio-Economic Information Management System), Statistics Canada's key socioeconomics database. Once the data are analysed, Statistics Canada produces a report, which is announced in its bulletin, *The Daily*.

The first national census, completed in 1851, asked questions about family, dwellings, religion, and origin. Census takers filled in this census by hand. Over the years, the questions changed relative to the times and the surveys are now fully computerized. What kind of data would it be important for Statistics Canada to gather today to help various government agencies with their planning?

Action!

Investigate 1 Explore Census Profiles

A census is a survey taken of every household in the country. It is mandatory that all households answer the questions in the census. The census occurs every five years, in the years ending in the digits 1 and 6.

Your teacher will direct you to the Statistics Canada website, where you can find results from the most recent census.

1. List which census results are available to view.

2. Census profiles are available for all cities across Canada. Explore this page and describe the steps you need to take to find the census profile of Kitchener, Ontario.

3. Select two cities of your choice and download the census profile for their census metropolitan areas.

4. Give a brief summary of the characteristics that are profiled.

5. Click on the **Download** tab. Select **CSV** format.

6. **Reflect** Select three characteristics and make a graphical and written comparison of your chosen cities.

7. **Extend Your Understanding** How could the city councils use this information in their planning?

Investigate 2 Use CANSIM Tables

Statistics Canada summarizes high-income earners by census metropolitan area (CMA). Your teacher will direct you to the Statistics Canada website, where you can find results from the most recent census.

1. Describe how Statistics Canada categorizes its data.

2. Search for **High Income Trends**. Click on the table number. Describe the data in the table.

3. Identify the source.

4. Identify the sample and sampling method.

5. Identify any possible sources of bias. How reliable would the data be?

6. Select **Add/Remove Data**. Describe the options available.

7. Select **Manipulate**. Describe the options available.

8. Select **Download**. Describe the options available.

9. If you wanted to use data from this table, describe how you would select the items you wish to include and how to download into a spreadsheet.

10. Download the appropriate items to compare the median after-tax income for the top 5% income group in each province and territory for the latest year.

Project Prep

You may decide to use the Statistics Canada website as a source of data for your culminating project. Remember to write down the table number and URL for future reference.

11. **Reflect** Use a spreadsheet or dynamic statistical software to produce graphs that would be useful in a report on the top 5% of income earners.

12. **Reflect** Rank the provinces and territories based on the top 5% of income earners.

13. **Extend Your Understanding** Explain why the rankings might be as they are.

Investigate 3 Analyse a Statistics Canada Report

Select one of the following articles. Your teacher will provide you with a file for either **Gender Differences in STEM Programs at University** or **Differences in Life Expectancy, Inuit vs. Rest of Canada**.

Read the article and perform a critical analysis.

1. What are the major findings of this study?

2. What types of graphs are used? How are the data displayed in graphs? Is there any bias in the graphs?

3. How are the data organized in charts? Is there any bias in how they are presented?

4. What are the sources of the data?

5. How big is the sample? Is it large enough to make inferences to the population?

6. How recent are the data? Are they recent enough for current use?

7. What methods were used to generate or obtain the data? Do the methods show any bias?

8. Does the article make reference to other sources?

9. Who conducted the study? Is there potential for bias due to influences by special interest groups?

10. **Reflect** Consider your answers to all of these questions. Describe your level of confidence that the findings of this study can be applied to the entire population.

11. **Extend Your Understanding** Describe some follow-up questions that might need to be answered if further studies were to be conducted.

Key Concepts

- Statistics Canada collects statistics on Canadians and Canadian issues through the national census and through regular surveys.

- Statistics Canada holds a national census every five years.

- Data are published online at CANSIM. The data are available in table form, and often in graphical form.

- Statistical reports are available online on the Statistics Canada website, and are summarized in their bulletin, *The Daily*.

- When reading a statistical report, it is important to perform a critical analysis.

Reflect

R1. A census profile includes such information as population, growth rates, population density, level of education, income, number of immigrants, and age distribution. Who could make use of this information?

R2. Statistics Canada is considered by many organizations to be one of the most reliable sources of data in the world. What factors would be considered in this rating?

R3. Why is it important to perform a critical analysis of a statistical report?

Practise

Choose the best answer for #1 and #2.

1. The national census is taken
   A every year
   B every 5 years
   C every 7 years
   D every 10 years

2. CANSIM stands for
   A Canadian Simulated Industrial Methodology
   B Canadian Association of National Statistical and Informational Marketers
   C Canadian Socio-Economic Information Management System
   D Canadian Annual National Study of Inferential Media

3. When reading a CANSIM data table,
   a) what does the **Add/Remove Data** tab allow you to do?
   b) what does the **Manipulate** tab allow you to do?

4. What kind of information is provided in a census profile of a particular city?

Apply

5. **Communication** Go to the Statistics Canada website. Select the **2006 Census of Population**. Select **Data Products**, then **Census Tract Profiles**. You will be able to enter a postal code and see its statistical profile.
   a) How is income related to educational attainment?

b) Collect data on median income, number of post-secondary degrees and diplomas, and size of the population age 15 or older for 5 to 10 different Ontario postal codes. Compare the profiles for these areas and state a hypothesis relating income to education.

6. Consider this Statistics Canada graph with the title **Prices increase in six of eight major components**.

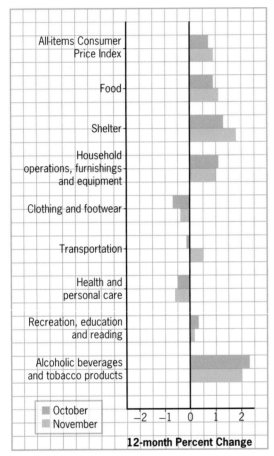

Source: Statistics Canada. *The Daily*, Friday, December 20, 2013: Consumer Price Index, November 2013: Chart 2

a) Which components of the Consumer Price Index increased in November? Which ones decreased?

b) Which components of the Consumer Price Index increased in October? Which ones decreased?

c) Describe the time frame for the percent change.

7. Communication Go to the Statistics Canada website. Select the **2011 Census**. Select **Data Products**, then **Historical Age Pyramid**.

Historical Age Pyramid for the Population of Canada, 1921 to 2011

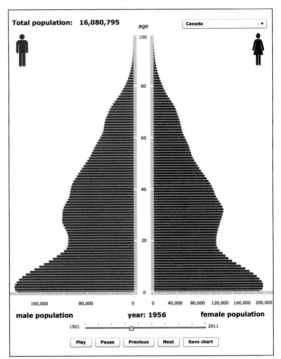

Source: Statistics Canada. Censuses of Population and Population Estimates Program, 1921 to 2011. December 23, 2013.

a) Describe the age pyramid in 1921.

b) Describe the age pyramid in 2011.

c) Describe the age pyramid in your year of birth.

d) The post-World War II baby boom occurred between 1946 and 1965. Use the animation feature to follow the baby boom. What does it look like on the age pyramid after 1965?

e) Estimate the male and female populations aged 10 and 50 in 2011.

8. **Application** Go to CANSIM on the Statistics Canada website. Select **Education, Training and Learning**, then **Students**. Select the table that provides data described as, **Weighted average tuition fee for full-time Canadian undergraduate students, by field of study**. Download data that allow you to compare tuition fees in Ontario to any two other provinces, by field of study, for the current and previous school years. Use the data to make appropriate graphs. Calculate measures of central tendency. Make appropriate comparisons between the selected provinces.

9. **Open Question** Choose a topic in the CANSIM category of the environment. Identify the table name and number. Collect data for all provinces and territories. Select the appropriate data, provide graphs, and calculate measures of central tendency and measures of spread where appropriate. Make comparisons to these measures for at least three provinces and territories.

10. Collect and summarize data from the latest edition of the National Household Survey (available on CANSIM) to compare the income distributions for males and females. Write a brief newspaper article on this issue, supported by graphs and summary statistics. Include an appropriate headline.

11. **Thinking** Do a critical analysis on the Statistics Canada article on the Consumer Price Index. Your teacher can provide you with the document entitled **Consumer Price Index**. Alternatively, go to the Statistics Canada website and search for Consumer Price Index. Refer to Investigation 3 for the steps involved in a critical analysis.

Literacy Link

The *Consumer Price Index (CPI)* is a weighted average of a "basket" of goods and services purchased by consumers. The weighting is relative to the level of use in the Canadian economy. The CPI is used as an indicator of changes in consumer prices over time.

12. **Thinking** Do a critical analysis of your choice of articles. Select a topic of interest from the Statistics Canada website. Select
    - English
    - Information for…
    - Analysts and Researchers
    - Click on the html or pdf link of the topic of interest to you.

    Refer to Investigation 3 for the steps involved in a critical analysis.

Extend

13. The first national census was taken in 1851, and occurred every 10 years until 1951. After 1951, a census was held every 5 years. Search for the 1851 census and select the file that compares the 1851 census with the most recent available. Use the download link in the top left corner of the page to download the data. Then use technology to answer the following questions.

    a) Calculate the growth rate for each decade.

    b) Make a time series graph of the population. Describe the graph.

    c) Make a time series graph of the population growth rates. Describe the graph and how it relates to the graph in part b).

Literacy Link

A *time series graph* is a line graph where time is measured on the horizontal axis and the variable being observed is measured on the vertical axis. The variable being observed is usually measured at successive points in time spaced at uniform time intervals.

Learning Goals

Section	After this section, I can
6.1	• interpret the mean, median, and mode of a set of data • choose the measure of central tendency that best describes the data
6.2	• describe the variability in a sample or population using measures of spread • calculate the range • understand how to use quartiles and percentiles to analyse data
6.3	• use technology to calculate the variance and standard deviation of a data set • calculate and understand the significance of a z-score • relate the positive or negative scores to their locations in a histogram • develop significant conclusions about a data set
6.4	• interpret statistical summaries to describe a one-variable data set and to compare two related one-variable data sets • understand whether the data presented are valid and reliable • describe how statistical summaries can misrepresent one-variable data • make inferences and make and justify conclusions from statistical summaries of one-variable data • interpret statistics in the media, assess the validity of conclusions made, and explain how statistics are used to promote a certain point of view
6.5	• collect data through secondary sources • generate, using technology, the relevant graphical summaries of one-variable data • interpret statistical summaries • assess the validity of conclusions presented in the media • draw conclusions from the analysis of data and evaluate the strength of the evidence

6.1 Measures of Central Tendency, pages 252–265

1. a) Define the three measures of central tendency.

   b) Explain how each measure is determined.

   c) Provide a real-life example of where each measure is most appropriate.

2. Calculate the mean, median, and mode of the data sets. Express your answers to one decimal place.

   a) 75 989 54 76 675 45 242 54
      85 342 12 931 2 37 675

   b) 7 19 21 5 17 31 62 7 50 10 7 34

   c) 1856 6754 2346 5200
      6754 9564 2346 1880

3. A softball player's slugging average is calculated using the formula

   $$SLG = \frac{S + 2D + 3T + 4H}{B},$$

   where S is the number of singles, D is the number of doubles, T is the number of triples, H is the number of home runs, and B is the number of times batting. Calculate each baseball player's slugging average.

   a) Jane, with 85 singles, 15 doubles, 1 triple, and 20 home runs, in 308 times at bat.

   b) Tonya, with 56 singles, 25 doubles, 0 triples, and 38 home runs, in 294 times at bat.

   c) Monique, with 112 singles, 10 doubles, 9 triples, and 6 home runs, in 315 times at bat.

4. a) Determine the mean, median, and modal interval of the data set.

b) Graph the data with a histogram and mark the measures of central tendency on the graph.

Salary Range ($ thousands)	Number of Employees
30–40	10
40–50	18
50–60	31
60–70	14
70–80	5
80–90	0
90–100	2
100–110	5

6.2 Measures of Spread, pages 266–277

5. a) Describe what is meant by percentiles and quartiles.

b) Explain how quartiles would be useful for a store ordering shoe sizes.

6. The table provides the number of Facebook friends for a sample of 50 people aged 18 to 25.

a) Determine the percentiles for each of the Number of Friends intervals.

b) Determine the quartiles and the interquartile range.

c) Make a box and whisker plot.

d) Determine whether there are any outliers.

Number of Friends	Frequency
0–25	3
25–50	18
50–75	16
75–100	35
100–125	62
125–150	23
150–175	14
175–200	0
200–225	5
225–250	2

6.3 Standard Deviation and *z*-Scores, pages 278–289

7. The table provides the full-time enrollments of Ontario universities for 2012–2013.

Selected Universities	Total Full-Time Enrollment
Algoma University	1 427
Brock University	15 678
Carleton University	21 988
University of Guelph	20 692
Lakehead University	7 046
Laurentian University	6 635
McMaster University	24 798
Nipissing University	3 757
OCAD University	3 570
University of Ontario Institute of Technology	8 469
University of Ottawa	33 581
Queen's University	19 901
Ryerson University	22 194
University of Toronto	69 081
Trent University	6 760
University of Waterloo	31 611
University of Western Ontario	29 108
Wilfrid Laurier University	15 984
University of Windsor	13 557
York University	44 492

a) Calculate the mean, variance, and standard deviation.

b) What is the *z*-score for York University?

c) Which universities have a *z*-score of –2 or less?

8. What does it mean to have a *z*-score of 1.5?

9. The quality control department of Cool Cola tested the bottle fillers and found them to fill 500 mL bottles to a mean of 501.1 mL, with a standard deviation of 0.48 mL. The company's standard is set at test results being within two standard deviations of the mean.

a) What is the acceptable range of fills?

b) Why would the company want to overfill the bottles?

c) Three bottles of Cool Cola were tested for fill volume. Which are acceptable?

i) 501.0 mL **ii)** 502.1 mL

iii) 500 mL

6.4 Interpreting Statistical Summaries, pages 290–301

10. The graph shows the voting intentions in four regions of Ontario, taken from a poll of 2000 voters three days before an election.

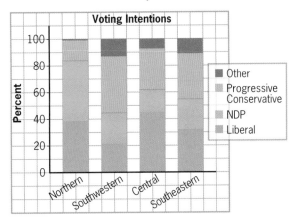

a) Identify three pieces of information that you can read from the graph.

b) Would you consider the graph to be a valid predictor of the outcome of the election? Explain.

11. The following information was collected by a large marketing firm interested in attracting individuals from Generation Y to apply for a position at the company. The firm surveyed its managers to develop a list of qualities and benefits that Generation Y employees bring to the workplace. The table shows the number of responses to the question, "What are the most important characteristics of a Generation Y employee?" Visually represent the data and provide a conclusion based on the inferences that can be made.

Characteristic	Frequency
Technological productivity	50
Global mindedness	35
Networking potential	35
Motivation through rewarding experiences	21
Innovative thinking	15
Openness	32
Flexibility	26
Confidence	6
Nothing	12

6.5 Analysing Data from Statistics Canada, pages 302–307

12. Go to CANSIM on the Statistics Canada website. Select **Travel and Tourism**, then **Domestic Travel**. Select the latest version of the file **Air passenger traffic and flights, annual**. Download the data that provide the total number of passengers enplaned and deplaned for each province for the latest year. Make a report that compares the number of airline passengers in each province. Include graphs, the mean, the standard deviation, and comparisons to the mean.

13. Your teacher will provide you with the Statistics Canada summary **Wage Growth Over the Past 30 Years: Changing Wages by Age and Education**. Perform a critical analysis by answering the following questions:

a) What are the major findings of this study?

b) How are the data displayed in graphs? Is there any bias in the graphs?

c) How are the data organized in charts? Is there any bias in how the data are presented?

d) What are the sources of the data?

e) How big is the sample? Is it large enough to make inferences to the population?

f) How recent are the data? Are they recent enough for current use?

g) What methods were used to generate or obtain the data? Do the methods show any bias?

h) Does the article make reference to other sources?

i) Who conducted the study? Is there potential for bias due to influences by special interest groups?

j) Is enough evidence presented to agree with the newspaper headline, "Wages have steadily increased over the past 30 years"? Explain.

Chapter 6 Test Yourself

Category	Knowledge/Understanding	Thinking	Communication	Application
Questions	1, 2, 3, 4, 5, 8, 11	6	6, 7	8, 9, 10, 11

Multiple Choice

Choose the best answer for #1 to #4.

1. The graph shows histograms of men's and women's heights in centimetres on the same set of axes.

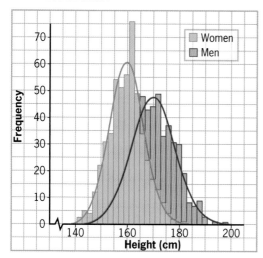

If the data sets were combined, the distribution of heights would have

   A no measures of central tendency

   B two modes

   C only one set of measures of central tendency

   D none of the above

2. Final marks in Maria's Data Management course are based on 70% for term work, 15% for the exam, and 15% for the final course project. What term mark did Maria receive if her final mark was 87 and she received 84 on the exam and 95 on her final project?

   A 87%   B 83%

   C 85%   D 86%

3. Find Q3 for the following masses of students in kilograms:

   70 74 78 80 81 84 90 92 94

   A 90

   B 87

   C 91

   D 92

4. What measure of central tendency is most appropriate to announce the most used bridge, on a daily basis, in Canada?

   A mean

   B mode

   C median

   D weighted mean

5. A set of nine different masses of pet cats are arranged in numerical order. The fifth mass is then increased by one. Which measure of spread for the data set could this change?

   A the range

   B the standard deviation

   C the interquartile range

   D all of the above

Short Answer

6. If you are given the data listed below and are asked to use the interquartile range, could you successfully determine which baseball player's home run season totals are more consistent? Explain why or why not.

   Ron: 20 21 23 25 18 19
   Joshua: 20 20 23 24 19 22

7. Explain why sampling bias is not a major concern for the national census conducted by Statistics Canada.

8. The mean daily temperature during January was –12.1 °C, with a standard deviation of 5.6 °C. Use z-scores to indicate which of the following daily mean temperatures is closest to the monthly mean.

   a) –17.4 °C

   b) –3.6 °C

   c) 0 °C

   d) –6.4 °C

9. For his culminating project, Asim referenced two sources as shown below. What information do these citations tell the reader?

   a) Statistics Canada. (2011). Table 109-0300 - Census indicator profile, Canada, provinces, territories, health regions (2011 boundaries) and peer groups, every 5 years, CANSIM [Database]. Retrieved from: http://cansim2.statcan.gc.ca/

   b) Statistics Canada. (2012). 2011 Census of Canada visual census, population change by broad age groups, Canada, 1996 to 2001, 2001 to 2006 and 2006 to 2011 [Graph]. Retrieved from http://www12.statcan.gc.ca/census-recensement/2011/dp-pd/vc-rv/index.cfm?Lang=ENG&TOPIC_ID=2&GEOCODE=01

Extended Response

10. The graph illustrates price fluctuations for three types of fruit. Each bar shows the mean price, with plus and minus one standard deviation superimposed. State the mean and interpret the standard deviation for each type of fruit.

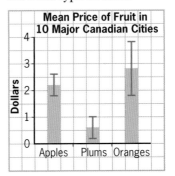

11. For a data management project, Ryan sent a survey to the teachers in his school, asking them how many years they have taught. Thirty teachers responded. Here are their responses:

    3, 12, 2, 2, 18, 27, 19, 0, 14, 15, 3, 17, 12, 37, 25, 17, 22, 1, 5, 5, 18, 13, 18, 6, 1, 10, 10, 4, 9, 28

    a) Calculate the mean, interquartile range, and standard deviation.

    b) Organize the data into a frequency distribution with five intervals.

    c) Estimate the mean, interquartile range, and standard deviation using the frequency distribution in part b). How do they compare to the true values?

    d) Illustrate all the calculations on appropriate graphs.

    e) What percentile rank is associated with 10 years of teaching?

    f) How many years of teaching are represented by the 90th percentile?

    g) Determine whether there are outliers. Identify any that are present.

    h) Analyse the validity of Ryan's sampling method.

Used Car Lot Business Report

The manager of a used car lot asks you to write a report on the average number of days the cars have been on the lot, along with the spread of the time. He provides you with the data in the table at the right, which represent the length of time, in days, the cars have been on the lot. *Note*: Measurements on an interval boundary are placed into the lower interval.

Time on the Lot (days)	Frequency
0–20	9
20–40	18
40–60	6
60–80	2
80–100	0
100–120	1

1. **a)** Determine the measures of central tendency.

   b) Plot a histogram of the data.

   c) Determine the interquartile range and make a box and whisker plot.

   d) Calculate the variance and standard deviation. Illustrate the standard deviation, along with the mean, on the histogram.

   e) How would this set of data compare to another set of data with a mean of 33.9 days and standard deviation of 18.9 days?

2. The original raw data for number of days on the lot are shown below.

17	22	27	41	34	118
45	19	32	8	12	49
12	22	29	53	28	29
31	25	50	21	38	2
20	27	45	1	24	74
30	33	21	61	12	38

   a) Calculate the measures of central tendency, the IQR, and the standard deviation.

   b) Compare these measures to those of the grouped data. Explain any differences.

   c) Identify any outliers.

   d) How would the mean, median, IQR, and standard deviation be affected if the outliers were removed from the data set?

3. Write a one-page report to the manager of the used car lot describing the time the cars spent on the lot. Make appropriate use of the measures of central tendency and spread, and support your findings with appropriate graphs.

Chapters 4 to 6 Cumulative Review

1. Two dice are rolled and the product of the upper faces is recorded. Show the probability distribution in table form and graphically.

2. A set of cards with the numbers 200 to 299 is used in a game. The cards are shuffled and the top card is turned up. Calculate the expectation and explain its meaning.

3. The serial numbers on $5 bills include three letters followed by seven digits. Assuming the digits are assigned at random, what is the probability that a serial number will contain

   a) exactly two 5s?

   b) at least four 5s?

   c) all 5s?

4. Five checkers are randomly placed on a checkerboard. What is the probability that three checkers are on squares of one colour and two checkers are on another colour?

5. a) Show the probability distributions, in table form and graphically, for the following distributions:

   i) Selecting a card four times, with replacement, from a standard deck, and recording the number of diamonds.

   ii) Selecting four cards at the same time, from a standard deck, and recording the number of diamonds.

   b) Compare the resulting graphs.

   c) Compare the expectations and comment on your findings.

6. **Thinking** In 2012, the musician Psy brought Korean pop music (K-Pop) to the world with his hit song "Gangnam Style." In 2013, he released another big hit, "Gentleman."

   a) The graph shows the number of Google searches related to "Gangnam Style" and "Gentleman." Which colour represents which search? Give reasons for your answer.

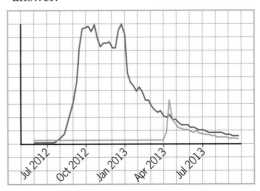

   b) The graphs below show the number of YouTube views of the videos for each song as of September 2013. Based on these data, do you think that "Gentleman" is doing better or worse than "Gangnam Style"? Justify your answer.

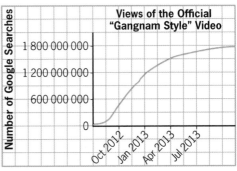

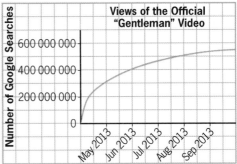

7. You are conducting a survey about one of the following topics: entertainment, sports, the environment, school, or technology.

  a) Discuss the methods you will use to conduct your survey.

  b) What questions will you ask?

  c) What types of data will you collect?

  d) How will you keep the data free of bias?

8. The table shows some data from *Romeo and Juliet*.

Character	Number of Words Spoken	Appearances
Romeo	4690	163
Juliet	4314	118
Friar	2624	52
Nurse	2223	91
Capulet	2156	50
Mercutio	2112	62
Benvolio	1157	64
Lady Capulet	874	45
Prince	590	16
Paris	542	23
Montague	319	10
Tybalt	263	17
Sampson	256	20
Peter	248	13
Balthasar	233	12

  a) How is the title of the play reflected in the data?

  b) Does it appear that the number of words spoken is related to the number of appearances? Justify your answer using the data.

  c) Who has the most spoken words in relation to their number of appearances?

  d) Create a graphical summary of the data. Your teacher may provide you with a file called **RomeoAndJuliet.csv**.

Use the following information to answer #9 to #13.

The chart shows the temperature, in degrees Celsius, of coffee in 30 recently tested coffee makers.

76	68	72	73	70	69	68	73	81	72
66	85	72	72	69	72	67	74	73	69
75	65	70	71	71	71	68	74	79	73

9. Calculate

  a) the mean, median, and mode

  b) the range, standard deviation, and variance

  c) the quartiles and interquartile range

10. a) Is there any value(s) in the data set that could potentially change the outcome of the measures of central tendency? Explain.

  b) Remove the value(s) identified in part a) and recalculate the mean, median, and mode. Which measure of central tendency is most appropriate to describe the distribution of the temperatures? Explain why.

  c) What makes the other two measures less appropriate? Explain why.

11. a) Create a frequency table by grouping the data into intervals.

  b) Create a histogram and a box and whisker plot of the data.

12. Coffee makers below the 5th and above the 95th percentiles are not recommended.

  a) How many of these coffee makers will this include?

  b) What are the temperatures of the coffee in the non-approved coffee makers?

13. You want to make a generalization about variability of coffee temperatures in coffee makers. Do you have enough information to make this claim? If not, explain what other pieces of information you would need.

Probability Distributions for Continuous Variables

Beekeepers remove honey from beehives, clarify it, and fill jars to sell to consumers. Processing engineers and technicians use probability distributions to ensure that the variation in the amount of honey in each jar falls within acceptable limits.

- What are some other food products sold in jars or bottles that are filled in a processing facility?
- Would you expect most of the jars to contain the amount stated on the label, more than this amount, or less than this amount?

Key Terms

attribute	margin of error
frequency histogram	confidence interval
frequency polygon	confidence level
normal distribution	continuity correction

Literacy Strategy

A frequency table provides a way to organize large amounts of data obtained from sampling. It simplifies analysis. For example, you can use a table to organize the amount of honey in 100 sample jars. Using the information in the table, you can generate a graph and determine probabilities.

Amount of Honey (g)	Number of Jars
145–149.9	1
150–154.9	3
155–159.9	9
160–164.9	17
165–169.9	26
170–174.9	25
175–179.9	17
180–184.9	2

Career Link

Mechanical Engineer

Doris plans to study mechanical engineering in preparation for a career in the food processing industry. She is working at a co-op position on a large farm that harvests and packages honey for sale in stores. The amount of honey in a jar varies, with a known mean and standard deviation. The mean can be adjusted on the filling machine.

- Why must the mean be set higher than the stated amount of honey in the jar?
- Why should the mean not be set too high?

Chapter Problem

Food Service Industry

In the food service industry, machines fill containers to a stated mean value with a known standard deviation. Engineers and technicians ensure that the machines are adjusted properly. The jar shown is labelled 500 g.

- Would you expect all jars to contain exactly this amount of honey?
- Why is it unwise, from a business point of view, for too many jars to contain less than this amount?
- Suggest a reason why a company would prefer not to have many containers with much more than this amount.
- How can technicians use a probability distribution to properly adjust the filling machine?

Prerequisite Skills

Areas of Rectangles and Trapezoids

1. Determine the area of each figure.

   a)

   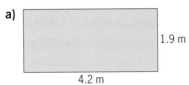

   1.9 m

   4.2 m

   b)

   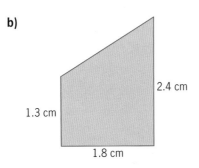

   2.4 cm

   1.3 cm

   1.8 cm

Organizing Data: Histogram, Mean, Standard Deviation, and z-Scores

A histogram is a graphical display that uses bars of varying heights to represent the frequency with which data occur.

If there are n data points in a data set, then

sample mean: $\bar{x} = \dfrac{\sum x}{n}$

sample standard deviation: $s = \sqrt{\dfrac{\sum (x - \bar{x})^2}{n-1}}$

The z-score is the number of standard deviations that the value of a continuous variable is from the mean.

z-score: $z = \dfrac{x - \bar{x}}{s}$

A data value below the mean has a negative z-score. A data value above the mean has a positive z-score.

2. Eighteen students counted the number of coins in their pockets.

Number of Coins					
3	1	4	3	1	2
4	6	3	5	3	6
5	6	3	2	4	7

   a) Sketch a histogram for the data.

   b) Sketch a relative frequency histogram for the data.

   c) Use technology to determine the mean and standard deviation for the number of coins.

   d) Determine the z-score for a student with two coins in her pocket.

3. On a final mathematics exam, the students in one class scored a mean of 74 with a standard deviation of 4. The students in another class scored a mean of 72 with a standard deviation of 6.

   a) What mark would result in the same z-score for each class?

   b) Are there any other marks that would work? Explain why or why not.

4. Thayer collected bonus bills from a hardware store for several months. He found that the 25-cent bill turned up with a relative frequency of 0.4. How many 25-cent bills would be expected in a sample of 80 bills?

Counting Principles: Permutations and Combinations

5. Evaluate.

   a) $5!$

   b) $_3P_3$

   c) $_{10}P_2$

   d) $_7C_4$

6. Farouk is visiting an amusement park. He has time to ride 5 of the 17 rides at the park. In how many ways can he choose his 5 rides?

7. Wayne is an author of 12 textbooks. He wants to display one copy of each book on a bookshelf.

  a) In how many ways can he arrange the 12 books from left to right?

  b) He has three books for each grade from 9 to 12. In how many ways can he arrange the books if they are clumped in groups of 3 for each grade in increasing order from left to right?

Probability

8. Sam purchases 5 green gumballs, 7 red gumballs, and 3 white gumballs. The gumballs are in a paper bag. He reaches into the bag and pulls out one gumball. What is the probability that it is green?

9. Six students are lined up to purchase tickets for a movie. What is the probability that they are lined up in alphabetical order by first name?

10. The Drama Club holds a draw at each performance to raise money for props and costumes. They sell 200 tickets at $2 each. There is one prize of each of $100, $75, and $25. What is the expected value of each ticket sold?

Discrete Probability Distributions

11. A board game uses a 12-sided die as shown. It is rolled 7 times. What is the probability that it comes up greater than 9 exactly 4 times?

12. The barriers at a commuter train crossing are down for a total of 12 min every hour. If 100 cars approach the barrier every hour, what is the probability that exactly 20 will find the barriers down?

13. A mathematics class has 4 students with red hair, 6 with black hair, 9 with brown hair, and 7 with blond hair. The teacher randomly chooses 4 students to plan a class pizza party. What is the probability that all 4 have red hair?

14. Of the 1000 students at Eastdale Secondary School, 420 are boys. For a promotion, the cafeteria manager selects 10 students at random to receive a free sample of a new wrap. Use technology to determine the probability that an equal number of boys and girls will receive a free sample.

We often calculate probabilities for a range of values. Keep in mind the differences among terms such as "at most," "less than," "greater than," and "at least."

15. A department store mails out Saturday-Scratch-n-Save cards to all of the households in a large city. One card in 100 offers a discount of 50%, while the rest offer 5%. Last Saturday, 250 customers used their cards.

  a) What is the probability that exactly 3 customers received a 50% discount?

  b) What is the probability that more than 1 but fewer than 4 customers received a 50% discount?

Continuous Random Variables

Learning Goals

I am learning to

- distinguish between discrete variables and continuous variables
- work with sample values for situations that can take on continuous values
- represent a probability distribution using a mathematical model
- represent a sample of values of a continuous random variable using a frequency table, a frequency histogram, and a frequency polygon

> ## Minds On...

A beekeeper collects data such as the number of bees in a hive or the amount of honey produced by the bees in a hive.

- Suggest some possible values for the number of bees in a hive and for the amount of honey produced in a hive. You may wish to use the Internet to help you provide reasonable estimates.

- What is different about the types of numbers used for each?

> ## Action!

Investigate Comparing Discrete and Continuous Random Variables

attribute

- a quality or characteristic given to a person, group, or object

Project Prep

The data in your project may take different forms. Make sure you identify your continuous and discrete variables appropriately.

1. Consider attributes of students in your class, such as number of siblings or height.

   a) List several attributes that are counted using discrete values.

   b) List several attributes that are measured using continuous values.

2. Some students were asked for the number of siblings in their families. The table shows the results.

   a) Classify the number of siblings as a discrete or a continuous variable. Explain your reasoning.

   b) Represent the data using a histogram.

Number of Siblings	Number of Students
0	3
1	5
2	7
3	3
4	2
5 or more	1

3. Students recorded the time, to the nearest minute, spent on math homework one evening. The table shows the results.

Time (min)	Number of Students
0–10	2
10–20	5
20–30	6
30–40	10
40–50	4
50+	1

If a data value falls on the boundary between two intervals, it is usually placed in the lower interval.

For example, a data value of 10 min is recorded in the 0–10 min interval.

a) Classify time as a discrete or a continuous variable. Explain your reasoning.

b) Why is the time shown in intervals?

c) Draw a scatter plot of these data. For the time value, use the midpoint of each interval. Sketch a smooth curve through the points on the scatter plot.

d) Reflect Does the shape of the curve make sense? Explain.

e) Extend Your Understanding Consider the choice of intervals in the table. Why must you be careful not to have too few or too many intervals?

You can represent a probability distribution by a table and a graph that relates each outcome to the probability that it occurs. For discrete data, the variable can take on only certain values, often whole numbers. For example, suppose you flip a coin twice, and count the number of heads.

Number of Heads	Probability
0	$\frac{1}{4}$ or 0.25
1	$\frac{1}{2}$ or 0.50
2	$\frac{1}{4}$ or 0.25

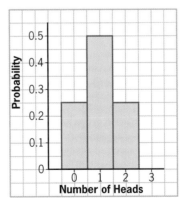

The first column of the table must include all possible outcomes.

- What is the sum of the numbers in the probability column?

- Will this always be the case, assuming that all possible outcomes have been considered?

Each rectangle in the graph has a width of one unit.

- What is the total area of the three rectangles?

- What does this area represent?

Processes

Connecting
Suggest two other examples of a discrete probability distribution that you have already encountered in this course.

For continuous data, you can group the outcomes into intervals. The variable can take on any value in the interval between two numbers, including decimal and fractional values. For example, suppose you measure the distances of various horseshoe throws, and group the distances in intervals.

Distance (m)	Probability
2–4	0.1
4–6	0.2
6–8	0.4
8–10	0.2
10–12	0.1

The first column must include all possible outcomes. What is the sum of the probabilities?

The probability density function defines the continuous probability distribution for a given random variable. The probability that a random variable assumes a value between a and b is the area under the curve between a and b. The total area under the probability distribution graph is equal to 1.

Example 1

Determine a Probability Using a Uniform Distribution

A survey at a doughnut shop shows that the time required for a customer to eat a doughnut varies from 30 sec to 3 min, with all times in between equally likely.

a) What kind of a distribution is this? How do you know?

b) Sketch a graph that illustrates this distribution. Place **Time** on the horizontal axis, and **Probability Density** on the vertical axis. Determine the vertical scale on the graph. Explain your reasoning.

c) What is the probability that a customer will eat a doughnut in 1 to 3 min?

d) How many values are possible for the time required to eat a doughnut? Explain your answer.

e) Is it possible to determine the probability that a customer will eat a doughnut in exactly 1 min using the area under the graph? Explain your answer.

Solution

a) Since all outcomes are equally likely, this is a uniform distribution.

b) All values from 0.5 min to 3.0 min are equally probable. The graph is a horizontal line from 0.5 min to 3.0 min.

The area under the graph represents the total of all of the probabilities. Therefore, the area must equal 1. The base of the rectangle has a length of 2.5.

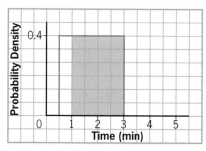

The total area of the probability density distribution will always be equal to 1 (or 100%). You can determine probabilities for a range of values by calculating the area under the graph.

$$bh = A$$
$$2.5h = 1$$
$$h = \frac{1}{2.5}$$
$$= 0.4$$

The top of the graph occurs at 0.4.

c) The probability that a customer will eat a doughnut in 1 to 3 min is equal to the shaded area under the graph from 1.0 min to 3.0 min.

$$P(1 \le X \le 3) = \text{area under the graph}$$
$$= 0.4(3.0 - 1.0)$$
$$= 0.8$$

The probability that a customer will eat a doughnut in 1 to 3 min is 0.8.

d) Since this is a continuous distribution, any real number between 0.5 and 3.0 is a possible value. An infinite number of possible values exist for the time required to eat a doughnut.

e) If you pick a single value such as 1 min, the rectangle under the graph will have a width of 0 min. The probability for a single value of a continuous distribution is 0. The area method cannot be used for single values of a continuous variable, only for a range of values.

It is tempting to want to say that the probability that it takes exactly 1 min to eat a doughnut is 0.4. However, this does not work for a continuous distribution. You must determine probabilities by using the area under the graph.

Your Turn

Chris works at a tire store. Chris can change a tire on a rim in 8 to 12 min, with all times in between equally likely.

a) What is the probability that Chris changes a given tire in less than 9 min?

b) What is the probability that it takes between 9 min and 11.5 min?

c) What is the probability that it takes exactly 10 min?

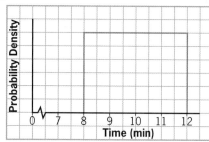

Example 2

Frequency Table, Frequency Histogram, Frequency Polygon

Many businesses use arrays of lights to attract customers. The life of a light bulb follows a continuous distribution. A technician sampled 40 light bulbs in a laboratory. The table shows the lifetime of each bulb, rounded to the nearest day.

Several versions of this sign at Sam the Record Man graced Yonge Street in Toronto from 1937 until 2007.

Life of Light Bulb (days)							
163	152	135	144	161	145	135	151
166	138	153	137	148	145	133	154
141	148	155	150	146	139	165	142
153	160	138	171	148	159	172	148
149	175	149	146	158	154	156	138

a) Can you use the data in the table to determine whether the data seem to follow a uniform distribution? Can you make a reasonable estimate of the mean lifetime of the bulbs?

b) Use a table like the one below to determine the frequency for each interval. The first two intervals have been completed for you.

Lifetime (days)	Tally	Frequency
120–130		0
130–140	ℍℍ |||	8
140–150		

c) Inspect the frequency table. Can you now answer part a) more easily?

d) How does a frequency table help you to analyse the raw data from a sampling experiment?

e) Use the frequency table to draw a **frequency histogram**. Then, add a **frequency polygon** to the histogram.

f) How is the shape of the frequency polygon related to the shape of the probability density distribution for the variable? Can you use the area under the frequency polygon to calculate probabilities for any range of values?

frequency histogram

- a graph with intervals on the horizontal axis and frequencies on the vertical axis

frequency polygon

- a segmented line that joins the midpoints of the top of each column in the frequency histogram

Solution

a) The data are difficult to analyse in this form. It is not obvious whether the distribution is uniform or not. Similarly, it is difficult to estimate the value of the mean with any accuracy.

b)

Lifetime (days)	Tally	Frequency
120–130		0
130–140	‖‖ ‖‖ ‖‖	8
140–150	‖‖ ‖‖ ‖‖‖	14
150–160	‖‖ ‖‖ ‖	11
160–170	‖‖‖‖	4
170–180	‖‖‖	3
180–190		0

You can check for errors by adding the numbers in the frequency column. What should be the total in this case?

c) From the frequency table, it appears that the frequencies vary from 0 to 14. The distribution is not uniform. The mean lifetime appears to be around 145 days.

d) The frequency table groups the raw data into intervals. The frequency in each interval makes the shape of the distribution more obvious, and gives an indication of the location of the mean.

e) Method 1: Use Paper and Pencil

- Draw axes on a piece of graph paper. Label the horizontal axis from 120 to 190. Label the vertical axis from 0 to 20.
- Use an interval width of 10 to draw the histogram.
- Mark the midpoint of the top of each bar on the histogram. Join the points with a segmented line to sketch the frequency polygon.

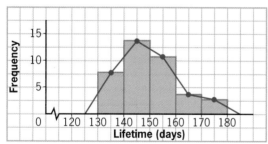

Method 2: Use a Graphing Calculator

- Turn on the calculator and clear all lists. Adjust the graphing **WINDOW** as shown.
- Enter the raw light bulb data in list **L1**. How many entries are there?
- Enter the midpoint of each interval in list **L2**. How many entries are there?

```
WINDOW
 Xmin=120
 Xmax=190
 Xscl=10
 Ymin=0
 Ymax=20
 Yscl=1
↓Xres=1
```

- Enter the frequency data in list **L3**.

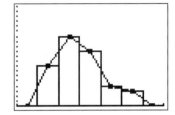

Why is the list in L1 not the same length as the lists in L2 and L3?

- Display the **STAT PLOT** screen. Turn on **Plot1**. Select the histogram. Ensure that **Xlist** is **L1**, and **Freq** is set to 1.

- Turn on **Plot2**. Select the line graph. Ensure that **Xlist** is **L2** and **Ylist** is **L3**.

- Press GRAPH to display the histogram and frequency polygon.

f) The shape of the frequency polygon gives an indication of the shape of the probability distribution for the variable. The total area under the frequency polygon is not equal to 1. You cannot calculate probabilities using areas under the frequency polygon. You need to use a probability distribution to determine probabilities.

Your Turn

A cubit measures the distance from the elbow to the tip of the outstretched middle finger. Ranjit's class has 30 students. Each student determines the length of a cubit using his or her arm. The frequency table shows the results.

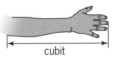

cubit

Cubit Length (mm)	Frequency
514–516	1
516–518	2
518–520	3
520–522	4
522–524	8
524–526	5
526–528	4
528–530	2
530–532	1

a) Sketch a frequency distribution histogram.

b) Add a frequency polygon to the histogram in part a).

c) Estimate the mean cubit length in the class.

d) Would this be considered a uniform distribution? Why?

Consolidate and Debrief

Key Concepts

- Some situations result in discrete data. These are often whole numbers.

- Some situations result in continuous data over a range. Continuous data include fractional or decimal values. Continuous distributions are often the result of measurements.

- The probability that a variable falls within a range of values is equal to the area under the probability density graph for that range of values.

- You can represent a sample of values for a continuous random variable using a frequency table, a frequency histogram, or a frequency polygon.

- The frequency polygon approximates the shape of the probability density distribution.

Reflect

R1. The manager of a hotel collects data about the operation of the hotel. Two examples include the number of guests that occupy the hotel each day and the time that a given guest waits for an elevator to arrive. Which of these is discrete and which is continuous? Is it possible to list all values of the discrete distribution? Is it possible to list all values of the continuous distribution? Explain.

R2. Three classmates measured Maya's height. The results are 154 cm, 155 cm, and 157 cm. Suggest reasons why the results are not all the same. Is this a measurement error or an example of bias? Explain.

R3. A classmate cannot accept that the probability that a bottle of juice from the cafeteria contains exactly 280 mL, as shown on the label, is zero. How can you convince him this is correct?

Practise

1. Which of these variables would be expected to result in a discrete distribution?

   a) the masses of the cupcakes for sale in the school cafeteria

   b) the value of a card drawn at random from a deck of 52 cards

   c) the daily barometric pressure measured in your city

2. Which of these variables would be expected to result in a continuous distribution?

   a) the number of students with blue eyes in each class in your school

   b) the weights of the police officers in the local police force

   c) the number of cartons of milk sold in the cafeteria vending machine

   d) the number of defective tablet computers in a shipment to an electronics store

3. A men's clothing store developed a customer waist size probability table from a sample of 300 customers, as shown.

Waist Size (in.)	Probability
26–28	0.000
28–30	0.025
30–32	0.175
32–34	0.295
34–36	0.300
36–38	0.160
38–40	0.045
40–42	0.000

a) Does the distribution appear to be uniform? Explain your answer.

b) What is the frequency associated with a waist size from 34 to 36?

c) If a new customer comes in with a waist size of 38, which interval should the data be placed in?

Literacy Link

Canada officially uses SI units for length, such as centimetres. However, in some industries—including the clothing industry—measurements are still recorded using imperial units, such as inches. 1 inch ≈ 2.54 cm.

Apply

4. Donna is monitoring nutrient levels in a local stream. She collects 44 samples of water from various locations. The table shows the volumes of the samples.

Volume of Sample (mL)			
55	63	56	64
55	62	61	65
57	62	59	63
55	65	60	62
58	62	56	61
63	60	64	57
57	64	60	59
55	61	56	56
58	58	65	64
58	57	60	65
63	61	59	59

a) Can you determine from the table if the distribution is uniform? Explain your answer.

b) Devise a plan to determine whether the distribution is uniform. Carry out your plan and draw a conclusion.

Processes

Representing
How did you choose to represent the data in the table to solve this problem? What are the advantages of your representation?

5. Thinking Air tanks used by scuba divers are typically filled to a pressure of 3000 psi (pounds per square inch). A sample of 32 tanks at a dive shop was selected, and the table shows the pressures.

Pressure (psi)			
3003	2999	2995	2999
3004	3001	3001	3000
2998	3000	2999	3000
3001	2997	2998	3003
3005	2995	3005	3002
2997	3004	2995	2997
2996	3001	3002	3002
2999	3003	2996	3003

a) Determine whether the distribution is uniform. Explain your method.

b) Is this distribution discrete or continuous? Give a reason for your answer.

c) Suggest a reason why are there no values in the table recorded with decimal places, such as 2998.347.

> **Literacy Link**
>
> In scuba diving, pressure is measured using the imperial unit of psi, which means pounds per square inch.

6. Consider the music produced by a piano.

a) How many keys are on a standard piano keyboard including both black and white keys?

b) The frequency of a piano note varies from a low of about 28 Hz at the left of the keyboard to a high of about 4100 Hz at the right of the keyboard. If you assign a number to each key, and count how many times that key is used in a piece of music, you will get a frequency distribution. Do you expect the distribution to be uniform? Explain your answer.

c) Is the distribution in part b) discrete or continuous? Give a reason for your answer.

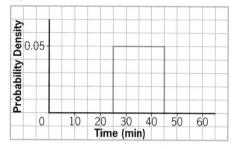

> **Literacy Link**
>
> The frequency of a sound is measured in units called *hertz* (Hz). Humans can hear from a low of about 20 Hz to a high of about 20 000 Hz.

7. The Ridgeway High School Paperman Triathlon consists of a 200-m swim, a 5-km bicycle ride, and a 1-km run. The graph shows the probability distribution for the time required to complete the triathlon.

a) What is the probability that a contestant will finish the triathlon in 30 min or less?

b) What is the probability that a contestant will finish the triathlon in 30 to 40 min?

c) Why was this type of distribution used? Explain.

8. A trombone can create musical notes like a piano. Because the musician uses a slider to control the frequency of the notes, the trombone can also play all of the frequencies between the notes that a piano is restricted to. A tenor trombone produces frequencies from a low of about 80 Hz to a high of about 600 Hz.

a) If a trombone player plays many notes at random frequencies, you can collect samples. Is this distribution discrete or continuous? Explain.

b) Suppose a trombone player plays a musical composition. If you measured the frequencies of the notes being played, would you expect the distribution to be discrete or continuous? Explain.

9. Sardines that will be canned are sorted from the main catch. Only fish that are 95 mm to 100 mm long are kept. The table shows the lengths of a sample of 24 sardines.

Length of Sardine (mm)			
99	98	100	95
98	95	95	96
97	100	100	99
100	99	97	97
98	99	97	96
96	99	99	98

a) Use the table to determine whether the distribution is uniform. Explain your method.

b) The plant manager would like to model these data with a uniform distribution. What should the manager use for the height of the probability density graph?

c) Sketch the probability density graph.

d) What is the probability that a sardine has a length less than or equal to 98 mm?

10. Communication Consider the uniform probability distribution shown. Jon says the shaded area represents the probability that the variable has a value of 3. Sunita says the shaded area represents the probability that the variable has a value of 2.5 to 3.5. Ahmed says the shaded area represents the probability that the variable has a value of 2 to 4. Who is correct? Give reasons for your answer.

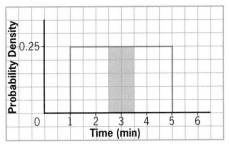

11. Carbon resistors are used in all types of electronic circuits including televisions, smartphones, and computers. Carbon resistors act to reduce current flow. They usually have a fixed resistance value measured in kilo-ohms (kΩ). When they are manufactured, those within 5% of a stated resistance value are set aside and form an approximately uniform distribution. Consider a 100 kΩ resistor.

a) What are the low and high cutoff values for this distribution?

b) Sketch a probability distribution for these resistors, assuming a uniform distribution.

c) What is the height of the probability distribution?

d) What is the probability that a given resistor has a resistance within 0.25% of the stated resistance value?

Literacy Link

Electrical resistance is measured in units called *ohms*, named after German high school teacher Georg Ohm (1789–1854). He developed the electrical theory of resistance that underlies most of the electrical and electronic devices that we are familiar with.

12. Doppler radar in a device similar to a police radar gun can be used to measure speeds of birds in flight. The table shows the measured speeds of 30 Canada geese.

Speed (km/h)				
78.5	68.0	64.7	75.1	68.3
76.6	76.6	71.2	73.7	73.5
76.7	64.6	66.7	68.8	73.6
80.2	72.4	69.6	77.3	74.8
72.5	66.1	73.5	75.0	68.9
71.7	65.7	67.4	70.9	73.0

a) Are these data discrete or continuous? Explain your answer.

b) Choose an appropriate interval width. Give a reason for your choice.

c) Construct a frequency table.

d) Use your frequency table to construct a frequency histogram.

e) Add a frequency polygon to the frequency histogram.

f) Estimate the mean of the speed data.

g) Estimate the probability that a goose is exceeding 80 km/h. Explain your thinking.

13. Thinking Should hair colour be considered discrete or continuous data? Give reasons for your answer.

Extend

14. Some musical instruments can play only certain frequencies, while others can play any frequency over a range.

a) Suggest three instruments that can play only discrete frequencies.

b) Suggest three instruments that can play any frequency over a range.

15. Thinking Most distributions are not uniform, but the probability that a value occurs between two boundary values is still equal to the area under the probability density curve. Study the probability density graph shown.

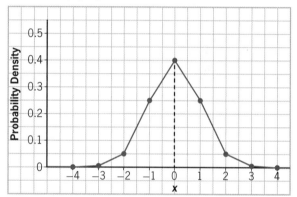

a) Develop a method for determining the area under the plot between any two points.

b) Use your method to determine the probability that the value of x lies between 0 and 3.

The Normal Distribution and z-Scores

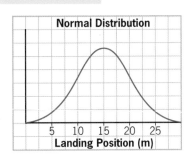

Learning Goals

I am learning to

- determine the theoretical probability for a continuous random variable over a range of values
- determine the mean and standard deviation of a sample of values
- calculate and explain the meaning of a z-score
- solve real-world probability problems involving normal distributions

 Minds On...

In a spot landing contest, airplane pilots take turns trying to land as close as possible to a line painted on the runway. Most will land close to the line, with fewer and fewer as the distance from the line increases. This kind of probability distribution is referred to as a **normal distribution**.

Suppose that the landing zone is 30 m long, with the target line at 15 m. The graph of a normal distribution for the spot landing contest would look something like this:

> Suggest two or three other situations that might reasonably be expected to form a normal distribution.

Normal Distribution

Landing Position (m)

normal distribution

- a probability distribution around a central value, dropping off symmetrically to the right and left, forming a bell-like shape

Study the shape of the normal distribution. What features can you see?

 Action!

Mathematically, the two "tails" of the normal distribution continue forever. In a real situation, the probability of finding a datum far from the central peak is essentially zero.

If you collect sample values of a variable that is expected to follow a normal distribution, the sample data will cluster around a central peak to form a bell-like shape, or "bell curve."

For a discrete distribution, you can calculate probabilities using counting techniques. For a continuous distribution, you can calculate probabilities by determining the area under a graph for a range of values. In this section, you will learn how to determine probabilities if you know that the distribution is a normal distribution.

Investigate The Effect of Interval Width on a Frequency Polygon

1. Review the frequency histogram and the frequency polygon from the light bulb data used in section 7.1. To estimate the mean, is one more useful than the other? Give a reason for your answer.

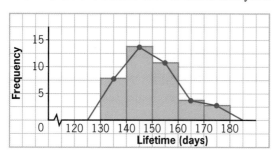

Life of Light Bulb (days)			
163	152	135	144
166	138	153	137
141	148	155	150
153	160	138	171
149	175	149	146
161	145	135	151
148	145	133	154
146	139	165	142
148	159	172	148
158	154	156	138

2. Work with a partner to construct a frequency table with intervals of 5 days, and another with intervals of 20 days.

3. The frequency polygon displays a segmented picture of the actual frequency distribution. Use the tables to produce frequency histograms and frequency polygons.

4. Compare the three frequency histograms. Which appears to display the data in the most useful way? Give a reason for your answer.

5. Compare the three frequency polygons. Which appears to follow the smoothest curve?

6. Reflect Would an interval width of 1 day be suitable for a frequency table in this case? Explain why or why not.

7. Extend Your Understanding Suppose the testing laboratory wanted to use an interval of 1 day to produce a very smooth frequency polygon. What changes would need to be made to the process of gathering data?

If you gather a large amount of data and use a small interval width, the frequency polygon looks like a smooth function.

Example 1

Use a Frequency Distribution to Estimate Probabilities

Fruityfizz Soft Drinks bottles its products in containers marked 500 mL. The table shows the frequency distribution for a sample of 200 bottles.

Volume (mL)	Frequency, f
490–492	0
492–494	0
494–496	2
496–498	11
498–500	43
500–502	81
502–504	48
504–506	14
506–508	1
508–510	0

a) Add a relative frequency column to the table.

b) Use the table to determine the probability that a given bottle will contain less than 500 mL of soft drink.

c) Use the table to determine the probability that a given bottle will contain between 498 mL and 502 mL of soft drink.

d) Is it possible to determine the probability that a given bottle will contain exactly 500 mL of soft drink using the table? Explain your answer.

e) Sketch a scatter plot of the frequency versus the volume. For the horizontal axis, use the midpoint of each interval.

f) Sketch a scatter plot of the relative frequency versus the volume. For the horizontal axis, use the midpoint of each interval. Sketch a smooth curve through the points. How does the shape of the graph of the frequency data compare to the shape of the graph of the relative frequency data?

g) Could you use the area under the relative frequency graph to answer parts b) and c)? Explain your answer.

h) Interpret the answers to parts b) and c) in relation to areas under a probability density graph.

Solution

a) To determine the relative frequency, divide each frequency by the total number of bottles tested.

Volume (mL)	Frequency, f	Relative Frequency, $rf = \dfrac{f}{200}$
490–492	0	0.000
492–494	0	0.000
494–496	2	0.010
496–498	11	0.055
498–500	43	0.215
500–502	81	0.405
502–504	48	0.240
504–506	14	0.070
506–508	1	0.005
508–510	0	0.000

b) To determine the probability, add the relative frequencies from 490 mL to 500 mL.

$0 + 0 + 0.010 + 0.055 + 0.215 = 0.280$

The probability that a given bottle will contain less than 500 mL of soft drink is 0.280.

c) To determine the probability, add the relative frequencies from 498 mL to 502 mL.

$0.215 + 0.405 = 0.620$

The probability that a given bottle will contain between 498 mL and 502 mL of soft drink is 0.620.

d) Probabilities for a continuous distribution cover a range of values. The probability that a given bottle will contain exactly 500 mL of soft drink would require an interval width of 0 mL, which is not available on the table. In fact, the probability that a given bottle will contain exactly 500 mL of soft drink is zero.

Consider the number of possible values that the volume of soft drink in the bottle could take. Can you use the definition of probability to explain why the answer to part d) makes sense?

e)

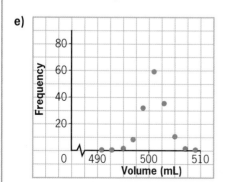

f)

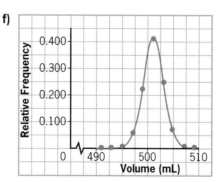

The graph of the relative frequency data has the same shape as the graph of the frequency data.

g) In order to use the area under a graph to calculate probabilities, the total area must be equal to 1. This is called a probability density graph. The relative frequency graph in part f) has the same general shape as the probability density graph, but the area under the graph is not equal to 1. You cannot use it to calculate probabilities by finding areas.

h) The probability that a bottle contains less than 500 mL is equal to the area under the probability density graph from the far left up to $x = 500$.

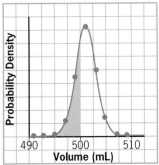

The probability that a bottle contains between 498 mL and 502 mL is equal to the area under the probability density graph from $x = 498$ to $x = 502$.

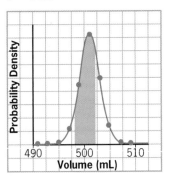

The vertical scale on the probability density graph must be chosen such that the total area under the graph is equal to 1. This is not easy to do. However, you can determine the area under a curve fairly easily if the distribution is normal.

Your Turn

A men's clothing store kept records of the waist sizes of a sample of their customers, measured to the nearest quarter of an inch. The table shows the relative frequencies.

What is the probability that a customer has a waist size

a) between 30 and 32 in.?

b) of more than 36 in.?

c) between 30 and 36 in.?

d) of exactly 38 in.?

Waist Size (in.)	Relative Frequency
26–28	0.000
28–30	0.025
30–32	0.175
32–34	0.295
34–36	0.300
36–38	0.160
38–40	0.045
40–42	0.000

Although Canada officially uses SI units for length, such as centimetres, clothing measurements are often recorded using imperial units, such as inches. 1 inch ≈ 2.54 cm.

If a variable is expected to follow a normal distribution, you can take a representative sample. You can use the mean and standard deviation of the sample to approximate the mean and standard deviation of the underlying normal distribution. The approximation becomes more accurate as more data are collected.

Example 2

Spot Landing Contest

Forty aircraft participated in a spot landing contest at the Wainfleet Ring Aerodrome. The landing zone was 30 m long, with the target line at the 15 m mark. The table shows the touchdown position of each aircraft along the landing zone. The data in the table are expected to follow a normal distribution.

Project Prep

Many continuous data sets are distributed normally. Consider including that in your data analysis.

Landing Zone Position (m)			
10.6	18.9	17.7	22.9
12.2	11.9	12.2	10.6
17.0	13.4	14.0	14.6
14.0	15.5	18.9	13.4
11.6	12.5	18.0	9.8
11.3	16.2	10.6	14.6
18.0	13.1	11.9	12.5
14.6	17.4	15.2	11.9
19.8	22.3	14.6	15.5
10.6	17.7	12.2	15.5

a) Determine the mean and the standard deviation of the spot landing data.

b) What is the z-score for a pilot who lands her plane at a position of 18.3 m?

c) What is the probability that a pilot lands at a position of 18.3 m or less?

d) What is the probability that a pilot lands at a position of more than 18.3 m?

e) What is the probability that a pilot lands at a position between 12.2 m and 18.3 m?

> Solution

a) Method 1: Use Paper and Pencil

Add the landing distances, and divide by 40.

$$\bar{x} = \frac{\sum x}{n}$$

$$= \frac{585.2}{40}$$

$$= 14.63$$

The mean of the landing distances is 14.63 m.

Use the equation for the standard deviation.

$$s = \sqrt{\frac{\sum x^2 - n(\bar{x})^2}{n - 1}}$$

$$= \sqrt{\frac{8975.68 - 40(14.63)^2}{40 - 1}}$$

$$\approx 3.259$$

The standard deviation is 3.259 m.

Method 2: Use a Graphing Calculator

- Turn on the calculator and clear all lists.
- Enter the landing distance data in list **L1**.
- Press **STAT** and scroll to **CALC**. Select **1:1-Var Stats**.
- Press **2ND**, then **1** to select **L1**. Press **ENTER**.

```
1-Var Stats
x̄=14.63
Σx=585.2
Σx²=8975.68
Sx=3.258928564
σx=3.21793412
↓n=40
```

The statistical summary will display as shown. The mean, $\bar{x}$, is 14.63 and the standard deviation, Sx, is 3.259.

b) Use the equation for a z-score:

$$z = \frac{x - \bar{x}}{s}$$

$$= \frac{18.3 - 14.63}{3.259}$$

$$\approx 1.12$$

The z-score for a landing at 18.3 m is 1.12.

The z-scores for a normal distribution follow a normal distribution themselves, with a mean of 0 and a standard deviation of 1. The area under the distribution of z-scores is equal to 1. It is possible to construct a probability table for these z-scores. You can find this table on pages 480–481.

c), d), e)

Method 1: Use a Table

To determine $P(X \le 18.3)$, start by moving down the z-column until you reach a z-score of 1.1. Then, move to the right until you reach a z-score of 1.12. Read the probability as 0.8686.

The entry in the table represents the probability that the variable has a value less than or equal to the value represented by the z-score.

z	0.00	0.01	0.02	0.03	0.
0.0	0.5000	0.5040	0.5080	0.5120	0.
0.1	0.5398	0.5438	0.5478	0.5517	0.
0.2	0.5793	0.5832	0.5871	0.5910	0.
0.3	0.6179	0.6217	0.6255	0.6293	0.
0.4	0.6554	0.6591	0.6628	0.6664	0.
0.5	0.6915	0.6950	0.6985	0.7019	0.
0.6	0.7257	0.7291	0.7324	0.7357	0.
0.7	0.7580	0.7611	0.7642	0.7673	0.
0.8	0.7881	0.7910	0.7939	0.7967	0.
0.9	0.8159	0.8186	0.8212	0.8238	0.
1.0	0.8413	0.8438	0.8461	0.8485	0.
1.1	0.8643	0.8665	0.8686	0.8708	0.
1.2	0.8849	0.8869	0.8888	0.8907	0.

The probability that a pilot lands at a position of 18.3 m or less is 0.8686.

Note that this is equal to the area under the normal distribution curve to the left of 18.3 m.

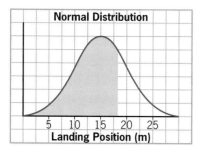

Normal Distribution

Landing Position (m)

Recall that the probability that a variable takes on a specific value is zero. Therefore, you get the same probability for $P(X \leq 18.3)$ as you do for $P(X < 18.3)$. The "extra" area for $P(X = 18.3)$ is equal to zero.

The probability that a pilot lands at a distance of more than 18.3 is equal to 1 minus the probability that the pilot lands at 18.3 m or less. These two probabilities are complements of one another.

$$P(X > 18.3) = 1 - P(X \leq 18.3)$$
$$= 1 - 0.8686$$
$$= 0.1314$$

The probability that a pilot lands at a distance of more than 18.3 m is equal to 0.1314. Note that this is equal to the area under the normal distribution curve to the right of 18.3 m.

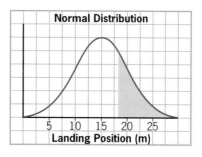

Normal Distribution

Landing Position (m)

The probability that a pilot lands at a position between 12.2 m and 18.3 m is equal to the probability that the pilot lands at 18.3 m or less minus the probability that the pilot lands at 12.2 m or less.

The z-score for a pilot landing at 12.2 m is

$$z = \frac{x - \overline{x}}{s}$$
$$= \frac{12.2 - 14.63}{3.259}$$
$$\approx -0.75$$

Use the table on pages 480–481 to determine the associated probability for a z-score of -0.75 as 0.2266.

$$P(12.2 \leq X \leq 18.3) = P(X \leq 18.3) - P(X \leq 12.2)$$
$$= 0.8686 - 0.2266$$
$$= 0.6420$$

The probability that a pilot lands at a position between 12.2 m and 18.3 m is equal to 0.6420. This is equal to the area under the normal distribution curve to the right of 12.2 m and to the left of 18.3 m.

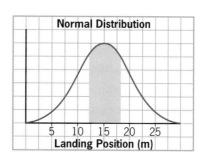

Normal Distribution

Landing Position (m)

c), d), e)

Method 2: Use a Graphing Calculator

- Press **2ND**, then **VARS** to access **DISTR**.
- Select **2:normalcdf(**.

The normal cumulative distribution function calculates the area under the normal curve from a lower to an upper bound. Choose −99999 as the lower bound and an upper bound of 18.3. Use the values for the mean and standard deviation that were calculated in parts a) and b). For example: **normalcdf(−99999, 18.3, 14.63, 3.259)**.

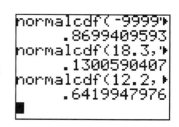

```
normalcdf(-9999▸
          .8699409593
normalcdf(18.3,▸
          .1300590407
normalcdf(12.2,▸
          .6419947976
```

The probability that a pilot lands at 18.3 m or less is 0.8699.

You can use a subtraction process to determine the probability that a pilot lands at more than 18.3 m, as in the table method. Alternatively, use the normal distribution function with a lower bound of 18.3 and an upper bound of 99999. The probability is 0.1301.

To determine the probability that a pilot lands at 12.2 m to 18.3 m, use a lower bound of 12.2 and an upper bound of 18.3. The probability is 0.6420.

Note that the graphing calculator solution gives slightly different results from those using the table, since the *z*-score values in the table are rounded to two decimal places.

The normal distribution curve continues to infinity in both directions. When determining a probability, sometimes you need to continue the area to infinity. The graphing calculator has no symbol for infinity, so a large number like 99 999 is used instead.

Your Turn

Kunal is trying out for the school football team. He wants to know how far he can kick the ball for a field goal. The table shows the data from 20 trials.

Field Goal Distance (yd)			
17	27	31	25
25	44	35	24
31	48	42	48
45	34	41	38
40	43	45	21

a) Determine the mean and standard deviation of the data.

b) What is the probability that Kunal kicks a distance of less than 30 yd?

c) What is the probability that Kunal kicks a distance of 20 yd to 40 yd?

In some sports, measurements are recorded using imperial units, such as yards. One yard is slightly shorter than one metre. 1 yd ≈ 0.9 m.

Processes

Selecting Tools and Computational Strategies

Did you have a choice of methods to use for this problem? If so, which did you choose? What were your reasons for the choice?

Consolidate and Debrief

Key Concepts

- The frequency polygon approximates the shape of the frequency distribution.

- You must use a range of values to determine the theoretical probability for a continuous random variable.

- The probability that a continuous random variable takes on any single value is zero.

- A normal distribution is a probability distribution around a central value, dropping off symmetrically to the right and left, forming a bell-like shape.

- You can determine the probability that a variable will lie within a range of values by finding an area under the normal distribution.

- You can use z-scores to determine probabilities, either from a table or by using technology.

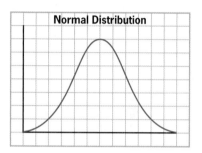

Reflect

R1. Consider the field goal distances in the Your Turn following Example 2. As Kunal practises and gains more skill, would you expect the mean and standard deviation to remain the same? Explain your answer.

R2. Relate to the graph of a normal distribution to explain why $P(z < -5)$ is almost zero.

Practise

Use this information to answer #1 to #4.

Roberta rides her bicycle to school. She records her times for one week, and determines a mean of 10.2 min and a standard deviation of 2.4 min. She believes the time follows a normal distribution.

Choose the best answer for #1 and #2.

1. What is the z-score for a trip that takes 13.8 min?

  A −3.6

  B −1.5

  C 1.5

  D 3.6

2. A trip has a z-score of −0.5. How long did the trip take?

  A 9.0 min

  B 9.7 min

  C 10.7 min

  D 11.4 min

3. What is the probability that a trip will take twice as long as the mean?

4. Communication Roberta makes similar measurements the following week, and calculates a different mean and standard deviation. Why did this happen? How can she obtain more reliable values for the mean and standard deviation?

Apply

5. The corner of Bloor and Bathurst streets in Toronto is the home of Honest Ed's, a huge discount store famous all over the world. The sign contains about 23 000 light bulbs.

The filament of an incandescent light bulb slowly evaporates, limiting the life of the bulb. Turning the bulb on and off also shortens its lifetime. Technicians tested a sample of 500 bulbs. The table shows the frequencies for the lifetime of the bulbs.

Lifetime (days)	Frequency
300–325	2
325–350	15
350–375	38
375–400	55
400–425	91
425–450	94
450–475	73
475–500	68
500–525	40
525–550	14
550–575	9
575–600	1

a) Sketch a frequency histogram and a frequency polygon for these data.

b) Estimate the mean life of these light bulbs.

c) Add a relative frequency column to the table.

d) What is the probability that a given light bulb will fail in 400 days or fewer?

e) If you want to be reasonably sure that there would never be a burned out bulb on the sign, how often should you replace all of the bulbs? Explain.

6. Mieke is using a tennis ball machine to launch tennis balls over the net at various speeds. The table shows the speeds from a sample of 40 launches.

Speed of Ball (km/h)			
63	69	62	63
60	62	58	63
59	65	67	64
51	57	58	57
63	60	62	61
58	68	61	53
60	56	50	59
60	66	62	69
61	55	57	65
61	63	63	71

a) Use an interval width of 5 km/h, starting at 49 km/h. Construct a frequency table.

b) Use your frequency table to construct a frequency histogram.

c) Add a frequency polygon to the frequency histogram.

d) Do the data appear to follow a normal distribution? Explain your answer.

e) Estimate the mean.

f) Add a relative frequency column to the table.

g) What is the probability that a given ball will launch at a speed of 59 to 69 km/h?

Processes

Selecting Tools and Computational Strategies
When dealing with large amounts of data, some methods are easier than others. What tools did you select to solve this problem? What were your reasons for the selection?

7. Refer to the tennis ball speed data in #6.

   a) Use an interval width of 2 km/h, starting at 49 km/h. Construct a frequency table.

   b) Use your frequency table to construct a frequency histogram.

   c) Add a frequency polygon to the frequency histogram.

   d) Estimate the mean.

   e) Which interval width made it easier to estimate the mean speed? Give a reason for your answer.

   f) Inspect the two frequency polygons. Which gives a clearer picture of the actual frequency distribution? Why is this so?

8. **Application** In the sport of archery, an archer controls the horizontal deviation of the arrow from the centre of the target by aiming the bow properly from left to right. Marian shot a total of 36 arrows toward a target and measured the horizontal deviation of each impact from the centre line of the target. A negative number indicates an error to the left, while a positive number indicates an error to the right.

Horizontal Error (cm)					
−2	5	−3	0	8	0
−5	−4	−1	−5	−3	−5
−1	0	0	−2	3	3
−6	2	−4	−1	6	3
−6	−1	−7	−4	2	−3
−8	1	−2	4	6	5

a) Use an interval width of 2 cm, starting at −10 cm. Construct a frequency table.

b) Add a relative frequency column to your frequency table.

c) What is the probability that the horizontal error is less than 4 cm to either side of the centre of the target?

d) Some archers use a sight to help them aim. Suppose an archer misadjusted the sight so that it had a bias to the left. How would this show up in the data?

9. **Application** Terry's Tree Farm planted Christmas tree seedlings last year. The table shows the current heights of a sample of 20 trees.

Tree Height (cm)			
37.4	35.0	34.8	35.7
32.4	35.2	38.0	36.1
32.8	38.0	38.5	37.6
32.0	36.3	31.1	35.5
30.4	34.1	36.2	35.8

a) Determine the mean height.

b) Determine the standard deviation of the heights.

c) Are there enough data to predict whether the distribution of the heights follows a normal distribution? Explain. Include a graph or table as part of your answer.

10. A student from region A scored 400 on a standardized math test with a mean of 350 and a standard deviation of 35. A student from region B scored 67 on a standardized math test with a mean of 62 and a standard deviation of 5. Both are being considered for a scholarship at the same university.

a) How can the university decide which candidate is the better student?

b) What assumptions must the university make?

c) Apply the method in part a), and determine which candidate is the better student. Give a reason for your answer.

11. Application In many cases, variables follow a distribution that falls off symmetrically to either side of a central maximum. Examples include heights of girls of the same age, lengths of parts produced by a machine, or blood pressures of a sample of patients. The British statistician Karl E. Pearson (1857–1936) suggested calling this curve the "normal distribution."

a) Suggest a practical example of a variable that you think should follow a normal distribution.

b) Search the Internet for measured values of your choice.

c) Copy the values into an appropriate technology.

d) Determine the mean and standard deviation of the data.

e) Select a value and determine the z-score for that value.

f) Determine the probability that the variable has a value greater than or equal to the value chosen in part e).

12. The Tuwheeler motorcycle factory produces pistons for motorcycle engines. The table shows the piston diameters for a production run of 20 pistons. The factory rejects pistons that have a diameter of less than 8.38 cm or more than 8.42 cm.

Diameter (cm)			
8.42	8.40	8.37	8.39
8.38	8.39	8.44	8.41
8.42	8.43	8.43	8.42
8.42	8.41	8.40	8.39
8.41	8.38	8.41	8.38

a) Determine the mean of these data.

b) Determine the standard deviation of these data.

c) Determine the z-scores that limit the acceptable range of diameters.

d) What is the probability that a given manufactured piston falls outside the acceptable range?

e) In a production run of 500 pistons, how many would be expected to be unacceptable?

13. Application A coal-fired power plant releases some radioactive substances into the air. For example, a 1000-MW coal plant releases a mean of 5200 kg of uranium per year, with a standard deviation of 1300 kg. The release of uranium follows a normal distribution.

a) What is the probability that the plant will release less than 4000 kg of uranium in a given year?

b) What is the probability that the plant will release more than 6000 kg of uranium in a given year?

c) What is the probability that the release will be within 10% of the mean?

Extend

14. Application A teacher has taught Grade 12 Mathematics for 25 years. He has kept records indicating that the long-term mean mark in his class is 72, with a standard deviation of 5. In his current class, the mean is 65, with a standard deviation of 7. He suspects that his tests have been harder this year, and decides to adjust all of the marks so that the mean becomes 72 with a standard deviation of 5. This process is known as "belling the marks," or "marking on the curve."

a) Suppose that you received a mark of 70 in this year's class. Devise a method to determine your mark after adjustment. Explain your method.

b) What is your adjusted mark?

c) Can you suggest any other reasons why the marks this year might be lower than expected?

15. Thinking Recall the soft drink volume data from Example 1. These data are already grouped, and the volumes of individual bottles are not known.

Volume (mL)	Frequency, f
490–492	0
492–494	0
494–496	2
496–498	11
498–500	43
500–502	81
502–504	48
504–506	14
506–508	1
508–510	0

a) How can you determine a more accurate estimate for the mean of these data? Devise an approach, and explain why you think it will work.

b) Carry out your plan. What is the mean?

c) Review the frequency polygon for these data. Does your mean make sense? Give a reason for your answer.

Applications of the Normal Distribution

Learning Goals

I am learning to

- recognize the general characteristics of a normal distribution
- use technology to simulate a normal distribution in order to investigate its properties
- determine probabilities for a normal distribution

> ## Minds On...

In the fall, apple picking is a popular activity in many orchards across Ontario.

- Would you expect that all of the apples on a tree have the same mass?

- Are the masses of the apples distributed normally? How can you tell?

- Are all distributions with a central maximum and a bell-like shape normal distributions?

> ## Action!

Investigate a Normal Distribution Using a Simulation

Materials

- computer with Fathom™

You can use technology such as Fathom™ or a graphing calculator to generate random values from a normal distribution. You can then increase the number of values to see what effect this has on the characteristics of the distribution.

A variety of apple has a mean mass of 150 g, with a standard deviation of 20 g. This is the underlying normal distribution.

Suppose you pick 20 of these apples from a tree, and determine the mean and standard deviation of your sample, $\bar{x}$ and s. How will these compare to the mean and standard deviation of the underlying normal distribution, μ and σ?

1. Open the Fathom™ file **AppleMasses.ftm** provided by your teacher. The data in this fil generated randomly from a distribution with a mean of 150 and a standard deviation of 20. You will see a collection, a case table with 20 random values from a normal distribution with a mean of 150 and a standard deviation of 20. You will also see a histogram of the data with the mean and median values displayed.

Apple Masses		
O a case	O a case	O a case
O a case	O a case	O a case
O a case	O a case	O a case
O a case	O a case	O a case

   Apple Masses

	Mass_g	<new>
=	randomNormal (150, 20)	
1	151.021	
2	144.209	
3	182.533	
4	124.535	
5	178.241	
6	174.852	
7	165.128	
8	134.738	
9	144.554	

   a) Do the data appear to lie around a mean of 150 g?

   b) Do most of the values fall within two standard deviations?

   c) How do the mean and standard deviation of the sample compare with those from the underlying normal distribution?

   d) Does the histogram approximate a normal distribution, with values symmetric about a central maximum? How do the mean and median compare?

   Apple Masses — Histogram

   median (Mass_g) = 152.3
   mean (Mass_g) = 152.337
   stdDev (Mass_g) = 18.0821
   — Density of Mass_g = normalDensity (x, 150, 20)

2. Press the **Rerandomize** button. This will select 20 different values for the masses of the apples. Press the **Rerandomize** button several times. Watch the effect on the graph and the measures.

   a) What changes do you see in the graph and in the measures? How do the mean and median compare?

   b) With a small number of values like this, how well does the sample approximate the underlying normal distribution?

3. Right click on the collection box, and select **New Cases…**. Add 80 more values for a total of 100. If necessary, adjust the scales of the axes on the graph.

   a) What differences can you see in the histogram with 100 cases?

   b) Press the **Rerandomize** button several times. Observe what happens to the measures and the histogram. How do the mean and median compare?

4. Repeat #3 for a total of 1000 cases, then a total of 10 000 cases. You can add only 5000 cases at a time, so you will need to perform this step twice to obtain a total of 10 000 cases.

5. **Reflect** Summarize how the number of data points in the sample affects the shape of the frequency histogram and the measures of sample mean and sample standard deviation.

6. **Extend Your Understanding** Suppose a sample of apples is taken from a different orchard, and more values appear to the left of the central peak than the right—that is, the distribution is skewed to the right. How would the values of the mean and median compare? How would they compare if the distribution were skewed to the left?

Example

Values Within One Standard Deviation of the Mean

Suppose the birth mass of a breed of guinea pig follows a normal distribution with a mean of 100 g and a standard deviation of 10 g.

a) What is the probability that a birth mass from a large sample lies within one standard deviation of the mean? two standard deviations?

b) Does the answer to part a) depend on the mean and standard deviation of the distribution?

Solution

a) Method 1: Use a z-Score Table

One standard deviation below the mean results in a z-score of -1, while one above the mean results in a z-score of $+1$. Two standard deviations below the mean results in a z-score of -2, while two above the mean results in a z-score of $+2$. Use the table on pages 480–481 to determine the probability that a value lies in each range.

$$P(-1 \leq z \leq 1)$$
$$= P(z \leq 1) - P(z \leq -1)$$
$$= 0.8413 - 0.1587$$
$$= 0.6826$$

$$P(-2 \leq z \leq 2)$$
$$= P(z \leq 2) - P(z \leq -2)$$
$$= 0.9772 - 0.0228$$
$$= 0.9544$$

The probability that a value lies within one standard deviation of the mean is about 68%, and within two standard deviations is about 95%.

Method 2: Use a Graphing Calculator

Use the **normalcdf(** function from the **DISTR** menu by inputting **normalcdf(−1,1,0,1)** and **normalcdf(−2,2,0,1)**. The probability that a value lies within one standard deviation of the mean is about 68% The probability that a value lies within two standard deviations of the mean is about 95%.

```
normalcdf(-1,1,▶
         .6826894809
normalcdf(-2,2,▶
         .954499876
```

b) Since one standard deviation from the mean will always result in z-scores of -1 and $+1$, the answer to part a) does not depend on the mean and standard deviation.

Your Turn

A sample of male patients at a hospital showed a mean systolic blood pressure of 124.7 mmHg with a standard deviation of 14.5 mmHg.

a) Use the z-score table on pages 480–481 to determine the probability that a measurement from a large sample lies within three standard deviations of the mean.

b) Use technology to determine the probability that a measurement from a large sample would lie within three standard deviations of the mean.

Key Concepts

- You can use the normal distribution to model the frequency and probability density distributions of continuous random variables.

- The normal distribution has a central peak, and is symmetric about the mean.

- The mean and median are equal.

- About 68% of the data values are within one standard deviation of the mean, about 95% of the data values are within two standard deviations of the mean, and about 99.7% are within three standard deviations of the mean.

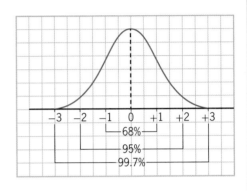

Reflect

R1. A factory produces bolts with a mean length of 5.0 cm and a standard deviation of 0.1 cm. You select a random sample from a batch and find that it has a length of 4.7 cm. Is this a surprising value? Explain your answer.

R2. Machine A fills 1000 one-kilogram honey jars using 1200 kg of honey. Machine B fills 1000 jars using 1050 kg of honey. When the jars are tested, 0.1% of the jars from each machine contain less than 1 kg of honey. Are these results possible? Explain your answer, using diagrams to help you.

Practise

Choose the best answer for #1 and #2.

1. Which of these situations might be reasonably expected to follow a normal distribution?

   A the heights of students in grade 3 at an elementary school

   B the mass of peanut butter in a sample of jars marked "1 kg"

   C the distance that a candidate for the football team can throw a football

   D all of these

2. Which statement is true concerning a normal distribution?

   A The curve is symmetrical about a central peak.

   B The median is always less than the mean.

   C All of the data values will occur within two standard deviations of the mean.

   D The mean of a sample always matches the mean of the underlying normal distribution.

3. A breed of adult cat has a mean mass of 4.2 kg with a standard deviation of 0.5 kg. An article in a pet magazine claims that 1 out of 40 such cats will have a mass of more than 5.2 kg. Does this make sense? Explain.

4. Communication A factory produces steel washers that will fit onto standard bolts. Why would a quality control engineer be interested in the mean and standard deviation of these washers?

Apply

5. Application A tire company produces bicycle tires with a mean outside diameter of 700 mm and a standard deviation of 13.2 mm.

a) Use technology to model a random sample of 10 tires from this company.

b) Determine the mean and standard deviation of your sample.

c) How closely do your mean and standard deviation match those of the underlying normal distribution?

d) Model random samples of 100 tires and 1000 tires.

e) Determine the sample mean and standard deviation for each sample in part d).

f) Summarize the values of $\bar{x}$, s, μ, and σ in a table for all three samples.

g) How do the values of the sample measures compare to the underlying normal distribution measures as the size of the sample increases?

6. To play an octave on a piano, your hand must span a distance of 16.4 cm. A sample of music students showed a mean hand span of 21.8 cm, with a standard deviation of 2.4 cm.

a) What is the probability that a student could not play an octave?

b) What is the probability that a student could play one and one-half octaves?

Literacy Link

If you start on any white key on a piano, such as C, and count up or down seven white keys, you will reach another C. This interval is known as an *octave*, because it contains eight notes.

7. Lithium cells used to power digital watches have a mean lifetime of 8 years with a standard deviation of 1.5 years. The Tempus Watch Company sells a sealed model of watch with power cells that are not replaceable. The watch costs $9.95, and the company offers a 5-year replacement warranty if the cell fails.

a) What percent of its watches would the company expect to replace under a 5-year warranty plan?

b) Assume that the company sells 100 000 watches this year, and it costs $5.00 to replace a defective watch, including shipping. How much should the company budget to replace watches under warranty?

c) An advertising executive suggests boosting sales by offering a 10-year warranty. Is this a reasonable idea? Use calculations similar to parts a) and b) to provide support for your answer.

8. The mean mark on a mathematics exam was 70%, with a standard deviation of 10%.

a) If 200 students wrote the exam, how many would be expected to score between 60% and 80%?

b) How many students would be expected to score above 90%?

c) How many students would be expected to score below 50%?

9. Thinking Precision racing pistons for a high-performance automobile engine need to have a diameter of 5 in. accurate to within 0.0001 in. A parts manufacturing company would like 95% of its pistons to fall within this range. What standard deviation is needed to meet this requirement?

✔ Achievement Check

10. Frank's Footlongs sells hot dogs at the beach. Analysis of his sales shows that the number of hot dogs sold on a given day follows a normal distribution with a mean of 120 and a standard deviation of 11.

a) Is it reasonable to treat these data as if they formed a continuous distribution? Give a reason for your answer.

b) What is a reasonable minimum number of hot dogs and buns for Frank to have on hand at the beginning of the day? Give reasons for your answer.

c) What is the probability that the stand will sell fewer than 25 hot dogs on a given day?

d) Frank's season lasts from May 1 until September 30. On how many days should he expect to sell between 100 and 140 hot dogs?

e) Should he expect to sell 200 or more hot dogs on at least one day during the season? Support your answer with numbers.

11. Application Honey jars from the farm where Doris works say they contain 500 g of honey. The table shows the actual amounts from a sample of 30 jars.

Mass of Honey (g)					
503	505	504	500	502	505
506	502	501	501	503	501
502	506	504	505	505	503
504	501	499	501	502	504
502	500	501	503	506	504

a) Determine the mean and standard deviation of the sample of honey jars.

b) What percent of the data in the table actually fall within one standard deviation of the mean?

c) How does the answer in part b) compare to the expected percent of the data within one standard deviation of the mean?

Extend

12. Rudy's Sandwich Shoppe sells corned beef sandwiches advertised to contain 200 g of corned beef. Rudy has set his slicing machine to a mean of 220 g. The actual amount follows a normal distribution. He ran a quality control check, and found that 5% of his sandwiches contained less than 200 g of corned beef.

a) What was the standard deviation of the amount of corned beef in the sandwiches?

b) Rudy would like to ensure that no more than 0.5% of the sandwiches contain less than 200 g of corned beef. Suggest two different actions that he can take.

c) From a business point of view, which action in part b) would be more desirable?

13. Communication Pafnuty Chebyshev was a Russian mathematician who worked in the field of statistics during the middle of the 19th century. Chebyshev's Theorem states that no more than $\frac{1}{k^2}$ of the values of a distribution lie more than k standard deviations from the mean. The value of k must be greater than 1. This theorem applies to all distributions, not just the normal distribution.

a) What is the maximum proportion of values that may lie more than two standard deviations from the mean?

b) Does this theorem agree with what you know about the normal distribution? Explain your answer, with examples.

c) Write an expression for the proportion of values that must lie within k standard deviations of the mean.

7.4

Confidence Intervals

Learning Goals

I am learning to

- distinguish among the meanings of common confidence levels such as 90%, 95%, and 99%
- determine the margin of error for a population mean estimated using a sample
- determine the upper and lower limits of the confidence interval

> ## Minds On...

Fishing is a popular activity in parks such as Algonquin Provincial Park. Many of the lakes in the park contain brook trout as well as lake trout. It is important to collect data on the fish populations and watch for any significant or sudden changes that may indicate problems with the health of the marine ecosystem.

- How can wildlife researchers determine reasonable estimates of the number and species distributions in a large lake?

- Why is it not possible to obtain exact numbers?

- How confident can researchers be that their estimates are close to the correct values?

> ## Action!

margin of error

- the range of values that a particular measurement is said to be within

- the smaller the margin of error, the greater the accuracy of the measurement

confidence interval

- the range of possible values of the measured statistic at a particular confidence level

A researcher might summarize the findings as "Lake trout make up 20.4% of the fish population in Lake Lavieille. This estimate is considered correct within ±3.0%, 19 times out of 20."

What does this statement mean?

Suppose the researcher samples the fish in the lake 20 times. The researcher is confident that the percent of lake trout found in the samples will be within 3% of 20.4% in 19 out of the 20 samples. The **margin of error** is 3% above or below the mean.

The **confidence interval** range is

$$20.4\% - 3\% = 17.4\% \quad \text{to} \quad 20.4\% + 3\% = 23.4\%$$

The **confidence level** is 19 out of 20, or 95%. How does this percent connect to the standard deviation of a normal distribution?

Investigate Simulating Fish Populations Using Game Chips

Complete this investigation as a class.

Materials

- bag
- 200 game chips (blue and other colours)

1. Use a bag containing 200 game chips. The bag contains a number of blue chips preselected by the teacher but unknown to the students, as well as other chips to make up a total of 200 in each bag.

2. Ensure that the chips are well mixed. Reach into the bag and pull out 30 chips at random, replacing the chosen chip each time. This is the sample size, n. Record the total number of blue chips chosen in the 30 trials. Determine the experimental probability, p, of getting a blue chip. Express p as a decimal.

Confidence Level	z-Score
90%	1.645
95%	1.960
99%	2.576

confidence level

- the probability that a particular statistic is within the range indicated by the margin of error
- commonly used confidence levels are 90%, 95%, and 99%

3. Calculate the margin of error, as a decimal, from the formula

$$E = z\sqrt{\frac{p(1-p)}{n}}$$

Use the z-score for a confidence level of 95%.

4. Use the margin of error to determine the confidence interval. Express the probability of getting a blue chip and the confidence interval as percents.

5. Have several class members take turns pulling 30 chips from the bag with replacement. Record the number of blue chips chosen in every 30 trials. Pool the class results for the total number of blue chips drawn. Determine the margin of error and the confidence interval for the class results using a confidence level of 95%.

6. **Reflect** Compare the individual confidence interval from #4 with that for the class results in #5. Why does the confidence interval decrease as the sample size n increases?

7. **Extend Your Understanding** You could use technology such as Fathom™ to simulate a large number of experiments.

   a) Open the Fathom™ file **FishSample.ftm** provided by your teacher. This data file simulates drawing 30 chips from a population with a proportion of blue chips equal to the value of p on the slider. The values plotted on the graph represent the proportion of blue chips in your sample, plus or minus the margin of error for a confidence level of 95%.

   b) Rerandomize the sample. How do the upper and lower bounds on the confidence interval change? Does the true proportion fall inside of your confidence interval?

   c) Right click on the sample and add another 30 cases. How do the upper and lower bounds on the confidence interval change?

   d) Add another 140 cases. How does the dot plot change? How do the upper and lower bounds on the confidence interval change?

e) Summarize the effect of increasing the number in the sample on the margin of error and the confidence interval. A sample Fathom™ screen for a 40% probability of getting a blue chip is shown.

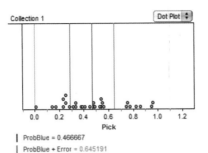

The minimum sample size required to obtain reliable results for the confidence interval is usually at least 30.

| ProbBlue = 0.466667
| ProbBlue + Error = 0.645191
| ProbBlue − Error = 0.288142

Inspect Collection 1

| Cases | **Measures** | Comments | Display | Categories |

Measure	Value	Formula
Count	30	count (Pick)
NumBlue	14	count (Pick ≤ V1)
ProbBlue	0.466667	$\dfrac{\text{NumBlue}}{\text{Count}}$
Error	0.178525	$1.96 \text{ sqrt } \left(\text{ProbBlue} \dfrac{(1 - \text{ProbBlue})}{\text{Count}}\right)$
<new>		

Example 1

Lake Trout in Lake Lavieille

Lake Lavieille is one of the largest lakes in Algonquin Park. In 2009, 234 lake trout were caught out of a total catch of 911. In 2012, 141 lake trout were caught out of a catch of 689.

a) Determine the percent of lake trout caught for each year.

b) Determine the margin of error for each year. Use a 95% confidence level.

c) Determine the confidence interval for each year.

d) Do the two confidence intervals overlap? Give a specific example.

e) Is it reasonable to conclude that the percent of lake trout in Lake Lavieille decreased from 2009 to 2012? Give a reason for your answer.

> Solution

a) For 2009:

$$p = \frac{234}{911}$$

$$\approx 0.257$$

For 2012:

$$p = \frac{141}{689}$$

$$\approx 0.205$$

The percent of lake trout caught is about 25.7% for 2009 and 20.1% for 2012.

b)

Confidence Level	z-Score
90%	1.645
95%	1.960
99%	2.576

For 2009:

$$E = z\sqrt{\frac{p(1-p)}{n}}$$

$$\approx 1.96\sqrt{\frac{0.257(1-0.257)}{911}}$$

$$\approx 0.028$$

For 2012:

$$E = z\sqrt{\frac{p(1-p)}{n}}$$

$$\approx 1.96\sqrt{\frac{0.205(1-0.205)}{689}}$$

$$\approx 0.030$$

The margin of error is about 2.8% for 2009 and 3.0% for 2012.

c) For 2009:

Lower limit = 25.7% − 2.8%
= 22.9%

Upper limit = 25.7% + 2.8%
= 28.5%

For 2012:

Lower limit = 20.5% − 3.0%
= 17.1%

Upper limit = 20.5% + 3.0%
= 23.1%

The confidence interval is 22.9% to 28.5% for 2009 and 17.1% to 23.1% for 2012.

d) The confidence intervals overlap; for example, both include 23.0%.

e) A 95% confidence level is used. The two confidence intervals overlap, meaning that the 2012 data could fall within the 2009 confidence interval. You cannot definitely conclude that the percent of lake trout has decreased.

How would the resulting intervals change if you used a different confidence interval?

Your Turn

An opinion poll surveyed 100 households who were watching television at a particular time. Of these, 75% were watching *Hockey Night in Canada*.

a) Determine the margin of error at a 99% confidence level.

b) Determine the confidence interval for this situation.

c) How would a news source state the results?

Example 2

Interpreting Survey Results

The first Major League Baseball franchise outside of the United States was the Montréal Expos, who played from 1969 to 2004. In 2005, the Expos moved to Washington, DC, and are now known as the Washington Nationals. A survey was conducted to determine whether a major league baseball team should come back to Montréal. Of the 1589 people surveyed, 69% were in favour of baseball coming back.

a) Determine the margin of error for this survey at a confidence level of 95%.

b) For what range of percents can you be 95% confident that people would be in favour of baseball returning to Montréal?

c) A second survey at a confidence level of 95% found that 56% were in favour, with a margin of error of 5.2%. Approximately how many people were surveyed?

Solution

a) In the first survey, $p = 69\%$.

$$E = z\sqrt{\frac{p(1-p)}{n}}$$

$$E = 1.96\sqrt{\frac{0.69(1-0.69)}{1589}}$$

$$E \approx 0.023$$

The margin of error is $\pm 2.3\%$.

b) The lower end of the range is $69\% - 2.3\% = 66.7\%$. The upper end of the range is $69\% + 2.3\% = 71.3\%$. There is a 95% chance that the percent of people in favour of another major league baseball team in Montréal is between 66.7% and 71.3%.

c) In the second survey, $p = 56\%$.

The margin of error is $E = 5.2\%$.

$$E = z\sqrt{\frac{p(1-p)}{n}}$$ Rearrange to solve for *n*.

$$E^2 = z^2\left(\frac{p(1-p)}{n}\right)$$ Square both sides to eliminate the square root.

$$n = \frac{z^2(p(1-p))}{E^2}$$ Multiply both sides by *n*. Divide both sides by E^2.

$$n = \frac{(1.96)^2(0.56(1-0.56))}{0.052^2}$$ Substitute and evaluate.

$$n \approx 350$$

The second sample surveyed about 350 people.

Your Turn

A pharmaceutical manufacturer makes more than 500 000 pills of a certain drug each day. The company randomly samples 400 pills daily to check that they meet the proper weight and size standards. On a given day, 52 pills were found to be substandard.

a) What is the margin of error for this sample at a confidence level of 90%?

b) If the company would like to cut the margin of error in half, how would the sample size have to change?

Repeated Sampling

Suppose that samples of the same size are repeatedly taken from a population that follows a normal distribution with a mean of μ and a standard deviation of σ. The means of the samples will be normally distributed with a mean of μ and a standard deviation of $\sigma_{\bar{x}} = \frac{\sigma}{\sqrt{n}}$.

Consider the role of the sample size n. If $n = 1$, the standard deviation of the sample means is the same as the standard deviation of the normal distribution. However, as the value of n increases, the standard deviation of the sample means decreases. The usual rule is that a value of $n = 30$ produces a reasonable estimate of the population mean.

You can calculate the margin of error for a sample mean from the formula $E = z\frac{\sigma}{\sqrt{n}}$ or $E = z\sigma_{\bar{x}}$. This is also known as the standard error.

Example 3

Determining Confidence Levels for a Sample Mean

At an agricultural fair, the masses of 8 giant pumpkins entered in a contest were 11 kg, 13 kg, 15 kg, 18 kg, 12 kg, 14 kg, 10 kg, and 16 kg. Results from past fairs suggest that the masses are normally distributed with a mean of 14.2 kg and a standard deviation of 2.5 kg. Determine a 90% confidence interval for the sample mean.

> ### Solution

Calculate the sample mean and standard deviation of the sample means.

$$\bar{x} = \frac{11 + 13 + 15 + 18 + 12 + 14 + 10 + 16}{8}$$

$$\approx 13.6$$

$$\sigma_{\bar{x}} = \frac{\sigma}{\sqrt{n}}$$

$$= \frac{2.5}{\sqrt{8}}$$

$$\approx 0.88$$

Project Prep

Does your project include continuous variables? Can you calculate and apply confidence intervals?

For a 90% confidence level, $z = 1.645$.

Lower limit $= \bar{x} - E$
$= \bar{x} - z\sigma_{\bar{x}}$
$\approx 13.6 - (1.645)(0.88)$
≈ 12.2

Upper limit $= \bar{x} + E$
$= \bar{x} + z\sigma_{\bar{x}}$
$\approx 13.6 + (1.645)(0.88)$
≈ 15.0

The 90% confidence interval for the mean mass is 12.2 kg to 15.0 kg. This means that with 90% confidence, you can predict that the mean mass of a pumpkin lies within the interval from 12.2 kg to 15 kg.

Your Turn

A consumers' group tested batches of light bulbs to see how long they lasted. The results, in hours, from one batch were 998, 1234, 1523, 1760, 937, 1193, 996, 1002, 986, 1285, 1163, and 1716. The manufacturer claims that the life of the light bulbs is normally distributed with a mean of 1200 h and a standard deviation of 420 h.

a) Calculate the mean of the sample and the standard deviation for the sample means.

b) Determine the 99% confidence interval for the sample mean.

Consolidate and Debrief

Key Concepts

- The confidence level is the probability that a particular statistic is within the range indicated by the margin of error.

- Commonly used confidence levels are 90%, 95%, and 99%. These are related to the z-scores of the distribution.

- A margin of error is the range of values that a particular statistic is said to be within. For a statistic with probability p, the margin of error is $E = z\sqrt{\dfrac{p(1-p)}{n}}$.

- The greater the sample size, the smaller the margin of error. The smaller the margin of error, the greater the accuracy of the measurement.

- The confidence interval is the range of possible values of the measured statistic.

- For repeated samples of the same size taken from the same population with a normal distribution, the standard deviation of the sample means is $\sigma_{\bar{x}} = \dfrac{\sigma}{\sqrt{n}}$ and the margin of error is $E = z\dfrac{\sigma}{\sqrt{n}}$.

Reflect

R1. Can you use the terms "confidence level" and "margin of error" interchangeably? Give reasons for your answer.

R2. A computer manufacturer found that a mean of 5.6% of a model of tablet computers were returned as defective within one year. The service department considered this number accurate within 1.4%, 9 times out of 10. What information does the confidence interval provide? What is the benefit of using the confidence interval?

R3. A 95% confidence interval can be stated as 19 times out of 20. Restate a 90% and a 99% confidence interval in a similar manner.

Practise

Choose the best answer for #2 and #3.

1. Common confidence levels are 90%, 95%, and 99%. A sample is taken from a population with a given mean and standard deviation. Within approximately how many standard deviations of the mean will the values in the confidence interval lie for a

   a) 90% confidence level?

   b) 95% confidence level?

   c) 99% confidence level?

2. A poll conducted by the student newspaper found that 78% of the students who ate lunch at the school cafeteria ordered a salad at least twice per week. The poll is considered accurate within ±5%, 17 times out of 20. What is the confidence level for the poll?

   A 75%

   B 85%

   C 95%

   D 98%

3. During a municipal election the local newspaper polled 251 people. The paper reported that 57% said they were in favour of candidate A for mayor. The result was considered accurate within 6.1%, 19 times out of 20. Which of the following statements is false?

   A The margin of error is 6.1%.

   B In a similar poll, 95% of the time between 50.9% and 63.1% of the people would be found in favour.

   C The confidence interval is 57% ± 6.1%.

   D In a similar poll, 95% of the time 57% or more of the people would be found in favour.

4. An automobile dealer offers a new line of tires. The tires last a mean of 75 000 km with a standard deviation of 5000 km, following a normal distribution. The tire life experienced by 100 customers is recorded. What is the expected standard deviation of the sample means?

Apply

5. The Canadian commercial pilot written exam consists of 100 multiple choice questions. Last year, the students enrolled in a community college aviation course recorded a mean mark of 82% among 25 candidates.

   a) Determine the margin of error at a 99% confidence level.

   b) Determine the confidence interval for the exam marks.

   c) State the results in the usual format for the course newsletter.

6. **Communication** A political party received an average of 34% support in recent polls plus or minus 3.4%, 19 times out of 20. Two subsequent polls showed 38% support and 27% support. How would you report on the meaning of these polls to the party membership?

7. **Application** A Single Crème cookie is made using a cream filling between two wafers. The amount of cream follows a normal distribution with a mean of 25 g and a standard deviation of 2.0 g. The company claims its new Double Crème line contains twice the amount of filling. A random sample of 20 such cookies were found to contain cream content as shown.

Mass of Cream (g)				
48.9	47.3	47.3	45.5	52.9
50.1	46.0	47.9	48.5	48.2
47.5	51.9	49.7	47.8	50.1
46.9	51.0	45.9	45.4	47.1

a) Calculate the mean of the sample and the standard deviation for the sample means. What assumption must you make?

b) Determine the 95% confidence interval for the sample mean.

c) Is the company justified in claiming that the Double Crème line contains twice the filling of the Single Crème line? Give reasons for your answer.

8. A concrete manufacturer knows from experience that setting times for concrete follow a normal distribution with a standard deviation of $\sigma = 8.5$ min. The manufacturer wants to use the slogan "Our concrete quick-sets in t minutes" in its advertising campaign. A technician pours 25 test squares of equal size and finds the mean setting time to be 72.2 min.

a) Determine a 95% confidence interval for the actual mean setting time of the concrete.

b) Advise the manufacturer on a reasonable value for t. Give a reason for your answer.

9. A honey farm rates its honey on a colour scale from 1 to 20, ranging from very light orange to deep orange. The colour of honey follows a normal distribution with a standard deviation of 2.5. A technician tests a sample of 50 jars of honey, resulting in a sample mean of 12. Determine a 95% confidence interval for the colour of the honey.

10. A survey of businesses showed that a mean of 17% of gross income was spent on office overhead, with a standard deviation of 5%, following a normal distribution. At a 99% confidence level, the margin of error was 10.5%. How many businesses were surveyed?

11. As part of Earth Day celebrations, an environmental scientist participated in a program to measure water clarity in 70 locations in Lake Ontario using a clarity measuring disk. The scientist reported that the lake water was clear to a mean depth of 5 m with a standard deviation of 1 m. The margin of error was 0.20 m. What confidence level was used?

12. A study of patients with low-back pain reported that the sample mean duration of the pain was 18.3 months. The duration follows a normal distribution in the population with a standard deviation of 5.9 months. The margin of error for the population mean was 1.5 months at a 95% confidence level. How many patients were in the study?

13. A manufacturer of computer hardware knows that the life of its hard drives follows a normal distribution with a standard deviation of 2400 h. Over the past three years, the mean life, based on a sample of 900 hard drives, was 16 000 h of use. What is the 95% confidence interval for the mean life of a hard drive?

✔ **Achievement Check**

14. When tomato farmers harvest their crop, they use an automated tomato picker that separates the tomato from the vine and eliminates any non-ripe tomatoes. The process of eliminating the non-ripe tomatoes is not perfect due to the speed with which the tomatoes are actually picked. Some green tomatoes get into the load. The buyer takes a single scoop of tomatoes from a random spot in the load. A sample of 300 tomatoes contains 92% of acceptable standard.

a) What is the confidence interval of the load if the confidence level is 95%?

b) The current load measures 41.992 tonnes. What is the interval for the mass of acceptable tomatoes?

c) Tomatoes sell for $94.40 per tonne. What is the range of values that this load is worth?

d) A load is accepted as long as the sample contains at least 67% acceptable tomatoes. How does the range of values change for a load at this level?

Literacy Link

The term *tonne* refers to the SI or metric unit equal to 1000 kg. The term *ton* refers to the imperial unit equal to 2000 lb.

15. A friend shows you a caption from the school newspaper:

"Two recent polls show that 57% of students would vote for Adam and 51% would vote for Meghan in the next student council election. These results are accurate to within ±3%, 19 times in 20."

Explain what the caption means.

Extend

16. Thinking Suppose you select 30 men from the entire population of 20-year-old men, and measure their weights.

a) Are you more likely to end up with men close to the population mean or far away from the population mean? Give a reason for your answer.

b) What effect does this have on the standard deviation of the sample mean compared to the population mean?

c) How does the formula for the standard deviation of the sample means, $\sigma_{\bar{x}} = \dfrac{\sigma}{\sqrt{n}}$, fit with the effect in part b)?

17. Consider the formula for the margin of error: $E = z\sqrt{\dfrac{p(1-p)}{n}}$. A poll is being conducted to determine the percent of voters who will vote for candidate Alpha with a confidence level of 95%. What is the minimum number of voters who must be interviewed to guarantee a margin of error of no more than 2%, regardless of the value of p? Explain your reasoning.

Connections to Discrete Random Variables

Learning Goals

I am learning to

- make connections between a normal distribution and a binomial distribution
- make connections between a normal distribution and a hypergeometric distribution
- recognize the role of the number of trials in these connections

 Minds On...

Recall from Chapter 4 that tossing a coin several times and recording the number of heads obtained is an example of a binomial distribution.

- How does the shape of the distribution depend on the number of times the experiment is tried?
- Predict the form of a graph of the number of heads possible when a coin is flipped five times. Make a sketch of your prediction.

Action!

Investigate 1 Compare the Binomial Distribution to the Normal Distribution

Materials

- computer with Fathom™

A coin is tossed five times, and the number of heads is recorded. What does the probability distribution look like? How does its appearance change as the number of tosses is increased?

1. Open the Fathom™ file **CoinToss.ftm** provided by your teacher. This file shows the probability distribution for the number of heads flipped on five trials. The binomial probability for each possible number of heads is shown in blue. The approximate normal distribution is shown in green superimposed over the binomial distribution.

   To approximate the binomial distribution with a normal distribution, you can calculate the mean from the formula $\mu = np$, and the standard deviation from the formula $\sigma = \sqrt{npq}$. The derivation of these formulas is beyond the scope of this course.

2. How well does the normal distribution match the binomial distribution?

Coin Toss | Rerandomize

Coin Toss

	numheads	P_numheads	<new>
=	caseIndex − 1	binomialProbability (numheads, n , p)	
1	0	0.03125	
2	1	0.15625	
3	2	0.3125	
4	3	0.3125	
5	4	0.15625	
6	5	0.03125	

Coin Toss | Scatter Plot ⬍

P_numheads vs numheads (0.35, 0.30, 0.25, 0.20, 0.15, 0.10, 0.05, 0.00 on y-axis; 0 1 2 3 4 5 6 on x-axis)

— P_numheads = binomialProbability (round (x), n , p)
— P_numheads = normalDensity (x , mean, stddev)

Inspect Coin Toss

Cases | **Measures** | Comments | Display | Categor…

Measure	Value	Formula
n	5	count ( ) − 1
p	0.5	
q	0.5	
mean	2.5	n • p
stddev	1.11803	sqrt (n • p • q)
<new>		

3. Right click on the collection box, and add 5 new cases. Adjust the scales on the axes of the graph if necessary. How is the fit with 10 tosses of the coin?

4. Right click on the collection box, and add 10 new cases. Adjust the scales on the axes of the graph if necessary. How is the fit with 20 tosses of the coin?

5. Reflect How does the fit of the normal distribution to the binomial distribution depend on the number of trials? Use your Fathom™ simulation to try a larger number of trials, such as 100 and then 1000.

6. Extend Your Understanding Suppose that a weighted coin is used in the coin toss. Now the probability of getting a head is only 0.3.

a) Predict the effect on the binomial distribution for a large number of trials. How would it compare to the normal distribution?

b) Adjust the probability values for p and q in the Fathom™ simulation, and check your prediction. Were you right? Explain your reasoning.

You can "step back" the Fathom™ simulation by choosing **Undo** from the **Edit** menu. Alternatively, you can use the keyboard shortcut **CTRL-z**.

Investigate 2 Compare the Hypergeometric Distribution to the Normal Distribution

Materials

• computer with Fathom™

A committee of 4 is chosen from a group of 200 people. How many males are on the committee? How does the distribution change as the size of the committee is increased? Does the population size have any effect?

1. Open the Fathom™ file **Committee.ftm** provided by your teacher. The file shows the probability distribution for the number of males selected in a committee of 4 people from a sample of 100 males and 100 females. The hypergeometric probability for each possible number of males is shown in blue. The approximate normal distribution is shown in green over the hypergeometric distribution.

   If the sample size is small compared to the population size, the probability of selecting a male is approximately equal to the number of males divided by the population size.

   To approximate the hypergeometric distribution with a normal distribution, you can calculate the mean from the formula $\mu = np$ and the standard deviation from the formula $\sigma = \sqrt{npq\left(\dfrac{NP - n}{NP - 1}\right)}$. The derivation of these formulas is beyond the scope of this course.

2. How well does the normal distribution match the hypergeometric distribution?

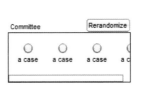

Committee			
	nummales	**P_nummales**	**<new>**
=	caseIndex – 1	hyperGeomProbability (nummale	
1	0	0.0606204	
2	1	0.249981	
3	2	0.378798	
4	3	0.249981	
5	4	0.0606204	

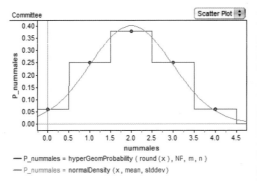

Committee

— P_nummales = hyperGeomProbability (round (x), NF, m, n)
— P_nummales = normalDensity (x, mean, stddev)

Inspect Committee

Cases **Measures** Comments Display Categories

Measure	Value	Formula
m	100	
f	100	
NP	200	m + f
n	4	count ( ) – 1
p	0.5	m
q	0.5	f
mean	2	n•p
stddev	0.992...	sqrt (n•p•q $\dfrac{(NP - n)}{(NP - 1)}$)
<new>		

3. Change the committee membership from 4 to 10. Right click on the collection box, and add 6 new cases. Adjust the scales on the axes of the graph if necessary. How is the fit with 10 members on the committee?

4. Change the committee membership to 20. Right click on the collection box, and add 10 new cases. Adjust the scales on the axes of the graph if necessary. How is the fit with 20 members on the committee?

5. **Reflect** The committee membership must remain a small fraction of the population size, typically less than one-tenth. Why is this necessary? Consider the values of p and q in the above investigation in your response.

6. **Extend Your Understanding** Suppose that a committee of 4 were chosen in a random selection from a very small population, say a club with 6 male members and 2 female members. Can you see any problems with calculating the number of males on the committee? Consider some extreme cases. Use the Fathom™ simulation from the investigation to explore different scenarios.

You can calculate a binomial probability using the formula from chapter 4. However, this formula requires the use of factorials. If the number of successes being considered is large, this can lead to a large number of computations. You can avoid this by using the approximation.

The normal approximation for a binomial distribution is usually considered reasonable if the values of np and nq are both greater than 5: $np > 5$ and $nq > 5$.

The normal approximation for a hypergeometric distribution is usually considered reasonable if the sample size is small compared to the size of the population, typically less than one-tenth: $n < \frac{1}{10}NP$, where n is the sample size and NP is the size of the population.

Since the binomial and hypergeometric distributions are discrete but the normal distribution is continuous, you must apply a **continuity correction** when using the approximation.

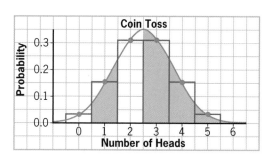

For example, suppose you want to determine the probability that, in 5 tosses of a coin, there is exactly 1 head. Refer to the graph shown.

The area under the normal distribution that represents this probability runs from 0.5 to 1.5. Therefore, you must calculate $P(0.5 \leq X \leq 1.5)$.

continuity correction

• a correction applied when using the normal approximation to correct for the difference between a discrete and continuous distribution

Similarly, if you want the probability of getting 3 or more heads, you need the area under the graph from 2.5 to infinity on the right, or $P(X \geq 2.5)$.

On the other hand, if you want to determine the probability of getting more than 3 heads, you need to calculate $P(X \geq 3.5)$.

Example 1

Normal Approximation for a Binomial Distribution

Suzette rolls a die 36 times. She records the number of times the die shows a 6.

a) Is it reasonable to approximate this distribution with a normal distribution? Give a reason for your answer.

b) Determine the mean and standard deviation of the normal approximation.

c) Determine the probability that the die will show a 6 at least 10 times.

d) What is the probability that the die will show a 6 more than 10 times, fewer than 10 times, and at most 10 times?

Solution

a) $np = 36 \times \dfrac{1}{6}$
   $= 6$

   $nq = 36 \times \dfrac{5}{6}$
   $= 30$

Recall that in a binomial distribution there are only two outcomes: success and failure. The probability of a success is p, and the probability of a failure is q.

Since both of these are greater than 5, the normal approximation is reasonable in this case.

b) $\mu = np$

   $= 36 \times \dfrac{1}{6}$

   ≈ 6

   $\sigma = \sqrt{npq}$

   $= \sqrt{36 \times \dfrac{1}{6} \times \dfrac{5}{6}}$

   ≈ 2.236

The mean is 6, and the standard deviation is 2.236.

c) Since you want the die to show 6 at least 10 times, you must apply a continuity correction and calculate $P(X \geq 9.5)$.

Method 1:
Use a Table

Calculate the z-score for 9.5.

$z = \dfrac{X - \mu}{\sigma}$

$\approx \dfrac{9.5 - 6}{2.236}$

≈ 1.565

Refer to the table on pages 480–481.

$P(X \geq 9.5) = 1 - P(x < 9.5)$
$= 1 - P(z < 1.57)$
$= 1 - 0.9418$
$= 0.0582$

The probability of 6 occurring 10 or more times is about 0.0582.

Method 2:
Use a Graphing Calculator

Use the **normalcdf(** function from the **DISTR** menu to calculate $P(X > 9.5)$ by inputting **normalcdf(9.5,999999, 6,2.236)**.

```
normalcdf(9.5,9▸
          .0587568658
```

The probability of 6 occurring 10 or more times is about 0.0588.

Processes

Reflecting
Why do the two methods in part c) not give exactly the same answer? Which method is more accurate? Why? Can you get a better answer from the table by interpolating between two probabilities? Try this, and see how the two methods compare.

d) If you want more than 10 successes, calculate $P(X \geq 10.5)$ by inputting normalcdf(10.5,999999,6,2.236). The probability is about 0.022.

```
normalcdf(10.5,▸
      .0220823814
normalcdf(-9999▸
      .9412431342
normalcdf(-9999▸
      .9779176186
```

If you want fewer than 10 successes, calculate $P(X \leq 9.5)$ by inputting **normalcdf(−999999,9.5,6,2.236)**. The probability is about 0.941.

If you want at most 10 successes, calculate $P(X \leq 10.5)$ by inputting **normalcdf(−999999,10.5,6,2.236)**. The probability is about 0.978.

Your Turn

The probability of rolling a 6 on a weighted die is 0.25. The die is rolled 25 times.

a) Is it reasonable to approximate this distribution with a normal distribution? Give reasons for your answer.

b) Determine the mean and standard deviation of the normal approximation.

c) Determine the probability that the die will show a 6 fewer than 8 times.

Example 2

Normal Approximation for a Hypergeometric Distribution

Chris works at a local daycare on a co-op work term. Chris plays a game with the children that involves pulling marbles from a bag. The bag contains 24 black marbles and 36 red marbles, well mixed. One of the children reaches in and takes out 5 marbles without looking. Chris records the number of black marbles.

a) Is it reasonable to approximate this distribution with a normal distribution? Give a reason for your answer.

b) Determine the mean and standard deviation of the normal approximation.

c) What is the probability that exactly 3 of the marbles are black?

d) What is the probability that a child pulls out at least 3 black marbles? more than 3 black marbles? fewer than 3 black marbles? at most 3 black marbles?

e) How does the answer to part c) compare with the probability calculated from the hypergeometric distribution?

Solution

a) There are 60 marbles in the bag, of which 5 are chosen. The number of trials is less than 10% of the population. The normal approximation is reasonable for this hypergeometric distribution.

b)
$$\mu = np$$
$$= 5 \times \frac{24}{60}$$
$$= 2$$

$$\sigma = \sqrt{npq\left(\frac{NP - n}{NP - 1}\right)}$$
$$= \sqrt{5 \times \frac{24}{60} \times \frac{36}{60}\left(\frac{60 - 5}{60 - 1}\right)}$$
$$\approx 1.058$$

The mean is 2, and the standard deviation is 1.058.

c) To determine the probability of 3 black marbles, you must calculate $P(2.5 \leq X \leq 3.5)$. Use the **normalcdf** function from the **DISTR** menu by inputting **normalcdf(2.5,3.5,2,1.058)**.

```
normalcdf(2.5,3▸
        .2401238396
```

If you prefer to use the table method for parts c) and d), follow steps similar to those used in Example 1, part c), Method 1. What z-score values will you use?

The probability of getting exactly 3 black marbles is about 0.240.

d) If you want at least 3 black marbles, calculate $P(X \geq 2.5)$ by inputting **normalcdf(2.5,999999,2,1.058)**. The probability is about 0.318.

```
normalcdf(2.5,9▸
        .3182529417
normalcdf(3.5,9▸
        .0781291021
```

If you want more than 3 black marbles, calculate $P(X \geq 3.5)$ by inputting **normalcdf(3.5,3.5,2,1.058)**. The probability is about 0.078.

If you want fewer than 3 black marbles, calculate $P(X < 2.5)$ by inputting **normalcdf(−999999,2.5,2,1.058)**. The probability is about 0.682.

```
normalcdf(-9999▸
        .6817470583
normalcdf(-9999▸
        .9218708979
```

If you want at most 3 black marbles, calculate $P(X < 3.5)$ by inputting **normalcdf(−999999,3.5,2,1.058)**. The probability is about 0.922.

To locate the nPr and nCr functions on some graphing calculators, select the MATH PRB functions. Explore your own calculator and record how to access these functions.

e) There is no hypergeometric probability function on a graphing calculator. You can use the combinatoric method from section 4.5.

$$P(X = 3) = \frac{{}_{24}C_3 \times {}_{36}C_2}{{}_{60}C_5}$$
$$\approx 0.233$$

```
24 nCr 3*36 nCr▸
        .2334738073
```

The probability of getting exactly 3 black marbles is about 0.23. The two answers are about the same.

Your Turn

Allison has a drawer full of unmatched socks. The drawer contains 30 blue socks, 30 green socks, and 30 yellow socks. She pulls seven socks from the drawer and records the number of blue socks in the sample.

a) Is it reasonable to approximate this distribution with a normal distribution? Give a reason for your answer.

b) Determine the mean and standard deviation of the normal approximation.

c) What is the probability that 3, 4, or 5 of the socks are blue?

Consolidate and Debrief

Key Concepts

- As the number of trials increases, a binomial distribution takes on the characteristics of a normal distribution.

- If the values of np and nq are both greater than 5, you can approximate the binomial distribution using a normal distribution.

- If the sample size is small compared to the population size, a hypergeometric distribution takes on the characteristics of a normal distribution.

- If the sample size is less than one-tenth of the population size, $n < \frac{1}{10} NP$, you can approximate the hypergeometric distribution using a normal distribution.

- You must use a continuity correction when approximating a discrete distribution with a normal distribution. For example, if you want the probability of rolling a 6 exactly 3 times, you must calculate $P(2.5 \leq X \leq 3.5)$. If you want the probability of rolling at least 3 sixes, you must calculate $P(X \geq 2.5)$. However, if you want the probability of rolling more than 3 sixes, you must calculate $P(X \geq 3.5)$.

Reflect

R1. Suggest another situation that is usually modelled with a binomial distribution but could reasonably be approximated with a normal distribution.

R2. Suggest another situation that is usually modelled with a hypergeometric distribution but could reasonably be approximated with a normal distribution.

R3. Suggest possible reasons why you might prefer to use a normal approximation rather than a binomial or hypergeometric distribution.

R4. Describe a situation where it is not possible to use a normal approximation for the binomial or hypergeometric distribution.

Practise

Choose the best answer for #1 and #2.

1. A card is randomly drawn from a deck of 52. Drawing a diamond is a success and anything else is a failure. The card is replaced and the deck is shuffled. The experiment is repeated 30 times. To model this experiment using a normal distribution, what mean and standard deviation should you use?

   A 7.5, 2.372

   B 7.5, 5.625

   C 2.739, 2.372

   D 2.739, 5.625

2. A bag of jellybeans contains 200 beans, of which 30 are red. Susan reaches into the bag and pulls out 15 beans at random. To model this experiment using a normal distribution, what standard deviation should you use?

   A 1.913

   B 1.778

   C 1.383

   D 1.333

3. Two dice are rolled. A double is considered a win, and anything else is a loss. What is the minimum number of rolls that should be made to model this situation using a normal distribution?

4. A barrel at the Pro Shop contains 30 white golf balls, 20 yellow golf balls, and 10 orange golf balls. A contest requires a contestant to blindly select several balls without replacement. The prize depends on the number of orange golf balls obtained. What is the maximum number of balls that could be selected to model the contest using a normal approximation?

5. Five cards are dealt from a deck of 52. The number of hearts is counted.

   a) Is it reasonable to model this distribution with a normal distribution? Explain.

   b) What mean should you use?

   c) What standard deviation should you use?

Apply

6. A special HOV (high-occupancy vehicle) lane along a highway is reserved for cars carrying two or more people. Police records indicate that 8% of the cars in the HOV lane are occupied by fewer than two people. A random police check observed 100 cars.

   a) Use the binomial distribution to determine the probability that exactly 10 of the cars contained one person.

   b) Use the normal approximation to determine the probability that exactly 10 of the cars contained one person.

   c) Compare the answers to parts a) and b).

7. **Thinking** A coin is tossed 12 times.

   a) Use technology to help you create a probability table for the number of heads using the binomial distribution.

   b) Construct a probability distribution.

   c) What does the height of each bar on the graph represent?

   d) Determine the total area under the probability distribution.

   e) Is it reasonable to model this experiment using a normal distribution? Explain.

   f) Construct the normal approximation.

   g) Devise a method to measure the area under the normal distribution as accurately as possible.

   h) How does the area under the normal distribution compare to the area under the probability histogram?

8. A card is drawn randomly from a deck and then replaced. The deck is shuffled. Ten trials are carried out.

   a) Use the binomial distribution to determine the probability that there are exactly 5 diamonds in 10 trials.

b) Could you reasonably model this distribution using a normal approximation? Explain.

c) Determine the mean and standard deviation of the normal approximation.

d) Use the normal approximation to determine the probability of getting exactly 5 diamonds.

e) How does the answer to part d) compare with the answer to part a)?

✓ **Achievement Check**

9. Microwave ovens made in China are packaged into containers and shipped to Canada. About 1% are expected to be dented during transport. A sample of five ovens is removed from a container that holds 200. If one is found dented, the container is rejected.

a) Use the hypergeometric distribution to determine the probability that no ovens in the sample are dented.

b) Determine the mean and standard deviation of a normal approximation to this distribution.

c) Use the normal approximation to determine the probability that no ovens in the sample are dented. How does the answer compare with the answer from part a)?

10. An insurance company knows that 12% of the homeowners in a town of 900 are customers. The marketing department calls 50 homes at random.

a) What is the probability that 10 or more of these are already customers?

b) What method did you choose to solve this problem? Give reasons for your choice.

11. Application Honey jars from the farm where Doris works say they contain 500 g of honey. A technician measures a sample of 30 jars. The mean content is 502.83 g, with a standard deviation of 1.95 g. The technician can adjust the machine that fills the jars to change the mean. Assume that the standard deviation remains unchanged.

a) Determine the probability that a honey jar contains less than 500 g of honey.

b) Do you need to use a continuity correction factor? Explain.

c) The owners of the company would like to ensure that the probability that a jar contains less than 500 g is at most 0.005. What setting for the mean is required?

Extend

12. A multiple choice test consists of 50 questions with 5 possible answers each. Students need 60% or more to pass.

a) Andre has not studied for the test and guesses randomly at the answers. What is the probability that he will pass the test?

b) Maria has done some studying, and can narrow down the choices to 2 of the 5 provided for each question. What is the probability that she will pass the test?

13. Thinking A police survey shows that 5% of drivers passing an intersection are distracted. The police initiate a public education program to inform drivers of the danger. After a month, the police observe 120 cars at the same intersection and find 4 drivers are distracted.

a) If the education program had no effect, how many drivers out of 120 would you expect to be distracted?

b) What is the probability that 4 or fewer drivers would be found distracted out of 120 by pure chance?

c) Would you conclude that the program was effective? Explain your answer.

Learning Goals

Section	After this section, I can
7.1	• distinguish between discrete variables and continuous variables • work with sample values for situations that can take on continuous values • represent a probability distribution using a mathematical model • represent a sample of values of a continuous random variable using a frequency table, a frequency histogram, and a frequency polygon
7.2	• determine the theoretical probability for a continuous random variable over a range of values • determine the mean and standard deviation of a sample of values • calculate and explain the meaning of a z-score • solve real-world probability problems involving normal distributions
7.3	• recognize the general characteristics of a normal distribution • use technology to simulate a normal distribution in order to investigate its properties • determine probabilities for a normal distribution
7.4	• distinguish among the meanings of common confidence levels such as 90%, 95%, and 99% • determine the margin of error for a population mean estimated using a sample • determine the upper and lower limits of the confidence interval
7.5	• make connections between a normal distribution and a binomial distribution • make connections between a normal distribution and a hypergeometric distribution • recognize the role of the number of trials in these connections

7.1 Continuous Random Variables, pages 320–331

1. Advanced scuba divers sometimes breathe enriched air called nitrox. Nitrox contains 32% or 36% oxygen rather than the usual 21% found in ordinary air. Nitrox is toxic to humans if breathed for too long. Before using a nitrox-filled tank, the diver must verify and record the actual percent of oxygen in the tank. The table shows the oxygen content of a sample of 15 tanks.

Percent Oxygen				
32.1	32.2	31.8	32.2	32.1
32.0	31.8	32.1	32.0	31.9
32.0	31.9	31.9	32.2	31.8

   a) Can you determine from the table whether the distribution is uniform? Explain your answer.

   b) Devise a plan to determine whether the distribution is uniform. Carry out your plan, and draw a conclusion.

2. A sporting goods company produces custom wooden arrows. Any arrows with a length less than 69.2 cm or greater than 73.0 cm are rejected. The remaining arrows follow an approximately uniform distribution.

   a) What is the height of the probability distribution?

   b) What is the probability that an arrow has a length less than 71.1 cm?

   c) What is the probability that an arrow has a length between 70.6 cm and 71.6 cm?

3. Ryan is raising fruit flies as a science project. The table shows the frequencies of the lifetimes of the flies.

Lifetime (days)	Frequency
5–7	1
7–9	3
9–11	13
11–13	24
13–15	27
15–17	20
17–19	9
19–21	3

a) Sketch a frequency histogram for these data.

b) Sketch a frequency polygon for these data.

c) Estimate the mean life of the fruit flies.

7.2 The Normal Distribution and z-Scores, pages 332–345

4. Refer to the fruit fly data in #3.

a) Add a column of relative frequencies to the table.

b) What is the probability that a given fruit fly will die before the end of the first week?

c) What is the probability that a fruit fly will live from 11 to 17 days?

5. Triple Q Farms grows soybeans. A farmer is testing a new strain of plant. After 3 months, 28 seeds produced plants with heights as shown.

Soybean Height (cm)			
25.1	48.8	41.0	47.4
39.7	40.2	41.1	41.6
44.2	49.5	36.9	30.0
32.0	36.8	36.1	37.1
37.6	34.4	44.6	45.8
38.7	38.8	32.0	44.0
42.9	34.9	43.3	33.8

a) Determine the mean height.

b) Determine the standard deviation of the heights.

c) Sketch a frequency histogram for these data.

d) Do the heights appear to be normally distributed? Explain.

6. Current engineering graduates earn a mean starting salary of $62 000 in Canada, with a standard deviation of $2500. Assuming that the salaries are normally distributed, what is the probability that a graduate will find a job with a starting salary of more than $65 000?

7.3 Applications of the Normal Distribution, pages 346–351

7. A police radar unit is set up to monitor vehicles on a stretch of highway with a speed limit of 100 km/h. Long-term records for this location show that speeds vary normally with a mean of 105 km/h and a standard deviation of 7 km/h. Drivers who exceed the speed limit by 20 km/h accumulate demerit points as well as pay a fine.

a) What percent of the drivers will accumulate demerit points?

b) What is the probability that a given vehicle has a speed between 99 km/h and 101 km/h?

8. An electric car requires a mean recharge time of 4.5 h if the batteries are fully discharged. The manufacturer guarantees that the car will fully recharge in no more than 5 h. If the probability that a recharge takes more than 5 h is to be kept to 0.0001%, what is the standard deviation of the battery recharge time?

7.4 Confidence Intervals, pages 352–361

9. Marketing analysts for a soft drink manufacturer conducted a survey in a large town. They determined that 42% of the 150 people surveyed regularly bought the soft drink.

a) Determine the margin of error at a 95% confidence limit.

b) Determine the confidence interval for the market share for the soft drink.

10. The mean lifetime expected from a model of automobile follows a normal distribution with a standard deviation of 9500 km. A sample of 100 cars showed a mean lifetime of 190 000 km.

a) Determine the margin of error at a 90% confidence limit.

b) Determine the confidence interval for the mean.

7.5 Connections to Discrete Random Variables, pages 362–371

11. A bus company has records showing that its buses arrive on time 95% of the time. Suppose the company operates 65 bus trips each day. The CEO has asked for the probability that 60 or more of these buses arrive on time.

a) Use the binomial distribution to determine the probability that 60 or more buses arrive on time.

b) Could this distribution be reasonably modelled using a normal approximation? Give reasons for your answer.

c) Determine the mean and standard deviation of the normal approximation.

d) Use the normal approximation to determine the probability that 60 or more buses arrive on time.

e) How does the answer to part d) compare with the answer to part a)?

12. A newspaper reports that 350 of the 3500 people living in a small town have the flu. The data management class at the local high school has 25 students.

a) Do you expect this to be a representative sample? Explain.

b) Could you reasonably model this distribution using a normal approximation? Give reasons for your answer.

c) Determine the mean and standard deviation of the normal approximation.

d) Use the normal approximation to determine the probability that at least 5 of the students have the flu.

e) Use technology to compare the answer in part c) to that calculated from the hypergeometric distribution.

Chapter 7 Test Yourself

Achievement Chart

Category	Knowledge/ Understanding	Thinking	Communication	Application
Questions	1, 2, 5	6, 10, 13	10, 11, 15	3, 4, 5, 7, 8, 9, 10, 11, 12, 13, 14, 15

Multiple Choice

Choose the best answer for #1 to #6.

1. Which of these variables would be expected to produce a discrete distribution?

   A the distance of a long jump during a track meet

   B the mass of a bolt produced by a factory

   C the number of students with the flu in a given class at your school

   D the total monthly rainfall at a weather station

2. Which of these variables would be expected to produce a continuous distribution?

   A the number of customers at a restaurant at a given time

   B the mass of a hawk recorded during a migration

   C the number of hamburgers sold each day in the school cafeteria

   D the number of defective watches in a shipment to a department store

3. The average speeds of five contestants in a bicycle race were 24.2 km/h, 28.1 km/h, 21.6 km/h, 22.0 km/h, and 31.2 km/h. What is the mean of these speeds?

   A 22.0 km/h   B 24.2 km/h

   C 25.4 km/h   D 31.2 km/h

4. What is the standard deviation of the speeds in #3?

   A 3.70 km/h   B 4.13 km/h

   C 4.4 km/h   D 5.04 km/h

5. One hundred twenty students qualified for the high jump event at a track meet. The table shows the probability distribution for first jumps.

Height of Jump (cm)	Probability
120–130	0.025
130–140	0.040
140–150	0.081
150–160	0.150
160–170	0.175
170–180	0.218
180–190	0.117
190–200	0.092
200–210	0.073
210–220	0.017
220–230	0.012

   What is the frequency associated with a jump between 180 cm and 190 cm?

   A 0

   B 0.117

   C 14

   D 120

6. Which statement is true concerning a normal distribution?

   A The curve may be skewed to the left or right.

   B The median is equal to the mean.

   C 95% of the data values will occur within one standard deviation of the mean.

   D The mean of a sample is always less than the mean of the underlying normal distribution.

Short Answer

7. An assembly line produces flip-flops of stated length 200 mm. The graph shows the probability distribution of the actual lengths. What is the probability that a given flip-flop will have a length greater than 203 mm?

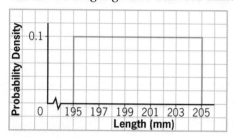

8. Karen's Zumba class has 50 students. She conducts a Zumba endurance contest. The table shows the probability distribution of the participants lasting increasing lengths of time.

Endurance (min)	Probability
30–35	0.04
35–40	0.04
40–45	0.10
45–50	0.20
50–55	0.24
55–60	0.16
60–65	0.10
65–70	0.08
70–75	0.04

a) How many students lasted between 45 min and 50 min?

b) What is the probability that a student lasted less than an hour?

9. When the ketchup dispenser at a fast-food restaurant is completely depressed, it dispenses a mean of 15 mL of ketchup with a standard deviation of 0.75 mL. Assuming that the distribution is normal, what is the probability that a hamburger will receive less than 14 mL of ketchup in one complete press?

10. Legs for a wooden dining room table are produced by a computer numerically controlled (CNC) lathe. The cutting blade lasts a mean time of 550 h with a standard deviation of 20 h. To avoid cutting errors, the shop manager would like to keep the probability of a failure to less than 0.002. How many hours should the blade be used before replacement? Explain.

11. A pharmaceutical company has determined the probability that a new antacid will relieve stomach distress is 75%. The antacid is given to 1000 patients. The number of patients who reported relief is recorded.

a) Could you reasonably model this distribution using a normal approximation? Explain.

b) Determine the mean and standard deviation of the normal approximation.

Extended Response

12. Students arrive at school at various times before the bell rings for the first class. The table shows data for 200 students.

Time (min)	Frequency
0–3	2
3–6	6
6–9	18
9–12	32
12–15	49
15–18	42
18–21	27
21–24	19
24–27	5
27–30	0

a) Sketch a frequency distribution histogram.

b) Add a frequency polygon to the histogram in part a).

c) Do the data appear to follow a normal distribution? Explain your reasoning.

13. Airliners taking off from City Central Airport produce a mean noise level of 108 dB (decibels), with a standard deviation of 6.7 dB. To encourage airlines to refit their aircraft with quieter engines, any airliners with a noise level above 120 dB must pay a "nuisance fee."

a) What percent of the airliners will be billed a nuisance fee?

b) After two years, a sample of 1000 airliners showed that 4 were billed the nuisance fee. Assuming that the program has been effective, and that the standard deviation has not changed, what is the new mean noise level?

14. A mail order company is planning to deliver small parcels using remote-controlled drones direct to households within 10 km of its warehouses, each located in a large city. As a test, drones delivered 500 parcels. A total of 420 parcels were delivered within the advertised time limit of 30 min. Determine a 99% confidence interval for the proportion of parcels delivered within 30 min.

15. A high school operates 450 computers. On a given day, an average of 15 of these computers are out of service. A computer lab contains 30 computers. A teacher would like to use the lab with her class of 27 students.

a) Is this a binomial or a hypergeometric distribution? Explain.

b) Could you reasonably model this distribution using a normal approximation? Explain.

c) Determine the mean and standard deviation of the normal approximation.

d) Use the normal approximation to determine the probability that there will be enough working computers.

Chapter Problem

Food Service Industry

The honey farm has installed a filling machine for honey jars that hold 500 g of honey. Doris is calibrating the new machine. She sets the machine to a mean of 500 g, and performs a test run of 48 jars, or two cases. The table shows the results.

Honey (g)					
499	501	498	497	499	500
501	499	501	501	498	502
498	498	502	500	499	499
496	503	500	501	499	498
498	501	499	502	500	500
500	502	501	500	500	500
500	501	500	500	500	503
499	499	497	502	499	502

a) Determine the mean and standard deviation of these data.

b) Assume that the distribution is normal. What is the probability that a jar contains less than 500 g of honey?

c) The probability that a jar contains less than 500 g is allowed to be at most 0.005. What setting for the mean should Doris try? What assumptions did you make?

d) How can Doris check that she has set the machine correctly?

e) Using the setting in part c), what is the probability that a jar might contain more than 510 g of honey?

f) As a manager of the company, what policy would you put in place to reassure any customers who receive less honey than expected?

CHAPTER 8

Two-Variable Data Analysis

Climate change is an area of increasing concern. Shrinking arctic ice caps pose a danger to both animals and people. Polar bears are losing their habitat, while human residents in low-lying coastal regions are at risk of flooding. Some argue that climate change is not a real threat. The use of data is important when trying to assess such an important issue. Do you think climate change is a natural occurrence, or has human behaviour contributed? What are some of the variables that could be measured and compared to help answer this question?

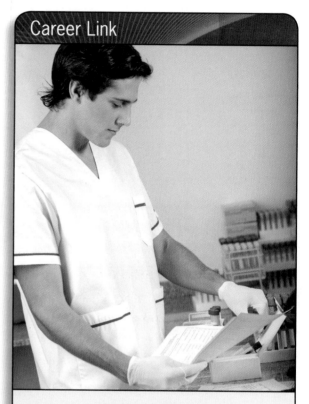

Key Terms

line of best fit

linear correlation

correlation coefficient

linear regression

cause and effect
   relationship

common cause
   relationship

presumed relationship

reverse cause and effect
   relationship

accidental relationship

residual plot

residual

outlier

hidden variable

Literacy Strategy

You can use concept circles to visually organize words and symbols that are related. As you work through the chapter, create concept circles to help you organize how different ideas relate to each other. An example is shown.

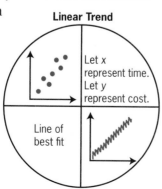

Linear Trend

Let x represent time.
Let y represent cost.

Line of best fit

Health Care Statistician

A health care statistician uses data management techniques to help advance medical treatments and educate the public. Responsibilities include analysing and interpreting health care data using statistical software. Managing and monitoring the integrity of data collection methods is also a significant part of this job. Health care statisticians usually have an advanced degree in statistics or mathematics and some leadership experience in health care. What are some factors that a health care statistician would be concerned about, and how could they be connected using two-variable data analysis?

Chapter Problem

Climate Change

Scientists generally agree that there is sufficient evidence to declare climate change is a real phenomenon with dangerous implications that need to be addressed. The graph shows the mean yearly temperature in degrees Fahrenheit (°F) and carbon dioxide (CO_2) concentration levels in parts per million (ppm) over time for Earth.

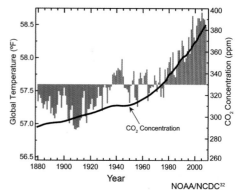

Source: United States Global Change Research Program

1. **a)** The mean temperature over this time period is approximately 57.6 °F. How is this represented in the graph?
   b) What do the blue bars represent?
   c) What do the red bars represent?

2. Did Earth's temperature change by the same amount from year to year? Is there a long-term trend over several decades? Explain your reasoning.

3. The solid black curve shows the carbon dioxide concentration level over time. Describe this trend.

4. Perform some research on climate change. Describe some of the physical, ecological, and social effects of climate change.

Literacy Link

In the United States, degrees Fahrenheit is used, so it is frequently seen in reports from the U.S., rather than degrees Celsius.

Prerequisite Skills

Scatter Plots

1. The graph shows a commuter's travel time in minutes versus the amount of daily precipitation in centimetres.

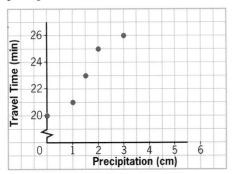

   a) Describe the trend in the data.

   b) Suggest why this trend may exist.

2. The table shows Anna-Marie's average speed for a number of running races.

Distance (m)	Average Speed (m/s)
100	8.1
200	7.5
500	6.6
1000	6.1
1500	5.2

   a) Create a scatter plot of the data.

   b) Describe the trend.

   c) Estimate Anna-Marie's speed for a 750-m race. Explain your method.

Use a Graphing Calculator to Create a Scatter Plot

3. a) Use a graphing calculator to create a scatter plot for the data.

   b) Is there a trend in the scatter plot? If so, describe it.

Goals	Assists
21	30
18	24
35	30
12	13
27	37
6	9
40	55
32	31

Use a graphing calculator to create a scatter plot of the data.

Age	Height (cm)
14	140
14	146
14	150
15	148
15	160
16	157
17	171
18	170

- Press **STAT** and choose **1:Edit**.
- Enter the data into lists **L1** and **L2**.

- Press **2ND** **STAT PLOT** .
- Set the parameters as shown.

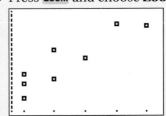

- Press **ZOOM** and choose **ZoomStat**.

Press **TRACE** and use the left and right arrows to read the coordinates of the data.

Linear Models

Use this information to answer #4 and #5.
Temperatures measured in Fahrenheit, F, and Celsius, C, are related by the following equation: $F = 1.8C + 32$.

4. a) Graph the relation for $C = 0°$ to $C = 100°$.

b) Identify the initial value. Explain what it means.

c) Identify the rate of change. What does it mean?

d) Use the graph to convert 25 °C to degrees Fahrenheit.

e) Check your answer using the equation.

f) Which method do you prefer, and why?

5. a) Use the equation to convert 50 °F to degrees Celsius.

b) Check your answer using the graph.

c) Which method do you prefer, and why?

Bias

Literacy Link

Bias occurs when data are collected or presented unfairly. It can lead to an inaccurate interpretation of the results of a statistical study.

6. A student council surveys the football team to see if they should ask the principal for an increase in the football program's budget.

a) How is bias present in this study?

b) What could be done to remove the bias?

7. A radio talk show host asks callers if they think the current government should be unseated. Identify any potential sources of bias.

Summary Statistics for One-Variable Data

8. The chart shows the heights of the players of a high school basketball team.

Player	Height (m)
Sarah	1.8
Jessica	1.5
Tina	1.5
Latisha	1.5
Uma	1.4
Kyla	1.9
Mina	1.4
Luisa	1.6
Sangita	1.5
Caroline	1.9

a) Determine the mean, median, and mode.

b) Explain why these measures of central tendency are not all equal.

c) Determine the standard deviation and z-score for a height of 1.9 m.

9. The box plot summarizes students' quiz scores out of 10.

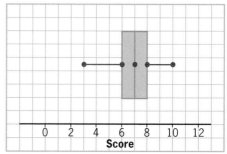

a) Determine the range of scores.

b) Determine the median score.

c) What is the interquartile range and what does it represent?

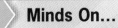

8.1

Line of Best Fit

Learning Goals

I am learning to

- classify a linear correlation between two variables
- determine a correlation coefficient using technology
- produce a line of best fit using linear regression

> ## Minds On...

Some parents like to track their children's growth over time. One way to do this is to measure the child's height on every birthday and record it on a wall or door frame.

- What are some other ways to record these data?

- Do you think a child grows by the same amount every year?

> ## Action!

Investigate Line of Best Fit

Materials

- transparent ruler

Darla's parents kept track of her height on her birthday every year from ages two through eight. The graph shows the measurements as a time series.

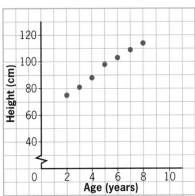

Literacy Link

A *time series* is a set of two-variable data in which a quantity is measured against time.

Literacy Link

An *independent variable* is a not affected by another variable. A *dependent variable* is affected by another variable.

1. Identify the independent and dependent variables. How do you know?

2. Does there appear to be a relationship between Darla's height and her age? If so, describe it.

382 MHR • Chapter 8

3. a) Sketch the graph and draw a line of best fit.

b) Does it make sense to draw a solid or a dashed line in this case? Explain why.

4. Extend the line to answer the following questions.

a) How tall will Darla be at age 10?

b) Estimate Darla's height when she was a newborn.

5. Reflect

a) How accurate do you think these estimates are? Explain.

b) Will this trend continue forever? If not, when will this linear model no longer be useful? Explain your reasoning.

Darla's parents also kept track of the number of baby teeth she still had, except for one year when they forgot. The data, collected on her birthdays, are shown.

6. Identify the independent and dependent variables.

7. Does there appear to be a correlation between the number of baby teeth Darla had and her age? If so, describe it.

8. a) Sketch the graph and draw a line of best fit.

b) Does it make sense to draw a solid or a dashed line in this case? Explain why.

c) Use the line to estimate how many baby teeth Darla had on her sixth birthday.

9. Reflect

a) How accurate do you think this estimate is? Explain.

b) Will this trend continue forever? Why or why not?

10. Reflect Compare the two lines of best fit that you drew in this investigation.

a) Was one easier to draw than the other?

b) Was one a better model for the data than the other? Justify your answers.

11. Extend Your Understanding Create a data table relating two variables for which it would be nearly impossible to draw a line of best fit that makes sense. Create a scatter plot and explain why a line of best fit does not make sense for the graph you created.

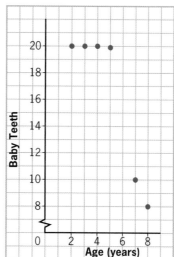

line of best fit

- a straight line that represents a trend in the scatter plot as long as the pattern is more or less linear
- should pass through as many points as possible, with about half the points above and half below the line
- a solid line represents continuous data that are constantly changing
- a dashed line represents discrete data that change only in steps

Literacy Link

Interpolation and *extrapolation* are important tools for two-variable data analysis. To interpolate, read a linear model between given data points. To extrapolate, read beyond given data points.

- a relationship in which a change in one variable tends to correspond to a proportional change in another variable

correlation coefficient

- a measure of how well a linear model fits a two-variable set of data
- values of r between -1 and 0 indicate a negative correlation, so the line of best fit has a negative slope
- an r value of 0 indicates that there is no linear correlation
- values of r between 0 and 1 indicate a positive correlation, so the line of best fit has a positive slope

In the Investigation, Darla's height changed largely in proportion to her age. As she got older, her height increased by an almost constant amount each year. This is an example of two variables that share a strong **linear correlation**. When two variables have a weaker linear correlation, a trend is still evident; however, a line of best fit is more difficult to recognize, as was the case in the number of Darla's baby teeth versus time. When two variables have no linear correlation, there is no recognizable linear pattern to the data.

The **correlation coefficient**, r, is a measure of the strength of the linear correlation between two variables. For a positive correlation, r can have values between 0, which represents no linear correlation, and 1, which represents a perfect positive linear correlation. For a negative correlation, 0 signifies no linear correlation and -1 indicates a perfect negative linear correlation.

	Negative Linear Correlation			**Positive Linear Correlation**		
Perfect						Perfect
	Strong	Moderate	Weak	Weak	Moderate	Strong
-1	-0.67	-0.33	0	0.33	0.67	1

Correlation Coefficient, r

Example 1

Strength of Correlation

Do the graphs below show a linear correlation? Describe the correlation for each relationship.

a)

$r = 1$

b)

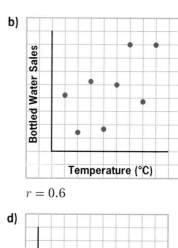

$r = 0.6$

c)

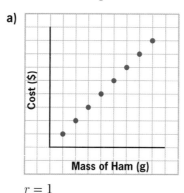

$r = -0.96$

d)

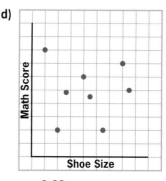

$r = 0.03$

e)

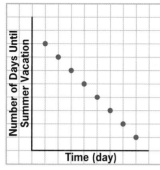

Number of Days Until Summer Vacation vs Time (day)

$r = -1$

f)

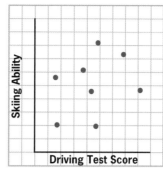

Skiing Ability vs Driving Test Score

$r = 0.29$

Solution

a) As the mass of ham increases, the cost increases by a proportional amount. This is an example of a perfect positive correlation.

b) As temperature increases, bottled water sales tend to increase; however, the trend is not obvious. The correlation coefficient of 0.6 suggests a correlation may exist.

c) A clear pattern is evident here. As practice time increases, the number of typing errors decreases. The correlation coefficient of –0.96 indicates that this relationship has a strong negative linear correlation.

d) There is little to indicate any linear pattern in this case. A correlation coefficient of 0.03 indicates there is definitely not a linear relation between math score and shoe size. The scatter plot does not appear to show any other type of relationship, so you can infer that math score is completely unrelated to shoe size.

e) The number of days until summer vacation is decreasing over time at a proportional rate. This is an example of a perfect negatively linear correlation.

f) Careful inspection reveals a slight upward trend in the data. Looking from left to right, as driving test scores increase there is a slight tendency for skiing ability to increase. The correlation coefficient of 0.29 suggests a weak linear correlation.

> **Project Prep**
>
> Note the minor difference between the graphs in parts d) and f). If you encounter a weak linear correlation when researching your project, try to find data that offer stronger evidence before claiming a correlational relationship.

Your Turn

Sketch a scatter plot relating two variables that have:

a) a strong positive correlation

b) a moderate weak correlation

c) no correlation

Indicate variables that could be correlated in this way for each case.

Example 2

Use Technology to Calculate the Correlation Coefficient

The table shows distance-time data for a student who is walking in front of a motion sensor.

d represents the distance between the walker and the motion sensor, in metres, after t seconds have passed.

Time, t (s)	Distance, d (m)
1	2.1
2	2.5
3	2.8
4	3.5
5	4.1

a) Create a scatter plot relating distance, d, and time, t.

b) Determine the strength of the linear correlation between these variables.

c) Determine the equation of the line of best fit and explain what it means.

Solution

Method 1: Use a Graphing Calculator

Refer to the Prerequisite Skills on page 195 for help creating a scatter plot using a graphing calculator.

a) • Enter the data into a table.

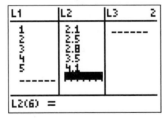

• Set the parameters as shown.

• Create a scatter plot of distance versus time.

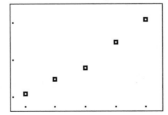

b) The scatter plot demonstrates a strong positive correlation between distance and time. Verify this by calculating the correlation coefficient.

- Press **STAT** and choose **CALC**.
- Select **4:LinReg(ax + b)**
- Press **2ND** **L1** , **2ND** **L2** , and then press **ENTER** .

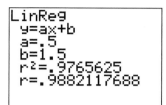

The correlation coefficient, r, is approximately 0.99, confirming a near perfect positive linear correlation between distance and time.

Processes

Selecting Tools and Computational Strategies

If r does not appear, the Diagnostics may be turned off. To turn them on,

- press **2ND** **CATALOG**
- press **2ND** **ALPHA** **D** to jump to commands beginning with D
- select **Diagnostics On** and press **ENTER**.

Method 2: Use Fathom™

a) • Open Fathom™ and create a table as shown.

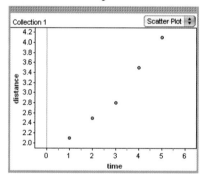

	time	distance
1	1	2.1
2	2	2.5
3	3	2.8
4	4	3.5
5	5	4.1

- Create a scatter plot of distance versus time.

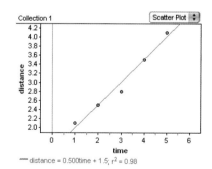

b) The scatter plot demonstrates a strong positive correlation between distance and time. Verify this by calculating the correlation coefficient. With the graph selected, choose the **Graph** menu and then choose **Least-Squares Line**.

The value of r^2 is 0.98. Take the square root to obtain $r = 0.99$. When you take the square root to determine the correlation coefficient, you must also analyse the graph to determine if it is positive or negative. The correlation coefficient, r, is approximately 0.99, confirming a strong positive linear correlation between distance and time.

Processes

Connecting

Fathom™ and the TI-83/84+ graphing calculators both generate r^2, which is called the coefficient of determination. While the correlation coefficient, r, measures how closely a set of data can be represented by a *linear* model, the coefficient of determination more generally measures how closely a set of data can be represented by either a linear model or a variety of *non-linear* models.

Method 3: Use a Spreadsheet

a) • Open a new spreadsheet.

• Label two columns and enter the data as shown.

• Create a scatter plot of distance versus time. Refer to the Prerequisite Skills on page 195 for help creating a scatter plot using a spreadsheet.

	A	B
1	Time	Distance
2	1	2.1
3	2	2.5
4	3	2.8
5	4	3.5
6	5	4.1

Distance vs. Time

b) The scatter plot demonstrates a strong positive correlation between distance and time. Verify this by calculating the correlation coefficient.

• Right click on one of the data points and choose **Add Trendline**.

• Choose **Linear**. Check the boxes to "Display Equation on chart" and "Display R-squared value on chart." Click **Close**.

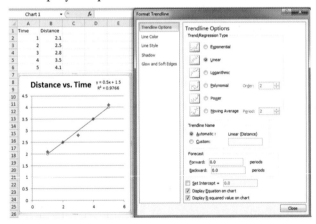

The value of r^2 is approximately 0.98. Take the square root to get $r = 0.99$.

The correlation coefficient, r, is approximately 0.99, confirming a strong positive linear correlation between distance and time.

Processes

Representing
The graphing calculator and spreadsheet used variables other than *d* and *t*. What variables were used in their place?

linear regression

• the formal process by which a line of best fit is mathematically determined

c) Each technology tool performed a linear regression. The equation of the line of best fit is $d = 0.5t + 1.5$, where d is the distance between the walker and the motion sensor after t seconds had passed. The fixed part of the equation, 1.5, gives the initial value of the walker's position. The variable part, $0.5t$, gives the rate of change. The equation shows that the walker started 1.5 m from the motion sensor and walked at a rate of 0.5 m/s away from the sensor.

Your Turn

The table shows distance from home for a cyclist over time.

Time (min)	Distance (km)
10	9.8
20	8.1
30	5.8
40	4.2
50	2.3

a) Create a scatter plot relating distance, d, and time, t.

b) Determine the strength of linear correlation.

c) Determine the equation of the line of best fit and explain what it means.

d) Why do the actual data points not always fall exactly on the line?

Consolidate and Debrief

Key Concepts

- When a change in one variable is accompanied by a proportional change in another variable, the variables share a linear correlation.

- The correlation coefficient, r, is a measure of the strength of linear correlation between two variables. The value of r, which can be between −1 and 1, gives an indication of how closely the data points relate to the line of best fit.

- The line of best fit can be used to model a linear correlation.

- Linear regression is the mathematical process that determines the line of best fit.

Reflect

R1. Two variables, X and Y, share a strong negative correlation.

a) Sketch what a scatter plot of Y versus X could look like.

b) Describe in words the correlation between X and Y.

R2. Repeat R1, assuming that X and Y have a moderate positive correlation.

R3. A student walking in front of a motion sensor generates distance-time data, where distance is in metres and time is in seconds. A linear regression on the data produces the information shown.

Describe everything you can about the motion of this walker and the relationship between distance and time.

```
LinReg
 y=ax+b
 a=.51
 b=.49
 r²=.9897260274
 r=.9948497512

■
```

Practise

Choose the best answer for #1 to #3.

1. Two variables have a linear correlation of –0.94. Which of the following is true?

   A The variables share a strong, positive correlation.

   B The variables share a moderate, positive correlation.

   C The variables share a strong, negative correlation.

   D The variables share a moderate, negative correlation.

2. The scatter plot shows the distance, d, in metres, and time, t, in seconds, for a student walking in front of a motion sensor.

   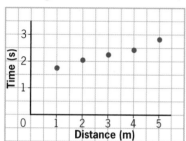

   Which equation represents the line of best fit?

   A $d = -0.25t + 1.5$

   B $d = 0.25t + 1.5$

   C $d = 0.5t + 1.5$

   D $d = 1.5t + 0.25$

3. The scatter plot shows the relationship between two variables, x and y. Which of the scenarios is most likely to have this relationship?

   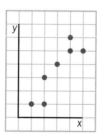

   A student's math score versus student's height

   B height above ground of a skydiver versus time

   C computer boot-up time versus unemployment rate

   D number of automobile accidents versus amount of snowfall

4. Compare the linear regression data for two students walking in front of a motion sensor:

   Bob's walk
   $d = 0.75t + 2$
   $r = 0.70$

   Tracey's walk
   $d = 0.75t + 2$
   $r = 0.95$

   a) How are the movements of these walkers similar? different?

   b) Sketch possible distance versus time graphs for Bob and Tracey.

Apply

Use the table to answer #5 and #6.

Number of Books Owned	Hours per Week Watching TV	Hours per Week Using Internet
25	16	8
44	20	12
12	22	16
16	25	13
78	8	20
112	2	15
56	10	11

5. **Application**

   a) Create a scatter plot of time spent watching television versus number of books owned.

   b) Characterize the correlation.

   c) Perform a linear regression and record the correlation coefficient. Does this support your answer to part b)? Explain.

6. Repeat the analysis performed in #5 for

   a) time spent on the Internet versus number of books owned

   b) time spent on the Internet versus time spent watching television

7. **Thinking**

   a) Use CANSIM or an alternate data source to find a time series that has a strong linear correlation.

   b) Create a scatter plot of the time series.

   c) Describe the correlation.

d) Construct a line of best fit. Explain what the equation means.

e) Why do you think the trend exists?

8. **Communication** In Fathom™, open the sample file found here: **Sample Documents/Statistics/Correlation and Regression/CorrelationPlay.ftm**. Drag the points to create each of the following. Then, describe or sketch the data pattern for each.

a) $r^2 = 1$ for a positive trend

b) $r^2 = 1$ for a negative trend

c) a moderate positive linear correlation

d) $r^2 = 0$

9. **Open Question** The result of a linear regression between two variables is:

$y = -0.25x + 15 \qquad r^2 = 0.75$

a) Sketch what the scatter plot of y versus x could look like.

b) Explain the reasoning behind your sketch.

✓ **Achievement Check**

10. Is there a linear correlation between body measures?

a) Pick three or four body measures, such as height, foot length, head circumference, hand span, forearm length, and so on. Measure and record data for yourself and several classmates.

b) Use technology such as Fathom™ or a spreadsheet to make two-variable comparisons using these strategies:
- scatter plot
- correlation coefficient
- line of best fit

c) Identify two or three strong linear correlations. In each case:
- describe the nature of the correlation
- identify and interpret the correlation coefficient
- write the equation of the line of best fit and explain what it means

11. **Thinking** The table shows Marley's distance from home.

Time (h)	Distance (km)
0.0	280
0.5	230
1.0	210
1.5	150
2.2	140
2.5	90

a) Create a scatter plot of distance versus time in Fathom™.

b) From the **Graph** menu, choose **Add Movable Line**. Adjust the line so that it is close to being a line of best fit:
- Click and drag it near one of the endpoints to adjust the slope.
- Click and drag it near the middle to translate the line vertically.

c) From the **Graph** menu, choose **Show Squares**. What happens?

d) Adjust the line so that the **Sum of Squares** value is as small as possible. Estimate when this occurs.

e) From the **Graph** menu, choose **Least-Squares Line**. Test your estimate. Explain what you observe.

Extend

12. The coefficient of determination, r^2, is a measure of how well a regression curve fits a set of data. When Y is the dependent variable, and X is the independent variable, r^2 represents how much variance in Y can be explained by X. If the curve of best fit is a perfect fit, $r^2 = 1$. The closer r^2 gets to 0, the poorer the curve of best fit. State the values of r^2 in some of the questions in this section and interpret their meanings.

13. Perform some research on the coefficient of determination, r^2.

a) How is it useful?

b) What values can it have?

c) How is it similar to the correlation coefficient? How is it different?

Cause and Effect

Learning Goals

I am learning to

- distinguish between correlation and causality
- identify the type of relationship between two variables

> ## Minds On...

When a lumberjack cuts down a tree, you can see its cross section, as shown in the image. Each ring in the cross section represents one year of the tree's growth.

- Do you think a tree grows by the same amount every year?

- What are some factors that might cause a tree to grow faster or slower?

> ## Action!

Investigate Cause and Effect

Materials

- ruler
- graphing calculator or software

1. Measure the radius of the tree for each ring shown. Call the smallest ring Year 1. Record radius versus year in a table.

Year	Radius (cm)
1	
2	

2. **a)** Create a scatter plot of radius versus time.

   b) Describe the correlation.

3. **a)** Perform a linear regression.

   b) What is the correlation coefficient? What does this suggest about the correlation?

4. **a)** What is the equation of the line of best fit?

   b) Interpret what this equation means.

5. **a)** Use your linear model to predict the radius of the tree at an age of
   - 25 years
   - 50 years

   b) Discuss any assumptions you must make and identify any factors that could affect the accuracy of your model.

6. **Reflect** Compare your linear models with those of your classmates. Are they identical? Are they close? Explain why there may be some inconsistency.

7. **Reflect** Identify the independent variable and the dependent variable in this study. Could they be reversed? Explain why or why not.

8. **Extend Your Understanding**

   a) Calculate the cross-sectional area of the tree after each year.

   b) Create a scatter plot of area versus time.

   c) Does the relationship appear to have a strong linear correlation? Explain.

   d) Use a spreadsheet or a graphing calculator to perform a quadratic regression. Comment on how well the curve that is generated fits the data. Why does this make sense?

Processes

Reflecting
Think about the data collection process. Would everyone have exactly the same data? Why or why not?

Data analysis involves much more than fitting a line or a curve to a set of data points. Establishing a linear correlation between a dependent variable and an independent variable is just the first step in understanding the true nature of a relationship. Once you know there is a correlation, it is important to consider how and why such a correlation exists. Finding the meaning behind a linear correlation is what distinguishes true mathematical modelling from simply fitting a line to a set of data.

Example 1

Analyse a Cause and Effect Relationship

The scatter plot and line of best fit show the relationship between the mark achieved and number of hours studied for a grade 12 data management final exam.

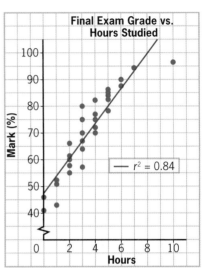

cause and effect relationship

- the correlation between two variables in which a change in one directly causes a change in the other

a) Does this correlation have a **cause and effect relationship**?

b) Interpret the line of best fit.

c) According to the linear model, for how many hours must a student study to achieve a perfect score of 100%? Comment on the validity of this answer.

Solution

a) Calculate the correlation coefficient to determine the strength of linear correlation. Then, consider whether a causal relationship is reasonable.

$r^2 = 0.84$ Take the square root.
$r \approx 0.92$

The correlation coefficient is about 0.92, suggesting a very strong correlation between mark and hours studied. Since most educational experts agree that strong study habits will result in higher achievement, and given the satisfactory sample size, it is reasonable to characterize this relationship as an example of cause and effect. The dependent variable is the student's mark, which is affected by the independent variable, number of hours studied.

b) The value of the correlation coefficient suggests that the line of best fit for these data is relatively good for predicting student performance. The equation relating mark, m, to hours studied, h, is $m = 6.5h + 47$.

Generally, you can predict a student's mark by substituting the number of hours studied into h in the equation and then calculating m.

Determine the vertical intercept and rate of change to develop a deeper interpretation of this linear model. The vertical intercept occurs when h is set to 0:

$m = 6.5(0) + 47$
$m = 47$

The linear model predicts a failing grade of 47 if a student does not study at all.

The rate of change is 6.5, which means that a student's mark will increase by approximately six and a half percentage points for each additional hour studied, according to the linear model.

c) The linear model can be applied to estimate the number of hours required to score a perfect exam. Substitute $m = 100$ and solve for h.

$$m = 6.5h + 47$$
$$100 = 6.5h + 47$$
$$100 - 47 = 6.5h$$
$$53 = 6.5h$$
$$\frac{53}{6.5} = h$$
$$8.2 = h$$

The linear model predicts that a score of 100% can be expected after a little more than eight hours of study. Care must be taken in making this prediction, however, particularly since one student who studied for 10 hours did not achieve a perfect exam. This example illustrates that linear models, while often useful, can have significant limitations.

Processes

Reasoning and Proving
Does the result $h = 8.2$ suggest that a student who studies for nine or more hours can expect a final mark above 100%? Explain.

Your Turn

The scatter plot and line of best fit show the relationship between the number of successful free throws made out of 10 attempts and the number of hours spent practising for members of a basketball team.

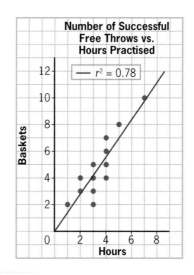

a) Characterize this correlation with regard to cause and effect.

b) Interpret the line of best fit.

c) Discuss any limitations of this linear model.

When analysing linear trends in data, it is important to distinguish between correlation and causality. Just because two variables share a strong linear correlation, it does not necessarily imply that a change in one variable is responsible for a change in the other. Inferring a cause and effect relation based strictly on correlational evidence is one of the most common errors in two-variable data analysis.

Sometimes two variables share a linear correlation because they both depend on another, third variable. This is known as a **common cause relationship**.

common cause relationship

- the correlation between two variables in which both variables change as a result of a third common variable

Example 2

Common Cause Relationships

The table and graph show a strong negative linear correlation between automobile sales and robberies from 1988 to 1993.

Year	Number of Robberies	Automobile Sales ($)
1988	6375	11 335 615
1989	6899	11 140 918
1990	8101	9 736 777
1991	9823	8 808 249
1992	9370	9 156 456
1993	8828	9 623 595

Source: CANSIM Table 079-0003, New motor vehicle sales, Canada, provinces and territories, Statistics Canada, April 11, 2014; CANSIM Table 252-0001, Crimes, by actual offences, Statistics Canada, November 15, 2001

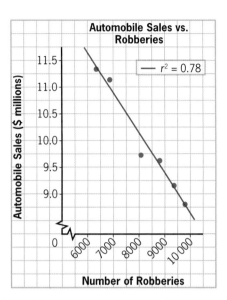

Is it likely that an increase in robberies would cause car sales to drop? Identify a possible common cause for these trends.

Solution

To conclude from these data that an increase in robberies could be responsible for a decrease in automobile sales does not make much sense. It is more likely that a common cause is involved.

What could cause both of these trends? When economic times are poor, families may be more likely to delay a major purchase such as an automobile. It is possible that robberies may be more likely to increase when people lose their jobs and become desperate to take care of their families. Is it possible that both of these trends are caused by high unemployment?

The table and graph show the average annual unemployment rate in Ontario.

Year	Percent Unemployment	Year	Percent Unemployment	Year	Percent Unemployment
1976	6.1	1988	5.0	2000	5.7
1977	6.9	1989	5.0	2001	6.3
1978	7.2	1990	6.2	2002	7.2
1979	6.6	1991	9.5	2003	6.9
1980	6.6	1992	10.8	2004	6.8
1981	6.9	1993	10.9	2005	6.6
1982	9.8	1994	9.6	2006	6.3
1983	10.4	1995	8.7	2007	6.4
1984	9.0	1996	9.0	2008	6.5
1985	7.9	1997	8.4	2009	9.0
1986	7.0	1998	7.2	2010	8.7
1987	6.1	1999	6.3	2011	7.8
				2012	7.8

Source: Labour Force Survey, Annual Average Unemployment Rate, Statistics Canada

Literacy Link

In economic terms, a *recession* refers to a poor time for business. Signs of a recession include low investments, low profits, and high unemployment. A *boom* is the opposite of a recession.

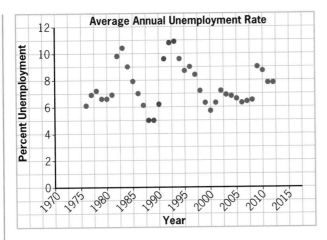

The unemployment rate spiked to a very high level during this same time period. It is quite possible that decreased automobile sales and increased counts of robbery could both be a result of a recession, or weak economy.

Your Turn

While performing research for his data management project, Aidan discovers a strong linear correlation between the number of forest fires per year and the yield of tomato harvest for the same region. He wonders if growing more tomatoes causes more forest fires. Do you agree with Aidan's line of reasoning? If so, explain why. If not, offer a more likely explanation for this correlation.

It is important not to jump to a conclusion too quickly when deciding on the type of relationship that exists between two variables. In the example above, a cause and effect relationship was ruled out because it did not make sense. A reasonable case was made for a common cause relationship; however, this still would not necessarily constitute proof.

Variables can be related in different ways. A **presumed relationship** can exist when it seems to make sense that two variables are related, and yet no causality can be inferred and it is also difficult to identify a clear common cause factor. An example of this would be a positive correlation between the number of books in children's homes and their math scores.

A **reverse cause and effect relationship** occurs when the assumed causation becomes reversed. Consider the positive correlation between severe illness and depression. A researcher might hypothesize that being severely ill is very emotionally difficult and so it causes depression. However, in reality, depressed people struggle to take care of themselves, so they are more likely to become severely ill.

Sometimes two variables share a strong linear correlation for no logical reason at all. This is called an **accidental relationship**. Suppose that a positive correlation was found between the local kitten birth rate and the price of eggs. It would be sensible to consider such a correlation purely coincidental.

<aside>

Project Prep

The data set in Example 2 was relatively small. To build a stronger case of automobile sales dropping and robberies increasing as a direct cause of high unemployment, more data from other recession periods could be studied. If similar results were replicated many times over, then a stronger argument could be made for a common cause relationship. When collecting data for your project, consider whether the size of the data set is sufficient to support your analysis.

---

presumed relationship

- a relationship that makes sense but does not seem to have a causation factor

reverse cause and effect relationship

- a relationship in which the independent and dependent variable are reversed

accidental relationship

- a relationship that is based purely on coincidence

</aside>

Example 3

Identifying Types of Relationships

Suggest the most likely type of relationship for each correlation.

a) The number of fire stations in a city is positively correlated with the number of parks.

b) The price of butter is positively correlated with fish population levels.

c) Seat belt infractions are positively correlated with traffic fatalities.

d) Self-esteem is positively correlated with vocabulary level.

e) Charged crimes is positively correlated with the size of the police force.

Solution

a) It does not seem to make sense that building more fire stations would cause an increase in the number of parks in a city. Both of these variables likely share a positive correlation with city population. This is most likely a common cause relationship.

b) No clear connection exists between the price of butter and fish population. When two variables share a strong linear correlation for no logical reason at all, it is an accidental relationship.

c) Seat belts are specifically designed to save lives in the event of an accident. A strong case can be made that this is a cause and effect relationship.

d) It makes sense that someone with strong language skills would tend to also have higher self-esteem. It would be difficult to suggest, however, that one causes the other, and it would also be challenging to identify a clear common cause factor. This is most likely a presumed relationship.

e) One hypothesis might be that when crimes increase, a police department responds by recruiting more officers. It could also be argued that as a police force is increased, there are more opportunities to catch and charge criminals. A reverse cause and effect relationship occurs when the assumed causation becomes reversed.

Your Turn

Classify the relationships and justify your choice in each case.

a) A patient's stress level is negatively correlated with the amount of exercise performed.

b) Student math scores are positively correlated with English scores.

c) Pancake sales are negatively correlated with amount of rainfall.

d) Job interview success rate is positively correlated with number of years a person has been married.

Project Prep

When searching for data for your project, you may discover a linear correlation between two variables. Could the correlation be explained by the presence of a common cause variable? Could a case be made for a cause and effect relationship? If no logical reason for the correlation can be inferred, the relationship may have to be dismissed as accidental. To answer these questions you will likely need to dig more deeply into the data.

Consolidate and Debrief

Key Concepts

- A cause and effect relationship exists when one variable is directly responsible for a change in another variable.

- If two variables share a strong correlation, it does not imply that a cause and effect relationship exists.

- A common cause relationship exists when a common third variable is responsible for the correlation between two other variables.

- Several types of relationships can exist between two variables, including cause and effect, common cause, presumed, reverse cause and effect, and accidental.

Reflect

R1. Explain why correlational evidence alone does not imply a cause and effect relationship.

R2. A positive correlation was discovered with each pair of the following variables:
- cases of the flu
- amount of severe winter weather
- tissue sales

What is the most likely type of relationship involved here? Explain.

R3. A study found that caffeine intake is positively correlated with nervousness.
  a) Suggest a cause and effect relationship that could explain this correlation.
  b) Suggest a reverse cause and effect relationship that could be argued.

R4. a) Make up an accidental relationship between two variables.
  b) Explain why the correlation is likely to be accidental.

Practise

Choose the best answer for #1 to #3.

1. As variable x increases, variable y decreases proportionately. Which of the following statements is definitely true?

  A This is a cause and effect relationship in which x is the dependent variable.

  B This is a cause and effect relationship in which y is the dependent variable.

  C These variables share a positive correlation.

  D These variables share a negative correlation.

2. Patients who participate in a new exercise program experience a drop in blood pressure over the same period of time. Which statement is most likely correct?

  A This is a cause and effect relationship, in which the dependent variable is amount of exercise.

  B This is a cause and effect relationship, in which the dependent variable is blood pressure.

  C This is an accidental relationship.

  D This is a presumed relationship.

3. In an economic study, average salaries were negatively correlated with the unemployment rate. Which of the following is most likely to be a common cause factor that accounts for this correlation?

   A the price of eggs

   B the strength of the economy

   C the current birth rate

   D movie industry revenue

4. At a ski resort, lift ticket sales were positively correlated with hot chocolate sales.

   a) Is this likely a cause and effect relationship? Explain why or why not.

   b) Suggest a common cause that could explain this relationship.

Apply

5. a) At a dance competition, how would you expect the relationship to look between dance performance score and number of hours practised? Sketch a graph to support your answer.

   b) Do you think this is a cause and effect relationship? Explain.

6. Identify the most likely type of relationship between the two variables for each scenario. Assume the independent variable is mentioned first. Justify your answers.

   a) Grass growth is positively correlated with amount of rainfall.

   b) Arm length is positively correlated with leg length.

   c) Sandwich sales are negatively correlated with dog bite incidents.

   d) Interest in televised sport is positively correlated with fitness level.

   e) Incidence of diabetes is negatively correlated with healthy eating habits.

   f) Heart disease is positively correlated with lung cancer.

7. A researcher wonders if people who do not get enough sleep also eat a lot of fast food.

   a) Explain why this is unlikely to be a cause and effect relationship.

   b) Suggest a common cause that could explain this correlation.

8. **Communication** A student discovers that ice-cream sales are positively correlated with occurrences of heat stroke. He suggests that ice-cream consumption could be a cause of heat stroke.

   a) Do you agree with the student? Why or why not?

   b) What advice can you offer to improve his analysis?

9. **Application** The number of deer in a region is positively correlated with the number of wolves.

   a) Explain how this could be a cause and effect relationship with the number of deer as the dependent variable.

   b) Explain how this could also be described as a reverse cause and effect relationship.

✔ **Achievement Check**

10. The table shows time series data for the population of two Ontario towns.

Year	Collingwood	Grimsby
1991	14 382	18 520
1996	15 596	19 585
2001	16 039	21 297
2006	17 290	23 937
2011	19 241	25 325

Source: Cities and Towns Table, City Populations

   a) Create a scatter plot of population of Collingwood versus population of Grimsby. Describe the correlation.

   b) Perform a linear regression. Interpret the equation of the line of best fit.

   c) Do you think this is a cause and effect relationship? Explain your thinking.

   d) What type of relationship do you think this is? Justify your answer with mathematical reasoning.

Use this information to answer #11 to #13.

The table shows the supply and demand for widgets at various selling price points. The demand represents the number of widgets expected to sell at a certain price. The supply represents the number that can be produced at a certain price.

Price ($)	Quantity Demanded	Quantity Supplied
10	18	8
11	17	9
12	15	11
13	14	12
14	12	14
15	10	16
16	9	17

11. Application

a) Create a scatter plot of price versus widget quantity demanded. Describe the correlation.

Processes

Representing

In economics, the independent variable is usually plotted on the vertical axis and the dependent variable on the horizontal axis, contrary to common mathematical convention.

b) Is this likely a cause and effect relationship? Explain.

c) Identify the independent and dependent variables. Explain your thinking.

12. a) Create a scatter plot of price versus widget quantity supplied. Describe the correlation.

b) Is this likely a cause and effect relationship? Explain.

c) Identify the independent and dependent variables. Explain your thinking.

13. Thinking

a) Perform a linear regression for the graphs in #11 and #12, and plot both functions on the same grid.

b) Identify the point of intersection. Explain what it signifies.

c) What will likely happen if the widget price is set
- above the intersection point?
- below the intersection point?

Explain your thinking.

Extend

14. The table shows a time series for the population of Brampton.

Year	1991	1996	2001	2006	2011
Population	234 445	268 251	325 428	433 806	523 911

Source: Cities and Towns Table, City Populations

a) Create a scatter plot of population versus time using technology.

b) Does the correlation appear to be linear? Explain.

c) Perform a linear regression. Describe the goodness of fit.

d) Perform an exponential regression on the data. Describe the shape of the curve that appears.

e) Compare the goodness of fit of the curve of best fit to that of the line of best fit.

f) Why might an exponential model be appropriate for this relationship?

Literacy Link

An *exponential regression* is the process of fitting an exponential curve of best fit to a set of data. To perform an exponential regression, use technology to carry out the same steps as a linear regression, but choose exponential regression instead of linear regression.

15. Investigate the population of a city or town in Ontario that is of interest to you. Graph the time series and compare linear and exponential regression models. Decide which is appropriate and justify your choice using mathematical reasoning.

Dynamic Analysis of Two-Variable Data

Learning Goals

I am learning to

- identify outliers and account for their impact on a data trend
- recognize the presence of extraneous variables
- identify a hidden variable and account for its impact on a correlation

> ## Minds On...

Suppose two athletes are competing for a position on the track and field team in the long jump event. The chart shows their tryout distances, in metres.

	Jump 1	Jump 2	Jump 3	Jump 4	Jump 5	Mean
Hank	4.5	4.0	4.3	4.2	4.0	4.2
Vito	4.9	5.1	4.8	1.2	4.7	4.1

- Which athlete do you think should make the team?
- Could you make an argument for either athlete?
- Is there anything that seems unusual in the data?
- Would more information be helpful?

> ## Action!

Investigate A Residual Plot

Materials

- computer with Fathom™ software

In the previous section, you compared the number of hours studied and final exam grades using a scatter plot and line of best fit. In this activity you will use that data set to perform a deeper analysis of the relationship between the line of best fit and the data that the line is fitted to.

1. a) Your teacher will provide you with a Fathom™ file called **InvestigateAResidualPlot.ftm**.

   b) Examine the scatter plot and line of best fit:
   - Click on a point to read its coordinates.
   - Repeat for a new point.

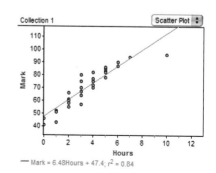

2. a) Identify the coordinates of some points that are right on the line or very close to it.

b) How good a predictor of performance is the linear model for these students? Explain your reasoning.

3. a) What are the coordinates of some points that are relatively far away from the line?

b) Is the linear model a good predictor for these students? Explain.

4. a) Create a residual plot. With the scatter plot selected, choose **Graph** and then **Residual Plot**.

b) Enlarge the graph by clicking and dragging one of the corners of the window frame.

c) Click on a point in the scatter plot and identify its corresponding point in the residual plot. The point (3, 80) is selected below:

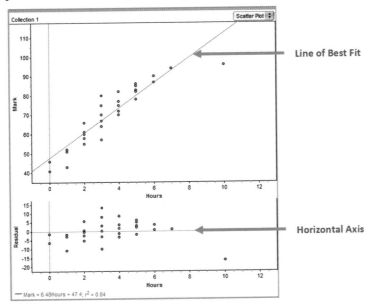

residual plot

• shows the value of each **residual** graphically as the vertical distance from a horizontal axis

residual

• the difference between a data point's actual dependent value and the dependent value predicted by the line of best fit

5. a) Click on a point in the scatter plot. Is it above or below the line of best fit? Is it close to or far from it?

b) Identify the corresponding point in the residual plot. Is it above or below the horizontal axis? Is it close to or far from it?

c) Compare your answers for a) and b).

d) Repeat for several other points.

6. Reflect How does a residual plot appear to be related to a scatter plot?

7. Extend Your Understanding Calculate the difference between the actual exam score and the score predicted by the linear model for several students. Explain how this difference is represented in the residual plot.

Example 1

Construct and Analyse a Residual Plot

Will an increase in recycling result in a reduction of landfill? The table compares the mass of garbage and recycling for a town during a recycling campaign.

Amount Recycled (kg)	Amount of Garbage (kg)
120	200
144	175
160	190
175	156
200	142
210	167
224	140
236	150

a) Create a scatter plot and perform a linear regression. Describe the trend. Is a linear model reasonable in this case?

b) Interpret the residuals for (120, 200) and (200, 142).

c) Construct a residual plot. Describe the pattern.

Solution

Processes

Reasoning and Proving
How do you know to include a negative sign with the correlation coefficient?

a) The scatter plot and linear regression show that as the mass of recycling increases, the mass of garbage decreases. The correlation coefficient of

$$r = -\sqrt{0.70}$$
$$\approx -0.84$$

confirms a strong negative correlation. A linear model is appropriate for describing this relationship.

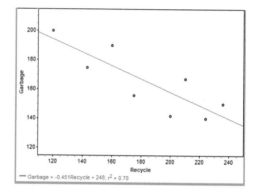

Garbage = -0.451Recycle + 248; r^2 = 0.70

b) The residual of (120, 200) is the difference between the actual mass of garbage (200 kg) and the amount predicted by the linear model. Use the equation of the line of best fit to calculate the amount predicted by the linear model. Let m represent the mass of recycled material and g the amount of garbage, both in kilograms.

$g = -0.451m + 248$ Substitute $m = 120$.
$ = -0.451(120) + 248$
$ = 193.88$

The linear model predicts that approximately 194 kg of garbage would be produced when the recycling amount is 120 kg. Subtract this value from the actual amount of garbage produced to determine the residual.

$200 - 194 = 6$

The residual for this datum is 6, which means that the actual mass of recycled material is 6 kg higher than what the linear model predicts.

Repeat this process for the datum (200, 142).

$g = -0.451(200) + 248$
$ = 157.8$

The actual value is 142. The linear model predicts approximately 158. So, the residual is 142 − 158 = −16.

The residual for this datum is −16, which means that the actual mass of recycled material is 16 kg lower than what the linear model predicts.

c) To construct a residual plot using Fathom™, select the scatter plot and choose **Graph** and then **Make Residual Plot**.

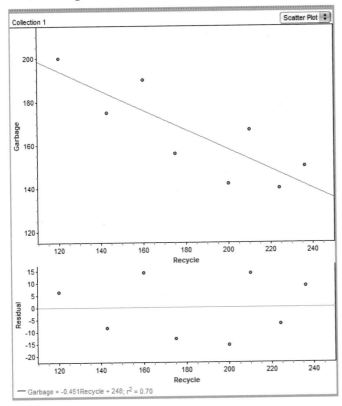

There is no clear pattern in the residual plot. Points seem to be randomly located above and below the horizontal axis. This is normal for a good linear model because there should be roughly the same number of data points above as below the line of best fit.

Your Turn

The table compares a jewellery store's weekly diamond ring sales to the minutes of radio advertising purchased for the same week.

a) Create a scatter plot and perform a linear regression. Describe the trend. Is a linear model reasonable in this case?

b) Interpret the residuals for (20, 7.9) and (18, 4.7).

c) Construct a residual plot. Describe the pattern in it.

Advertising (min)	Diamond Ring Sales ($1000s)
7	1.6
12	4.4
20	7.9
32	10.6
22	6.0
18	4.7
26	7.6

A residual plot can be helpful for deciding how well a linear model fits a set of data. If there is a pattern or irregularity in a residual plot, the linear model may have to be re-evaluated.

Example 2

Account for Outliers

The table shows repair costs over the course of a year for several cars of the same model.

a) Create a scatter plot of repair costs versus age.

b) Perform a linear regression and discuss the goodness of fit.

c) Construct a residual plot and identify any **outliers**.

d) Repeat the regression with the outlier removed.

e) Compare the two linear models.

Age of Car (years)	Repair Costs ($1000s)
4	0.6
4	0.8
4	3.2
5	1.1
6	1.2
6	1.5
7	1.4
8	1.8
9	1.9
10	2.1

outlier

- a data point that does not fit an otherwise clear trend
- in a scatter plot, the outlier is relatively far from the line of best fit
- in a residual plot, the outlier is either relatively far above or below the horizontal line

Solution

Method 1: Use Fathom™

a) Import or enter the data into Fathom™. Select the case table and drag a **New Graph** into the workspace. Drag the **Age** attribute onto the horizontal axis and the **Repairs** attribute onto the vertical axis.

b) With the graph selected, choose **Graph** and then **Least-Squares Line**.

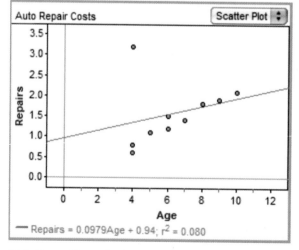

This line of best fit does not appear to serve as a very good model for the data. The relatively high extrapolated vertical intercept suggests around a thousand dollars of repairs for a brand-new vehicle, which does not sound right.

The correlational coefficient,

$r = \sqrt{0.08}$

$\approx 0.28,$

suggests a weak linear correlation, but, except for one point, the data appear to form a strong linear trend. Could the point (4, 3200) be an outlier? Could it be responsible for the construction of a weak linear model?

c) Construct a residual plot and click on the suspected outlier. The residual of (4, 3200) is much farther from the residual line than the other residuals, which appear to have a pattern. This suggests that the outlier has a strong influence on the linear model.

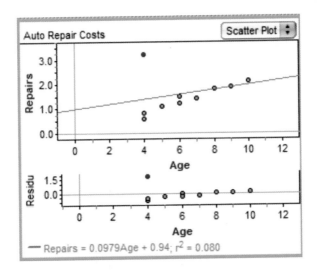

d) Repeat the analysis with the outlier removed. With the point (4, 3200) selected, choose **Edit** and then **Cut Case**. The linear model will be automatically updated.

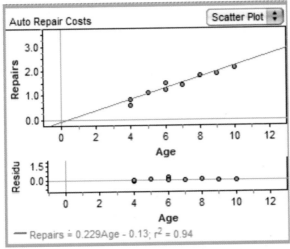

The new line of best fit fits the remaining data very well. The predicted initial repair cost is nearly zero. The correlational coefficient,

$r = \sqrt{0.94}$

$= 0.97,$

suggests a very strong linear correlation. There is no obvious pattern to the residuals and none appear overly far from the residual line. This appears to be a strong linear model for predicting repair costs for this type of vehicle.

Method 2: Use a Graphing Calculator

a) Create a scatter plot of repair costs versus age. Refer to the Prerequisite Skills on page 195 for help.

- Enter the data in the lists.
- Set up the parameters as shown.

- The scatter plot will appear.

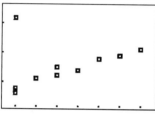

b) Perform a linear regression and store it as function Y1:

- Press **2ND** **QUIT** to go to the home screen.
- Press **STAT**. Then, choose **CALC** and **4:LinReg(ax+b)**.
- Press **2ND** **L1** , **2ND** **L2** , **VARS**. Choose **Y-VARS**. Then, choose **1:Function** and then **Y1**. Press **ENTER**.
- Press **GRAPH** to see the line of best fit.

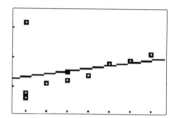

Press **ZOOM** and choose **3:Zoom Out** to see where the line of best fit crosses the vertical axis.

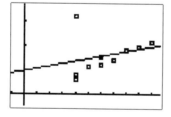

This line of best fit does not appear to serve as a very good model for the data. The relatively high extrapolated vertical intercept suggests around a thousand dollars of repairs for a brand-new vehicle, which does not sound right. The correlational coefficient, $r = 0.28$, suggests a weak linear correlation, but, except for one point, the data appear to form a strong linear trend. Could the point (4, 3200) be an outlier? Could it be responsible for the construction of a weak linear model?

c) Construct a residual plot and look for the suspected outlier:

- Press **STAT** and choose **1:Edit**.
- Move to the top of L3. Press **2ND** **INS** . Type **RESID** and press **ENTER**.
- Press **2ND** **STAT PLOT** . Turn Plot1 off and turn Plot2 on.
- Set the parameters as shown.

- Press **ZOOM** and choose **9:ZoomStat**.

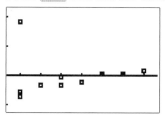

The residual of (4, 3200) is much farther from the residual line than the other residuals which appear to have a pattern. This suggests that the outlier has a strong influence on the linear model.

d) Repeat the analysis with the outlier removed.

- Press **STAT** and choose **1:Edit**.
- Delete the table entries corresponding to (4, 3200).
- Repeat the linear regression analysis.

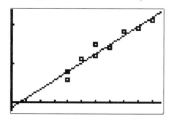 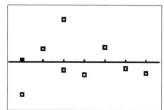

The new line of best fit fits the remaining data very well. The predicted initial repair cost is nearly zero. The correlational coefficient, $r = 0.97$, suggests a very strong linear correlation. There is no obvious pattern to the residuals and none appear overly far from the residual line. This appears to be a strong linear model for predicting repair costs for this type of vehicle.

e) The original linear model was heavily influenced by the presence of an outlying point: a four-year-old car needing $3200 in repairs in one year. This seems quite high compared to the other data; however, there may be other factors involved.

- Was the car involved in a serious collision?
- Did the owner neglect to perform preventive maintenance?
- Was the vehicle just a lemon?

After the outlier was removed from the analysis, the linear model appeared to be quite strong, suggesting that it was the superior model for predicting repair costs for this type of vehicle. The size of the data set, however, is quite small in terms of statistical reliability. A much larger sample size not only would reduce the likelihood of sample bias, but also would lessen the influence of a single outlier.

Your Turn

The table shows the sale price for several used motorcycles of the same model and their age.

Age (years)	Price ($1000s)
1	15
2	13
2	12
3	2
3	10
4	8
4	7.5
4	7
5	6.5
5	6
6	5
7	4

a) Create a scatter plot of sale price versus age.

b) Perform a linear regression and discuss the goodness of fit.

c) Construct a residual plot and identify any outliers. Suggest reasons why any outliers may exist.

d) Repeat the regression with the outlier removed.

e) Compare the two linear models.

Example 3

Account for a Hidden Variable

Is absenteeism among professional workers on the rise in Canada? Are there similar trends for males and females? The contingency table shows the average number of absences for all Canadian males and females who have at least one university degree. Perform dynamic statistical analysis to determine any absenteeism trends.

Literacy Link

A *contingency table* subdivides data into two or more categories.

Absences					
Year	Males	Females	Year	Males	Females
1990	3.7	11	2002	5.2	8.6
1991	3.6	11.1	2003	5.2	8.5
1992	3.6	10.3	2004	5.5	8.7
1993	3.6	11.3	2005	6.4	8.8
1994	3.3	11.5	2006	6.0	9.4
1995	3.1	12.1	2007	5.3	9.9
1996	3.2	12.0	2008	5.7	9.2
1997	4.1	7.7	2009	5.5	9.3
1998	3.8	7.6	2010	5.1	8.8
1999	4.5	7.0	2011	5.4	9.5
2000	4.5	6.8	2012	5.3	8.7
2001	4.6	7.7			

Source: CANSIM Table 279-0036, Absence rates of full-time employees, by sex and education, Canada, Statistics Canada, September 18, 2013

Solution

- In Fathom™, open a new **Collection** and paste the cases. Drag a **New Graph** into the workspace and plot **Males** versus **Year**. From the **Graph** menu, choose **Least-Squares Line**.

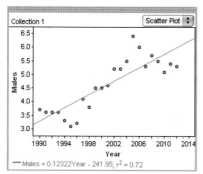

There appears to be an upward trend between male absenteeism and year, with a correlation coefficient of $\sqrt{0.72} \approx 0.85$. Male absenteeism appears to be strongly correlated with time. Professional male worker absenteeism is increasing at a rate of approximately 0.12 days per year.

- Drag a **New Graph** into the workspace and plot **Females** versus **Year**. Then, construct a line of best fit. Examine the data for females.

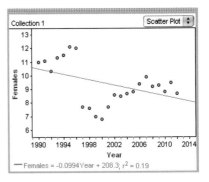

There appears to be a slight downward trend between female absenteeism and year. The correlation coefficient of $-\sqrt{0.19} \approx -0.44$ suggests, however, that this correlation is barely moderate. A closer inspection of this graph reveals two distinct trends, between 1990 and 1996 and between 1997 and 2012. There appear to be two distinct positive trends. What could possibly account for this strange pattern? The following excerpt was taken from the data source:

Footnotes:

1. Data from 1987 to 1996 include maternity leave. Also, men using paid paternity (in Quebec only) and parental leave are included in the calculation till 2006.

Maternity leave is included in absence tallies until 1996 only. This **hidden variable** could account for the fragmented pattern in the data. Remove the data points from 1990 to 1996 and repeat the analysis.

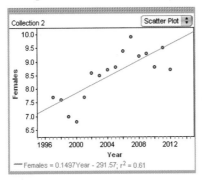

Now the trend for females more closely resembles the male data. A correlational coefficient value of $\sqrt{0.61} \approx 0.78$ confirms that female absence is strongly correlated with time. Absenteeism among female professional workers is increasing at a rate of approximately 0.15 days per year.

The data in this analysis suggest that absenteeism among Canadian professionals is on the rise. A desire to identify possible causes for this could prompt further study.

Your Turn

Do you think men using paid paternity leave in Quebec until 2006 is a significant hidden variable in this analysis? Why or why not?

Key Concepts

- A residual is the difference between the actual dependent value of a datum and the value predicted by a line of best fit.

- A residual plot shows how close each data point is to a line of best fit.

- An outlier is a data point that does not fit well in an otherwise linear trend.

- An outlier can have a strong impact on a linear regression model if the number of data points is relatively small.

- A hidden variable can distort or obscure a linear correlation between two other variables.

- It is important to consider the impact of outliers and hidden variables when conducting a correlational study. It may help to remove or account for them when analysing the data.

Reflect

R1. Explain what a residual plot shows for a set of two-variable data. Draw a sketch to support your answer.

R2. a) What is an outlier?

b) Describe two ways of identifying an outlier in a set of two-variable data.

Practise

Choose the best answer for #1 to #3.

1. Consider the correlation.

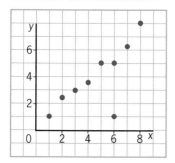

Which statement is most accurate?

A There is a strong positive correlation.

B There is a moderate positive correlation.

C There is a strong positive correlation with an outlier.

D There is a strong positive correlation with a possible hidden variable.

2. Consider the correlation.

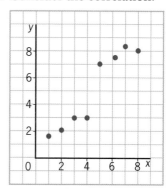

Which statement is most accurate?

A There is a strong positive correlation.

B There is a moderate positive correlation.

C There is a strong positive correlation if the outlier is disregarded.

D There is a strong positive correlation with a hidden variable.

3. What impact can a hidden variable have on a linear trend?

    A It can hide or obscure the linearity.

    B It can cause an irregularity in an otherwise linear trend.

    C Both A and B are possible.

    D It cannot have an impact on the trend.

Use this information to answer #4 to #6.
Is science ability related to math ability? The table shows a set of final grades for a number of intermediate students.

Math Grade	Science Grade
80	75
72	76
84	52
67	70
58	62
90	88
75	77

4. **a)** Create a scatter plot of science marks versus math marks. Perform a linear regression.

    b) Is this a good linear model? Explain why or why not.

5. **a)** Create a residual plot.

    b) Determine the residual for (84, 52).

    c) How does this residual compare to the others?

6. **a)** Repeat the analysis of the previous two questions after removing (84, 52).

    b) Compare the new linear model to the original. Which do you think is better and why?

Apply

7. **Communication** Jonathon's test scores are 80%, 84%, 83%, 40%, and 83%.

    a) Which score appears to be an outlier? Explain.

    b) Determine Jonathon's mean, median, and mode scores.

    c) Remove the outlier. Discuss the impact this has on Jonathon's
    - mean score
    - median score
    - mode score

Use this information to answer #8 and #9.
The table shows the weekly earnings of a restaurant server, including tips.

Time Worked (h)	Earnings ($)
30	540
25	510
33	605
26	780
35	620
29	525

8. **a)** Construct a scatter plot of earnings versus time worked. Describe the correlation.

    b) Perform a linear regression. Interpret the meaning of the equation of the line of best fit.

    c) Is this a useful linear model? Explain.

9. **a)** Construct a residual plot.

    b) Identify an outlier in the data. What could account for the unusual data point?

    c) Repeat the analysis of #8 with the outlier removed.

10. **Open Question**

    a) A set of two-variable data has no outliers. Draw a sketch that shows what its residual plot could look like.

    b) Repeat part a) for a data set that has an outlier.

Use this information to answer #11 to #13.
The graph illustrates the number of Stanley
Cup wins by the Montréal Canadiens over time,
measured in decades. For these questions, 1950
refers to the 1949–50 season, and so on.

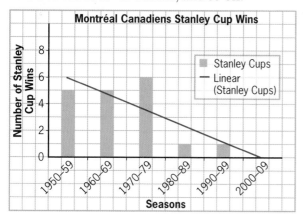

11. a) What does this graph suggest about
the performance trend of the Montréal
Canadiens over the 50-year period?

b) Any team in the National Hockey League
(NHL) is eligible to win the Stanley Cup.
Consider the table, which shows how the
number of teams in the NHL changed
over time. Identify a possible hidden
variable related to the correlation shown
in the graph.

Year	Number of Teams	Year	Number of Teams
1940	7	1980	21
1943	6	1992	22
1968	12	1993	24
1971	14	1995	26
1973	16	1999	27
1975	18	2000	28
1979	17	2001	30

12. The Stanley Cup was not awarded in the
2004–05 season due to a labour disruption.
Discuss how this could also represent a
hidden variable in this study.

13. Based on the given data, could you make
an argument that the Montréal team of the
1970s was a better hockey team than those
of the 1950s or 1960s? Explain.

✔ Achievement Check

14. The table shows the average annual
attendance for a minor league baseball team.

Year	Attendance (thousands)
2001	5.6
2002	5.8
2003	6.3
2004	6.5
2005	6.7
2006	6.8
2007	4.9
2008	5.3
2009	6.5
2010	7.0
2011	7.2
2012	7.4

a) Construct a scatter plot of this time
series. Is baseball interest on the rise?

b) Perform a linear regression. Describe the
strength of correlation.

c) What graphical evidence is there of a
hidden variable?

d) In 2007, a large factory shut down due to
the poor economy. How do you think this
affected this correlational study?

e) What do you think happened over the next
few years following the plant closure?

f) Repeat the linear regression with the data
points for 2007–2009 removed. Compare
this linear model to the previous one.

g) Reflect on the interest in baseball now.

Extend

15. Conduct some research on residuals.

a) How can you tell if a point will have a
positive or negative residual?

b) What is the sum of all residuals for a set
of data? Why does this make sense?

16. Choose a set of data in this section.
Calculate the residuals manually. Then,
Construct a residual plot without using
technology. Explain your method.

Uses and Misuses of Data

Learning Goals

I am learning to

- recognize that the same data can be presented in different ways
- see that the way data are presented can have an impact on how the data are interpreted
- recognize when, how, and why data are deliberately distorted in order to influence the perception of the reader

> ## Minds On...

Data can help us make wise decisions. But data can also cause damage if not used properly. The Education Quality and Assurance Office (EQAO) provides detailed data related to the performance of Ontario students in reading, writing, and mathematics. Educators can use these data to identify areas of strength and weakness in their students' achievement.

- In what ways could educators use these data to help children with their learning?

- Are there any ways that this type of data could be misused?

> ## Action!

Investigate Bias in Two-Variable Data

Materials

- ruler

The graphs represent Ontario's grade 3 EQAO reading scores for the school years from 2008–09 to 2012–13. Each bar represents the number of students who met or exceeded the provincial standard in reading.

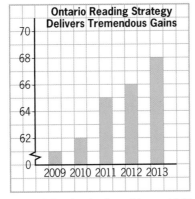

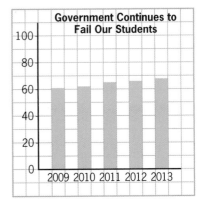

Source: Education Quality and Accountability Office

1. What is the same about the numerical information in these graphs? What is different? Explain.

2. Identify any elements of bias present in these two graphs.

3. a) Do you think the title of the first graph is appropriate? Why or why not?

   b) Do you think the title of the second graph is appropriate? Why or why not?

   c) Write a more appropriate title for these graphs. Explain why your title is a better one.

4. **Reflect** Suggest a particular group that might have constructed each graph, and explain why that group might have presented the graph in the way that it did.

5. **Extend Your Understanding** Read and reflect on the following quotes. What do you think these authors are suggesting or implying?

   "Be able to analyze statistics, which can be used to support or undercut almost any argument."
   Marilyn vos Savant

   "There are two ways of lying. One, not telling the truth, and the other, making up statistics."
   Josefina Vazquez

   "Statistics: the only science that enables different experts using the same figures to draw different conclusions."
   Evan Esar

Processes
Connecting
The authors of these quotes are interesting people. Use the Internet to research them. Also look up other interesting quotes on statistics.

How you choose to display data can have a significant impact on how a reader is likely to interpret them. By changing the vertical scale on a graph, a relatively small trend can be made to appear much larger, and vice versa. The intentional use of biased words can influence the interpretation of data. As a critical user of data, it is important to recognize when, how, and why data are being distorted.

Example 1

Distorting Data to Sway Opinion

Is fighting in hockey on its way out in the NHL? The graph and table illustrate the total number of fights per season in NHL hockey games over time.

Season	Games	Fights
2012–2013	720	347
2011–2012	1230	546
2010–2011	1230	645
2009–2010	1230	714
2008–2009	1230	734

Source: NHL Fight Stats Table, hockeyfights

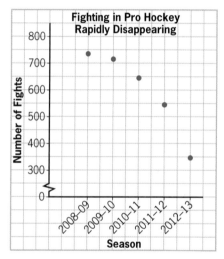

a) Identify the sources of bias in the graph.

b) Present the data in an unbiased way and reinterpret the data.

Solution

Processes

Reflecting
Look at the dramatic drop in fights from 2011–12 to 2012–13. What happened there?

a) Bias exists in both the data and the title of the graph.

Source of Bias	Explanation	Probable Intended Effect
Title	The language is not neutral.	• to convince that fighting is on the decline
Vertical scale	The scale does not start at zero.	• to exaggerate the downward trend
Outlier (2012–13, 720) due to a hidden variable	Only 720 games were played during this season due to a labour disruption.	• to exaggerate the downward trend
Sample size	Only five points were chosen.	• to hide that the trend is less downward over a longer period of time

b) To present the data more fairly, remove the outlier, use a larger sample size, start the vertical scale at zero, and give the graph a title that has neutral language.

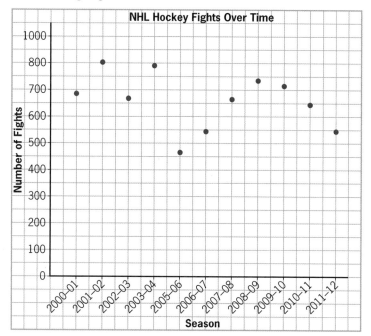

This graph illustrates the data in an unbiased way. While there still seems to be a slight downward trend in the number of fights over time, it appears to be much more gradual than the way it was originally presented. There is little in this graph to suggest that fighting will disappear from the NHL any time soon.

Your Turn

Is the number of multiple-fight NHL games on the decline? The table shows the number of games per season with more than one fight over time.

Season	Games With More Than One Fight
2012–13	66
2011–12	98
2010–11	117
2009–10	171
2008–09	173

Source: NHL Fight Stats Table, hockeyfights

a) Create a scatter plot that shows the number of games with more than one fight as a time series.

b) Is there an outlier in the data? If so, should it be removed? Explain.

c) Identify any other sources of bias that could be distorting the linear correlation.

Example 2

Sensational Use of Data

The following article was taken from an Internet news blog.

The aliens are getting braver: UFO sightings in Canada doubled last year

By Lindsay Jolivet | Daily Buzz

The alien invasion has arrived at Earth's doorstep.

Canadian reports of UFO sightings more than doubled between 2011 and 2012, according to a report released this week by Ufology Research.

People look at the night sky using night vision goggles during a UFO tour (Reuters)

Sure, the skies have become more and more crowded with space junk and debris. And yes, it's possible that we're all getting just a little bit crazier.

However it's safest for everyone if we interpret the data as irrefutable evidence of an imminent attack from extra terrestrials that are swarming our skies in greater numbers than ever.

Canadians reported 1,981 UFO sightings in 2012, according to the report, which analyzed data of reported sightings from researchers and websites that monitor UFOs.

About 40 per cent of last year's reported sightings took place in Ontario.

Library and Archives Canada keeps a database of historical UFO sightings, including a case in 1969 when residents of Prince George, B.C. saw a round, glowing object ascending into the sky. An official RCMP investigation, detailed in a report, found the object was a plastic laundry bag and candles converted into a makeshift hot air balloon.

Well, you can't be too careful with these things.

The report says only a tiny fraction of cases involved close encounters with UFOs and in fact, most were merely sightings of lights in the sky. The report speculates on several explanations, including an increase of secret military exercises or a lack of knowledge about objects frequenting our skies that are not exactly "unidentified."

Chris Rutkowski, Ufology's research director, told the *Winnipeg Sun* last year there was no definitive evidence that any of the people reporting sightings have been in contact with aliens.

But what if he's one of *them*?

Source: Yahoo! News Canada, October 12, 2013

---

a) Discuss how data are used in this article in a questionable way.

b) What inappropriate conclusions are drawn?

c) What is the probable intent of the article?

a) The author does not explain how the data were collected, nor is it made clear what constitutes a "UFO sighting." It may be possible that people who claim sightings are more likely to believe in extra-terrestrial beings and therefore more likely to misinterpret a normal event as a UFO sighting. The data may be subject to voluntary response bias.

b) The title of the article draws an inappropriate conclusion that UFO sightings imply the existence and nearby presence of extra-terrestrial beings. This false conclusion is further established in the third paragraph where the author infers that an invasion is imminent.

c) The article does go on to offer alternative explanations for the reported sightings, and offers a reputable quote suggesting no definite evidence of alien contact. This, combined with the playful opening and final sentences and overall sensational tone of the article, suggest that this was written as a piece of satire, more to entertain than inform.

Literacy Link

In literature, *satire* refers to a written piece that uses sarcasm and other forms of humour to make fun of something. *Sensationalism* is a type of bias where a piece of work uses tactics such as over-exaggeration to provoke an emotional response. The author probably hopes she will increase her readership by generating controversy in these ways.

Your Turn

Consider the following statement taken from the article:

About 40 per cent of last year's reported sightings took place in Ontario.

Does this suggest that aliens are more interested in Ontario than they are in other provinces? Explain your thinking.

Consolidate and Debrief

Key Concepts

- You can display data in multiple ways. Sometimes data are deliberately distorted to make an argument more convincing.

- The media often sensationalize data to generate public interest.

Reflect

R1. a) In what ways can data be deliberately distorted?

  b) List some motives someone could have to deliberately distort data.

R2. A juice company shares data in a television commercial that suggest its brand of juice is twice as popular as a competing brand.

  a) Why would this company want to share this information?

  b) What information would you like to know before making an informed interpretation of the study's findings?

R3. a) What is meant by the sensational use of data?

  b) What is the purpose of using data in a sensational way?

Practise

Choose the best answer for #1 to #3.

1. The graph shows a sales trend over the past six months. Which of the following is the most appropriate title for this graph?

A Sales in sharp decline

B Sales holding steady

C Sales poised to bounce back

D Sales trend over the past six months

2. On a television commercial, three enthusiastic parents claim that a new home study program has done wonders for their children's progress in math. This correlational evidence is likely subject to which of the following biases?

A sample size bias

B random sample bias

C both

D neither

3. Which statement is least likely to have been made for a sensational purpose?

A Human and chimpanzee DNA differ by 0.7%.

B 80% of all automobile accidents occur within 40 kilometres of home.

C The unemployment rate rose this month by 0.5%.

D Three out of four people are easily impressed by statistics.

4. In the supermarket, you see a tabloid newspaper with the following headline: "20% of America convinced the King still lives!" This headline is in reference to Elvis Presley, commonly known as the King of Rock 'n Roll, who died in 1977.

a) How reliable do you consider the data referenced in this headline to be?

b) What questions would you like answered about how the data were collected?

c) What is the likely intended use of the data?

Apply

Use this information to answer #5 to #7.

The data show monthly reported UFO sightings for the period from January 1, 2010 to October 12, 2013.

Reports	Count	Reports	Count
Oct-13	34	Nov-11	440
Sep-13	723	Oct-11	634
Aug-13	850	Sep-11	546
Jul-13	947	Aug-11	634
Jun-13	609	Jul-11	749
May-13	515	Jun-11	393
Apr-13	405	May-11	315
Mar-13	383	Apr-11	315
Feb-13	275	Mar-11	328
Jan-13	369	Feb-11	270
Dec-12	654	Jan-11	325
Nov-12	766	Dec-10	302
Oct-12	664	Nov-10	358
Sep-12	747	Oct-10	465
Aug-12	884	Sep-10	448
Jul-12	919	Aug-10	524
Jun-12	741	Jul-10	833
May-12	511	Jun-10	372
Apr-12	495	May-10	327
Mar-12	527	Apr-10	293
Feb-12	387	Mar-10	261
Jan-12	574	Feb-10	186
Dec-11	530	Jan-10	291

Source: National UFO Reporting Center Report Index by Month

5. Application

a) There is a clear outlier in this data set. Identify it and explain why it should be excluded from the analysis.

b) Create a scatter plot of UFO sightings versus time.

c) Does the number of UFO sightings appear to be on the rise? Explain.

6. Thinking

a) Describe any seasonal trends in the data.

b) Does this suggest that we are more or less likely to be visited by extra-terrestrial beings at different times of the year? Explain your thinking.

7. Communication

a) Do you think there is bias in these data? Why or why not?

b) Identify some questions you would like answered about how the data were collected.

✓ Achievement Check

8. Are Canadian citizens politically involved? The graph below compares voter turnout for Canadian and US citizens over time.

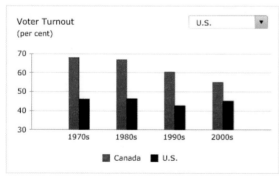

Source: Conference Board of Canada

a) **Open Question** Write a title for this graph that suggests Canada's political interest is consistently strong.

b) How could you adjust the vertical scale of the graph to emphasize your point?

c) **Open Question** Write a title for this graph that suggests Canada's political interest is declining.

d) How could you adjust the vertical scale of the graph to support your point?

Extend

9. The graphs below compare voter turnout for Canadian, Swiss, and Australian citizens over time.

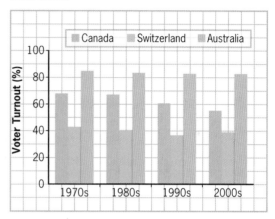

Source: Conference Board of Canada

a) Identify any trends that you see. Suggest some possible reasons for these.

b) Perform some research on the political situation of these countries. Identify and report on any hidden variables that you discover. Your teacher can direct you to some helpful websites.

10. Search the Internet or print media for an example of a sensational use of data.

a) What statistical claim(s) are being made?

b) What is the likely purpose of the article?

c) Why would you consider the data to be unreliable?

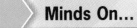

8.5

Advanced Techniques for Data Analysis

Learning Goals

I am learning to

- organize and display data using a variety of tools and strategies
- analyse various representations of data

Minds On...

People who exercise regularly get many health benefits such as lower body fat, higher muscle mass, and better respiratory health.

- How does regular exercise affect resting heart rate?
- How could you use data analysis to find out?

Action!

Example 1

Use a Filter to Compare Groups

The heart rates for two groups of women in their thirties are shown below. The women in Group A train to run marathons. The women in Group B do not exercise regularly.

Group	Resting Heart Rate (bpm)	Working Heart Rate During Exercise (bpm)	Heart Rate 1 Min After Exercise (bpm)	Heart Rate 30 Min After Exercise (bpm)
A	55	175	117	77
B	76	187	125	96
A	59	184	115	85
B	74	189	128	92
B	67	182	134	87
B	80	193	131	90
A	64	179	126	72
A	52	173	121	80
B	65	198	137	96
A	57	186	114	74
B	71	186	134	87
A	59	181	119	79

a) Summarize and compare the resting heart rate and working heart rate of Group A and Group B.

b) Identify any potential bias in the analysis of these data.

Solution

a) You are comparing quantitative, or numerical, data across different categorical groups. One strategy to do this is to run the quantitative data through a categorical filter, training.

Method 1: Analyse Side-by-Side Box Plots Using Fathom™

Import or enter the data into Fathom™. Construct and analyse box plots to compare aggregate resting heart rate and maximum heart rate scores.

- Drag a **New Graph** into the workspace.
- Click and drag the Resting Heart Rate attribute onto the horizontal axis.
- Click on the pull-down menu to change the **Dot Plot** to a **Box Plot**.
- Click and drag the Group attribute onto the vertical axis.
- Repeat these steps for Working Heart Rate.
- Align the graphs vertically.

Adjust the vertical scales to eliminate data distortion.
- Drag the ends of the scale to stretch or compress it.
- Drag the middle of the scale to slide it.

Processes

Representing
In chapter 6, box plots were called box and whisker plots. Both names are commonly used.

Collection 1

Collection 1

	Group	Resting...	Workin...	Heart_R...	Heart_R...
1	A	55	175	117	77
2	B	76	187	125	96
3	A	59	184	115	85
4	B	74	189	128	92
5	B	67	182	134	87
6	B	80	193	131	90
7	A	64	179	126	72
8	A	52	173	121	80
9	B	65	198	137	96
10	A	57	186	114	74
11	B	71	186	134	87
12	A	59	181	119	79

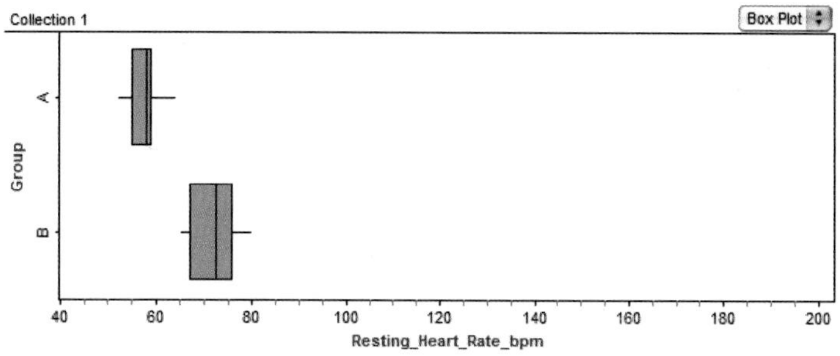

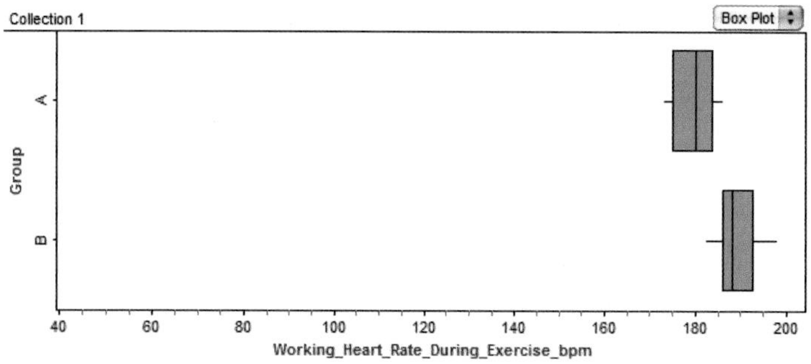

Collection 1

The side-by-side box plots show that Group A had both a lower resting heart rate and a lower working heart rate than Group B.

Filter the table data to compare the summary statistics by group.

- Drag a new **Summary Table** into the workspace.
- Drag the Resting Heart Rate attribute to the right arrow on the summary table.
- Repeat for Working Heart Rate.
- Click and drag the Group attribute to the down arrow of the summary table.

Collection 1

		Resting_Heart_Rate_bpm	Working_Heart_Rate_During_Exercise_bpm
Group	A	57.6667 6	179.667 6
	B	72.1667 6	189.167 6
Column Summary		64.9167 12	184.417 12

S1 = mean ( )
S2 = count ( )

Literacy Link

A *contingency table* shows the frequency distribution of variables in different categories.

The contingency tables show that the marathon runners had a mean resting heart rate of 57.7 bpm compared to a rounded mean of 72.2 bpm for those who did not exercise. The maximum heart rate of the marathon runners had a mean of 179.7 bpm compared to a mean of 189.2 bpm for the group that did not exercise.

Method 2: Analyse a Pivot Table Using a Spreadsheet

A pivot table summarizes data by sorting, giving count totals, or averaging data found in large data tables. Pivot charts provide a visual representation of the summary in the pivot table.

Import or enter the data into a spreadsheet. Use cells A1 to C13. Create a pivot chart and pivot table to compare resting heart rates and working heart rates.

- Select the entire data set.
- From the **Insert** ribbon, click on **PivotTable** and choose **PivotChart** from the drop-down menu.
- Choose **Existing Worksheet** and type A15 into the Location field. Click **OK**.

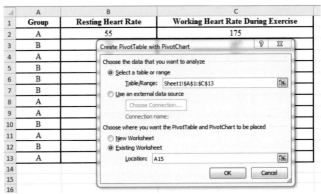

Customize the pivot table to calculate and display the mean heart rates.

- In the **PivotTable Field List**, check the boxes for Group, Resting Heart Rate, and Working Heart Rate During Exercise.

- In the $\sum$**VALUES** section, click on **Sum of Resting Heart Rate** and then choose **Value Field Settings**.

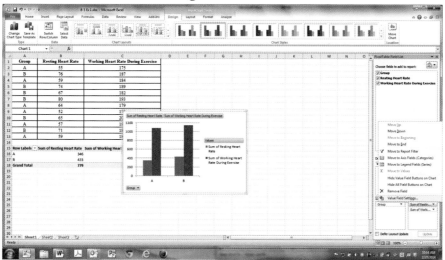

- Change **Sum** to **Average** and click **OK**. Repeat for **Sum of Working Heart Rate**.
- Click **OK**.
- Close the **Pivot Chart Fields** window. The graph will look like this:

Row Labels ▼	Average of Resting Heart Rate	Average of Working Heart Rate During Exercise
A	57.66666667	179.6666667
B	72.16666667	190.1666667
Grand Total	64.91666667	184.9166667

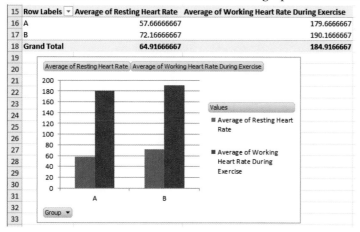

Both the pivot table and chart show that marathon runners had a lower average resting heart rate than non-runners, with an average of 57.7 bpm compared to 72.2 bpm. They also show that marathon runners had a lower average working heart rate than non-runners with an average of 179.7 bpm compared to 190.2 bpm.

b) The analysis of the data in this example is subject to sample size bias. This could be addressed by including additional cases in the study.

Your Turn

Open a new spreadsheet. Summarize and compare the performance of both groups in this example in heart rate after 30 min of exercise and heart rate after 1 min of exercise.

Example 2

Use Graphing Tools to Uncover a Hidden Variable

The table shows distance-time data for a number of bicycle runs. The altitude data represent the net change in altitude over the course of the run.

Distance (km)	Time (min)	Altitude (m)
14.9	37	−80
13.6	28	−200
12.1	42	110
15.7	57	170
20.0	35	−350
15.7	42	100
12.6	37	170
15.3	50	80
14.8	40	−80
11.2	25	−100
14.6	50.3	340

Determine if there is a correlation between distance and time.

Solution

Method 1: Use a Bubble Plot in a Spreadsheet

A bubble plot can show the influence of a third variable in a correlational study. In a bubble plot, each point becomes a bubble whose size corresponds to the value of the third variable. In the case of positive and negative values, the colour of the bubble becomes significant.

Enter the data in a spreadsheet. Create a scatter plot of time versus distance and perform a linear regression.

Processes

Reasoning and Proving
Usually distance is plotted against time. Why does it make sense to plot time versus distance in this case?

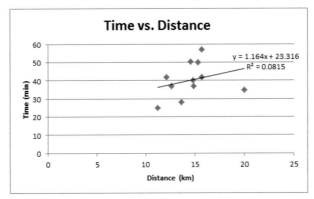

There does not appear to be a strong linear correlation between run time and distance, which seems unusual. The correlation coefficient $r = 0.29$ suggests a weak linear correlation.

Consider the altitude data. Could this be a hidden variable obscuring the linear correlation?

Construct a bubble plot to see if altitude change has an impact on the trend.

- Select the entire data set. From the **Insert** ribbon, click on **Other Charts** and choose **Bubble Chart**.
- Right click on one of the bubbles and choose **Format Data Series**.
- Under **Series Options**, check **Show negative bubbles**.
- Close the **Format Data Series** window.

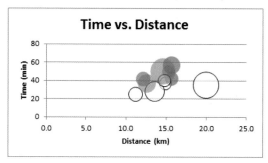

The bubble plot confirms that change in altitude is obscuring the linear correlation between run time and distance. The uphill runs, represented by the blue bubbles, tend to have longer run times than the downhill runs, represented by the white bubbles.

Method 2: Use a Legend Attribute in Fathom™

In Fathom™, you can identify the impact of a third variable by analysing a legend attribute. A legend attribute adds a colour scale to the data points, which corresponds to the value of the third variable being measured.

Enter the data into a Fathom™ table. Create a scatter plot of time versus distance and perform a linear regression.

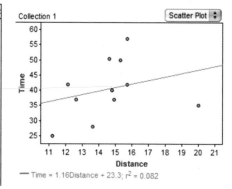

There does not appear to be a strong linear correlation between run time and distance, which seems unusual. The correlational coefficient $r = 0.29$ suggests a weak linear correlation.

Consider the altitude data. Could this be a hidden variable obscuring the linear correlation?

Add a legend attribute scale to see if altitude change has an impact on the trend.

- From the **Graph** menu, uncheck **Least-Squares Line**.
- Click and drag the Altitude attribute onto the middle of the graph.

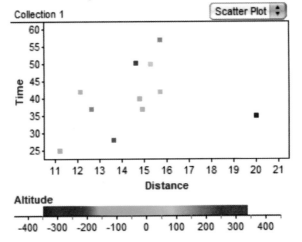

The altitude attribute scale confirms that altitude is obscuring the linear correlation between run time and distance. The uphill runs, represented by the yellow, orange, and red points, tend to have longer run times than the downhill runs, represented by the purple, blue, and bright green points.

To account for this hidden variable, it would make sense to collect and analyse more distance-time data for runs with identical altitude changes.

Your Turn

a) In Fathom™, open the sample file found here: **Sample Documents/Sports/Bicycling.ftm**. Repeat the analysis performed in this example using the data. A sample of the data is shown.

Distance (km)	Time (min)	Altitude (m)
14.5	33.7	−80
9.7	15.2	−270
8.9	14.4	−130
12.0	58.0	600
14.4	20.0	−600
17.9	31.0	−350
10.3	27.0	0
5.6	15.0	70
10.3	31.0	155
9.5	31.0	125
9.2	17.5	−125
5.4	15.8	45
7.9	36.2	380
6.4	19.2	−160
14.5	38.4	−140

b) Are your results consistent with those in the example? Discuss.

Key Concepts

- Raw data can be awkward to work with. Software progams have tools to filter, organize, present, and analyse data.

- Contingency tables, side-by-side box plots, pivot tables, and pivot charts are methods for comparing quantitative data across different categories.

- Bubble plots and legend attributes are tools that can be used to recognize the possible impact of a hidden variable in a correlational study.

Reflect

R1. a) What is a contingency table?

    b) How can a contingency table be useful?

R2. Refer to Example 1.

    a) How were side-by-side box plots used?

    b) What did they illustrate?

R3. Refer to Example 2. What information did the bubble plot and the legend attribute provide that the scatter plot did not?

R4. Consider the tools and strategies used in this section. Write a summary of their advantages and disadvantages. Use examples to support your points.

Practise

Choose the best answer for #1 to #3.

Use this information to answer #1 and #2.

The contingency table shows the unemployment rate for non-student youths aged 15 to 24.

Year	Male Unemployment Rate (%)	Female Unemployment Rate (%)
2008	14.9	11.3
2009	19.8	11.6
2010	19.8	13.2
2011	15.6	12.2
2012	17.5	13.3

Source: CANSIM Table 282-0095, Labour force survey estimates (LFS), by full- and part-time students during school months, sex and age group, Statistics Canada, January 9, 2014

1. What are the mean unemployment rates for the time period shown?

  A 15.6 for males and 12.2 for females

  B 17.5 for males and 12.3 for females

  C 19.8 for males and 13.25 for females

  D 14.9 for males and 11.6 for females

2. Which of the following characterizes the linear correlation between male and female unemployment rates?

  A strong positive

  B strong negative

  C moderate positive

  D moderate negative

Use this information to answer #3 and #4.

The graph shows the winning times for the New York Marathon from 1970–1999.

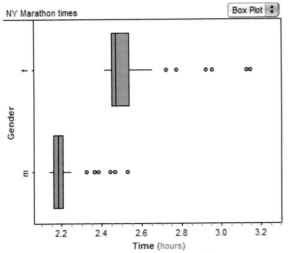

Source: Fathom™: Sample Documents/Sports/MarathonTimes

3. Which of the following statements is true?

   A The fastest female time is about 2.5 hours and the fastest male time is about 3.2 hours.

   B The mean male winning time is about 2.2 hours and the mean female time is about 2.5 hours.

   C The median male winning time is about 0.3 hours faster than the median female time.

   D None of the above is true.

4. What are the fastest winning times shown for males and females?

Apply

Use the data in Example 1 on page 424 for #5 and #6.

5. **Application** In Fathom™, select a summary table. From the **Summary** menu, choose **Add Basic Statistics**. What summary statistics are generated?

6. **Application** In Fathom™, select a summary table. From the **Summary** menu, choose **Add Five Number Summary**. What summary statistics are generated?

Use the data in Example 2 Your Turn on page 430 for #7 and #8.

7. **a)** Use a filter in Fathom™ to separate the downhill runs from the uphill runs.
   - Create a scatter plot of time versus distance, as in the example.
   - From the **Object** menu, choose **Add Filter**.
   - Choose **Attributes** and double click on **Altitude**.
   - Type < 0 m and click **OK**.

   The uphill runs will be filtered out leaving only the downhill runs.

   b) Perform a linear regression and interpret the equation of the line of best fit.

8. **a)** Repeat the analysis filtering out the downhill runs.

   b) Compare the two linear models. Does it make sense for them to differ in this way? Explain.

Use this information to answer #9 to #11.

Your teacher will provide you with a Fathom™ file called **Hotdogs.ftm**.

9. **Thinking** Is there a correlation between sodium and fat content in hot dogs?

   a) Create a scatter plot of number of calories versus amount of sodium.

   b) Perform a linear regression. Describe the correlation.

   c) Repeat the analysis separately for each type of meat. Compare the linear models and the strength of correlation to the original model in each case.

   d) Is the type of meat a hidden variable in the correlation between calories and sodium? Explain why or why not.

> **Processes**
>
> **Selecting Tools and Computational Strategies**
> To analyse only beef hot dogs, you can use a filter:
> - With the scatter plot selected, click on **Object** and choose **Add Filter**.
> - Choose **Attribute** and double-click on **Type**.
> - Type = "Beef" and click on **OK**.

10. Communication Which types of hot dogs have the least amount of sodium?

a) Create side-by-side box plots to compare the amount of sodium in each type.

b) Create summary statistics and interpret the results.

11. Which types of hot dogs have the lowest number of calories? Repeat the analysis from the previous question for number of calories.

✓ Achievement Check

12. The table provides preparation and performance data for a number of students at a driving school.

Gender	Study Hours	Road Hours	Written Test (%)	Road Test (%)
M	4	9	80	95
M	6	8	70	90
F	6	5	75	80
F	7	6	80	85
F	8	5	95	85
F	7	7	85	85
M	5	8	80	85
M	4	6	75	70
F	8	7	90	85
M	3	8	75	90
M	5	7	85	80
F	9	4	70	75
M	2	5	85	80
F	8	7	80	85
M	4	9	90	95
F	7	9	90	95

a) Use tools and strategies from this section to compare the average number of hours studied and written test score for males and females.

b) Compare the performance of the two gender groups.

c) Repeat the analysis for average number of road hours and road test score for both genders.

13. Application A group of elementary students were chosen at random to write a literacy test. Their results are shown.

Grade	Score
4	7
3	6
5	8
2	3
2	4
6	6
5	7

a) Use Fathom™ to construct a scatter plot. Describe the correlation.

b) Construct a dot plot with a grade legend attribute.
  • Drag a **New Graph** into the workspace.
  • Drag the **Score** attribute onto the horizontal axis.
  • Drag the **Grade** attribute onto the middle of the graph.

c) How does the second graph represent the correlation between grade and score?

Extend

Use this information to answer #14 and #15.

The table shows the popularity of four Ontario political parties over the course of five surveys.

Conservative	34	35	35	35	34
Liberal	31	29	31	30	47
NDP	29	28	27	25	16
Green	6	8	5	6	2

Source: Ontario Voter Support Separated by Party, Laurier Institute for the Study of Public Opinion

14. Application

a) Enter the data into a spreadsheet. Create a column of sparklines.
  • Highlight the numerical data.
  • From the **Insert** ribbon, choose **Line** from the Sparklines menu.
  • To enter a Location Range, highlight four empty cells in a column beside the data table. Click OK.

b) Describe what appears.

15. Communication

a) What do the sparklines illustrate?

b) What do they not show clearly?

c) Do any sparklines distort the data? Explain.

Learning Goals

Section	After this section, I can
8.1	• classify a linear correlation between two variables • determine a correlation coefficient using technology • produce a line of best fit using linear regression
8.2	• distinguish between correlation and causality • identify the type of relationship between two variables
8.3	• identify outliers and account for their impact on a data trend • recognize the presence of extraneous variables • identify a hidden variable and account for its impact on a correlation
8.4	• recognize that the same data can be presented in different ways • see that the way data are presented can have an impact on how the data are interpreted • recognize when, how, and why data are deliberately distorted in order to influence the perception of the reader
8.5	• organize and display data using a variety of tools and strategies • analyse various representations of data

8.1 Line of Best Fit, pages 382–391

1. Match each scatter plot with its correct correlation coefficient.

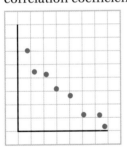 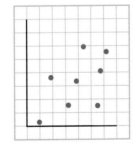

Correlation coefficients:
−0.97, −0.56, 0.56, 0.97

2. The table shows a trucker's distance from home over time.

Time, t (h)	Distance, d (km)
0.5	500
1.0	425
1.5	360
2.0	280

a) Use graphing technology to create a scatter plot of the data.

b) Determine the strength of linear correlation between these variables.

c) Perform a linear regression. Interpret the meaning of the equation of the line of best fit.

8.2 Cause and Effect, pages 392–401

3. Children's self-esteem is positively correlated with their level of achievement.

a) Suggest a cause and effect relationship that could account for the results.

b) What reverse cause and effect relationship could also account for the results?

4. Characterize each of the relationships. The independent variable is listed first.

a) Computer sales are negatively correlated with the unemployment rate.

b) The price of gas is positively correlated with the performance of a football team.

c) Running speed is positively correlated with heart rate.

8.3 Dynamic Analysis of Two-Variable Data, pages 402–415

Use this information to answer #5 and #6.

The table shows student population data for a new high school. The school wants to project the school's population growth over time.

Year	Population
2007	778
2008	984
2009	998
2010	1010
2011	1018
2012	1026

5. a) Create a scatter plot of population versus time. Call 2007 year 0. Describe the correlation.

   b) Perform a linear regression. Interpret the equation of the line of best fit.

   c) Create a residual plot. Does this appear to be a good linear model? Explain.

6. Grade 12 was not offered until 2008.

   a) How does this information affect the correlational study? Does it make sense to remove the 2007 datum? Explain.

   b) Repeat the analysis with the outlier removed. Compare the two models.

   c) Use both models to predict the school's population in 2016. Which model should the principal rely on and why?

Use this information to answer #7 to #9.

The graph shows a newspaper's annual average circulation data.

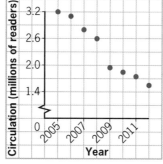

7. a) Describe the trend in sales.

   b) Is there evidence of a hidden variable?

   c) When do you think the newspaper raised its price from $1 to $1.50? Explain.

   d) Explain how the price change represents a hidden variable in this correlation.

8.4 Uses and Misuses of Data, pages 416–423

8. How does the vertical scale in the newspaper circulation graph distort the linear trend?

9. Suppose this graph were published with the headline "Newspaper circulation in free fall."

   a) Explain how this title is biased.

   b) Write an unbiased title for this graph.

8.5 Advanced Techniques for Data Analysis, pages 424–433

Use this information to answer #10 to #12.

The table shows a group of students' grade 12 calculus marks and first year university marks. Half took a summer prep course.

Yes Prep.		No Prep.	
Grade 12	First Year	Grade 12	First Year
80	77	77	65
70	72	74	68
92	86	68	60
84	84	70	64
85	84	81	72

10. a) Create a scatter plot that compares first year marks to grade 12 marks.

   b) Perform a linear regression. Interpret the correlation coefficient.

   c) Was the summer prep course helpful?

11. a) Create a contingency table and side-by-side box plots or a pivot table and pivot chart to compare the two groups.

   b) Use summary statistics to determine if the summer prep course is helpful.

12. a) Use a bubble plot or a legend attribute to compare the two groups.

   b) Does the graph show that the prep course is helpful? Explain.

✓ **Achievement Chart**

Category	Knowledge/ Understanding	Thinking	Communication	Application
Questions	1, 2, 3	7	4, 5	6

Multiple Choice

Choose the best answer for #1 to #3.

1. Classify the nature of each linear correlation.

   a)

   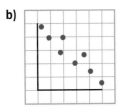

   A moderate positive correlation

   B strong positive correlation

   C moderate negative correlation

   D strong negative correlation

   b)

   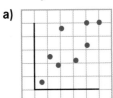

   A moderate positive correlation

   B strong positive correlation

   C moderate negative correlation

   D strong negative correlation

2. Consider the scatter plot relating two variables.

   Which of the following best characterizes this correlation?

   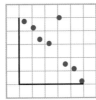

   A strong positive correlation

   B strong negative correlation

   C strong negative correlation with a hidden variable

   D strong negative correlation with an outlier

3. The graph shows the unemployment rate over a five-month period.

   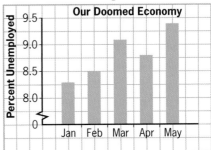

   Which of the following contribute to bias in this graph?

   A the title

   B the sample size

   C the choice of vertical scale

   D all of the above

Short Answer

4. Classify each of the relationships. The independent variable is listed first.

   a) Snow tire sales are positively correlated with hot chocolate sales.

   b) Movie box office sales are negatively correlated with ticket price.

   c) Driving test scores are negatively correlated with driver height.

   d) Cheeseburger sales are negatively correlated with pita sales.

5. Attendance at football games is positively correlated with a team's position in the league standings.

   a) Suggest a cause and effect relationship that could account for the results.

   b) Pose and defend an argument for a reverse cause and effect relationship.

Extended Response

6. The table shows the speed of a skydiver as she falls from the instant she leaves a plane.

Time (s)	Speed (m/s)
0	0.0
1	5.0
2	9.1
3	12.5
4	15.8

a) Construct a scatter plot of speed versus time. Describe the correlation.

b) Perform a linear regression. Interpret the equation of the line of best fit.

7. The number of users of a social networking website is shown as a time series.

Time (months)	Users (millions)	Time (months)	Users (millions)
1	1.2	7	3.3
2	1.5	8	1.7
3	2.0	9	1.6
4	2.4	10	1.3
5	2.7	11	1.1
6	3.1	12	0.9

a) Construct a scatter plot of this time series. Describe the trend.

b) Perform a linear regression. Interpret the equation of the line of best fit.

c) Construct a residual plot. Do you think this is a good model for this correlation? Explain why or why not.

d) Is there evidence of a hidden variable? Explain.

e) Initially this website was free. When did the website start charging a fee? How do you know? Explain the effect this had on the linear trend.

f) Use a graph to illustrate the impact of this hidden variable on the time series correlation.

g) Construct a new linear model that will do a better job of predicting the future popularity of this website. Discuss your reasoning, including any assumptions you make.

Chapter Problem

Climate Change

Present your findings on climate change in one of the following formats:
- written report
- electronic slideshow
- podcast
- poster or infographic

Consider your culminating project. What elements of two-variable data could be relevant? Will your project involve exploring multiple data sets? What tools and strategies from this chapter will you use to organize, filter, display, and analyse your data? How will you identify and account for outliers and hidden variables?

Chapters 7 and 8 Cumulative Review

1. The chart shows systolic blood pressure measurements for a sample of 30 athletes.

Systolic Blood Pressure (mmHg)					
120	118	118	115	120	119
124	120	115	122	121	117
121	124	116	123	118	121
117	123	116	116	123	122
119	115	124	117	122	119

a) Is the distribution uniform?

b) What is the height of the probability distribution?

c) What is the probability that an athlete's blood pressure is 120 mmHg or less?

d) How would you expect the distribution to differ if the general population was measured instead of a select group? Give reasons for your answer.

2. At a provincial high school track meet, 40 contestants participated in the discus event. The table shows the results.

Distance (m)	Frequency
25–30	1
30–35	3
35–40	5
40–45	9
45–50	6
50–55	6
55–60	5
60–65	3
65–70	1
70–75	1

a) Sketch a frequency histogram for these data.

b) Sketch a frequency polygon.

c) Estimate the mean distance thrown.

d) Add a relative frequency column to the table.

e) What is the probability that a contestant throws the discus more than 60 m?

f) How would you expect the distribution to differ if the data were taken from students in a physical education class instead of those who were participating in a track meet? Give reasons for your answer.

3. A large number of airplanes in Canada are built from kits. A company advertises that building its kit takes a mean time of 300 h, with a standard deviation of 40 h. The company has sold 120 such kits.

a) What percent of the builders are expected to take longer than 400 h to complete their kits?

b) How many builders are expected to finish their kits in less than 250 h?

c) If 120 kits were given to people selected at random from the community, how would the distribution of times change? Give reasons for your answer.

4. An industrial wind turbine is designed to produce a maximum of 1.8 MW of power in a 60 km/h wind. Lab tests of 120 turbines showed that seven did not meet this standard.

a) Determine a 99% confidence interval for the proportion of turbines from the plant that do not meet the standard.

b) Use a standard statistical format suitable for a report to state the results of the lab tests.

5. A drug prescribed to prevent gout produces side effects in 2% of patients who take it. A new formulation is tested on 1500 patients, and 20 suffer side effects.

a) Could this distribution be reasonably modelled using a normal approximation? Give reasons for your answer.

b) Determine the mean and standard deviation of the normal approximation.

c) What is the probability that the new formulation is no better than the original? Use the normal approximation to determine the probability that at most 20 patients suffered side effects.

d) Is the company justified in claiming that the new formulation results in side effects in about 1.3% of the patients who take it? Give reasons for your answer.

6. The table gives the distance of a hiker from camp over time.

Time (min)	Distance (km)
10	0.5
20	1.1
30	1.4
40	1.7
50	2.4

a) Create a scatter plot of distance versus time. Describe the correlation.

b) Perform a linear regression. Interpret the equation of the line of best fit.

7. A study found that worker absenteeism is negatively correlated with income level.

a) Do you think this is a cause and effect relationship? Explain.

b) Suggest a possible common cause factor that could account for this relationship.

8. Characterize each type of relationship.

a) Automotive sales is positively correlated with amount of rainfall.

b) Number of hours practised is negatively correlated with number of musical errors.

9. The table shows student achievement for the grade 9 applied EQAO assessment over time.

Year	Percent Achieving at or Above Provincial Standard
2001–2002	21
2002–2003	21
2003–2004	25
2004–2005	27
2005–2006	35
2006–2007	35
2007–2008	34
2008–2009	38
2009–2010	40
2010–2011	42
2011–2012	44
2012–2013	44

Source: Education Quality and Accountability Office

a) Create a scatter plot for this time series. Call 2001–2002 year 0. Describe the correlation.

b) Perform a linear regression. Interpret the equation of the line of best fit.

c) Construct a residual plot. Does there appear to be any evidence of a hidden variable in the data? Explain.

d) In 2005, the math curriculum was revised. Could this fact be considered a hidden variable? Why or why not?

e) Repeat the analysis performed in parts a) to c) for 2005–06 to 2012–2013.

f) Is there evidence that this linear model is better than the original one? Explain.

10. The graph shows the point totals for a hockey player's first five seasons.

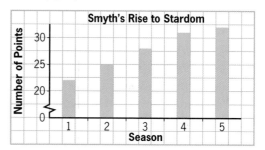

a) Identify any sources of bias in the graph.

b) Smyth's contract is up for renewal. Do you think the graph was made by the team manager or by Smyth's agent? Explain your thinking.

c) How could you remove all bias in the graph?

11. Research the gender income gap (GIG) and report on the following:

- What initiatives have been put in place to try to eliminate the GIG in Canada?

- Has the Canadian GIG been increasing, decreasing, or stayed constant over time?

- How does the Canadian GIG compare to that of other countries?

Use graphs, summary statistics, and the tools from this section to support your points.

CHAPTER
9

Culminating Investigations

In every province and territory except Nunavut, it is illegal to use a hand-held wireless communication device while driving. Why are these laws put in place? How are data collected to justify the laws? How do insurance companies apply probability theory to calculate insurance rates?

In this chapter, you will learn how to design and complete culminating projects for probability and statistics. Sections 9.1 and 9.2 will show you how to apply probability concepts to design a culminating probability project. Sections 9.3 and 9.4 will demonstrate how to use the research process to complete a culminating statistics project. Both of these projects will require you to design a framework for planning, completing, and presenting your work. Your teacher will provide you with a timeline for your project. Section 9.5 will review how your project will be evaluated and how you will evaluate your peers' projects.

Career Link

Statistician

People who effectively collect, analyse, summarize, and represent data can support law reform, social change, health education, business growth, and more. Samuel Perreault is a statistician who collects data on the incidence of impaired driving rates across the country. The information he collects helps police forces and educators target impaired driving. Statisticians study statistics in a mathematics or social science program at university. How might data collection and analysis be helpful in other sectors, such as marketing, environmental science, health and wellness, travel and tourism, technology, manufacturing, or transportation?

Key Terms

research question
hypothesis

Planning and Carrying Out a Culminating Probability Project

Learning Goals

I am learning to

- assess games for elements of chance or randomness
- critique games for fairness
- plan a game of chance for a culminating probability project

Board games, lotteries, sweepstakes, and other contests have varying degrees of elements of chance. How can you calculate the probability of winning those games to become an informed player?

You can also use probability to simulate real-life events. For example, you could use Sidney Crosby's historical shooting percentage and simulate him taking 300 shots per season for 10 seasons to see what type of variation there would be in his goal-scoring totals. What are some other ways you could use probability or simulations in a culminating project?

Investigate A Game of Chance

Materials

- 3 dice per group
- 10 counters per player
- 100 counters per dice roller
- playing board with numbers 3 to 18

Triple Your Chances, Double Your Counters is a dice game in which players guess the sum of a roll of three dice.

3	5	7	9	11	13	15	17	18
	4	6	8	10	12	14	16	

1. Read the instructions for the game. In a group, play a few sample rounds, and record your data as you play. One person will be the dice roller and the rest will be players.

   Instructions:
   - Each player has 10 counters.
   - The dice roller has 100 counters.
   - A player places **one** counter on a sum on the game board.
   - The dice roller rolls the dice.
   - If the sum of the dice matches the sum chosen by a player, the player wins. The table on the next page shows the number of counters a player wins for a given sum.

- If the sum of the dice does not equal the sum chosen by the player, the dice roller wins those counters. The game ends when the players have no counters left.

Outcome of the Dice Roll	Counter Payout to the Player
Sum of 9, 10, 11, or 12	1 (win back the counter, plus one more)
Sum of 7, 8, 13, or 14	2 (win back the counter, plus two more)
Sum of 5, 6, 15, or 16	3 (win back the counter, plus three more)
Sum of 3, 4, 17, or 18	9 (win back the counter, plus nine more)

2. In your group, discuss and rank the game for each criterion in the chart.

Criteria	Ranking		
Description of game	Poorly described	Somewhat clear	Makes sense
Uniqueness of game	Not unique	Somewhat unique	Very unique
Complexity	Not complex	Somewhat complex	Very complex
Clarity of rules	Not clear	Somewhat clear	Very clear
Fun factor	Not fun	Somewhat fun	Very fun
Fairness toward players	Hard to win	Some chance to win	Easy to win
Chance vs. skill	All skill	Some chance	All chance

3. For your probability project, you could conduct a number of trials of a game and analyse the experimental and theoretical probability of the player winning. What are the pros and cons of using this game for a probability project, based on your assessment so far?

Investigate Creating a Game of Chance

1. Work with a partner or in a small group. Brainstorm a list of board games, card games, or computer games you have played.

2. Research various kinds of lottery games (Lotto 649), sweepstakes (Heart & Stroke Lottery, Princess Margaret Home Lottery), television game shows (*Deal or No Deal*), or other board games (Monopoly, Risk) to add to your list.

3. Sort the games in your list based on how you win: purely on chance, purely on skill, or both chance and skill.

4. Consider the games in your list that are based purely on chance. Choose one game and answer the following questions to analyse it.

  a) How do you play? Are the rules clearly described? How do you win?

  b) How complex is the game?

  c) How fun is the game?

  d) How is the game marketed to consumers?

  e) Is the probability of winning reported on the game? If so, report the probability of winning.

  f) Does the game seem fair to the players? Why or why not?

  g) What kind of data might the game generate?

  h) What other interesting information do you notice about this game?

  i) What elements/materials from this game could be used to create a new game of chance?

5. a) Is it possible to represent all the outcomes for your game in a chart or diagram? Why or why not?

> **Example:** In the lottery game Lotto 649, players choose six numbers between 1 and 49. They can choose repeat digits, so there are 49^6 or 13 841 287 201 total six-number combinations possible. There are too many outcomes to show them all in a list, chart, or diagram.

  b) Brainstorm how to calculate the theoretical probability of winning the grand prize.

> **Example:** In Lotto 649, only one set of six numbers wins the grand prize. There is only one way to win the game out of 13 841 287 201 possible outcomes.
>
> So, the theoretical probability of winning is $\dfrac{1}{13\ 841\ 287\ 201}$.

  c) If probability cannot be calculated based on the information given, what additional information is necessary?

  d) Could the game be changed to simplify the probability calculations?

6. Reflect What game ideas could you incorporate into your game of chance project? What tools, such as dice, could you use to generate random numbers?

7. Extend Your Understanding How could you change the game you analysed to increase the players' chance of winning? How about to decrease the players' chance of winning?

Step 1: Prepping for Game Construction

1. Create a mind map to brainstorm ideas about a game of chance you could create. Consider the games you investigated above, as well as any games discussed in class. Include details about how your data, calculations, and analysis might look.

Project Prep

Refer to the analysis of a game of chance in section 9.2 for more ideas.

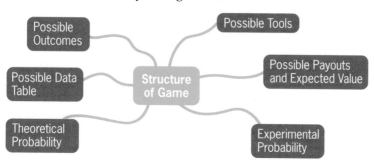

2. Create a list of materials needed to construct your game.

3. Brainstorm the instructions for your game and how you will share them with players.

4. Decide on an appropriate payout structure for the winners.

5. What kind of data will your game generate? Design a chart you can use to record your data.

Round of Play	Desired Outcome	Actual Outcome	Number of Counters Won	Your Running Balance
1				
2				
3				

6. Simulate your game and record the data to test your instructions and data collection chart. Edit your instructions and chart if necessary.

7. Work with a partner to determine what probability calculations you can perform on the data generated. If you cannot calculate the theoretical probability of winning your game, you may need to change its structure. Does your game need to be
   • simplified? more complex?
   • easier to play? easier to track?
   • more fair to the players? more fair to you?

8. If your class is having a game day or fair to collect data, determine
   • how you will attract people to your game and how you will manage the data collection process
   • how you will educate people about games of chance in the real world and their probability of winning and fairness compared to your game

Step 2: Assessing Your Plan

Use the checklist to determine whether your game of chance plan is on track.

The Game	Yes	No
Is your game based solely on chance?		
Is your game • unique • fun • easy to understand • quick to play?		
Have you collected or created all the materials for your game?		
Have you prepared a chart to record data while playing your game?		
Have you calculated the theoretical probability of winning your game and planned an appropriate payout for the winners?		
If your class is having a game day or fair, have you developed a marketing strategy to attract players to your game?		
Are the rules clearly outlined and available to players? If your class is having a game day or fair, consider sharing the rules of the game as a poster, a short explanation, or a soft copy via LCD.		
If you are working with a partner, do you each have roles for game day?		
If your class is not having a game day or fair, have you determined how you will collect data for your game?		

Step 3: Collecting Your Data

1. Collect data for your game, either on a game day or by playing or simulating your game multiple times.

2. Be sure to keep track of all outcomes and payouts.

Analysing a Culminating Probability Project

Learning Goals

I am learning to

• critique a game of chance and the related analysis

Investigate Analysing a Culminating Probability Project

Kaelyn and Emma presented the following information about Triple Your Chances, Double Your Counters in a culminating project report. See section 9.1 for the game instructions.

Read Kaelyn and Emma's report. Then, complete the questions to critique and analyse it. Consider how you might analyse your game of chance and what elements you would include in your report. Record your ideas.

Triple Your Chances, Double Your Counters: Student Analysis of the Game

Theoretical Distribution of the Sum of Three Dice

There are 216 total possible sums when three dice are rolled at once.

		1						2						3						4						5						6				
	1	2	3	4	5	6	1	2	3	4	5	6	1	2	3	4	5	6	1	2	3	4	5	6	1	2	3	4	5	6	1	2	3	4	5	6
1	3	4	5	6	7	8	4	5	6	7	8	9	5	6	7	8	9	10	6	7	8	9	10	11	7	8	9	10	11	12	8	9	10	11	12	13
2	4	5	6	7	8	9	5	6	7	8	9	10	6	7	8	9	10	11	7	8	9	10	11	12	8	9	10	11	12	13	9	10	11	12	13	14
3	5	6	7	8	9	10	6	7	8	9	10	11	7	8	9	10	11	12	8	9	10	11	12	13	9	10	11	12	13	14	10	11	12	13	14	15
4	6	7	8	9	10	11	7	8	9	10	11	12	8	9	10	11	12	13	9	10	11	12	13	14	10	11	12	13	14	15	11	12	13	14	15	16
5	7	8	9	10	11	12	8	9	10	11	12	13	9	10	11	12	13	14	10	11	12	13	14	15	11	12	13	14	15	16	12	13	14	15	16	17
6	8	9	10	11	12	13	9	10	11	12	13	14	10	11	12	13	14	15	11	12	13	14	15	16	12	13	14	15	16	17	13	14	15	16	17	18

Possible Sums (x)	Probability $P(x)$	Expected Sum $x \cdot P(x)$	Counter Payout to Player (X)	Probability $P(X)$	Expected Payout $X \cdot P(X)$
3	$\frac{1}{216}$	$\frac{3}{216}$	9	$\frac{1}{216}$	$\frac{9}{216}$
4	$\frac{3}{216}$	$\frac{12}{216}$	9	$\frac{3}{216}$	$\frac{27}{216}$
5	$\frac{6}{216}$	$\frac{30}{216}$	3	$\frac{6}{216}$	$\frac{18}{216}$
6	$\frac{10}{216}$	$\frac{60}{216}$	3	$\frac{10}{216}$	$\frac{30}{216}$
7	$\frac{15}{216}$	$\frac{105}{216}$	2	$\frac{15}{216}$	$\frac{30}{216}$
8	$\frac{21}{216}$	$\frac{168}{216}$	2	$\frac{21}{216}$	$\frac{42}{216}$
9	$\frac{25}{216}$	$\frac{225}{216}$	1	$\frac{25}{216}$	$\frac{25}{216}$
10	$\frac{27}{216}$	$\frac{270}{216}$	1	$\frac{27}{216}$	$\frac{27}{216}$
11	$\frac{27}{216}$	$\frac{297}{216}$	1	$\frac{27}{216}$	$\frac{27}{216}$
12	$\frac{25}{216}$	$\frac{300}{216}$	1	$\frac{25}{216}$	$\frac{25}{216}$
13	$\frac{21}{216}$	$\frac{273}{216}$	2	$\frac{21}{216}$	$\frac{42}{216}$
14	$\frac{15}{216}$	$\frac{210}{216}$	2	$\frac{15}{216}$	$\frac{30}{216}$
15	$\frac{10}{216}$	$\frac{150}{216}$	3	$\frac{10}{216}$	$\frac{30}{216}$
16	$\frac{6}{216}$	$\frac{96}{216}$	3	$\frac{6}{216}$	$\frac{18}{216}$
17	$\frac{3}{216}$	$\frac{51}{216}$	9	$\frac{3}{216}$	$\frac{27}{216}$
18	$\frac{1}{216}$	$\frac{18}{216}$	9	$\frac{1}{216}$	$\frac{9}{216}$
		$\sum x \cdot P(x) = \frac{2268}{216}$ $= 10.5$			$\sum X \cdot P(X) = \frac{416}{216}$ ≈ 1.9

The expected sum of three dice in this game on any given roll is 10.5, which means we expect the average sum of three dice will be 10.5.

The expected payout shown in the table is 1.9. So, we should expect to pay about 1.9 counters to players for each round of play. Assume one counter is placed on each sum in any given round. This means we would collect 16 counters from players and keep an average of 14.1 or 88% of the counters, suggesting this game is not very fair to the players.

Processes

Connecting
How would this calculation change if players could place 5 counters on the board? 10 counters? between 1 and 10 counters?

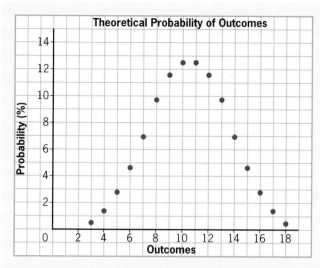

Notice the pattern. Sums of 3 and 18 have the least chance of occurring in the game because there is only one way to make each sum with three dice. Sums of 10 and 11 can each be made 27 ways with three dice, so they have the highest probability of occurring.

We used the probability of each possible outcome to help us decide how many counters to pay out when a player landed on a sum. Sums that are highly likely pay out fewer counters, compared to sums that are less likely.

Experimental Data: Sample of 10 Die Rolls Out of 120 Rounds of Play

Outcomes Chosen by Player	Actual Sum of Dice Rolled	Player Loss	Player Win	Number of Counters Won by Player	Balance of Counters for Die Roller (started with 100)
18	12	X		−1	101
17	10	X		−1	102
5	5		X	+3	99
16	10	X		−1	100
14	14		X	+2	98
8	8		X	+2	96
13	9	X		−1	97
6	10	X		−1	98
14	12	X		−1	99
4	4		X	+9	90

Kaelyn and Emma collected 120 rounds of experimental data. The table shows a sample of only the first 10 rounds to highlight how they recorded their data.

Calculating Experimental Probability for Sums

To collect data for our game, we played the game for 120 rounds and recorded our data.

Sum	3	4	5	6	7	8	9	10	11	12	13	14	15	16	17	18
Number of Times Sum Occurred	0	1	2	5	7	9	12	21	21	19	8	11	1	3	0	0

To calculate the experimental probability of each sum, we used the number of times a sum occurred out of the total number of rounds played.

$$P(9) = \frac{\text{\# of times occurred}}{\text{\# of rounds played}} \times 100$$
$$= \frac{12}{120} \times 100$$
$$= 10\%$$

The calculations shown are a sample of experimental probability calculations done for each of the possible sums.

$$P(12) = \frac{\text{\# of times occurred}}{\text{\# of rounds played}} \times 100$$
$$= \frac{19}{120} \times 100$$
$$\approx 16\%$$

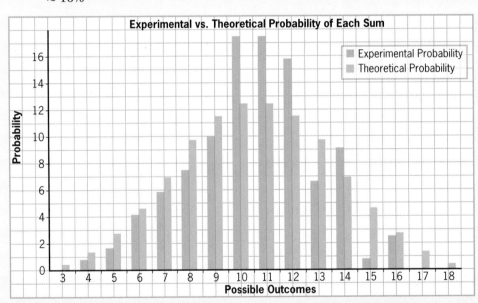

Calculating Counter Payout Based on Experimental Probability From 120 Rounds

Sum	3	4	5	6	7	8	9	10	11	12	13	14	15	16	17	18
Number of Times Sum Occurred	0	1	2	5	7	9	12	21	21	19	8	11	1	3	0	0
Number of Matches With Player	0	1	1	2	5	6	0	0	0	0	6	7	0	2	0	0
Payout Factor	9	9	3	3	2	2	1	1	1	1	2	2	3	3	9	9
Total Payout		9	3	6	10	12					12	14		6		

After playing 120 rounds, we had to pay out a total of 72 counters. This means we paid out $0.6 \left(\frac{72}{120}\right)$ counters for every round played in our game.

Conclusions

The Experimental vs. Theoretical Probability of Each Sum graph shows which sums occurred more often than expected in our game. Sums of 9, 10, 11, and 12 occurred most often. Since these sums can be made in many ways with three dice, this is not a surprise. However, we would have expected sums 8, 13, and 15 to occur more often based on their theoretical probability.

In the experimental distribution, sums of 3, 17, and 18 show a probability of zero, which is also not a surprise because each of these sums also has the lowest theoretical probability. The theoretical probability suggests many of the outcomes should have occurred more often, even if only a little more often.

We would expect the theoretical and experimental probabilities to become more similar with more rounds of play.

In reality, the game was not very fair, as we had a significant advantage for winning counters. To make the game more fair we could alter the payout structure to provide greater payouts or allow players to put counters on more than one sum. For example, provide a grouping of {3, 4, 17, 18} with a 9 : 1 payout ratio. If a player placed a counter on the {3,4,17,18} group, the payout would be 9 counters if one of those sums were rolled.

1. What are the key elements of Kaelyn and Emma's analysis?

2. Could a tree diagram represent the possible outcomes of their game?

3. Does their analysis fully examine the probability of winning and any pros and cons of their game?

4. Does 120 rounds of play to calculate experimental probability seem large enough? What might happen if they played 500 or 1000 rounds?

5. **a)** Refer to page 15 for instructions on how to create a random number generator on a graphing calculator, or download an app. Simulate the outcomes of the game using 1000 and 5000 rounds of play.

   b) Compare the results to the experimental probability distribution for 120 plays. What do you notice?

6. Does the title of the game Triple Your Chances, Double Your Counters describe the probability of winning this game? Why might this title have been chosen?

7. Why do you think Kaelyn and Emma chose the payout structure they did? Do you agree with the counter payout offered to the player for each possible sum?

8. Do the charts and graphs provide a clear and accurate representation of their game and calculations?

9. What elements could be added or changed to more clearly explain the game, outcomes, and probability calculations?

Step 4: Planning Your Report

1. Are there any similarities between Kaelyn and Emma's game and your game of chance?

2. How might you represent the key elements of your analysis?

3. What graphs or charts could you use to represent data collected in your game?

4. What calculations could you include in your game of chance analysis? How will you show these calculations?

5. Would you make any adjustments to the payout structure in your game to ensure you win, or to make it more enticing for the player to continue playing?

6. What amount of data would you collect for your game of chance?

7. Could you use a random number generator to represent your data? If so, how many plays might you simulate? What results would you expect compared to the theoretical probability of winning your game, and to your experimental distribution if you simulated more rounds of play?

8. What would be an effective title for marketing your game of chance?

9. What elements of Kaelyn and Emma's game and analysis would you keep, change, or add to make a better game and report for your culminating probability project?

Step 5: Writing Your Report

> **Project Prep**
>
> Refer to section 9.5 for tools to self-assess your probability report.

A well-written report is organized, logical, and includes the necessary information with appropriate headings. Pull all the pieces together to tell the story of your game and its analysis in the form of a report. Your report should include

- a description of the game, rules, and required materials

- data from the game day or simulation

- calculations of the theoretical distribution, experimental distribution, and expected value

- comparison of the theoretical and experimental distributions

- summary of conclusions, including discrepancies in the results and insights and reflections about the game

Step 6: Finalizing Your Project

Look back at the theoretical probability for the game Triple Your Chances, Double Your Counters. Were the results very likely, given the number of trials Kaelyn and Emma ran?

While the game was being played, Logan was overhead saying, "This game is so easy! I could win five times in just five rounds! All I have to do is put my counters on 10!" Kaelyn and Emma did not agree and did the following calculations to disprove the statement.

Since a sum of 10 has the highest probability of occurring, we assumed that Logan will place his counter on 10 for all five plays. We can use a binomial distribution to represent the number of wins that occur out of five games because:

- Each roll of the dice is an independent event.
- There is a fixed number of dice being rolled.
- There are two possible outcomes: success or failure (either the sum on the dice is 10 or it is not).
- The chances of success remain constant, assuming Logan places his counter on 10 for all five rounds.

The table shows the chances of winning on each of the five rounds.

Number of Wins Out of Five Rounds	Probability of Winning Out of Five Rounds, $P(x) = {}_nC_x p^x q^{(n-x)}$
0	$P(x) = {}_5C_0(0.125)^0(0.875)^{(5-0)}$ $= 0.512\ 91$
1	$0.366\ 36$
2	$0.104\ 68$
3	$0.014\ 95$
4	$0.001\ 068$
5	$0.000\ 030\ 5$

Theoretical probability of rolling a sum of

$10 = \dfrac{27}{216}$

$= 0.125.$

Our calculations show that Logan has a 51.3% chance of winning 0 out of 5 rounds played, assuming the same outcome is chosen for each of the five rounds.

Also, Logan's chance of winning 1, 2, 3, 4, or all 5 times out of five rounds gets progressively lower, suggesting that our game is actually not very easy to win.

1. Was a binomial distribution an appropriate choice to show the chances of winning from 0–5 times in five rounds?

2. Under what conditions does a binomial distribution model not work for this game?

3. Would another distribution model fit the data from this game better? Explain how you know.

4. What kind of distribution model might best fit the data from your game of chance? Include this information in your report and justify your calculations.

Step 7: Assessing Your Probability Project

Use the checklist to ensure your probability project is on track.

The Report	Yes	No
Does your report include: • Title page • Appropriate use of headings • Description of the game and relevant background information • Outline of the rules, including how to win • Explanation of the fee structure (cost to play) • Data table representing actual data from the game day • Actual winnings earned in the game based on your data table		
Have you calculated and/or graphed: • Theoretical distribution (possible outcomes vs. probability) • Experimental distribution (actual outcomes vs. probability) • Expected value of the game (profit based on your theoretical calculations)		
Does your analysis of the results: • Compare and contrast the theoretical and actual distributions • Discuss any discrepancies in the results • Provide insights and reflections about the game • Summarize your conclusions		
Review the following elements of your report: • Terminology: Are mathematical terms used correctly? • Neatness: Is your font clear and readable? Does your report look professional? • Writing Skills: Have you followed proper writing conventions? • Organization: Are key ideas presented logically, clearly, and concisely? Is your report focused and on topic? • Creativity: Have you included pictures or diagrams that make the report interesting? • Technology Skills: Are your visuals easily understood? Are your graphs clearly labelled?		

9.3

Planning and Carrying Out a Culminating Statistics Project

Learning Goals

I am learning to

- pose research questions and state hypotheses
- design a plan to investigate a research question
- gather, organize, and represent data

Does
level of education
affect earning
potential?

Does
a part-time job
affect a student's
marks?

Does
living in a city with
high pollution increase
my chances of having
asthma?

How
does the number
of followers a celebrity has
on social media affect
earnings?

In 2009, legislation was passed in Ontario making it illegal to use hand-held devices while driving. What prompts the need for such a law? As cell phone use increases, police officers are reporting that more accidents are occurring while drivers are texting. Does texting while driving increase your chances of being in an accident? To answer this question, researchers are collecting data to look for trends.

Overview of the Research Process

research question

- a question about a topic, problem, or area that can be investigated or solved

hypothesis

- a prediction about the relationship between variables or about the outcome of a research question
- used to guide an investigation or experiment

Questions or ideas arise in nature, health, science, and various other fields.
Does texting while driving increase your chances of having an accident?
Does exercise reduce your risk of heart disease?

↓

Researchers explore the question further. They use the Internet, libraries, government publications, databases, and all other available resources.

↓

Based on the information found in their search, researchers revise the initial **research question** into a prediction statement called a **hypothesis**.
Texting while driving increases your risk of having an accident.
Regular exercise reduces your risk of heart disease.

↓

Researchers gather data to find out whether the prediction is accurate. They may use existing sources such as Statistics Canada or collect data via surveys, games, simulations, or experiments.

↓

Researchers use charts, graphs, pictures, or tables to organize the data. Then, they use statistical tools, calculations, or equations to see what story the data tell.

↓

Researchers summarize the story and share it with other researchers for critiquing. The validity of the research method and analysis is assessed.

↓

The results of research projects can affect policies and programs.

Step 1: Defining and Posing the Problem

Materials

• computer with Internet access

A good research question explores a relationship between two variables.

For example:
• What is the relationship between car insurance premiums and a driver's age?
• What is the relationship between education and income level?

1. Consider your interests and search for current issues or controversies in newspapers, magazines, or on the Internet.

2. Construct a graphic organizer showing your areas of interest, related issues, and possible research questions. You could use a concept map, a mind map, a graffiti sheet, or a chart.

3. Add a hypothesis to your graphic organizer for each research question in your list. Write your hypothesis as a prediction statement. The chart shows some examples. The dependent variable is underlined. The independent variable is italic. Identify the dependent and independent variable for each of your research questions.

Possible Research Questions	Hypothesis Written as Prediction Statement
What is the relationship between *homework completion* and grades in math?	Completing more homework questions will raise your math mark.
What is the relationship between the amount of *exercise* a person gets and their resting heart rate?	Regular cardiovascular exercise leads to a lower resting heart rate.
What is the relationship between *time spent playing video games* and fitness level?	As time spent playing video games increases, fitness level decreases.

4. a) Choose a question from the graphic organizer that you wish to use as your project question.

   b) What kind of data would help you investigate your question?

   c) Who is the population and sample for your research question?

Once you have chosen a research question and determined your hypothesis, you will need to collect some data to support your hypothesis. In some cases, data on your variables may already exist. If you cannot find existing data, you can alter your research question to match available data, or you might collect your own survey data.

Example 1

Searching for Data

Search for data on the following research question: What is the relationship between texting while driving and being in a collision?

Solution

An Internet search on texting, driving, and collisions suggests that texting while driving is becoming a problem and is a topic worthy of investigation.

"Instead of drinking, drivers are now distracting themselves to death."

Source: "How the War on Drunk Driving Distracts from the Real Danger," *Maclean's*, October 21, 2013.

"According to the Ontario Provincial Police, as of the beginning of September, 32 deaths in the province this year are attributable to impaired driving, while 47 were caused by distracted driving."

Source: "How the War on Drunk Driving Distracts from the Real Danger," *Maclean's*, October 21, 2013.

"Texting is the most deadly of these distractions. The Canadian Automobile Association claims texting drivers are 23 times more likely to be in an accident than a driver who's paying attention to the road."

Source: "How the War on Drunk Driving Distracts from the Real Danger," *Maclean's*, October 21, 2013.

"Experiments have also shown drivers who are actively texting have reaction times substantially slower than someone legally impaired by alcohol."

Source: "How the War on Drunk Driving Distracts from the Real Danger," *Maclean's*, October 21, 2013.

"Analysis of driving performance revealed that participants responded more slowly to the onset of braking lights while texting and driving. Moreover, text-messaging drivers were involved in more crashes than drivers not engaged in text messaging. Text messaging while driving has a negative impact on simulated driving performance. This negative impact appears to exceed the impact of conversing on a cell phone while driving."

Source: Drews, Frank A., et al., "Text Messaging During Simulated Driving," *Human Factors: The Journal of the Human Factors and Ergonomics*, December 16, 2009.

"Rigging a car with a red light to alert drivers when to brake, *Car and Driver* tested how long it takes to hit the brake when sober, when legally drunk at .08, when reading an e-mail, and when sending a text.

The results:
Unimpaired: .54 seconds to brake
Legally drunk: add 4 feet
Reading e-mail: add 36 feet
Sending a text: add 70 feet"

Source: LeBeau, Philip, "Texting and Driving Worse Than Drinking and Driving," Behind the Wheel, CNBC, June 2009.

After doing this initial research, you might hypothesize that texting while driving increases the chance that the driver will be in a collision. You could then collect data on how often people text while driving and on how often texting is listed as the cause of an accident. You might search websites such as Transport Canada, Statistics Canada, Traffic Injury Research Foundation (TIRF), or Canadian Automobile Association (CAA) to find this information.

Suppose that after extensive searching you cannot find the data you need to answer your research question, but instead find data on deaths and injuries from collisions and data on wireless subscribers for the same time period.

You could alter your research question to investigate the relationship between the number of cell phones in use and the number of accidents during the same time period. You might hypothesize that as cell phone purchases increase, accidents also increase because more cell phones likely means more opportunities for distracted driving and related accidents to occur.

Consider the table. You can use these data to calculate one-variable and two-variable statistics because they come from Canadians over the same time period.

Year	Total Deaths or Injuries From Collisions in Canada	Number of Wireless Phone Subscribers in Canada
1991	249 217	771 060
1992	249 823	1 023 810
1993	247 593	1 321 387
1994	241 899	1 868 882
1995	238 458	2 584 387
1996	227 283	3 414 711
1997	217 401	4 207 019
1998	213 319	5 317 247
1999	218 457	6 883 195
2000	222 869	8 731 220
2001	216 489	10 678 560
2002	222 707	11 934 565
2003	216 210	13 442 350
2004	206 229	14 984 396
2005	204 764	16 809 988
2006	199 970	18 425 194
2007	192 744	19 919 512
2008	176 455	21 513 862
2009	171 415	22 850 757
2010	170 629	24 567 947

Sources: Collision and Casualties 1991–2010, Transport Canada
Mobile Wireless Subscribers in Canada, Canadian Wireless Telecommunications Association

The graph shows injuries or deaths from collisions as a function of the number of wireless phone subscribers.

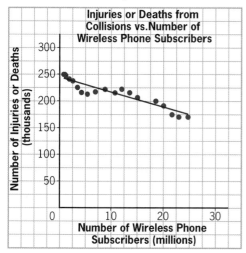

According to the graph, as the number of wireless phone subscribers increases, the accident rate appears to decrease.

With a correlation coefficient of –0.94 and an r^2 value of 0.88, there appears to be a strong negative linear correlation. This result **contradicts** the hypothesis that as the number of cell phone subscribers increases, accidents will also increase.

When unexpected results arise, researchers must consider what other factors could account for the results.

Consider the following graphs. What trends do you notice?

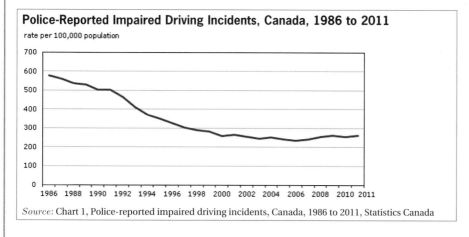

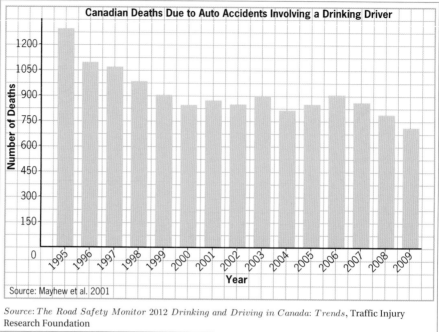

Canadian Deaths Due to Auto Accidents Involving a Drinking Driver

Source: Mayhew et al. 2001

Source: The Road Safety Monitor 2012 *Drinking and Driving in Canada: Trends*, Traffic Injury Research Foundation

The graphs show a decline in both impaired driving incidents and deaths resulting from a drinking driver. Education about the risks of impaired driving may have reduced the frequency of impaired driving, which could result in a fewer accidents.

Further, graduated licensing programs adopted starting in 1994 allow for more driving practice before full driving privileges are granted. Studies have shown that this contributes to the decrease in the overall accident rate.

Increased enforcement of speed limits and increased levels of fines and licence suspensions might be another factor contributing to the decreasing number of accidents.

Lastly, in recent years more drivers might be using Bluetooth technology leading to fewer accidents resulting from cell phone use.

To summarize, the negative correlation between the number of cell phones in use and accident rates could have occurred because accident rates are dropping for a variety of reasons.

Some important information is missing from the data that were collected:
- How many of the accidents were actually the result of cell phone use in the first place?
- Of these accidents, how many can be attributed to texting?
- Have either of these variables changed over time?

Without knowing the answers to these questions, the result of the regression analysis is not reliable. Even though the relationship has a correlation coefficient of –0.94 and an r^2 value of 0.88, **no conclusions** can be drawn about accident rates and cell phones in use, or about accidents resulting from texting while driving, because so many other variables could have been responsible for the decrease in accident rates.

Further investigation is required to support the hypothesis that increased cell phones in use leads to an increased accident rate.

If your research and analysis also lead to unexpected results, you don't need to start over. Instead, consider possible explanations for your results and discuss ideas for future study.

In terms of texting and driving research, teens participated in a plan to investigate distracted driving behaviours as follows:

"[H]igh school students in 10 Canadian cities [were asked] to conduct a national distracted-driving blitz. The students staked out major intersections and toted-up drivers doing things they shouldn't. Nearly 20 per cent of all drivers were spotted either talking or texting on their cell phones, something that's illegal in all provinces."

Source: "How the War on Drunk Driving Distracts from the Real Danger," *Maclean's*, October 21, 2013.

In the absence of ideal data, you may still be able to present a convincing argument if you apply your critical thinking skills.

Step 2: Finding and Collecting Secondary Data

1. Search the Internet for websites related to your question of interest.

2. Search the Statistics Canada website to determine whether data on your variables have already been collected.

3. Search newspapers, magazines, journals, or other literature for more background information or data. If you cannot find data, or if the amount of data is overwhelming, consider revising your research question.

4. Keep track of the websites you use and cite your online references properly.

APA Style

Format for referencing an article from a website:

Organization or Author's Last Name, Author's First Initial. (Year, Month Day Published). *Website Title*. Retrieved Month Day, Year, from URL.

Example:

Canadian Automobile Association. (2014). *CAA Bike Safety*. Retrieved Feb. 21, 2014 from URL.

Format for referencing a data set from a website:

Organization or Author's Last Name, First Initial. (Year). Table name [Data file], Retrieved from URL.

Example:

Statistics Canada. (2014). Labour Force Survey January 2014 [Data file]. Retrieved from URL.

---

5. a) Are the data you found valid and related to your research question?

b) What is the source of the data? Is this a reliable source for data? How do you know?

c) How were the data collected?

d) What was the sample for this data set? Will it allow you to make predictions about the larger population?

e) Is there any evidence of bias in the data collection method?

f) Can the data be organized to facilitate retrieval and analysis?

g) How much and what kind of data do you need for your project?

h) Do you need to revise your research question?

Example 2

Surveying for Data

Secondary data are not always available, so researchers may need to collect their own data. Surveys are a common tool for collecting primary data. Cassie wants to investigate the relationship between time spent using technology (cell phones, texting, social media sites, video games, and so on) and students' academic performance.

a) Create a paper survey to help Cassie determine which questions to use. Consider what kind of data the survey questions could generate.

b) If Cassie wants to use an electronic survey, what criteria should she first consider?

Solution

a) Read each question and consider the response the question would generate.

Cassie's Survey

For #1 to #6, circle one answer per question.

1. What is your gender?	Male Female
2. What grade are you in?	9 10 11 12 12+
3. Do you own a cell phone?	Yes No
4. Do you use text messaging?	Yes No
5. Do you use social media websites?	Yes No
6. Do you play video games?	Yes No

Each question generates categorical data that would allow Cassie to compare results across a category. For example, she might compare the technology use of males and females, or of students by grade.

For #7 and #8, circle one answer per question.

7. How much time did you spend on your cell phone yesterday?

0-1 hrs	1-2 hrs	2-3 hrs	3-4 hrs	4-5 hrs	5-6 hrs	6-7 hrs	7-8 hrs	8-9 hrs	9-10 hrs	10-11 hrs	11-12 hrs

8. How many texts did you send yesterday?

0-20	20-40	60-80	80-100	100-120	120-140	140-160

For each question, the data generated will fall into one of the given ranges. Providing ranges on a survey can help respondents consider a wider variety of responses. However, the midpoint of each range would have to be used to calculate measures of central tendency, which could diminish the level of accuracy of the calculations and results.

For #9 and #10, think about a typical week and answer as accurately as possible.

9. How many hours did you spend on social media websites yesterday? _____

10. How many hours did you spend playing video games yesterday? _____

11. What is your current math mark? _____

12. What was your overall average mark on your last report card? _____

Why is this better than asking how many hours you spend on social media websites per day?

Processes

Connecting
What data management tools can you use to investigate numerical data such as the answers for #9 to #12?

These questions allow respondents to enter their own data. The questions are open-ended with no restrictions, which can generate more accurate results as long as respondents answer truthfully.

b) In chapter 5, you created a survey using Fathom™ and Google Docs. You can also create a survey using online survey tools. Before committing to an electronic survey, you need to be sure the technology fits your purpose.

Consider the following criteria to help you determine which type of electronic survey best meets your needs. Cassie's responses are shown.

Criterion	Cassie's Response
Is there a fee to use the service?	Fees may make it harder for me to get participants.
Is there a limit to how many survey questions can be asked?	10 to 20 questions should be enough.
Does the tool allow for open and closed questions?	Questions can be framed either way to get the data I need.
How is the survey sent out? Examples: email, telephone, posted for the public	It would be easiest to give the survey website to participants
Can anyone respond?	I will limit my sample to participants from school.
How is anonymity protected?	Accuracy may not be compromised since data I am collecting are not personal or sensitive.
Is there a time limit or expiration on the survey site?	As long as I get participants right away, this will not matter.
How are the survey data organized?	I can change the format if I need to.
When are the data available?	Right away is best.
How easy is the survey to use, for both the surveyor and respondents?	If it is too hard to complete, no one will participate.

Before doing a paper or electronic survey, test your survey on a small sample to check whether your questions make sense.

Step 3: Gathering Primary Data

If you cannot find secondary data to help answer your research question, you may need to create your own survey to collect primary data. Refer back to Cassie's survey in Example 2 on page 463. What kinds of questions did Cassie ask?

1. Brainstorm a list of questions for your survey.

2. How will you structure your questions to maximize clarity and minimize bias? Decide the best way to ask each of your survey questions. For example, open response, multiple choice, a scale, or a scale with intervals.

3. Construct your survey. Remember to protect the anonymity of survey respondents by avoiding questions that reveal their identity.

4. Do the survey to see how long it takes to answer. Check for errors.

5. Give a few copies of your survey to a small sample to ensure your survey questions make sense and provide appropriate, valid responses.

6. Edit your survey as required.

7. Determine what amount of data is required for your project. Decide who you will survey, and how you will distribute your survey to ensure valid results.

8. If your survey questions will allow you to graph your data, calculate one and two variable statistics, and tell a meaningful story, then it is time to collect your data.

Step 4: Graphing Your Data

Once you have collected data, it is helpful to see the data summarized in a graphical format, such as a table, chart, or graph.

1. What kind of graph would best represent your data?

2. Graph your data using more than one type of graph. This will allow you to determine which visual best represents your data. Be sure to consider the most appropriate scales and labels for your graph and variables.

3. What are the advantages or disadvantages of each type of graph?

4. Examine your graphs. Do you see any patterns?

5. Are there any outliers? How might these outliers affect your one-variable and two-variable statistics calculations?

Step 5: Assessing Your Project So Far

Use this checklist to ensure your statistics project is on track.

Defining the Problem	Yes	No
The chosen topic is relevant and appropriate.		
The hypothesis is clearly stated and justified.		
The dependent and independent variables are clearly defined.		
The population of interest is clearly identified.		
Background information is used to introduce the research question.		

Secondary Data Collection	Yes	No
The source of data (URL) is provided.		
The sampling technique is described and justified.		
Sources of sampling bias are identified.		
Sufficient data are collected.		
The raw data are effectively represented.		

Primary Data Collection	Yes	No
The sample survey is included in the report.		
The survey contains an appropriate introduction.		
The survey questions are well designed.		
The data are collected in a timely and responsible manner.		
Survey participants' anonymity is clearly protected.		
Sufficient survey data are collected.		
Raw survey data are effectively represented.		

Data Analysis	Yes	No
The data are represented using appropriate charts and graphs.		

Analysing a Culminating Statistics Project

Learning Goals

I am learning to

- represent and interpret one- and two-variable statistics from a data set
- evaluate the impact of outliers on my calculations and justify my results
- organize, summarize, and interpret the key results of my data analysis

Mean, median, and mode are three common statistical calculations used to provide a snapshot or quick summary of a data set. The range, interquartile range, standard deviation, and variance also help describe the general distribution of a data set.

- How will you share your measures of central tendency and dispersion in your statistics project?

- What might be an effective and interesting way to summarize these calculations?

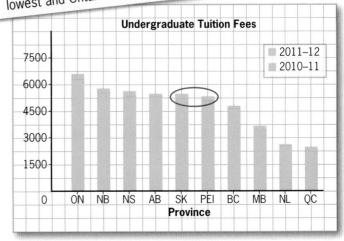

Median: Saskatchewan and PEI tuition fees fall in the middle, with Quebec at the lowest and Ontario at the highest end.

Source: CNW Group/Canadian Federation of Students

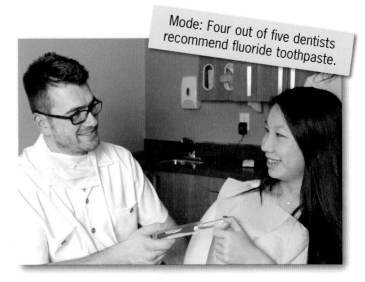

Mode: Four out of five dentists recommend fluoride toothpaste.

Mean: Canadians consume an average of 26 teaspoons of sugar per day.

Step 6: Digging In to the Centre of Your Data

Telling the story of data begins with assessing the distribution of the data.

1. Consider the data you collected. Would it be useful to look at the mean, median, mode, standard deviation, or variance? Perform the relevant calculations and record your results in a table like the one below.

	Mean	Median	Mode	Standard Deviation	Variance
Independent Variable					
Dependent Variable					

2. What do these calculations tell you about your data?

3. Are there any data values for which you might wish to calculate a z-score? If so, calculate it now.

4. Do your data values appear to follow the pattern of a normal distribution? If not, what does this mean?

5. Test for outliers using a modified box and whisker plot or the 1.5 IQR test described in chapter 6. If your data contain outliers, describe their impact on the mean, median, mode, range, interquartile range, standard deviation, and variance.

Step 7: Searching for Patterns

Now it is time to determine whether your data follow a specific pattern or model, or whether a specific mathematical relationship exists among your variables.

1. Enter your data into appropriate lists using the technology of your choice.

2. Perform a regression analysis to determine whether a linear correlation represents your data. Record and interpret the r and r^2 values.

3. You may also wish to perform an additional regression analysis to see whether a quadratic, cubic, or exponential model fits your data better than a linear model. Record and interpret the r^2 values. Remember that the r or r^2 values on their own do not indicate which model is best, just if the model is a good fit. In addition, it does not imply cause and effect.

4. Represent your regression analysis on a scatter plot to show the line (or curve) of best fit.

5. If you had any outliers in your data set, describe their impact on the line (or curve) of best fit.

6. Show how the line (or curve) of best fit changes if you remove any outliers. Decide whether you should remove outliers from the data set. Justify your choice.

7. What might be an interesting way to share or represent these results in your project?

8. Are there any other statistical calculations you can include to further describe the story of your data?

Step 8: Assessing Your Data Analysis

Revisit the work you have done so far. Use the checklist to ensure you are on track.

Data Analysis	Yes	No
The data are represented using appropriate charts and graphs.		
The measures of central tendency are calculated and interpreted clearly.		
The measures of spread or dispersion are calculated and interpreted clearly.		
The appropriate tests have been done for outliers.		
Relevant z-score calculations are included and explained.		
The impact of any outliers on the results is thoroughly analysed.		
For the regression analyses: • all relevant models of best fit are explored, discussed, and reported. • the most appropriate model is chosen and justified. • the r and r^2 values are reported and explained. • a scatter plot shows a line (or curve) of best fit and the impact of potential outliers.		

Step 9: Assessing the Validity of Your Process and Results

Now that you have completed your statistical analysis, it is time to assess your research method and the validity of your results and sources.

1. Examine each of your statistical calculations. Do your results and conclusions support or refute your hypothesis?

2. How strong is the evidence?

3. Are there limitations to the evidence? Discuss bias, cause and effect, hidden variables, and how well your sample represents the population.

4. What questions arose that might require further investigation?

5. What might you do differently if you were to complete a similar project in the future?

Step 10: Assessing Your Results

Use this checklist to ensure your statistics project is on track.

Evaluating Your Results	Yes	No
Sources of bias (beyond sampling bias) are examined and discussed.		
Conclusions are reported and justified.		
Reflections on the methodology and improvements for future studies are thorough and insightful.		
References are appropriately sourced.		

> **Project Prep**
>
> Refer to section 9.5 for tools to self-assess your culminating project report and presentation.

A well-written report is organized, logical, and includes the necessary information with appropriate headings. Pull together all the pieces to tell the story of your data in the form of a report and/or presentation.

9.5

Creating a Report, Presenting, and Critiquing Other Projects

Learning Goals

I am learning to

- critique my own research report or presentation constructively
- critique the research reports or presentations of my peers based on predetermined criteria

Think of a time when you received constructive feedback. What was helpful? Did anything make you feel uncomfortable?

Assessing Your Culminating Probability Project

Materials

- criteria for effective feedback generated by class
- Probability Project Self-Assessment Checklist
- Probability Project Content Rubric
- Probability Project Presentation Rubric
- Probability Project Peer Critique Form
- Statistics Project Self-Assessment Checklist
- Statistics Project Content Rubric
- Statistics Project Presentation Rubric
- Statistics Project Peer Critique Form
- video recorder (optional)

1. Use the Probability Project Self-Assessment Checklist to ensure you have included all relevant elements in your project.

2. Use the Probability Project Content Rubric to assess the depth and quality of your report.

3. If you will be presenting your project to the class, consider recording your presentation on video and use the Probability Project Presentation Rubric to assess the quality of your presentation.

4. With a partner, brainstorm criteria for effective constructive feedback. Write a list of at least five tips to follow when providing feedback to a peer.

5. Trade projects with another peer or team. Use the Probability Project Self-Assessment Checklist and Probability Project Content Rubric to critique their work.

6. Use the Probability Project Peer Critique Form to provide written feedback. Keep in mind the criteria you brainstormed in #4 for effective feedback.

Reflect

a) Are there any aspects of your peers' projects you could incorporate into your project?

b) What feedback from your peers can you incorporate into your project/report?

c) What changes or improvements will you make before submitting your final project?

Assessing Your Culminating Statistics Project

1. Use the Statistics Project Self-Assessment Checklist to ensure you have included all relevant elements in your project.

2. Use the Statistics Project Content Rubric to assess the depth and quality of your report.

3. If you will be presenting your project to the class, consider recording your presentation on video and use the Statistics Project Presentation Rubric to assess the quality of your presentation.

4. With a partner, brainstorm criteria for effective constructive feedback. Write a list of at least five tips to follow when providing feedback to a peer.

5. Trade projects with another peer or team. Use the Statistics Project Self-Assessment Checklist and Statistics Project Content Rubric to critique their work.

6. Use the Statistics Project Peer Critique Form to provide written feedback. Keep in mind the criteria you brainstormed in #4 for effective feedback.

Reflect

a) Are there any aspects of your peers' projects you could incorporate into your project?

b) What feedback from your peers can you incorporate into your project/report?

c) What changes or improvements will you make before submitting your final project?

Probability Project Self-Assessment Checklist

The Game	Yes	No
Is your game based solely on chance?		
Is your game • unique • fun • easy to understand • quick to play?		
Have you collected or created all the necessary materials for your game?		
Have you prepared a table to record your data during the playing of your game?		
Have you calculated the theoretical probability of winning your game and planned an appropriate payout for the winners?		
If your class is having a game day or fair, have you developed a marketing strategy to attract players to your game?		
Are the rules clearly outlined and available to players? If your class is having a game day or fair, consider sharing the rules of the game as a poster, succinct explanation, or soft copy via LCD.		
If you are working with a partner, do you each have roles for game day?		
If your class is not having a game day or fair, have you determined how you will collect data for your game?		
The Report	**Yes**	**No**
Does your report include: • Title page • Appropriate use of headings • Description of the game and relevant background information • Outline of the rules, including how to win • Explanation of the fee structure (cost to play) • Data table representing actual data from the game day • Actual winnings earned in the game based on your data table		
Have you calculated and/or graphed: • Theoretical distribution (possible outcomes vs. probability) • Experimental distribution (actual outcomes vs. probability) • Expected value of the game (profit based on your theoretical calculations)		
Does your analysis of the results: • Compare and contrast theoretical and actual distributions • Discuss any discrepancies in the results • Provide insights and reflections about the game • Summarize your conclusions		
Review the following elements of your report: • Terminology: Are mathematical terms used correctly? • Neatness: Is your font clear and readable? Does your report look professional? • Writing Skills: Have you followed proper writing conventions? • Organization: Are key ideas presented logically, clearly, and concisely? Is your report focused and on topic? • Creativity: Have you included pictures or diagrams that make the report interesting? • Technology Skills: Are your visuals easily understood? Are your graphs clearly labelled?		

Probability Project Content Rubric

	Level 1 (50–59%)	Level 2 (60–69%)	Level 3 (70–79%)	Level 4 (80–100%)
Knowledge and Understanding				
Introduction • Description of the game and rules, relevant background information	• Limited information about the game	• Sufficient information about the game	• Detailed description of most elements of the game	• Clear and detailed description of all elements of the game
Data Collection • Data table represents actual data from the game day or simulation	• Insufficient data collected	• Sufficient data collected	• Sufficient data collected; data are appropriate to the task	• Extensive data collected; data are appropriate to the task and clearly represented
Mathematical Understanding • probability calculations and data analysis	• Reflects limited mathematical understanding	• Reflects some mathematical understanding	• Generally reflects mathematical understanding	• Reflects thorough mathematical understanding
Application				
Data Analysis • theoretical distribution • experimental distribution • expected value	• Limited use of appropriate mathematical procedures and strategies	• Mathematical strategies and procedures generally appropriate and sometimes correct	• Appropriate strategies used most of the time • Mathematical procedures generally correct/appropriate	• Mathematical strategies and procedures always correct/appropriate and are highly detailed
Thinking				
Summary and Conclusions • compare/contrast theoretical and actual distributions • discuss discrepancies in the results • provide insights and reflections about the game and clear conclusions	• Performs limited comparisons • Uses mathematical reasoning to justify few conclusions	• Performs some comparisons • Uses mathematical reasoning to justify some conclusions	• Performs detailed comparisons • Uses mathematical reasoning to justify all conclusions	• Performs and mathematically justifies conclusions based on insightful comparisons and reflections
Communication				
Clarity • explanations clear, accurate, and thorough	• Explanations are incomplete, inaccurate, and/or lack clarity	• Explanations are somewhat clear and accurate	• Explanations are mostly clear and accurate	• Explanations are clear, accurate, and thorough
Math Terminology and Writing • mathematical terms used correctly • proper writing conventions followed	• Limited use of correct terminology and notation • Proper writing conventions followed to a limited extent	• Some use of correct terminology and notation • Proper writing conventions followed sometimes	• Considerable use of correct terminology and notation • Proper writing conventions mostly followed	• Thorough and meticulous use of correct terminology and notation • Proper writing conventions extensively followed
Organization • key ideas presented logically • appropriate headings (title page, table of contents, etc.)	• Report not clear or logical; ideas rarely connect	• Report somewhat clear or logical; ideas connect sometimes	• Report most often clear, logical; ideas mostly connect	• Report clear, logical; ideas thoroughly connect

Probability Project Presentation Rubric

	Level 1 (50–59%)	Level 2 (60–69%)	Level 3 (70–79%)	Level 4 (80–100%)
Introduction				
Game Description • rules, objectives, and key information about the game	• Provides an unclear description of the game	• Provides a somewhat focused description that states the objective and some of the key points about the game	• Provides a focused description that clearly states the objective and the key points of the game	• Provides an effective description that captures the attention of the audience and clearly states the objective and the key points of the game
Visual Aids				
Visuals (graphs and slides) • clear/readable • neatly presented • easy to understand • graphs clearly labelled	• Visual aids do not support the conclusions or are almost non-existent	• Visual aids sometimes support the conclusions	• Visual aids generally support the conclusions	• Visual aids used consistently and thoroughly support the conclusions
Presentation Skills				
Communication • voice is clear, relaxed, audible • appropriate eye contact/body language • appropriate pace • clear, concise explanations • engaging and enthusiastic	• Presenter's voice rarely clear/audible • Presenter frequently reads from the screen or notes • Presentation is slow and choppy	• Presenter's voice somewhat clear • Presenter sometimes reads from the screen or notes • Presentation flows but moves slowly	• Presenter's voice usually clear • Presenter occasionally reads from the screen/notes • Presentation flows well; pace keeps the audience interested	• Presenter's voice always clear/audible • Presenter maintains eye contact with the audience • Presentation is highly engaging
Organization • key ideas presented logically • focused and on topic	• Not very clear or logical; ideas rarely connect • Few aspects are organized	• Somewhat clear or logical; ideas connect sometimes • Some aspects are organized	• Often clear, logical; ideas mostly connect • Many aspects are well-organized	• Clear, logical; ideas thoroughly connect • Presentation is well-organized
Ability to Engage the Audience				
Response to Audience Questions	• Responds to few audience questions, with limited justification or mathematical reasoning	• Responds to some audience questions, with somewhat detailed justification or mathematical reasoning	• Responds to most audience questions, with detailed justification or mathematical reasoning	• Responds to all audience questions, with very detailed justification or mathematical reasoning

Probability Project Peer Critique Form

Rate the quality of the presentation or report in each category using the following scale:

1 = poor   2 = fair   3 = good   4 = very good   5 = outstanding

	1	2	3	4	5
Description of game • outline of the rules, including how to win • explanation of the probability of the player winning					
Data table representing actual data from the game day or simulation					
Data analysis: • theoretical distribution (possible outcomes vs. probability) • experimental distribution (actual outcomes vs. probability) • expected value of the game (profit based on your theoretical calculations)					
Visuals (graphs and slides)					
Organization					
Communication					
Technology					
Conclusions					

Highlights:	Things to improve or add:

Statistics Project Self-Assessment Checklist

Defining the Problem	Yes	No
The chosen topic is relevant and appropriate.		
The hypothesis is clearly stated and justified.		
The dependent and independent variables are clearly defined.		
The population of interest is clearly identified.		
Background information is used to introduce the research question.		
Secondary Data Collection	**Yes**	**No**
The source of data (URL) is provided.		
The sampling technique is described and justified.		
Sources of sampling bias are identified.		
Sufficient data are collected.		
The raw data are effectively represented.		
Primary Data Collection	**Yes**	**No**
The sample survey is included in the report.		
The survey contains an appropriate introduction.		
The survey questions are well designed.		
The data are collected in a timely and responsible manner.		
Survey participants' anonymity is clearly protected.		
Sufficient survey data are collected.		
Raw survey data are effectively represented.		
Data Analysis	**Yes**	**No**
The data are represented using appropriate charts and graphs.		
The measures of central tendency are calculated and interpreted clearly.		
The measures of dispersion are calculated and interpreted clearly.		
The appropriate tests have been done for outliers.		
Relevant z-score calculations are included and explained.		
The impact of any outliers on the results is thoroughly analysed.		
For the regression analyses: • all relevant models of best fit are explored, discussed, and reported. • the most appropriate model is chosen and justified. • the r and r^2 values are reported and explained. • a scatter plot shows line (or curve) of best fit and the impact of potential outliers.		
Evaluating Your Results	**Yes**	**No**
Sources of bias (beyond sampling bias) are examined and discussed.		
Conclusions are reported and justified.		
Reflections on the methodology and improvements for future studies are thorough and insightful.		
References are appropriately sourced.		

Statistics Project Content Rubric

	Level 1 (50–59%)	Level 2 (60–69%)	Level 3 (70–79%)	Level 4 (80–100%)
Knowledge and Understanding				
Topic Question and Introduction	• Hypothesis stated, but not clear or justified • Background knowledge stated to a limited extent	• Hypothesis makes sense but could be more clear • Background knowledge somewhat evident	• Clear hypothesis • Background knowledge evident	• Clear, justified hypothesis • Background knowledge clearly evident and extensive
Data Collection and Sampling Method • understands methods for collecting and validating data	• Insufficient data collected • Data limited to one element of the course • Inadequate validation of the data source	• Some data collected • Data limited to few aspects of the course • Some validation of the data source	• Sufficient data collected • Data mostly appropriate to the task • Adequate validation of the data source	• Extensive data collected • Data appropriate to the task • In-depth validation of the data source
Mathematical Understanding • calculations and data analysis	• Reflects limited mathematical understanding	• Sometimes reflects mathematical understanding	• Generally reflects mathematical understanding	• Reflects thorough mathematical understanding
Application				
Data Analysis • central tendency • spread or dispersion • outliers • z-scores • regression • graphs	• Statistical tools incorporated to a limited extent • Limited use of appropriate mathematical procedures	• Statistical tools incorporated sometimes • Mathematical procedures sometimes appropriate and sometimes correct	• Statistical tools incorporated most of the time • Mathematical procedures generally correct/appropriate	• Statistical tools incorporated extensively • Mathematical procedures always correct/appropriate and highly detailed
Communication				
Math Terminology and Writing Conventions • uses proper math conventions for graphs, calculations, tables, etc. • uses proper writing conventions	• Limited use of correct math terminology and notation • Proper writing conventions followed to a limited extent	• Some use of correct math terminology and notation • Proper writing conventions followed sometimes	• Considerable use of correct math terminology and notation • Proper writing conventions mostly followed	• Thorough and meticulous use of correct math terminology and notation • Proper writing conventions followed extensively
Organization • key ideas presented logically • appropriate headings (title page, table of contents, etc.) • sources cited appropriately	• Report not clear or logical; ideas rarely connect • Few aspects are organized • Some references included • Sources cited incorrectly	• Report somewhat clear or logical; ideas connect sometimes • Some aspects are organized • Some references missing • Sources cited mostly following proper format (few errors)	• Report mostly clear, logical; ideas mostly connect • Many aspects are well-organized • All references included • Sources cited mostly following proper format (few errors)	• Report clear, logical; ideas thoroughly connect • Most aspects are well-organized • All references included • Sources cited following proper format
Thinking				
Conclusions, Assumptions, Limitations, and Reflection	• Identifies few assumptions, limitations, or ideas for future study • Conclusions supported minimally by the mathematical analysis and reasoning	• Identifies some assumptions, limitations, or ideas for future study • Conclusions somewhat justified by the mathematical analysis and reasoning	• Identifies many assumptions, limitations, and viable ideas for future study • Conclusions generally justified and supported by the mathematical analysis and reasoning	• Assumptions, limitations thoroughly discussed; detailed suggestions for future study included • Conclusions consistently justified by the mathematical analysis and reasoning

Statistics Project Presentation Rubric

	Level 1 (50–59%)	Level 2 (60–69%)	Level 3 (70–79%)	Level 4 (80–100%)
Hypothesis and Introduction				
Topic Question and Introduction	• Hypothesis stated, but not clear or justified • Background knowledge stated to a limited extent	• Hypothesis makes sense; could be more clear • Background knowledge somewhat evident	• Clear hypothesis • Background knowledge usually evident	• Clear, justified hypothesis • Background knowledge of topic clearly evident
Technology Skills (If Technology Is Used in the Presentation)				
Technology	• Uses technology with difficulty	• Uses technology with some proficiency, or overuses it	• Makes effective use of technology	• Technology enhances the quality of the presentation
Visual Aids				
Visuals (graphs and slides) • clear/readable • neatly presented • easy to understand • graphs clearly labelled	• Visual aids do not support the conclusions or are almost non-existent	• Visual aids sometimes support the conclusions	• Visual aids generally support the conclusions	• Visual aids are used consistently and thoroughly support the conclusions
Presentation Skills				
Communication • voice is clear, relaxed, audible • appropriate eye contact/body language • appropriate pace • clear, concise explanations • engaging and enthusiastic	• Presenter's voice rarely clear/audible • Presenter frequently reads from the screen or notes • Presentation slow and choppy	• Presenter's voice somewhat clear • Presenter sometimes reads from the screen or notes • Presentation flows, but moves slowly	• Presenter's voice usually clear • Presenter occasionally reads from the screen/notes • Presentation flows well; pace keeps the audience interested	• Presenter's voice always clear/audible • Presenter maintains eye contact with the audience, rarely reading from the screen/notes • Presentation is highly engaging
Organization • key ideas presented logically • focused and on topic	• Not very clear or logical; ideas rarely connect • Few aspects are organized	• Somewhat clear or logical; ideas connect sometimes • Some aspects are organized	• Often clear, logical; ideas mostly connect • Many aspects are well-organized	• Clear, logical; ideas thoroughly connect • Presentation is well-organized
Ability to Engage the Audience				
Response to Audience Questions	• Responds to few audience questions, with limited justification or mathematical reasoning	• Responds to some audience questions, with somewhat detailed justification or mathematical reasoning	• Responds to most audience questions, with detailed justification or mathematical reasoning	• Responds to all audience questions, with very detailed justification or mathematical reasoning

Statistics Project Peer Critique Form

Rate the quality of the presentation or report in each category using the following scale:

1 = poor   2 = fair   3 = good   4 = very good   5 = outstanding

	1	2	3	4	5
Introduction					
Hypothesis					
Description/justification of sampling technique and population					
Data analysis: • central tendency • spread or dispersion • outliers • z-scores • regression					
Visuals (graphs and slides)					
Organization					
Communication					
Technology					
Conclusions					

Highlights:	Things to improve or add:

Areas Under the Normal Distribution Curve

The table lists the shaded area for different values of z.
The area under the entire curve is 1.

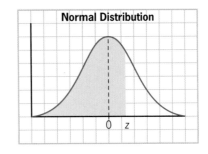

Normal Distribution

z	0.00	0.01	0.02	0.03	0.04	0.05	0.06	0.07	0.08	0.09
−2.9	0.0019	0.0018	0.0018	0.0017	0.0016	0.0016	0.0015	0.0015	0.0014	0.0014
−2.8	0.0026	0.0025	0.0024	0.0023	0.0023	0.0022	0.0021	0.0021	0.0020	0.0019
−2.7	0.0035	0.0034	0.0033	0.0032	0.0031	0.0030	0.0029	0.0028	0.0027	0.0026
−2.6	0.0047	0.0045	0.0044	0.0043	0.0041	0.0040	0.0039	0.0038	0.0037	0.0036
−2.5	0.0062	0.0060	0.0059	0.0057	0.0055	0.0054	0.0052	0.0051	0.0049	0.0048
−2.4	0.0082	0.0080	0.0078	0.0075	0.0073	0.0071	0.0069	0.0068	0.0066	0.0064
−2.3	0.0107	0.0104	0.0102	0.0099	0.0096	0.0094	0.0091	0.0089	0.0087	0.0084
−2.2	0.0139	0.0136	0.0132	0.0129	0.0125	0.0122	0.0119	0.0116	0.0113	0.0110
−2.1	0.0179	0.0174	0.0170	0.0166	0.0162	0.0158	0.0154	0.0150	0.0146	0.0143
−2.0	0.0228	0.0222	0.0217	0.0212	0.0207	0.0202	0.0197	0.0192	0.0188	0.0183
−1.9	0.0287	0.0281	0.0274	0.0268	0.0262	0.0256	0.0250	0.0244	0.0239	0.0233
−1.8	0.0359	0.0351	0.0344	0.0336	0.0329	0.0322	0.0314	0.0307	0.0301	0.0294
−1.7	0.0446	0.0436	0.0427	0.0418	0.0409	0.0401	0.0392	0.0384	0.0375	0.0367
−1.6	0.0548	0.0537	0.0526	0.0516	0.0505	0.0495	0.0485	0.0475	0.0465	0.0455
−1.5	0.0668	0.0655	0.0643	0.0630	0.0618	0.0606	0.0594	0.0582	0.0571	0.0559
−1.4	0.0808	0.0793	0.0778	0.0764	0.0749	0.0735	0.0721	0.0708	0.0694	0.0681
−1.3	0.0968	0.0951	0.0934	0.0918	0.0901	0.0885	0.0869	0.0853	0.0838	0.0823
−1.2	0.1151	0.1131	0.1112	0.1093	0.1075	0.1056	0.1038	0.1020	0.1003	0.0985
−1.1	0.1357	0.1335	0.1314	0.1292	0.1271	0.1251	0.1230	0.1210	0.1190	0.1170
−1.0	0.1587	0.1562	0.1539	0.1515	0.1492	0.1469	0.1446	0.1423	0.1401	0.1379
−0.9	0.1841	0.1814	0.1788	0.1762	0.1736	0.1711	0.1685	0.1660	0.1635	0.1611
−0.8	0.2119	0.2090	0.2061	0.2033	0.2005	0.1977	0.1949	0.1922	0.1894	0.1867
−0.7	0.2420	0.2389	0.2358	0.2327	0.2296	0.2266	0.2236	0.2206	0.2177	0.2148
−0.6	0.2743	0.2709	0.2676	0.2643	0.2611	0.2578	0.2546	0.2514	0.2483	0.2451
−0.5	0.3085	0.3050	0.3015	0.2981	0.2946	0.2912	0.2877	0.2843	0.2810	0.2776
−0.4	0.3446	0.3409	0.3372	0.3336	0.3300	0.3264	0.3228	0.3192	0.3156	0.3121
−0.3	0.3821	0.3783	0.3745	0.3707	0.3669	0.3632	0.3594	0.3557	0.3520	0.3483
−0.2	0.4207	0.4168	0.4129	0.4090	0.4052	0.4013	0.3974	0.3936	0.3897	0.3859
−0.1	0.4602	0.4562	0.4522	0.4483	0.4443	0.4404	0.4364	0.4325	0.4286	0.4247
−0.0	0.5000	0.4960	0.4920	0.4880	0.4840	0.4801	0.4761	0.4721	0.4681	0.4641

z	0.00	0.01	0.02	0.03	0.04	0.05	0.06	0.07	0.08	0.09
0.0	0.5000	0.5040	0.5080	0.5120	0.5160	0.5199	0.5239	0.5279	0.5319	0.5359
0.1	0.5398	0.5438	0.5478	0.5517	0.5557	0.5596	0.5636	0.5675	0.5714	0.5753
0.2	0.5793	0.5832	0.5871	0.5910	0.5948	0.5987	0.6026	0.6064	0.6103	0.6141
0.3	0.6179	0.6217	0.6255	0.6293	0.6331	0.6368	0.6406	0.6443	0.6480	0.6517
0.4	0.6554	0.6591	0.6628	0.6664	0.6700	0.6736	0.6772	0.6808	0.6844	0.6879
0.5	0.6915	0.6950	0.6985	0.7019	0.7054	0.7088	0.7123	0.7157	0.7190	0.7224
0.6	0.7257	0.7291	0.7324	0.7357	0.7389	0.7422	0.7454	0.7486	0.7517	0.7549
0.7	0.7580	0.7611	0.7642	0.7673	0.7704	0.7734	0.7764	0.7794	0.7823	0.7852
0.8	0.7881	0.7910	0.7939	0.7967	0.7995	0.8023	0.8051	0.8078	0.8106	0.8133
0.9	0.8159	0.8186	0.8212	0.8238	0.8264	0.8289	0.8315	0.8340	0.8365	0.8389
1.0	0.8413	0.8438	0.8461	0.8485	0.8508	0.8531	0.8554	0.8577	0.8599	0.8621
1.1	0.8643	0.8665	0.8686	0.8708	0.8729	0.8749	0.8770	0.8790	0.8810	0.8830
1.2	0.8849	0.8869	0.8888	0.8907	0.8925	0.8944	0.8962	0.8980	0.8997	0.9015
1.3	0.9032	0.9049	0.9066	0.9082	0.9099	0.9115	0.9131	0.9147	0.9162	0.9177
1.4	0.9192	0.9207	0.9222	0.9236	0.9251	0.9265	0.9279	0.9292	0.9306	0.9319
1.5	0.9332	0.9345	0.9357	0.9370	0.9382	0.9394	0.9406	0.9418	0.9429	0.9441
1.6	0.9452	0.9463	0.9474	0.9484	0.9495	0.9505	0.9515	0.9525	0.9535	0.9545
1.7	0.9554	0.9564	0.9573	0.9582	0.9591	0.9599	0.9608	0.9616	0.9625	0.9633
1.8	0.9641	0.9649	0.9656	0.9664	0.9671	0.9678	0.9686	0.9693	0.9699	0.9706
1.9	0.9713	0.9719	0.9726	0.9732	0.9738	0.9744	0.9750	0.9756	0.9761	0.9767
2.0	0.9772	0.9778	0.9783	0.9788	0.9793	0.9798	0.9803	0.9808	0.9812	0.9817
2.1	0.9821	0.9826	0.9830	0.9834	0.9838	0.9842	0.9846	0.9850	0.9854	0.9857
2.2	0.9861	0.9864	0.9868	0.9871	0.9875	0.9878	0.9881	0.9884	0.9887	0.9890
2.3	0.9893	0.9896	0.9898	0.9901	0.9904	0.9906	0.9909	0.9911	0.9913	0.9916
2.4	0.9918	0.9920	0.9922	0.9925	0.9927	0.9929	0.9931	0.9932	0.9934	0.9936
2.5	0.9938	0.9940	0.9941	0.9943	0.9945	0.9946	0.9948	0.9949	0.9951	0.9952
2.6	0.9953	0.9955	0.9956	0.9957	0.9959	0.9960	0.9961	0.9962	0.9963	0.9964
2.7	0.9965	0.9966	0.9967	0.9968	0.9969	0.9970	0.9971	0.9972	0.9973	0.9974
2.8	0.9974	0.9975	0.9976	0.9977	0.9977	0.9978	0.9979	0.9979	0.9980	0.9981
2.9	0.9981	0.9982	0.9982	0.9983	0.9984	0.9984	0.9985	0.9985	0.9986	0.9986

Answers

Chapter 1 Introduction to Probability

Prerequisite Skills, pages 4–5

1. a) 0.25, 25%　　**b)** 0.833..., 83.$\overline{3}$%
　c) 0.666..., 66.$\overline{6}$%　**d)** 0.65, 65%

2. a) $\frac{3}{4}$　**b)** $\frac{1}{4}$　**c)** $\frac{22}{35}$　**d)** $\frac{4}{9}$

3. a) $\frac{1}{2}$, 0.5, 50%　**b)** $\frac{11}{12}$, 0.91$\overline{6}$, 91.$\overline{6}$%

　c) $\frac{5}{12}$, 0.41$\overline{6}$, 41.$\overline{6}$%　**d)** $\frac{3}{4}$, 0.75, 75%

4. a) $\frac{1}{12}$, 0.08$\overline{3}$, 8.$\overline{3}$%　**b)** $\frac{1}{6}$, 0.1$\overline{6}$, 16.$\overline{6}$%

　c) $\frac{5}{9}$, 0.$\overline{5}$, 55.$\overline{5}$%　**d)** $\frac{1}{8}$, 0.125, 12.5%

5. a) 3 : 10
　b) blue : total = 2 : 10 = 1 : 5; yellow : total = 5 : 10 = 1 : 2
　c) red: 30%, blue: 20%, yellow: 50%

6. a) $\frac{\text{hits}}{\text{times at bat}} = \frac{10}{35}$　**b)** $\frac{10}{35} \approx 0.286$
　c) about 114 hits

7. a) random: The coin is equally likely to land on heads or tails.
　b) non-random: The intersection is not entered unless it is safe.
　c) non-random: You select exactly what you want.
　d) random: Without looking, each candy is equally likely to be chosen.

8. Answers may vary.
　a) rolling a die
　b) selecting your favourite pair of jeans to wear

9. a) $\frac{1}{4}$ of the deck　**b)** about 11.5% of the deck

10. a) 1 way: 1 and 1
　b) 6 ways: 6 and 1, 5 and 2, 4 and 3, 3 and 4, 2 and 5, 1 and 6
　c) 0 ways
　d) 6 ways: 1 and 1, 2 and 2, 3 and 3, 4 and 4, 5 and 5, 6 and 6
　e) 7 ways: 1 and 3, 2 and 2, 3 and 1; 3 and 6, 4 and 5, 5 and 4, 6 and 3

11.

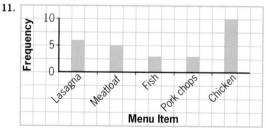

12 a) chicken; about 37%　**b)** $\frac{21}{27}$ or $\frac{7}{9}$
　c) Answers may vary. What percent of the class chose fish? $\frac{3}{27}$, or $\frac{1}{9}$ of the class chose fish.

1.1 Simple Probabilities, pages 6–15

Example 1 Your Turn

a) orange: $\frac{1}{4}$, 0.25, 25%; red: $\frac{1}{8}$, 0.125, 12.5%;

　purple: $\frac{1}{4}$, 0.25, 25%; green: $\frac{3}{8}$, 0.375, 37.5%

b) Answers may vary. The spinner could be one-quarter orange, one-eighth red, one-quarter purple, and three-eighths green.
c) It is possible that there is a fifth colour, but that the arrow did not land on it in any of these 32 spins.

Example 2 Your Turn
a) cable: about 42%, satellite: about 37%, Internet: about 13%, antenna: about 3%, none: about 5%
b) Answers may vary. The cable company would be interested for marketing. They can claim to be the most popular.
c) Answers may vary. Internet TV service will increase and cable/satellite will decrease. Access to Internet TV will increase with sales of smart TVs and as networks make more programming available.

Example 3 Your Turn
Answers may vary.
a) 0.01; In Ontario, July is a summer month so the probability of a snow day in July is highly unlikely.
b) 1; The sun always sets in the west so the probability of the sun setting in the west tonight is guaranteed.
c) 0.5; The next person to enter the school cafeteria will be male or female.

Reflect
R1. a) Experimental probability is probability based on experimental trials. It is calculated as the number of times an outcome happens divided by total number of trials.
　b) Experimental probability is a useful tool for making predictions. It can tell you what might happen and how likely it is to occur based on what has been observed.
　c) While experimental probability can be close enough to help with decision making, it is based on an experiment. Conditions or circumstances may change and the next experiment could result in different experimental probabilities.
R2. a) The event is impossible.
　b) The event is certain to happen.
　c) This is the range representing impossible to certain.
R3. a) #probability is an estimate of how likely something will occur based on intuition
　b) Answers may vary. I think there is a 0.95 probability that Canada will win the gold medal in women's hockey.

Practise
1. C
2. a) 0.4　　　　　　　**b)** 0.6

Apply
3. a) 0.7　　　　　　　**b)** 0.65
　c) Since the two experimental probabilities of her scoring were both less than 80% (70% and 65%), her statement is not accurate. She has over-estimated her scoring ability.

4. a) yellow: $\frac{1}{2}$, green: $\frac{1}{6}$, purple: $\frac{1}{4}$, blue: $\frac{1}{12}$
　b) Answers may vary. It could be one-half yellow, one-sixth green, one-quarter purple, and one-twelfth blue.
　c) Yes, because it is based on experimental probability.

5. Answers may vary.

   a) The table shows the results for a mystery spinner.

Colour	Favourable Outcomes, $n(A)$
Green	8
Orange	4

   b)

6. a) vanilla: about 6%, chocolate: about 14%, raspberry ripple: about 28%, pralines and cream: about 52%

   b) The stand sells about the same number of pralines and cream cones as all the other flavours together. The owner can use this information to ensure that there is enough pralines and cream.

7. 21 rainy days

8. a) fast ball: about 91%, curve ball: about 9%, knuckle ball: 0%

   b) Answers may vary. The batter would know that the pitch will most likely be a fast ball.

9. a) straight down the line: 7.5%, middle: 30%, outside: 62.5%

   b) Answers may vary. Sandeep's opponent would know that the serve will most likely end up in the outside region.

10. Answers may vary.

   a) 0.9; I study a lot and do all the homework assignments.

   b) 0.9; I study a lot, do all the homework assignments, and have passed all the exams.

   c) 0.7; We are currently in the middle of a record snowfall period.

   d) 0.99; My favourite song is currently number one on the charts, and I listen to the radio every day for several hours.

11. Answers may vary. 0.9; They have won more than any other team since the competition first started, and this year they are the host country.

12. 2 male puppies

14. 3 times

15. Answers may vary.

   a) `randInt(1,8,20)`
    `{1 3 1 1 5 7 7` ...

   b)

Random Number	Tally
1	4
2	0
3	2
4	2
5	3
6	2
7	4
8	3

   c) rolling a 1: 20%, rolling a 2: 0, rolling a 3: 10%, rolling a 4: 10%, rolling a 5: 15%, rolling a 6: 10%, rolling a 7: 20%, rolling an 8: 15%

   d) The values are not equal. I think they should be equal with repeated experiments. Each number should have the same likelihood of being generated.

16. Answers may vary.

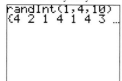

`randInt(1,4,10)`
`{4 2 1 4 1 4 3` ...

rolling a 2: 10%

17. Answers may vary.

18. Answers may vary. Staffing is appropriate for the morning, understaffed for the afternoon, and overstaffed for the evening. The afternoon should increase to 11 open cash registers, and the evening should be reduced to 3 open cash registers.

1.2 Theoretical Probability, pages 16–25

Example 1 Your Turn
about 33%

Example 2 Your Turn
about 67%

Example 3 Your Turn

a) $3:2$ **b)** $4:1$

Reflect

R1. a) The set of all possible outcomes is the sample space. An event is a set of outcomes in the sample space that have a common characteristic. Then, the probability of an event A happening is the number of outcomes in that subset divided by the total number of outcomes in the sample space. Diagrams may vary.

   b) Answers may vary. There are 3 red, 2 blue, and 1 yellow marbles in a bag. What is the theoretical probability of randomly picking a red one? Sample space: R, R, R, B, B, Y; Event of picking red: R, R, R; Theoretical probability of picking red: 0.5.

R2. a) The complement of an event is the set of possible outcomes not included in an event.

   b) Answers may vary. There are 3 red, 2 blue, and 1 yellow marbles in a bag. What is the theoretical probability of randomly picking a red one? The event, A, is picking red. The complement, A', is not picking red. The theoretical probability of the complement, not picking a red marble, is $1 - 0.5$, or 0.5.

R3. a) A ratio of the probability that an event will happen to the probability that it will not happen.

   b) A ratio of the probability that an event will not happen to the probability that it will happen.

   c) The concepts are similar in that they are a ratio of the same probabilities. The difference is the order in which they are presented.

Practise

1. D   **2.** A   **3.** C

Apply

4. a) $\frac{1}{12}$ **b)** $\frac{1}{6}$ **c)** $\frac{1}{2}$ **d)** $\frac{31}{36}$ **e)** $\frac{29}{36}$

5. a) $S = \{B_1B_2, B_1B_3, B_1W, B_1G_1, B_1G_2, B_2B_1, B_2B_3, B_2W, B_2G_1, B_2G_2, B_3B_1, B_3B_2, B_3W, B_3G_1, B_3G_2, WB_1, WB_2, WB_3, WG_1, WG_2, G_1B_1, G_1B_2, G_1B_3, G_1W, G_1G_2, G_2B_1, G_2B_2, G_2B_3, G_2W, G_2G_1\}$

   b) $A = \{B_1B_2, B_1B_3, B_2B_1, B_2B_3, B_3B_1, B_3B_2, G_1G_2, G_2G_1\}$

   c) $\frac{4}{15}$ **d)** $4:11$

6. a) 0.75   **b)** about 0.66

7. a) about 0.033   **b)** about 0.967

   c) Answers may vary. The monkey has associated red with no reward.

8. a) subjective probability **b)** $\frac{1}{5}$

9. a) $4:1$ **b)** $3:1$

11. Answers may vary.

12. Answers may vary.

   a) $\frac{1}{9}$ **b)** 8 times

13. If there are k possible outcomes to a certain probability experiment, all equally likely, then the theoretical probability of any one outcome is $\frac{1}{k}$. Then, the sum of theoretical probabilities of the outcomes is

$$\text{Sum} = \underbrace{\frac{1}{k} + \frac{1}{k} + \frac{1}{k} + \cdots + \frac{1}{k}}_{k \text{ times}}$$

$$= k\left(\frac{1}{k}\right)$$
$$= 1$$

14. $P(\text{Canadiens winning}) = \frac{1}{1+8} \approx 0.111$

   $P(\text{Canucks winning}) = \frac{2}{2+17} \approx 0.105$

   So, the Canadiens are more likely to win.

15. **a)** The reporter has expressed the odds against incorrectly as $n(S):n(A)$ instead of $P(A'):P(A)$.

   b) The odds against the Ottawa Senators winning against the Vancouver Canucks are $2:1$ because they have won only one of their three meetings so far this year.

Extend

16. **a)** $P(n \text{ heads}) = \left(\frac{1}{2}\right)^n$ **b)** $\left(\frac{1}{2}\right)^{10} \approx 9.766 \times 10^{-4}$

17. **a)** The odds in favour of A are equal to the reciprocal of the odds against A.

   b) Answers may vary. The odds in favour of the Canadian women's hockey team winning the gold medal at the next Winter Olympics are $3:1$. Then, the odds against the Canadian women's hockey team winning the gold medal at the next Winter Olympics are $1:3$.

   c) odds in favour of $A = \dfrac{P(A)}{P(A')}$

$$= \frac{1}{\dfrac{P(A')}{P(A)}}$$

$$= \frac{1}{\text{odds against } A}$$

1.3 Compare Experimental and Theoretical Probabilities, pages 26–33

Reflect

R1. Theoretical probability cannot predict the actual outcome of a probability experiment, but it can give you an idea of what is likely to happen. Experimental probability is not a perfect predictor of the outcome of a probability experiment because results of experiments can change.

R2. If the number of times an outcome occurs is observed over a very large number or trials, you can be more certain of the likelihood of its occurrence.

Practise

1. A   **2.** B

Apply

3. Answers may vary.

4. Answers may vary.

5. a)

Sum, x	Frequency	Theoretical Probability
2	1	$\frac{1}{64}$
3	2	$\frac{1}{32}$
4	3	$\frac{3}{64}$
5	4	$\frac{1}{16}$
6	5	$\frac{5}{64}$
7	6	$\frac{3}{32}$
8	7	$\frac{7}{64}$
9	8	$\frac{1}{8}$
10	7	$\frac{7}{64}$
11	6	$\frac{3}{32}$
12	5	$\frac{5}{64}$
13	4	$\frac{1}{16}$
14	3	$\frac{3}{64}$
15	2	$\frac{1}{32}$
16	1	$\frac{1}{64}$

b)

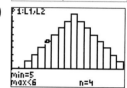

c) In a few trials, the statistical and theoretical probabilities vary greatly. After a very large number of trials, the statistical probabilities are much closer to the theoretical probabilities.

d) Answers may vary.

7. Answers may vary.

   a) Two 4-sided dice are rolled and the sum is recorded.

Sum, x	Frequency	Theoretical Probability
2	1	$\frac{1}{16}$
3	2	$\frac{1}{8}$
4	3	$\frac{3}{16}$
5	4	$\frac{1}{4}$
6	3	$\frac{3}{16}$
7	2	$\frac{1}{8}$
8	1	$\frac{1}{16}$

c) As the number of trials increases, the statistical probability values approach the theoretical probability values.

8. a) No. There are 36 possible outcomes for the sum of two dice. With 20 trials, it is mathematically impossible for the statistical probabilities to equal the corresponding theoretical probabilities.

   b) In theory, the minimum number of trials necessary would be 36. However, it is almost impossible for the statistical and theoretical probabilities to agree in this case.

Extend

9. Answers may vary.
   a) I chose 5. Draw Cards. You can choose from 1 to 3 decks, with or without replacement, and a 52-card deck or a 32-card deck. Each card is shown in a table along with number and suit.
   b) What is the theoretical probability of drawing a heart from a deck of cards, with replacement? Conduct a large number of trials. How does the experimental probability of drawing a heart from a deck of cards, with replacement, compare? The theoretical probability of drawing a heart from a deck of cards, with replacement, is $\frac{1}{4}$.

   For the experimental probability, run repeated trials, save the data, check for the number of hearts ($= 1$) in the list and divide by the number of trials.

10. Answers may vary.

1.4 Mutually Exclusive and Non-Mutually Exclusive Events, pages 34–43

Example 1 Your Turn
60%

Example 2 Your Turn
50%

Example 3 Your Turn
about 67%

Example 4 Your Turn
50%

Reflect

R1.

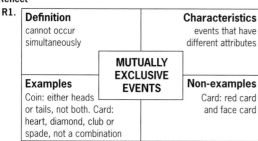

Definition	Characteristics
cannot occur simultaneously	events that have different attributes

MUTUALLY EXCLUSIVE EVENTS

Examples	Non-examples
Coin: either heads or tails, not both. Card: heart, diamond, club or spade, not a combination	Card: red card and face card

R2. **a)** If A and B are non-mutually exclusive events, then the total number of favourable outcomes is: $n(A \text{ or } B) = n(A) + n(B) - n(A \text{ and } B)$.
   b) When events are non-mutually exclusive. It ensures that items are not counted twice.

R3. Answers may vary. Rolling doubles or a sum 6.

Practise

1. C   2. D

Apply

3. **a)** pink shirt or purple shirt: $\frac{3}{5}$,
      pink shirt or a short-sleeved shirt: $\frac{4}{5}$
   b) first scenario: mutually exclusive events. The shirt cannot be pink and purple.
      second scenario: non-mutually exclusive events. One shirt is pink and short-sleeved.

4. about 36%

5. about 78%

6. **a)** 37.5%   **b)** 50%   **c)** 62.5%

7. **a)** 50%

   b) I used the principle of inclusion and exclusion.

8. **a)** 20%   **b)** 40%
   c) There are five possible outcomes to this game: 8 same, 7 same, 6 same, 5 same, or 4 same. If there are 3 the same, then there are 5 of the other colour, and so on. So, the probability of 8 buttons the same colour is 20%. Scoring at least 4 points means 7 or 8 buttons the same colour. So, the probability of 7 or 8 buttons the same colour is 40%.

10. Answers may vary.
   a) Since there are 3 blue marbles and the probability of green or yellow is 50%, there must be at least 3 marbles that belong to the mutually exclusive event of "green or yellow." This could mean that there is 1 green and 2 yellow marbles along with the 3 blue marbles.
   b) Two green and 1 yellow marble along with the 3 blue marbles.

11. $11:7$

12. Answer may vary. What is the probability of rolling either doubles or a sum of 5 with a standard pair of dice? $\frac{5}{18}$

Extend

13. From the principle of inclusion and exclusion,
    $n(A \text{ or } B) = n(A) + n(B) - n(A \text{ and } B)$.
    $$P(A \text{ or } B) = \frac{n(A \text{ or } B)}{n(S)}$$
    $$= \frac{n(A) + n(B) - n(A \text{ and } B)}{n(S)}$$
    $$= \frac{n(A)}{n(S)} + \frac{n(B)}{n(S)} - \frac{n(A \text{ and } B)}{n(S)}$$
    $$= P(A) + P(B) - P(A \text{ and } B)$$

14. **a)** $\frac{1}{3}$
   b) Answers may vary. I solved this using a tree diagram with four time periods and looked for outcomes that included B and C in periods one and two or B and C in periods three and four.
   c) Answers may vary. I assumed that any of Renzo's classes could be in any time period.

15. **a)** Starting with $n(A) + n(B) + n(C)$, regions A and B, B and C, and A and C will be counted twice, while region A and B and C is counted three times.

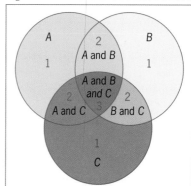

Subtract the regions
$n(A \text{ and } B) + n(B \text{ and } C) + n(A \text{ and } C)$:
$n(A) + n(B) + n(C) - n(A \text{ and } B) - n(B \text{ and } C)$
$- n(A \text{ and } C)$

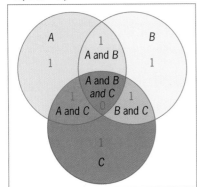

This results in excluding the count for region A and B and C altogether. Add the region A and B and C.
$n(A \text{ or } B \text{ or } C) = n(A) + n(B) + n(C) - n(A \text{ and } B)$
$- n(B \text{ and } C) - n(A \text{ and } C) + n(A \text{ and } B \text{ and } C)$
Then, divide both sides by $n(S)$.
$P(A \text{ or } B \text{ or } C) = P(A) + P(B) + P(C)$
$- P(A \text{ and } B) - P(B \text{ and } C) - P(A \text{ and } C)$
$+ P(A \text{ and } B \text{ and } C)$

b) Answers may vary. What is the probability of rolling a sum of 6 or doubles or an even sum?
In this case, $n(A) = 5$, $n(B) = 6$, $n(C) = 18$, $n(A \text{ and } B) = 1$, $n(B \text{ and } C) = 6$, $n(A \text{ and } C) = 5$, $n(A \text{ and } B \text{ and } C) = 1$, and $n(S) = 36$.
$P(A \text{ or } B \text{ or } C)$
$= P(A) + P(B) + P(C) - P(A \text{ and } B)$
$\quad - P(B \text{ and } C) - P(A \text{ and } C) + P(A \text{ and } B \text{ and } C)$
$= \frac{5}{36} + \frac{6}{36} + \frac{18}{36} - \frac{1}{36} - \frac{6}{36} - \frac{5}{36} + \frac{1}{36}$
$= \frac{18}{36}$
$= 0.5$
The probability of rolling a sum of 6 or doubles or an even sum is 50%.

1.5 Independent and Dependent Events, pages 44–55

Example 1 Your Turn
6.25%

Example 2 Your Turn
24%

Example 3 Your Turn
25%

Example 4 Your Turn
10%

Example 5 Your Turn
15 sales

Reflect
R1. a) Independent events have no influence on each other's probability of occurring, while dependent events do influence the probability of the other event occurring.
b) Answers may vary. Drawing two cards from a deck with replacement versus drawing two cards from a deck without replacement.

R2. The second scenario is more likely, because the first scenario involves multiple events while the second only involves a single event.
R3. a) Conditional probability is the probability of a second event occurring, given that a first event occurred.
b) Answers may vary. Three green marbles and two yellow marbles are placed into a bag. What is the probability of randomly drawing a second green marble given that a green marble was already chosen?
What is the probability of randomly drawing a green marble followed by a green marble, assuming that the first marble is replaced before the second marble is drawn?
R4. Answers may vary. A probability tree diagram makes it easier to see the event branch of interest and aids in the calculation of probabilities.

Practise
1. C   **2.** B   **3.** D
Apply
4. a) 12.5%   **b)** about 16.7%
c) Part a) involves independent events, while part b) involves dependent events.
5. a) Yes; both players have the same probability of winning a point on a given trial (about 4.2%).
b) Answers may vary. Player A wins a point if the result is Red-1. Player B wins a point if the result is Green or Blue-4. Then, player A has about a 4.2% probability of winning and player B has a $\frac{1}{16}$, or 6.25% of winning.
6. 4 sales
7. a) 6.25%
b) first path decision is correct: 12.5%, first two path decision are correct: 25%
8. a) about 9.1%   **b)** about 0.43%
c) 0%
10. a) about 0.14, assume that the crowd's experimental probability of 85% is accurate
b) about 9 times
Extend
11. a) 1:7   **b)** 11:5
12. Answers may vary. In part a), the superior team would have a higher probability of winning. In part b), the probability of playing seven games would decrease.
13. No. In general, $P(A|B)$ will not equal $P(B|A)$.
14. Answers may vary.

Chapter 1 Review, pages 56–57

1. a) blue: $\frac{24}{149} \approx 16.11\%$, green: $\frac{48}{149} \approx 32.21\%$, yellow: $\frac{51}{149} \approx 34.23\%$, purple: $\frac{26}{149} \approx 17.45\%$
b) Answers may vary. blue sector: about 58°, green sector: about 116°, yellow sector: about 123°, purple sector: about 63°.
c) Yes; it is based on experimental probability.
2. a) 0.6   **b)** 168 throws

3. a) 0.9; Since Canada has won at least one medal since 1900, the probability is high that we will win at least one medal in the next Olympics.
  b) 0.1; About 10% of the population is left-handed.
  c) 0.25; There are typically four grades in a high school.

4. a) $\frac{1}{36}$ **b)** $\frac{1}{9}$ **c)** $\frac{5}{6}$ **d)** $\frac{29}{36}$

5. a) 25% **b)** $\frac{1}{13}$ **c)** $\frac{3}{13}$

6. 3 : 1

7. a) 25% **b)** $\frac{1}{6}$
  c) Experimental probability is not a perfect predictor of the outcome of a probability experiment because results of experiments can change. Experimental probability approaches theoretical probability as a very large number of trials are conducted.

8. a) outcomes: (H, H), (H, T), (T, H), (T, T)
  b)
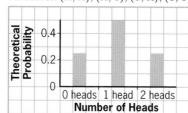
  c) The probability of 1 head is twice that of 0 or 2 heads.

9. a) 25% **b)** 62.5% **c)** 62.5% **d)** 62.5%

10. a) 62.5% **b)** 50% **c)** 50% **d)** 75%

11. a) The first scenario of an even value and a heart will be drawn is more likely to occur.
  b) $P(\text{even number}) = \frac{1}{2}, P(\text{heart}) = \frac{1}{4}.$
    So, $P(\text{even number and heart}) = \frac{1}{2} \times \frac{1}{4} = \frac{1}{8}.$
    $P(\text{composite number}) = \frac{1}{3}, P(\text{face card}) = \frac{3}{13}.$
    So, $P(\text{composite number and face card})$
    $= \frac{1}{3} \times \frac{3}{13} = \frac{1}{13}$

12. a) 25% **b)** 20%
  c) Part a) involves independent events, while part b) involves dependent events.

13. 6 times

Chapter 1 Test Yourself, pages 58–59

1. C **2.** C **3.** B **4.** 25%
5. a) Since this is Marlis's opinion, it is subjective probability. **b)** 4 : 1
6. a) about 8.7% **b)** about 45.6%
7. a) 11 : 7
  b) These are mutually exclusive events. There are 6 ways to roll seven, 2 ways to roll 11, and 6 ways to roll doubles. 36 outcomes are possible.
    So, $P(A) = \frac{6}{36} + \frac{2}{36} + \frac{6}{36},$ or $\frac{14}{36}.$
    Then, $P(A') = 1 - \frac{14}{36},$ or $\frac{22}{36}.$
8. a) 25% **b)** 87.5% **c)** 62.5% **d)** 37.5%
9. a) $\frac{1}{12}$ **b)** $\frac{1}{3}$
10. a) $\frac{1}{3}$ **b)** $\frac{1}{20}$ **c)** $\frac{1}{15}$

Chapter 2 Permutations

Prerequisite Skills, pages 62–63

1. a) 0.039, 0.24, 0.5, 0.718 **b)** 3.0078, 3.078, 3.78
  c) $\frac{1}{6}, \frac{1}{5}, \frac{1}{4}, \frac{1}{3}, \frac{1}{2}$ **d)** $\frac{7}{12}, \frac{5}{8}, \frac{3}{4}, \frac{5}{6}$
2. a) 27.5% **b)** 490% **c)** 12 562%
  d) 40% **e)** 475%
3. $\frac{57}{36}$
4. a) Starting with one triangle, add an increasing number of odd triangles to form a larger triangle.

  b) Starting with 12, subtract 3 continuously.
    $12, 9, 6, 3, 3 - 3 = 0, 0 - 3 = -3, -3 - 3 = -6, \dots$
  c) Starting with the expression $n - 2$, subtract 1 continuously.
    $n - 2, n - 3, n - 4, n - 4 - 1 = n - 5, n - 5 - 1 = n - 6, n - 6 - 1 = n - 7, \dots$
  d) Starting with $\frac{1}{2}$, multiply the denominator by 2 continuously.
    $\frac{1}{2}, \frac{1}{4}, \frac{1}{8}, \frac{1}{8 \times 2} = \frac{1}{16}, \frac{1}{16 \times 2} = \frac{1}{32}, \frac{1}{32 \times 2} = \frac{1}{64}, \dots$
5. Answers may vary.
  a) If you view the diagrams as stairs, start with 2 steps then add 1 step continuously to get the next diagram in the pattern. 2, 3, 4, …
    Starting with a perimeter comprised of 6 line segments, add 2 line segments continuously to get the next diagram in the pattern. 6, 8, 10, …
  b) 2, 3, 4, 5, 6, …; 6, 8, 10, 12, 14, …
6. a) 816 **b)** 30 **c)** 15 120
  d) 2850 **e)** $\frac{65}{81}$ **f)** $\frac{1}{256}$
7. a) 360 **b)** 1716
  c) 35 **d)** approximately 0.005 530
8. a) 60 **b)** 63 **c)** 15 **d)** 722
9. a) $x^3 - 3x^2 + 2x$ **b)** $2x^2 + 4$
  c) $x + 5$ **d)** $x^2 - 5x + 6$
10. a) 336 **b)** 5040 **c)** 6 **d)** 2772
11. a) $\frac{1}{6}$ **b)** $\frac{5}{36}$ **c)** $\frac{1}{2}$ **d)** $\frac{1}{4}$ **e)** $\frac{1}{6}$
12. a) independent, the outcome of flipping a coin does not affect the outcome of rolling a die
  b) dependent, the outcome of dealing a first card affects the second card dealt
  c) independent, the outcome of first die does not affect the outcome of the second die
  d) independent, the outcome of randomly selecting a date does not affect the outcome of randomly selecting someone's name
13. a) $\frac{1}{20}$ **b)** $\frac{1}{20}$ **c)** $\frac{2}{20}$ or $\frac{1}{10}$
  d) $\frac{10}{20}$ or $\frac{1}{2}$ **e)** $\frac{8}{20}$ or $\frac{2}{5}$ **f)** $\frac{14}{20}$ or $\frac{7}{10}$
14. a) mutually exclusive
  b) non-mutually exclusive
  c) mutually exclusive
  d) non-mutually exclusive
  e) non-mutually exclusive

15.

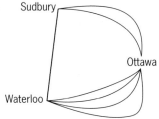

Tree diagram outcomes: (WOS), (WOS), (WOS), (WOS), (WOS),(WOS), (WOS), (WOS), (WS)

16.

Second Die \ First Die	1	2	3	4	5	6
1	2	3	4	5	6	7
2	3	4	5	6	7	8
3	4	5	6	7	8	9
4	5	6	7	8	9	10
5	6	7	8	9	10	11
6	7	8	9	10	11	12

36 possible outcomes

2.1 Organized Counting, pages 64–69

Example 1 Your Turn

a)

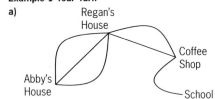

Tree diagram outcomes: (A, R, C, S), (A, R, C, S), (A, R, C, S), (A, R, C, S), (A, R, C, S), (A, R, C, S)

b) six routes

Example 2 Your Turn

a) 24 possible outcomes

b) (Z, B, R, D)

c) 24

Reflect

R1. Answers may vary. While a tree diagram does show all possible outcomes, the actual drawing gets more complicated with more stages. For three stages, a tree diagram is an efficient way to illustrate the outcomes of three spins.

R2. Answers may vary.

a) A table of values is faster to create.

b) When there are three or fewer stages.

Practise

1. 32

T, T, T, T, T	T, F, F, T, T	T, T, F, F, F	T, F, F, T, F
T, T, T, T, F	F, F, T, T, T	T, F, F, F, T	T, F, T, F, F
T, T, T, F, T	F, T, F, T, T	F, F, F, T, T	F, F, F, F, T
T, T, F, T, T	F, T, T, F, T	F, F, T, F, T	F, F, F, F, T
T, F, T, T, T	F, T, T, T, F	F, F, T, T, F	F, F, F, T, F
F, T, T, T, T	T, T, T, F, F	T, F, T, T, F	F, T, F, F, F
T, T, T, F, F	T, F, T, T, F	T, F, T, F, T	T, F, F, F, F
T, T, F, F, T	T, T, F, T, F	F, T, T, T, F	F, F, F, F, F

2. a) 9 outcomes: (1, 1), (1, 2), (1, 3), (2, 1), (2, 2), (2, 3), (3, 1), (3, 2), (3, 3)

b) 27 outcomes: (1, 1, 1), (1, 1, 2), (1, 1, 3), (1, 2, 1), (1, 2, 2), (1, 2, 3), (1, 3, 1), (1, 3, 2), (1, 3, 3), (2, 1, 1),

(2, 1, 2), (2, 1, 3), (2, 2, 1), (2, 2, 2), (2, 2, 3), (2, 3, 1), (2, 3, 2), (2, 3, 3), (3, 1, 1), (3, 1, 2), (3, 1, 3), (3, 2, 1), (3, 2, 2), (3, 2, 3), (3, 3, 1), (3, 3, 2), (3, 3, 3)

3. B   **4.** C

Apply

5. Answers may vary.

6. a) 20 possible outcomes: (A, A, A), (A, A, B, A), (A, A, B, B, A), (A, A, B, B, B), (A, B, A, A), (A, B, A, B, A), (A, B, A, B, B), (A, B, B, A, A), (A, B, B, A, B), (A, B, B, B), (B, A, A, A), (B, A, A, B, A), (B, A, A, B, B), (B, A, B, A, A), (B, A, B, A, B), (B, A, B, B), (B, B, A, A, A), (B, B, A, A, B), (B, B, A, B), (B, B, B)

b)

AAA	ABAA	ABBAB	BAABB	BBAAA
AABA	ABABA	ABBB	BABAA	BBAAB
AABBA	ABABB	BAAA	BABAB	BBAB
AABBB	ABBAA	BAABA	BABB	BBB

c) 20

7. a)

Member 1	Member 2
A	B or C or D or E or F
B	A or C or D or E or F
C	A or B or D or E or F
D	A or B or C or E or F
E	A or B or C or D or F
F	A or B or C or D or E

b) 30

c) 15 outcomes

Member 1	Member 2
A	B or C or D or E or F
B	C or D or E or F
C	D or E or F
D	E or F
E	F

8. No. Tree diagram outcomes for die, then coin: (1, H), (1, T), (2, H), (2, T), (3, H), (3, T), (4, H), (4, T), (5, H), (5, T), (6, H), (6, T)
Tree diagram outcomes for coin, then die: (H, 1), (H, 2), (H, 3), (H, 4), (H, 5), (H, 5), (T, 1), (T, 2), (T, 3), (T, 4), (T, 5), (T, 6)

9. Answers may vary. Assume that the possible test results are letter grades A, B, and C and that a student stops testing once she/he receives an A grade.
Tree diagram outcomes: (A), (B, A), (B, B, A), (B, B, B), (B, B, C), (B, C, A), (B, C, B), (B, C, C), (C, A), (C, B, A), (C, B, B), (C, B, C), (C, C, A), (C, C, B), (C, C, C)
15 sets of results are possible.

10. Answers may vary.

a)

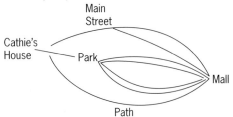

Tree diagram outcomes: (Cathie, Main, Mall), (Cathie, Main, Mall), (Cathie, Park, Mall), (Cathie, Park, Mall), (Cathie, Park, Mall), (Cathie, Park, Mall), (Cathie, Path, Mall)

b) 7

12. a) 45 configurations

b) Adding a siding colour results in an increase of 15 choices. An additional trim colour results in only 9 more choices.

13. a) 2   **b)** 19   **c)** 4

Extend

14. There are 1 190 000 different local phone numbers Sarah can call.

15. Assume rows on checkerboard are numbered 0 to 7. The portion of the tree diagram that starts with a move diagonally left has 49 possible paths to the opposite side. Similarly, the portion of the tree diagram that starts with a move diagonally right has 54 possible paths to the opposite side. The total number of possible paths to the opposite side is 49 + 54, or 103.

16. a) 8   **b)** 16   **c)** 2^n

2.2 The Fundamental Counting Principle, pages 70–75

Example 1 Your Turn

60

Example 2 Your Turn

a) 308 915 776   **b)** 19 770 609 664

Example 3 Your Turn

13 800

Reflect

R1. Johnny is wrong. He should apply the fundamental counting principle: $4 \times 8 \times 3 = 96$.

R2. Answers may vary. The fundamental counting principle is the product of the number of ways multiple events can occur. For example, there are 3 flavours of ice cream and 6 choices of toppings to create a sundae. Event one, choose ice cream flavour, can happen in 3 ways. Event two, choosing a topping, can happen in 6 ways. The result in 3×6, or 18 different 1-topping ice cream sundaes.

Practise

1. a) 4   **b)** 8   **c)** 16   **d)** 2^n

2. a) 210   **b)** 2730

3. 240

4. a) 3   **b)** appetizers: 4, main course: 5, dessert: 3

c) 60

5. C

6. B

7. a) 25   **b)** 20

Apply

8. a) 16   **b)** 64   **c)** 64   **d)** 4096

e) 144   **f)** 248 832   **g)** n^k

9. 19 000

10. 90

11. 7776

12. a) 12 960 000   **b)** 11 703 240

13. a) 216 000   **b)** 205 320

15. a) 456 976 000   **b)** 17 576 000   **c)** 1 000 000

16. An Alberta licence plate will have much fewer choices than an Ontario licence plate. There are 26 choices for a letter, while there are only 10 choices for a digit.

17. 24

18. The same. In event one and two, the colour of the dice does not affect the choices for a die, and rolling three dice once has the same results as rolling one die three times.

19. Answers may vary.

a) My security code is 325. I pressed ENTER 145 times before I saw my code. The actual number of possible outcomes for a three-digit security is 1000.

b) It might take 100 times longer to break a five-digit code versus a three-digit code. The actual number of possible outcomes for a five-digit security is 100 000. Using a graphing calculator to randomly generate a five-digit code could possibly take more than 10 000 presses of ENTER because of duplicates or your code may never be generated.

20. Answers may vary. To find the number of choices for each of the three toppings, factor 4080: $2 \times 2 \times 2 \times 2 \times 3 \times 5 \times 17$. Using all the factors, create three values. For example, there could be $(2 \times 2 \times 2)$ choices for sauce, $(2 \times 3 \times 5)$ choices for actual topping ingredient, and 17 choices for cheese. Another possibility is that this includes four different sizes (S, M, L, XL). Then, there are actually 1020 $(2 \times 2 \times 3 \times 5 \times 17)$ topping options.

21. a) 1 048 576   **b)** 9 756 625

Extend

22. 52 400 215 plates

23. a) 60   **b)** 52

24. 8223

25. 1 275 120

2.3 Permutations and Factorials, pages 76–81

Example 1 Your Turn

a) 24   **b)** 720

c) 7920   **d)** 144

Example 2 Your Turn

40 320

Example 3 Your Turn

59 280

Example 4 Your Turn

240

Reflect

R1. Arranging r people from a group of n people with regard to order will have more possibilities. For example, ABC can be arranged in 6 ways: ABC, ACB, BAC, BCA, CAB, CBA. Without regard for order these arrangements are the same.

R2. Answers may vary. Using a calculator, 0! has a value of 1. Look at the formula for permutations. Suppose three people are awarded first, second, and third prize. So, $r = n = 3$ and the formula becomes $\frac{3!}{0!}$. In order for this to make sense, choose 0! to be defined as 1.

Practise

1. a) 362 880   **b)** 3 991 680   **c)** 5040   **d)** 6720

2. a) $\frac{6!}{2!}$ **b)** $\frac{15!}{9!}$ **c)** 7!   **d)** $\frac{8!}{4!}$

e) $\frac{n!}{(n-4)!}$ **f)** $(n+1)!$

3. a) $_6P_6$ **b)** $_{91}P_6$ **c)** $_{18}P_6$

4. C   **5.** B   **6.** 2730   **7.** 73 440

Apply

8. $_{22}P_9$, or 180 503 769 600

9. a) 10!   **b)** 99!   **c)** 10!

d) $n!$ **e)** $(n+2)!$

10. a) 15!, or 1 307 674 368 000   **b)** 32 760
  c) 13 650
11. a) 3 628 800   **b)** 604 800
12. 3 720 087   **14.** 3 628 800   **15.** 207 3660 000

Extend
16. a) $n = 11$ **b)** $n = 6$
17. 371 589 120
18. 23!, or 25 852 016 738 884 976 640 000
19. a) $\dfrac{9!}{8!!}$ **b)** $\dfrac{(2k+1)!}{2k!!}$ **c)** $2^n n!$
20. 6

2.4 The Rule of Sum, pages 82–87

Example 1 Your Turn
a) 408 240
b) 46 080

Example 2 Your Turn
a) $_{13}P_3$
b) $_4P_3$
c) 1739

Example 3 Your Turn
480

Reflect
R1. It is simpler to calculate the number of executives without any males or females than all the possibilities for at least one male and one female.
R2. Use the fundamental counting principle when the events are independent. For example, rolling a die twice. The outcome of the first event does not affect the second. Use the rule of sum when events are mutually exclusive. For example, rolling a 1 or a 2. Both events cannot happen at the same time.

Practise
1. 2016
2. a) 8   **b)** 18
3. A   **4.** D

Apply
5. a) 130   **b)** 78
6. 182 520 000   **7.** 173 659 200
8. a) 120 100   **b)** 980 200
  c) When the answers in parts a) and b) are expanded into factorial form, all three expressions in part b) are at least 2 times as big as those in part a). So, the result is more than $2^3 = 8$ times the answer in part a).
9. a) 60
  b) Answers may vary. Question: Five speakers, P, Q, R, S, and T, are available to address a meeting. The organizer must decide whether to have four or five speakers. How many options would the organizer have for the meeting? Answer: 5! + 4! = 144. There are 144 options.
10. 61 328   **11.** 3 628 799
12. a) 48   **b)** 126
13. Answers may vary. For each roll of two dice, there are six ways to get doubles. There are 6 + 6 + 6, or 18 ways to get doubles in one or two or three rolls.
14. Morse code is used to represent 26 letters, 10 digits, and 8 punctuation symbols, or a total of 44 symbols. Since each character has two options (dot or dash), a maximum of six characters is needed: $2^6 = 64$.

Extend
16. 82
17. a) 9   **b)** 44
18. a) 265   **b)** 455   **c)** 1

2.5 Probability Problems Using Permutations, pages 88–95

Example 1 Your Turn
a) $P(\text{all same}) = \dfrac{1}{10\ 000\ 000\ 000}$
b) $P(\text{all 6s}) = \dfrac{1}{7776}$
  For independent trials,
  P(all the same) = (P(a success))$^{\#\ \text{trials}}$.

Example 2 Your Turn
$P(\text{in grade order}) = \dfrac{1}{24}$

Example 3 Your Turn
a) $P(\text{ace, ace, ace, jack, jack}) = \dfrac{1}{1\ 082\ 900}$
b) $P(\text{heart, heart, club, club, club}) = \dfrac{143}{166\ 600}$

Example 4 Your Turn
a) approximately 0.7164   **b)** approximately 0.2836

Reflect
R1. No. The probability that at least two people have the same birthday is approximately 0.6269.
R2. Answers may vary. If the trials are dependent, permutations can be used. Look for restrictions such as, "without replacement" or "alphabetical order."
R3. Answers may vary. The first represents 3 of 12 objects being arranged. The second is 3 times 1 of 12 objects being arranged.

Practise
1. $P(\text{king, queen, jack}) = \dfrac{8}{16\ 575}$
2. $\dfrac{1}{15}$ **3.** A   **4.** C

Apply
5. $\dfrac{1\ 307\ 674\ 367\ 999}{1\ 307\ 674\ 368\ 000} \cdot \dfrac{1}{1\ 307\ 674\ 368\ 000}$
6. a) approximately 0.000 505
  b) $\dfrac{_{30}P_3}{_{365}P_3} \approx 0.000\ 505$
7. a) $P(\text{doubles}) = \dfrac{1}{6}$ **b)** $P(\text{doubles twice}) = \dfrac{1}{36}$
  c) They are the same.
8. a) $P(\text{3 boys}) = \dfrac{1}{8}$ **b)** $P(\text{4 boys}) = \dfrac{1}{16}$
  c) $P(\text{5 boys}) = \dfrac{1}{32}$ **d)** $P(n\text{ boys}) = \dfrac{1}{2^n}$
9. a) $P(\text{MATH}) = \dfrac{1}{3024}$ **b)** $P(\text{M,A,T,H}) = \dfrac{1}{126}$
  c) $P = \dfrac{4}{9}$
10. a) $P(\text{ascending order}) \approx 4.1697 \times 10^{-5}$
  b) $P(\text{no same denomination}) \approx 0.2102$
11. $P(\text{at least two the same}) \approx 0.4114$
12. 23
13. a) $P(\text{songs in order}) = \dfrac{1}{3\ 628\ 800}$
  b) $P = \dfrac{1}{45}$
14. a) 0.8203 : 0.1797   **b)** 0.4160 : 0.5840
15. Answers may vary. Example: 7

16. a) i) $\dfrac{1}{38\,955\,840}$ ii) $\dfrac{1}{78\,960\,960}$ iii) $\dfrac{1}{146\,611\,080}$

b) The probability of cracking the safe decreases as the five different numbers are chosen from a greater range of number.

18. The probability that at least two people have the same birthday as you is approximately 0.5687.

19. a) not throwing a sum of 7 on consecutive rolls

b) three different letters being arranged in alphabetical order

c) two out of five friends having the same birth month

Extend

20. 3.1664×10^{-7}

21. Answers may vary. Any scenario that has $n(A) = 1$ and $n(S) = {}_{15}P_7$. For example, winning first prize similar to question 20.

22. a) approximately 0.0947
b) approximately 6.9613×10^{-5}

23. a) approximately 0.0188
b) approximately 0.1004

24. a) approximately 2.2355×10^{-6}
b) approximately 0.0026

Chapter 2 Review, pages 96–97

1. 27 possible outcomes

2.

First Die / Second Die	1	2	3	4	5	6	7	8
1	2	3	4	5	6	7	8	9
2	3	4	5	6	7	8	9	10
3	4	5	6	7	8	9	10	11
4	5	6	7	8	9	10	11	12
5	6	7	8	9	10	11	12	13
6	7	8	9	10	11	12	13	14
7	8	9	10	11	12	13	14	15
8	9	10	11	12	13	14	15	16

The sum of 9 occurs eight times. There is only one occurrence of the sum 2 and sum 16.

3. a) 60 possible outcomes **b)** (Q, K, A) **c)** 60

4. a) 100 000 **b)** 800 000 s, or about 9.3 days

5. a) 360
b) Ryan has 432 choices to configure his computer. Increasing the number of choices for any option will increase the total number of possible configurations.

6. 150

7. 60

8. a) and b)

```
            1
          2   2
        3   6   6
      4   12  24  24
    5   20  60 120 120
  6   30 120 360 720 720
```

The first term in row n is n. To obtain the remaining terms in row n, multiply all the terms in the row above by n.

c) Answers may vary. The last term in row n equals $n!$. The last two terms in each row are equal.

9. 87 091 200

10. a) 144 **b)** 576 **c)** 5040

11. 576

12. 60

13. a) approximately 2.7557×10^{-7}
b) $1 - 2.7557 \times 10^{-7}$

14. a) $\dfrac{1}{30}$ **b)** $\dfrac{2}{15}$ **c)** $\dfrac{29}{30}$

15. a) approximately 8.4165×10^{-8}
b) $1 - 8.4165 \times 10^{-8}$

Chapter 2 Test Yourself, pages 98–99

1. C **2.** D **3.** A

4. ${}_9P_{10}$ is not defined, $n < r$.

$$
\begin{aligned}
{}_9P_{10} &= \frac{9!}{(9-10)!} \\
&= \frac{9!}{(-1)!}
\end{aligned}
$$

5. a) 24 possible outcomes **b)** 6

6. 1152 **7.** 95 040 **8.** $\dfrac{1}{56}$

9. a) 40 320 **b)** 25 200

10. 32 659 200

11. a) 3 575 880 **b)** 3 156 000 **c)** 1 806 000

12. a) $\dfrac{1}{456\,976}$ **b)** $\dfrac{1}{358\,800}$

13. approximately 0.9345

14. a) 311 875 200 **b)** 158 146 560
c) approximately 3.6938×10^{-6}
d) approximately 3.5013×10^{-5}

Chapter 3 Combinations

Prerequisite Skills, pages 102–103

1. a) 40 320 **b)** 60 480 **c)** 144 **d)** 151 200
e) 1320 **f)** 35 **g)** 330 **h)** 504 504

2. a) $n!$ is a product of sequential natural numbers with the form $n! = n(n-1)(n-2) \times \ldots \times 2 \times 1$.

b) The number of permutations of r items from a collection of n items is written as ${}_nP_r$ or $P(n, r)$.
$$ {}_nP_r = \frac{n!}{(n-r)!}, \ n \geq r $$

3. a) $\dfrac{7!}{4!}$ **b)** $\dfrac{100!}{8!}$ **c)** $\dfrac{n!}{(n-6)!}$ **d)** $\dfrac{15!}{(15-r)!}$

4. a) 40 320 **b)** 6720 **c)** 1716

5. a) 39 916 800 **b)** 86 400

6. a) 40 320 **b)** 336

7. a) The first and last terms are 1. The remaining terms are the sum of the two adjacent terms in the row above.

```
              1
            1   1
          1   2   1
        1   3   3   1
      1   4   6   4   1
    1   5  10  10   5   1
  1   6  15  20  15   6   1
```

b) Answers may vary. Consider the top of the triangle row 0. Then, the sum of entries in row n equals 2^n. The second diagonal contains the counting numbers 1, 2, 3, 4, 5, ….

8. a) $\dfrac{1}{8}$ **b)** $\dfrac{1}{8}$ **c)** $\dfrac{1}{8}$ **d)** $\dfrac{3}{8}$

9. a) approximately 0.0060 **b)** approximately 0.2549
c) approximately 0.3077

10. a) $\dfrac{1}{18}$ **b)** $\dfrac{1}{18}$ **c)** $\dfrac{1}{9}$
d) approximately 1.5619×10^{-16}

11. a) It could have six faces, two of each colour.

b) 18   **c)** $\frac{1}{18}$ **d)** $\frac{2}{3}$

12. The events A and B are not mutually exclusive, since the overlap shows there are common elements. If A and B are non-mutually exclusive events, then the total number of favourable outcomes is:
$n(A \text{ or } B) = n(A) + n(B) - n(A \text{ and } B)$.

13. 7

14. a)

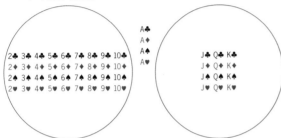

b)

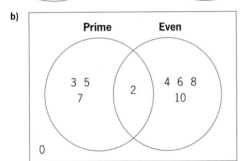

c)

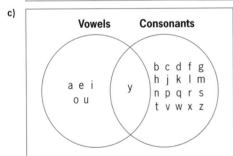

d)

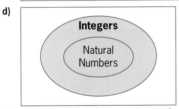

15. a) x^6 **b)** $4a^2$ **c)** $25m^6$ **d)** $81k^{12}$

16. a) $x^2 + 2xy + y^2$ **b)** $a^3 + 3a^2b + 3ab^2 + b^3$
c) $4p^2 + 4pq + q^2$

17. a) $(n-1)(n-2)$ **b)** $n(n-1)$ **c)** n

3.1 Permutations With Non-Ordered Elements, pages 104–109

Example 1 Your Turn
a) In each case, there are 3! permutations.
b) In each case, there are 2!2! permutations.

Example 2 Your Turn
I would expect the number of orders of the second team to be higher.

Example 3 Your Turn
840

Reflect
R1. There are four identical 2s.
R2. No. The number of permutations of three girls and four boys, or seven people, is 7!
The number of permutations of three red balls and four green balls is $\frac{7!}{3!4!}$. All red balls are identical and all green balls are identical.
R3. Answers may vary. It is much quicker to use the formula. Drawing a tree diagram or chart may not be practical and takes longer.

Practise
1. a) 2520   **b)** 1680
c) 420   **d)** 1 905 780 240
2. B
3. D
4. a) 20 160   **b)** 420   **c)** 415 800   **d)** 180
5. a) 60   **b)** 20   **c)** 30   **d)** 5

Apply
6. a) 369 600   **b)** 34 650   **c)** 924
7. 70   **8.** 2520   **9.** 9 459 450
10. Since it is not possible to have 0 or a fractional number of ways to do something, the number of permutations involving identical objects will always be a natural number. The denominator must be a factor of the numerator.
11. 462; Assume that the streets are laid out in a grid pattern, and that all of the streets are continuous between his school and his home.
12. a) 369 600   **b)** 7 484 400
13. 42
14. 24
16. a) 10 764 000   **b)** 43 056 000   **c)** 1 794 000
d) The number of licence plates in part c) is about 0.4% of the total licence plates without restrictions.
17. Answers may vary. How many arrangements are there of 12 flags in a row if two are red, three are green, four are blue, and three are yellow?

Extend
18. 1320   **19.** 60   **20.** 185 794 560

3.2 Combinations, pages 110–115

Example 1 Your Turn
a) 210   **b)** 252   **c)** 210

Example 2 Your Turn
525

Example 3 Your Turn
35

Reflect
R1. Answers may vary.
a) For permutations, order matters. For example, select five out of eight for five different offices of the committee.
b) For combinations, order does not matter. For example, select five out of eight for a committee.

R2. Answers may vary. Examples: selecting groceries, selecting toppings for a sandwich

R3. A situation in which order matters (permutations) will have more possibilities. $_nC_r = \dfrac{_nP_r}{r!}$

For each combination of r items there are $r!$ permutations. So, the number of combinations is $r!$ times smaller than the number of permutations.

Practise

1. **a)** 126   **b)** 70   **c)** 220
   d) 462   **e)** 420   **f)** 27 772 222 500
2. B   **3.** B   **4.** 210   **5.** 330   **6.** 1
7. **a)** 1   **b)** 1   **c)** 1   **d)** 1   **e)** 1

Apply

8. 168
9. **a)** 65 780   **b)** 792   **c)** 575 757
   d) 845 000   **e)** 1 096 680
10. **a)** 5 586 853 480   **b)** 3 838 380
    c) There is a larger number of ways to choose a 12-person jury than a 6-person jury. The denominator in part a) (28!12!) is smaller than that in part b) (34!6!).
11. **a)** 330   **b)** 150   **c)** 60   **d)** 5   **e)** 15
    f) Parts b) to e) are subsets of part a). The combinations add to 230. With the inclusion of a three truck and one car option, the total is 330.
12. **a)** This is a combination situation, since the order does not matter.
    b) $_{14}C_2 = 91$
13. **a)** 210   **b)** 252
    c) $_{10}C_n, 3 \le n \le 10$
14. **a)**   i) $_7C_2 = 21, _7C_5 = 21$
         ii) $_4C_3 = 4, _4C_1 = 4$
         iii) $_{12}C_4 = 495, _{12}C_8 = 495$
       The values in each pair are the same.
    b) $_nC_r = _nC_{n-r}$. The only difference is the order of the terms in the denominator. The number of combinations of n items taken r at a time is equivalent to the number of combinations of n items taken $n - r$ at a time.
    c) $_nC_r = \dfrac{n!}{(n-r)!r!}$
       $= \dfrac{n!}{r!(n-r)!}$
       $= \dfrac{n!}{(n-(n-r))!(n-r)!}$
       $= _nC_{n-r}$
15. **a)** 6 126 120   **b)** 6 126 120
    c) The results for parts a) and b) are the same. The order in which the jobs are assigned is irrelevant.
16. **a)** 20
    b) The general formula for the number of diagonals in a polygon with n sides is $\dfrac{n(n-3)}{2}$. Using combinations, select two points from the n vertices: $_nC_2$. However, this also includes consecutive vertices that form a side of the polygon. So, subtract n, the number of sides. There are $_nC_2 - n$ diagonals in an n-sided convex polygon.
18. 756 756
19. 2 375 880 867 360 000
20. The techniques from the two sections result in the same answer.

21. There are $_{30}C_5 \times _{25}C_5 \times _{20}C_5 \times _{15}C_5 \times _{10}C_5 \times _5C_5$ ways to divide a class of 30 students into six teams of five members.
    The number of ways to arrange a total of 30 balls with six different colours is also $_{30}C_5 \times _{25}C_5 \times _{20}C_5 \times _{15}C_5 \times _{10}C_5 \times _5C_5$.
22. For $r > 0$, there will always be more r-permutations of n items than r-combinations or n items.
    $$_nC_r = \dfrac{_nP_r}{r!}$$
    In permutations order matters, not in combinations. For each combination of r items there are $r!$ permutations. So, the number of combinations is $r!$ times smaller than the number of permutations.
23. 42

Extend

24. **a)** Let the three consecutive numbers be represented by $n, n-1$, and $n-2$.
    $$\dfrac{n(n-1)(n-2)}{3!} = \dfrac{n(n-1)(n-2)(n-3)!}{(n-3)!3!}$$
    $$= _nC_3$$
    b) Let the r consecutive numbers be represented by $n, n-1, n-2, ..., (n-r+1)$.
    $$\dfrac{n(n-1)(n-2)\cdots(n-r+1)}{r!}$$
    $$= \dfrac{n(n-1)(n-2)\cdots(n-r+1)(n-r)!}{(n-r)!r!}$$
    $$= _nC_r$$
25. $n = 5$
26. 816

3.3 Problem Solving With Combinations, pages 116–121

Example 1 Your Turn
Combinations:
$$_8C_1 + _8C_2 + _8C_3 + _8C_4 + _8C_5 + _8C_6 + _8C_7 + _8C_8$$
$$= \dfrac{8!}{(8-1)!1!} + \dfrac{8!}{(8-2)!2!} + \dfrac{8!}{(8-3)!3!} + \dfrac{8!}{(8-4)!4!}$$
$$+ \dfrac{8!}{(8-5)!5!} + \dfrac{8!}{(8-6)!6!} + \dfrac{8!}{(8-7)!7!} + \dfrac{8!}{(8-8)!8!}$$
$$= 255$$
Indirect Method:
$2^8 - 1 = 256 - 1$
$\qquad\quad = 255$

Example 2 Your Turn
a) 576 050 767 488   **b)** 2 672 060
c) 4 306 559 400   **d)** 181 823 183 256
e) 158 362 127 352

Example 3 Your Turn
a) 2 052 000   **b)** 307 800

Reflect
R1. When determining the total number of subsets of a set, you add the number of possibilities in each case because the events are mutually exclusive.
R2. When using cases to determine the number of ways of selecting objects from different sets, you add because the events are mutually exclusive.

R3. Answers may vary.

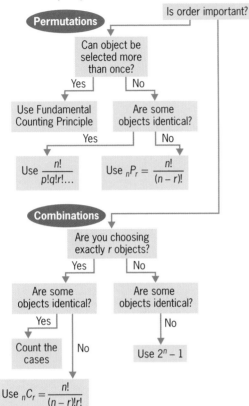

Practise
1. 15   2. B   3. C
4. a) 6720   b) 5880   c) 2016   d) 14 826

Apply
5. a) combinations; The order in which the 5 members are chosen does not matter.
   b) permutations; Order matters, since each position holds an office.
   c) both; The order in which the members of the team are chosen does not matter. When arranging for a photo, order matters.
   d) permutations; Order matters because there are 3 different prizes.
6. 32 767   7. 92   8. 63   9. 15   10. 14 400
11. a) 1 237 792   b) 6 799 260   c) 3 219 112
12. a) 5 326 270   b) 6 864 396 000
13. 600   14. 2 041 200 000   15. 160

Extend
17. 968   18. 2 560 481 280

3.4 Combinations and Pascal's Triangle, pages 122–127

Example 1 Your Turn
$1 + 7 + 28 + 84 + 210 = 330$.
Comparing the terms in Pascal's triangle to combinations gives $_6C_6 + _7C_6 + _8C_6 + _9C_6 + _{10}C_6 = _{11}C_7$.

Example 2 Your Turn
Pascal's Method:
School

210	84	28	7	1
126	56	21	6	1
70	35	15	5	1
35	20	10	4	1
15	10	6	3	1
5	4	3	2	1
1	1	1	1	Home

Bill can take 210 different routes to school.
Combinations: $_{10}C_4 \times _6C_6 = 210$

Example 3 Your Turn
a) $(a + b)^4 = _4C_0a^4b^0 + _4C_1a^3b^1 + _4C_2a^2b^2 + _4C_3a^1b^3 + _4C_4a^0b^4$
   $= a^4 + 4a^3b + 6a^2b^2 + 4ab^3 + b^4$
   The terms $_4C_r$, where $r = 0$ to 4 correspond to row 4 in Pascal's triangle. The degree of each term is 4.
b) $(p + q)^5 = _5C_0p^5q^0 + _5C_1p^4q^1 + _5C_2p^3q^2 + _5C_3p^2q^3 + _5C_4p^1q^4 + _5C_5p^0q^5$
   $= p^5 + 5p^4q + 10p^3q^2 + 10p^2q^3 + 5pq^4 + q^5$
   The terms $_5C_r$, where $r = 0$ to 5 correspond to row 5 in Pascal's triangle. The degree of each term is 5.

Reflect
R1. Answers may vary. The term labels begin with $t_{0,0}$. This maintains the pattern of first and last terms in each row both being 1, since there is only one term.
R2. The terms in row n of Pascal's triangle correspond to the combinations $t_{n,r} = _nC_r$. Each row in Pascal's triangle represents the combinations of choosing 0 items, 1 item, 2 items, and so on, out of n items.
R3. Yes. Finding the number of arrangements of n items with p of one type identical and q of another type identical is a valid solution. The result is the same $\frac{9!}{4!5!}$.

Practise
1. a) $_9C_0$ $_9C_1$ $_9C_2$ $_9C_3$ $_9C_4$ $_9C_5$ $_9C_6$ $_9C_7$ $_9C_8$ $_9C_9$
   b) $_4C_4$ $_5C_4$ $_6C_4$ $_7C_4$ $_8C_4$
2. $a = 286 + 78$ $b = 1001 - 286$ $c = a + 1001$
   $= 364$ $= 715$ $= 364 + 1001$
                                 $= 1365$
3. D
4. B
5.

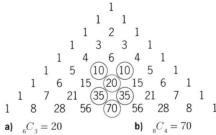

a) $_6C_3 = 20$ b) $_8C_4 = 70$

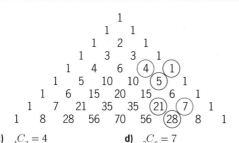

$$\begin{array}{ccccccccccccccccc}
&&&&&&&&1\\
&&&&&&&1&&1\\
&&&&&&1&&2&&1\\
&&&&&1&&3&&3&&1\\
&&&&1&&4&&6&&④&&①\\
&&&1&&5&&10&&10&&⑤&&1\\
&&1&&6&&15&&20&&15&&6&&1\\
&1&&7&&21&&35&&35&&㉑&&⑦&&1\\
1&&8&&28&&56&&70&&56&&㉘&&8&&1
\end{array}$$

c) $_4C_3 = 4$ d) $_7C_6 = 7$

Apply

6. a) i) 4   **ii)** 9   **iii)** 16
  b) They are perfect squares.
  c) These occur in diagonal 2.
  d) Each perfect square greater than 1 is equal to the sum of a pair of adjacent terms on diagonal 2 of Pascal's triangle: $n^2 = {}_nC_2 + {}_{n+1}C_2, n > 1$

7. a) 165; $_7C_7 + {}_8C_7 + {}_9C_7 + {}_{10}C_7 = {}_{11}C_8$
  b) $_rC_r + {}_{r+1}C_r + {}_{r+2}C_r + \ldots + {}_{r+k-1}C_r = {}_{r+k}C_{r+1}$

8. 35   **9.** 27   **10.** 180

11. a) 32; Since this is a triangular array, combinations can be used to solve this question.
  b) 20; Since this is not a triangular array, combinations cannot be used.

12. a) diagonal 2
  b) $1 + 2 = {}_3C_2$ $1 + 2 + 3 = {}_4C_2$ $1 + 2 + 3 + 4 = {}_5C_2$
  The sum of the first n natural numbers is $_{n+1}C_2$.
  c) Example 1 involved sums of terms in diagonal 2. This question involves sums of terms in diagonal 1.

13. a) $x^8 + 8x^7y + 28x^6y^2 + 56x^5y^3 + 70x^4y^4 + 56x^3y^5 + 28x^2y^6 + 8xy^7 + y^8$
  b) $x^5 - 5x^4y + 10x^3y^2 - 10x^2y^3 + 5xy^4 - y^5$
  c) $16a^4 + 32a^3b + 24a^2b^2 + 8ab^3 + b^4$
  d) $x^6 - 6x^4 + 12x^2 - 8$

14. a)

Number of Lines	Number of Regions	Rewrite the Number of Regions
0	1	1
1	2	1 + 1
2	4	1 + (1 + 2)
3	7	1 + (1 + 2 + 3)
4	11	1 + (1 + 2 + 3 + 4)
⋮		⋮
n		1 + (1 + 2 + 3 + … + n)

The values being added represent the triangular numbers, whose sum is $\dfrac{n(n + 1)}{2}$. The formula for the number of regions is $R(n) = 1 + \dfrac{n(n + 1)}{2}$.
The sum of the first n natural numbers is $_{n+1}C_2$.
So, $R(n) = 1 + {}_{n+1}C_2$.
  b) 211

15. a)

n	Sum of Squares $1^2 + 2^2 + … + n^2$	$t_{n+1,3} + t_{n+2,3}$
1	$1^2 = 1$	
2	$1^2 + 2^2 = 5$	$t_{3,3} + t_{4,3} = 1 + 4 = 5$
3	$1^2 + 2^2 + 3^2 = 14$	$t_{4,3} + t_{5,3} = 4 + 10 = 14$
4	$1^2 + 2^2 + 3^2 + 4^2 = 30$	$t_{5,3} + t_{6,3} = 10 + 20 = 30$
5	$1^2 + 2^2 + 3^2 + 4^2 + 5^2 = 55$	$t_{6,3} + t_{7,3} = 20 + 35 = 55$
6	$1^2 + 2^2 + 3^2 + 4^2 + 5^2 + 6^2 = 91$	$t_{7,3} + t_{8,3} = 35 + 56 = 91$

  b) The values in columns two and three are the same.

c) The sum of the first n squares is $_{n+1}C_3 + {}_{n+2}C_3$, $n > 1$.
  d) 42 925

16. a)

Layer, n	Total Number of Oranges	$t_{n+1,2} + t_{n+1,3}$
1	1	
2	1 + 3 = 4	$t_{3,2} + t_{3,3} = 3 + 1 = 4$
3	1 + 3 + 6 = 10	$t_{4,2} + t_{4,3} = 6 + 4 = 10$
4	1 + 3 + 6 + 10 = 20	$t_{5,2} + t_{5,3} = 10 + 10 = 20$

  b) The total number of oranges needed for a stack of n layers can be found in diagonal 3 of Pascal's triangle.
  c) $_{n+1}C_2 + {}_{n+1}C_3, n > 1$ **d)** 220

18. $(h + t)^5 = {}_5C_0h^5t^0 + {}_5C_1h^4t^1 + {}_5C_2h^3t^2 + {}_5C_3h^2t^3 + {}_5C_4h^1t^4 + {}_5C_5h^0t^5$
  $= 1h^5t^0 + 5h^4t^1 + 10h^3t^2 + 10h^2t^3 + 5h^1t^4 + 1h^0t^5$
If a coin is tossed five times, there is
1 way to get 5 heads and 0 tails
5 ways to get 4 heads and 1 tail
10 ways to get 3 heads and 2 tails
10 ways to get 2 heads and 3 tails
5 ways to get 1 head and 4 tails
1 way to get 0 heads and 5 tails

Extend

19. a) $p^5 - 5p^3 + 10p - \dfrac{10}{p} + \dfrac{5}{p^3} - \dfrac{1}{p^5}$
  b) $81m^8 + 216m^4 + 216 + \dfrac{96}{m^4} + \dfrac{16}{m^8}$

3.5 Probabilities Using Combinations, pages 128–133

Example 1 Your Turn
a) approximately a 0.000 113% chance
b) approximately a 0.015 765% chance
c) approximately 0.999 841 22
d) Answers may vary. It is extremely unlikely that anyone will win the lottery prizes.

Example 2 Your Turn
a) approximately 0.36   **b)** approximately 0.28
c) It is more likely that there will be equal numbers of male and female students than more female than male students.

Example 3 Your Turn
Slots A and F: 0; Slots B and E: $\dfrac{1}{8}$; Slots C and D: $\dfrac{3}{8}$

Reflect
R1. Answers may vary. A student selects three cards in order, without replacement, from a standard deck. What is the probability that the student selects a king, then two queens? What is the probability that a hand of three cards contains only face cards?
R2. If you interpret the language to mean Jake is first and Hamid is second, order matters. So, the probability that two are the top two finishers is $\dfrac{_2P_2}{_8P_2}$.
If you interpret the language to mean Jake and Hamid are top two with no assigned place (first or second), order does not matter. So, the probability that two are the top two finishers is $\dfrac{_2C_2}{_8C_2}$. Both expressions result in the same probability of $\dfrac{1}{28}$.

1. a) approximately 0.000 495
   b) approximately 0.025
   c) approximately a 0.000 305
2. $\frac{1}{3}$ 3. B   4. C

Apply

5. a) approximately 0.006   b) approximately 0.076
   c) approximately 0.002   d) approximately 0.7
6. approximately 1.575×10^{-12}
7. approximately 0.303
8. approximately $0.145 : 0.855$
9. approximately 0.167
10. a) space D at about 0.38
    b) If the checker begins in a different location, the number of possible paths ending at each destination will be different.
11. approximately 0.908
12. Answers may vary. The probability of the disc landing in each slot at the bottom of the board depends on its starting slot. Dropping the ball from one of two centre slots (3 or 4) will give the most paths, so that is the best strategy. Starting in slot 3, the probability of the ball landing in A or F: $\frac{1}{32}$; B or E: $\frac{5}{32}$; C or D: $\frac{5}{16}$; G: 0.
13. approximately 0.54
14. approximately 0.476

Extend

16. $\frac{7}{9}$
17. a) approximately 0.952   b) approximately 0.952
    c) approximately 0.548
18. 0.225

Chapter 3 Review, pages 134–135

1. 840
2. a) 840   b) 3 326 400   c) 277 200
3. 1001
4. a) i) $r = 4$ ii) $r = 5$
      iii) $r = 3$ or $r = 4$ iv) $r = 7$ or $r = 8$
   b) The greatest number of combinations when n is even occurs at $r = \frac{n}{2}$. The greatest number of combinations when n is odd occurs at $r = \frac{n}{2} \pm 0.5$.
5. a) 352 800   b) 210
6. a) 210
   b) Answers may vary. A committee has 10 people. In how many ways could a president and vice president be chosen?
   c) Answers may vary. From a committee of 10 people, there are $_{10}P_3$, or 90 ways to choose a president and vice president.
7. 300
8. 31
9. a) 30 257 175   b) 22 120 065   c) 22 116 900
10. $a = 792$, $b = 462$
11. a) i) 1 ii) 5 iii) 15
    b) They are entries in diagonal 4 of Pascal's triangle.
    c) They are represented by $_nC_4$.
    d) 495
12. a) row 9   b) row 12

13. Pascal's Method:

Home	1	1	1	1
1	2	3	4	5
1	3	6	10	15
1	4	10	20	35
1	5	15	35	70
1	6	21	56	126
1	7	28	84	210
1	8	36	120	330

School

Stephen can take 330 different routes to school.
Combinations: $_{11}C_2 \times _7C_7 = 330$

14. a) $a^5 + 5a^4b + 10a^3b^2 + 10a^2b^3 + 5ab^4 + b^5$
    b) $16x^4 + 32x^3y + 24x^2y^2 + 8xy^3 + y^4$
15. a) approximately 0.000 285
    b) approximately 0.000 495
16. a) approximately 0.005   b) approximately 0.587
17. a) approximately 0.004   b) approximately 0.496
    c) 0.504

Chapter 3 Test Yourself, pages 136–137

1. C   2. B   3. B   4. A
5. 1001   6. 35   7. 70   8. 15 120
9. a) $_8C_3 = \frac{_8P_3}{3!}$
   b) Both $_8C_3$ and $_8P_3$ represent the number of arrangements of 3 items from 8. However, combinations have no regard for order, while permutations do. Combination: A committee of three people can be chosen from a list of 8 people in $_8C_3$, or 56 ways. Permutation: From a committee of 8 people, there are $_8P_3$, or 336 ways to choose a president, vice president, and secretary.
10. approximately 0.396
11. 210
12. Permutations With Like Objects:
    $\frac{18!}{3!3!3!3!3!3!} = 137\,225\,088\,000$
    Combinations:
    $_{18}C_3 \times _{15}C_3 \times _{12}C_3 \times _9C_3 \times _6C_3 \times _3C_3 = 137\,225\,088\,000$
13. a) Each row in Pascal's triangle represents the combinations of choosing 0 items, 1 item, 2 items, and so on, out of n items.
    b) The terms of Pascal's triangle are generated by adding two adjacent terms and placing the result immediately below them in the next row.
    $t_{n,r} + t_{n,r+1} = t_{n+1,r+1}$
    Using combinations, $_nC_r + _nC_{r+1} = _{n+1}C_{r+1}$.
14. a) Alternately subtracting and adding successive terms in a row of Pascal's triangle results in 0.
    b) For $n > 0$, $_nC_0 - _nC_1 + _nC_2 - \ldots _nC_n$.
15. a) 169
    b) It would be greater, since there are more chances to get olives or mushrooms. $_{15}C_4 - _{13}C_4 = 650 > 169$
16. a) approximately 0.81   b) approximately 0.008
    c) approximately 0.184
17. a) approximately 0.0002   b) approximately 0.043
    c) approximately 0.381   d) approximately 0.624
    e) approximately 0.351

Chapters 1 to 3 Cumulative Review, pages 138–139

1. a) $\frac{2}{3}$ b) $\frac{1}{3}$

2. a) $1:4$ b) $1:1$

3. a) Experimental probability is based on experimental trials, while theoretical probability is based on the analysis of all outcomes.

   b) Experimental probability approaches theoretical probability as a very large number of trials are conducted.

4. $\frac{2}{9}$ 5. $\frac{7}{13}$

6. a) $\frac{9}{25}$ b) $\frac{3}{10}$

   c) The answers to parts a) and b) are different because one deals with replacement and the other does not.

7. Map:

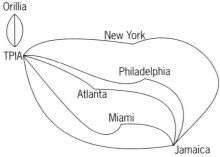

Tree diagram outcomes: (O, D, NY, J), (O, D, M, J), (O, D, A, J), (O, D, P, J), (O, D, J), (O, B, NY, J), (O, B, M, J), (O, B, A, J), (O, B, P, J), (O, B, J), (O, T, NY, J), (O, T, M, J), (O, T, A, J), (O, T, P, J), (O, T, J)

List:

OT_cNJ	OT_cPJ	OT_cAJ	OT_cMJ	OT_cJ
OT_bNJ	OT_bPJ	OT_bAJ	OT_bMJ	OT_bJ
OT_tNJ	OT_tPJ	OT_tAJ	OT_tMJ	OT_tJ

8. a) 216   b) 1296   c) 64   d) 1728

9. a) 1680

   b) Adjacent countries share boundaries. These boundaries are more visible if the countries are different colours. With only 8 colours available, there could be many countries that are coloured the same colour, but adjacent countries should not be.

10. 124 251 000   **11.** 1680   **12.** 399 168 000

13. a) $\frac{1}{120}$

   b) Winning would be less probable if the digits could be repeated, because there would be more possible outcomes.

14. 63   **15.** 1 646 400

16. a) 210

   b) Answers may vary. $_{10}C_6 = 210$. Pascal's method will arrive at the same result by adding the number of paths to the adjacent grid points to determine the number of paths to the given point.

17. a)

n	$_nC_2 \div {_nC_1}$	Result
2	$1 \div 2$	0.5
3	$3 \div 3$	1
4	$6 \div 4$	1.5
5	$10 \div 5$	2
6	$15 \div 6$	2.5
7	$21 \div 7$	3
8	$28 \div 8$	3.5
9	$36 \div 9$	4

   b) When n is odd, $_nC_2$ is divisible by $_nC_1$.

   c) When n is odd, $_nC_2$ is divisible by $_nC_1$. These rows have an even number of terms.

   d) Yes, $_{15}C_2$ is divisible by $_{15}C_1$, because n is odd.

18. 56

19. a) 31   b) 31

20. a) 6

   b) Yes. Let the three directions the spider can move be right, left, and down. The spider needs to travel 3 edges to its destination. Select any one of these three edges to travel, say right. From two remaining edges, select another direction, say left. Then, the last edge travel down.

$$_3C_1 \times {_2C_1} \times {_1C_1} = \frac{3!}{2!1!} \times \frac{2!}{1!1!} \times \frac{1!}{0!1!}$$
$$= 6$$

21. a) approximately 0.190   b) approximately 0.9903

Chapter 4 Probability Distributions for Discrete Variables

Prerequisite Skills, pages 142–143

1. a) $\frac{4}{52}$ or $\frac{1}{13}$ b) $\frac{26}{52}$ or $\frac{1}{2}$ c) $\frac{13}{52}$ or $\frac{1}{4}$

2. a)

Sum	Possible Groupings	Number of Outcomes	Probability
3	(1,1,1)	1	$\frac{1}{216}$
4	(1,2,1)	3	$\frac{3}{216}$
5	(1,3,1), (1,2,2)	6	$\frac{6}{216}$
6	(1,4,1), (1,3,2), (2,2,2)	10	$\frac{10}{216}$
7	(1,4,2), (1,3,3), (5,1,1), (3,2,2)	15	$\frac{15}{216}$
8	(1,4,3), (1,2,5), (1,1,6), (4,2,2), (3,3,2)	21	$\frac{21}{216}$
9	(6,2,1), (5,3,1), (5,2,2), (4,4,1), (4,3,2), (3,3,3)	25	$\frac{25}{216}$
10	(6,3,1), (6,2,2), (5,3,2), (5,4,1), (4,4,2), (4,3,3)	27	$\frac{27}{216}$
11	(6,4,1), (6,3,2), (5,5,1), (5,4,2), (5,3,3), (4,4,3)	27	$\frac{27}{216}$
12	(6,5,1), (6,4,2), (6,3,3), (5,5,2), (5,4,3), (4,4,4)	25	$\frac{25}{216}$
13	(6,6,1), (6,5,2), (6,4,3), (5,5,3), (5,4,4)	21	$\frac{21}{216}$
14	(6,4,4), (6,5,3), (5,5,4), (6,6,2)	15	$\frac{15}{216}$
15	(6,6,3), (6,4,5), (5,5,5)	10	$\frac{10}{216}$
16	(6,6,4), (6,5,5)	6	$\frac{6}{216}$
17	(6,6,5)	3	$\frac{3}{216}$
18	(6,6,6)	1	$\frac{1}{216}$

   b) The sum of the probabilities is 1.

3. a) $\frac{3}{8}$ **b)** $\frac{1}{8}$

4. a) $\frac{1}{2}$ **b)** $\frac{2}{7}$

5. a) $\frac{8}{12}$ or $\frac{2}{3}$ **b)** $\frac{7}{12}$ **c)** 0

6. a) independent **b)** dependent
  c) independent **d)** dependent

7. a) Tree diagram outcomes: (H, H, H), (H, H, T),
  (H, T, H), (H, T, T), (T, H, H), (T, H, T), (T, T, H),
  (T, T, T)
  b) independent; the outcome of flipping a coin does
  not affect the outcome of flipping another coin.

8. a) $\frac{1}{156}$ **b)** $\frac{1}{78}$ **c)** $\frac{15}{26}$

9. a) 26 400 **b)** 31 119

10. a) 108 **b)** 252 **c)** 894

11. a) $\frac{15!}{3!3!3!3!3!}$ or $_{15}C_3 \times {}_{12}C_3 \times {}_9C_3 \times {}_6C_3 \times {}_3C_3$
  or 168 168 000
  b) $_{15}C_5 \times {}_{10}C_5 \times {}_5C_5$ or 756 756

12. a) 44 352 **b)** 0.0707… **c)** 0.3426 …
  d) 0.2304 **e)** 0.0823 …

13. a) $x^4 + 4x^3y + 6x^2y^2 + 4xy^3 + y^4$
  b) $1024x^5 + 3840x^4y + 5760x^3y^2 + 4320x^2y^3 + 1620xy^4$
  $+ 243y^5$
  c) 1 **d)** 1

14.

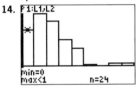

4.1 Probability Distributions, pages 144–153

Example 1 Your Turn
a) the number of rooms in apartments in a particular
complex
b)

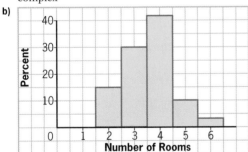

c) The area of each bar represents its probability, as a
percent. The width of each bar is 1, so the probability,
as a percent is shown on the vertical axis.
d) Four-room apartments occur most frequently, and the
probability decreases as the room value increases or
decreases from four.
e) Sum of the probabilities is 1. Yes.

Example 2 Your Turn
a) Tree diagram outcomes:
  (R, R, R, R), (R, R, R, B), (R, R, B, R), (R, R, B, B),
  (R, B, R, R), (R, R, R, B), (R, B, B, R), (R, B, B, B),
  (B, R, R, R), (B, R, R, B), (B, R, B, R), (B, R, B, B),
  (B, B, R, R), (B, B, R, B), (B, B, B, R), (B, B, B, B)

b)

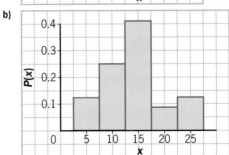

c) 2
d) On average, the spinner would land on blue 2 out of the
4 spins.

Example 3 Your Turn
a) −$2.25
b) Answers may vary. No; You lose money if you buy a ticket.
c) Answers may vary. The price could be reduced or more
prizes could be given away.

Reflect
R1. While it is impossible to have 1.8 children, expected
values are predicted average values and should not be
rounded.
R2. Answers may vary. The number of email messages
you receive each day of the week and the number of
students in each mathematics class at your school.
These examples are discrete because each must be a
whole number.
R3. Answers may vary. Create a table showing all
possible sums of the two 12-sided dice. Determine
the frequency of each sum and its probability. Then,
construct a histogram to illustrate the probability
distribution.

Practise
1. a) discrete **b)** continuous **c)** discrete
  d) discrete **e)** continuous
2. A
3. C
4. a)

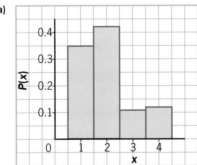

b)

5. a) 2.6 **b)** 3.8

Apply

6. a) the diameter of the marbles in a bag

b) discrete; the number of marbles in a bag is a whole number

c)

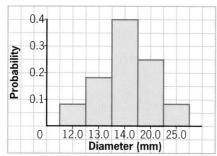

d) The area of each bar represents its probability. The width of each bar is 1, so the probability is shown on the vertical axis.

e) about 16.067; the weighted mean of the outcomes equals the expectation

7. a)

Sum, x	Frequency
2	1
3	2
4	3
5	4
6	5
7	6
8	7
9	8
10	7
11	6
12	5
13	4
14	3
15	2
16	1

b)

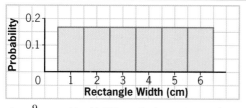

c) 9; On average, the expected sum of two dice is 9.

8. Answers may vary. Perimeter = 24 cm.

Rectangle Width (cm), x	Distribution of Dimensions	Frequency	Probability, P(x)
1	1 by 11	1	$\frac{1}{6}$
2	2 by 10	1	$\frac{1}{6}$
3	3 by 9	1	$\frac{1}{6}$
4	4 by 8	1	$\frac{1}{6}$
5	5 by 7	1	$\frac{1}{6}$
6	6 by 6	1	$\frac{1}{6}$

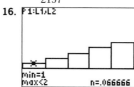

9. a) $\frac{9}{2000}$ **b)** $0.525 **c)** $4.475 **d)** $5.03

11. a) Let D represent rolling doubles and ND represent not rolling doubles. Tree diagram outcomes: (D, D, D), (D, D, ND), (D, ND, D), (D, ND, ND), (ND, D, D), (ND, D, ND), (ND, ND, D), (ND, ND, ND)

b)

Number of Doubles	Distribution of Doubles	Probability
0	(ND,ND,ND)	$\frac{125}{216}$
1	(D,ND,ND) (ND,D,ND) (ND,ND,D)	$\frac{75}{216}$
2	(D,D,ND) (D,ND,D) (ND,D,D)	$\frac{15}{216}$
3	(D,D,D)	$\frac{1}{216}$

c) 0.5

12.

Sum	Possible Groupings	Number of Outcomes	Probability
3	(1,1,1)	1	$\frac{1}{216}$
4	(1,2,1)	3	$\frac{3}{216}$
5	(1,3,1), (1,2,2)	6	$\frac{6}{216}$
6	(1,4,1), (1,3,2), (2,2,2)	10	$\frac{10}{216}$
7	(1,4,2), (1,3,3), (5,1,1), (3,2,2)	15	$\frac{15}{216}$
8	(1,4,3), (1,2,5), (1,1,6), (4,2,2), (3,3,2)	21	$\frac{21}{216}$
9	(6,2,1), (5,3,1), (5,2,2), (4,4,1), (4,3,2), (3,3,3)	25	$\frac{25}{216}$
10	(6,3,1), (6,2,2), (5,3,2), 5,4,1), (4,4,2), (4,3,3)	27	$\frac{27}{216}$
11	(6,4,1), (6,3,2), (5,5,1), (5,4,2), (5,3,3), (4,4,3)	27	$\frac{27}{216}$
12	(6,5,1), (6,4,2), (6,3,3), (5,5,2), (5,4,3), (4,4,4)	25	$\frac{25}{216}$
13	(6,6,1), (6,5,2), (6,4,3), (5,5,3), (5,4,4)	21	$\frac{21}{216}$
14	(6,4,4), (6,5,3), (5,5,4), (6,6,2)	15	$\frac{15}{216}$
15	(6,6,3), (6,4,5), (5,5,5)	10	$\frac{10}{216}$
16	(6,6,4), (6,5,5)	6	$\frac{6}{216}$
17	(6,6,5)	3	$\frac{3}{216}$
18	(6,6,6)	1	$\frac{1}{216}$

13. Answers may vary.

14. a) Answers may vary. There are many more values in these data sets that start with one compared to other digits.

b) 3.441

15. a) $\frac{4}{52}$ or $\frac{1}{13}$ **b)** $\frac{12}{169}$

c) $\frac{144}{2197}$ **d)** $\left(\frac{48}{52}\right)^{n-1} \times \frac{4}{52}$

16.

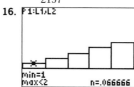

17. approximately 7.02

4.2 Uniform Distributions, pages 154–159

Example 1 Your Turn

a) Yes. Each randomly generated radius is equally likely and there is a single trial.

b)

Random Number, x	P(x)	x • P(x)
1	$\frac{1}{8}$	$\frac{1}{8}$
2	$\frac{1}{8}$	$\frac{2}{8}$
3	$\frac{1}{8}$	$\frac{3}{8}$
4	$\frac{1}{8}$	$\frac{4}{8}$
5	$\frac{1}{8}$	$\frac{5}{8}$
6	$\frac{1}{8}$	$\frac{6}{8}$
7	$\frac{1}{8}$	$\frac{7}{8}$
8	$\frac{1}{8}$	$\frac{8}{8}$

c)

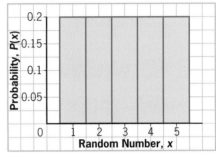

d) 4.5; On average, the expected radius length will be 4.5.

Example 2 Your Turn

No. A fair game will have an expectation equal to 0. This is not a fair game because the player will win 0.75 point on each turn, on average.

Reflect

R1. Yes, randomly selecting students by their student number is uniform. Each randomly generated student number is equally likely in a single trial.

R2. a) **b)**

R3. The expected profit per ticket is $2 – $0.75 = $1.25. This gives an advantage to the school.

Practise

1. a) no; there are different probabilities for different sums in a trial
   b) yes; there is an equal probability of selecting each card in a trial
   c) yes; there is an equal probability of each song being randomly selected in a trial
   d) no; there are different probabilities for different numbers of boys in a family of five
   e) yes; there is an equal probability of each person being randomly selected in a trial

2. C

3. D

4. 6 green balls

5. a) 15   **b)** 3.5

Apply

6. a) 6.5
   b) No. The expectation is simply the predicted average of all outcomes. Each number between 1 and 12 is equally likely.

7. a) $\frac{1}{52}$
   b) yes; there is an equal probability of selecting any specific card in a trial
   c) $\frac{1}{51}$
   d) no; the probability of any specific card changes after a card is removed

8. Let A = 1, B = 2, C = 3, D = 4, and E = 5.

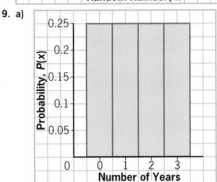

9. a)

b) Answers may vary. The only chance of going free is if prisoner P confesses. Prisoner P should confess. If Q confesses, then P should also confess. If Q denies, then P should confess because he will be set free.

10. a) Answers may vary. 2.5, 3.5, 4.5, 6.5, and 10.5 (the average of the face values for each platonic solid).
   b) four faces: 2.5; six faces: 3.5; eight faces: 4.5; twelve faces: 6.5
   c) Answers may vary. My findings in part b) confirm my prediction for the icosahedron.

11. $700.

12. a) The areas of the three regions are not equal so this is not a uniform distribution.
   b) Answers may vary. Let A be worth 5 points, B be worth 16 points, and C be worth 20 points.
   c) Answers may vary. A similar target with a uniform distribution would have regions of equal area.

13. –$1.3726   **14.** $5.55

16. Answers may vary.

Extend

17. The expected outcome is $\frac{n+1}{2}$.

18. Choosing 1 gives the greatest expected outcome at $70.50.

4.3 Binomial Distribution, pages 160–169

Example 1 Your Turn

a) $_{10}C_1\left(\dfrac{1}{13}\right) \times _9C_9\left(\dfrac{12}{13}\right)^9$ or approximately 0.3743

b) $_{10}C_3\left(\dfrac{1}{13}\right)^3 \times _7C_7\left(\dfrac{12}{13}\right)^7$ or approximately 0.0312

Example 2 Your Turn

a) X = the number of occurrences of a girl

b)

Number of Girls, x	Probability, $P(x)$	$x \cdot P(x)$
0	$_6C_0(0.5)^0(0.5)^6 = 0.015\ 625$	0
1	$_6C_1(0.5)^1(0.5)^5 = 0.093\ 75$	0.093 75
2	$_6C_2(0.5)^2(0.5)^4 = 0.234\ 375$	0.468 75
3	$_6C_3(0.5)^3(0.5)^3 = 0.3125$	0.9375
4	$_6C_4(0.5)^4(0.5)^2 = 0.234\ 375$	0.9375
5	$_6C_5(0.5)^5(0.5)^1 = 0.093\ 75$	0.468 75
6	$_6C_6(0.5)^6(0.5)^0 = 0.015\ 625$	0.093 75

c) The probabilities sum to 1.

d) 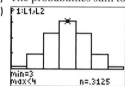 This probability distribution is more closely bell-shaped with the mode at $x = 3$ girls. It is slightly skewed to the left.

e) 3; On average, you can expect to have three girls in a family of six children.

Example 3 Your Turn

a) about 95.02% **b)** 3.2 days

Reflect

R1. $_nC_x$ represents the number of ways each of the number of successes can happen.

R2. Answers may vary. In a binomial distribution, p and q represent the probability of success and failure, respectively. The probability of drawing a heart (success) from a deck of cards is 0.25, while the probability of not drawing a heart (failure) is 0.75.

R3. Answers may vary. In a group of 25 people, the expected number of left-handed people is 2.75. However, the probability of one person in 25 being left-handed is $_{25}C_1(0.11)^1(0.89)^{24}$, or about 16.78%.

Practise

1. A **2.** B **3.** D

4. a) Tree diagram outcomes:
(1, 1, 1, 1), (1, 1, 1, 2), (1, 1, 2, 1), (1, 1, 2, 2),
(1, 2, 1, 1), (1, 2, 1, 2), (1, 2, 2, 1), (1, 2, 2, 2),
(2, 1, 1, 1), (2, 1, 1, 2), (2, 1, 2, 1), (2, 1, 2, 2),
(2, 2, 1, 1), (2, 2, 1, 2), (2, 2, 2, 1), (2, 2, 2, 2)

b) In the tree diagram, each roll of 1 has probability of 0.75 and each roll of 2 has probability of 0.25.

c) 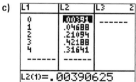 Assume a success is a rolling a 1. Use a graphing calculator to determine all $P(x) = _nC_x p^x q^{n-x}$, where $n = 4$, $x = 0, 1, 2, 3, 4$, $p = 0.75$, and $q = 0.25$.

d) The expansion contains the same terms as determined using the binomial distribution formula, but in reverse order.

5. a)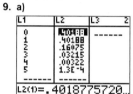

b)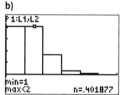

6. about 333.33

7. a) $_5C_2(0.5)^2(0.5)^3$ or 0.3125

b) $_5C_3(0.5)^3(0.5)^2$ or 0.3125.

Apply

8. a) 0.0305 **b)** 0.0328

9. a)

b)

c) 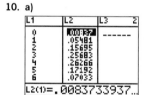 The expected number of sums of 7 in five rolls is about 0.8333.
$E(X) = np$
$= \dfrac{5}{6}$
≈ 0.8333

10. a)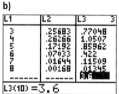

b)

The expected number of bull's-eyes is 3.6.

c) $P(8) = 0.001\ 68$, so it is highly unlikely.

11. a) $_5C_2\left(\dfrac{1}{6}\right)^2\left(\dfrac{5}{6}\right)^3$ or about 0.1608

b) $\left(\dfrac{1}{6} + \dfrac{5}{6}\right)^5 = 1\left(\dfrac{1}{6}\right)^5\left(\dfrac{5}{6}\right)^0 + 5\left(\dfrac{1}{6}\right)^4\left(\dfrac{5}{6}\right)^1 + 10\left(\dfrac{1}{6}\right)^3\left(\dfrac{5}{6}\right)^2$
$+ 10\left(\dfrac{1}{6}\right)^2\left(\dfrac{5}{6}\right)^3 + 5\left(\dfrac{1}{6}\right)^1\left(\dfrac{5}{6}\right)^4 + 1\left(\dfrac{1}{6}\right)^0\left(\dfrac{5}{6}\right)^5$

c) The fourth term: $_5C_2\left(\dfrac{1}{6}\right)^2\left(\dfrac{5}{6}\right)^3$.

d) The general term, $_nC_x p^x q^{n-x}$, in the binomial expansion represents the probability of x successes in n independent trials, where p is the probability of success on an individual trial and q is the probability of failure on that same individual trial.

12. a) about 0.0168 **b)** about 2.7901×10^{-7}

c) about 0.018 84

d) Answers may vary.

e) Answers may vary. Yes. The expected number of bulbs that do not meet specification out of 10 bulbs is $10(0.06)$, or 0.6.

13. Calculate the expectation. Points received indicate a positive value for the random variable, x. Each point represents a car given away.

Number of Cars That Start	Point Value, x	$P(x)$	$x \cdot P(x)$
0	0	$_5C_0\left(\frac{1}{10}\right)^0\left(\frac{9}{10}\right)^5$	0
1	0	$_5C_1\left(\frac{1}{10}\right)^1\left(\frac{9}{10}\right)^4$	0
2	2	$_5C_2\left(\frac{1}{10}\right)^2\left(\frac{9}{10}\right)^3$	0.1458
3	3	$_5C_3\left(\frac{1}{10}\right)^3\left(\frac{9}{10}\right)^2$	0.0243
4	4	$_5C_4\left(\frac{1}{10}\right)^4\left(\frac{9}{10}\right)^1$	0.0018
5	5	$_5C_5\left(\frac{1}{10}\right)^5\left(\frac{9}{10}\right)^0$	0.00005
		Sum	0.17195

A fair game will have an expectation equal to 0. This game favours the contestant, on average.

14. a) $_{10}C_8(0.8)^8(0.2)^2$ or about 0 30.2%
  b) about 67.8%
16. a) The probability of success changes with each trial.
  b) Answers may vary. A jar contains 12 red balls and eight green balls. Six balls are removed with replacement. What is the probability that four of the balls are red?
  c) 0.311 04
17. a) sample of 7: approximately 0.1998; sample of 100: approximately 7.3783×10^{-4}; sample of 1000: 0
  b) The probability of the majority of people approving the transit system decreases with the increase in sample size.
18. $3700
19. Answers may vary.
20. Answers may vary. 19% of the Canadian population live in rural areas. A group of 30 Canadians is selected at Pearson International Airport. What is the probability that more than two of them live in a rural area? What is the expected number of rural citizens?

Extend
21. a) $P(\text{outcome 1, outcome 2, outcome 3}) = \frac{n!}{a!b!c!}p^aq^br^c$
  where
  P is the probability of outcome 1, outcome 2, and outcome 3
  a is the number of times outcome 1 occurs
  b is the number of times outcome 2 occurs
  c is the number of times outcome 3 occurs
  p is the probability of outcome 1
  q is the probability of outcome 2
  r is the probability of outcome 3
  b) about 0.0427

22. $E(X)$

$$= \sum_{i=1}^{n} x_i \cdot P(x_i)$$

$$= \sum_{x=0}^{n} x \cdot {_nC_x}p^xq^{n-x}$$

$$= \sum_{x=0}^{n} x\frac{n!}{(n-x)!x!}p^x(1-p)^{n-x}$$

$$= \sum_{x=1}^{n} x\frac{n!}{(n-x)!x(x-1)!}p^x(1-p)^{n-x}$$

$$= \sum_{x=1}^{n} \frac{n!}{(n-x)!(x-1)!}p^x(1-p)^{n-x}$$

$$= np\sum_{x=1}^{n} \frac{(n-1)!}{(n-x)!(x-1)!}p^{x-1}(1-p)^{n-x}$$

$$= np\sum_{x=1}^{n} \frac{(n-1)!}{((n-1)-(x-1))!(x-1)!}p^{x-1}(1-p)^{(n-1)-(x-1)}$$

Let $m = n - 1$ and $y = x - 1$.

$$= np\sum_{y=0}^{m} \frac{m!}{(m-y)!y!}p^y(1-p)^{m-y}$$

This is a form of the binomial theorem $(x + y)^n$ with $x = p$, $y = 1 - p$, and $n = m$.

$$= np(p + (1-p))^m$$
$$= np(1)^m$$
$$= np$$

4.4 Hypergeometric Distributions, pages 170–179

Example 1 Your Turn
about 39.56%

Example 2 Your Turn
a)

L1	L2	L3	2
0	.00476	------	
1	.11429		
2	.42857		
3	.38095		
4	.07143		
------	------	------	

L2(1)=.0047619047...

b)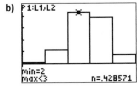

min=2
max<3   n=.428571

c) The probability is less bell-shaped with the mode at $x = 2$. It is skewed to the left.
d) $P(0) = 0.00476$ or 0.476%, which means that getting no green jelly beans is very unlikely.
e) 2.4; On average, there will be 2.4 green jelly beans in four selections.

Example 3 Your Turn
a) approximately 0.6430
b) about 2.9167

Example 4 Your Turn
about 1176 foxes

Reflect
R1. a) The random variable is the number of red marbles selected. The size of the sample space is 5 marbles. The size of the population is 10 marbles. The range of the random variable is 0 to 5.
  b) The random variable is the number of hearts selected. The size of the sample space is 7 cards. The size of the population is 52 cards. The range of the random variable is 0 to 7.
R2. Since the trials are independent, this is not a hypergeometric probability situation.

Practise

1. D   **2.** A

3. a) $n = 6 + 9$, or 15, and $r = 3 + 2$, or 5

   b) $a = 10 - 7$, or 3, and $b = 6 - 5$, or 1

   c) $c = 25 - 6$, or 19, and $d = 3 + 2$, or 5

4. a)   **b)**

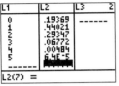

Apply

5. a)

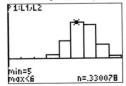

   b) $E(X) = \dfrac{ra}{n}$

$$= \dfrac{5(5)}{20}$$

$$= 1.25$$

6. a) about 0.6009   **b)** 0.75

   c) The probability that all three light bulbs are defective is about 0.88%, which is very unlikely.

7. a) about 0.0026   **b)** about 0.6962

   c) about 2.6084×10^{-6}

8. The probability of fewer than three means $P(0) + P(1) + P(2)$.

The probability of more than seven typically means $P(8) + P(9) + P(10)$. However, there are only 8 mice with a defective mutation. So, the probability of more than seven means $P(8)$. Knowing the shape of the distribution, the ends are highly unlikely.

There is a greater probability of the mice having the genetic mutation in fewer than three.

9. about 1429 foxes

10. a) about 17

   b) Yes. The expected number of tagged deer is 17.

11. a) Answers may vary. A five-card hand will have a greater probability of no spades.

   b) For a seven-card hand,

$$P(\text{no spades}) = \dfrac{_{13}C_0 \times \, _{39}C_7}{_{52}C_7}$$

$$= 0.114\,967\ldots$$

For a five-card hand,

$$P(\text{no spades}) = \dfrac{_{13}C_0 \times \, _{39}C_5}{_{52}C_5}$$

$$= 0.221\,533\ldots$$

As the number of cards in a hand increases, so does the possibility that it contains a spade.

13. a)

   b) Answers may vary.   **c)** Answers may vary.

Extend

14. about 0.0263   **15.** about 0.0182

4.5 Comparing and Selecting Discrete Probability Distributions, pages 180–187

Example Your Turn

a)

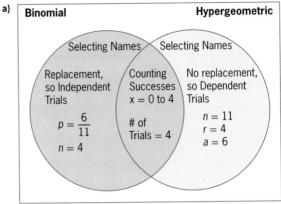

b)

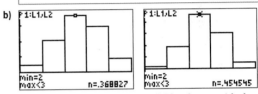

c) The graphs have the same bell-like shape, with the $x = 2$ female names being the most likely outcome. The hypergeometric graph is slightly taller than the binomial graph at $x = 2$ and $x = 3$, and shorter at the other values of x.

Reflect

R1. Answers may vary.

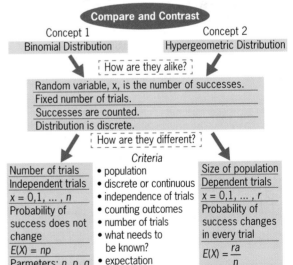

R2. No. For a binomial distribution, the probability of each *success* is the same, but with hypergeometric the probability of success changes with each trial.

Practise

1. a) hypergeometric; the trials are dependent
b) binomial; the trials are independent and given the probability of failure
c) hypergeometric; the trials are dependent
d) uniform; the trials are independent and all outcomes are equally likely

2. C

3. C

4. Answers may vary.
a) the number of cards of a particular suit or denomination, $x = 0$ to 5
b) the number of grade 11 students or grade 12 students, $x = 0$ to 4
c) the value of the outcome (a particular suit or denomination)
d) the number of a particular digit, $x = 0$ to r
e) the number of defective bottles, $x = 0$ to r
f) the value of the outcome (winning square)

Apply

5. Answers may vary.

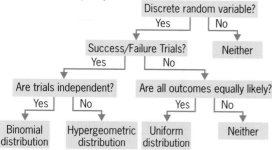

6. a) uniform; each outcome is equally likely
b) Answers may vary. Six people are asked to choose a number between 1 and 15. What is the probability that two people choose the number 13?
7. a) binomial; these are independent success/failure trials
b) Answers may vary. At Bill's Burger Barn, there is a hat with five free hamburger tickets and ten free fries tickets. If three tickets are drawn, what is the probability of winning a free hamburger?
8. a) hypergeometric; these are dependent success/failure trials
b) Answers may vary. For a random draw, 20 slips of paper containing people's names are placed into a bin, 20% of which are her friends. What is the probability that at least one friend's name will be drawn?
c) In the first scenario, $P(x \geq 1) \approx 0.7183$
In the second scenario, $P(x \geq 1) \approx 0.6723$
d) Since there is a higher probability of a friend winning in the first scenario, Barb would be happier with the hypergeometric distribution.
9. Answers may vary.
10. a) about 0.3077 **b)** 2 **c)** 1
12. Answers may vary.
a) Show the probability distribution for the number of successful ring-tosses in eight attempts.
b) There are 15 bottles, with five green and ten clear. Show the probability distribution for the number of successful ring-tosses onto green bottles in four attempts.

c) There are eight bottles numbered 1 to 8, and the probability of a successful ring-toss on any one is equally likely. Show the probability distribution for the bottle number.

13. a) population of 10:   population of 200:

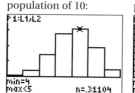 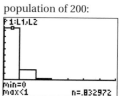

b) population of 10:   population of 200:

c) The two distributions for $n = 10$ both have somewhat similar bell shapes, with a mode of $x = 4$. The hypergeometric graph is slightly taller than the binomial graph at $x = 3$ and $x = 4$, and shorter at the other values of x.
The two distributions for $n = 200$ both have almost identical half-bell shapes, with a mode of $x = 0$. The hypergeometric graph is slightly taller than the binomial graph at $x = 1$, and slightly shorter at the other values of x.
d) The binomial distribution gives a close approximation of a hypergeometric distribution when r is small in relation to n.

Extend

14. L2 shows $P(x) = \dfrac{e^{-np}(np)^x}{x!}$, where $n = 2000$, $p = 0.015$, $x = 0, 1, 2, 3, 4, 5, 6, 7, 8, 9$.
L3 shows $P(x) = {}_nC_x p^x q^{n-x}$, where $n = 2000$, $x = 0, 1, 2, 3, 4, 5, 6, 7, 8, 9$, $p = 0.015$, and $q = 0.985$.

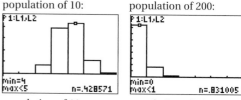

The Poisson distribution gives approximately 7.1×10^{-6}, where as the binomial distribution gives approximately 6.4×10^{-6}.

15. a) i) $E(X) = \dfrac{n+1}{2}$ **ii)** $E(X) = a$ **iii)** $E(X) = a$
b) The expected value for the binomial distribution equals that of the hypergeometric distribution.
16. a) i) 0.4 **ii)** 0.24 **iii)** 0.144 **iv)** $(0.6)^{n-1}(0.4)$
b) (probability of failure)^n × (probability of success)
c) The probability of success after a waiting time of x failures is $P(x) = q^x p$, where p is the probability of success in each single trial and q is the probability of failure.

d)

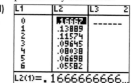 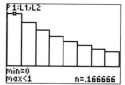

e) All three distributions have two possible outcomes, success or failure. The geometric and binomial distributions involve independent trials where the probability of success is the same in every trial. This is in contrast to the hypergeometric distribution, where trials are dependent and the probability of success is not the same in every trial. Binomial and hypergeometric distributions involve a fixed number of trials, whereas geometric distributions involve continued trials until success.

Chapter 4 Review, pages 188–189

1. a) continuous   **b)** discrete
    c) discrete   **d)** continuous

2. a)

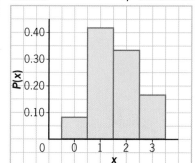

    b)

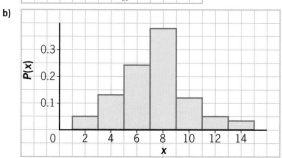

3. a) about 1.58   **b)** 7.32

4. A uniform distribution occurs when, in a single trial, all outcomes are equally likely.

5. a)

Random Number, x	$P(x)$	$x \cdot P(x)$
1	$\frac{1}{6}$	$\frac{1}{6}$
2	$\frac{1}{6}$	$\frac{2}{6}$
3	$\frac{1}{6}$	$\frac{3}{6}$
4	$\frac{1}{6}$	$\frac{4}{6}$
5	$\frac{1}{6}$	$\frac{5}{6}$
6	$\frac{1}{6}$	$\frac{6}{6}$

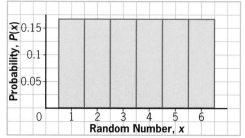

    b) 3.5; the predicted average value of the random number will be 3.5.

6. a) Amounts received indicate a positive value for the random variable, x. Amounts lost indicate a negative value for x.

Number of Green Balls	Amount ($), x	$P(x)$	$x \cdot P(x)$
0	−360	$_3C_0(0.4)^0(0.6)^3$	−77.76
1	−40	$_3C_1(0.4)^1(0.6)^2$	−17.28
2	280	$_3C_2(0.4)^2(0.6)^1$	80.64
3	600	$_3C_3(0.4)^3(0.6)^0$	38.40
		Sum	24

This is not a fair game because the player will win $24 on each turn, on average.

    b)

Number of Green Balls	Amount ($), x	$P(x)$	$x \cdot P(x)$
0	−360	$_3C_0\left(\frac{15}{25}\right)\left(\frac{14}{24}\right)\left(\frac{13}{23}\right)$	−71.22
1	−40	$_3C_1\left(\frac{10}{25}\right)\left(\frac{15}{24}\right)\left(\frac{14}{23}\right)$	−18.26
2	280	$_3C_2\left(\frac{10}{25}\right)\left(\frac{9}{24}\right)\left(\frac{15}{23}\right)$	82.17
3	600	$_3C_3\left(\frac{10}{25}\right)\left(\frac{9}{24}\right)\left(\frac{8}{23}\right)$	31.30
		Sum	23.99

This is not a fair game because the player will win $23.99 on each turn, on average.

7.

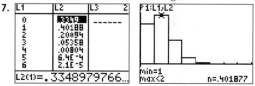

8. a) 55.2; the probability of success (type O) does not change with each trial.
    b) Type A: 50.4; Type B: 10.8; Type AB: 3.6

9. a) about 0.3798   **b)** about 0.1087   **c)** 1.2

10. a)

    b) $E(X) = \dfrac{ra}{n}$
$$= \frac{7(10)}{25}$$
$$= 2.8$$

11. a) approximately 1.228×10^{-6}
    b) about 0.0133   **c)** about 0.9043

12. 1000 seals

13. a) binomial   **b)** hypergeometric
    c) none   **d)** uniform

14. a) $\dfrac{_{12}C_5 \times {}_{40}C_2}{_{52}C_7}$, or about 0.0046

    b) $_7C_5\left(\dfrac{3}{13}\right)^5\left(\dfrac{10}{13}\right)^2$, or about 0.0081

    c) There is a greater probability of five face cards with replacement because the trials are independent and the probability of a face card does not change.

1. C **2.** D **3.** A **4.** A **5.** B
6. 4 **7.** about 0.4632
8. a) hypergeometric distribution; the trials are
dependent (without replacement)
  b) make it with replacement
9. 29 beavers
10. a)

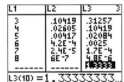
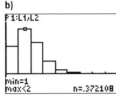

  b)

  c)

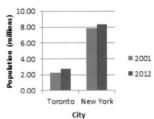

The expected number
of sums of 7 is about
1.3333.

11. a) about 0.9945 **b)** 14.25
12. $P(0 \text{ women}) = \dfrac{{}_5C_0 \times {}_{10}C_4}{{}_{15}C_4}$

≈ 0.1538

$P(\text{at least 1 woman}) = 1 - P(0)$

≈ 0.8462

There is a much greater chance that at least one female
was promoted, so the committee's claim is unfounded.
13. a) about 0.1556 **b)** 0.72
14. a) about 0.0082 **b)** about 0.0156.
  c) about 0.7335
15. Answers may vary. The binomial distribution gives a
close approximation of a hypergeometric distribution
when r is small in relation to n. If n is very large, non-
replacement of successes will not change the ratio of
successes to the population that much, and a binomial
distribution will be a good approximation to the
hypergeometric distribution.
16. a) about 0.5045 **b)** about 0.2003

Chapter 5 Organization of Data for Analysis

Prerequisite Skills, pages 194–195

1. a) line graph **b)** double bar graph
  c) scatter plot **d)** circle graph
  e) bar graph **f)** histogram
2. a) 10 to 14, 15 to 19, 20 to 24
  b) a little over $100 per address
  c) Incidents of crime seem to increase with an
increase in officers.
  d) Xbox 360 **e)** November
  f) Breaking Dawn - Part 2
3. bar graph: shows the frequencies of the values of the
variable with disconnected bars, represents non-
numeric or unordered data; histogram: uses connected
bars, represents a continuous range of values in
numeric order

4. Number of Viewers for Four TV Shows

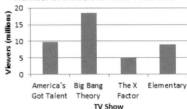

5. Favourite Food

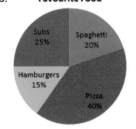

6. Car Values

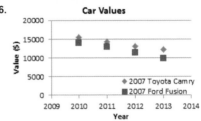

7. Population Comparison

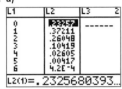

5.1 Data Concepts and Graphical Summaries, pages 196–205

Example 1 Your Turn
Answers may vary. Climate change: 97% of climate
scientists agree that climate-warming trends are very likely
due to human activities. Others argue that the warming is
attributable to natural causes.

Example 2 Your Turn
categorical, ordinal
data:

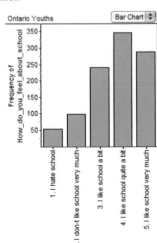

numerical, continuous data:

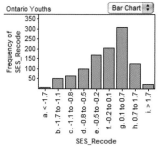

numerical, discrete data:

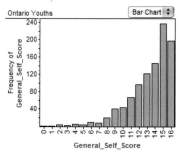

categorical, nominal data:

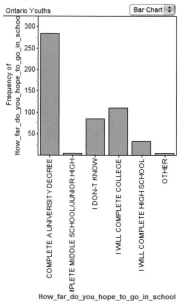

The only data that cannot be represented as a graph is the child ID number. There is simply one per student.

Example 3 Your Turn
Answers may vary.
a) #vacation: tweets go up and down; #math: tweets go up and down; #Junos: tweets are almost non-existent until 4:00 p.m., then there is a peak at 8:00 p.m., dropping to nothing again by 12:00 a.m.
b) #math and #vacation are not that common (low constant volume) and only peak when there is an interest.
c) 8:00 pm, because that hashtag was tweeted less often from then on.
d) No; there were so many more tweets in the #Junos graph. Even at 12:00 p.m., when the number of tweets for #Junos was near its lowest, there were more #Junos tweets than there were at any time for #math.

Reflect
R1. Answers may vary. Predictions made by political experts are not reliable. They are only correct about half the time.
R2. Answers may vary. Positive: Availability, ease of backup, lower risk of loss, and not susceptible to viruses. Negative: Access speed, requires Internet connection, environmental impact with electricity use and carbon emissions of data centres.

Practise
1. Answers may vary.
   a) Continuous and discrete data can be numeric, but continuous data can have any value within a given range. Discrete data can have only certain separate values. Heights of students is continuous but the number of students enrolled in each class is discrete.
   b) Ordinal and nominal data are qualitative, but ordinal data can be ranked and nominal data cannot. A rating scale for a taste test shows ordinal data, while the type of cookie preferred shows nominal data.
   c) Numerical data is quantitative and can be continuous or discrete, while categorical data is qualitative. How many movies you see in a year shows numerical data, and the types of movies you like shows categorical data.
2. a) numerical data: armspan, height; the remaining columns contain categorical nominal data.
   b) continuous data: reaction time, travel time; discrete data: number of languages spoken, number of siblings; the remaining columns contain categorical nominal data.
3.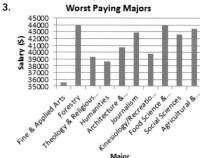
4. a)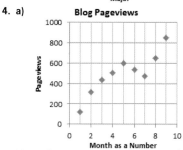
   b) an increase in pageviews over the first few months
   c) School is not in session in June and July.
   d) Answers may vary. About 1100.
5. a) There are different scales on the two vertical axes (one for Canada, one for the U.S.), but they both show that auto sales are nearing pre-crisis levels. If there was only one scale used, Canada's auto sales would look like a relatively flat horizontal line.
   b) Answers may vary. This graph does not show a dramatic drop in sales as well.

6. Answers may vary.
- **a)** It reveals underlying trends in data that seasonal movements tend to mask.
- **b)** To reveal an underlying trend.

Extend
8. a) Answers may vary.
- **b)** Answers may vary.
- **c)** Answers may vary. Examples: Roy peaked in the 1890s. Marilyn and Joan both peaked in the 1930s.
- **d)** Answers may vary. Examples: Madison, Jackson, Avery

9. a) School A appears to be doing the best because the results steadily increased each year.
- **b)** Answers may vary. School A: 84% maintained standard but 5% dropped from standard. School B: 26% rose to standard but 19% never met standard. School C: 80% maintained standard but 13% dropped from standard. Based on the cohort data, School B appears to have the best results; it has the greatest percent that rose to standard.

5.2 Principles of Data Collection, pages 206–211

Example Your Turn
- **a)** convenience sample
- **b)** stratified sample
- **c)** cluster sample
- **d)** simple random sample
- **e)** systematic sample
- **f)** voluntary response
- **g)** multistage sample

Reflect
R1. Answers may vary. Both divide the population into groups, just differently. In a cluster sample, a number of groups are chosen randomly, and each member of the chosen groups is sampled. In a multistage sample, the group is subdivided further by creating a hierarchy and choosing a random sample at each level.

R2. Answers may vary. If a population is biased one way or another, that will be evident in the smaller sample size.

Practise
1. a) systematic sample
- **b)** simple random sample
- **c)** voluntary response
- **d)** stratified sample

2. A population is all the individuals in a group being studied (all students in a school), while a sample is a group selected from the population (one class in the school).

3. Answers may vary.
#SimpleRandomSample each member of population has equal chance of being selected.
#SystematicSample orders population and people are chosen at regular intervals.
#StratifiedSample has same proportion of members from each group as population does.
#ClusterSample divides population into groups, randomly selects groups, and samples each member of chosen groups.
#MultistageSample divides population into a hierarchy and chooses random sample at each level.
#ConvenienceSample choose members of population who are easy to access.
#VoluntarySample people choose whether to participate so contains members heavily for or against topic.

4. Answers may vary. Stratified: use grade level or gender. Cluster: use random class sample at each grade level. Voluntary: allow students to choose whether to respond.

5. Answers may vary. Systematic sample: randomly select a time each hour and then test the next 10 batches of candy mix on the factory line.

6. Answers may vary. Audrey Tobias is an 89-year-old peace activist who refused to fill out the 2011 census because of its link to a U.S. military contractor. She faced a criminal charge and her lawyer argued that forcing her to complete the census would violate her freedoms of conscience and free expression. She was acquitted due to reasonable doubt as to her intent at the time of refusal.

7. a) These are both random sampling techniques that divide the population into groups, but differently. Stratified sampling uses the same proportions as the proportions in the entire population (when surveying teachers, use gender groups). Multistage sampling uses sequential levels of sampling by subdividing the group into smaller groups (select from a group of high schools, then departments, then teachers).
- **b)** These are both non-random sampling techniques that can produce unreliable results because people who respond are not necessarily representative of the entire population. Convenience sampling bases selection on easy access (poll people at a movie theatre about the best movie). Voluntary sampling is comprised of only those who choose to participate (ask people to vote online about the best movie).

8. a) customers of the car dealership
- **b)** SUV/truck: 57 calls; Minivan: 81 calls; Midsize car: 32 calls, Economy car: 65 calls; Sports car: 15
- **c)** Answers may vary. They might hope to get more responses by calling, it might be more cost effective.
- **d)** Answers may vary. Ensure actual customer is surveyed not just a person living at that household.

Extend
10. Answers may vary. Pros: Canadians are not forced to divulge detailed personal information under threat of prosecution. Cons: Since it is not mandatory, data collected on a voluntary basis will not be as accurate and there will most likely be fewer respondents.

11. Aerial surveys estimate the number of moose. The park is divided into 57 plots representing either high-quality or low-quality winter moose habitat. Twenty percent of the 57 blocks are randomly selected and moose are counted to estimate the population. This is similar to cluster sampling. The habitat is divided into areas, a number of areas are randomly chosen, and population is counted in those areas.

5.3 Collecting Data, pages 212–221

Example 1 Your Turn
1. a) there are no controls for the number of colds and the subjects are not randomized
- **b)** Answers may vary. Add a control group that does not go to the gym.

2. a) control group: plants growing in water with neutral pH; experimental groups: plants grown using water with increasingly acidic pH levels.
- **b)** Answers may vary. To help eliminate any previously diseased plants.

Example 2 Your Turn

a) Answers may vary. There are only three options.
   What is your favourite game system?

b) It is biased. It suggests that leadership training is necessary to run a business.
   Do you think that leadership training would help you run a business?
   ■Yes ■No ■No opinion

c) Asks for an opinion about two things.
   How important do you think speed of service is?
   ■Very Important ■Important ■Somewhat Important
   ■Of Little Importance ■Not important

   How important do you think quality of service is?
   ■Very Important ■Important ■Modestly Important
   ■Of Little Importance ■Not Important

Example 3 Your Turn

Answers may vary.

Reflect

R1. Answers may vary. To get accurate and unbiased information.

R2. Answers may vary. To account for effects from treatment that do not depend on the treatment itself, such as knowledge and expectations of treatment. A placebo group gives researchers a comparison group to determine whether the treatment itself had any effect.

R3. Answers may vary. Informed consent, voluntary participation, avoidance of harm.

Practise

1. C

2. B

3. a) Ask two separate questions.
   Do you exercise daily? ■Yes ■No
   Do you get enough sleep at night? ■Yes ■No

   b) Rephrase to make it neutral.
   Do you think that the Star Wars saga is one of the best science fiction stories of all time?
   ■Strongly agree ■Agree ■Don't know ■Disagree
   ■Strongly disagree

   c) Make it an open question.
   What is your favourite type of music?

   d) Make more concise.
   How do you feel about the following statement: We should increase the number of recycling days in the school.
   ■Strongly agree ■Agree ■Don't know ■Disagree
   ■Strongly disagree

4. Answers may vary. How often do you walk to school?

5. a) observational study; whether magnetic therapy reduces pain

   b) observational study; whether lying in bed for an extended period of time exhibits similar issues to weightlessness in space

   c) experimental study; whether handedness affects math grades

Apply

6. a) 410 people

   b) They have not used the Internet.

   c) Answers may vary. I think that the 0 computer category will either not exist or be very small, and the 1 and 2 computer categories will greatly increase. The no for connected to the Internet will either disappear or be very small, and the yes will greatly increase. Also, all of the red portions should be much smaller, because most people have used the Internet.

   d) Answers may vary.

7. Answers may vary.
   Which is your favourite sport?
   ■Tennis ■Hockey ■Basketball

   How do you like K-pop music?
   ■Pretty Good ■Good ■Great ■Fantastic ■Awesome

   How important do you think exercise and eating healthy are?
   ■Very important ■Important ■Somewhat important
   ■Of little importance ■Unimportant

8. Answers may vary.

   a) A list and description of 43 attributes from Statistic Canada's 2001 Census of Population for Canada.

   b) and c) Answers may vary.

   d) To study cultural trends, health care needs, and other social-economic issues.

9. Answers may vary.
   How concerned are you about safety in sports?
   ■No opinion ■Not concerned ■A little concerned
   ■Concerned ■Very concerned

   What is your favourite classification of sports?
   ■Endurance sports ■Team sports ■Target sports
   ■Strength sports ■Athletics ■Other

   How many hours a week do you watch sports?
   ■0–5 ■6–10 ■11–15 ■16–20 ■more than 20

   What sport do you play?

   What is your level of expertise in your sport on a scale of 1 to 5 with 1 being poor and 5 being an expert?

10. Answers may vary.
    Do you agree that cell phones should be silenced in movie theatres?
    ■Strongly agree ■Agree ■Undecided ■Disagree ■Strongly disagree

    How often do you see a person using a cell phone while he or she is driving?
    ■Very frequently ■Frequently ■Occasionally ■Rarely ■Never

    I find my mathematics class interesting.
    ■Almost always true ■Usually true ■Occasionally true
    ■Sometimes true ■Never true

    How well do you like the latest sci-fi movie release?
    ■Like a lot ■Like a little ■Do not like or dislike
    ■Dislike a little ■Dislike a lot

    How important do you think global warming is?
    ■Very important ■Important ■Modestly important
    ■Of little importance ■Unimportant

11. Answers may vary.

12. a) observational study

    b) Answers may vary. A control crop that uses chemical fertilizers is needed, then the treatment crop uses natural fertilizers. The effect being studied is whether natural organic crops yield less than traditional crops.

14. Answers may vary. The subjects cannot be randomly assigned to a treatment group or control group. It is not feasible to assign the "treatment" of academic success.

Extend

15. a) Answers may vary. Studies may seem questionable if the source does not seem reliable, if the sample seems skewed, or if the methods seem biased.

    b) Answers may vary.

    c) observational study. It found a positive association between coffee consumption and all-cause mortality in men and in men and women younger than 55 years. This group should avoid drinking more than four cups of coffee a day. The study population included a range of ages all of which completed a medical history and lifestyle questionnaire, were given a baseline examination for mortality, and present findings for all-cause mortality are consistent with those of earlier studies. However, the results of recent studies have been highly variable. The non-coffee-drinking group may have had a higher mortality risk not related to the consumption of coffee.

16. Answers may vary.

5.4 Interpreting and Analysing Data, pages 222–232

Example 1 Your Turn
Answers may vary.
a) The average domestic fare decreased from 2008 to 2009 by around $30.
b) The average domestic fares for 2008 and 2011 by individual city, by province, by cities within a province, or for Canada

Example 2 Your Turn
a) name, artist, composer, album, genre, size of the file, length of the song, year it was released, sampling bit rate, number of times it was played
b) Answers may vary. The most common length for a song is from 210 s to less than 230 s.
c) No.
d) Answers may vary. If you know how long the song is *and* the sampling rate, you can determine the size of the file.

Example 3 Your Turn
a) experiment; the student is controlling the drop height of the ball
b) Drop height of the ball is controlled, and the different bounce heights are recorded.
c) Bounce height appears to be about 70% of the drop height.
d) The relationship appears to be linear.

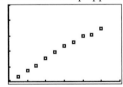

e) Yes, use a line of best fit.

Reflect
R1. Each provides an organized store of records containing information on players, teams, and games.
R2. Secondary data; we typically are exposed to someone else's use of primary data.

Practise
1. B   **2.** C
3. Table 128-0014: Electricity generated from fossil fuels
Table 203-0026 : Survey of household spending (SHS), household spending, by age of reference person.
Table 427-0004: Number of international tourists entering or returning to Canada, by province of entry.
Table 361-0013 : Spectator sports, event promoters, artists and related industries, summary statistics, by North American Industry Classification System (NAICS)
4. a) primary data   **b)** secondary data
    c) primary data   **d)** secondary data
    e) primary data   **f)** secondary data.

Apply
5. Answers may vary.
6. a) about 21%
    b) Queen Charlotte Islands. It was the largest in North or South America in 2012.
    c) Dot plot compares magnitudes.

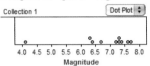

    d) Answers may vary. Colour shows the severity of magnitude.

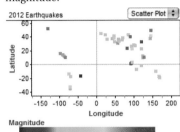

    e) South America
    f)

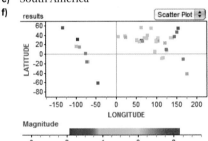

There were more larger magnitude earthquakes in 2013.

7. a) date, time, exposure time, F-stop, Exp program, metering mode, whether flash was used, focal length, ISO speed, orientation, dimensions, total pixels, file size in kilobytes
    b) Answers may vary.
    c)

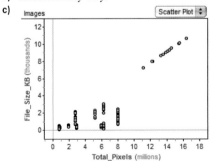

Number of pixels determines the file size, then divide the remaining storage capacity by the file size and estimate how many more photos can be taken at that setting.

8. a) The numbers in the table are primary data from weather stations. The table represents secondary data for anyone else who uses it.
    b) Stratford: 1064 mm of rain, Hartley Bay: gets over 4 times more rain at 4549 mm per year,

Henderson Lake: gets over 8 times more rain at 9082 mm per year

c) With locations organized by region, it is easy to see that the six highest rainfall locations are all in BC.

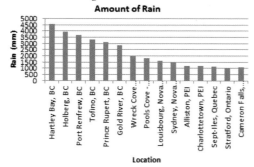

Amount of Rain

Location

Extend

10. Answers may vary.

a) The various sizes and colours of dots begin to change size and location to show that income per person and life expectancy increased over time.

b) size: population of the country, colour: geographic region. The size is in relation to the world population.

c) Each country's story is told in regards to income per person and life expectancy over time. Canada for the most part has continuously increased in both income per person and life expectancy.

d) Answers may vary.

5.5 Bias, pages 233–243

Example 1 Your Turn

a) response bias
b) sampling bias
c) non-response bias
d) measurement bias

Example 2 Your Turn

Answers may vary.

a) no vertical scale, the points suggest a linear relationship, but the number of jobs lost does not change by a constant amount. The horizontal scale is not consistent.

b) The rate did not drop in October. Also, the vertical scale does not start at 0.

c) This information is most likely anecdotal and cannot be verified. In addition, no actual data on the amount of weight lost is given or whether consumers were on a diet and exercise regimen.

Example 3 Your Turn

Answers may vary.

a) The amount spent is about $62.23 per household. For countries that do not celebrate Halloween, this is a lot to spend on candy, costumes, and decorations. However, for many Canadians and Americans this is not a lot of money.

b) Apple's gross profit in 2010 was $26.71 billion and in 2011 it was $45.63 billion, so a $19 billion is a large increase of about 59%.

Example 4 Your Turn

a) The Canadian teams have a white background and the logo is inserted inside the bar.

b) It would have the smallest percent of Canadians and Americans.

c) Answers may vary. There are more Canadian-born players in the NHL and on each team.

d) Answers may vary. The actual percent of American-born players on each team.

e) No. The presentation and information given slants it towards Canadian-born players.

f) Answers may vary.

Reflect

R1. Answers may vary. Yes, by displaying it in a distorted fashion.

R2. Answers may vary. By omitting other information basing the statistics on faulty experiments or studies.

R3. Answers may vary. The consumer is at fault. Just because the product is called *vitamin*water® this in no way should imply that it contains vitamins and consumers must read the fine print labels.

Practise

1. D

2. Answers may vary.

a) response bias; make the response anonymous

b) non-response bias and sampling bias; hold several open public meetings to gather a more accurate opinion.

c) sampling bias; make the poll available in other ways

d) response bias; ask how often the person exercises

e) sampling bias; make the petition available in other ways

3. Answers may vary. Measurement bias. A survey question asks, "Who is the best supercross rider of all time, Ricky Carmichael or James Stewart?

4. Answers may vary.

a) The statement does not explain what the typical number of headaches was, nor does it identify other potential factors (diet, water consumption, weather).

b) The two sections that indicate people like math look significantly larger than the two sections that indicate people do not like math.

c) The break in the vertical scale exaggerates the change in population.

d) It is very difficult to determine actual values from the use of icons.

e) The break in the vertical scale exaggerates the change in units sold, and the horizontal scale does not show consistent monthly increments.

6. a) This number represents about three pieces of mail per dwelling per day, which seems typical. So, the number 9.8 billion is not significant.

b) If each viewer watches about 5.8 h of video each year which does not seem like a lot. So, the number 70 billion is not significant.

c) Since Clayton Kershaw is the highest paid player in Major League history, and he earns more than 15% more than the next highest paid player, this number is significant.

d) Compare this with last year's national debt of $602.4 billion, it is an increase of about 8%. This is a significant number.

Apply

7. a) Answers may vary. The sun-like design and bright colours.

b) 29th. Answers may vary. Environmental conditions, lack of federal spending, public attitudes, and other cheaper forms of generating electricity.

c) The sun-like shape and use of "sun" colours.

d) Answers may vary. They are trying to imply that Canada is far behind in its use of solar energy and needs to improve its standing.

8. Answers may vary. Shocking: Cancer rates up by 25%. Neutral: Cancer rate changes from 1.6% in 2013 to 2% in 2014.

9. Answers may vary. The push poll is a form of telemarketing-based propaganda disguised as a poll that attempts to influence or alter the view of voters.

10. Answers may vary. The Hawthorne effect refers to the fact that people will modify their behavior simply because they are being observed. Example: a typically slow worker who works faster and does a better job when his or her boss is watching.

11. Answers may vary.
a) Confirmation bias is a tendency for people to favour information that confirms their preconceptions regardless of whether the information is true or not. For example, watching certain TV news programs or only visiting websites that express your opinion.
b) Observational selection bias is the effect of suddenly noticing things you did not notice that much before and you wrongly assume that the frequency has increased. For example, when one of your car's headlights is out and suddenly you notice other cars with the same problem.

12. Answers may vary.
a) measurement bias. How important is it for you to use high-tech farming methods?
b) The firm presents the information in this misleading manner to exaggerate their growth and to try to convince potential new clients to "get onboard."

13. Answers may vary.
a) The majority of movies are sci-fi/fantasy, the highest ranked movie has made over $100 million more than the movie ranked at number two.
b) The greatest number of movies were released after 2010. These movies have an unfair advantage over much older movies, which had cheaper ticket prices.
c) This graph is almost the reverse of the other one. Adjusting for inflation negates the effect of higher ticket prices in more recent years.
d) Answers may vary. The top movie on the unadjusted list drops to number three on the adjusted list. Also, the adjusted list contains quite a few different movies and only five movies were released in the 2000s.
e) Answers may vary.

Extend

14. Answers may vary.
a) There is an anti-vaccination movement with celebrity supporters who believe there is a link between vaccines and autism.
b) The possible link between vaccines and autism is in part based on a very small and flawed study published in the UK in 1998. The study was retracted in 2004, and several major health services have all concluded that there is no evidence of a link between the MMR vaccine and autism.

15. Answers may vary. In a double blind study, neither the subjects nor the scientists know who is receiving

the medication and who is receiving a placebo. This helps to prevent results from being influenced by the placebo effect or observer bias.

Chapter 5 Review, pages 244–245

1. Answers may vary.
a) numerical, discrete: number of students in a class
b) numerical, continuous: height of students in a class
c) categorical, ordinal: answers to a question that uses a rating scale
d) categorical, nominal: eye colour of students in a class

2. a) The peaks coincide with weekends, since they occur on a regular weekly basis.
b) Answers may vary. Yes, they used about 102 Gb.
c) Using the sum function in a spreadsheet, the family actually used 104.73 Gb.
d) The average daily Internet usage of the family is 3.491 Gb. Answers may vary. It is not useful. They almost always use less than this on weekdays, and significantly more on weekends.

3. a) voluntary response survey
b) convenience sample

4. a) There are two possible responses for age 15, 20, and 35.
How old are you?
■15 and below ■16–19 ■20–34 ■35–60 ■Above 60
b) This question is biased.
How do you feel about a violence rating system for video games?
■Strongly agree ■Agree ■Agree a little ■Don't agree
c) Give a range of responses.
Do you like the new logo for the school?
■Like it a lot ■Like it ■Do not like or dislike
■Dislike a little ■Dislike a lot

5. a) experimental   **b)** observational

6. a) The table is primary data for whoever collected it. The table represents secondary data for anyone else who uses it.
b) primary   **c)** secondary

7. Answers may vary.
a) Any scenario where a small group that is not representative of the population is surveyed.
b) Any scenario where a limited list of answer choices is given or an opinion is stated before asking the question.
c) Any scenario that influences an answer so as to avoid embarrassment or please the questioner.
d) Any scenario where a response is voluntary.

8. a) The size of the fruit icons is misleading. The rows are basically the same length, but due to the size of the icons used each line actually represents a different number.
b) It is difficult to judge the sizes of each sector and no percent data is given.

9. Answers may vary.

Chapter 5 Test Yourself, pages 246–247

1. A   **2.** B   **3.** B   **4.** B
5. Answers may vary.
a) Each household varies in is electricity usage. The sales representative cannot guarantee anything

and should instead offer an assessment of what is needed and the payback timeline.

b) Response bias, because a student may respond falsely to avoid embarrassment. The teacher could make the response anonymous by asking students to rate their understanding on a scale of 1 to 5 on a piece a paper, all of which are collected in a bag.

6. Answers may vary.

a)

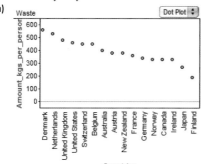

b) The amount of waste in kilograms per person per year by country. A person in Denmark creates the most waste, while a person in Finland creates the least.

7. Answers may vary.

8. Answers may vary.

a)

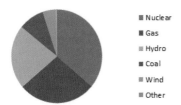

Energy Production in Ontario

b) **Energy Production in Ontario**

Legend: Nuclear, Gas, Hydro, Coal, Wind, Other

It does not show the percent for each section.

9. Answers may vary.

a) **Province a Person Was Born In**

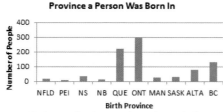

b) stratified sample; the number of people born in each province approximately matches the percent of Canada's population in each province.

c) The percent of Ontarians travelling is slightly higher than their relative percent of the population. The percent of people from New Brunswick travelling is much greater relative to their percent of the population.

d) Provide the percent of the population that travels rather than just the number of trips.

10. a) Answers may vary.

b) Answers may vary. Highly credible: sample should reflect the characteristics of the population, use a non-biased sampling, and use survey questions free of bias. Not very credible: sample that reflects only some portion of the population, use a biased sampling technique, and use survey questions that contain bias.

Chapter 6 One-Variable Data Analysis

Prerequisite Skills, pages 250–251

1. a) mean: about 45.7, median: 44, mode: 12
 b) mean: about 12.7, median: 14, mode: 14
 c) mean: about 13.5, median: 12.85, no mode
 d) mean: about 147.2, median: 142, mode: 134

2. 12

3. a) categorical   **b)** numerical
 c) categorical   **d)** ordinal data
 e) numeric   **f)** numeric data

4. a) bar graph   **b)** stem and leaf plot
 c) pictograph   **d)** circle graph
 e) histogram   **f)** circle graph
 g) bar graph

5. the bar graph gives a visual representation of the nominal data

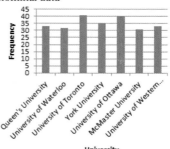

the circle graph allows for easier comparison to the whole

University Choices

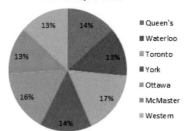

Legend: Queen's 14%, Waterloo 13%, Toronto 13%, York 17%, Ottawa 14%, McMaster 16%, Western 13%

6. a) A stem and leaf plot preserves each data value, whereas a histogram does not with class intervals.

Stem	Leaf
4	3
5	2 5 9
6	1 5 7
7	3 7 8 9
8	0 3
9	9

b) The stems will be the whole number values and the leaves will be the decimal values. This is not practical or useful. Using class intervals of a histogram is a much better choice.

Stem	Leaf
44	5
45	
46	
47	
48	
49	
50	0
51	
52	
53	
54	9

6.1 Measures of Central Tendency, pages 252–265

Example 1 Your Turn

a) mean: about 31.7 °C, median: 29 °C, mode: 29 °C
b) The weather forecast does not match any of the calculated measures of central tendency. However, the mean is affected by the outlier, 45 °C, and the median and mode are the same. Therefore, the weather forecast is not accurate.
c) The outlier of 45 °C causes the mean to be inflated. It does not affect the median or mode.
d) The mean is significantly affected by the outlier. So, the median or mode is more representative of the data.

Example 2 Your Turn

a) estimated mean: about 4 h, median: 3 h, modal interval: 2–4 h
b) Since the data are positively skewed, the modal interval is the least appropriate measure of central tendency. The mean is the greatest of the measures. The median would be an appropriate measure.

Example 3 Your Turn

a) about 84%
b) No, she would have to score 103.17% on the exam. This is not possible, so she cannot receive a final mark of 90% based on the final exam score alone.

Reflect

R1. The mean; an outlier skews the distribution, pushing the mean away from the centre.
R2. Answers may vary.
  a) Assignment grade data when you are looking for the average mark.
  b) A final course grade that is comprised of a number of categories with varying percents.
  c) The results of a survey on how many hours a week students spend on homework.
R3. Answers may vary.
  a) Mode: The "model" that occurs most often. Most people have two hands, two eyes, and two legs.
  b) Mean: The sum of the travel times divided by the number of trips. The mean time it takes to get to school is 38 min.
  c) Median: The middle student in an ordered list. Johnny is an above median student.

Practise

1. a) mean: about 8.7, median: 8, modes: 4, 7, and 15
  b) mean: about 13.3, median: 12, mode: 9
  c) mean: about 125.9, median: 121, mode: 110

2. a) mean: about 1.45 min, median: about 1.44 min
  b) The median best describes Nina's average time. Half of her times are below this and half are above.
3. C
4. D

Apply

5. 80
6. 4.5 cm
7. a) invalid; the mean is not necessarily in the centre of the data. So, the company cannot claim that half the team members sold more than $16 235.
  b) invalid; outliers could cause the mean to be inflated and the distribution to be positively skewed. Thus, resulting in 78% of the salaried to be below the mean.
  c) valid; if the class sizes are the same, or invalid if the class sizes are different
  d) invalid; the median value times 12 does not equal the sum of the monthly expenses for the year. The total expenses for the year is the mean times 12.
8. a) median; The mode could occur anywhere, and not necessarily near the centre of the data. The small size of the sample means that outliers would have a greater effect on the mean than on the median.
  b) mode; This would result in the movie chosen most often.
  c) mean; By definition, the mean times the number of employees is the necessary budget.
  d) median; The mode could occur anywhere, and not necessarily near the centre of the data. Also, any outliers would have a greater effect on the mean than on the median.
9. Answers may vary.
  a) Ice time, in minutes, for a hockey player.
    15 18 13 15 15 14 16
  b) Used car values, in thousands, sold during the first eight days of a month.
    25 36 42 8 5 4 7 7
  c) The temperatures on March 1st for 10 consecutive years.
    16, 17.5, 3.5, 15, 5, −1, 16.5, −2.5, −14.5, 16.5
  d) It affects the mean the most by making it too small or too large. The location of the median in a data set is not affected by outliers.
10. a) and **c)**

Frequency of Length of Sleep

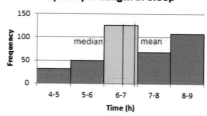

  b) mean: about 6.9 h, median: 6.5 h, modal interval: 6–7 h
  d) Since the data are negatively skewed, the modal interval is the least appropriate measure of central tendency. The median and mean are very close together, so either one would be an appropriate measure.

11. a)

Canadian or Canadian-born Nobel Prize Winners

b) mean: about 62, median: 61, mode: 61

c) The "average" age of a Canadian Nobel Prize winner is 61 years old. Recognition does not occur until the achievement has been widely accepted, and this sometimes takes decades.

12. a) Russia drops from first to 12th. This moves Norway from 2nd to 1st. Canada drops from 3rd to 10th.

b) Answers may vary. Russia stays 1st. Canada moves from 3rd up to 2nd. Norway moves from 2nd to 3rd.

c) Answers may vary.

13. a) 76%   **b)** 92%   **c)** at least 59%

d) No. Karen would need an exam score of 102%.

14. Answers may vary. A sample of car owners categorized by age.

16. approximately 1.85 kg

17. Answers may vary.

Extend

18. a) Competitor B

b) Both competitors would have a mark of 8.5.

19. a) $\frac{84}{39}$ **b)** $\frac{84}{39}$ **c)** $1.31/kg

20. a) about 5.24   **b)** about 2.88%

6.2 Measures of Spread, pages 266–277

Example 1 Your Turn

a) 40th percentile: 16.55 min, 95th percentile: 23.85 min.

b) **i)** 7th percentile   **ii)** 82nd percentile   **iii)** 61st percentile

Example 2 Your Turn

a) median: 22.5 m, range: 45 m, Q1: 17.5 m, Q3: 27.5 m, interquartile range: 10 m

b) 25% of the data are contained in each of the intervals 0 to 17.5 m, 17.5 to 22.5 m, 22.5 to 27.5 m, and 27.5 to 45 m.

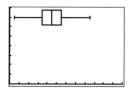

c) no outliers

Example 3 Your Turn

Answers may vary. The median birth length for boys is 0.5 cm greater than the median birth length for girls. The middle 50% of the birth lengths for boys lie between 48.5 cm and 52 cm, for an IQR of 3.5 cm. The middle 50% of the birth lengths for girls lie between 47.5 cm and 51 cm, for an IQR of 3.5 cm. Both the range and IQR for boys is greater than for girls. So, the birth lengths for boys are more spread out.

Reflect

R1. The median for Data Set 1 is 0.8 less than the median for Data Set 2. The middle 50% for Data Set 1 lie between 60.2 and 43.2, for an IQR of 17. The middle 50% for Data Set 2 lie between 63.2 and 34.5, for an IQR of 28.7. Both the range and IQR for Data Set 2 is greater than for Data Set 1. So, the values for Data Set 2 are more spread out.

R2. The range only gives information about the extreme values, not how closely the data is clustered around its centre.

R3. The interquartile range contains the middle 50% of the data. The smaller this value, the more closely the data is clustered around the centre.

Practise

1.

Mark	Percentile Rank
4.0	about 3rd
5.0	about 13th
6.0	about 32nd
7.0	about 59th
8.0	about 82nd
9.0	about 91st
10.0	about 97th

2. 62

3. a) median: 51, range: 77, Q1: 35.5, Q3: 62, interquartile range: 26.5, outliers: 87, 99

b) median: 233, range: 340, Q1: 214, Q3: 264, interquartile range: 50, outliers: 127, 467

c) median: 4.5, range: 9, Q1: 3, Q3: 6, interquartile range: 3, no outliers exist

d) median: 5968, range: 4559, Q1: 3567, Q3: 7659, interquartile range: 4092, no outliers exist

4. D

5. D

6. a)

Infant Mortality Rate by Province and Territory	2011
Yukon	0.0
New Brunswick	3.5
British Columbia	3.8
Prince Edward Island	4.2
Québec	4.3
Ontario	4.6
Nova Scotia	4.9
Alberta	5.3
Newfoundland and Labrador	6.3
Saskatchewan	6.7
Northwest Territories	7.2
Manitoba	7.7
Nunavut	26.3

b) Answers may vary. New Brunswick: 12th percentile, Prince Edward Island: 27th percentile, Ontario: 42th percentile, Alberta: 58th percentile, and Northwest Territories: 81st percentile.

7. a)

	2007	2008	2009	2010	2011
Median	5.2	5.3	5.8	5	4.9
Interquartile Range	3.2	2.75	3.25	2.2	2.95

b) Answers may vary. The median infant mortality rate increased from 2007 to 2009, and then decreased through 2011. The interquartile range of the infant mortality rates seem to cycle.

c) Answers may vary. Because of outliers.

8. a) Nunavut is an outlier.

b) Answers may vary. This could be due to low birth weight, lack of hospitals, or population prone to respiratory-track infections.

9. Answers may vary.

a)

Population of Canada by Age Group	
Age Group (years)	**2009**
100 or over	5474
90 to 100	180 409
80 to 90	1 075 522
70 to 80	1 994 853
60 to 70	3 299 618
0 to 10	3 626 272
10 to 20	4 253 528
30 to 40	4 534 301
20 to 30	4 608 623
50 to 60	4 798 598
40 to 50	5 251 373

Population of Canada by Age Group	
Age Group (years)	**2013**
100 or over	6 911
90 to 100	242 124
80 to 90	1 181 124
70 to 80	2 202 364
0 to 10	3 804 924
60 to 70	3 857 403
10 to 20	4 048 205
30 to 40	4 762 084
20 to 30	4 855 939
40 to 50	4 940 356
50 to 60	5 256 870

2009: 80 to 90: 2nd percentile, 0 to 10:
25th percentile, 50 to 60: 77th percentile
2013: 80 to 90: 2nd percentile, 0 to 10:
16th percentile, 50 to 60: 93rd percentile

b) Age groups 60 to 70 and 0 to 10 swapped positions from 2009 to 2013, as well as age groups 50 to 60 and 40 to 50. In particular, the 0 to 10 age group went from being in the 25th percentile in 2009 to the 16th percentile in 2013, and the 50 to 60 age group went from being in the 77th percentile in 2009 to the 93rd percentile in 2013.

10. a) A quintile divides a data set into five equal groups.

b) Answers may vary. While the percent of total net worth remained the same for the first quintile, all others changed. The second and third quintiles saw declines in the percent of total net worth, while the fourth and fifth quintiles saw increases. Basically, the wealthiest 20% of Canadians increased their share of the total wealth at the expense of the second the third quintiles.

12. December is an outlier. This is most likely caused by a combination of bad weather and increased number of flights due to the holiday season.

Extend

13. Answers may vary.

a) Locate the age of the child along the horizontal axis and follow the line up to the BMI. Interpret the percentile using the following table.

Weight Status Category	Percentile
Underweight	Less than 5th percentile
Healthy weight	5th percentile to less than 85th percentile
Overweight	85th to less than 95th percentile
Obese	Equal to or greater than 95th percentile

b)

	BMI Range by Age		
Percentile	**2**	**10**	**20**
$p < 5$th	BMI < 14.7	BMI < 14.2	BMI < 19.1
5th $\leq p <$ 10th	14.7 $\leq$ BMI < 15.1	14.2 $\leq$ BMI < 14.6	19.1 $\leq$ BMI < 19.8
10th $\leq p <$ 25th	15.1 $\leq$ BMI < 15.8	14.6 $\leq$ BMI < 15.5	19.8 $\leq$ BMI < 21.2
25th $\leq p <$ 50th	15.8 $\leq$ BMI < 16.6	15.5 $\leq$ BMI < 16.6	21.2 $\leq$ BMI < 23
50th $\leq p <$ 75th	16.6 $\leq$ BMI < 17.6	16.6 $\leq$ BMI < 18.2	23 $\leq$ BMI < 25.4
75th $\leq p <$ 85th	17.6 $\leq$ BMI < 18.2	18.2 $\leq$ BMI < 19.4	25.4 $\leq$ BMI < 27
85th $\leq p <$ 90th	18.2 $\leq$ BMI < 18.6	19.4 $\leq$ BMI < 20.3	27 $\leq$ BMI < 28.3
90th $\leq p <$ 95th	18.6 $\leq$ BMI < 19.3	20.3 $\leq$ BMI < 22.1	28.3 $\leq$ BMI < 30.6
95th $\leq p$	19.3 $\leq$ BMI	22.1 $\leq$ BMI	30.6 $\leq$ BMI

14. Answers may vary.

6.3 Standard Deviation and z-Scores, pages 278–289

Example 1 Your Turn

Answers may vary.

Set A	
Height (cm)	**Frequency**
150–155	1
155–160	2
160–165	4
165–170	2
170–175	1
175–180	0
180–185	0

Set B	
Height (cm)	**Frequency**
150–155	2
155–160	3
160–165	2
165–170	1
170–175	1
175–180	0
180–185	1

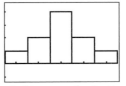 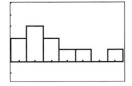

The histogram for Set B will have a greater standard deviation.

Example 2 Your Turn

a) Answers may vary.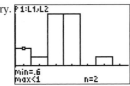

b) mean: about 1.8 dB, standard deviation: approximately 0.447 dB

c) The standard deviation would increase because 1.5 dB is farther from the mean and the spread of the data would increase.

d) The standard deviation would decrease because 1.7 dB is closer to the mean and the spread of the data would decrease.

e) Since values decrease by the same amount, the spread will not change. The standard deviation would be unchanged.

f) levels less than 2.3 dB or greater than 1.3 dB

Example 3 Your Turn

a) mean: about 1.53 mm, standard deviation: approximately 0.2196 mm

b) about 0.3188; A gap of 1.6 mm is about 0.3188 standard deviations greater than the mean.

c) about −0.5920; A gap of 1.4 mm is about 0.5920 standard deviations less than the mean. A gap of 1.4 mm is farther from the mean than a gap of 1.6 mm, and is to the left of the means instead of to the right.

d) Any gaps that are less than 1.0908 mm or greater than 1.9692 mm would be rejected. None of the cars in this sample would be rejected.

Reflect

R1. a) A data point is two standard deviations below (less) the mean. In this case, 17.3 has a z-score of –2.

b) A data point is 1.5 standard deviations above (greater) the mean. In this case, 28.15 has a z-score of 1.5.

R2. Answers may vary. Since stock A has a smaller standard deviation, its price is more consistent, or reliable, than stock B. If you are a cautious investor, stock A is less risky than stock B. However, the potential for greater profit is with stock A.

R3. a) x is greater than the mean
   b) x is less than the mean
   c) x is equal to the mean

R4. Answers may vary. Use population formulas when all values of a population are included. Use sample formulas when only a sample of the population is taken.

Practise

1. D   **2.** A

3. a) about 0.5288; A value of 27.2 is about 0.5288 standard deviations greater than the mean.
   b) about −0.3333; A value of 24.1 is about 0.3333 standard deviations less than the mean.
   c) about −0.9444; A value of 21.9 is about 0.9444 standard deviations less than the mean.
   d) 1.25; A value of 29.8 is 1.25 standard deviations greater than the mean.

4. a) approximately 2.6092 cm
   b) approximately 8.5201 home runs
   c) approximately a 17.2620 points

5. a) Sample: Researchers are studying a sample of the population, females ages 35 to 50 years old.
   b) Population: This is a national survey for which researchers want to describe the variability in all ages.
   c) Population: The teacher wants to summarize the results of all the students in her class.

6. a) years worked that are greater than 6 years and less than 15 years
   b) about 97%
   c) Answers may vary. The graph visualizes the number of standard deviations an observation is from the mean.

7. a) mean: approximately 45.24 min, standard deviation: approximately 7.831 min
   b) Answers may vary. Sample formulas, since 93 customers is likely a sample from one day.
   c)

Time Midpoint	z-Score
32.5	about −1.63
37.5	about −0.99
42.5	about −0.35
47.5	about 0.29
52.5	about 0.93
57.5	about 1.57
62.5	about 2.20

   d)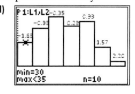

8. a) Mississauga-Erindale: about 1.8632, Parkdale-High Park: about −0.0228
   b) Answers may vary. They are underrepresented.

9. 92%

10. a) mean: approximately 1.007 L, standard deviation: approximately 0.014 L
   b) Sample formulas, since volume is checked using a selection of 102 cartons.
   c) Yes, it is within two standard deviations of the mean.
   d) Answers may vary. The mean volume of milk increased from 1.007 L on the first day to 1.012 L on the second day. However, the standard deviation decreased from 0.014 L on the first day to

0.009 L on the second day. The data is less spread out from the mean on the second day.

11. a) mean: approximately 7.336 m, standard deviation: approximately 1.570 m
   b) Answers may vary. The mean length of logs decreased from 8.44 m on the previous day to 7.336 m on this day. In addition, the standard deviation decreased from 1.836 m on the previous day to 1.570 m on this day. The data is less spread out from the mean on this day.
   c) Answers may vary. For quality control purposes. It would help identify any problems in sawing-machine centres, sawing systems, or set repeatability systems.

13. The standard deviation is the square root of the variance. In other words, the standard deviation squared equals the variance. A value between 0 and 1, when squared results in a smaller value. So, the standard deviation will be larger than the variance when it is between 0 and 1. If $s = 0.99$ then $s^2 = 0.9801$.

14. Answers may vary. In the case of a career with a standard deviation of $15 000, the salary range is more spread out and includes a potential high salary of $86 000 but also a low salary of $26 000. Compare this to the case of a career with a standard deviation of $5000, where the salary range is more clustered around the mean. Here a potential high salary may be only $66 000 but a low salary of $46 000 is far above that of the other career.

15. a) Answers may vary. The uncertainty of the investment, or the difference between observed and expected rate of returns.
   b) The standard deviation would increase for a risker investment.

16. Answers may vary. Since quartiles divide a set of ordered data into four groups with equal numbers of values, the interquartile range will not change. For a set of five values, Q1 still falls between data values one and two and Q3 still falls between data values four and five. The standard deviation will change because the new value is closer to the mean.

Extend

17. mean: $\bar{x} + a$, standard deviation remains unchanged.

18. mean: $c\bar{x}$, standard deviation: becomes cs.

19.
$$\sigma = \sqrt{\frac{\sum (x_i - \mu)^2}{N}}$$
$$= \sqrt{\frac{\sum (x_i^2 - 2x_i\mu + \mu^2)}{N}}$$
$$= \sqrt{\frac{\sum x_i^2 - \sum 2x_i\mu + \sum \mu^2}{N}}$$
$$= \sqrt{\frac{\sum x_i^2 - 2\mu \sum x_i + N\mu^2}{N}}$$
$$= \sqrt{\frac{\sum x_i^2}{N} - \frac{2\mu \sum x_i}{N} + \frac{N\mu^2}{N}}$$
$$= \sqrt{\frac{\sum x_i^2}{N} - 2\mu^2 + \mu^2}$$
$$= \sqrt{\frac{\sum x_i^2}{N} - \mu^2}$$
$$= \sqrt{\frac{\sum x_i^2 - N\mu^2}{N}}$$

6.4 Interpreting Statistical Summaries, pages 290–301

Example 1 Your Turn
Answers may vary.
a) the median and mean for a particular Internet service provider, the IQR for the industry
b) For a claim that this ISP is "always" faster, they are using their mean data most of the time. When the mean is greater than the median, the median must be what they are using.
c) The claim is inaccurate. The mean is influenced by outliers, so extremely fast response times will significantly decrease the mean. Since the industry IQR does not include the median, it is not possible to compare this provider's response time to the industry.
d) The vertical scale does not start at 0 and the choice of units is milliseconds. As a result, the differences between the graphs seem to be greater than in reality.

Example 2 Your Turn
a)

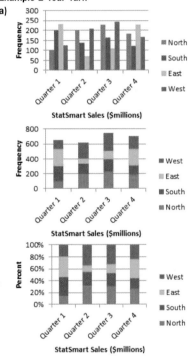

StatSmart Sales ($millions)

StatSmart Sales ($millions)

StatSmart Sales ($millions)

b) Answers may vary. The multiple bar graph and the split bar graph both show the breakdown of sales within the regions. In the situations where the sales values are not that different, it is easier to see the difference in the multiple bar graph. However, total sales are different each quarter, so the relative frequency graph needs to be used to compare how well each region did.

Example 3 Your Turn
Answers may vary.
a) While Facebook is a critical tool for communicating, shopping, and listening music, privacy settings are not seen as important.
b) Use of a different colour to circle one statistic for emphasis. Graphics are used to signify each statistic. Various font sizes and font colours are used to catch the eye.

c) How large was the sample? How was the sample chosen and was it a random selection? What questions were asked in the survey?
d) What was the source of the data? Were the data primary or secondary? Who sponsored the survey?

Reflect
R1. Answers may vary. All three types use different colours and length of bars to represent data. However, a multiple bar graph and split bar graph show different quantities, where as a relative split bar graph shows different percents. Only the multiple bar graph displays bars side by side, while the other two types use bars placed one above the other.
R2. Answers may vary.
  a) To determine whether you can make valid generalizations. Statistics are often used to represent certain points of view by manipulating graph axes, by citing only one measure of central tendency, or through measurement or sampling bias.
  b) How large was the sample? How was the sample chosen and was it a random selection? What questions were asked in the survey? What was the source of the data? Were the data primary or secondary? Who sponsored the survey?

Practise
1. Answers may vary. No. The sample sizes appear to be the same, 100 of each gender. So, the graph shows that a slightly higher percent of grade 12 males have their G2 driver's licence. However, more than 50% of both females and males have their G2 licences.
2. Answers may vary.
  a) No. The sample size is too small and was collected during a particular season when it is most likely to be a popular item.
  b) increase the sample size and ensure that the sample accurately represents the entire population.
3. D
4. B
5. sample size of trout, the mean length, and the standard deviation for the length
6. **a)**

Eat Lunch in Cafeteria?

b) Since the sample sizes are not the same for each grade level, the relative split bar graph can be used to compare grade levels.

Apply

7. Answers may vary. Using 2013 data, "2% of the world's population has more than half the world's wealth" translates to "142 000 people have more than $115.5 trillion in wealth." In contrast, "half the world's population has only 1% of the world's wealth" translates to "3 550 000 people have only $2.31 trillion in wealth."

8. Answers may vary.
  a) That climate change must not be important (or not being taken seriously). The graph shows that more countries have increased their greenhouse gas emissions than reduced them.
  b) No. While Russia is the second largest producer of greenhouse emissions in this graph, the country has reduced emissions from 1990 to 2004, while others have increased. Compared to countries not included in this graph, say China and India, Russia is most likely lower on the list.
  c) No. While Russia shows the largest decrease in emissions, the graph contains no information on how this was accomplished.
  d) The headline implies that climate change must not really be happening since very few countries have attempted to reduce their greenhouse emissions. The graph does show very few countries have decreased their greenhouse gas emissions, but the graph includes only nine countries.

9. Answers may vary.
  a) Boys: median: 50%, IQR: 20%, range: 85%
  Girls: median: 55%, IQR: 20%, range: 60%
  The median for girls is greater than for boys, 55% compared to 50%. While the IQR is the same for both genders, the range for boys is considerable greater than the girls. This means that the data values are more spread out.
  b) The median, Q1, and Q3 values for the girls are greater than the corresponding values for the boys. However, the maximum score for boys is 95% compared to girls at 90%. For this data set, I think the evidence supports that on average girls are better than boys at math.

10. The difference between a z-score of –2 and a z-score of –1 represents one standard deviation. As well, the difference between a z-score of 0 and a z-score of 1 is also one standard deviation. So, the statement means that the mean height is 96 cm with a standard deviation of 3.8 cm.

11. a)

Measure of Central Tendency	Male	Female
Mean	68.1 min	93.4 min
Median	65 min	98 min
Mode	none	none

b)
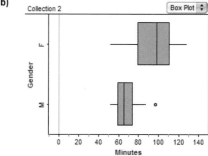
Collection 2   Box Plot

c) Answers may vary.

12. Answers may vary. While Fox has the heavy coverage of the Western Conference, it has little coverage of the Eastern Conference. NBC has heavy coverage of the Eastern Conference and little coverage of the Western Conference. CBS is the only network with equal coverage of both Conferences.

13. Answers may vary.
  a) Life Sciences is the fastest growing industry.
  b) Statistics Canada (Labour Force Survey) and Ontario Ministry of Finance

14. mean depth: approximately 1.23 m, standard deviation: approximately 1.03 m

15. Answers may vary. Determine the size of the sample, how the sample chosen and if it was a random selection, what was measured, the source of the data and whether it was primary or secondary, if any sponsors were involved.

16. a)
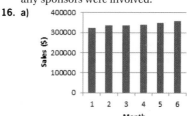

b)
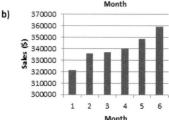

18. Answers may vary.
  a) The North American Growth Fund. Returns have been in Q3 for three of the five years and Q2 for the two years. The other two funds showed returns in three or four different quartiles, indicating that they are more volatile.
  b) For the long haul, I would recommend the North American Growth Fund because of its consistency, although it does not have high returns. For a short term riskier investment, I would recommend the Canadian Mineral Resource Fund because it appears to cycle to a high every third year.

19. Answers may vary.

20. a)

Phase of Flight	Percent of Bird Strikes
Descent	2
Enroute	5
Climb	8
Approach	21
Land & Taxi	27
Takeoff	37

b)

Phase of Flight	Percent of Bird Strikes	Percentile
Descent	2	1
Enroute	5	4.5
Climb	8	11
Approach	21	25.5
Land & Taxi	27	49.5
Takeoff	37	81.5

c)

Phase of Flight	Bird Strike Percent Phase Flight Percent	Risk Percent
Takeoff	37	55.9
Climb	0.533	0.8
Enroute	0.088	0.1
Descent	0.182	0.3
Approach	1.4	2.1
Land & Taxi	27	40.8

Phase of Flight	Risk Percent	Percentile
Enroute	0.1	0.05
Descent	0.3	0.25
Climb	0.8	0.8
Approach	2.1	2.25
Land & Taxi	40.8	23.7
Takeoff	55.9	72.05

6.5 Analysing Data From Statistics Canada, pages 302–307

Reflect

R1. Answers may vary. The data are used by all levels of government, the private sector, and social and community groups.

R2. Answers may vary. Factors to be considered include sample design, questionnaire design, and data collection.

R3. Answers may vary. In order to evaluate the strength of the evidence and draw conclusions on that basis.

Practise

1. B   **2.** C

3. a) customize the data according to how data is represented over time
   b) customize the data according to which groups and areas are represented

4. population and dwelling counts, age characteristics, marital status, family characteristics, household and dwelling characteristics, detailed mother tongue, knowledge of official languages, first official language spoken, detailed language spoken most often at home, and detailed other language spoken regularly at home

Apply

5. Answers may vary.

6. a) increase: food, shelter, household operations, furnishings and equipment, transportation, recreation, education and reading, and alcoholic beverages and tobacco products
   decrease: clothing and footwear and health and personal care
   b) increase: food, shelter, household operations, furnishings and equipment, recreation, education and reading, and alcoholic beverages and tobacco products
   decrease: clothing and footwear, transportation, and health and personal care
   c) 12 months

7. Answers may vary.
   a) The pyramid is wider at the base, with the maximum number of males and females at about age 5. In the late 30s to late 70s, there are more males than females. From there, the age population is split between the genders.
   b) The pyramid is the widest around age 50. In general, the two genders mirror each other in growth and decline until the mid 60s. From there, the age population is comprised of more females than males.
   c) Descriptions may vary. Any birth year in the late 1990s has a similar shape to 2011 but is the widest in the mid 30s.
   d) The width of the base goes from about 240 000 people in 1946 to almost double that 480 000 people.
   e) male aged 10: 270 000, male aged 50: 180 000, female aged 10: 280 000, female aged 50: 180 000

8. Answers may vary.   **9.** Answers may vary.
10. Answers may vary.   **11.** Answers may vary.
12. Answers may vary.
13. Answers may vary.

a)

Period	Census Population (1000s)	Growth	Growth Rate (%)
1851–1861	3230	793	24.55
1861–1871	3689	459	12.44
1871–1881	4325	636	14.71
1881–1891	4833	508	10.51
1891–1901	5371	538	10.02
1901–1911	7207	1836	25.48
1911–1921	8788	1581	17.99
1921–1931	10377	1589	15.31
1931–1941	11507	1130	9.82
1941–1951	13648	2141	15.69
1951–1961	34319	4590	13.37
1961–1971	41583	3330	8.01
1971–1981	48270	2859	5.92
1981–1991	54132	3211	5.93
1991–2001	60632	2990	4.93

b) The graph appears to show continued growth from 1851 to 2001. There was a big jump in the population from 1951 to 1961.

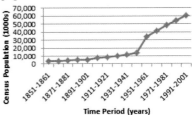

c) While the population from 1851 through 2001 was growing steadily, the rate of growth was increasing and decreasing in a fluctuating manner. During almost the entire time period from 1911 to 2011, the rate of growth was declining. During these 100 years, the rate of growth increased once from 1941 to 1951. From 1981, the population is growing at an almost steady rate of about 5%.

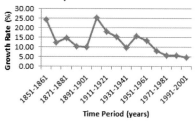

6. a)

Number of Friends	Percentile
0–25	0.8
25–50	6.7
50–75	16.3
75–100	30.6
100–125	57.9
125–150	81.7
150–175	92.1
175–200	96.1
200–225	97.5
225–250	99.4

b) Q1: 87.5 friends, Q3: 112.5 friends, Interquartile range: 25 friends

c) 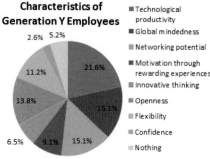 **d)** 42 outliers

Chapter 6 Review, pages 308–310

1. a) mean: the average of a set of data; median: the middle number when the numbers are arranged in numerical order; mode: the number that occurs most often

b) mean: the sum of the data entries divided by the number of entries.
median: for an odd number of data, the median is the middle value of all the data points when the data values are listed in order from least to greatest. For an even number of data, the median is the average between the two middle values.
mode: found by inspection

c) Answers may vary. Mean: the average length of time it takes to get to school. Median: to represent a typical salary among employees. Mode: to represent the most popular song.

2. a) mean: about 286.3, median: 76, modes: 54 and 675
b) mean: 22.5, median: 18, mode: 7
c) mean: 4587.5, median: 3773, modes: 2346 and 9564

3. a) approximately 0.643 **b)** approximately 0.878
c) approximately 0.581

4. a) mean: approximately $57 235, median: $55 000, mode: 50–60 salary interval

b)

5. a) A percentile is the percent of all the data that are less than or equal to the specific data point. Quartiles divide the data set into four equal parts. Q1 is the 25th percentile, Q2 is the median (or 50th) percentile, and Q3 is the 75th percentile.

b) Answers may vary. A shoe store may use the IQR to determine the typically sold sizes. Then, use this information to order shoe sizes.

7. a) standard deviation: approximately 15 895 students, variance: 252 651 025 students^2
b) about 1.5398
c) No universities have a z-score of –2 or less.

8. To have a z-score of 1.5 means that the value is 1.5 standard deviations above the mean.

9. a) 500.14 mL to 502.06 mL
b) Answers may vary. The company may want to overfill the bottles to account for air in the dispensing of the drink liquid.
c) The bottles with volumes of 501.0 mL and 500 mL are acceptable.

10. Answers may vary.
a) each region's information is represented by one of the stacked bars, each stacked bar shows which parties are be considered in that region, and each stacked bar shows the percent of the sample of voters that intend to vote those parties
b) No; this is only a sample of 2000 voters from across all of Ontario.

11. Answers may vary. From a manger's perspective, the most important characteristic of a Generation Y employee is his or her technological productivity.

12. Answers may vary.
13. Answers may vary.
a) there was markedly different wage growth across age groups and that there was narrowing of wage differences across education levels during the 2000s

b) and **c)**
The article contains two multiple line graphs and one multiple bar graph. Without grid backgrounds, the values are difficult to read. The vertical scale of charts 1 and 3 (line graphs) does not start of 0 and may exaggerate the results.

d) Statistics Canada surveys

e) and **f)** No specifics are given on sample size, though it covers full-time workers aged 17 to 64 from 1981 to 2011.

g) No actual methods are listed. However, it is secondary data.

h) The article gives references for information on previous trends.

i) René Morissette, Garnett Picot, and Yuqian Lu of the Economic Analysis Division at Statistics Canada

j) No. Technically, wages did not *steadily* increase of the past 30 years. Chart 1 shows that while overall hourly wages continued to increase, there were various times over the 30-year period that wages decreased.

Chapter 6 Test Yourself, pages 311–313

1. C   **2.** D   **3.** C   **4.** B   **5.** B

6. Yes. The IQR is the spread of the middle 50% of the data. The smaller this range, the smaller the spread of the central half of the data or the more consistent the player. In this case, Joshua is the more consistent player with an IQR of 3 compared to Ron with an IQR of 4.

7. The national census is sent to every household in Canada and completion is mandatory, so there is no concern that any parts of the population will not be represented.

8. −17.4 °C is the closest to the monthly mean

9. a) the source, date published, table number, table title and content, database, and URL
b) the source, date, graph title and content, and URL

10. Answers may vary. Apples: mean: approximately $2.20, standard deviation: approximately $0.40
Plums: mean: approximately $0.60, standard deviation: approximately $0.40
Oranges: mean: approximately $2.80, standard deviation: approximately $1

11. a) mean: approximately 12.43 years, standard deviation: approximately 9.38 years, Q1: 4 years, Q3: 18 years, Interquartile range: 14

b)

Number of Years Teaching	Frequency
0–8	11
8–16	8
16–24	7
24–32	3
32–40	1

c) mean: approximately 13.33 years, standard deviation: approximately 9.18 years, Q1: 4 years, Q3: 20 years, Interquartile range: 16
The mean and the IQR have increased, but the standard deviation has decreased.

d) vertical lines represent one standard deviation below the mean (3.05),

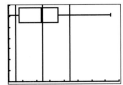

the mean (12.43), and one standard deviation above the mean (21.81):

vertical lines represent one standard deviation below the mean (4.15), the mean (13.33), and one standard deviation above the mean (22.51):

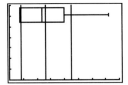

e) 43rd percentile
f) 26 years of teaching
g) no outliers exist in this data set
h) Answers may vary. Ryan's data is not valid because the results do not accurately represent the entire population. Since Ryan sent the survey to the teachers, each chooses whether or not to respond. It is a voluntary response survey. Not knowing how many teachers are at Ryan's school, I assume that the entire population is not represented in the sample.

Chapters 4 to 6 Cumulative Review, pages 314–315

1. a)

Product, x	Frequency	Probability, P(x)
1	1	$\frac{1}{36}$
2	2	$\frac{1}{18}$
3	2	$\frac{1}{18}$
4	3	$\frac{1}{12}$
5	2	$\frac{1}{18}$
6	4	$\frac{1}{9}$
8	2	$\frac{1}{18}$
9	1	$\frac{1}{36}$
10	2	$\frac{1}{18}$
12	4	$1/9$
15	2	$\frac{1}{18}$
16	1	$\frac{1}{36}$
18	2	$\frac{1}{18}$
20	2	$\frac{1}{18}$
24	2	$\frac{1}{18}$
25	1	$\frac{1}{36}$
30	2	$\frac{1}{18}$
36	1	$\frac{1}{36}$

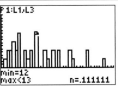

2. 249.5. The predicted average value of the card turned up will be 249.5.

3. a) about 0.1240   **b)** about 0.0027

    c) 1×10^{-7}

4. about 32.27%

5. a)

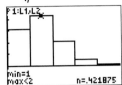

    i)   **ii)**

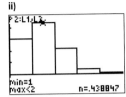

    b) The graphs have the same bell-like shape, with the $x = 1$ diamond being the most likely outcome. The hypergeometric graph is slightly taller than the binomial graph at $x = 1$ and $x = 2$, and shorter at the other values of x.

    c) The expected value for the binomial distribution is $4(0.25)$, or 1. The expected value for the hypergeometric distribution is $\frac{4(13)}{52}$, or 1. On average, there will be 1 diamond in a four-card selection, with or without replacement.

6. a) Since the blue graph shows the greatest number of searches from August 2012 to Jan 2013, it represents the Google search data related to "Gangnam Style." Since the yellow graph shows a spike in searches about mid-April 2013, it represents the Google search data related to "Gentleman."

    b) The scale on the two graphs are very different. In the first five months, "Gangnam Style" had over 900 000 000 reviews, while "Gentleman" had only about 550 000 000 views. So, "Gentleman" is doing worse than "Gangnam Style."

7. Answers may vary.

    a) I would use a sample that is representative of the population. So, selection for the sample must be random.

    b) I would ask questions that are anonymous, clear, concise, and free of bias.

    c) I would collect both continuous (e.g., hours) and discrete (e.g., number of people) numerical data, as well as categorical ordinal (e.g., rating scale) and nominal (e.g., type of sport) data.

    d) I will keep the data free of bias by using a collection method that is free from sampling, measurement, response, or non-response bias. I will also display the data in an unbiased fashion.

8. a) Those two characters have the most appearances and largest speaking roles.

    b)

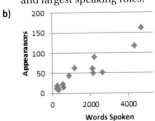

There appears to be an upward trend. As the number of words spoken increases, so does the number of appearances.

c) the Friar

d)

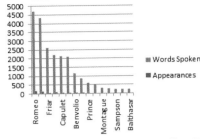

9. a) mean: approximately 71.93 °C, median: 72 °C, mode: 72 °C

    b) range: 20 °C, standard deviation: approximately 4.28 °C, variance: 18.3184 °C^2

    c) Q1: 69 °C, Q2: 72 °C, Q3: 73 °C, Interquartile range: 4

10. a) Two outliers exist in this data set: 81 and 87.

    b) mean: approximately 71.1 °C, median: 71.5 °C, mode: 72 °C. The median is in the middle of the data, so it would be the best measure to represent the average temperature of the coffee.

    c) The mean is not appropriate because it is affected by the outliers and it is the least of the three measures. The mode is not appropriate because it is now the greatest measure.

11. Answers may vary.

a)

Coffee Temperature (°C)	Frequency
65–69	9
69–73	14
73–77	4
77–81	2
81–85	1

b)

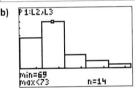 

12. a) 2   **b)** 65 °C, 85 °C

13. Yes. The middle 50% of the coffee temperatures lie between 69 °C and 73 °C.

Chapter 7 Probability Distributions for Continuous Variables

Prerequisite Skills, pages 318–319

1. a) 7.98 m^2 **b)** 3.33 cm^2

2. a)

b)

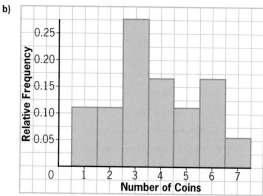

c) mean: about 3.7778 coins, standard deviation: about 1.7675 coins.

d) about −1.0058

3. a) 78   **b)** No.

4. 32

5. a) 120   **b)** 6   **c)** 90   **d)** 35

6. 6188

7. a) 479 001 600   **b)** 1296

8. $\frac{1}{3}$ **9.** $\frac{1}{720}$ **10.** −$1

11. about 0.0577   **12.** about 0.0993

13. $\frac{1}{14\ 950}$ **14.** about 0.217

15. a) about 0.2149   **b)** about 0.4750

7.1 Continuous Random Variables, pages 320–331

Example 1 Your Turn

a) 0.25   **b)** 0.625   **c)** 0

Example 2 Your Turn

a) and **b)**

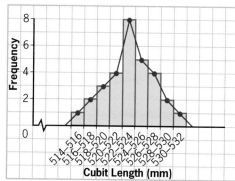

c) around 523 mm

d) All outcomes are not equally likely. So, this is not a uniform distribution.

Reflect

R1. The number of guests that occupy the hotel each day is discrete data, while the time a guest waits for an elevator is continuous data. It is possible to list all values of the discrete distribution, since these would be values from 0 up to the maximum capacity of the hotel. It is not possible to list all values of the continuous distribution, since time can be recorded in fractions of a second.

R2. Answers may vary. Maya could be standing differently each time, bad measuring technique, and misreading the measuring device. This is most likely measurement error, not bias.

R3. Answers may vary. The probability that a variable falls within a range of values is equal to the area under the probability density graph for that range of values. The area method cannot be used for single values of a continuous variable, only for a range of values. A continuous random variable can take on an infinite number of values. The probability that it will equal a specific value is always zero.

Practise

1. a) No; mass represents a continuous variable

     b) Yes; the value of a card represents a discrete variable

     c) No; barometric pressure represents a continuous variable

2. a) No; the number of students with blue eyes represents a discrete variable

     b) Yes; weight represents a continuous variable

     c) No; the number of cartons of milk represents a discrete variable

     d) No; the number of defective tablets represents a discrete variable

3. a) No; each waist size interval is not equally likely

     b) 90

     c) 36–38 interval

Apply

4. a) It is not obvious whether the distribution is uniform or not.

     b) Use a table to determine the frequency for each interval. If all frequencies are equal, then the distribution is uniform.

Volume of Sample (mL)	Frequency
54–55	4
55–56	4
56–57	4
57–58	4
58–59	4
59–60	4
60–61	4
61–62	4
62–63	4
63–64	4
64–65	4

This distribution is uniform.

5. a) Use a table to determine the frequency for each interval. If all frequencies are equal, then the distribution is uniform. The distribution is not uniform.

Pressure (psi)	Frequency
2995–2997	8
2997–2999	6
2999–3001	7
3001–3003	7
3003–3005	4

     b) In general, pressure is a continuous variable. So, the distribution is continuous.

     c) Answers may vary. The gauge used to measure the pressure only has a whole-number scale.

6. a) 0.25   **b)** 0.5

     c) This type of distribution was used because all times are equally likely.

7. a) 88 keys

     b) Answers may vary. No, because I doubt that all keys will be used in a piece of music.

c) Answers may vary. Since each key represents a specific note (frequency), the distribution in part b) is discrete.

8. Answers may vary.

a) If a trombone player plays many notes at random frequencies, I would guess that he is constantly moving the slider to new positions while blowing. Since the trombone can play all frequencies between notes, I would expect the distribution to be continuous.

b) If a trombone player plays a musical composition, he plays specific notes. I would expect the distribution to be discrete.

9. a) There are six possible lengths for the sardines. There are six occurrences of 99 mm. So, it is not possible for the 24 sardine sample to be a uniform distribution.

b) 0.2

c)

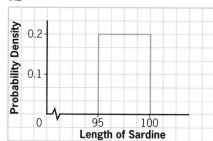

d) 0.6

10. The area method cannot be used for single values of a continuous variable. So, Jon is incorrect. The probability that a variable falls within a range of values is equal to the area under the probability density graph for that range of values. The area shaded is from 2.5 to 3.5. So, Sunita is correct.

12. a) Speed is a continuous variable, so the data is continuous.

b) The data ranges from 64.6 to 80.2. So, I chose intervals of width two, starting at 64.5.

c)

Speed (km/h)	Frequency
64.5–66.5	4
66.5–68.5	4
68.5–70.5	3
70.5–72.5	5
72.5–74.5	5
74.5–76.5	3
76.5–78.5	5
78.5–80.5	1

d) 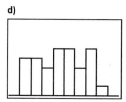 **e)**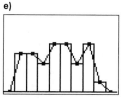

f) The mean appears to be around 72.5 km/h.

g) Answers may vary. Since only one speed was recorded over 80 km/h, my estimate is $\frac{1}{30}$, or about 0.033.

13. Answers may vary. I think that hair colour should be considered continuous, since there are unlimited numbers of shades between blonde, red, brown, and black.

Extend

14. Answers may vary.

a) Three instruments that can play only discrete frequencies are electric piano, organ, and harp.

b) Three instruments that can play any frequency over a range are bass, cello, violin.

15. Answers may vary.

a) Use the formula for the area of a trapezoid with height 1 to calculate a probability to the left or right of 0. Then, determine the sum if needed.

b) 0.5

7.2 The Normal Distribution and z-Scores, pages 332–345

Example 1 Your Turn

a) 0.175   **b)** 0.205

c) 0.770   **d)** 0

Example 2 Your Turn

a) mean: 35.2 yd, standard deviation: about 9.567 yd

b) about 0.2934

c) about 0.6360

Reflect

R1. Answers may vary. As Kunal practises and gains more skill, I expect the mean and standard deviation to change. As he improves and becomes more consistent, I expect the mean to increase and the standard deviation to decrease.

R2. The z-scores for a normal distribution follow a normal distribution themselves, with a mean of 0 and a standard deviation of 1. From the graph, $P(z < -5)$ is located far in the left tail. So, the probability that far from the central peak is essentially zero.

Practise

1. C   **2.** A   **3.** 0

4. Answers may vary. Data collected one week could be different from another because of the path chosen, traffic lights, or weather condition. Roberta could obtain more reliable values for the mean and standard deviation by combining the data from the two weeks.

Apply

5. a)

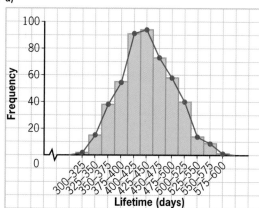

b) around 437.5 days

c)

Lifetime (days)	Frequency	Relative Frequency
300–325	2	0.004
325–350	15	0.030
350–375	38	0.076
375–400	55	0.110
400–425	91	0.182
425–450	94	0.188
450–475	73	0.146
475–500	68	0.136
500–525	40	0.080
525–550	14	0.028
550–575	9	0.018
575–600	1	0.002

d) 0.220

e) Answers may vary. Replace the light bulbs every 437.5 days, the estimated mean, to be reasonably sure that there would never be a burned out light bulb.

6. a)

Speed of Ball (km/h)	Frequency
49–54	3
54–59	10
59–64	19
64–69	7
69–74	1

b) and c)

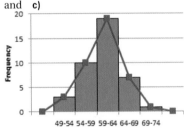

d) Answers may vary. While the distribution is centred around a central value, it does not drop off symmetrically to the left and right.

e) around 61.5 days

f)

Speed of Ball (km/h)	Frequency	Relative Frequency
49–54	3	0.075
54–59	10	0.250
59–64	19	0.475
64–69	7	0.175
69–74	1	0.025

g) 0.65

7. a)

Speed of Ball (km/h)	Frequency
49–51	2
51–53	1
53–55	1
55–57	4
57–59	5
59–61	8
61–63	10
63–65	3
65–67	2
67–69	3
69–71	1

b) and c)

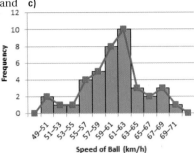

d) around 61 km/h

e) Answers may vary. I think the smaller interval width made it easier to estimate the mean.

f) Answers may vary. The smaller interval width gives a clearer picture of the actual distribution because it better approximates the shape of the frequency distribution.

8. a)

Horizontal Error (cm)	Frequency
(–10)–(–8)	1
(–8)–(–6)	3
(–6)–(–4)	6
(–4)–(–2)	6
(–2)–0	8
0–2	3
2–4	4
4–6	4
6–8	1

b)

Horizontal Error (cm)	Frequency	Relative Frequency
(–10)–(–8)	1	0.0278
(–8)–(–6)	3	0.0833
(–6)–(–4)	6	0.1667
(–4)–(–2)	6	0.1667
(–2)–0	8	0.2222
0–2	3	0.0833
2–4	4	0.1111
4–6	4	0.1111
6–8	1	0.0278

c) 0.5833

d) Answers may vary. A misadjusted sight with a bias to the left would result in more negative values.

9. a) 35.145 cm   **b)** about 2.3612 cm

c) Answers may vary. If a variable is expected to follow a normal distribution, you can take a representative sample. However, there is not enough data to predict whether the distribution is normal. The data given shows that distribution may be centred, but it is unclear whether it will drop off symmetrically to the left and right.

Tree Height (cm)	Frequency
30–32	3
32–34	2
34–36	7
36–38	7
38–40	1

10. a) Calculate the z-score for each student. Determine which student is performing at a higher number of standard deviations from the respective means.
b) Answers may vary. The university must assume that the test are comparable in material and level of difficulty.
c) z-score of region A ≈ 1.4286; z-score of region B $= 1$. Since $1.429 > 1$, the student from region A performed at a level that is further above average than the student from region B.
11. Answers may vary.
a) marks on an exam, heights of plants, battery life, shoe size, masses of infants. Once data is collected and entered into technology, the remaining parts follow a similar procedure to #12.
13. a) 0.1788   **b)** 0.2676   **c)** 0.3108

Extend
14. Answers may vary.
a) To compare the two distributions, use the z-score. Determine the z-score for this year's class and then use that to determine the equivalent score using the historical mean and standard deviation.
b) 76
c) Marks this year might be lower than expected because the calibre of the students has declined.
15. a) Consider the formula for the mean of grouped data, which is the same as the sum of the product of the midpoint of each interval, m_i, and the relative frequency of each interval, rf_i.

$$\bar{x} = \frac{\sum f_i m_i}{\sum f_i}$$
$$= \frac{f_1 m_1 + f_2 m_2 + \cdots f_n m_n}{\sum f_i}$$
$$= \frac{f_1 m_1}{\sum f_i} + \frac{f_2 m_2}{\sum f_i} + \cdots \frac{f_n m_n}{\sum f_i}$$
$$= m_1 \frac{f_1}{\sum f_i} + m_2 \frac{f_2}{\sum f_i} + \cdots m_n \frac{f_n}{\sum f_i}$$
$$= m_1 rf_1 + m_2 rf_2 + \cdots m_n rf_n$$
$$= \sum m_i rf_i$$

b) Determine the midpoint of each interval.

Volume (mL)	Frequency, f	Midpoint, m_i	Relative Frequency, $rf = \dfrac{f}{200}$
490–492	0	491	0.000
492–494	0	493	0.000
494–496	2	495	0.010
496–498	11	497	0.055
498–500	43	499	0.215
500–502	81	501	0.405
502–504	48	503	0.240
504–506	14	505	0.070
506–508	1	507	0.005
508–510	0	509	0.000

$\bar{x} = \sum m_i rf_i$
$= 491(0) + 493(0) + 495(0.10) + \cdots + 509(0)$
$= 501.08$
The mean soft drink volume is 501.08 mL.
c) The value of the mean makes sense. It occurs in the centre of the bell-shaped frequency polygon.

7.3 Applications of the Normal Distribution, pages 346–351

Example Your Turn
a) about 99.7%
b)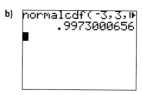

Reflect
R1. Answers may vary. Determine the z-score for a length of 4.7 cm. Use $x = 4.7$, $\bar{x} = 5$, and $s = 0.1$.
$$z = \frac{x - \bar{x}}{s}$$
$$= \frac{4.7 - 5.0}{0.1}$$
$$= -3$$
The probability that the length of a bolt is 4.7 cm or less is only about 0.1%, so this would be a surprising value.
R2. Answers may vary. Each machine produces a normal distribution for the mass of honey in a jar. The distributions have different means, one at 1.05 kg and the other at 1.2 kg. Each also produces a "tail" to the left of 1.0 kg. If the standard deviations are correct, the two tail areas will be equal, i.e., 0.001. Under these conditions, the results are possible.

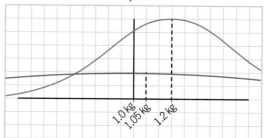

Practise
1. D   **2.** A
3. The probability that a mass is greater than two standard deviations is about 2.3%. Since this represents approximately 1 cat, this claim makes sense.
4. Answers may vary. A quality control engineer would want to ensure that they will actually fit onto the standard bolts. In particular, the internal diameter of the washer must not be smaller the exterior diameter of the bolt shaft.

Apply
5. Answers may vary.
a)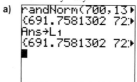
b) mean: about 701 mm, standard deviation: about 20.1 mm
c) They are fairly close to the underlying normal distribution.

d)–f)

Sample Size	Mean (mm)	Standard Deviation (mm)
population	$\mu = 700$	$\sigma = 13.2$
10	$\bar{x} = 701$	$s \approx 20.1$
100	$\bar{x} = 700$	$s \approx 14.9$
1000	$\bar{x} = 700$	$s \approx 13.1$

g) The larger the sample, the closer the sample measures are to the underlying normal distribution.

6. a) 0.0122   **b)** 0.121

7. a) 2.5%   **b)** $11 400

   c) No, 90.82% of the watches fail within 10 years.

8. a) 136 students   **b)** 190 students

   c) about 5 students

9. 0.000 05 in.

11. a) mean: about 503 g, standard deviation: about 2 g

   b) 80%

   c) The expected percent of the data within one standard deviation is 68%. So, these values are more clustered around the mean.

Extend

12. a) about 12.1 g

   b) To ensure that no more than 0.5% of the sandwiches contain less than 200 g of corned beef, Randy could buy a better slicing machine. New standard deviation: about 7.8 g. Randy could increase the slicing machine mean. New mean: about 231.2 g.

   c) Answers may vary. Most likely increasing the slicing machine mean will be more cost effective than buying a new machine.

13. a) For two standard deviations from the mean, $k = 2$. According to Chebyshev's Theorem, no more than $\frac{1}{2^2}$, or 25% of the values lie more than two standard deviations from the mean.

   b) Since 95% of the data values lie within two standard deviations of a normal distribution, then 5% of the data lie outside this range. Chebyshev's Theorem does not exactly agree, but could since the 25% value is a maximum.

   c) The proportion of values that must lie within k standard deviations of the mean is given by $1 - \frac{1}{k^2}$.

7.4 Confidence Intervals, pages 352–361

Example 1 Your Turn

a) about 11.2%   **b)** 63.8% to 86.2%

c) Answers may vary. *Hockey Night in Canada* is watched by 75% of households. This estimate is considered correct within ±11.2%, 99 times out of 100.

Example 2 Your Turn

a) about 2.8%   **b)** increase to about 1561 pills

Example 3 Your Turn

a) mean: 1232.75 h, standard deviation: about 121.24 h

b) about 920.44 h to 1545.06 h

Reflect

R1. No. The confidence level is the probability that a particular statistic is within the range indicated by the margin of error. The confidence level's related z-score is used to calculate the margin of error.

R2. The lower end of the range is 4.2%. The upper end of the range is 7%. The 90% confidence interval for the mean defective tablets within one year is 4.2% to 7%. This is the range of possible percents of defective tablets. This would help the manufacturer budget for returns and provide information on the reliability of the manufacturing process.

R3. 90% confidence interval: 9 times out of 10
99% confidence interval: 99 times out of 100

Practise

1. a) about 1.6   **b)** about 2   **c)** about 2.6

2. B   **3.** D   **4.** 500 km

Apply

5. a) about 19.8%   **b)** 62.2% to 101.8%

   c) Answers may vary. Students recorded a mean mark of 82% ± 19.8%, 99 times out of 100.

6. Answers may vary. For the original poll, the lower end of the range is 30.6%. The upper end of the range is 37.4%. The 95% confidence interval for the average percent of support is 30.6% to 37.4%. The other two polls are both outside of this range, suggesting that support is not consistent.

7. a) mean: about 48.3 g, standard deviation: about 0.45 g. I assumed that the standard deviation stayed the same as the Single Crème line.

   b) about 47.4 g to 49.2 g

   c) Answers may vary. No. The company is not justified in claiming the line contains twice the filling. The Double Crème line contains twice the filling when compared to approximately the lower half of the Single Crème line distribution. So, for only less than half of the cookies is the claim valid.

8. a) about 68.9 min to 75.5 min

   b) Answers may vary. I would advise the manufacturer that 70 min is a reasonable value for t, since it lies within the 95% confidence interval.

9. about 11 to 13

10. about 2

11. 90.5%

12. approximately 59 patients

13. 15 843.2 h to 16 156.8 h

15. Anywhere from 54% to 60% of students would vote for Adam and anywhere from 48% to 54% of students would vote for Meghan with a 95% confidence level.

Extend

16. Answers may vary.

   a) Since the masses of 20-year-old men most likely follow a normal distribution, I would expect to end up with more men close to the population mean, which is consistent with the bell-shaped curve.

   b) This results in the standard deviation of the sample mean being smaller than that of the population.

   c) The effect in part b) fits with the formula for the standard deviation of the sample, $\sigma_{\bar{x}} = \frac{\sigma}{\sqrt{n}}$. The standard deviation of the population is divided by $\sqrt{n}$, thus decreasing the value.

17. $z = 1.960$, $E \le 0.02$

$$E = z\sqrt{\frac{p(1-p)}{n}}$$

$$0.02 \ge 1.960\sqrt{\frac{p(1-p)}{n}}$$

$$\frac{0.02}{1.960} \ge \sqrt{\frac{p(1-p)}{n}}$$

$$\left(\frac{0.02}{1.960}\right)^2 \ge \frac{p(1-p)}{n}$$

$$n \ge p(1-p)\left(\frac{1.960}{0.02}\right)^2$$

$$n \ge 9604p(1-p)$$

The minimum number of voters who must be interviewed is 2401.

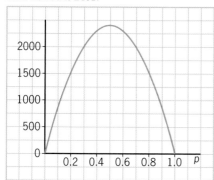

7.5 Connections to Discrete Random Variables, pages 362–371

Example 1 Your Turn

a) $np = 6.25$ and $nq = 18.75$. Since both are greater than 5, the normal approximation is reasonable in this case.

b) mean: 6.25, standard deviation: about 2.165

c) about 0.718

Example 2 Your Turn

a) There are 90 sock in the drawer, of which 7 are chosen. The number of trials is less than 10% of the population. The normal approximation is reasonable for this hypergeometric distribution.

b) mean: about 2.333, standard deviation: about 1.204

c) about 0.441

Reflect

R1. Answers may vary. For example, number of heads when flipping a coin or failure rate for quality control.

R2. Answers may vary. For example, choosing certain people to be on a committee or the number of a particular type of card in a five-card hand.

R3. Answers may vary. Using the approximation allows the probabilities of value ranges to be calculated more easily than with the binomial or hypergeometric formulas.

R4. Answers may vary. In the case of the normal approximation for a binomial distribution, any scenario where $np \le 5$ or $nq \le 5$. In the case of the normal approximation for a hypergeometric distribution, any scenario where the number of dependent trials is greater than or equal to 10% of the population.

Practise

1. A   **2.** D   **3.** 31 rolls   **4.** 5 balls

5. a) Technically, 10% of the population is 0.10(52), or 5.2. So, five cards meets the restriction.

b) 1.25   **c)** about 0.930

Apply

6. a) about 0.1024   **b)** about 0.1118

c) Answers may vary. Since both np and nq are greater than five, I would expect close agreement between the two methods.

7. a)

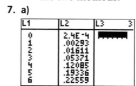

b)

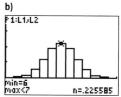

c) the probability of a particular number of heads

d) 1

e) Yes; the probability distribution is centred around a value and drops off symmetrically to the right and left forming a bell-like shape.

f)

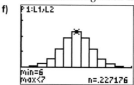

g) When tossing coins, the mean is $\mu = 6$ and the standard deviation is

$$\sigma = \sqrt{(npq)}$$
$$= \sqrt{12 \times 0.5 \times 0.5}$$
$$\approx 1.732$$

Using normalcdf(–0.5,12.5,6,1.732), the probability is about 0.9998.

h) The areas are the same, 1.

8. a) about 0.0584

b) Since np is less than 5, it is not reasonable to model this distribution using a normal approximation.

c) mean: 2.5, standard deviation: about 1.369

d) about 0.0578.

e) The answers to parts a) and d) are very close. They both round to 5.8%.

10. a) about 0.0586

b) Answers may vary. I chose to use the normal approximation for a hypergeometric distribution because of the number of calculations needed to calculate $P(X \ge 10)$ using the hypergeometric distribution.

11. a) 0.0735

b) No; the population mean and standard deviation are given for the normal distribution.

c) about 505.02 g

Extend

12. a) about 0   **b)** about 0.1016.

13. a) 6   **b)** about 0.2649

c) Answers may vary. No. With a probability of 26.5% that this scenario could happen by chance, there is not enough information to conclude that the program was effective. More data needs to be collected. If the program was effective, I would expect the probability of 4 or fewer drivers being distracted to be higher.

Chapter 7 Review, pages 372–374

1. **a)** The data are difficult to analyse in this form. It is not obvious whether the distribution is uniform or not.
   b) Use a table to determine the frequency for each interval. If all frequencies are equal, then the distribution is uniform.

Percent Oxygen	Frequency
31.7–31.8	3
31.8–31.9	3
31.9–32.0	3
32.0–32.1	3
32.1–32.2	3

This distribution is uniform.

2. **a)** approximately 0.263 **b)** 0.4997 **c)** 0.263
3. **a)** and **b)**

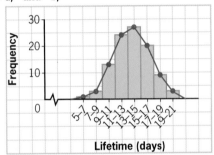

Lifetime (days)

   c) 14 days
4. **a)**

Lifetime (days)	Frequency	Relative Frequency
5–7	1	0.01
7–9	3	0.03
9–11	13	0.13
11–13	24	0.24
13–15	27	0.27
15–17	20	0.20
17–19	9	0.09
19–21	3	0.03

   b) 0.01 **c)** 0.71
5. **a)** mean: 39.225 cm
   b) standard deviation: about 5.8260 cm
   c)

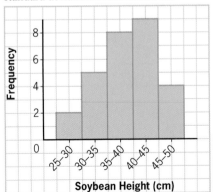

Soybean Height (cm)

   d) Answers may vary. No. While the distribution is somewhat bell-shaped, it is negatively skewed.
6. 0.1151
7. **a)** about 1.6% **b)** 0.0894

8. about 0.1052
9. **a)** about 7.9% **b)** 34.1% to 49.9%
10. **a)** 1562.75 km
    b) 188 437.25 km to 191 562.75 km
11. **a)** about 0.8941
    b) Since nq is less than 5, it is not reasonable to model this distribution using a normal approximation.
    c) mean: 61.75, standard deviation: about 1.757.
    d) about 0.8834
    e) The answer to part a) is slightly higher than that of part d), approximately 89% compared to 88%.
12. **a)** Answers may vary. No; the class is not a representative sample of the population of the town because it is only comprised of high school students.
    b) The number of trials is less than 10% of the population. The normal approximation is reasonable for this hypergeometric distribution.
    c) mean: 2.5, standard deviation: about 1.4948
    d) about 0.0905
    e) In this situation, $n = 3500$, $r = 25$, and $a = 350$.
    $$P(x \geq 5) = 1 - P(0) - P(1) - P(2) - P(3) - P(4)$$
    $$\approx 0.6430$$

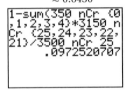

The probability that at least five students have the flu is about 0.0973.
The normal approximation results in a higher probability, about 9.7% versus 9.0%.

Chapter 7 Test Yourself, pages 375–377

1. C **2.** B **3.** C **4.** B **5.** C **6.** B **7.** 0.2
8. **a)** 10 students **b)** 0.78
9. 0.0918
10. 492.4 h
11. **a)** Since np and nq are both greater than 5, it is reasonable to model this distribution using a normal approximation.
    b) mean: 750, standard deviation: about 13.693
12. **a)** and **b)**

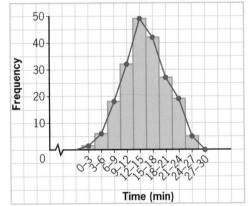

Time (min)

c) Yes. Since the probability distribution is centred around a value and drops off mostly symmetrically to the right and left forming a bell-like shape, the data appear to follow a normal distribtion.

13. a) about 3.7%   **b)** about 102 dB

14. 79.8% to 88.2%

15. a) hypergeometric probability distribution; there are two outcomes, success and failure, and all trials are dependent.
   b) Yes; the number of trials is less than 10% of the population.
   c) mean: 29.01, standard deviation: about 0.9463.
   d) about 0.9383

Chapter 8 Two-Variable Data Analysis

Prerequisite Skills, pages 380–381

1. a) upward and positive
   b) Answers may vary. As precipitation increases, visibility and speed decrease, so travel time increases.

2. a)

   b) downward and negative
   c) Answers may vary. Using a line of best and interpolate: about 6.4 m/s.

3. a)
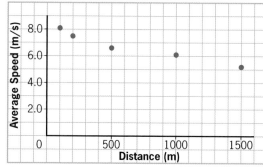
   b) Answers may vary. With the exception of two outliers, the general trend is upward and positive.

4. a)
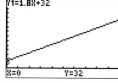
   b) $F = 32$. This is the vertical intercept and means that 0° C equals 32° F.

   c) 1.8° F/°C. Every 1° C change results in a 1.8° F.
   d) 25° C = 77° F
   e) $F = 1.8C + 32$
      $= 1.8(25) + 32$
      $= 77$
   f) Answers may vary.

5. a) 50° F = 10° C   **b)** 50° F = 10° C
   c) Answers may vary.

6. a) Because only the football team are asked, it is likely the respondents will overwhelmingly want to increase the football program's budget. This is sampling bias.
   b) Answers may vary. Survey the entire student body.

7. Usually, the people who call in to radio shows are those with extreme opinions. People who are indifferent or do not think the topic is important may not vote, so a large proportion of listeners choose not to respond. This is non-response bias. Also, since only listeners of the radio show will call in, sampling bias is present, too; the respondents likely would not properly represent the entire population.

8. a) mean: 1.6 m, median: 1.5 m, mode: 1.5 m
   b) Outliers have a greater effect on the mean than other measures. In this case, they increase the value of the mean.
   c) standard deviation: about 0.1844 m; z-score: about 1.63

9. a) 7   **b)** 7
   c) 2; it represents the "middle half" of the data.

8.1 Line of Best Fit, pages 382–391

Example 1 Your Turn
Answers may vary.
a)   **b)**
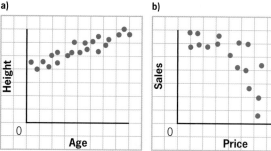

c)
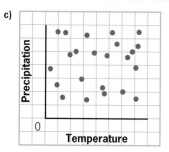

Example 2 Your Turn
a)
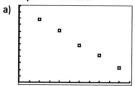

   b) $r \approx -0.999$
   c) $d = -0.189t + 11.71$; the cyclist started 11.71 km from home and cycled at a rate of 0.189 km/min toward home.
   d) Answers may vary. The value of r, which can be between −1 and 1, gives an indication of how closely the data points relate to the line of best fit.

Reflect

R1. a)

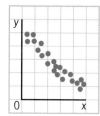

b) The correlation coefficient, r, would be somewhere between -0.67 and -1.

R2. a)

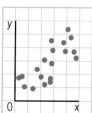

b) The correlation coefficient, r, would be somewhere between 0.33 and 0.67.

R3. Answers may vary. $r \approx 0.995$, so there is a near perfect positive linear correlation between distance and time. The equation of the line of best fit is $d = 0.51t + 0.49$. The equation shows that the student started 0.49 m from the motion sensor and walked at a rate of 0.51 m/s away from the sensor.

Practise

1. C   **2.** B   **3.** D

4. Answers may vary.

a) same: equation of line of best fit, initial distance, walking away at same rate
different: Tracey's pace is more consistent

b)

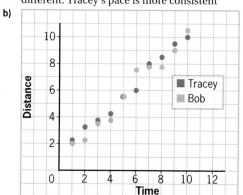

Apply

5. a)

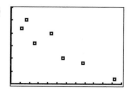

b) strong negative linear correlation

c) $r \approx -0.93$. Yes, r is between -1 and -0.67.

6. a) a weak moderate linear correlation. $r \approx 0.39$

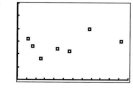

b) a weak linear correlation. $r \approx -0.27$

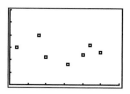

7. Answers may vary.

8. Answers may vary.

a)

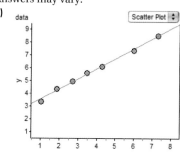

$y = 0.781x + 2.8; r^2 = 1.00$

b)

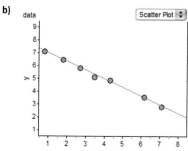

$y = -0.675x + 7.6; r^2 = 1.00$

c)

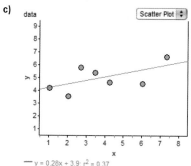

$y = 0.28x + 3.9; r^2 = 0.37$

d)

$y = -0.000223x + 5.6; r^2 = 0.000000050$

9. Answers may vary.

a)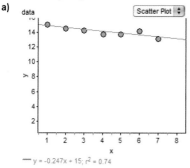
— $y = -0.247x + 15$; $r^2 = 0.74$

b) The line of best fit starts at the point where $x = 0$ and $y = 15$. The line drops 0.25 on the y-axis for each incremental increase on the x-axis. Because $r^2 = 0.75$, $r \approx -0.866$. There is a strong linear correlation, so the data points are close to the line of best fit.

11. a)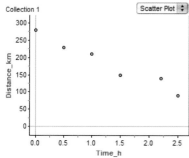

b) and c) Several boxes appear. An equation for the line and the sum of squares appear.

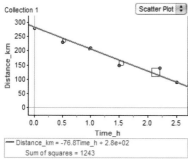
— Distance_km = -76.8Time_h + 2.8e+02
  Sum of squares = 1243

d) Estimates may vary. 1103
e) The sum of squares for the line of best fit is 990.7.

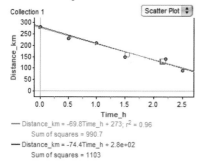
— Distance_km = -69.8Time_h + 273; $r^2 = 0.96$
  Sum of squares = 990.7
— Distance_km = -74.4Time_h + 2.8e+02
  Sum of squares = 1103

Extend

12. Answers may vary. From #5, $r^2 \approx 0.86$. Since the value is fairly close to 1, the choice of linear regression is a pretty good fit. From #6, $r^2 \approx 0.15$. Since the value is much closer to 0 than 1, linear regression is a poor fit.

13. Answers may vary.
a) The coefficient of determination allows you to check the closeness of fit for non-linear regression situations.
b) values from 0 to 1
c) Both coefficients test how well a model fits the data. The correlation coefficient only applies to linear regression, while the coefficient of determination applies to any type of regression curve. The coefficients also take on different values: $-1 \le r \le 1$ and $0 \le r^2 \le 1$.

8.2 Cause and Effect, pages 392–401

Example 1 Your Turn
a) $r \approx 0.88$, suggesting a strong correlation between number of successful free throws and hours spent practising. Since most coaches agree that long practise hours will result in higher scoring, it is reasonable to characterize this relationship as an example of cause and effect.
b) The value of the correlation coefficient suggests that the line of best fit for these data is relatively good for predicting a team member's free throw performance. The equation relating free throws, n, to hours studied, h, is $n = 1.4h$. The linear model predicts no successful free throws if a team member does not practise at all. The rate of change is 1.4, which means that successful free throws will increase by approximately 1.4 for each additional hour practised.
c) This model suggests that continually increasing practice will result in more than 10 successful attempts out of 10 tries, which is impossible.

Example 2 Your Turn
Answers may vary. It is more likely that a common cause is involved, such as climate change.

Example 3 Your Turn
Answers may vary.
a) cause and effect; Many studies have shown that a patient's stress level can be reduced by exercise.
b) common cause relationship; Both of these variables likely share a positive correlation with strong study habits.
c) accidental relationship; No clear connection exists between pancake sales and the amount of rainfall.
d) presumed relationship; It seems logical that a person from a stable relationship with assumed good communication skills would interview well. It would be difficult to suggest that one causes the other.

Reflect
R1. It does not explain how and why such a correlation exists.
R2. Answers may vary.
Cases of the flu and the amount of severe winter weather most likely have a presumed relationship. Cold weather does not cause the flu.
Cases of the flu and tissue sales most likely have a reverse cause and effect relationship. More tissues are purchased when more people are sick.
The amount of severe winter weather and tissue sales most likely have a common cause effect relationship. More people are sick during the winter and sick people buy more tissues.

R3. Answers may vary.
  a) caffeine consumption causes nervousness
  b) nervous people are more likely to drink coffee
R4. Answers may vary.
  a) The number of females enrolled in undergraduate engineering programs and the number of reality shows on TV both increased for several years.
  b) These are likely to be coincidental.

Practise
  1. D   **2.** B   **3.** B
  4. a) No. More people at the ski resort most likely results in increased sales of many items, not just hot chocolate.
     b) An increase in the number of customers.

Apply
  5. a) Answers may vary.   **b)** Yes; many hours of dedicated practise typically results in better performance.

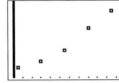

  6. Answers may vary.
     a) reverse cause and effect: grass growth is directly affected by the amount of rainfall
     b) common cause: arm length and leg length are typically related to height
     c) accidental: there is no obvious connection between sandwich sales and dog bites
     d) presumed: it seems logical that sports would be of interest to fit people but difficult to prove one variable affects the other
     e) presumed: it seems logical that cases of diabetes would decrease with healthy eating habits, however this only lowers the risk as other factors also play a role
     f) common cause: both heart disease and lung cancer can be tied to smoking
  7. a) It is unlikely that eating more fast food would cause a person to sleep less.
     b) Answers may vary. The person's overall health.
  8. a) No. Ice cream consumption is not likely to cause heat stroke. Heat stroke is generally caused by extremely hot weather.
     b) This relation is likely a common cause relationship; incidents of heat stroke and ice cream sales are likely to increase when the weather is hot.
  9. a) The deer population sustains the wolf population.
     b) Wolf population would decline as its source of food declines.
  11. a) 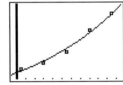 strong negative correlation
     b) By definition of demand, the variables are directly related, so it is reasonable to characterize this relationship as likely cause and effect.

  c) Because price affects demand, price is the independent variable and demand is the dependent variable.
  12. a) strong positive correlation
     b) By definition of supply, the variables are directly related, so it is reasonable to characterize this relationship as likely cause and effect.
     c) Because price affects supply, price is the independent variable and supply is the dependent variable.
  13. a) **b)** (13, 13.36). This shows the quantity for which demand and supply are the same price.

Intersection
X=13   Y=13.360656

  c) Answers may vary. Above $13.36: supply increases but demand drops. Below $13.36: demand increases but supply drops.

Extend
  14. a) **b)** Yes. The relationship appears to show a strong positive linear correlation.

  c) $r \approx 0.98$, indicating a very good linear fit.
  d) The shape of the curve passes very close to the data points.
  e) $r^2 \approx 0.99$, indicating that this is a better model for the data.
  f) As new housing developments are constructed, the population increases at a faster rate.
  15. Answers may vary.

8.3 Dynamic Analysis of Two-Variable Data, pages 402–415

Example 1 Your Turn
  a) and **c)**

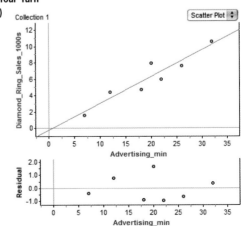

As advertising increases, diamond ring sales increase. $r = \sqrt{0.89} \approx 0.94$ confirms a strong positive correlation. A linear model is appropriate.

b) For (20, 7.9), the residual is 1.65, which means that the actual duration of advertising is 1.65 min greater than what the linear model predicts.
For (18, 4.7), the residual is –0.894, which means that the actual duration of advertising is 0.894 min less than what the linear model predicts.

c) There is no clear pattern in the residual plot.

Example 2 Your Turn

a)–c)

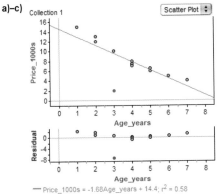

Price_1000s = -1.68Age_years + 14.4; r^2 = 0.58

This line of best fit is not a good model for the data. The extrapolated vertical intercept suggests around $15 500 for a brand-new motorcycle, which does not sound right if a 1-year bike is $15 000. The correlational coefficient, $r = -\sqrt{0.58} \approx -0.76$, suggests a moderately strong linear correlation, but, except for one point, (3, 2), the data appear to form a much stronger linear trend.
The residual of (3, 2) is much farther from the residual line than the other residuals which appear to have a pattern. This suggests that the outlier has a strong influence on the linear model.

d)

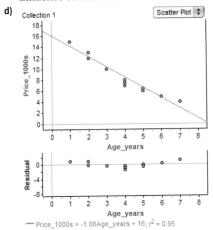

Price_1000s = -1.88Age_years + 16; r^2 = 0.95

e) The original linear model was influenced by the outlier. After the outlier was removed from the analysis, the linear model appeared to be quite strong.

Example 3 Your Turn

Answers may vary. No. Looking at the data points from 1996 to 2006, only (2005, 6.4) appears to be a possible outlier. If the paternity leave had a significant effect, I would expect the correlation coefficient to be closer to the low end of the moderate range.

Reflect

R1. Answers may vary. A residual plot shows the value of each residual graphically as the vertical distance from a horizontal axis.

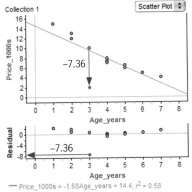

Price_1000s = -1.68Age_years + 14.4; r^2 = 0.58

R2. a) A data point that does not fit well in an otherwise linear trend.

b) In a scatter plot, the outlier is relatively far from the line of best fit. In a residual plot, an outlier is either relatively far above or below the horizontal line.

Practise

1. C   2. D   3. C

4. a)

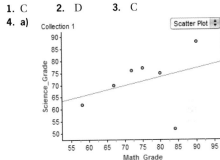

Science_Grade = 0.36Math_Grade + 44.4; r^2 = 0.11

b) No. $r \approx 0.33$, which suggests weak linear correlation, but, except for one point, (84, 52), the data appear to form a much stronger linear trend.

5. a)

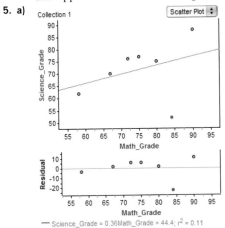

Science_Grade = 0.36Math_Grade + 44.4; r^2 = 0.11

b) –22.64.

c) It is much farther from the residual line than the other residuals.

6. a) This line of best fit appears to serve as a very good model for the data. $r \approx 0.96$, which suggests a strong linear correlation.

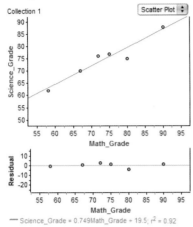

Science_Grade = 0.749Math_Grade + 19.5; r^2 = 0.92

This appears to be a strong linear model for predicting the science grade based on a math grade.

b) The original linear model was influenced by an outlier. After the outlier was removed from the analysis, the linear model appeared to be quite strong.

Apply

7. a) 40%; all of Jonathon's other marks were in the 80s.

b) mean: 74%, median: 83%, mode: 83%

c) In this case, removing the outlier only impacted the mean, which is now 83%, the same as the median and the mode.

8. a) and **b)** With the exception of one point, (26, 780), the data appear to have a strong positive linear correlation.

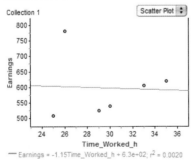

Earnings = -1.15Time_Worked_h + 6.3e+02; r^2 = 0.0020

b) $r \approx -0.04$, which suggests a very weak linear correlation.
The equation of the line of best fit is $e = -1.15t + 630$. The equation shows that earnings start at $630 and decrease at a rate of $1.15 per hour worked.

c) No. This model makes no sense and is unrealistic.

9. a)

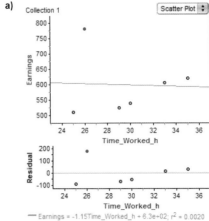

Earnings = -1.15Time_Worked_h + 6.3e+02; r^2 = 0.0020

b) The residual of (26, 780) is much farther from the residual line than the other residuals. This suggests that the outlier has a strong influence on the linear model. This unusual data point could be caused by overly generous tippers.

c) This line of best fit appears to serve as a very good model for the data. $r \approx 0.95$, which suggests a strong linear correlation.

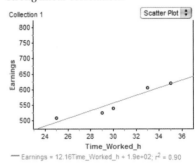

Earnings = 12.16Time_Worked_h + 1.9e+02; r^2 = 0.90

The equation of the line of best fit is $e = 12.16t + 190$. The equation shows that earnings start at $190 and increase at a rate of $12.16 per hour worked. This is a useful linear model that is realistic.

10. Answers may vary.

11. a) An overall negative trend over the 50-year period.

b) Answers may vary. There are two distinct trends, between 1940 and 1943 and between 1968 and 2001, with the first being negative and the second positive.

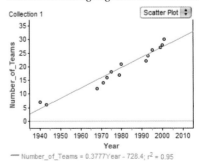

Number_of_Teams = 0.3777Year - 728.4; r^2 = 0.95

From 1968 on, the league added teams. The expansions of the league could be a hidden variable that might account for the correlation shown in the Montréal Canadiens Stanley Cup Wins graph.

12. Answers may vary. While a lockout cancelled the entire 2004–05 NHL season, it is only one season in the decade and may not invalidate the general trend shown in this study.

13. Answers may vary. Yes. During the 50s and 60s, the Canadiens competed in a league of six teams. However, in the 1970s they competed in a league ranging from 12 to 18 teams and managed to win the greatest number of Stanley Cups during that time.

Extend

15. **a)** Any points above the line of best fit will have a positive residual and any below the line will have a negative residual.
    b) 0. By definition, the line of best fit typically has a number of points above and below it, so the positive error will balance out the negative error, resulting in a sum of 0.

16. Answers may vary.

8.4 Uses and Misuses of Data, pages 416–423

Example 1 Your Turn

a)

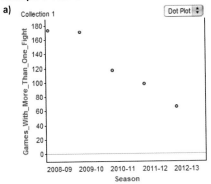

b) There is an outlier (2012-13, 66) due to a hidden variable. Only 720 games were played during this season due to a labour disruption. It should be removed because it exaggerates the downward trend.

c) Sample size is another source of bias. Only five points were chosen, perhaps to hide that the trend is less downward over a longer period of time.

Example 2 Your Turn

Answers may vary. No. This could be a typical percent of UFO sightings for Ontario, since approximately 40% of the population of Canada resides in Ontario.

Reflect

R1. Answers may vary.
  a) choice of scales or titles on a graph, sample size, use of outliers, making inappropriate conclusions
  b) to grab the attention of the viewer, for humour, to sway opinion, or to exaggerate a point

R2. Answers may vary.
  a) To get more sales.
  b) how the data were collected, the sample size, and what exactly "twice as popular" means

R3. Answers may vary.
  a) Sensationalism is a type of bias where a piece of work uses tactics such as over-exaggeration to provoke an emotional response.
  b) to provoke controversy or discussion or to gain attention

Practise

1. D   2. A   3. B

4. **a)** not reliable
   b) the sample size, whether there was any bias in the survey of sampling technique.
   c) to sell more tabloid newspapers

Apply

5. **a)** (Oct-13, 34). It should be excluded from the analysis since it does not include the whole month of October's data.

   b)

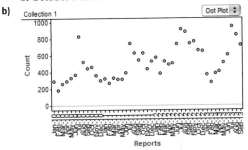

   c) Answers may vary. No, it appears to rise and fall with some regularity each year.

6. **a)** Sightings reach a maximum in the summer months and a minimum in the winter months.
   b) Answers may vary. No. People probably spend more time outside in the evenings during the summer months than in the winter months.

7. Answers may vary.
   a) Yes. There may be voluntary response bias as those who claim sightings are more likely to believe in extra-terrestrial beings and therefore more likely to misinterpret a normal event as a UFO sighting.
   b) Is the sample representative of the population? What type of sampling technique and data collections methods were used? Are the data verified?

Extend

9. Answers may vary.
   a) and **b)** Voter turnout in Australia seems very consistent at just over 80%. This is due to a compulsory voting system in which electors are obliged to vote. Voter turnout for Canada appears to be declining slightly. According to the Conference Board of Canada, this may be due to lower participation of young people. Voter turnout for Switzerland appears to remain at about the 40% mark. The Swiss government is highly decentralized with limited powers, and referendums for important decisions are common, so individual votes for the federal legislature are less likely to have a significant effect on the nation.

10. Answers may vary.

8.5 Advanced Techniques for Data Analysis, pages 424–433

Example 1 Your Turn

Row Labels	Average of Heart Rate 1 Min After Exercise (bpm)	Average of Heart Rate 30 Min After Exercise (bpm)
A	118.6	77.6
B	131.5	91.33333333
Grand Total	125.6363636	85.09090909

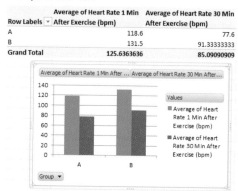

Both the pivot table and chart show that marathon runners had a lower average heart rate 1 min after exercise than non-runners, with an average of 118.6 bpm compared to 131.5 bpm. They also show that marathon runners had a lower average heart rate 30 min after exercise than non-runners with an average of 77.6 bpm compared to 91.3 bpm.

Example 2 Your Turn

a) There appears to be a fairly strong linear correlation between run time and distance. $r \approx 0.76$, which suggests a mildly strong linear correlation.

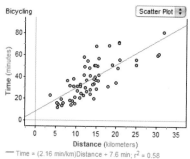

The altitude attribute scale confirms that altitude is obscuring the linear correlation between run time and distance. The uphill runs tend to have longer run times than the downhill runs.

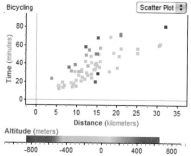

b) With the exception of (18.2 km, 69 min, –60 m) and (31.8 km, 81 min, –860 m), the results are consistent with those in the example. Perhaps something occurred on those two runs to cause the unusual times, like an accident, construction, or flat tire.

Reflect

R1. a) a table which subdivides data into two or more categories
   b) for comparing quantitative data across different categories

R2. a) to compare aggregate resting heart rate and maximum heart rate scores
   b) Group A had both a lower resting heart and a lower working heart rate than Group B.

R3. They showed the influence of a third variable by confirming that change in altitude was obscuring the linear correlation between run time and distance.

R4. Answers may vary.

Practise

1. B   2. C   3. C
4. males: about 2.15 h, females: about 2.4 h

Apply

5. standard deviation [StdDev()], standard error [StdError()], and the count for the number of cases for which a value of a specified attribute is missing [count(missing())]

6. minimum value [min()], first quartile [Q1()], median [median()], third quartile [Q3()], and maximum value [max()]

7. a) and b)

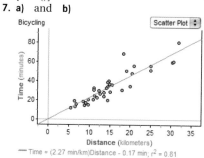

b) $r = 0.9$, which suggests a strong linear correlation. The equation of the line of best fit is $t = 2.27d - 0.17$. The equation shows that time starts at –0.17 min, which makes no sense, and increases at a rate of 2.27 min/km.

8. a) and b) $r \approx 0.89$, which suggests a strong linear correlation. The equation of the line of best fit is $t = 3.23d + 4.4$. The equation shows that time starts at 4.4 min and increases at a rate of 3.23 min/km.

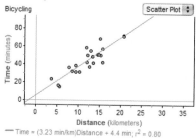

b) While the two linear models differ, it makes sense that the rate for the downhill runs (2.27 min/km) would be less than the rate for the uphill runs (3.23 min/km).

9. a) and b)

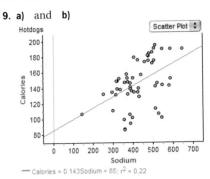

— Calories = 0.143Sodium + 85; r^2 = 0.22

$r \approx 0.47$, which suggests a barely moderate linear correlation.

c) beef: $r \approx 0.89$, which suggests a fairly strong linear correlation.

meat: $r \approx 0.87$, which suggests a fairly strong linear correlation.

poultry: $r \approx 0.66$, which suggests a solid moderate linear correlation.

Each of the individual meat types has an improved linear correlation compared to the original model.

d) Yes. This can be confirmed with the legend attribute.

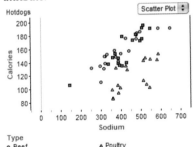

Type	
o Beef	▲ Poultry
▪ Meat	

10. a)

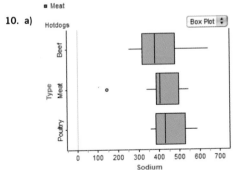

b)

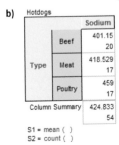

		Sodium
Type	Beef	401.15 20
	Meat	418.529 17
	Poultry	459 17
Column Summary		424.833 54

S1 = mean ( )
S2 = count ( )

Beef hotdogs have the lowest mean sodium of about 401 mg compared to about 418 mg for meat and 459 mg for poultry.

11. a)

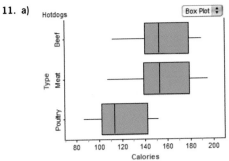

b)

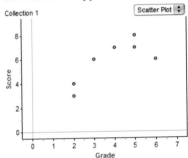

		Calories
Type	Beef	156.85 20
	Meat	158.706 17
	Poultry	118.765 17
Column Summary		145.444 54

S1 = mean ( )
S2 = count ( )

Poultry hotdogs have the lowest mean calories of about 119 calories per hotdog compared to about 157 calories per beef hotdog and about 159 calories per meat hotdog.

13. a) The correlation appears to be a strong positive one.

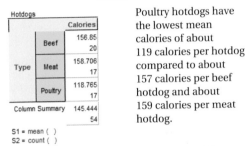

b)

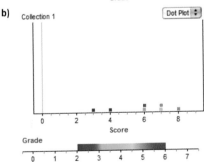

c) The colour trend in the dot plot shows the correlation between grade and score; the purple and blue dots represent younger grades and they tend to have lower scores than the orange and red dots that represent older grades.

Extend

14. a)

b) A tiny line graph representing each row of data appears.

15. a) data trends

b) Answers may vary. They do not include actual data values, so it is difficult to compare with other data sets.

c) The sparkline for the Green party distorts the data. These mini-graphs are each absolute, not relative.

Chapter 8 Review, pages 434–435

1. graph on the left: –0.97; graph on the right: 0.56

2. a)

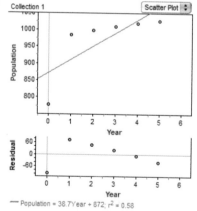

b) strong negative correlation between distance and time

c) $r \approx -0.999$, which suggests a strong linear correlation. The equation of the line of best fit is $d = -145t + 572.5$. The equation shows that the initial distance from home was 572.5 km and the distance decreases at a rate of –145 km/h.

3. a) As self-esteem increases, so does the level of achievement.

b) As the level of achievement increases, so does self-esteem.

4. a) reverse cause: it is more likely that computer sales drop with increased unemployment

b) accidental: there is no obvious connection between the price of gas and the performance of a football team

c) cause and effect: heart rate is directly affected by running speed

5. a)–c)

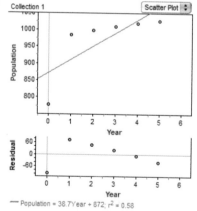

Population = 38.7Year + 872; r^2 = 0.58

With the exception of (0, 778), the data appear to have a strong positive linear correlation.

b) $r \approx 0.76$, which suggests a mildly strong linear correlation. The equation of the line of best fit is $p = 38.7y - 872$. The equation shows that the population started in year zero at about 872, and increased at a rate of 38.7 students per year. This is not very accurate and is likely due to the outlier at (0, 778).

c) The residual of (0, 778) is much farther from the residual line than the other residuals and the other points form a pattern. This suggests that this is not a good linear model.

6. a) An outlier can have a strong impact on a linear regression model if the number of data points is relatively small. The outlier is due to a hidden variable, only three grade levels. It should be removed because it exaggerates the upward trend.

b) This line of best fit appears to serve as a very good model for the data. $r \approx 0.99$ which suggests strong linear correlation.

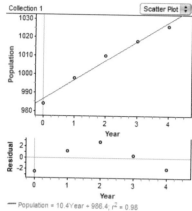

Population = 10.4Year + 986.4; r^2 = 0.98

The equation of the line of best fit is $p = 10.4y + 986.4$. The equation shows that the population started in year zero at about 986, and increased at a rate of 10.4 students per year. This is an accurate reflection of the school's initial population and rate of growth.

There is no obvious pattern to the residuals and none appear overly far from the residual line. This appears to be a strong linear model for predicting the population based on year.

c) original model: about 1220 students; corrected model: about 1080 students

The principal should rely on the corrected model because it is more accurate.

7. a) a general downward trend between circulation andyear

b) Yes, there are two distinct trends, from 2005 to 2008 and from 2009 to 2012, which suggests a hidden variable.

c) In 2009, and that is what likely caused the sudden drop in circulation.

d) The price change is what caused the fragmented trend.

8. Since the vertical scale does not start at 0, it exaggerates the downward trend.

9. Answers may vary.

a) The language is not neutral.

b) "Newspaper circulation declines"

10. a) and b)

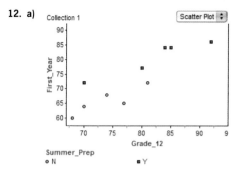

Collection 1 — Scatter Plot

First_Year = 1.054Grade_12 - 9.1; $r^2 = 0.78$

$r \approx 0.88$, which suggests a strong linear correlation.

c) Answers may vary. It is unclear whether the summer prep course was helpful. It is most likely a hidden variable that is obscuring the linear correlation.

11. a)

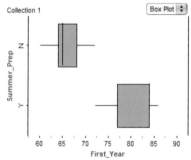

Collection 1 — Box Plot

(Summer_Prep vs Grade_12)

Collection 1 — Box Plot

(Summer_Prep vs First_Year)

Collection 1

Summer_Prep		Grade_12	First_Year
N		74	65.8
		5	5
Y		82.2	80.6
		5	5
Column Summary		78.1	73.2
		10	10

S1 = mean ( )
S2 = count ( )

b) Students who took the summer prep course had higher mean grade 12 calculus marks of about 82 compared to a mean of 74 for students that did not take the summer prep course. Students that took the summer prep course had higher mean first year university marks, with a mean of about 81 compared to a mean of about 66 for students that did not take the summer prep course, so the summer prep course seems to have been helpful.

12. a)

Collection 1 — Scatter Plot

(First_Year vs Grade_12)

Summer_Prep
o N   ■ Y

b) The summer prep attribute scale confirms that students who took the summer prep course had higher marks than those who did not. This confirms that the summer prep course is helpful.

Chapter 8 Test Yourself, pages 436–437

1. a) A   **b)** D
2. D   **3.** D
4. Answers may vary.
  a) common cause: snow tire sales and hot chocolate sales are typically related to winter
  b) reverse cause and effect: it is more likely that box office sales drop with increased ticket prices
  c) presumed: it seems logical that height can play a role in driving safely but difficult to prove one variable affects the other
  d) accidental: there is no obvious connection between cheeseburger sales and pita sales
5. Answers may vary.
  a) As a team's position in the league standings increases, so does attendance at games. People like to support and watch winning teams, so the better the team, the better the support by fans willing to attend games.
  b) As attendance at games increases, so does a team's position in the league standings. As the team gets more support and encouragement, they improve and move up in the standings.
6. a)

a strong positive correlation between speed and time

b) $r \approx 0.996$. The equation of the line of best fit is $s = 3.91t + 0.66$. The equation shows the skydiver's speed started as 0.66 m/s and increased at a rate of 3.91 m/s.

7. a) and b)

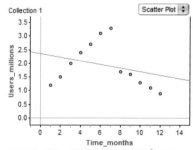

Collection 1 — Scatter Plot

Users_millions = -0.065Time_months + 2.3; $r^2 = 0.085$

There are two separate trends, one upward and one downward.

b) $r \approx 0.29$, which suggests a fairly weak linear correlation. The equation of the line of best fit is $u = -0.065t + 2.3$. The equation shows that the number of users started at 2 300 000 and decreased at a rate of –0.065 million users per month.

c)

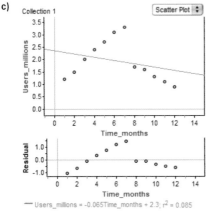

—Users_millions = -0.065Time_months + 2.3; r² = 0.085

The residuals form two linear patterns which suggests that this is not a good linear model.

d) The fragmented trend is evidence of a hidden variable. Something happened in month 8.

e) The website started charging a fee in month 8. That is what caused the break in the trend, and changed it from positive to negative.

f)

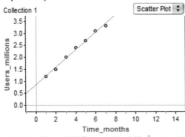

g) The equation of the line of best fit for the positive trend is $u = 0.364t + 0.86$ shows that the number of users started at 860 000 and increased at a rate of 0.86 million users per month. Analyse the sets separately.

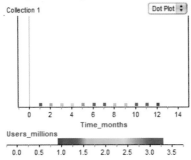

—Users_millions = 0.364Time_months + 0.86; r² = 0.99

Time_months < 8

The line of best fit for the latter negative trend, $u = -0.21t + 3.4$, indicates that the social networking site is headed towards no users within another five months.

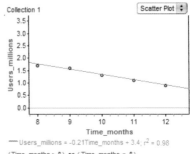

—Users_millions = -0.21Time_months + 3.4; r² = 0.98
(Time_months > 8) or (Time_months = 8)

The most common way for social networking sites to make money is by allowing companies to advertise on their site. If the website wants to grow its user base, I think they should drop the fee. Then, the first positive trend can be used to predict the future popularity of this website, assuming that the users return.

Chapters 7 and 8 Cumulative Review, pages 438–439

1. a) Yes. **b)** about 0.1 **c)** 0.5
   d) Answers may vary. I expect the distribution to no longer be uniform if the general population was measured due to the wide range of wellness.

2. a) and **b)**

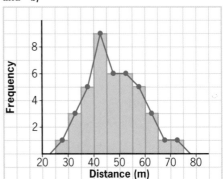

c) around 42.5 m

d)

Distance (m)	Frequency	Relative Frequency
25–30	1	0.025
30–35	3	0.075
35–40	5	0.125
40–45	9	0.225
45–50	6	0.150
50–55	6	0.150
55–60	5	0.125
60–65	3	0.075
65–70	1	0.025
70–75	1	0.025

e) 0.125

f) Answers may vary. The entire distribution would move to the left. This would be due to the reduced skill level in throwing a discus.

3. a) 0.62%
   b) 10.56%
   c) Answers may vary. I would expect the entire distribution to move to the right. The mean would increase as well as the standard deviation. This

would be due to the reduced skill level in building airplane kits.

4. a) 3.7% to 7.9%
   b) Answers may vary. 5.8% of industrial wind turbines will not meet the standard. This estimate is considered correct within ±2.1%, 99 times out of 100.

5. a) Since np and nq are both greater than 5, it is reasonable to model this distribution using a normal approximation.
   b) mean: 30, standard deviation: about 5.422
   c) about 0.04.
   d) Answers may vary. Since the probability is higher, the company is not justified in its new claim.

6. a)

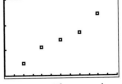 a strong positive correlation

   b) $r \approx 0.987$. The equation of the line of best fit is $d = 0.044t + 1$. The equation shows the hiker started 1 km from camp and hiked at a rate of 0.044 km/min away from camp.

7. Answers may vary.
   a) No. It seems unlikely that a higher income level would directly decrease absenteeism. Just because you earn more does not mean you work more days. Both of these variables likely share a negative correlation with an external variable.
   b) Possible common causes that explain this relationship are job satisfaction, financial wellness, or family factors.

8. a) accidental: there is no obvious connection between automobile sales and rainfall
   b) cause and effect: long practise hours typically will result in fewer musical errors

9. a)–c)

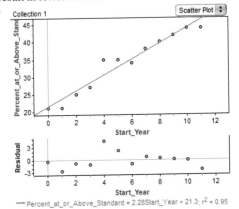

— Percent_at_or_Above_Standard = 2.28Start_Year + 21.3; r^2 = 0.95

   There are two separate trends, both upward, between the percent achieving at or above provincial standard and the year.
   b) $r \approx 0.97$ which suggests a strong linear correlation. The equation of the line of best fit is $p = 2.28y - 21.3$. The equation shows that the percent achieving at or above provincial standard started at 21.3 in year zero and increased at a rate of 2.28 percent per year.

c) The residuals in the middle seem to form a linear pattern. This suggests that this is not a good linear model and that there is possible evidence of a hidden variable.
   d) Yes. The curriculum perhaps became better aligned with the content of the exam.
   e)

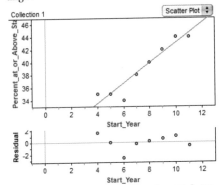

— Percent_at_or_Above_Standard = 1.6Start_Year + 27; r^2 = 0.91

Start_Year > 3
   The correlational coefficient, $r \approx 0.95$, still suggests a strong linear correlation. The equation of the line of best fit is $p = 1.6y + 27$. The equation shows that the percent achieving at or above provincial standard started at 27 and increased at a rate of 1.6 percent per year. There is no obvious pattern to the residuals and none appear overly far from the residual line.
   f) From the residual plot, this appears to be a stronger linear model for predicting the percent achieving at or above provincial standard based on time, in years.

10. a) There is bias in the title that is not neutral, the sample size is only five seasons, and the vertical scale does not start at 0.
   b) Since the graph exaggerates Smyth's skills, it was made by Smyth's agent, most likely in hopes of getting his client a better contract.
   c) Bias can be removed by using a neutral title and starting the vertical axis at 0.

11. Answers may vary.

Glossary

A

accidental relationship A relationship that is based purely on coincidence.

aggregate data Data that are combined or summarized in such a way that the individual microdata can no longer be determined.

arrangement An ordered list of items.

attribute A quality or characteristic given to a person, group, or object.

B

bias Occurs when there is a prejudice for or against an idea or response. Biased samples can result from problems with either the sampling technique or the data collection method.

binomial probability distribution A distribution with independent trials whose outcomes are either success or failure.

binomial theorem A formula used to expand $(a+b)^n$.

$$(x+y)^n = {}_nC_0x^ny^0 + {}_nC_1x^{n-1}y^1 + {}_nC_2x^{n-2}y^2 + \dots \\ + {}_nC_{n-1}x^1y^{n-1} + {}_nC_nx^0y^n$$

The general term is ${}_nC_rx^{n-r}y^r$.

C

categorical (qualitative) data Data that can be sorted into distinct groups or categories.

cause and effect relationship The correlation between two variables in which a change in one directly causes a change in the other.

combination A selection from a group of objects without regard to order. The number of r object chosen from a set of n items is

$${}_nC_r = \frac{n!}{(n-r)!\,r!}.$$

common cause relationship The correlation between two variables in which both variables change as a result of a third common variable.

complement A set of possible outcomes not included in an event.

compound events Multiple events in a probability experiment which may or may not affect each other.

conditional probability The probability of a second event occurring, given that a first event occurred. The sample space for the second event is reduced from the first event.

confidence interval The range of possible values of a measured statistic at a particular confidence level.

confidence level The probability that a particular statistic is within the range indicated by the margin of error.

continuity correction A correction applied when using the normal approximation to correct for the difference between a discrete and continuous distribution.

continuous random variable A variable that can have an infinite number of possible values in a given range.

control group The participants in an experiment who do not receive the specific treatment being measured.

correlation coefficient A measure of how well a linear model fits a two-variable set of data.

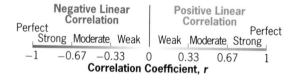

D

dependent events The occurrence or non-occurrence of one event influences the probability of the other event occurring.

discrete random variable A variable that can have only certain values within a given range.

E

event A set of outcomes that have a common characteristic.

expectation (expected value) The predicted average of all possible outcomes in a probability distribution.

$$E(X) = x_1 \cdot P(x_1) + x_2 \cdot P(x_2) + \dots x_n \cdot P(x_n)$$

$$= \sum_{i=1}^{n} x_i \cdot P(x_i)$$

experimental probability Probability based on experimental trials.

$P(A) = \dfrac{n(A)}{n(T)}$, where $P(A)$ is the probability that outcome A occurs, $n(A)$ is the number of times that outcome A occurred, and $n(T)$ is the total number of trials.

F

factorial A product of sequential natural numbers with the form
$n! = n(n-1)(n-2) \dots \times 2 \times 1$.

frequency histogram A graph with intervals on the horizontal axis and frequencies on the vertical axis.

frequency polygon A segmented line that joins the midpoints of the top of each column in a frequency histogram.

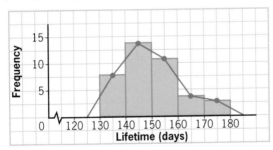

fundamental counting principle If one event can occur in m ways and a second event can occur in n ways, then together they can occur in $m \times n$ ways.

H

hidden variable A variable that affects or obscures the relationship between two other variables.

hypergeometric probability distribution A distribution with dependent trials whose outcomes are either success or failure.

hypothesis A prediction about the relationship between variables or about the outcome of a research question.

I

independent events Situations in which the occurrence or non-occurrence of one event has no influence on the probability of the other event occurring.

indirect method A method of solving a permutation where you subtract the number of unwanted outcomes from the total number of outcomes without restrictions.

interquartile range (IQR) The difference between the first and third quartiles.

L

line of best fit A straight line that represents a trend in the scatter plot as long as the pattern is more or less linear.

linear correlation A relationship in which a change in one variable tends to correspond to a proportional change in another variable.

linear regression The formal process by which a line of best fit is mathematically determined.

M

margin of error The range of values that a particular measurement is said to be within.

mean The sum of the data entries divided by the number of entries.

measurement bias When the survey collection method is such that the characteristics are consistently over- or under-represented.

median The middle value of all the data points when the data values are listed in order from least to greatest.

microdata An individual set of data about a single survey respondent.

mode The data value that occurs most often in a data set.

multiple bar graph A graph in which different quantities are represented by different colours and lengths of bars that are placed side-by-side.

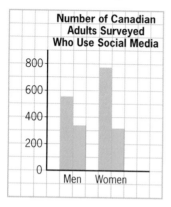

mutually exclusive events Events that have different attributes and cannot occur simultaneously.

N

nominal data Qualitative data that cannot be ranked.

non-mutually exclusive events Different events that can happen at the same time.

non-response bias When the opinions of survey respondents differ in meaningful ways from those of non-respondents.

normal distribution A probability distribution around a central value, dropping off symmetrically to the right and left, forming a bell-like shape.

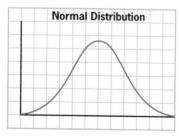

null set A set with no elements.

numerical (quantitative) data Data in the form of any number.

O

odds against The ratio of the probability that an event will not happen to the probability that it will.

$$A = P(A) : P(A')$$

odds in favour The ratio of the probability that an event will happen to the probability that it will not.

$$A = P(A') : P(A)$$

ordinal data Qualitative data that can be ranked.

outcome A possible result of an experiment.

outlier An element of the data set that is significantly different from the rest of the data points.

P

Pascal's triangle A triangular array of numbers in which each term is the sum of the two terms above it.

```
            1
          1   1
        1   2   1
      1   3   3   1
    1   4   6   4   1
```

percentile The percent of all the data that are less than or equal to a specific data value.

$p = 100\dfrac{(L + 0.5E)}{n}$, where p is the percentile, L is the number of data less than the data point, E is the number of data equal to the data point, and n is the size of the population.

permutation An arrangement of n distinct items in a definite order. The total number of these permutations is written nPn or $P(n, n)$. The number of permutations of n items is ${}_nP_n = n!$.

population All the individuals in a group that is being studied.

presumed relationship A relationship that makes sense but does not seem to have a causation factor.

primary source data Data that have been collected directly by the researcher and have not been manipulated or summarized.

probability The likelihood of something occurring.

probability distribution The probabilities for all possible outcomes of an experiment or sample space.

probability histogram A graph of a probability distribution in which equal intervals are marked on the horizontal axis and the probabilities associated with these intervals are indicated by the areas of the bars.

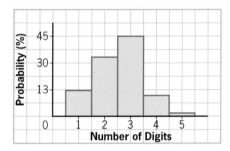

Q

quartiles Three points that divide the data set into four equal groups. The first quartile (Q1) is the middle number between the smallest number and the median. The second quartile (Q2) is the median of the data set. The third quartile (Q3) is the middle number between the median and the largest number in a data set.

R

random variable A quantity that can have a range of values. Designated by X, with individual values designated by x.

range The difference between the highest value and the lowest value of a data set.

relative split bar graph A graph in which different percents, totalling 100, are represented by different colours and lengths of bars that are placed one above the other.

Percent of Canadian Adults Who Use Social Media

reliable data Results of a study that can be duplicated in another study.

research question A question about a topic or problem that can be investigated or solved.

residual The difference between a data point's actual dependent value and the dependent value predicted by the line of best fit.

residual plot A graph which shows the value of each residual graphically as the vertical distance from a horizontal axis.

response bias When survey respondents change their answers to influence the results, to avoid embarrassment, or to give the answer they think the questioner wants.

reverse cause and effect relationship A relationship in which the independent and dependent variable are reversed.

S

sample A group of items or people selected from the population.

sample space A collection of all possible outcomes. Sometimes called a sample set.

sampling bias When the sample does not closely represent the population.

secondary source data Data used by someone other than those who actually collected them.

split bar graph A graph in which different quantities are represented by different colours and lengths of bars that are placed one above the other.

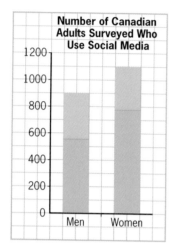

standard deviation The average distance of the scores from the mean.

population standard deviation:

$$\sigma = \sqrt{\frac{\sum(x-\mu)^2}{N}}$$

sample standard deviation:

$$s = \sqrt{\frac{\sum(x-\overline{x})^2}{n-1}},$$ where the population deviation is represented by $(x-\mu)$ and the sample deviation is represented by $(x-\overline{x})$.

subjective probability A probability estimate based on intuition.

T

theoretical probability A probability based on analysis of all possible outcomes.

$$P(A) = \frac{n(A)}{n(S)},$$ where $P(A)$ is the probability that event A can occur, $n(A)$ is the number of ways it can occur, and $n(S)$ is the total number of possible outcomes in the sample space.

treatment group The participants in an experiment who receive the specific treatment being measured.

U

uniform distribution Occurs when, in a single trial, all outcomes are equally likely.

$$P(x) = \frac{1}{n},$$ where n is the number of possible outcomes in the experiment.

V

valid data Results that accurately represent the entire population.

variability (in samples) Shows how samples are different from each other. The more similar the samples are, the lower the variability and the more accurately they represent the population.

variance The average squared difference of the scores from the mean.

population variance:

$$\sigma^2 = \frac{\sum(x-\mu)^2}{N}$$

sample variance:

$$s^2 = \frac{\sum(x-\overline{x})^2}{n-1},$$

where the population deviation is represented by $(x-\mu)$ and the sample deviation is represented by $(x-\overline{x})$.

W

weighted mean The mean of a set of numbers that are given weightings based on their frequency.

Z

z-score The number of standard deviations an observation is from the mean.

population z-score:

$$z = \frac{x-\mu}{\sigma}$$

sample z-score:

$$z = \frac{x-\overline{x}}{s}$$

Index

A

accidental relationship, 397

additive principle for mutually exclusive events, 37

    see also rule of sum

adjust for inflation, 243

aggregate data, 224

airline flight delays, 277

APA style, 461

arrangement, 76–77, 119

attribute, 320

average net worth, 276

B

bar graph, 31, 195, 250

    cluster bar graph, 195

    multiple bar graph, 290, 291, 294, 295

    relative split bar graph, 290, 291

    split bar graph, 290, 291, 295

    stacked bar graph, 294

bell curve, 332

bias, 216, 381

    big numbers, 237

    identification of, 234

    infographics, interpretation of, 238–239

    measurement bias, 233

    misleading statistics, 235–236

    non-response bias, 233

    response bias, 233

    sampling bias, 233

    in two-variable data, 416–417

    type of bias, 233

big numbers, 237

binomial probability distribution, 160, 163–165, 184

    application, 166

    counting successes, 162

    and hypergeometric distributions, comparison of, 180

    independent trials, 170

    investigation of, 160–161

    normal approximation, 365, 366–367

    and normal distribution, comparison of, 362–363

    outcomes, 366

    probability in a binomial distribution, 162

binomial theorem, 124–125, 143

the birthday problem, 92, 95

box and whisker plot, 269, 270–273

    see also side-by-side box plots

box office hits, 242

box plot. *See* box and whisker plot; side-by-side box plots

bubble plot, 428–429

C

Canadian census, 211, 302–303, 307

CANSIM, 222, 302, 303–304

capital sigma, 149, 279

careers

    computer programmer, 60

    data miner, 192

    health care statistician, 378

    insurance underwriter, 2

    management science, 100

    mechanical engineer, 316

    meteorologist, 140

    risk assessment manager, 248

    statistician, 440

categorical (qualitative) data, 198, 225, 250

categorical nominal data, 198

categorical ordinal data, 198

cause and effect, 392–399

cause and effect relationship, 394–395

cell phones, and driving, 440, 455

census, 211, 222, 302–303, 307

census metropolitan area, 303

census profiles, 302–303

central tendency, measures of. *See* measures of central tendency

chances of winning, 129

Chebyshev, Pafnuty, 351

Chebyshev's Theorem, 351

checklists

    probability project self-assessment checklist, 472

    statistics project self-assessment checklist, 476

choose, then arrange, 119

choose from groups, 130

circle graph, 251

clinical trials, 221

cluster bar graph, 195

cluster sample, 207

clustered column graph, 294

coefficient of determination, 387, 391

combination, 111

    choose, then arrange, 119

    counting cases, 118–119

    diagram, interpretation of, 112

    items from a set, 111

    more than one group, 112

    non-ordered selections, 110–111

    number of sums of money, 116

    and Pascal's triangle, 122–125

    probabilities using combinations, 128–132

    problem solving with, 116–120

    solving counting problems with, 100

    total number of subsets, 117

combination of real trials, 31

comma-separated values, 303

common cause relationship, 395–397

comparison

    discrete distributions, 180–184

    experimental and theoretical probabilities, 26–32

    filter, 424–427

    graphical comparison of groups, 294–295

    normal distribution and binomial distribution, 362–363

    normal distribution and hypergeometric distribution, 364–365

    two similar distributions, 181–183

    types of data, 199

complement, 20–21

compound events, 44

    compound independent events, 47

    different compound events, 47–49

    simple compound events, 44–45

computer programmer, 60

concave, 115

concept circles, 378

conditional probability, 51–52

confidence intervals, 352–358

confidence level, 352, 353, 357–358, 359

Consumer Price Index (CPI), 223, 307

contingency table, 411

continuity correction, 365

continuous data, 198, 322

continuous numerical data, 198

continuous probability distributions

    calculation of probabilities, 332

    confidence intervals, 352–358

    connections to discrete random variables, 362–369

    normal distribution, 344, 346–349, 362–369

    probability density function, 322

    uniform distributions, 322–323

continuous random variable, 146, 320–327

continuous sample space, 146

control, 213

control group, 213

convenience sample, 207

convex, 115

convex octagon, 115

correlation coefficient, 384, 386–388

correlation strength, 384–385

statistical summaries
    critical analysis of media claims,
        296–297
    graphical comparison of groups,
        294–295
    interpretation of, 290–298
    measures of central tendency,
        interpretation of, 292–293
    statistical claims in the media,
        290–291
statistician, 440
Statistics Canada, 222–223, 224–225, 292,
    302–305
Statistics Canada report, 304
statistics project. *See* culminating
    statistics project
statistics project content rubric, 477
statistics project peer critique form, 479
statistics project presentation rubric, 478
statistics project self-assessment
    checklist, 476
stem and leaf plot, 31
stratified sample, 207
studies, 212–214, 219, 220, 243
subjective probability, 11–12, 22
subset, 117
sum of probabilities, 9
summary, 100, 250
    see also statistical summaries
survey, 212, 215–216, 217–218, 291,
    356–357
systematic sample, 207

T

table, 338–339
technology
    see also Fathom™; graphing
        calculator; scientific calculator;
        spreadsheet
    simulation of probability
        experiment, 26
    survey, creation of, 217–218
tetrahedral dice, 167
tetrahedron, 158

theoretical probability, 16
    see also probability
    calculation of, 18–20
    complement, 20–21
    and experimental probability,
        comparison of, 26–32
    odds against, 21
    odds in favour, 21
    odds of an event, 22–23
    outcomes and events, 17
    probability, use of term, 34, 35
time graph, 228–229
time series, 382
time series graph, 307
total number of subsets, 117
treatment group, 213
tree diagram, 18, 45, 46, 48, 103
trend on a time graph, 228–229
trials
    clinical trials, 221
    combination of real trials, 31
    dependent trials, 90, 170
    independent trials, 89, 170
    repeated independent trials, 72
    repeated trials without replacement,
        72
trimmed mean, 265
Triple Your Chances, Double Your
    Counters, 442–443, 447–449
two-variable data analysis
    advanced techniques, 424–431
    bias, 416–417
    cause and effect, 392–399
    dynamic analysis, 402–412
    hidden variable, 411–412
    line of best fit, 382–389
    outliers, accounting for, 406–410
    residual plot, 402–405
    uses and misuses of data, 416–421

U

uniform distributions, 154–157, 184,
    322–323

union set, 39
US Census Bureau, 292

V

valid data, 292
variability (in data), 197
variability (in samples), 206
variables
    accidental relationship, 397
    cause and effect relationship,
        394–395
    common cause relationship, 395–397
    continuous random variable, 146,
        320–327
    data with more than one variable,
        200–202
    dependent variable, 382, 401
    discrete random variable, 146, 320–
        321, 362–369
    hidden variable, 411–412, 428–430
    independent variable, 382, 401
    presumed relationship, 397
    random variable, 145, 184
    relationships, 394–398
    reverse cause and effect relationship,
        397
variance, 279, 281–282, 466
    calculation of, 281–282
    population variance, 279
    sample variance, 279
Venn diagram, 2, 18, 21, 35, 181
visual representation, 21
volatility, 289
voluntary sample, 207

W

weighted mean, 148, 149, 261–262

Z

z-score, 283–285, 318, 338–339

Credits

Photo Credits

p2 ValeStock/Shutterstock; p3 top Jason Weingart Photography, Westend61 GmbH/All Canada Photos; p6 David Tanaka; p10 FoodCollection; p13 top Websubstance/dreamstime/GetStock, PCN Photography/All Canada Photos; p15 CandyBox Studio/All Canada Photos; p16 top Caro/All Canada Photos, David Tanaka; p17 David Tanaka; p18 Jeff Greenberg/All Canada Photos; p20 David Tanaka; p22 Paul Chiasson/The Canadian Press; p26 Photo by ESA-T. Peake/Rex Features/The Canadian Press; p34 Brian McEntire/iStock; p43 age fotostock/Alamy; p44 nautilus_shell_studios/iStock; p55 4x6/iStock; p60 Jack Hollingsworth/Getty Images; p61 Bernd Thissen/dpa/Corbis; p64 AdamGregor/iStock; p70, 72 David Tanaka; p74 Ann E Parry/All Canada Photos; p75 David Tanaka; p76 David Tanaka; p81 Prisma Bildagenter AG/All Canada Photos; p82 top B.O'Kane/Alamy, Jo Miyake/All Canada Photos; p83 Design Pics/Alan Marsh; p88 YinYang/iStock; p91 monkeybusinessimages/iStock; p96 left David Tanaka, veryan dale/All Canada Photos; p97 Jeff Greenberg/All Canada Photos; p98 The Canadian Press/HO, COC/Mike Ridewood; p100 Pavel L Photo and Video/Shutterstock; p101 Steve Skjold/All Canada Photos; p104 Glow Images; p106 PCN Photography/All Canada Photos; p108 Arthur Baensch/Corbis; p109 Stockbyte; p110 Newscast/All Canada Photos; p114 Image Source/Getty Images; p116 Radius Images/All Canada Photos; p119 wonderlandstock/Alamy; p121 Digitalexpressionimages/Dreamstime.com/GetStock.com; p128 Phovoir/All Canada Photos; p135 Design Pics Inc./Alamy; p139 Brand X; p140 "Kim MacDonald from The Weather Network/MétéoMédia"; p141 CBS via Getty Images; p144 Getty Images; p152 David Tanaka; p154 WireImage/Getty Images; p160 Photo courtesy of Third Dimension and Accurex Measurement; p168 x3rviar/iStock; p170 NPS Photo/All Canada Photos; p180 Lokibaho/iStock; p186 Outline 205/Dreamstime; p196 Radius Images/All Canada Photos; p206 David R. Frazier Photolibrary, Inc/All Canada Photos; p210 gillmar/Shutterstock; p211 David Petro; p212 Jim West/All Canada Photos; p233 PictureGroup [2008] all rights reserved/The Canadian Press; p242 Graphic by Amanda Shendruk. Used by permission; p247 Solidago/Getty Images; p248 YanLev/iStock; p249 top clockwise Sisoje/iStock, Gabriel Grams/Getty Images, PCN Photography/All Canada Photos; p264 PA Photos Limited [2001] all rights reserved; p266 Don Mason/Corbis; p278 NASA; p300 Christopher Futcher/iStock; p302 Library and Archives Canada; p316 SafakOguz/iStock; p317 top ClarkandCompany/iStock, David Tanaka; p319 left yelo34/iStock, David Tanaka; p320 vikif/iStock; p324 The Canadian Press/Michael Hudson; p328 Adamgregor/GetStock; p329 powerofforever/iStock; p330 David Tanaka; p331 scol22/iStock; p332 Paneuropean/Copyright 2008 Viking Air; p334 Boarding1Now/iStock; p337 tomprout/iStock; p340 B. Leighty/Photri Images/All Canada Photos; p342 left Fred Lum/The Globe and Mail, The Image Bank/Getty Images; p343 left Mutlu/iStock, KeithSzafranski/iStock; p344 left Science Photo Library, David Tanaka; p345 Boarding1Now/iStock; p346 John Lehmann/The Globe and Mail; p348 Danny Xu/Shutterstock; p350 top left clockwise Constantine Pankin/Shutterstock, David Tanaka, Vladimir Volodin/Shutterstock; p352 Nick Moore/All Canada Photos; p354 mackflix/iStock; p356 AP Photo/Ed Betz; p360 left David Tanaka, Chris Linder/Visuals Unlimited/Science Photo Library; p361 Photo Researchers/Getty Images; pp362, 366 David Tanaka; p370 Floydian/Creative Commons License 3; p371 lagereek/iStock; p373 The Canadian Press/Mario Beauregard;

p374 Michael Matthews/All Canada Photos; p377 top AP Photo/Jae C. Hong, Richard Gross/Corbis; p378 Montgomery Martin/All Canada Photos; p379 Wayne Lynch/All Canada Photos; p382 Peter Burnett/iStock; p392 Chris Pearsall/All Canada Photos; p402 Mark Herreid/Shutterstock; p416 StHelena/iStock; p420 Reuters/Mike Blake; p422 Michael Ochs Archives/Getty Images; p424 lightpoet/Shutterstock; p440 Ted Rhodes-Windsor Star/The Canadian Press; p441 top clockwise egd/Shutterstock, mtsyri/Shutterstock, Cisco Freeze/Shutterstock; p442 David Tanaka; p447 Ebby May/Stone Collection/Getty Images; p455 visual7/iStock; p466 top LSOphoto/iStock, Dominik Pabis/iStock; p470 PhotoAlto sas/All Canada Photos.

Text Credits:

Chapter 5

5.1 Investigate table: "Statistics of Passengers Rescued and Lost," *White Star Mementos Ltd.*, n.d. www.whitestarmomentos.co.uk/disaster_statistics.html (Apr 15, 2014).

5-1 Example 1: Silver, Nate. *The Signal and the Noise: Why So Many Predictions Fail—But Some Don't*. New York, U.S.A.: The Penguin Press, 2012.

5.1 Example 3 table: OECD Health Data, "Table 2: Total expenditure on health per capita," *OECDilibrary*, October 11, 2013 www.oecd-ilibrary.org/social-issues-migration-health/total-expenditure-on-health-per-capita_20758480-table2 (Apr 15, 2014).

OECD Health Data, "Table 11: Life expectancy at birth, total population," *OECDilibrary*, December 6, 2013 www.oecd-ilibrary.org/social-issues-migration-health/life-expectancy-at-birth-total-population_20758480-table8 (Apr 15, 2014).

5.1 #3 table: Council of Ontario Universities, "Average Annual Salaries of 2010 Graduates Employed Full-Time," *2012 Grad Survey*, n.d. http://cou.on.ca/publications/reports/pdfs/cou-gradsurvey_nov2013-final-final-s (Apr 15, 2014).

5.1#5: "Chart of the Week," *Maclean's*, September 30 2013, p. 36

5.4 Minds on…: Free material from www.gapminder.org

5.4 Example 3: Dlugokencky, E.J., P.M. Lang, K.A. Masarie, A.M. Crotwell, and M.J. Crotwell (2013), Atmospheric Carbon Dioxide Dry Air Mole Fractions from the NOAA ESRL Carbon Cycle Cooperative Global Air Sampling Network, 1968-2012, Version: 2013-08-28, ftp://aftp.cmdl.noaa.gov/data/trace_gases/co2/flask/surface/.

5.4 #6: National Geophysical Data Center / World Data Service (NGDC/WDS): Significant Earthquake Database. National Geophysical Data Center, NOAA. doi:10.7289/V5TD9V7K (Apr 15, 2014)

5.4 #8: Osborn, Liz. "Rainiest Places in Canada," Current Results, n.d., http://www.currentresults.com/Weather-Extremes/Canada/wettest.php (Apr 15, 2014).

5.5, Example 4: Data source: NYTimes.com, Amitabh Chandra, Harvard University. Photo from http://thedailyviz.com/2012/05/12/how-common-is-your-birthday/

5.5, Example 4 Your Turn: CBC Sports, "Infographic: The Most Canadian Team," CBC Sports, October 25, 2013, www.cbc.ca/sports-content/hockeynightincanada/bio/infographics/most-canadian-nhl-team/ (Apr 15, 2014).

5.5 R3: Gleeson, John, "Memorandum and Order," CV-09-0395 (JG) (RML), http://cspinet.org/new/pdf/order_on_m-dismiss_doc_44.pdf (Apr 15, 2014).

5.5 #9: Graphic by Amanda Shendruk. Used by permission.

Chapter 6

Section 6.2, Investigate: "Fuel Consumption Ratings," Natural Resources Canada, February 5, 2014, http://oee.nrcan.gc.ca/transportation/tools/fuelratings/ratings-search.cfm (Jan 6, 2014).

Section 6.2, Apply question 10: Drummond, Don and David Tulk, "Lifestyles of the Rich and Unequal: An Investigation Into Wealth Inequality in Canada," TD Economics Special Report, December 13, 2006, http://www.td.com/document/PDF/economics/special/td-economics-special-dt1206-wealth.pdf (Jan 11, 2014).

Section 6.2, Extend Question 13: National Center for Health Statistics and National Center for Chronic Disease Prevention and Health Promotion, "2 to 20 years: Boys Body mass index-for-age-percentiles," CDC, May 30, 2000, http://www.cdc.gov/growthcharts/data/set2clinical/cj41c073.pdf (Jan 11, 2014).

Section 6.4 Example 3: Cooper, Belle Beth. "10 Surprising Social Media Statistics That Will Make You Rethink Your Social Strategy." FastCompany. November 18, 2013. http://www.fastcompany.com/3021749/work-smart/10-surprising-social-media-statistics-that-will-make-you-rethink-your-social-stra (Jan 13, 2014).

Section 6.4 Example 3, Your Turn: Cooper, Belle Beth. "10 Surprising Social Media Statistics That Will Make You Rethink Your Social Strategy." FastCompany. November 18, 2013. http://www.fastcompany.com/3021749/work-smart/10-surprising-social-media-statistics-that-will-make-you-rethink-your-social-stra (Jan 13, 2013).

Section 6.4 Apply question 17: World Health Organization. *World Health Statistics* 2013: *A Wealth of Information on Global Public Health*. Geneva, Switzerland: WHO Document Production Services, 2013. http://apps.who.int/iris/bitstream/10665/82058/1/WHO_HIS_HSI_13.1_eng.pdf (Jan 13, 2014)

Chapter 6 Review Question 10: "Feasibility Studies," *Green Energy Technologies*, www.getsmartenergy.com/feasibility-study/ (Feb 8, 2014)

Chapter 6 Review Question 12: Used by permission of L2, Inc.

Chapter 8

8.4, Ex. 2: Used by permission of Yahoo Canada October 12, 2013

8.2 #13 AC: "Cities and Towns," *City Populations*, www.citypopulation.de/Canada-Ontario.html (Apr 16, 2014).

8.2 Extend: "Cities and Towns," *City Populations*, www.citypopulation.de/Canada-Ontario.html (Apr 16, 2014).

8.4 Ex. 1: "NHL Fight Stats," *hockeyfights.com*, hockeyfights.com/stats (Apr 16, 2014).

8.4 Apply section: "National UFO Reporting Center Report Index by Month," *National UFO Reporting Center*, http://www.nuforc.org/webreports/ndxevent.html (Apr 16, 2014).

8.4 Apply Achievement Check: "Voter Turnout," *Conference Board of Canada*, http://www.conferenceboard.ca/hcp/details/society/voter-turnout.aspx (Apr 16, 2014).

8.4 Extend #9: "Voter Turnout," *Conference Board of Canada*, http://www.conferenceboard.ca/hcp/details/society/voter-turnout.aspx (Apr 16, 2014).

8.5 Apply #9: "Datafiles: Hotdogs," *Data and Story Library*, http://lib.stat.cmu.edu/DASL/Datafiles/Hotdogs.html (Apr 16, 2014).

8.5 Extend: "Ontario Voter Support Separated by Party", *Laurier Institute for the Study of Public Opinion and Policy*, http://www.lispop.ca/ontariotrendgraph.html (Apr 16, 2014).

Chapter 9

9.3 Ex. 1 quotes: "How the War on Drunk Driving Distracts from the Real Danger," *MacLean's*, October 21, 2013. www2.macleans.ca/2013/10/21/how-the-war-on-drunk-driving-distracts-from-the-real-danger/

Drews, Frank A. et al., "Text Messaging During Simulated Driving," *Human Factors: The Journal of the Human Factors and Ergonomics*, December 16, 2009. www.psych.utah.edu/lab/appliedcognition/publications/texting.pdf (Apr 16, 2014).

Austin, Michael. "Texting While Driving: How Dangerous is it?," *Car and Driver*, June 2009. www.caranddriver.com/features/texting-while-driving-how-dangerous-is-it (Apr 16, 2014).

9.3-Ex. 1 Table: "Collision and Casualties 1991–2010," Transport Canada, www.tc.gc.ca/eng/roadsafety/tp-1317.htm#5 (Apr 16, 2014).

"Mobile Wireless Subscribers in Canada," Canadian Wireless Telecommunications Association, cwta.ca/facts-figures/ (Apr 16, 2014).

9.3 Ex. 1 Graphs: Perreault, Samuel. "Impaired Driving in Canada, 2011," Chart 1 Police-reported impaired driving incidents, Canada, 1986 to 2011, Statistics Canada, January 10, 2013. www.statcan.gc.ca/pub/85-002-x/2013001/article/11739-eng.pdf (Apr 16, 2014).

"Drinking and Driving in Canada," *The Road Saftey Monitor* 2012, Traffic Injury Research Foundation, December 2012, www.tirf.ca/publications/PDF_publications/RSM_2012_Drinking_Driving_Eng_2.pdf (Apr 16, 2014).

9.3, Ex. 1: "How the War on Drunk Driving Distracts from the Real Danger," *MacLean's*, October 21, 2013, http://www2.macleans.ca/2013/10/21/how-the-war-on-drunk-driving-distracts-from-the-real-danger/ (Apr 16, 2014).

Technical Art

Tom Dart, Kim Hutchinson, and Brad Smith of First Folio Resource Group, Inc.